Accounting Information Systems

SEVENTH EDITION

Accounting Information Systems

George H. Bodnar

Duquesne University

William S. Hopwood

Florida Atlantic University

Prentice Hall
Upper Saddle River, New Jersey 07458

To Donna, Kendra, Andy, and Debbie
To Kathi and Beth Hopwood, and Pepe the rascal

Executive Editor: Annie Todd
Editor-in-Chief: P. J. Boardman
Assistant Editor: Natacha St. Hill
Editorial Assistant: Elaine Oyzon-Mast
Marketing Manager: Deborah Hoffman Emry
Marketing Assistant: Bob Prokop
Production Editor: Marc Oliver
Production Coordinator: Cindy Spreder
Managing Editor: Katherine Evancie
Senior Manufacturing Supervisor: Paul Smolenski
Manufacturing Manager: Vincent Scelta
Design Director: Pat Smythe
Cover Design/Illustration: Marjory Dressler
Composition: Digitype

Materials from Uniform CPA Examination, Questions and Unofficial Answers, Copyright © 1981, 1982, 1983, 1984, 1985, 1986, 1987, 1988, 1989, 1990, 1991, 1992, and 1993 by the American Institute of Certified Public Accountants, Inc., is reprinted (or adapted) with permission.

Materials from the Certificate in Management Accounting Examinations, Copyright 1977, 1978, 1979, 1980, 1982, 1983, 1984, and 1986 by the National Association of Accountants are reprinted and/or adapted with permission.

Copyright © 1998, 1995 by Prentice-Hall, Inc.
A Simon & Schuster Company
Upper Saddle River, New Jersey 07458

Library of Congress Cataloging-in-Publication Data
Bodnar, George H.
   Accounting information systems / George H. Bodnar, William S.
Hopwood.—7th ed.
    p.   cm.
   Includes index.
   ISBN 0-13-750978-2
   1. Accounting—Data processing.   2. Information storage and
retrieval systems—Accounting.   I. Hopwood, William S.   II. Title.
HF5679.B59   1998
657′.0285—dc21   97-38248
                                       CIP

Prentice-Hall International (UK) Limited, *London*
Prentice-Hall of Australia Pty. Limited, *Sydney*
Prentice-Hall Canada, Inc., *Toronto*
Prentice-Hall Hispanoamericana, S.A., *Mexico*
Prentice-Hall of India Private Limited, *New Delhi*
Prentice-Hall of Japan, Inc., *Tokyo*
Simon & Schuster Asia Pte. Ltd., *Singapore*
Editora Prentice-Hall do Brasil, Ltda., *Rio de Janeiro*

Printed in the United States of America

10 9 8 7 6 5 4 3 2 1

Contents

v

PART II: CONTEMPORARY INFORMATION TECHNOLOGY   428

Preface

The seventh edition of *Accounting Information Systems* is suitable for courses at either the undergraduate or graduate level. The text's emphasis on transaction cycles and internal controls makes it ideal for courses taken at the sophomore or junior level as preparation for the auditing course.

The seventh edition stresses information, communication, and networking technology applied within the context of transaction cycles and internal control structure. Transaction cycles are a conceptual approach to the study of accounting information systems. The first edition was the first text to emphasize a transaction cycle approach to the study of accounting information systems. Detailed material on business functions and internal control structure is central to the textbook's organization.

The viability of the transaction cycle approach is evident as one considers the enormous technological change that has occurred in information systems since the first edition was published in 1980. Although technical knowledge that was gained a decade ago has little current value, knowledge gained a decade ago concerning transaction cycles has increased in importance. An understanding of transaction cycles is fundamental to contemporary auditing, professional, and legal considerations relating to an organization's internal control structure. Each transaction cycle is subject to loss exposures. Management should develop detailed control objectives for each transaction cycle. Such control objectives provide a basis for analysis and audit of an organization's internal control structure as well as a basis for managing the loss exposures that are associated with an organization's dependence on information systems.

This book provides the most complete and comprehensive coverage of material relevant to transaction cycles. Transaction cycles are a specific subtopic on the Content Specification Outline for the auditing section of the Uniform CPA Examination. The text contains an extensive CPA examination problem set pertaining to transaction cycles and internal controls (both multiple-choice and essay questions), with complete answers and explanations in the *Instructor's Manual*.

This book also provides comprehensive coverage of contemporary information technology. Topics covered include communication and networking technology, EDI, EFT, paperless accounting systems, computer security, and disaster planning. The seventh edition provides revised and greatly expanded coverage of the Internet and electronic commerce. Many chapters have been updated to reflect recent technical and professional developments. Chapter 5 has been completely rewritten and reorganized to reflect the current professional definition of internal control.

OUTLINE OF THE TEXT

Each chapter contains the following instructional aids:

- Learning Objectives
- Glossary

- Ten-Question Chapter Quiz
- Review Problem

The chapters in Part I survey information technology, electronic commerce, transaction processing, transaction cycles, internal control, computer security, systems development, and reporting systems. Chapter 1 surveys the relationships between accounting and information technology and thus serves as a general introduction to the text. Chapter 2 provides detailed coverage of flowcharting and other systems documentation techniques. Chapter 3 provides a comprehensive survey of the Internet, electronic commerce, and information technology. Chapter 4 discusses the basic elements of accounting systems—journals, ledgers, charts of accounts, standard journal entries, coding systems, and records-retention requirements. Chapters 5 and 6 provide a foundation in internal controls and computer security. Principles of internal control are illustrated in Chapters 7 and 8 in terms of fundamental transaction-cycle application systems such as sales order and purchasing. Chapter 9 provides a one-chapter survey of the systems development life cycle and systems development technologies. Chapter 10 discusses accounting information systems and managerial decision making.

Part II covers contemporary information technology, with separate chapters on file processing and data management concepts (Chapter 11) and distributed information systems and electronic data interchange (Chapter 12).

Part III covers contemporary applications of information technology. Chapter 13 stresses control principles in computer-based application systems. Discussion includes paper-based batch and on-line systems, and also paperless processing systems. Chapter 14 discusses quick-response sales and manufacturing systems—state-of-the-art applications of information technology. Chapter 15 examines information technology from an EDP auditing viewpoint.

Part IV covers the systems development life cycle, with separate chapters on systems planning and analysis (Chapter 16), systems design (Chapter 17), and systems implementation, operation, and control (Chapter 18).

SUGGESTED TEACHING APPROACHES

There is no one "best" approach to teaching systems. Our text is designed to allow for any one of several approaches to be followed.

1. General coverage of information technology, transaction processing, internal controls, systems development, and reporting systems. Although the seventh edition contains 18 chapters, it is not necessary to cover all of them to deal adequately with the areas of internal controls, reporting systems, information technology, and systems development. Each of these areas is covered in a comprehensive survey chapter designed to act as stand-alone coverage for those not wishing to pursue a special emphasis. Instructors should assign Chapters 1 and 2 as a general introduction to all major topics in the book. After this, students can complete the five functional areas in five comprehensive survey chapters:

   A. Chapter 3 provides a complete foundation in information technology. Topics include the Internet, electronic commerce, and hardware and software issues relating to personal computers, midrange computers, and mainframes, as well as communication networks.
   B. Chapter 4 provides a summary of transaction processing and related technology.

C. Chapter 5 provides comprehensive coverage of internal controls.
D. Chapter 9 surveys the theory and practices relating to systems development.
E. Chapter 10 surveys reporting practices as they relate to accounting information systems.

Most instructors will probably want to cover Chapters 3, 4, and 5 because these chapters are essential for auditing. Many instructors will also want to cover systems development, and Chapter 9 will allow them to provide their students with a one-chapter survey of this important area. Still other instructors will want to cover reporting practices as they relate to accounting information systems. This material is covered in Chapter 10.

The additional chapters beyond the foundation chapters give the instructor considerable flexibility in providing concentrated coverage in a particular area. Various concentrations are discussed in the following sections.

2. An emphasis on internal control and flowcharting. The seventh edition provides considerable support for this approach. The instructor can cover internal control in great detail by covering Chapter 5. Many instructors might find that no additional coverage of controls is necessary beyond this point.

The instructor can then cover Chapter 6, which provides comprehensive treatment of computer and information security. There are also two chapters (7 and 8) that deal specifically with internal accounting controls for revenue, expenditure, production, and finance cycle application systems. These chapters contain extensive flowcharts and case materials. In addition, there is a rich set of CPA exam questions included in the problem materials.

3. An emphasis on systems development. Part IV provides a comprehensive treatment of systems development. However, the concepts of the life cycle, structured analysis, and even logical data flow diagrams are introduced in Chapters 1 and 2. Again, this allows the instructor great flexibility, because many will find the introductory material to provide adequate coverage of systems development. However, those desiring more in-depth coverage of the systems life cycle have the option of choosing this focus right from the beginning.

Chapter 9 provides a complete introduction to systems development and discusses all major phases of the life cycle, emphasizing structured development, modularity, and documentation. This chapter should be adequate for a comprehensive introduction to the topic.

Those who wish to cover the systems life cycle and systems development more thoroughly may want to include Chapters 16 through 18, which examine systems planning, analysis, design, implementation, operation, evaluation, control, and auditing. Some instructors may wish to cover only one or several of these topics.

All chapters relating to systems development and the life cycle include a wide variety of questions, problems, and cases.

4. An emphasis on information technology. Six chapters are devoted to computer-related technology and computer-based systems. Chapter 3 provides the basic foundation in information technology. Chapters 11 and 12 provide more advanced topics, including database systems and distributed information systems. Chapter 13 covers the fundamental procedures for transaction processing common to all automated systems. Chapter 14 deals with completely paperless accounting systems that rely on electronic data interchange, source data automa-

tion, and specialized networking technology. Chapter 15 deals with auditing computerized systems.

5. An emphasis on decision support and reporting. The introductory chapters treat the entire information system from the decision support view. Managers and other recipients of information are treated as more than just receivers of the system's output. They are integral components of the system itself. This is supported by Chapter 10, which provides a thorough coverage of reporting systems from the standpoint of decision support.

Part IV, relating to systems development, treats the user as the reason for the system's existence. Decision analytic techniques such as decision flow diagrams and input/output matrices are used extensively.

G. H. B.
W. S. H.

CHAPTER 1

Accounting Information Systems: An Overview

LEARNING OBJECTIVES

Careful study of this chapter will enable you to:

- Understand the related concepts of transaction cycles and internal control structure.

- Describe the organizational structure of the information system function in organizations.

- Discuss applications of information technology in organizations.

- Characterize the development of information systems.

ACCOUNTING INFORMATION SYSTEMS AND BUSINESS ORGANIZATIONS

Organizations depend on information systems in order to stay competitive. Information is just as much a resource as plant and equipment. Productivity, which is crucial to staying competitive, can be increased through better information systems. Accounting, as an information system, identifies, collects, processes, and communicates economic information about an entity to a wide variety of people. Information is useful data organized such that correct decisions can be based on it. A system is a collection of resources related such that certain objectives can be achieved.

An **accounting information system (AIS)** is a collection of resources, such as people and equipment, designed to transform financial and other data into information. This information is communicated to a wide variety of decision makers. Accounting information systems perform this transformation whether they are essentially manual systems or thoroughly computerized.

Information and Decisions

An organization is a collection of decision-making units that exist to pursue objectives. As a system, every organization accepts inputs and transforms them into outputs that take the form of products and services. A manufacturing firm transforms raw material, labor, and other scarce resource inputs into tangible items, such as furniture, that are subsequently sold in pursuit of the goal of profit. A university accepts a variety of inputs, such as faculty labor and student time, and transforms these inputs into a variety of outputs in pursuit of the broad goals of education and the promotion of knowledge. Conceptually, all organizational systems seek objectives through a process of resource allocation, which is accomplished through the process of managerial decision making. Information has economic value to the extent that it facilitates resource allocation decisions, thus assisting a system in its pursuit of goals. Indeed, information may be the most important organizational resource.

The users of accounting information fall into two broad groups: external and internal. External users include stockholders, investors, creditors, government agencies, customers and vendors, competitors, labor unions, and the public at large. External users receive and depend on a variety of outputs from an organization's accounting information system. Many of these outputs are of a routine nature. Accounts payable transactions with suppliers, for example, require outputs such as purchase orders and checks from an organization's accounting information system. Customers receive bills and make payments, which are processed by the accounting information system. Employees receive paychecks and other payroll-related data; stockholders receive dividend checks and routine information concerning stock transactions.

The information needs of external users are varied. The publication of general-purpose financial statements, such as balance sheets and income statements, and other nonroutine outputs assist in meeting these needs. Stockholders, investors at large, creditors, and other external users utilize a firm's general-purpose financial statements to evaluate past performance, predict future performance, and gain other insights into an organization.

Internal users comprise managers, whose requirements depend on their level in an organization or on the particular function they perform. Figure 1.1 is a schematic of the different levels of managerial interest in information. The diagram emphasizes that there are different information needs and demands at different managerial levels in an organization. The accounting information system summarizes and filters the data available to decision makers. By processing the data, the accounting information system influences organizational decisions.

Figure 1.2 presents information characteristics relevant to lower-level, middle, and top-level managers in an organization. Top-level management is generally concerned with long-run strategic planning and control. Accounting reports to top-level management accordingly consist largely of aggregated and summarized items such as total quarterly sales by product line or division. Middle managers need more detail, such as daily or weekly sales by product line, as their scope of control is narrower. Lower-level managers typically receive information relevant

FIGURE I.I Pyramid of Information Levels in an Organization.

	Lower-Level Managers	Middle Managers	Top-Level Managers
Characteristics of Information	Operational Control	Management Control	Strategic Planning
Source	Largely Internal	- - - - - ->	External
Scope	Well-Defined, Narrow	- - - - - ->	Very Wide
Level of Aggregation	Detailed	- - - - - ->	Aggregate
Time Horizon	Historical	- - - - - ->	Future
Currency	Highly Current	- - - - - ->	Quite Old
Required Accuracy	High	- - - - - ->	Low
Frequency of Use	Very Frequent	- - - - - ->	Infrequent

FIGURE I.2 Information Qualities.

only to their particular subunit, such as the total sales of Department A. Personnel in the lower levels of an organization, such as clerks processing payroll or sales transaction data, constantly interact with the detailed transaction data.

The production of useful information is constrained by the environment of an accounting information system and the cost-benefit structure inherent in users' decisions. The uncertainty of the environment in which information is developed and presented means that estimates and judgments must be made. No information system can ignore the practicality of presenting information. If information costs more to provide than it is worth to the user, it is not practical to provide this information.

From an organization's viewpoint, a distinction might be drawn between two broad classes of accounting information: mandatory and discretionary. Various government agencies, private agencies, and legislation set statutory requirements for record keeping and reports. Reports, for example, are required for federal and state income taxes, social security taxes, and by the Securities and Exchange Commission, Federal Trade Commission, and the like. In addition, certain basic accounting functions are essential to normal business activity. Payroll and accounts receivable are prime examples. These functions must be performed in any organization if the organization is to survive. Budgetary systems, responsibility accounting systems, and specific reports for internal management are examples of discretionary information. Conceptually, information should satisfy a cost-benefit criterion. Although the criterion theoretically applies to all the outputs of an accounting information system, the typical organization does not have control over all its information requirements. In meeting mandatory information requirements, the primary consideration is minimizing costs while meeting minimum standards of reliability and usefulness. When the provision of information is discretionary, the primary consideration is that the benefits obtained exceed the costs of production.

Information Systems

The term *information system* suggests the use of computer technology in an organization to provide information to users. A "computer-based" information system is a collection of computer hardware and software designed to transform data

INFORMATION SYSTEMS
Electronic Data Processing System (EDP)
Data Processing System (DP)
Management Information System (MIS)
Decision Support System (DSS)
Expert System (ES)
Executive Information System (EIS)
Accounting Information System (AIS)

FIGURE 1.3 Types of Information Systems.

into useful information. As indicated in Figure 1.3, one might distinguish several types of computer-based information systems.

Data Processing

Electronic data processing (EDP) is the use of computer technology to perform an organization's transaction-oriented data processing. EDP is a fundamental accounting information system application in every organization. As computer technology has become commonplace, the term **data processing (DP)** has come to have the same meaning as EDP.

Management Information Systems

Management information systems (MIS) describes the use of computer technology to provide decision-oriented information to managers. An MIS provides a wide variety of information beyond that which is associated with DP in organizations. MIS recognizes that managers within an organization use and require information in decision making, and that computer-based information systems can assist in providing information to managers.

Functional MIS Subsystems.   Many organizations apply the MIS concept to specific functional areas within the organization. Terms such as *marketing information system, manufacturing information system,* and *human resources information system* indicate the tailoring of the MIS concept to the development of specific information systems to support decision making in a particular, well-defined organization subunit.

A **marketing information system** is an MIS that provides information to be used by the marketing function. Much of the information is provided by the organization's accounting information system. Examples are sales summaries and cost information. Other information must be collected from the organization's environment. Examples of environmental information would include consumer preference data, customer profiles, and information on competitors' products.

A **manufacturing information system** is an MIS that provides information to be used by the manufacturing function. Much of the information is provided by the organization's accounting information system. Examples are inventory summaries and cost information. Other information must be collected from the organization's environment. Examples of environmental information would include raw material data, potential new vendor profiles, and information on new manufacturing techniques.

A **human resource information system** is an MIS that provides information to be used by the human resource (i.e., personnel) function. Much of the information is provided by the organization's accounting information system. Examples are wage and payroll tax summaries and benefit information. Other information must be collected from the organization's environment. Examples of environmental information would include government regulation data and general labor market information.

A **financial information system** is an MIS that provides information to be used by the finance function. Much of the information is provided by the organization's accounting information system application. Examples are cash flow summaries and payment information. Other information must be collected from the organization's environment. Examples of environmental information would include interest rate data, lender profiles, and information on credit markets.

The functional information systems discussed before are found in many organizations. Any well-defined application area in an organization might develop its own MIS. An internal audit information system might be developed for use by the internal audit function. A corporate quality information system might be developed for use by an organization's corporate quality group.

It is important to note that functional MIS subsystems are not physically independent. They share common information system resources in an organization. In particular, they all depend on an organization's accounting information system for important inputs concerning the results of operations and other matters. Functional MIS subsystems represent a logical rather than physical way of implementing the MIS concept in organizations.

Decision Support Systems

In a **decision support system (DSS),** data are processed into a decision-making format for the end user. A DSS requires the use of decision models and specialized databases, and differs significantly from a DP system. A DSS is directed at serving ad hoc, specific, nonroutine information requests by management. DP systems serve routine, recurring, general information needs. A DSS is designed for specific types of decisions for specific users. A familiar example is the use of spreadsheet software to perform what-if analyses of operating or budget data, such as sales forecasting by marketing personnel.

Expert Systems

An **expert system (ES)** is a knowledge-based information system that uses its knowledge about a specific application area to act as an expert consultant to end users. Like DSS, an ES requires the use of decision models and specialized databases. Unlike DSS, an ES also requires the development of a knowledge base—the special knowledge that an expert possesses in the decision area—and an inference engine—the process by which the expert makes a decision. An ES attempts to replicate the decisions that would be made by an expert, human decision maker in the same decision situation. An ES differs from a DSS in that a DSS assists a user in making a decision, whereas an ES makes the decision.

Executive Information Systems

An **executive information system (EIS)** is tailored to the strategic information needs of top-level management. Much of the information used by top-level management comes from sources other than an organization's information systems. Examples are meetings, memos, television, periodicals, and social activities. But some information must be processed by the organization's information systems. An EIS provides top-level management with easy access to selective information that has been processed by the organization's information systems. This selective information concerns the key success factors that top-level management has identified as being critical to the organization's success. Actual versus projected market share for product groups and budget versus actual profit and loss data for divisions might be key success factors for a top-level executive.

Accounting Information Systems

Analogous to the preceding definitions, we might define an **accounting information system (AIS)** as a computer-based system designed to transform accounting data into information. However, we use the term *accounting information system* more broadly to include transaction processing cycles, the use of information technology, and the development of information systems.

TRANSACTION PROCESSING CYCLES

The term *accounting information system* includes the variety of activities associated with an organization's **transaction processing cycles.** Although no two organizations are identical, most experience similar types of economic events. These events generate transactions that may be grouped according to four common cycles of business activity (Figure 1.4):

- **Revenue cycle.** Events related to the distribution of goods and services to other entities and the collection of related payments

FIGURE 1.4 Transaction Cycle Model of an AIS.

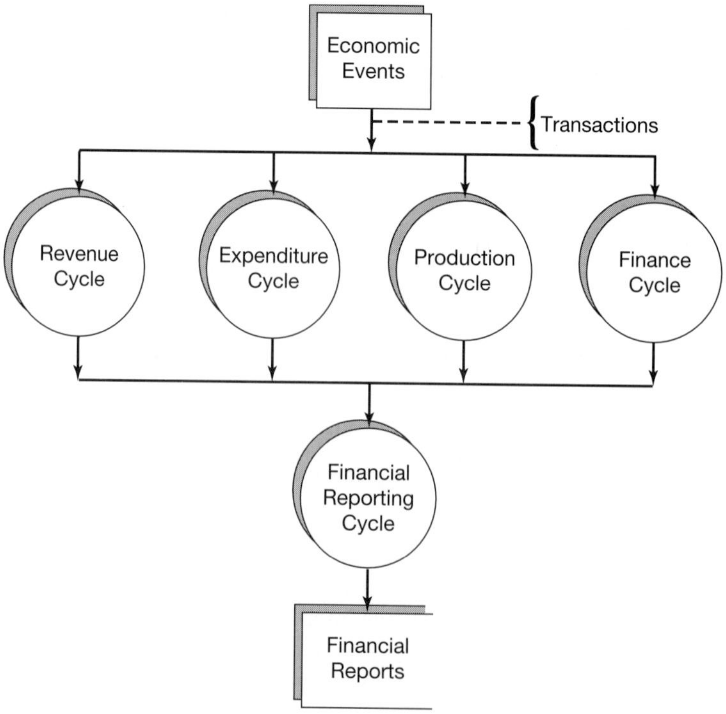

- **Expenditure cycle.** Events related to the acquisition of goods and services from other entities and the settlement of related obligations
- **Production cycle.** Events related to the transformation of resources into goods and services
- **Finance cycle.** Events related to the acquisition and management of capital funds, including cash

A transaction processing cycle consists of one or more application systems. An application system processes logically related transactions. An organization's revenue cycle might commonly include application systems involving customer order entry, billing, accounts receivable, and sales reporting. An expenditure cycle might commonly include application systems involving vendor selection and requisitioning, purchasing, accounts payable, and payroll. A production cycle might include application systems involving production control and reporting, product costing, inventory control, and property accounting. An organization's finance cycle might include application systems concerned with cash management and control, debt management, and the administration of employee benefit plans.

Although usually financial in nature, most transactions also generate statistical data of interest to management. The receipt of a sales order and a notice of the arrival of goods from a supplier are examples of business transactions. Accounting information systems are designed and implemented not only to produce the ledger balances from which financial statements are prepared, but also to produce a wide variety of management and operational information in nonaccounting terms.

The initial task of an accounting information system is to recognize transactions that should be processed by the system. All financial exchanges with other entities should be reflected in an organization's financial statements. An accounting information system routinely processes these monetary transactions, as well as internal transactions. Examples of internal economic events that may be processed by an accounting information system are the transfer of assets from inventory to a production process, depreciation calculations, and adjustments to customer invoices and other documents. Accounting information systems also process transactions that are not directly reflected in those ledger balances that are the basis of financial statements. Customer address changes and employee pay rate changes are examples of important accounting information system-processed transactions that do not directly affect an organization's financial statements.

The transaction cycle model of an organization includes a fifth cycle—the **financial reporting cycle.** The financial reporting cycle is not an operating cycle. It obtains accounting and operating data from the other cycles and processes these data in such a manner that financial reports may be prepared. The preparation of financial reports in accordance with generally accepted accounting principles requires many valuation and adjusting entries that do not directly result from exchanges. Depreciation and currency translation are two common examples. Such activities are part of an organization's financial reporting cycle.

The concept of transaction processing cycles provides a framework for analyzing an organization's activities. Although different organizations may not include the same application systems within a given transaction processing cycle, the cycle concept provides a basis for categorizing the flow of economic events that are common to all organizations. Transaction cycles offer a systemic framework for the analysis and design of accounting information systems in that there is a similar objective for each of the various cycles. This objective is to be an integral part of an organization's internal control structure.

Internal Control Process

Perhaps the most important aspect of an accounting information system is the role it plays in an organization's **internal control process.** The term *internal control process* suggests actions taken within an organization to regulate and direct the activities of the organization.

Much information needed by management to control finances and operations comes from the accounting information system. One of management's major responsibilities is stewardship. Management must protect the resources of an organization against possible losses ranging from embezzlement to careless use of supplies or productive materials, unwarranted extension of credit, failure to purchase from the lowest-cost supplier, inefficient workers, and outright theft.

Control assures that management policies and directives are properly adhered to. Management is far removed from the scene of operations in a large organization, and personal supervision of employees is impossible. As a substitute, management must rely on various control techniques to implement its decisions and goals and to regulate the activities for which it has ultimate responsibility. Control extends over a wide range of activities, such as the maintenance of inventory quantities, the consumption of supplies in production and administration, and the payment of bills within allowed discount periods. Good internal control is a key factor in the effective management of an organization.

Elements of Internal Control Process

Internal control is a process designed to provide reasonable assurance regarding the achievement of objectives in (a) reliability of financial reporting, (b) effectiveness and efficiency of operations, and (c) compliance with applicable laws and regulations. An organization's internal control process consists of five elements: the control environment, risk assessment, control activities, information and communication, and monitoring. These elements are defined and discussed in Chapter 5. The present discussion seeks only to introduce the notion of internal control. The concept of internal control structure is based on two major premises, these being management's responsibility and reasonable assurance.

Internal control should require the establishment of responsibilities within an organization. A specific person should be responsible for each task or job function. The reason is twofold: Responsibilities must be clearly assigned in order to delineate problem areas and direct attention to them; and once employees have a clear understanding of the scope of their responsibilities, they tend to work harder toward controlling these responsibilities.

Internal control also calls for the maintenance of adequate records in an effort to control assets and analyze the assignment of responsibility. Good documentation means that records should be maintained by all parties involved in a transaction. Accordingly, all records should allow cross-referencing from one area of responsibility to another. Along this same line, responsibilities for related transactions should be divided. In the process, one area of responsibility will provide a check on the other and vice versa. The people responsible for the custody of assets should not be responsible for recording the assets in the books of record. Employees are less likely to misappropriate or waste assets if they realize that others are recording their use. This does not mean that work should be duplicated, although in many cases some duplication is unavoidable. Ideally, a task can be so divided as to make job functions natural checks on each other.

For example, the inventory records maintained by an inventory application system establish accountability over goods in a store. Periodic physical inventory counts will reveal shortages or errors that may creep into the records, and the knowledge that the results of their activities will be compared gives the stock clerks and the inventory clerk an incentive to work carefully. The stock clerks will watch the accuracy of receiving room counts as goods are transferred to their custody because the receiving records will be the basis for charging the inventory records for the goods the stock clerks must account for.

Segregation of Accounting Functions

Of primary importance is the segregation of duties so that no individual or department controls the accounting records relating to its own operation. A common violation of this principle is the delegation of both accounting and financial responsibilities to the same individual or department. Both the accounting and finance functions are primarily concerned with money, so "logical" thinking places both responsibilities under one person. The financing function of a business is just as much an operating responsibility as the manufacturing or sales function. Recognizing this fact suggests the need for segregation of the accounting and finance functions.

A common approach is to delegate the accounting function to a controller or similar office and the finance function to a treasurer. Typically, the controller and treasurer are top-management officials, functioning on an equal plane with other executives who report directly to the president. The organization chart in Figure 1.5 illustrates such an arrangement.

The accounting function involves several subfunctions. In a small business, the controller is likely to handle these personally, but in a large concern, the duties are ordinarily delegated to staff assistants or department heads.

Figure 1.5 shows several normal staff positions that commonly report to the controller. The budgeting function involves the preparation of operating budgets, capital expenditure budgets, and the related forecasts and analyses used by man-

FIGURE 1.5 Organization Chart.

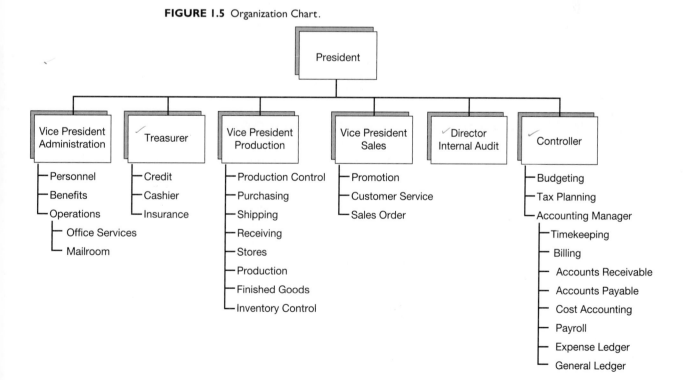

agement in planning and controlling the operations of the organization. The tax planning function concerns the administration of tax reporting and the analysis of transactions that have significant tax consequences for the organization. The accounting manager supervises the routine operating functions of the accounting department, such as posting the general ledger and preparing financial reports.

The treasurer is responsible for the finances of the business. He or she arranges to obtain the funds necessary to finance operations and is charged with securing any required funds under the best terms commensurate with the needs of the business. In addition, the treasurer is responsible for the liquid assets of the business—cash, receivables, and investments. Records of these assets are maintained under the controller in order to obtain the desired segregation of accounting and operations. Under the treasurer is the credit manager, who is responsible for credit and collections even though the original charge to accounts receivable and the accounting for receivables are both handled by the accounting department. Cash collections on these receivables are placed in the custody of a cashier, who is also responsible to the treasurer. Accountability over the cashier is established through the accounts receivable records and the general ledger record of cash. The credit to receivables that relieves the credit manager of responsibility when cash is received on an account is offset by the debit to cash that charges the cashier with the collected funds.

Internal Audit Function

Recognizing the need for and complexity of adequate internal control in a large organization has led to the evolution of internal auditing as a control over all other internal controls. Internal audit is charged with monitoring and assessing compliance with organizational policies and procedures.

Internal audit is an independent appraisal activity within an organization. The organizational level of the internal audit function must be high enough to enable it to operate independently. Figure 1.5 shows the director of internal audit at the vice-presidential level. This placement of internal audit responsibilities is now common in large organizations because it enhances the independence of internal audit, although historically most internal audit functions have been subject to the authority of the controller or other chief accounting officer. Whatever its organizational status, the internal audit function must be segregated from the accounting function and also have neither responsibility nor authority for any operating activity.

ACCOUNTING AND INFORMATION TECHNOLOGY

The term *accounting information system* includes the use of information technology to provide information to users. Computers are used in all types of information systems. Information technology includes computers, but it also includes other technologies used to process information. Technologies such as machine-readable bar codes and scanning devices, and communications protocols and standards such as ANSI X.12, are essential to office automation and quick-response systems.

The Information System Function

Every organization that uses computers to process transactional data has an information system function. The **information system function** is responsible for data processing (DP). DP is a fundamental accounting information system application in every organization. The information system function in organizations has evolved from simple organizational structures involving few people to complex structures involving many qualified specialists.

Organizational Location

Figure 1.6 shows the head of the information systems function titled as **chief information officer (CIO)** and an advisory group called a steering committee. Each of these functions represents a common response to the issues related to the organizational placement of responsibility for the overall information system function. The location of the information system function in the organization has become important as computer applications have become common and essential in all parts of an organization. As computer applications have crossed functions and the computer system's budget has increased in size, there has been a trend toward elevating the information system function in the organization. In many firms, the chief information officer reports to the firm's vice-presidential level or is in a position at the vice-presidential level. However, many information system departments still report to a senior financial officer such as the controller. This is often true in small firms and among relatively new users.

Regardless of the organizational location of the information system function, a **steering committee** or other advisory group is the means by which managers of other areas can influence the policies, budget, and planning of information services. A steering committee consists of high-level members of user functions such as manu-

FIGURE 1.6 Functional Organization Structure of an Information Systems Department.

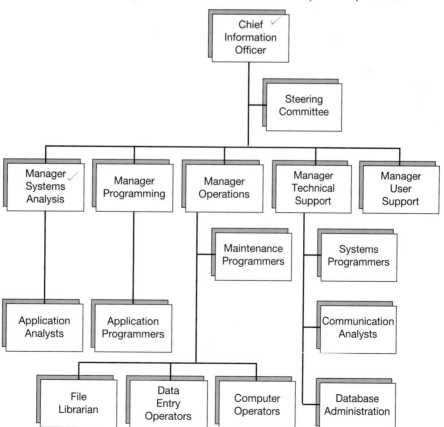

facturing and marketing, as well as the head of the information system function and several of his or her staff. The steering committee meets periodically to set and review important policy, budget, and project decisions relating to information systems. Because the members are consumers of the product of the information system, a steering committee provides user feedback in controlling the information system function. A member of the internal audit function might also participate on the steering committee, or the audit function might advise and review the information system function through a different channel.

Functional Specializations

The most prevalent information system departmental structure is the assignment of responsibilities and duties by area of technical specialization, that is, function. The larger the information system department, the more specialized functions are likely to be.

A large information systems department with functional organization is shown in Figure 1.6. The department is organized into five major functions: systems analysis, programming, operations, technical support, and user support. The **analysis function** focuses on identifying problems and projects for computer processing and designing systems to satisfy these problems' requirements. The **programming function** is responsible for the design, coding, testing, and debugging of computer programs necessary to implement the system designed by the analysis function. The **operations function** is charged with data preparation, the operation of the equipment, and system maintenance. The **technical support function** allows specialization in areas such as operating systems and software, data management and database design, and communications technology. The **user support function** services end users, much as the technical support function services personnel of the information systems department.

Each of these major functions may be subdivided as the size and technical sophistication of the information system function increase. The analysis function might be factored into specialties concerning the identification of user information requirements (information analyst), and the translation of these needs into computer application systems (systems designer). The programming function might be subdivided into systems, application, and maintenance programming specialties. The operations function might be subdivided into computer operations, data preparation, and a librarian function responsible for program and data files.

Technical support specializations include systems programming, which concentrates on software development. This allows the systems analysis function to concentrate on identifying user information requirements and conceptual system design. Data administration as a technical support function coordinates data storage and usage among system users and assumes responsibility for the integrity of the corporate database. Communication analysts specialize in data communications technology, the means by which data are transferred among networks for processing.

Specializations within the technical support function can vary greatly depending on the information system environment. This is true for the analysis, programming, operations, and user support functions as well. For example, note that in Figure 1.6 maintenance programmers report to the manager of operations rather than to the manager of programming. Assigning several maintenance programmers to the operations function often occurs in organizations that depend heavily on their computer-based information systems. The large number of programs makes maintenance a continuous activity and one on which the operation function becomes highly dependent.

The user support function is necessitated by distributed processing technology, which fosters end-user computing. The manager of user support works with the chief information officer to plan the supply of computing services to end users. The user support function often functions as an information center. An **information center** is a support facility for end users in an organization. It assists users in developing their own computer processing applications. An information center might provide users with equipment and software as well as with consulting support. In many organizations, the information center helps end users evaluate microcomputer hardware and software for their particular computing requirements. The user support function might also serve as a place where users can make comments and suggestions concerning the operation of the information systems department.

Although the functional form of organization is prevalent, a common variation is to structure the analysis and programming functions by project. In **project organization,** analysts and programmers are assigned to specific application projects and work together to complete a project under the direction of a project leader. Project organization focuses responsibility for application projects on a single group, unlike functional organization, in which responsibility for a specific project is spread across different functional areas.

End-User Computing

In information systems terminology, an end user is an organizational function other than the information system function that requires computer data processing. The sales or marketing function is an end user that requires computer processing for sales reports, market analyses, sales projections, sales budgets, and so forth. The accounting function is an end user that requires computer processing support for posting of journals and preparation of reports.

End-user computing (EUC) is the hands-on use of computers by end users. Functional end users do their own information processing activities with hardware, software, and professional resources provided by the organization. A common EUC application is information retrieval from the organization's database using the query language feature of database management systems (DBMS).

For example, a user such as an accountant might access accounts receivable data from a company's centralized database, manipulate them, and then print a report. This might occur as shown in Figure 1.7. Using an on-line data terminal and the query language software, the user prepares and submits a report request to the mainframe database access control software. The job is processed by the query language processor against the database, and the report is distributed to the user. As just illustrated, the end user has bypassed direct use of information systems specialists by developing his or her own data processing application and then directly implementing it with the query language software. This direct, hands-on use of computers by users to perform functions that previously had to be performed by information systems specialists is the distinguishing feature of EUC (Figure 1.8). Prior to facilities for EUC, the end user would have had to specify his or her processing request to the organization's information systems department and then await the outcome. If the request was denied or delayed, the user might perform the task manually, if possible.

Personal computers (PCs) give end users their own processing power. Once users have obtained data, they may perform their own processing without being dependent on a centralized computer facility. For example, a user might access

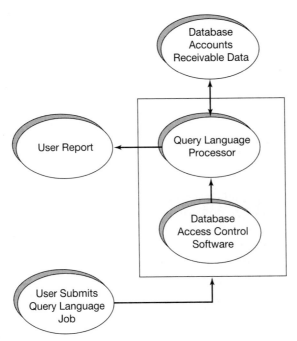

FIGURE 1.7 EUC: Mainframe Application.

data from a centralized database as described before, but then enter these data along with other data into his or her own PC and process the data using spreadsheet software (Figure 1.9). Rather than manually input the data obtained from the central computer, a more sophisticated end-user application might directly download these data into a PC. In either case, the significant impact of distributed information technology within organizations is this capability of end users to perform independent computer processing. End users can participate in applications development without the direct involvement of information systems specialists.

FIGURE 1.8 Data Processing for the End User.

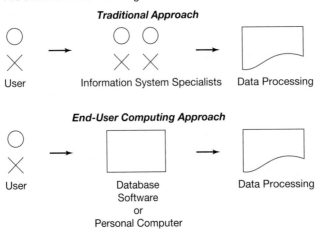

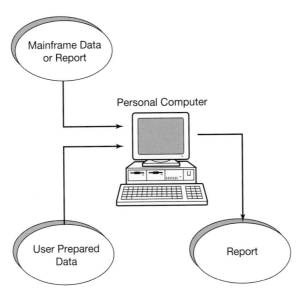

FIGURE 1.9 EUC: Stand-alone PC Application.

Risks of End-User Computing

The growth of EUC poses some problems and risks to an organization. Controlling the hardware, software, people, and data resources used in EUC is a large task. All aspects from user training to security to hardware and software usage need to be properly integrated for EUC to operate effectively. Both management and end users themselves must develop and enforce policies and procedures to minimize these risks. Several problems associated with EUC are inadequate systems development, ineffective use of resources, and data integrity and security problems.

The development and use of end-user applications by end users themselves pose inherent risks in that end users are not themselves specialists in systems development. Inadequate analysis may result in solving the wrong problem. Poor design and lack of basic controls and documentation may easily result from a user's haste to develop an application. The risks associated with inadequate development increase significantly when the output of an EUC application is shared with other users.

Ineffective use of resources in EUC might easily result if not carefully controlled. Relatively expensive equipment, such as PCs, might be underutilized. A mainframe computer system might be overloaded as it processes frivolous EUC requests or poorly designed and hence very inefficient EUC applications or queries. Unauthorized use of e-mail or fax can cause increased cost for these services. Junk fax—unsolicited transmissions received by fax machines—can hinder operations. Increased costs might be caused by duplicate machinery, incompatible software packages, or several different users independently and simultaneously solving the same problem.

The development and use of end-user applications by end users themselves pose inherent data integrity and security risks in that end users are not themselves specialists in data integrity and security problems. When accessing a DBMS, files may be inadvertently altered, or data may be changed or deleted. Although DBMS contain security features, end users may fail to implement them or may implement them incorrectly. Similarly, when end users develop their own applications, they may fail to implement data integrity and security controls or may implement them incorrectly.

Quick-Response Technology

The term *quick-response system* is seemingly self-explanatory. Certainly such systems are "quick" and "responsive." But much more is implied in the quick-response concept. Quick-response systems are essential to the **total quality performance (TQP)** movement in business. TQP (also called **TQM—total quality management**) is a philosophy that one should do *the right thing right the first time.* TQP requires high-quality production, operational efficiency, and continuous improvement in operations. TQP emphasizes "customer satisfaction" to the point of "customer obsession." In the extremely competitive environment of the business world, TQP is a strategy for survival.

Several technologies interact to make quick-response systems feasible. Hardware and software standardization and the movement toward open systems have made the interconnection of computer systems easier. Electronic data interchange (EDI) is essential to quick-response systems. Although EDI is essential to the "quick" in quick-response systems, it alone is not sufficient. Universal product code (UPC) bar code identification of products and scanning technology, such as point-of-sale (POS) retail terminals, are other essential technologies. The UPC bar code scanned by POS technology at the checkout counter of a retail store is the initial event in a chain of events that ends with the item, *the right item,* being quickly replenished in the store's inventory so that it can be sold again (Figure 1.10). This is critical in retailing, where fads (i.e., customer demand for certain products) can and do change rapidly. What

FIGURE 1.10 Chain of Events in a Quick-Response Sales System.

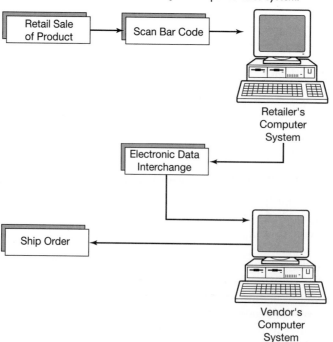

sold last year, last month, or maybe even last week may no longer be what the customer wants.

Just-in-Time

A quick-response retail sales system is the retailing equivalent of **just-in-time (JIT)** inventory systems used in manufacturing. Purchase orders for inventory items are made on a "demand–pull" basis rather than a fixed interval (e.g., monthly or weekly) "push" basis to restock store inventory levels.

In a non-JIT environment, process activity is intermittent. Batches of similar products are periodically processed to satisfy present and planned future needs. "Setup" activity costs are usually incurred every time a batch is processed, and these costs are typically the same regardless of the proposed size of the batch processing run. As the word *planned* indicates, a batch environment fosters a push concept of efficiency. Economic (i.e., efficient) batch size is derived by using formulas, such as those provided in EOQ (economic order quantity) models. In a non-JIT, retail sales environment, for example, orders for new products are periodically processed as a batch and sent to vendors to replenish inventory stocks. Inventory stocks are kept at levels adequate to satisfy anticipated future needs. Ordering (setup) costs are minimized by applying EOQ concepts to reordering decisions.

A JIT environment is a continuous flow environment rather than a batch process environment. A JIT environment requires operation of a process on a continuous basis, to minimize or totally eliminate inventories. JIT also advocates the elimination of waste in the manufacturing process and stresses continuous improvement in operation. JIT is similar in concept to TQM, and is considered by many to be an essential aspect of TQM.

In a JIT environment, process activities occur under a pull concept. Activity (i.e., ordering new product) occurs only when it is needed to satisfy customer demand. Customer demand, as evidenced by current sales, pulls orders from the reordering process; in effect, demand causes orders to be placed to vendors. Orders to vendors are placed on the basis of actual sales to quickly replenish stocks of items that are selling. Current sales demand pulls (i.e., automatically generates) orders for inventory. Retailers can order on the basis of current buying trends.

Electronic Mail

Electronic mail (e-mail) involves the sending of text and files via electronic communications. Almost any kind of information can be sent as e-mail, including accounting transactions. The specific software for formatting, sending, and receiving e-mail messages and files varies from one network to the next.

Electronic Data Interchange

Electronic data interchange (EDI) is the direct computer-to-computer exchange of business documents via a communications network (Figure 1.11). EDI differs from electronic mail in that electronic mail messages are created and interpreted by humans (person-to-person), whereas EDI messages are created and interpreted by computers. Public EDI standards, in particular ANSI X.12, have had great impact on the development of quick-response systems. Public EDI standards provide a common architecture for data interchange, and thus eliminate costly and error-prone cross-referencing of codes by parties to an EDI transaction.

An EDI link between a retailer's computer system and a vendor's computer system eliminates paper processing and allows near instantaneous placing and

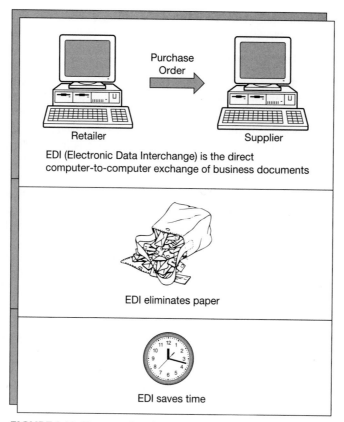

FIGURE 1.11 Electronic Data Interchange (EDI).

processing of purchase orders, facilitating quick-response shipment. The vendor might also invoice the retailer using EDI. In some cases, electronic funds transfer (EFT) payment might be made by the retailer to the vendor's account. All of these events, including the picking of the order from the vendor's inventory, might take place without any human intervention.

Computer-Integrated Manufacturing

Computer-integrated manufacturing (CIM) is an integrated approach to the use of information technology in manufacturing enterprises. Components of a CIM system typically include computer-aided design (CAD) workstations, real-time production monitoring and control systems, and order and inventory control systems. CIM components are connected by a computer network and equipped with software systems designed to support distributed operation. CIM reduces information costs and, through EDI, brings the producer, the supplier, and the customer closer together.

Source data automation of production activities is essential to CIM, thus machine-readable bar codes and scanner technology are critical system components. If you look under the hood of a new car, you will see bar code symbols on many parts, the bar symbol being similar to the UPC bar code that is commonplace on consumer products. The bar codes, which are as commonplace on factory goods as they are on consumer goods, allow a computer or robot to identify materials, process information, and initiate whatever procedures are necessary.

Electronic Funds Transfer

Electronic funds transfer (EFT) systems are payment systems in which processing and communication are primarily or totally electronic. EFT systems provide electronic movement of funds between organizations based on customer instructions. Banks can interface with corporate EDI applications.

The banking and financial industry uses FedWire, Clearing House Interbank Payment System (CHIPS), and Clearing House Automated Payment System (CHAPS). FedWire is an electronic payment and communications system. Banks holding reserve accounts with the U.S. Federal Reserve Bank use FedWire to transfer funds among themselves. CHIPS is an automated clearing house system used for the clearing of Eurodollar payments between U.S. and non-U.S. financial institutions. CHAPS provides same-day settlement of sterling funds transfer and is used primarily by the major United Kingdom clearing banks and the Bank of England.

Retail EFT systems include the telephone wire transfers and telephone payment systems, preauthorized payment systems, POS applications, and automated teller machines (ATMs). Telephone wire transfer is the oldest form of funds movement, and is primarily a manual system. Telephone payment systems, often referred to as "pay-by-phone" applications, are similar to wire transfers in that the telephone is the primary medium for data communications. In pay-by-phone systems, customers can call their bank and direct payments to merchants via a touch tone phone. Preauthorized payment systems are used when both the creditor and customer hold accounts at one bank. Preauthorized payment systems allow automatic payment of recurring items with no manual intervention. POS systems allow the electronic approval and debiting of customer accounts at the merchant's site. POS systems can have a direct telecommunications interface with the credit and debit card databases, thus eliminating the courier costs of physically transporting receipts and totals. ATMs perform banking transaction tasks rapidly with reduced manual intervention. ATMs connect to computer networks that process financial transactions and, in the case of shared networks, provide settlement clearing functions with other banks. Common customer uses for ATMs include depositing or withdrawing cash, transferring funds from one account to another, and making payments.

THE ACCOUNTANT AND SYSTEMS DEVELOPMENT

The term *accounting information system* includes system development activities that an accountant or auditor might expect to encounter professionally. Accountants may undertake systems development activities either internally for their company or externally as consultants. Systems development activities are often encountered by internal and external auditors during reviews of information systems controls conducted as part of an audit.

The Nature of Systems Development

A systems development project ordinarily consists of three general phases: systems analysis, systems design, and systems implementation. Systems analysis involves formulating and evaluating solutions to systems problems. The emphasis of systems analysis is on the objectives of the entire system under consideration. Basic to this is an analysis of trade-offs between system objectives. The general objectives of systems analysis can be summarized as follows:

- To improve the quality of information
- To improve internal control
- To minimize cost, where appropriate

These objectives are interrelated and often conflicting. Trade-offs must often be made between such qualities as economy and usefulness, or between simplicity and a realistic but complex system. Frequently, the only method of evaluating such trade-offs is subjective because the factors involved defy quantification.

Systems design is the process of specifying the details of the solution selected by the systems analysis process. Systems design includes the evaluation of the relative effectiveness and efficiency of alternative system designs in light of the overall system requirements. Systems implementation is the process of placing the revised or newly designed procedures and methods into operation. Systems implementation includes testing the solution prior to implementation, documenting the solution, and reviewing the system when it actually begins operation to verify that the system functions according to the design specifications.

The **systems approach** is a general procedure for the administration of a systems project. Its purpose is to assist in the orderly development of effective systems. The systems approach can be viewed as a process that consists of six steps:

1. Statement of system objective(s)
2. Creation of alternatives
3. Systems analysis
4. Systems design
5. Systems implementation
6. Systems evaluation

The systems approach, like a system itself, is composed of subsystems. Thus, each step in the process can itself be subjected to the systems approach. For example, the first step requires that the system objective(s) be stated. Solving this problem by the systems approach involves all six steps. A defined systems objective is the purpose being pursued. To achieve this purpose, alternatives can be created. The system might, for example, seek objective A, B, or C, or some combination of them. These alternative objectives can then be analyzed and the one that seems most suitable can be designed, implemented, and evaluated.

Executing each subsequent step in the systems approach can also be viewed as a process that involves all six steps. Figure 1.12 illustrates this with respect to the system design step. Top-down design with successive refinement is the essence of a systems approach to problem solving. Each successive refinement adds a finer level of detail to system plans, and a top-down approach to successive refinement structures this process in an orderly fashion.

Behavioral Considerations in Systems Development

Management, users, and systems personnel are necessarily involved in the design and subsequent operation of an information system. Typically, a design group or project team consisting of users, analysts, and management representatives is formed to identify needs, develop technical specifications, and implement a new system.

Technical, organizational, and project management problems are encountered in the implementation of an information system. A new information system

Define Objectives of Design	Develop simple, clear, and precise specifications for effective and efficient systems implementation
Plan Alternative Possible Designs	Develop alternative design plans that meet design objectives
Analyze Alternative Possible Designs	This includes a. Separating plans into logical parts b. Evaluating the relative effectiveness and efficiency of alternatives against system output requirements c. Using a team approach in many cases d. Selecting the best alternative to form a design strategy
Develop Detailed Design Specifications	They should include a. Enough detail to serve as the basis for the implementation process b. Identification of system inputs c. Identification of system outputs d. Strategies for producing system outputs
Document Design Specifications	This should include specifications for every input and output data element and all circumstances for their uses
Evaluate Design Specifications	This involves testing for the desired output of the design process (specification of an effective and efficient design). The evaluation of the design should consider whether it is a. Developed according to the systems approach model b. Based on effective systems strategy produced by a careful and detailed systems analysis c. Effective, efficient, simple, clear, easy to build, easy to change, and easy to test or evaluate

FIGURE 1.12 The Systems Approach to Design.

creates new work relationships among existing personnel, changes in job content, and perhaps a change in the formal organizational structure. The related technical, behavioral, situational, and personnel factors should all be considered. Failure to do so may lead to the output of the system not being used, even if the system itself is technically sound. Furthermore, users' cooperation is continually required to operate the system (provide inputs, verify outputs) after its implementation.

The user cooperation needed to operate the system successfully should be ensured during the design of a system, not afterward. Most accounting applications are routine. To ensure adherence to production schedules, ongoing relationships between users and information system personnel are important. Schedules for inputs, reports, and other items are usually the responsibility of the systems group, but to implement and maintain these schedules, cooperation is required from users.

A philosophy of **user-oriented** design fosters a set of attitudes and an approach to systems development that consciously considers the organizational context. Users should be involved in the design of applications. Careful attention to output, both in quantity and format, in the design phase will prevent users having to rework data or request new reports once the system is in operation. Outputs should be directed toward decisions; users must understand the nature and purpose of outputs to be able to use them. Personnel training should be included in the design phase, not initiated after the system is installed. Finally, the system must be prepared to accept and make changes after operation begins. Users will usually request changes; anticipation of this possibility and the other factors mentioned is essential to a user-oriented philosophy of systems design.

SUMMARY

An accounting information system is a collection of resources designed to transform data into information. This information is communicated to a wide variety of decision makers. We use the term *accounting information system* broadly to include transaction processing cycles, the use of information technology, and the development of information systems.

Most organizations experience similar types of economic events. These events generate transactions that may be grouped according to four common cycles of business activity: revenue cycle, expenditure cycle, production cycle, and financial cycle. An internal control structure consists of the policies and procedures established to provide reasonable assurance that specific organizational objectives will be achieved. Transaction cycles offer a systemic framework for the analysis and design of information systems in that there is a similar objective for each of the various cycles. This objective is to be an integral part of an organization's internal control structure.

The information system function is responsible for data processing. The organizational structure and location of a large information systems department with functional organization were discussed, and common functions within the department were described. Office automation describes the use of electronic technology in the office or workplace. Office automation systems consist of computer-based technologies that allow processing of a variety of electronic messages and documents. Three technologies interact to make quick-response systems feasible. These technologies are EDI (electronic data interchange), UPC bar code identification, and scanning technology, such as POS (point-of-sale) retail terminals. Just-in-time (JIT), computer-integrated manufacturing (CIM), and electronic funds transfer (EFT) are also relevant to quick-response systems.

A systems development project ordinarily consists of three general phases: systems analysis, systems design, and systems implementation. The systems approach is a general procedure for the administration of a systems project. Its purpose is to assist in the orderly development of effective systems. Technical, organizational, and project management problems are encountered in the implementation of an information system. A philosophy of user-oriented design fosters a set of attitudes and an approach to systems development that consciously considers the organizational context.

Glossary

accounting information system (AIS): a collection of resources designed to provide data to a variety of decision makers according to their needs and entitlement.

analysis function: focuses on identifying problems and projects for computer processing and designing systems to satisfy these problems' requirements.

application system: processes logically related transactions.

chief information officer (CIO): has overall responsibility for the information system function.

computer-integrated manufacturing (CIM): an integrated approach to the use of information technology in manufacturing enterprises.

data processing (DP): the use of computers to perform an organization's transaction-oriented data processing.

decision support system (DSS): data are processed into a decision-making format for the end user.

document imaging systems: the use of computers to digitally capture, store, manipulate, and display documents, pictures, graphs, and other illustrations in the same fashion that word processing makes it possible to process text.

electronic data interchange (EDI): the direct computer-to-computer exchange of business documents via a communications network.

electronic data processing (EDP): synonym for data processing.

electronic funds transfer (EFT): payment systems in which processing and communication are primarily or totally electronic.

electronic mail (e-mail): the sending of text and files via electronic communications.

end-user computing (EUC): the direct, hands-on use of computers by end users to perform their own data processing.

executive information system (EIS): an MIS tailored to the strategic information needs of top management.

expenditure cycle: events related to the acquisition of goods and services from other entities and the settlement of related obligations.

expert system (ES): a knowledge-based information system that uses its knowledge about a specific application area to act as an expert consultant to end users.

finance cycle: events related to the acquisition and management of capital funds, including cash.

financial reporting cycle: obtains accounting and operating data from the other cycles and processes these data in order that financial statements can be prepared.

information center: a support facility for the computer users in an organization.

information system function: responsible for data processing (DP) and information systems in an organization.

internal control process: a process designed to provide reasonable assurance regarding the achievement of objectives in (a) reliability of financial reporting, (b) effectiveness and efficiency of operations, and (c) compliance with applicable laws and regulations.

just-in-time (JIT): a continuous flow environment that seeks to minimize or totally eliminate inventories.

management information system (MIS): the use of computers to provide decision-oriented information to managers.

office automation (OA): the use of electronic technology in the office or workplace.

operations function: charged with data preparation, operation of the data processing equipment, and system maintenance.

production cycle: events related to the transformation of resources into goods and services.

programming function: responsible for the design, coding, testing, and debugging of computer programs.

project organization: analysts and programmers are organized by application projects rather than by organizational function.

revenue cycle: events related to the distribution of goods and services to other entities and the collection of related payments.

steering committee: an advisory group consisting of high-level members of user functions that influences the policies, budget, and planning of information services.

systems approach: a general procedure for the administration of a systems project.

technical support function: specialists in areas of computer expertise such as software, data management, and database design.

telecommuting: the use of telecommunication and information technology to allow employees to work at home yet still have direct interaction with the organization's information systems.

total quality management (TQM): synonym for TQP (total quality performance).

total quality performance (TQP): a philosophy that one should do the right thing right the first time.

transaction processing cycle: consists of one or more application systems.

user-oriented: a philosophy of design that fosters a set of attitudes and an approach to systems development that consciously considers organizational context.

user support function: services and supports end users and end-user computing.

Chapter Quiz

Answers to the Chapter Quiz appear on page 30.

1. The term (_____) describes the use of computer technology to provide decision-oriented information to managers.
   (a) data processing
   (b) electronic data processing
   (c) expert system
   (d) management information system

2. The text groups economic events into how many basic transaction cycles?
   (a) one
   (b) two
   (c) three
   (d) four

3. Which of the following indicates a satisfactory situation from the viewpoint of good internal control?
   (a) The cashier reports to the treasurer.
   (b) Payroll accounting reports to the controller.
   (c) Both of the above indicate an unsatisfactory situation.
   (d) Both of the above indicate a satisfactory situation.

4. The statement "Amounts due to vendors should be accurately and promptly classified, summarized, and reported" might serve as a control objective in which of the following transaction cycles?
   (a) revenue cycle
   (b) expenditure cycle
   (c) production cycle
   (d) finance cycle

5. Which of the following information system functions is generally responsible for the design, coding, and debugging of computer programs?
   (a) technical support
   (b) programming
   (c) operations
   (d) systems analysis

6. Which of the following information system functions focuses on the identification of problems and projects for computer processing?
   (a) user support
   (b) programming
   (c) operations
   (d) systems analysis

7. Which of the following is a general term that is used to describe the use of electronic technology for business documents?
   (a) telecommuting
   (b) information system
   (c) office automation
   (d) electronic data interchange

8. (_____) is the direct computer-to-computer exchange of business documents via a communications network.
   (a) electronic data interchange
   (b) electronic funds transfer
   (c) telecommuting
   (d) e-mail

9. The three general phases of analysis, design, and implementation are part of a (_____).
   (a) system development study
   (b) systems approach
   (c) expert system
   (d) decision support system

10. (_____) is the first step in the systems approach.
    (a) systems design
    (b) stating objectives
    (c) systems analysis
    (d) systems evaluation

Review Questions

1. What is an accounting information system?
2. What groups need the outputs of an accounting information system?
3. Identify and describe several types of computer-based information systems.
4. Identify the four common operating cycles of business activity.
5. Characterize an organization's internal control structure.
6. Distinguish between a controller and a treasurer.
7. Describe the purpose of the internal audit function.
8. Characterize the organizational structure of the information system function.
9. Identify several functions that may be specialized areas of expertise in an information system department.
10. How does project organization differ from functional organization in an information system department?
11. What is the purpose of a steering committee?
12. Describe several components of office automation.
13. Give an example of end-user computing (EUC).
14. Identify several components of quick-response technology.
15. How does EDI differ from e-mail?
16. Identify several components of computer-integrated manufacturing (CIM).
17. List the six steps in the systems approach.
18. What is meant by user-oriented systems design?

19. "A credit sale is not a complete transaction." Discuss.

20. Discuss factors that should be considered in the organizational location of the internal audit function.

21. Apply the systems approach to the following objectives:
    (a) to improve the quality of an accounting information system
    (b) to improve the image of a university
    (c) to better the competition

22. Identify several accounting-related decisions that you feel might be made by the following personnel. Do the information needs of these positions differ?
    (a) president of a company
    (b) controller
    (c) accounting manager

23. Discuss briefly the importance in systems design of good communication among systems analysts, management, and systems operating personnel.

24. An internal control structure is an organizational plan to protect assets, ensure the integrity of accounting information, and promote operational efficiency. Indicate whether each of the following situations is satisfactory or unsatisfactory in a manufacturing company from the viewpoint of good internal control. If the situation is unsatisfactory, suggest an improvement.
    (a) Purchase requisitions are made verbally by departments to the purchasing agent.
    (b) The clerk who is responsible for maintaining raw material inventory records does not have access to the storeroom where the raw materials are kept.
    (c) All receiving operations related to shipments from vendors are handled by the clerks who are responsible for managing the storeroom where goods are kept.
    (d) Purchase orders are prepared by the clerks who are responsible for managing the storeroom where goods are kept.
    (e) Employees who are responsible for counting the shipments of goods received from vendors do not have access to the information concerning how many units were ordered from the vendor.
    (f) A periodic physical inventory is taken and reconciled to the materials inventory records by the same clerks who are responsible for managing the storeroom where goods are kept.
    (g) Purchase orders must be compared to receiving reports before a vendor can be paid.
    (h) Copies of purchase orders are sent to the personnel who originally requested the material.
    (i) A firm employs personnel whose only function is to move materials and supplies as needed by the production departments.

25. The accounting information system of an organization may be simple or it may be massive and complex. Accounting information systems are designed and implemented not only to maintain the ledger balances from which financial statements and reports are prepared but also to produce other types of management and operating information that are essential to the operation of a business. Regardless of how large and complex—or how simple—an organization's accounting information system is, accountants, auditors, and other parties are required to study the internal controls periodically. Without such studies it would be impractical or impossible in many cases to acquire a detailed knowledge of the processing procedures that affect all types of transactions. Simplification is not only acceptable but is both desirable and necessary.

    Transaction processing cycles can be used to simplify this task. Although all entities differ, they experience similar economic events, which can be classified into one of the four cycles of business activity: the revenue cycle, the expenditure cycle, the production cycle, and the finance cycle. Each cycle should be an integral part of an organization's internal control structure.

Required

In periodic studies of the internal controls in an organization's accounting information system, accountants and auditors often develop control objectives for each transaction processing cycle. The control objectives provide a basis for analysis. The accountants or auditors collect information to determine the extent to which control objectives are being achieved in each of the organization's transaction processing cycles.

Classify each of the following statements as a revenue cycle objective, expenditure cycle objective, production cycle objective, or finance cycle objective.

(a) Vendors should be authorized in accordance with management's criteria.

(b) The prices and terms of goods and services provided should be authorized in accordance with management's criteria.

(c) All shipments of goods and services provided should result in a billing to the customer.

(d) Customers should be authorized in accordance with management's criteria.

(e) Employees should be hired in accordance with management's criteria.

(f) The production plan should be authorized in accordance with management's criteria.

(g) The amounts and timing of debt transactions should be authorized in accordance with management's criteria.

(h) Compensation rates and payroll deductions should be authorized in accordance with management's criteria.

(i) Amounts due to vendors should be accurately and promptly classified, summarized, and reported.

(j) Cost of goods manufactured should be accurately and promptly classified, summarized, and reported.

(k) Billings to customers should be accurately and promptly classified, summarized, and reported.

(l) Access to cash and securities should be permitted only in accordance with management's criteria.

(m) Access to personnel, payroll, and disbursement records should be permitted only in accordance with management's criteria.

26. The Cheery Kooler Company manufacturers wine coolers. The company began operations several years ago and has experienced rapid sales growth. The company is organized by business function, with vice presidents for manufacturing, marketing, finance, accounting, and general administration. The firm operates a medium-sized mainframe computer, which supports a variety of batch processing applications for manufacturing, marketing, finance, accounting, and general administration. Manufacturing and marketing also utilize several on-line computer applications relating to inventory control and shipment information. The manager of EDP reports to the vice president of general administration.

The company's rapid growth has strained the firm's computer resources, and the number of complaints concerning inadequate support and service from EDP have increased dramatically in the past year. The vice presidents for manufacturing and marketing have taken their complaints about EDP directly to the company president. Citing inadequate EDP support of the on-line computer applications relating to inventory control and shipment information, manufacturing and marketing have requested that the firm purchase a minicomputer that would be used exclusively to support these systems. The president is somewhat perplexed by this request because she recently received a request from the vice president of general administration to fund a significant upgrading of the firm's mainframe computer system. The president is also aware that the finance and accounting divisions have recently purchased several microcomputers and are planning to request funds for additional purchases of microcomputer hardware in their next budget submissions. The president realizes the importance of adequate computer resources to the firm's operations, but given the recent complaints about EDP support and these seemingly contradictory requests for additional computer hardware, she has begun to wonder whether there is sufficient control and adequate planning for the acquisition and use of computer resources at Cheery Kooler. The president thinks forming a steering committee might help solve these problems.

Required

What is a steering committee? Discuss the role of a steering committee in planning for the acquisition and use of computer resources at the Cheery Kooler Company.

27. *Robinson Industries: Organization of the EDP Function[1]*

Introduction

Robinson Industries is a loosely knit conglomerate that offers centralized data processing services to its affiliated companies. To improve the attractiveness of its services, the data processing department this past year introduced on-line service. Several affiliates have become or are becoming users of this service. It has resulted in a reorganization of the data processing department that concerned Mat Dossey, the senior on the audit. Dick Goth, the semi-senior on the engagement, reported that the client had not prepared a new organization chart but agreed to see what he could find out. His report is as follows:

Data Processing Department Organization

The data processing department now consists of 25 people reporting to the president through the director of data processing. In addition to these data processing department employees, key committees perform important roles, as do the internal and external auditors for the company. The internal auditors now report operationally to the board of directors and functionally to the president.

Committees

Selected functions of key committees that are important to the management and control of the data processing department are described briefly in the following:

Data Processing Committee

This committee, composed of three members of the board of directors, meets as required to review and evaluate major changes in the data processing area and to review approval of all pricing of services offered. Their responsibilities also include a review of major agreements with hardware and software vendors.

Audit Committee

In its oversight of the audit function, this committee of the board of directors is directly concerned with the quality of the records and reports processed by the department and the controls employed.

User Groups

These groups consist of representatives from on-line users within a specific geographic area. They meet periodically throughout the year to discuss common areas of interest, possible enhancements, and current problems related to the on-line system.

[1]Prepared by Frederick L. Neumann, Richard J. Boland, and Jeffrey Johnson; funded by The Touche Ross Foundation Aid to Accounting Education Program.

The results of these group meetings are reported directly to the data processing department through a user advisory committee.

Data Processing Department

Data processing department management consists of five managers who report to the director through an assistant director. The department management meets weekly to review the status of projects, customer service levels, and any problems. Weekly status reports are then prepared and distributed to each level of line management. Formal meetings with Robinson's president are held quarterly, or more often if required, to review future plans and past performance.

The following describes the sections within the department under the direction of each of the five managers.

On-Line Services

On-Line Technical Staff

This staff conducts all user training, conversions, and parameter definitions necessary to set up a new user. Training classes are conducted at the data processing center. Conversion assistance is provided to the user prior to the initiation of on-line services. If conversion programs are required, these are defined by the on-line services section to the on-line analyst programmers for program preparation. During the first month after conversion of a new user, calls are directed to on-line services; thereafter, user calls are directed to the user liaison section.

Applications Coordinator

This person is responsible for coordinating the approval of user and data processing department project requests, assisting in the requirements definition of a systems maintenance project, monitoring ongoing projects, and approving project test results.

Operations

Data Communications Coordinator

This person monitors all service levels and response time related to the communications network and terminals. The coordinator receives all user calls regarding communications problems. The coordinator logs all calls, identifies the nature of the problem, and reports the status of the problems until they are corrected.

Computer Operators

This section consists of operators, supervisors, and librarians who execute, review, and service the daily computer production runs, special computer runs, and program compilations and tests. The operations are scheduled on a 24-hour basis for six days a week. Shift supervisors review all on-line operations and prepare written documentation of each problem encountered.

Scheduler

This person is responsible for setting up the computer job runs and adjusting them for on-line special requests.

User Liaison

This staff consists of four people who receive, log, and report all questions of potential problems, other than communications problems, by on-line users. User input is obtained through telephone calls, letters, and on-line messages over the communications network and notes from user committee meetings.

On-Line Reports Control

This staff is responsible for the distribution of all hard copy output to all users. Microfiche are sent directly to users from the outside processing vendor. Logs are maintained where appropriate to control distribution and to reconcile items such as check numbers and dividend totals.

Systems and Programming

On-Line Analyst Programmers

This staff is responsible for all the applications and system software programming required for the on-line system. Systems analysis and programming consist primarily of maintenance to existing computer programs, correction of problems, and enhancements to the current applications.

In-House Analyst Programmer

This staff is responsible for all applications and system software programming not on-line.

Research and Development

This staff evaluates and conducts preliminary investigations into new applications such as electronic funds transfers.

Marketing

This staff responds to requests for information regarding the services provided by the data processing department. Once a user signs an on-line service agreement as a new user, that member is turned over to on-line services for training and conversion.

Required

Based on Dick Goth's report, prepare an organization chart of the data processing department and of its relationships to the rest of the organization affecting it.

Answers to Chapter Quiz

1. D	**4.** B	**7.** D	**10.** B
2. D	**5.** B	**8.** A	
3. D	**6.** D	**9.** A	

CHAPTER 2

Systems Techniques and Documentation

LEARNING OBJECTIVES

Careful study of this chapter will enable you to:

■ Characterize the use of systems techniques by auditors and systems development personnel.

■ Describe the use of flowcharting techniques in the analysis of information processing systems.

■ Define common systems techniques, such as HIPO charts, systems flowcharts, and logical data flow diagrams.

USERS OF SYSTEMS TECHNIQUES

Systems techniques are tools used in the analysis, design, and documentation of system and subsystem relationships. They are largely graphical (pictorial) in nature. Systems techniques are essential to both internal and external auditors and are indispensable to systems personnel in the development of information systems. Systems techniques are also used by accountants who do systems work, either internally for their company or externally as consultants.

Use of Systems Techniques in Auditing

Most auditing engagements are divided into two basic components. The <u>first</u> component, usually called the interim audit, has the objective of establishing the degree to which the organization's internal control structure can be relied upon. This usually requires some type of compliance testing. The purpose of compliance testing is to confirm the existence, assess the effectiveness, and check the continuity of operation of those internal controls on which reliance is to be placed. The <u>second</u> component of an audit, usually called the financial statement audit, involves substantive testing. Substantive testing is the direct verification of financial statement figures, placing such reliance on internal control as the results of the interim audit warrant. For example, substantive testing of cash would involve direct confirmation of bank balances. Substantive testing of receivables would involve direct confirmation of balances with customers. Both compliance testing and substantive testing might be undertaken by internal auditors as well as external auditors.

✓ Internal Control Evaluation

As indicated before, auditors are often involved in the evaluation of internal controls. In evaluating internal controls, auditors are typically concerned with the flow of processing and distribution of documents within an application system. Because segregation and division of duties is an important aspect of internal control, the auditor needs techniques that systematically structure the system under study with respect to the distribution of documents and division of processing duties among personnel and/or departments. Several systems techniques, in particular analytic flowcharts, document flowcharts, and forms distribution charts may be used by auditors to analyze the distribution of documents in a system. These charts are organized into columns to group the processing functions performed by each entity. Several other system techniques, such as questionnaires and matrix methods, might also be used in the evaluation of internal controls.

✓ Compliance Testing

Auditors undertake compliance testing to confirm the existence, assess the effectiveness, and check the continuity of operation of internal controls on which reliance is to be placed. Compliance testing requires an understanding of the controls that are to be tested. When the controls to be tested are components of an organization's information system, the auditors must also consider the technology employed by the information system. This requires understanding of the systems techniques that are commonly used to document information systems.

Thus, auditors must have a basic understanding of systems techniques used in systems analysis and design. Input–process–output (IPO) and hierarchy plus input–process–output (HIPO) charts, program flowcharts, logical data flow diagrams (DFDs), branching and decision tables, and matrix methods are systems techniques that are commonly used in systems analysis and design. Auditors will often encounter these techniques as they review systems documentation. This is why familiarity with such techniques is desirable. However, auditors usually have little need to prepare IPO or HIPO charts, program flowcharts, DFDs, branching and decision tables, and matrix methods in the course of an audit, because these techniques are useful primarily in planning or designing a system. The usual focus of an audit is to review an existing system rather than design a new system.

✓ Working Papers

Working papers are the records kept by an auditor of the procedures and tests applied, the information obtained, and conclusions drawn during an audit engagement. The auditor is required by professional standards to maintain working papers, and these constitute the principal record of work done.

Auditors use systems techniques to document and analyze the content of working papers. Internal control questionnaires, analytic flowcharts, and system flowcharts appear frequently in working papers because they are commonly used by auditors in the evaluation of internal controls. Data flow diagrams, HIPO charts, program flowcharts, branching and decision tables, and matrix methods might appear in working papers if they are part of the documentation of a system that is being reviewed.

Use of Systems Techniques in Systems Development

A systems development project generally consists of three phases: systems analysis, systems design, and systems implementation. Systems development personnel include systems analysts, systems designers, and programmers. Systems analysis involves formulating and evaluating solutions to systems problems. Systems design is the process of specifying the details of the solution selected by the systems analysis process. Systems design includes the evaluation of the relative effectiveness and efficiency of alternative system designs in light of the overall system requirements. Systems implementation is the process of placing the revised or newly designed procedures and methods into operation. Systems implementation includes testing the solution prior to implementation, documenting the solution, and reviewing the system when it actually begins operation to verify that the system functions according to the design specifications.

Systems Analysis

Much of a systems analyst's job involves collecting and organizing facts. Systems techniques assist the analyst in performing these tasks. Interviewing techniques, questionnaires, document reviews, and observation are useful in collecting facts. Formal techniques for organizing facts include work measurement analysis, work distribution analysis, and other matrix techniques. Information flow analysis is also an important part of system analysis. Many systems techniques are useful for this kind of analysis. Logical data flow diagrams and analytic flowcharts can be helpful in giving an overall picture with regard to transaction processing within the organization.

Systems Design

Systems design must formulate a blueprint for a completed system. As an artist needs special tools for painting, the designer needs certain tools to assist in the design process. Many of these tools are also used in systems analysis. These include such techniques as input/output (matrix) analysis, systems flowcharting, and data flow diagrams. Many design problems concern information systems design, such as forms design for input documents and database design. IPO and HIPO charts, program flowcharts, branching and decision tables, and other systems techniques are used extensively in documenting information systems design.

Systems Implementation

Systems implementation involves the actual carrying out of the design plan. Typical activities during execution include selecting and training personnel, installing new computer equipment, detailed systems design, writing and testing computer programs, system testing, standards development, documentation, and file conversion. Detailed design execution during the implementation phase often involves computer programming.

Documentation is one of the most important parts of systems implementation. Computer programs in particular should be adequately documented. Systems techniques such as program flowcharts and decision tables serve as documentation tools as well as tools used for analysis by programmers. Good documentation, a result of the use of systems techniques in analysis and design, assists in training new employees, and generally assists in assuring that systems design specifications are met.

SYSTEMS TECHNIQUES

Flowcharts are probably the most common systems technique. A **flowchart** is a symbolic diagram that shows the data flow and sequence of operations in a system.

Flowcharting Symbols

Flowcharts are used by both auditors and systems personnel. Flowcharts became widespread when business data processing became computerized. As the importance of flowcharts as a communication device increased with the growth and complexity of computer processing, a need for standard symbols and usage conventions became apparent. In the United States, this need was largely filled by the publication of *American National Standard Flowchart Symbols and Their Usage in Information Processing* in the mid-1960s. ANSI X3.5-1970 is the current version.[1]

ANSI X3.5 defines four groups of flowchart symbols and illustrates conventions governing their use. The four groups of symbols are basic symbols, specialized input/output symbols, specialized process symbols, and additional symbols. ANSI X3.5 defines the shape of each symbol but not its size.

The **basic symbols** (Figure 2.1) include the input/output symbol, the process symbol, the flowline symbol, and the annotation, comment symbol. These correspond to the basic data processing functions and can always be used to represent these functions. A specialized symbol may be used in place of a basic symbol to give additional information.

The input/output symbol represents an input/output (I/O) function, that is, the making available of data for processing (input) or the recording of processed information (output). For example, manual input or magnetic disk can be used to input data for processing; the processed data can be output to paper or to another magnetic disk. The process symbol represents any kind of processing function, for example, executing a defined operation or group of operations resulting in a change of value, form, or location of information, or in determining which of several flow directions is to be followed.

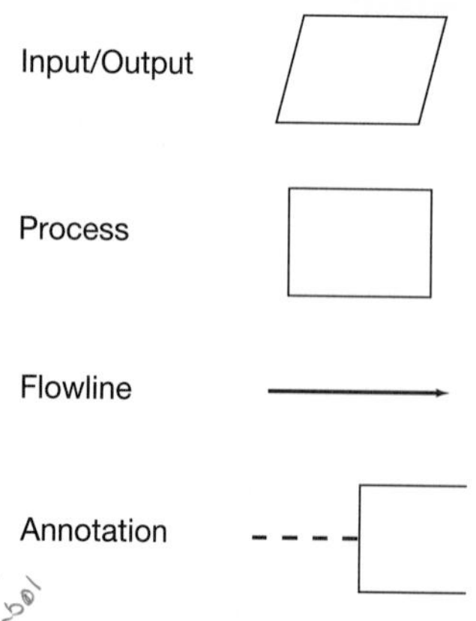

Input/Output

Process

Flowline

Annotation

FIGURE 2.1 Basic Symbols.

---

[1]ANSI X3.5-1970. *American National Standard Flowchart Symbols and Their Usage in Information Processing.* New York: American National Standards Institute, Inc., 1971.

The flowline symbol is used to link other symbols. Flowlines indicate the sequence of available information and executable operations. Flowlines can cross or form a junction. A crossing of flowlines means that they have no logical interrelation. A junction of flowlines occurs when two or more flowlines join with one outgoing flowline. Every flowline entering or leaving a junction should have arrowheads near the junction point.

The annotation, comment symbol represents the addition of descriptive comments or explanatory notes as clarification. The broken (dashed) line is connected to any symbol where the annotation is meaningful by extending the broken line in whatever fashion is appropriate. A brace (connected to a symbol by a broken line) may also be used to indicate an annotation or comment.

Specialized input/output symbols (Figure 2.2) can represent the I/O function and, in addition, denote the medium on which the information is recorded, or the manner of handling the information, or both. If no special symbol exists, the basic I/O symbol is used.

The punched card symbol represents an I/O function in which the medium is punched cards, which are seldom used these days. The on-line storage symbol represents an I/O function using any type of on-line storage, for example, magnetic disk or optical disk. The magnetic tape symbol, the punched tape symbol, the magnetic drum symbol, the magnetic disk symbol, and the document symbol each represent an I/O function utilizing a particular medium.

The manual input symbol represents an input function in which the information is entered manually at the time of processing, for example, by means of online keyboards, switch settings, or touch screens. The display symbol represents an I/O function in which the information is displayed for human use at the time of processing, by means of video devices, console printers, plotters, and so forth. The

FIGURE 2.2 Specialized Input/Output Symbols.

Punched Card

Document

On-Line Storage

Manual Input

Magnetic Tape

Display

Punched Tape

Communication Link

Magnetic Disk

Off-Line Storage

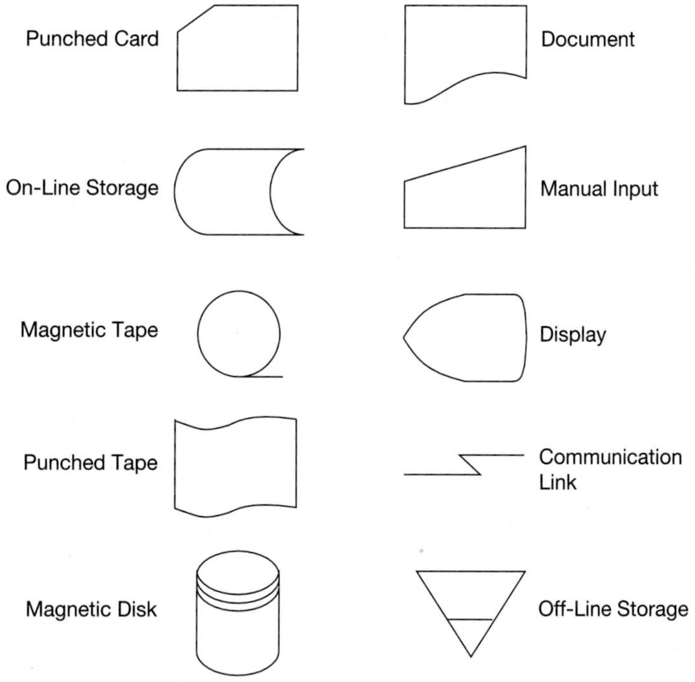

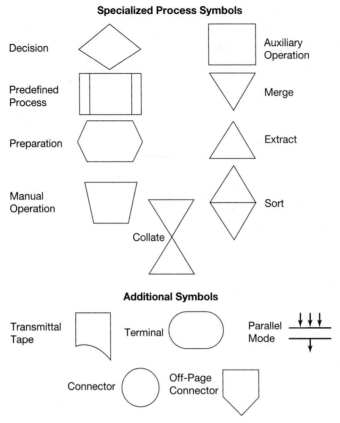

FIGURE 2.3 Specialized Process and Additional Symbols.

communication link symbol represents a function in which information is transmitted by a telecommunication link. The off-line storage symbol represents the function of storing information off-line, regardless of the medium on which the information is recorded.

Specialized process symbols (Figure 2.3) can represent the processing function and, in addition, identify the specific type of operation to be performed on the information. If no specialized symbol exists, the basic process symbol is used.

The decision symbol represents a decision or switching type operation that determines which of a number of alternative paths is to be followed. The predefined process symbol represents a named procedure consisting of one or more operations or program steps that are not specified within this set of flowcharts. The preparation symbol represents modification of an instruction or group of instructions that changes the program itself, for example, set a switch, modify an index register, or initialize a routine.

The manual operation symbol represents any off-line process geared to the speed of a human being, without using mechanical aid. The auxiliary operation symbol represents an off-line operation performed on equipment not under direct control of the central processing unit. The merge, extract, sort, and collate symbols can each be used to represent the associated specific type of processing function.

Additional symbols (Figure 2.3) can be used to clarify a flowchart or to make the flowcharting of a complete process more convenient. The connector symbol represents an exit to or an entry from another part of the flowchart. A set of two connectors is used to represent a continued flow direction when the flow is broken by any space or stylistic limitation. The terminal symbol represents a terminal point in a flowchart, for example, start, stop, halt, or interrupt. The parallel mode symbol represents the beginning or end of two or more simultaneous operations. The off-page connector symbol is not in the ANSI X3.5 standard but is commonly used to represent an exit to or entry from another page of a flowchart. The transmittal tape symbol is commonly used to represent a manually prepared batch control total.

Symbol Use in Flowcharting

Symbols are used in a flowchart to represent the functions of an information or other type of system. Flow direction is represented by lines drawn between symbols. Normal direction of flow is from left to right and top to bottom. When the flow direction is not left to right or top to bottom, open arrowheads should be placed on reverse-direction flowlines. When increased clarity is desired, open arrowheads can be placed on normal-direction flowlines. When flowlines are broken due to page limitation, connector symbols should be used to indicate the break. When flow is bidirectional, it can be shown by either single or double lines, but open arrowheads should be used to indicate both normal-direction flow and reverse-direction flow.

Figure 2.4 contains four illustrations that correctly use symbols, flowlines, arrowheads, and the connector symbol. In the first illustration, notice that the document symbol is used for an invoice, which is shown as input to a manual operation symbol. The text inside the manual operation symbol indicates that the invoice is to be reviewed and approved. The approved invoice is output from this process. Because the direction of flow is normal in this illustration (left to right and top to bottom), no arrowheads are necessary.

The next illustration is a different flowchart for the same process of approving an invoice. In this case, the reverse flow of the approved invoice is indicated with arrowheads.

The third illustration in Figure 2.4 shows how the connector symbol is used to flowchart the transmission of a requisition from the stores department to the purchasing department. The connector symbol is used instead of a flowline to indicate this transmission.

The fourth illustration shows the manual preparation of a purchase order. The document symbol is used to represent the requisition, which is shown as input to a manual operation symbol. Notice that the annotation (comment) symbol is used to indicate what operations are to occur in the manual operation. The annotation symbol is used here because it is not feasible to enter all the text necessary for a complete description within the manual operation symbol. The basic input/output symbol is used to represent the vendor files. Assuming that the files were on paper or cards, it would also be correct to represent the vendor files with the document symbol. It is always correct to use the basic input/output symbol for any input or output, regardless of its physical form. Notice that arrowheads are used to indicate the bidirectional (both normal and reverse) flow between the manual operation and the vendor files. This indicates that the vendor files are

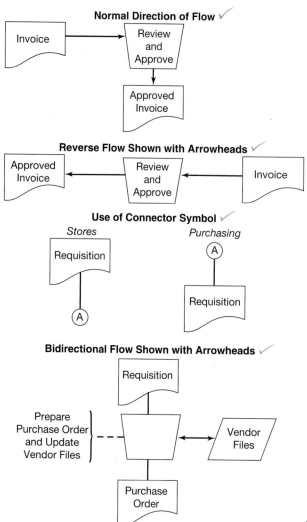

FIGURE 2.4 Symbol Usage Illustration.

both used in the operation and modified (updated) by the operation. The document symbol is used to represent the purchase order that is output from the manual operation.

IPO and HIPO Charts

IPO and HIPO charts are used primarily by systems development personnel. It is customary to distinguish as to the level of system detail described in a flowchart. At the most general level of analysis, only the basic input–process–output relations in a system are of concern. An input–process–output, or IPO, chart (Figure 2.5) can be used to provide a narrative description of the inputs needed to generate desired system outputs. An **IPO chart** provides very little detail concerning the processing function but is a useful technique for analyzing overall information requirements. Additional processing detail is provided by hierarchy plus input–process–output, or HIPO, charts (Figure 2.6). A HIPO consists of a series of charts that represent systems at increasing levels of detail, where the level of detail depends on the needs of users.

Author: Mr. Foxx Chart Number: 3.1	System: Payroll Description: Calculate Gross Pay	Date: 6/9/9X
Input	Process	Output
Payroll job record Payroll master file	Accumulate hours worked Find correct pay rate Compute gross pay	Gross pay records Payroll master file Error messages

FIGURE 2.5 IPO Chart. ✓ 1|19|99

A **HIPO chart** contains two segments: the hierarchy chart that factors the processing task into various modules or subtasks and an IPO chart to describe the input–process–output requirements of each module. The hierarchy chart describes the overall system and provides a "table of contents" to the detailed IPO charts, usually through a numbering scheme, as shown in Figure 2.6. The IPO part of a HIPO is usually in narrative form, as shown in Figure 2.5, but other descriptive techniques can be used as well. In a complex system, the initial HIPO chart is factored into a set of HIPO rather than IPO charts, and then each separate sub-HIPO chart is factored into IPO diagrams. The progression of charts is always from the general to the specific; thus, HIPO structures a top-down strategy in structured system analysis and design.

HIPO charts are a design aid and a documentation tool. They are useful for identifying what is to be done in a problem; they are limited, however, for specifying how or when processing is to be accomplished. Graphic flowcharts using the symbols discussed previously are better suited to specifying information system functions and processing logic.

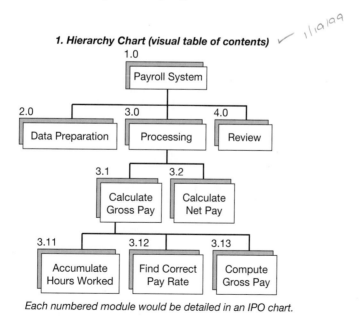

1. Hierarchy Chart (visual table of contents) ✓ 1|19|99

Each numbered module would be detailed in an IPO chart.

2. IPO Charts (one for each module)

HEADER

INPUT   PROCESS   OUTPUT

FIGURE 2.6 HIPO Illustration.

Systems and Program Flowcharts

Systems flowcharts are used by both auditors and systems personnel. A **systems flowchart** identifies the overall or broad flow of operations in a system. A systems flowchart shows where inputs originate, the sequence and mode (manual or machine) of processing, and the disposition of outputs. The focus of systems flowcharting concerns media and processing functions rather than the detailed logic of individual processing functions.

Program flowcharts are used primarily by systems development personnel. A **program flowchart** (also called a **block flowchart**) is more detailed concerning individual processing functions than a systems flowchart. Each of the processing functions depicted in a systems flowchart is further detailed in a program flowchart, similar to the successive layering of IPO charts in HIPO.

Systems flowcharts are associated with the analysis phase of a systems project and program flowcharts with the design phase. A program flowchart is the design step between overall system design and coding the system for computer processing.

Logical Data Flow Diagrams

Logical data flow diagrams or **data flow diagrams** (both abbreviated as **DFD**) are used primarily by systems development personnel in systems analysis. A systems analyst often acts as the communication link between a user who desires some type of computer-based processing and the programmers/systems support staff who will actually prepare the physical design of a system to satisfy the user's need. Explicit documentation of the user/systems analyst interface is a major systems development control concern. DFDs are used by systems analysts to document the logical design of a system to satisfy the user's request. The DFD helps ensure that the systems analyst has understood the user's request by providing the user with a picture of the systems analyst's conception of the user's problem.

The emphasis here is on the word *logical*. The intent of using DFDs is to clearly separate the logical process of systems analysis from the physical process of systems design. The systems analyst provides a logical description to the systems designer/programmer, who then designs the physical specifications.

Table 2.1 illustrates the DFD symbols that will be used in this book. Although the symbology of DFDs is simple, a total standardization of usage does

TABLE 2.1 Logical Data Flow Diagram Symbols

Name	Symbol	Meaning
Terminator		Represents sources and destinations of data
Process		Task or function being done
Data store		A repository of data
Data flow		Communication channel

not exist in the literature. This, of course, is also the case with traditional flow-charting symbols.

There are four symbols. The *terminator* is used to indicate a source or a destination of data. The *process* indicates a process that transforms data. The *data store* is used to indicate a store of data. The *data flow* is used to indicate a flow of data. Although these terms and symbols are representative, many variations exist.

Note here the similarity between the four DFD symbols and the four basic flowcharting symbols, which can be used to prepare any type of flowchart. Although a DFD could reasonably be drawn with the four basic flowcharting symbols, the DFD symbols serve two purposes. The first is to emphasize the analysis of data flows. The second is to emphasize logical rather than physical design. The criticism of and dissatisfaction with traditional flowcharting symbols arise because many of the traditional flowcharting symbols represent data processing operations or physical media. The use of such symbols by a systems analyst necessarily causes a blurring of the separation of logical analysis from physical design. This is not quite true if only the four basic flowcharting symbols are used. Nevertheless, this reasoning is the major argument offered by those who support the use of DFDs.

Logical Data Flow Diagrams and Structured Analysis

This section illustrates the construction of DFDs and their role in structured systems analysis. As indicated earlier, structured systems analysis is characterized by top-down design and successive refinement. We will illustrate these ideas in the context of a payroll application system.

Figure 2.7 illustrates a DFD for a top-level view of a payroll system. This DFD illustrates a very general description of a payroll system. Payroll data supplied by timekeeping are processed against a store or file of payroll data to generate paychecks that are given to the employees. The pointed flowlines indicate the flow of data. Notice that the store of payroll data is both used in the payroll process (the flowline payroll details) and updated by the payroll process (the flowline payroll data).

Several points about the construction of a DFD as illustrated in Figure 2.7 can be made:

- The DFD should consist solely of DFD symbols.
- Each symbol in the DFD, including each pointed flowline, should be labeled.
- The flow of logic should be clear, with all source and destinations of data indicated on the DFD.

FIGURE 2.7 DFD for Payroll Processing.

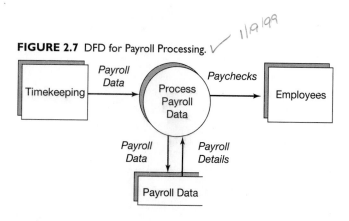

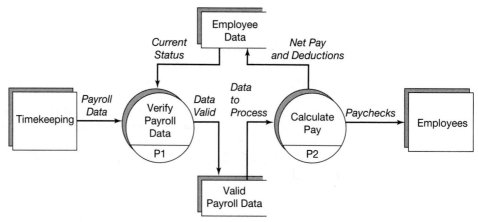

FIGURE 2.8 Expansion of the DFD of Payroll Processing.

Successive refinement of the payroll DFD in Figure 2.7 is required to attain a more meaningful description of the system. Figure 2.8 illustrates an "expansion" of the initial payroll DFD to incorporate more detail. Note that the source and destination are the same as in Figure 2.7. But a new store—employee data—has been added, and the process payroll data in Figure 2.8 has been factored into two processes: verify payroll data and calculate pay. Each of these processes has been numbered so it may be easily referenced. This process can continue until the analyst is satisfied that all major processing modules have been identified.

When the analyst is satisfied that all major modules have been identified,

FIGURE 2.9 Explosion of Process P2.

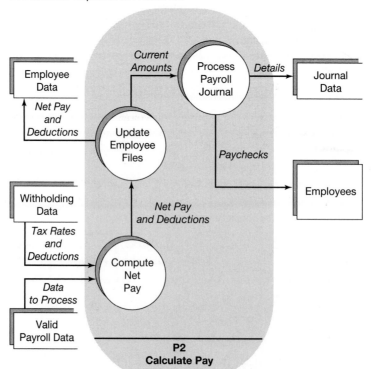

structured analysis proceeds with successive refinement of each of the major processing modules. Figure 2.9 illustrates the "explosion" of P2 in Figure 2.8. This explosion adds more detail. Notice the new stores of data and the new processing modules. Explosion of each of these new modules can be then undertaken as necessary to complete the description of the system.

The expansion and explosion process just described is conceptually identical to that used in the HIPO charts discussed earlier in this chapter. Expansion and explosion of modules generate a hierarchical collection of processing modules that is very useful in providing a description of a proposed or existing system. An important aspect of DFDs, however, is that they concentrate on stores of data and decision logic. When the DFD is complete, the systems analyst can proceed to analyze the stores of data identified as required for the application.

Analytic, Document, and Forms Distribution Flowcharts

These types of flowcharts are used by both auditors and systems personnel. Auditors are often concerned more with the flow and distribution of documents in an application system than with the mode of processing, particularly when evaluating the internal controls in an existing or proposed system. Because the segregation and division of duties compose an important element of internal control, the auditor needs techniques that systematically structure the system with respect to the distribution of processing duties among personnel and/or departments.

Analytic flowcharts, document flowcharts, and forms distribution charts can be used to analyze the distribution of documents in a system. These charts are organized into columns to group the processing functions performed by each entity. Flowcharting across the separate columns, which represent the entities in the system, is an effective way to evaluate segregation of duties. This form of flowcharting also highlights the interfaces between entities. These interfaces—such as sending a document from one department to another—are important control points in an application system.

An **analytic flowchart** (Figure 2.10) is similar to a systems flowchart in level of detail and technique. The flow of processing is depicted using symbols connected with flowlines. An analytic flowchart identifies all significant processing in an application, emphasizing processing tasks that apply controls. Note the organization of the chart by columns. All of the activities of the purchasing department are collected in one column so titled. A **document flowchart** (Figure 2.11) is similar in format to an analytic flowchart but contains less detail about the processing functions of each entity shown on the chart. Strictly speaking, the only symbol used in a document flowchart is the document symbol. However, other symbols can be used as necessary for clarity. The intent is to take each document used in an application system and identify its point of origination, distribution, and ultimate disposition. Comments should be added as necessary to clarify the illustration. Each document symbol generally represents a batch of documents rather than a single document.

Closely related to the document flowchart is the **forms distribution chart** (Figure 2.12). A forms distribution chart illustrates the distribution of multiple-copy forms within an organization. The emphasis is on who gets what forms rather than on how these forms are processed. Forms may be represented by symbols, reduced photos of the forms themselves, or simply word descriptions. The form is pictured or designated on the left side of the chart and usually progresses horizontally through the various columns allotted to organizational units. Analysis may be directed toward eliminating unnecessary copies, unnecessary filing of copies, unauthorized distribution, and so on.

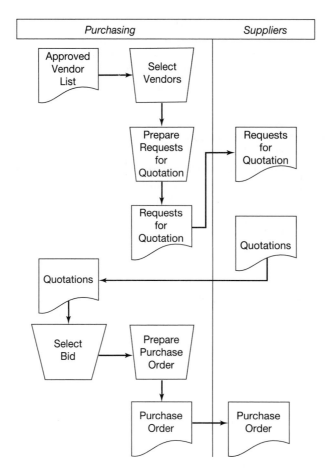

FIGURE 2.10 Analytic Flowchart.

FIGURE 2.11 Document Flowchart.

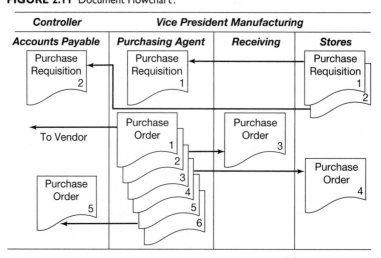

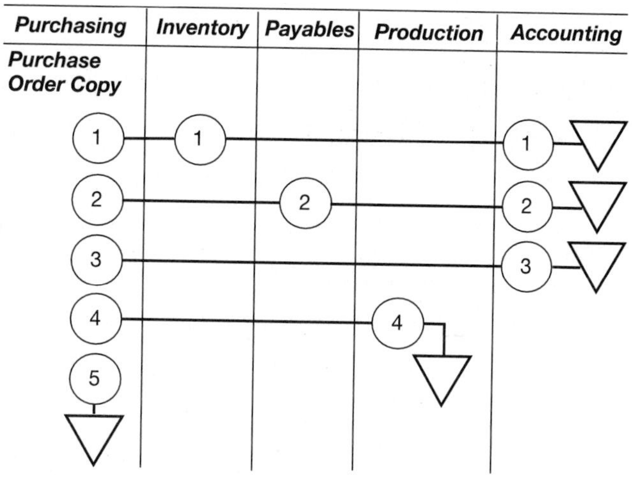

Purchasing	Inventory	Payables	Production	Accounting
Purchase Order Copy				

FIGURE 2.12 Forms Distribution Chart for a Purchase Order.

These techniques structure data concerning application systems in a format that is suitable to analyzing the segregation of duties within the system and the controls that are administered at the interfaces between various entities. It is these features that the analyst is interested in when reviewing the internal controls in a system.

Analytic Flowcharting Illustration

The objective of this section is to illustrate the preparation of an analytic flowchart of a transaction processing system. We wish to flowchart the following system:

> The cashier opens the mail containing cash payments and remittance advices that have been forwarded by customers as payments on their accounts. The cashier prepares a batch control total of the mail receipts and sends this document to the general ledger clerk for posting to the general ledger. The remittance advices are sent to the accounts receivable clerk for posting to the accounts receivable ledger. The cashier then prepares two copies of a deposit slip, deposits the cash at the bank, and files the second copy of the deposit slip, which has been validated at the bank, by date.
>
> The general ledger clerk posts the batch control total to the general ledger and then files the batch control total by date. The accounts receivable clerk posts the remittance advices to the accounts receivable ledger and then files the remittance advices by date.

Planning the Flowchart

First, the materials that will be needed, such as paper, pencils, eraser, and a flowcharting template, must be obtained. In some cases, a PC with a software package that draws and stores flowcharts might be used. It is then necessary to determine which type of flowchart should be drawn, which should be determined by the intended purpose of the flowchart. Here we are drawing an analytic flowchart.

Symbol Selection

After determining which type of chart is required, it is necessary to determine which symbols will be used in the actual construction. ANSI X3.5 standard symbols as discussed and illustrated in this chapter are recommended, but in some cases organizations have their own symbol definitions, which should then be used.

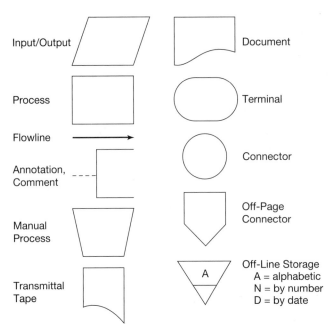

FIGURE 2.13 Symbols for Flowcharting Manual Procedures.

Figure 2.13 illustrates several flowchart symbols that are commonly used in preparing analytic flowcharts that depict manual processing operations. All the symbols illustrated in Figure 2.13 have been defined in this chapter. The symbols are reproduced here to emphasize their importance in preparing analytic flowcharts. Auditors and accountants frequently prepare such flowcharts for the purpose of analyzing internal controls in a system.

Figure 2.13 contains the four basic flowcharting symbols, the manual process symbol, the transmittal tape symbol, the document symbol, the terminal symbol, the connector symbols, and the off-line storage symbol. Note the letter *A* that appears inside the off-line storage symbol in Figure 2.13. A letter may be included inside the off-line storage symbol to indicate the manner in which documents are filed. The letter *A* indicates that documents are filed alphabetically. The letter *N* indicates that documents are filed by number. The letter *D* indicates that documents are filed by date.

System Analysis

In preparing any type of flowchart, it is important to carefully review the material to be charted to obtain a good understanding of the description of the system. In preparing an analytic flowchart, it is necessary to determine what entities will be represented as separate columns. Usually, only entities for which some detailed processing activities are described need to be represented as separate columns. Using this criterion, analyzing the system to be charted reveals discussion of processing by three entities: the cashier, the general ledger clerk, and the accounts receivable clerk. Our flowchart will therefore have three columns—one for each of these entities. Because no processing activities are described for the other two entities in the description—customers and the bank—they will not be represented as separate columns in the flowchart but in ways discussed in what follows.

The next step in the analysis is to identify the documents involved in the system. There are six: cash payments, remittance advices, batch control total, deposit slip, general ledger, and accounts receivable ledger. Each of these should appear in the flowchart as appropriate.

Drawing the Flowchart

Our intent here is to chart the flow of documents in the system, using appropriate flowchart symbols, flowlines, and style. The first step described is the opening of the mail that contains cash payments and remittance advices by the cashier. This is a manual operation and may be charted as in Figure 2.14. The terminal symbol is used to indicate the source of the mail (customers). It also indicates the starting point in the flowchart. The mail is represented by a document symbol. The basic input/output symbol could also be used here. The manual operation symbol is used to represent the "open-mail" process. The basic process symbol could also be used to represent this process. In both cases a specialized symbol was selected because it more clearly describes the system. For the same reason, the special document symbol is used to represent the cash payments and remittance advices. Although cash payments (cash and/or checks) are not documents in the same sense as remittance advices, they are an important flow in this transaction processing system and should be clearly identified in the flowchart. Flowlines are used to indicate the flow of action. This portion of the flowchart would be placed in a column labeled "cashier" because the cashier is performing this process.

The next step described is the preparation of a batch control total of the mail receipts. This also is a manual operation and can be charted as in Figure 2.15. The manual operation system is used to represent the "prepare-batch-control-total" process, and the document symbol is used to represent the cash payments and the remittance advices. The document symbol has also been selected to represent the batch control total. The transmittal tape symbol shown in Figure 2.13 could also be used to represent the batch control total. This portion of the flowchart would also be placed in the column labeled "cashier" because it is a continuation of the flowchart of the cashier's activities.

Sandwich Rule

Notice the similarity of construction between the two portions of the flowchart that have been described. In both cases, inputs (documents) flow into a process symbol and outputs (documents) flow out of the process symbol. Every process symbol should have its inputs and outputs clearly specified. This has been called the **sandwich rule;** every process symbol should be "sandwiched" between an input symbol and an output symbol.

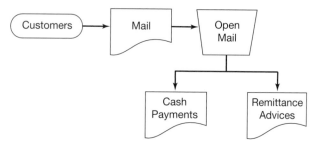

FIGURE 2.14 Open-Mail Portion of an Analytic Flowchart.

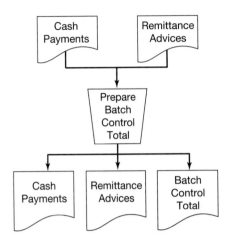

FIGURE 2.15 Prepare-Batch-Control-Total Portion of an Analytic Flowchart.

Use of Connector Symbol

The cashier forwards the batch control total to the general ledger clerk and the remittance advices to the accounts receivable clerk. This can be flowcharted as in Figure 2.16. Connector symbols are used here to eliminate long flowlines. The matching connector symbols appear in the columns for the general ledger clerk and the accounts receivable clerk in the complete flowchart, which is shown in Figure 2.18.

This is a question of style that affects the overall appearance and clarity of the flowchart. One important advantage connector symbols have over long flowlines that cross over columns of a flowchart is that they add flexibility in that the flowchart becomes modular. Notice that the absence of long flowlines that cross over columns of the flowchart in Figure 2.18 make it possible to add or move columns without affecting the logical clarity or actual physical construction of the flowchart. There would be no need to erase and redraw flowlines in either case. This feature is especially appreciated when making changes to an existing flowchart.

Entity–Column Relations

The cashier prepares two copies of a deposit slip, deposits the cash at the bank, and files the second copy of the deposit slip, which has been validated by the bank, by date. This can be charted as in Figure 2.17. The manual operation system is used to represent the "prepare deposit slip" process, and the document symbol is used to represent the cash payments and the deposit slips. This portion of the flowchart would also be placed in the "cashier" column because it is a continuation of the flowchart of the cashier's activities.

The bank is a separate entity, yet the process of depositing the cash payments at the bank is shown as a manual operation in the cashier column of the

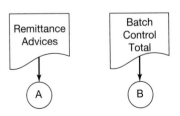

FIGURE 2.16 Use of a Connector Symbol.

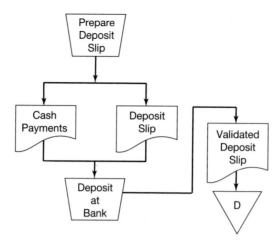

FIGURE 2.17 Cashier Activities Flowchart.

FIGURE 2.18 Analytic Flowchart Illustration.

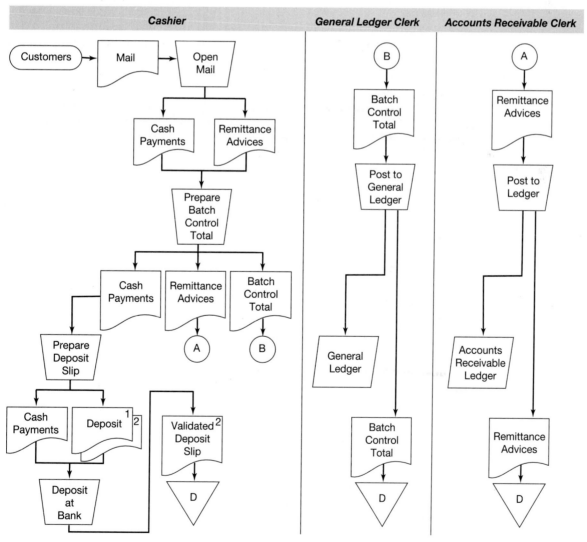

flowchart. The bank could be shown as a separate column and the flow of the deposit slip to and from the bank could be charted. The method shown was chosen because the narrative description being charted does not contain any discussion of processing at the bank. This is a question of style that affects the overall appearance and clarity of the flowchart. This same point is true for the customers, who are also separate entities. The terminal symbol rather than a separate column was used to indicate the source of the mail (customers) because the narrative description being charted does not contain any discussion of processing by the customers.

Because the narrative contains a description of the processing by the general ledger clerk and the accounts receivable clerk, both of these entities are shown as separate columns. The charting of the manual processing activities performed by the general ledger clerk and the accounts receivable clerk is very similar to that of the cashier's activities. The completed flowchart is shown in Figure 2.18. Notice that the basic input/output symbol has been used to represent the general ledger and the accounts receivable ledger. The document symbol or off-line storage (file) symbol could be used in either or both cases. The basic input/output symbol has been used to emphasize that it is always correct to represent input or output with this symbol.

The previous points have been discussed to emphasize that preparing flowcharts is more art than science. Many choices must be made when preparing a flowchart. Choices should be made such that the end result—the flowchart—is clear in appearance and effectively conveys the functioning of the system. Five general guidelines are as follows:

1. Analyze the system to identify entities and documents, as done in this illustration.
2. Select the symbols to be used in accordance with the general guidelines described in this chapter.
3. Sketch a rough first draft of the system to organize the entity columns and flow of documents.
4. Review this sketch for major omissions or errors.
5. Finalize the flowchart, making sure that comments are added as necessary to clarify the flowchart.

Narrative Techniques

Narrative techniques are often useful, particularly in the fact-finding stage of system analysis. Interviews are useful for familiarizing the analyst with individual decision makers and their problems. Depth interviews allow the systems analyst to establish a personal working relationship with the manager. Structured interviews might be used to answer a specific set of questions.

Open-ended questionnaires are a fact-gathering technique where persons provide written answers to general rather than specific questions. Open-ended questionnaires serve the same purpose as depth interviews, asking very general questions such as, "Do you have any suggestions for improving the system? Please explain." Closed-ended questions are a useful technique for gathering answers to a large number of questions. They require considerably less time on the part of the systems analyst than interviewing techniques do. Such questionnaires are very effective in many situations, including collecting information about internal control.

Narrative techniques include document reviews. Often a large number of documents are available for review by the analyst or auditor, such as flowcharts, organization charts, procedure manuals, operation manuals, reference manuals, and historical records. These documents can assist the analyst or auditor in gaining an overall understanding of the organization.

Resource Utilization Analysis

The techniques we have discussed assume an existing or proposed flow or structure of operations and do not directly address the question of system resource utilization requirements. For example, assume that you had prepared flowcharts for a particular procedure, identified the changes necessary to accomplish the task at hand, and obtained approval to prepare (design) the detailed plan of operation and/or implement the newly designed procedure. Clearly, further analysis would be required to match the resources at hand with the task at hand. How many clerks or machines will be required to process the data? What type or size of machine is required? And, concerning people, who gets what task?

Resource utilization analysis must always be considered by systems development personnel in implementing systems. Auditors should consider resource utilization when they plan an audit. Tasks such as assigning staff to particular audit functions can be facilitated with systems techniques. Thus, systems techniques for resource utilization analysis can be used by both auditors and systems personnel.

Work Measurement

Questions of this type fall under the broad topic of **work measurement** techniques. Work measurement is based on a simple premise: Quantitative measurement is essential to the design of efficient procedures. Work measurement includes the variety of techniques used to model, measure, or estimate clerical or other activities in a production framework. In an accounting framework, work measurement is similar to the concept employed in standard cost systems. The essential ingredient is the development of a standard, a yardstick, that can be used to gauge the efficiency of actual operation.

Work measurement involves four basic steps:

1. Identify the tasks.
2. Obtain time estimates for performing the tasks, utilizing the time-and-motion studies, test runs, historical data, or some other source.
3. Adjust these time estimates for idle time and similar considerations.
4. Analyze requirements based on these data.

The following are general examples of step 4:

(Average time/unit + idle time/unit) × average volume = total task time

Total time available/total task time = capacity utilization

To illustrate the general idea, consider the following excerpt from an actual system analysis:

> Our desire to evaluate the relative costs associated with various operating configurations for the CVU Unit led to the programming of a computational model of the CVU operation. The model is essentially a personnel cost model. A constant volume is passed through the CVU operation under certain assumptions as to operating configuration. Costs are accumulated and reported. Costs are calculated in terms of the work hours needed to perform a given operation. A standard computation would appear as follows:

- X = volume to be processed
- R = processing rate (volume/hour)
- C = average hourly personnel cost for this processing rate
- Y = resulting cost

Then

1/19/09 ✓

$$Y = C(X/R)$$

The standard above includes such operations as counting, bundle and strap counts, verification, and destruction. In most cases, certain fixed costs are added, such as the cost of observers. As several days are lapsed in processing a given lot, the assumption of a constant volume allows us to calculate the cost/lot. The constant volume used is the average daily volume for the preceding year.

1/19/09 ✓

Work measurement techniques have two major areas of application in systems work. The first is in evaluating the technical feasibility or technical requirements of a system design. Examples of this usage are determining the number of magnetic disks needed to store a specific number of documents, determining the size of computer system necessary to process a proposed workload, and determining the number of clerks necessary to input data. The second major area of application is in performance evaluation of system-related tasks such as computer programming and project development. Performance evaluation requires the definition of performance standards in terms of some directly measurable criterion such as "number of lines coded" or "hours of project work," so that actual performance can be quantified and evaluated with respect to managerial expectations for the task.

1/19/09 ✓ **Work Distribution Analysis** who does what?

After the operational characteristics of a system have been identified and selected through some form of work measurement, a **work distribution analysis** must be undertaken to assign specific tasks to employees. This analysis may take several forms, but conceptually the problem may be represented as a matrix. Table 2.2 illustrates a work distribution table.

A work distribution analysis requires detailed information about the functions and responsibilities of all employees involved in the analysis. A task list is used to record each separate item of work performed by an individual and the average number of hours spent on each task per week. The detail of tasks considered depends on the level of work measurement analysis. Table 2.2 portrays the assignment of several tasks (left-hand column) to employees. Each employee (or

TABLE 2.2   Sample Work Distribution Table

Task	Estimated Hours per Day	Assignment to Employees		
		Lola	Dale	Neil
Open mail	2	1	1	0
Sort advices	6	2	2	2
Batch control	2	0	0	2
File advices	8	4	4	0

department, and so on) is represented by a column; the work assignments are spread across the table to employees. The method of assignment should be rational; that is, employee qualifications, internal control, scheduling, timing of events, and so forth should be considered. The method of assignment is the choice of the analyst. Formal techniques, using mathematical programming or similar algorithms, can be found in management science and industrial engineering literature.

Decision Analysis Techniques

Branching and Decision Tables

Branching and decision tables are used primarily by systems development personnel. Often the decision logic required in a computer program is sufficiently complex to mitigate the usefulness of the standard decision flowcharting symbol. In such cases a **branching table** can be used to depict a decision function. The table is composed of a statement of the decision to be made, a list of the conditions that can occur, and the path to be followed for each condition. The "Go to" section contains either an inconnector (connector symbol) reference or a single flowline exiting to another symbol. Examples of branching table formats are shown in Figure 2.19.

A **decision table** is a tabular representation of a decision-making process (see Figure 2.20). It is similar to a branching table but more complex in that it incorporates multiple-decision criteria. Decision tables are constructed on an IF–THEN premise and appear as a two-dimensional matrix in general form. The table is divided into four areas: the condition stub, the condition entries, the action stub, and the action entries. Conditions are listed on horizontal rows in the condition stub area and are read as "IF condition 1 And condition 2 ... And con-

FIGURE 2.19 Branching Table Formats.

Code Equal to	1	2	3	4
Go to		Inconnector reference	Inconnector reference	

Code Equal to	Go to
1	
2	Inconnector reference
3	Inconnector reference
4	

Table Title	Rules				
	1	2	3	· · ·	N
If: Condition stub	Condition entry				
Then: Action stub	Action entry				

FIGURE 2.20 Decision Table Format.

dition N, THEN Action 1, Action 2, Action N." Rules are numbered horizontally across the top of the table and represent the logical combinations of condition entries and action entries that constitute the decision process. There is one vertical row for each combination.

A decision table example is shown in Figure 2.21. As the figure shows, condition entries are usually limited to Y (for "true"), N (for "false"), or − (for "not applicable"). Action entries are listed as applicable or not applicable—the presence or absence of an "x" in Figure 2.21. The interpretation of rule 1 in Figure 2.21 is: IF conditions 1, 2, and 3 are Y, then take actions 10, 11, 12, and 14. The other rules are interpreted in the same manner.

FIGURE 2.21 Decision Table.

Organization ABC Company   Page ___1___ Of ___1___

System Labor Distribution   Project No. ____123____

Program Name Labor Dist. Print   No. ___LD01___   Revision Date ___3/26___

Prepared by W. Smith   Date ___2/26___   Approved by ____J. Jones____

Table Name:

Line	Condition Action Rule →	1	2	3	4	5	6	7	8		
1	15 Regular Hours	Y	–	–	–	N					
2	15 Overtime Hours	Y	–	N	–	Y	–	N			
3	15 Shift Bonus Hours	Y	N	Y	N	Y	N	Y	N		
10	Regular Dollars = Reg. Hours x (Hourly + .115)	x	x	x	x						
11	Overtime Dollars = Overtime Hrs. 150%	x	x								
12	Shift Dollars = Shift Bonus Hours = $10 x .10	x		x							
13	Error No Shift or OT without Reg. Hours					x	x	x			
14	Next Record	x	x	x	x	x	x	x			

If { lines 1–3 }
Then { lines 10–14 }

Go to - F (Function); R (Rule, Same Table); T (Table)

Notes: The error message at line 13 should be displayed in the "Dollars" area of the report, to the right of a dump of the 501 Record.

Condition Entries ("If")   { Y = True   N = False   − = Not applicable }   Action Entry ("Then")   { x = Take Action }

LIMITED ENTRY TABLE
Fig. 2.21

The type of decision table just discussed is called a limited-entry table because condition and action entries are restricted to Y, N, or not applicable. An extended-entry decision table might also be used where the entries indicate specific types of actions to be taken, specific conditions, or references to other decision tables. Decision tables might be used in lieu of program flowcharts to analyze and document the logic of an application program. The structure of the tabular format of a decision table is an important advantage compared to graphic flowcharts as the complexity of a decision process increases.

Matrix Methods

Matrix methods are used by both auditors and systems personnel. A decision table is essentially a matrix presentation. Matrices and array forms of presentation have many uses in systems work because they are a convenient method for analyzing and displaying a large volume of data. The "worksheets" or "spreadsheets" used in accounting systems to spread or distribute account balances through different subclassifications or to facilitate the closing process are common examples of matrix techniques. The essential analytical feature of matrix techniques is the spreading of the row entries through the various column entries. This assures that each row/column combination is explicitly analyzed and documented.

In an application control matrix, the row entries are controls, and the column entries are processing actions. This technique may be used systematically to evaluate the internal controls in an application system. In a data control matrix, the row entries are data elements, and the column entries are forms or reports. Analysis may be directed toward the elimination of redundant data on a set of forms or to the commonality of data on a set of reports.

SUMMARY

Systems techniques are used by both auditors and systems personnel as tools for analysis and documentation. Table 2.3 summarizes the many techniques described in this chapter and indicates the primary users of the technique. Systems techniques are necessary to a structured systems approach to the analysis and design of information systems. One popular and widely used system technique is flowcharting. Several different types of flowcharts were discussed and illustrated. Standard flowcharting symbols were defined and illustrated. Even though standard symbols are in widespread usage, flowcharting is more art than science.

Many other system techniques are used in addition to flowcharts. Logical data flow diagrams (DFDs) are frequently used in systems analysis and design. DFDs can be used to successively refine the design of a system. Branching and decision tables, IPO and HIPO charts, and matrix methods were also discussed and illustrated as they are used in system analysis and design.

Techniques used in resource utilization analysis and decision analysis were also illustrated. Although flowcharts, DFDs, and other graphic techniques are very useful, these techniques do not consider the question of system resource utilization. Work measurement techniques are necessary to address the important questions concerning how much or how many resources will be required for the operation of a system.

TABLE 2.3	Primary Users of Systems Techniques	
Analytic flowchart	Charts the flow of documents and processing between different entities, which are represented by separate columns in the chart	Auditor Systems analyst
Block flowchart	Synonym for program flowchart	Systems designer Programmer
Branching table	A tabular technique used to represent a decision function in a flowchart	Systems designer Programmer
Data flow diagram	A charting technique used to document the logical design of a system	Systems analyst Systems designer
Decision table	Used to supplement or replace the preparation of flowcharts when there are a large number of alternative decision paths	Systems designer Programmer
Document flowchart	A flowchart of document flow in which the only symbol used is the document symbol	Auditor Systems analyst
Flowchart	A symbolic diagram that shows the data flow and sequence of operations in a system	Auditor Systems analyst Systems designer Programmer
Forms distribution chart	Illustrates the distribution of multiple-copy documents within an organization	Auditor Systems analyst Systems designer
HIPO chart (Hierarchy plus Input–Process–Output)	An organized collection of IPO charts	Systems analyst Systems designer
IPO chart (Input–Process–Output)	Describes the inputs necessary to produce certain outputs, and generally provides very little detail concerning the required processing	Systems analyst Systems designer
Logical data flow diagram	Synonym for data flow diagram	Systems analyst Systems designer
Program flowchart	A flowchart indicating detailed processing functions	Systems designer Programmer
Systems flowchart	A pictorial or graphical representation of the overall flow of work, documents, and operations in an application system	Auditor Systems analyst Systems designer
Work measurement	Techniques used to measure activities in a production framework	Systems analyst Systems designer
Work distribution analysis	Techniques used to rationally assign work to entities	Auditor Systems analyst System designer

Glossary

additional symbols: a group of flowchart symbols in ANSI X3.5, consisting of miscellaneous symbols that make flowcharting more convenient.

analytic flowchart: charts the flow of documents and processing between different entities—which are represented by separate columns in the chart—in a system.

basic symbols: one of the four groups of flowchart symbols in ANSI X3.5, consisting of symbols that correspond to the basic data processing functions.

block flowchart: synonym for program flowchart.

branching table: a tabular technique used to represent a decision function in a flowchart.

data flow diagram (DFD): a charting technique used to document the logical design of a system.

decision table: used to supplement or replace the preparation of flowcharts when there are a large number of alternative decision paths.

document flowchart: a flowchart of document flow in a system in which the only symbol used is the document symbol.

forms distribution chart: illustrates the distribution of multiple-copy documents within an organization.

HIPO chart (hierarchy plus input–process–output): an organized collection of IPO charts.

IPO chart (input–process–output): describes the inputs necessary to produce certain outputs, and generally provides very little detail concerning the required processing.

logical data flow diagram (DFD): synonym for data flow diagram.

program flowchart: a flowchart indicating detailed processing functions.

sandwich rule: the flowcharting principle that every process symbol should be "sandwiched" between an input symbol and an output symbol.

specialized input/output symbols: a group of flowchart symbols in ANSI X3.5, consisting of symbols that can be used to represent input/output and also the medium on which the information is recorded.

specialized process symbols: a group of flowchart symbols in ANSI X3.5, consisting of symbols that can be used to represent processing and, in addition, identify the specific type of operation to be performed.

systems flowchart: a pictorial or graphical representation of the overall flow of work, documents, and operations in an application system.

systems techniques: tools used in the analysis, design, and documentation of systems.

work distribution analysis: techniques used to rationally assign work to entities.

work measurement: techniques used to measure activities in a production framework.

Chapter Quiz

Answers to the Chapter Quiz appear on page 70.

1. The group concerned with establishing standards for flowchart symbols is
   (a) ASCII.
   (b) EBCDIC.
   (c) ANSI.
   (d) AICPA.

2. A pictorial or graphical representation of the overall flow of work, documents, and operations in an application system is shown in a(n)
   (a) IPO chart.
   (b) forms distribution chart.
   (c) systems flowchart.
   (d) process chart.

3. Which type of diagram emphasizes the physical description of a system?
   (a) analytic flowchart
   (b) logical data flow diagram (DFD)
   (c) HIPO
   (d) IPO

4. ANSI X3.5-1970—the information system flowcharting standards published by the American National Standards Institute—defines four groups of flowchart symbols and illustrates conventions regarding their use. Which of the following is *not* one of these groups?
   (a) specialized input/output symbols
   (b) specialized processing symbols
   (c) branching and decision table symbols
   (d) basic symbols

5. Structured systems analysis can best be referred to as
   (a) a process of increasingly complex sets of controls.
   (b) a process of successive refinement.
   (c) a procedure for documenting process logic.
   (d) a statement of decision tables.

6. An important omission from flowcharts and matrix techniques is
   (a) the ability to represent decisions.
   (b) the ability to include internal control considerations.
   (c) the ability to incorporate error conditions.
   (d) the ability to specify systems resource requirements.

7. Which of the following items would be most useful in analyzing the separation of duties and functions in an application system?
   (a) document flowchart
   (b) program flowchart
   (c) HIPO chart
   (d) source document

8. In the preparation of a logical data flow diagram for a payroll processing application, which of the following symbols should be used to indicate the payroll data?
   (a) terminator symbol
   (b) data store symbol
   (c) process symbol
   (d) input/output symbol

9. In the preparation of an analytic flowchart for a payroll processing application, which of the following symbols could be used to indicate the payroll data?
   (a) connector symbol
   (b) decision symbol
   (c) process symbol
   (d) input/output symbol

10. In the preparation of an analytic flowchart, which of the following symbols should be used when flowlines are broken due to a page limitation?
    (a) terminal symbol
    (b) connector symbol
    (c) manual operation symbol
    (d) input/output symbol

Review Problem

This review problem involves a manual system. A service request form (two copies) is prepared in the production department. Copy 2 is forwarded to the repair and maintenance department. Copy 1 is filed in the production department.

In the repair and maintenance department, copy 2 of the service request is used to manually prepare a four-part work order form. Copy 2 of the service request form is then filed in the repair and maintenance department. Copy 4 of the work order form is forwarded to the production department to acknowledge the service request. Copy 3 of the work order form is filed in the repair and maintenance department. Clerks in the repair and maintenance department manually record actual materials and supplies used and labor time required onto copies 1 and 2 of the work order. When the work order is completed, copy 1 is filed in the repair and maintenance department, and copy 2 is forwarded to the accounting department.

Clerks in the accounting department manually complete a detailed costing of copy 2 of the work order and prepare a work order summary report (three copies). Copy 2 of the work order is filed in the accounting department. Copy 1 of the work order summary is forwarded it to the production department. Copy 2 of the work or-

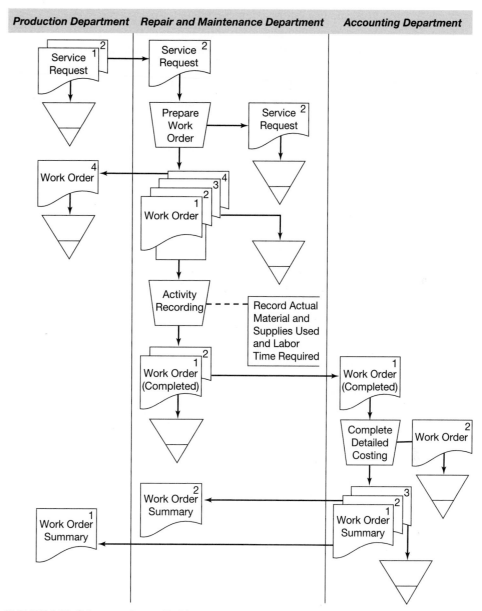

FIGURE 2.22 Solution to Review Problem.

der summary is forwarded to the repair and maintenance department. Copy 3 of the work order summary is filed in the accounting department.

Required
Prepare an analytic flowchart of the previous procedures. (See Figure 2.22 for the solution.)

Review Questions

1. Define flowcharting.
2. List and draw the basic flowchart symbols.

3. Flowchart symbols represent what aspect of a system?
4. Distinguish between IPO and HIPO charts.
5. What is the difference between a systems flowchart and an analytic flowchart?
6. A logical data flow diagram can be used to document what aspect of a system?
7. Why do auditors prepare analytic flowcharts of processing systems?
8. What important feature is common to analytic, document, and forms distribution charts?
9. Identify the symbols that are used to construct logical data flow diagrams.
10. Is flowcharting useful in analyzing the resources required to implement a system?
11. Relate the concept of work measurement to the system implementation process.
12. Outline the steps involved in a work distribution analysis.

Discussion Questions and Problems

Questions 13 through 15 are based on the section of a system flowchart for a payroll application shown in Figure 2.23.

13. Symbol A could represent
    (a) computation of gross pay.
    (b) input of payroll data.
    (c) preparation of paychecks.
    (d) verification of pay rates.
14. Symbol B could represent
    (a) computation of net pay.
    (b) separation of erroneous time cards.
    (c) validation of payroll data.
    (d) preparation of the payroll register.

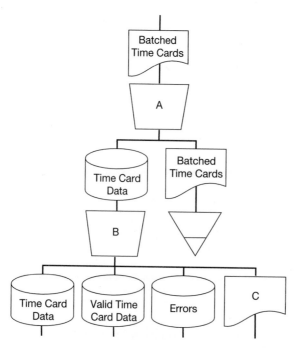

FIGURE 2.23 Section of a System Flowchart for a Payroll Application.

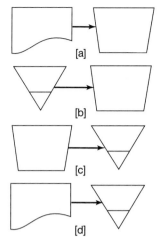

FIGURE 2.24 Symbolic Representations for Problem 16.

15. Symbol C could represent
    (a) batched time cards.
    (b) unclaimed payroll checks.
    (c) erroneous time cards.
    (d) an error report.

(CPA)

16. Which of the symbolic representations in Figure 2.24 indicates that a sales invoice has been filed?

(CPA)

17. During the review of an EDP internal control system an auditor may review decision tables prepared by the client. A decision table is usually prepared by a client to supplement or replace the preparation of
    (a) an internal control questionnaire when the number of alternative responses is large.
    (b) a narrative description of a system where transactions are not processed in batches.
    (c) flowcharts when the number of alternatives is large.
    (d) an internal control questionnaire not specifically designed for an EDP installation.

(CPA)

18. Which of the symbolic representations in Figure 2.25 indicate that a file has been consulted?

(CPA)

19. The XYZ Company distributes three product lines to seven customers. Sales are manually recorded on invoices. Separate invoices are always used to record sales of product line number 1. Sales of the other two product lines are always recorded together on a single invoice.

    The manager would like to know the total daily sales of each product line in dollars and also the daily sales total for each product line sold to each customer.

    To develop this information manually, the manager will collect all the invoices at the end of each day. A separate worksheet will be used to record the daily sales total for each product line. Each worksheet will have seven columns with separate headings—one for each customer. The manager will record each day's sales totals on a separate line of each worksheet.

    Design a system with the specific steps necessary to develop and record the desired information from the daily batch of sales invoices.

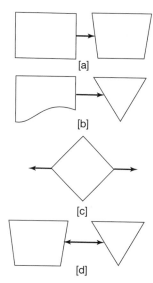

FIGURE 2.25 Symbolic Representations for Problem 18.

20. The HRZ Company maintains a perpetual inventory system. Clerks in the accounting department post the data manually from receiving reports, materials requisition forms, copies of purchase orders, and other transactions, such as returns and adjustments to the inventory records. The source documents are filed by posting date. The inventory records are analyzed after each posting to determine if the item should be reordered. If an item needs to be reordered, a purchase requisition (one copy) is prepared and sent to the purchasing department. There, clerks select a vendor from a master vendor file, prepare a purchase order (four copies), and update the vendor file to reflect the order. The purchase order is approved and distributed as follows: original copy to the vendor; copy 2 is filed numerically with the corresponding purchase requisition attached; copy 3 is forwarded to the receiving department; copy 4 is sent to the accounting department.

    Required
    (a) Prepare an analytic flowchart of the previous procedures.
    (b) Prepare a logical data flow diagram of the previous procedures.

21. Prepare a logical data flow diagram for each of the following application systems. Your chart should include the major processing modules you feel should be identified with each application system. Be sure to label all data flows between modules and to include all relevant sources and destinations of data.
    (a) sales order application system
    (b) purchase application system
    (c) production control application system
    (d) cash disbursement application system

22. A systems analyst has asked you for advice concerning the construction of a logical data flow diagram for the process of validating a user ID, which is input from a data terminal, to request access to a computer system. Criticize the DFD that has been prepared by the systems analyst (see Figure 2.26).

23. You are reviewing audit work papers containing a narrative description of the Tenney Corporation's factory payroll system. A portion of that narrative is as follows:

    Factory employees punch time clock cards each day when entering or leaving the shop. At the end of each week the timekeeping department collects the time cards and prepares duplicate batch control slips by department, showing total hours and number of employees. The time cards and original batch control slips are sent to the

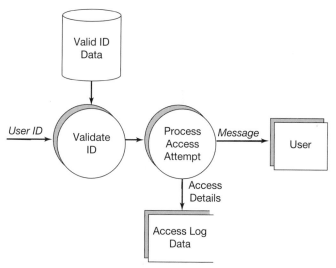

FIGURE 2.26 DFD for Problem 22.

payroll accounting section. The second copies of the batch control slips are filed by date.

In the payroll accounting section, payroll transaction records are input from the information on the time cards, and a batch total record for each batch is input from the batch control slip. These records are input to magnetic disk. The time cards and batch control slips are then filed by batch for possible reference. The payroll transaction file is sent to data processing, where it is sorted by employee number within batch. Each batch is edited by a computer program, which checks the validity of employee number against a master employee disk file and the total hours and number of employees against the batch total record. A detailed printout by batch and employee number is produced, which indicates batches that do not balance and invalid employee numbers. This printout is returned to payroll accounting to resolve all differences.

In searching for documentation you found a flowchart (Figure 2.27) of the payroll system, which included all appropriate symbols (American National Standards Institute) but was only partially labeled.

Required

(a) Number your answer 1 through 16. Next to the corresponding number, supply the appropriate labeling (document name, process description, or file order) applicable to each numbered symbol on the flowchart.

(b) Flowcharts are one of the aids an auditor can use to determine and evaluate a client's internal control system. List advantages of using flowcharts in this context.

(CPA)

24. Harvard Square Software Company uses a manual sales order processing system. Sales order forms (three copies) are prepared by the sales department and forwarded to the accounting department. In the accounting department, an invoice (three copies) and a shipping order (four copies) are manually prepared on the basis of the sales order. One copy each of the sales order, the invoice, and the shipping order are forwarded to the sales department. A copy of the sales order is attached to two copies of the shipping order and then forwarded to the shipping department. One copy of the invoice is forwarded to the customer. The remaining documents are attached to each other and then filed in the accounting department by sales order number.

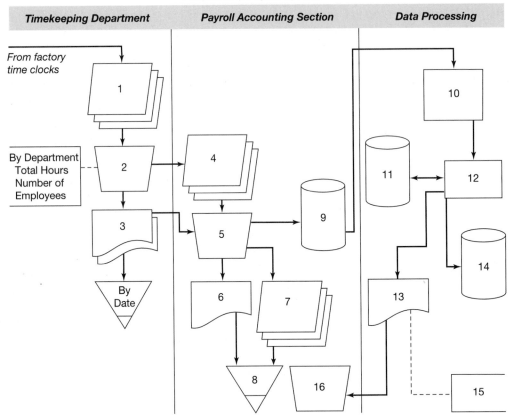

Tenney Corporation
Flowchart of Payroll System

FIGURE 2.27 Flowchart for Problem 23.

Required
Prepare an analytic flowchart of the previous procedures.

25. Batches of customer payments on account are manually processed in the cashier's office. Clerks open the payments, separate the checks and the remittance advices, and prepare a batch control total (two copies) of the remittances. The checks are manually processed to prepare a deposit slip (two copies). Copy 1 of the deposit slip and the batch of checks are forwarded for deposit at the bank. Copy 2 of the deposit slip is verified to copy 1 of the batch control total, attached to it, and then filed in the cashier's office, by date. Copy 2 of the batch control total is forwarded to the general ledger department. The remittance advices are forwarded to the accounts receivable department.

Clerks in the accounts receivable department manually post the remittance advices to the accounts receivable ledger. The remittance advices are then filed in the accounts receivable department by customer number.

Required
Prepare an analytic flowchart of the previous procedures.

26. Production workers prepare materials requisition forms (four copies) and forward them to the production supervisor for approval. The materials requisition form is then forwarded to stores. In stores, the order is filled and the materials requisition form is signed by a clerk. The clerk then returns copy 1 of the materials requisition form along with the materials to the production workers. Copy 2 of the materials req-

uisition form is forwarded to the production supervisor. Copy 4 is forwarded to the cost accounting department. Copy 3 of the materials requisition form is used in stores to manually post the materials that were issued to the perpetual inventory records. Copy 4 is then filed in stores by number.

Required

Prepare an analytic flowchart of the previous procedures.

27. Collateral Deposit (Part 1).[2] (This case is continued as Problem 59 in Chapter 5.)

Dan Matt, a junior auditor for Kramp and Company, was assigned the responsibility of conducting a preliminary application review of a client bank's loan department operations.

Dan had completed his flowchart and explanation of the loan process and turned it over to his senior. He was writing up his assessment of the process from his notes when his senior interrupted and asked what happened to the collateral received on loans. Dan recognized the significance of this omission and agreed to check it out right away.

Collateral can be anything of value acceptable to the bank but is typically some type of security. Dan found that customers turn over any collateral to their loan officer, who prepares and signs the next in sequence of a prenumbered four-part form that describes the collateral and serves as a receipt. Each copy of the form is a different color to facilitate identification. The customer receives the original of the collateral receipt form, which is pink. The second, or white, copy of the form is sent directly to the collateral records clerk, who logs it in. The loan officer takes the blue, or third, copy to the vault custodian along with the collateral. The final, or yellow, copy is canceled and discarded. The vault custodian compares the blue copy of the receipt with the collateral in the loan officer's presence. If they agree, the vault custodian signs the blue copy. He or she then attaches a tag to the collateral and carries it and the blue copy of the collateral receipt to the vault attendant. The vault attendant also compares the description on the blue copy with the tagged collateral. If they match, the vault attendant opens the vault and jointly with the vault custodian deposits the collateral within. The vault attendant notes the location on the blue copy and signs it. The completed blue copy is then taken by the vault attendant to the collateral clerk. Until the blue copy is received, the collateral clerk keeps the unmatched white copy, filed numerically in a suspense file as a reminder for follow-up purposes.

Upon receiving the blue copy from the vault attendant, the collateral clerk compares it to the white copy previously received directly from the loan officer. If the blue and white copies match, the collateral clerk completes the entry in the collateral register in numerical order. The white copy and the blue copy of the collateral receipt are placed in a permanent file by name. Any differences are resolved with the loan officer's assistance.

List of Procedures

Customer

1. Brings in collateral to loan officer
2. Receives receipt for collateral

Loan Officer

3. Receives collateral from customer
4. Removes prenumbered four-part form from file
5. Completes form describing collateral and signs it

---

[2]Prepared by Frederick L. Neumann, Richard J. Boland, and Jeffrey Johnson: funded by The Touche Ross Foundation Aid to Accounting Education Program.

6. Gives pink copy to customer
7. Sends white copy to collateral clerk
8. Takes blue copy to vault custodian
9. Cancels and discards yellow copy
10. Takes collateral in sealed bags to vault custodian

Vault Custodian

11. Receives blue copy of collateral receipt from loan officer
12. Receives collateral from loan officer
13. Reads description and instructions regarding collateral on blue copy
14. Compares collateral with blue copy
15. Signs blue copy
16. Gives blue copy to vault attendant
17. Opens vault jointly with vault attendant
18. Deposits collateral in vault

Vault Attendant

19. Receives blue copy from vault custodian
20. Compares blue copy to collateral being deposited
21. Assists vault custodian in opening vault
22. Signs blue copy upon witnessing deposit of collateral
23. Takes blue copy to collateral clerk

Collateral Clerk

24. Receives white copy from loan officer
25. Makes entry in numerical sequence in log book
26. Holds white copy until later receipt of blue copy
27. Matches blue copy when received to white copy and notes appropriate signatures
28. Records deposit of collateral in collateral register
29. Files collateral receipt copies in permanent file

Required

Prepare a flowchart of the collateral receipt process and cross-reference it to the list of procedures provided.

28. A partially completed charge sales systems flowchart is shown in Figure 2.28. The flowchart depicts the charge sales activities of the Bottom Manufacturing Corporation.

A customer's purchase order is received and a six-part sales order is prepared from it. The six copies are initially distributed as follows:

Copy 1—Billing copy—to billing department
Copy 2—Shipping copy—to shipping department
Copy 3—Credit copy—to credit department
Copy 4—Stock request copy—to credit department
Copy 5—Customer copy—to customer
Copy 6—Sales order copy—file in sales order department

When each copy of the sales order reaches the applicable department or destination, it calls for specific internal control procedures and related documents. Some of the procedures and related documents are indicated on the flowchart. Other procedures and documents are labeled letters *a* to *r*.

Required

List the procedures of the internal documents that are labeled letters *c* to *r* in the flowchart of Bottom Manufacturing Corporation's charge sales system.

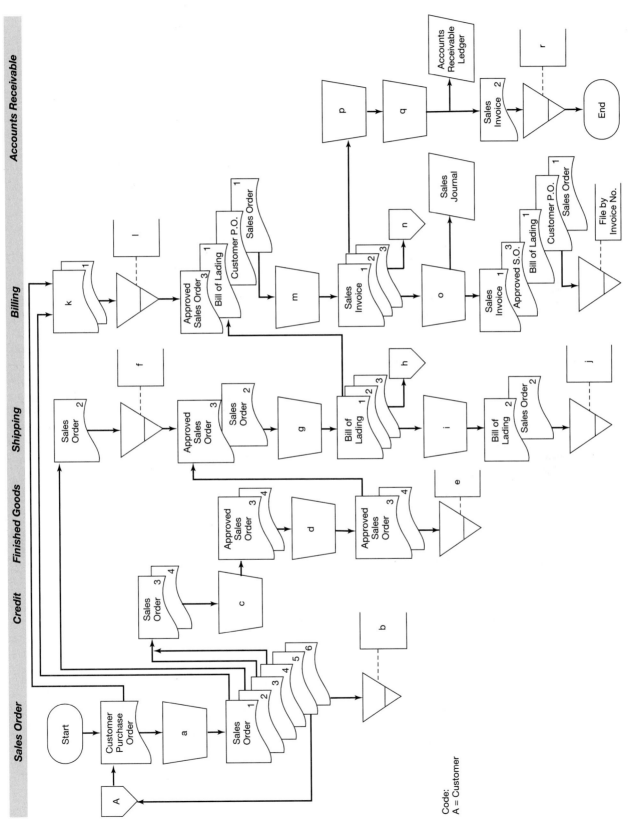

FIGURE 2.28 Flowchart for Problem 28.

Organize your answer as follows (explanations of the letters *a* and *b*, which appear in the flowchart, are entered as examples):

Flowchart Symbol Letter	Procedures or Internal Document
a	Prepare six-part sales order
b	File by order number

(CPA)

29. Figure 2.29 illustrates a manual system for executing purchases and cash disbursements transactions.

    Required
    Indicate what each of the letters *A* through *L* represents.

(CPA)

30. An analyst wishes to prepare a decision table for purchase order procedures. First, there is a credit check of the customer. If credit is approved, the order is accepted. If the order calls for 0–25 units, there is no discount on the order. If the order calls for 26–55 units, it is eligible for a 5% discount; if more than 55 units are ordered, the discount is 10%.

    Required
    (a) Prepare a limited-entry decision table.
    (b) Prepare an extended-entry decision table.

31. An analyst wishes to document credit card purchase authorization procedures in a decision table. A purchase under $50 is approved automatically. Purchases between $50 and $100 are given an authorization number. For purchases over $100 a "hold" is placed on the customer's account in addition to an authorization number being assigned to the purchase.

    Required
    (a) Prepare a limited-entry decision table.
    (b) Prepare an extended-entry decision table.

32. Analyze the following data incident to machine posting of checks drawn by bank depositors:

Number of checks posted	570
Total elapsed minutes	480
Rest period minutes	20
Interruption and delay minutes	20

    Develop a standard time per check. In terms of percentage, what is the rest and delay allowance?

33. The Big Plastic Company manufactures a variety of plastic utensils, employing approximately 400 factory workers. Supervisors are paid a salary for a 40-hour week but receive overtime for hours worked in excess of 40. Supervisors record hours worked on a weekly time card, clocking in and out at the beginning and end of each day.

    Factory workers are paid on an hourly basis. Activity rates are assigned to the operation of various machines in the factory; a worker assigned to a machine is paid the higher of either the machine's activity rate or the standard hourly pay rate. Workers clock in and out of each assigned activity on a daily basis. Supervisors record the activity code and elapsed time for each entry on a machine operator's daily time card. Supervisors maintain a record of machine operator overtime. All workers must account for 8 hours a day, and receive time-and-a-half for hours worked in excess of 8 per day.

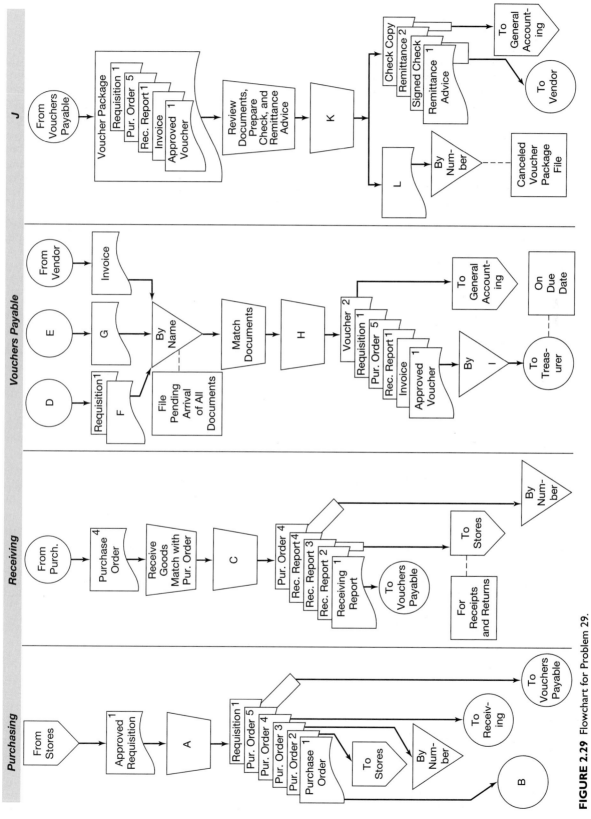

FIGURE 2.29 Flowchart for Problem 29.

A timekeeper collects time cards on a daily basis. Supervisors' time cards are collected at the end of each week. Time cards are compared to an authorized employee list, initialed by the timekeeper, and forwarded to the payroll department.

In the payroll department, a clerk verifies the timekeeper's initials, batches the cards in groups of 40 or fewer cards, and prepares a prenumbered batch control form for each batch. This form contains total regular hours, overtime hours, date, and number of documents in the batch. The payroll clerk transcribes the contents of each batch control form onto an input batch control log to record and maintain control of each batch. The time cards are then submitted to the computer processing department, where they are key-transcribed, verified, and processed by a payroll system edit program to produce a detailed listing of the input items. At the end of the listing, control totals are printed for the valid and rejected items. If any item in a batch is rejected, then all items in the batch are rejected to maintain batch integrity. The payroll clerk corrects rejected items, prepares a new batch control form, using the original batch number and a suffix to identify the batch as a correction batch, and resubmits the batch to the computer processing department. This procedure is repeated throughout the week until all errors have been corrected.

The payroll is processed weekly to produce an updated payroll master file, employee checks, and payroll register. These reports are distributed to the payroll department, where a reconciliation with the input controls is performed.

Required
Flowchart the preceding payroll procedure.

34. Prepare a program flowchart for the following application. This application calculates straight-line depreciation for a file of fixed assets. The fixed-asset file consists of the following record types:

   (a) A header record, which contains the file ID number and a hash total of all of the record ID (key) values.

   (b) A record for each fixed asset. Each record contains the following fields: ID number, a location code, original cost, useful life in months, depreciation taken to date, and salvage value.

   The program should read each fixed-asset record, compute the amount of depreciation for the year (12 months), update the necessary fields, and write the updated record. End-of-job processing should print the number of assets processed, print the total depreciation computed, and verify the hash total for this run.

35. Modify the previous problem to compute depreciation by the double-declining balance method.

Answers to Chapter Quiz

1. C	**4.** C	**7.** A	**10.** B
2. C	**5.** B	**8.** B	
3. A	**6.** D	**9.** D	

CHAPTER 3

The Internet, Intranets, and Electronic Commerce

LEARNING OBJECTIVES

Careful study of this chapter will enable you to:

- Explain the history of the Internet and how it works.

- Describe intranets and explain how they are made secure.

- Explain client-server technology and how it applies to electronic financial transactions.

- Describe various approaches to securing electronic financial transactions.

ELECTRONIC COMMERCE

Electronic Networks

A great many of the business transactions in today's business environment are transmitted over some type of electronic network. The network may be very small and involve only a handful of computers within a single business, or it may be so large that it encompasses the entire globe. Either way, **electronic networks** are groups of computers that are connected together electronically. They make it possible for companies to conveniently assemble transaction data and distribute information across multiple physical locations.

LANs, MANs, and WANs

Networks are sometimes classified according to the distance they span. **Local area networks (LANs)** are networks that span a single site, such as a building or a group of buildings that are in close proximity to one another. **Metropolitan area networks (MANs)** are networks that span a single city or metropolitan area, and, finally, **wide area networks (WANs)** are networks of computers that span at least two metropolitan areas. From a practical point of view, the main difference between these three types of networks is the rate at which data flow through them. Due to hardware technology, data flow the fastest through local area networks and the slowest through wide area networks. But from the standpoint of the processing of accounting transactions, these differences in the rates of the flows of data are not usually critical because individual accounting transactions involve only small amounts of data. For example, the data in a typical sales order might amount to only a couple of hundred characters of data. Accordingly, in less than 1 second the typical sales transaction can just as easily move from one state to the next as it can from one building to the next.

In the past, each of the three types of networks used its own hardware and software standards, and in practice such standards even varied from one computer vendor to the next. The result was an environment in which companies more often chose to communicate with each other via the U.S. mail rather than by computer. But the Internet has brought universal standards of communication to all networks, and with today's technology it is possible for any type of computer in any type of network to conveniently exchange information with any other computer in the world.

The Internet

The **Internet** is an electronic highway, consisting of various standards and protocols, that allows computers everywhere to communicate with each other. The best way to fully explain the Internet is to explain some of its history. The roots of the Internet go all the way back to the 1960s during the Cold War era when the U.S. government was in search of a means of maintaining military communications in the event of a nuclear war.

The government's problem was tackled by the RAND Corporation, which came up with two amazing suggestions: (1) The network should have no central command-and-control center, and (2) the network should be able to operate in tatters from the very beginning. These goals were achieved by making every node (i.e., computer) in the network operate independently. Furthermore, the physical path connecting one computer to another was considered unimportant. Specifically, computers in Boston and New York could communicate directly with each other, or alternatively, they could just as easily communicate with each other through an intermediate computer in, say, Chicago, Los Angeles, or Miami. This way, if one link in the network were destroyed, the computers in the network could continue to communicate with each other through the remaining links. Therefore, the network would be able to withstand a nuclear attack.

The earliest practical version of the Internet was created in the early 1970s by the Pentagon's Advanced Research Projects Agency (ARPA); it was called ARPANET. Originally, this network was used to allow the military to spread its computing tasks across several computers, but soon something unexpected happened: Users of the network began sending each other electronic mail containing news and personal messages.

While ARPANET grew, others networks (such as Bitnet, MILnet, and NSFnet) sprung up. Eventually they adopted a common set of communications protocols called TCP/IP (Transmission Control Protocol/Internet Protocol). **TCP** is a protocol for dividing electronic messages into "packets" of information and then reassembling these packets at the receiving end. **IP,** on the other hand, is an addressing protocol that assigns a unique address to each computer on the Internet. The TCP/IP protocols soon spread throughout the entire world and now constitute the universal standard for virtually all long-distance Internet communications.

Despite the universality of its communication protocols, the Internet has developed very much into the type of network that the RAND Corporation envisioned decades ago. That is, the Internet has no central command-and-control structure, and it operates more or less under the principle of anarchy. There is no

"Internet Corporation" or "Internet Agency." Rather, the Internet operates more like a public park, where anyone can come and talk to anyone else in the park, using any language he or she chooses.

Still, many groups of individuals have found it desirable to adopt their own special technologies for communicating across the Internet. Some of these technologies are discussed later. First, some basics of Internet addresses are discussed.

Internet Addresses. Every computer or user on the Internet needs an **IP (Internet Protocol) address** to communicate with other computers on the Internet. The IP address consists of a long number separated by periods. For example, a typical IP address will look something like 207.49.159.2. IP addresses are typically obtained from an organization such as InterNIC, which manages and distributes them to the general public. Most organizations obtain a group of IP addresses that they in turn allocate to their individual users. In some cases, organizations permanently allocate each user a personal IP address. From the user's standpoint, his or her IP address always remains the same. Such an IP address is called a **fixed IP address.** Fixed IP addresses are generally necessary for users whose computers are connected to the Internet 24 hours per day, or for very long periods of time. On the other hand, some organizations only temporarily allocate IP addresses to users. This is helpful when an organization has, say 100 users and only ten IP addresses to allocate. In this case the organization will allocate IP addresses to users only while they are accessing the Internet. When a individual user disconnects from the Internet, his or her IP address is returned to the pool for someone else to use. This type of IP address is called a **dynamic IP address,** which is one that is temporarily assigned to a user while he or she is accessing the Internet.

Since IP addresses are long and difficult to remember, procedures have been created whereby easy-to-remember alias names can be used instead. For example, the name www.bodhop.ais.com, might be used in place of 131.91.120.68. This name, www.bodhop.ais, is called the **domain name,** which is simply an alias name that can be used in place of the IP number. Domain names and their corresponding IP addresses are kept in electronic "phone books" at many sites on the Internet. These electronic phone books are called **domain name servers** (DNSs).

Most Internet-related software allows the user to address another computer by its domain name. The user's software then automatically contacts a nearby DNS and finds the related IP number, which is then used to complete the user's request. This whole lookup process normally takes only a fraction of a second and the user rarely needs to be concerned with it.

Intranets

The various protocols and technologies relating to the Internet have become so popular that many companies have adopted them for in-house communications over local area networks. This phenomenon has given rise to self-contained, in-house internets, or **intranets.**

For those inside the organization the intranet may appear to be part of the Internet. That is, employees of the organization may access the company's repositories of information in the same way they access similar resources anywhere on the Internet. The only difference is that the entire intranet may be completely invisible or unavailable to outsiders. Alternatively, all or part of the intranet may be available to outsiders only after they are properly authenticated.

A variation on the intranet is the extranet. **Extranets** exist when the intranets of two or more companies are linked together. Typical extranets involve the linking of a company's intranet with the intranets of its suppliers or customers.

Intranet Security Issues. Needless to say, intranets pose considerable security risks by potentially exposing the organization's sensitive information to everyone on the Internet. For this reason, many companies use combinations of hardware and software called firewalls to limit access from outsiders. **Firewalls** (Figure 3.1) limit access to information on the company's servers from the rest of the world. Specifically, in the typical situation the only way an outsider can access information in the company's intranet is through a single point guarded by a firewall.

Firewalls typically filter each packet of incoming information to ensure that it has originated from an authorized source. One common approach to such packet filtering is IP filtering, which blocks out incoming packets that don't originate from preauthorized IP addresses. The list of preauthorized IP address is an example of an **access control list.** This list is normally maintained by network administrators.

Firewalls can also filter packets based on their content or destination. But unfortunately, like all security measures, filtering-type firewalls can be defeated. For example, outsiders with the right combination of hardware and software can **"spoof"** an IP address. That is, they can send incoming information requests that falsely appear to come from an authorized IP address. For this reason firewalls should serve only as the first line of defense in a system of layered defenses. The additional layers will normally include encryption and access limits through password control.

Another type of security device used with intranets is the proxy server. **Proxy servers** are typically used on the inside of the company's firewall and serve

FIGURE 3.1 Firewall.

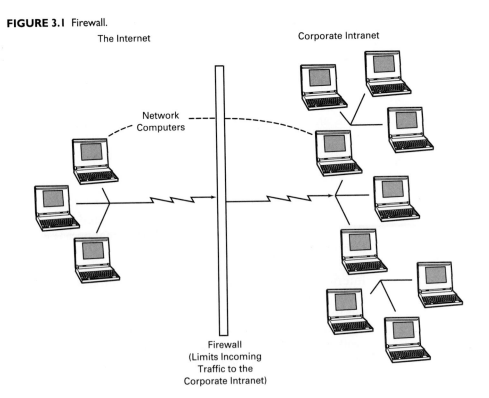

The Internet

Corporate Intranet

Network Computers

Firewall
(Limits Incoming
Traffic to the
Corporate Intranet)

as filters for all outgoing requests for information. Specifically, all requested accesses to addresses outside of the company are sent to the proxy server. The proxy server then analyzes each request and determines if it is being made by an authorized individual to an authorized site on the Internet. (The list of authorized individuals and sites is maintained on an access control list.) If the request is valid, it is then passed through the proxy server; otherwise the request is blocked. For example, consider the situation in which a company employee requests a Web page located at www.games.fun. If the company doesn't want its employees playing games, the proxy server can block the request, and the employee will receive an error message indicating that the requested Internet address is not available.

Proxy servers can also operate in reverse, filtering incoming requests, thus preventing access to specific locations inside the organization. Reverse proxying provides a type of firewall. As compared to firewalls, proxy servers tend to be more sophisticated and support features such as password authentication and sophisticated transaction logging.

Proxy servers are useful not only for security but also for efficiency because proxy servers can store frequently requested information in a cache. This allows the proxy server to quickly supply information that is already in the cache; there is no need for the server to forward the request to the destination site on the Internet. One major Internet service provider (ISP) uses a proxy server for all its subscribers, and about 50% of all requests for information come from the proxy server's cache.

Commerce on the Internet

Client-Server Technology

The Internet can be used to transmit almost any kind of information between two points. However, certain important patterns of usage have emerged that evolved around client-server technology. A **server** is a robot-type program that constantly runs on some computer and exchanges information with users who request it. Users' programs that access and exchange information with servers are called **clients.**

A great many of the business transactions that occur on the Internet take place in client-server environments. There are several reasons for this:

1. Being robots, servers don't get paid by the hour and don't require fringe benefits.
2. Servers can, in some cases, deal with hundreds or even thousands of users (clients) at one time. Most humans, on the other hand, can deal with only one user at a time.
3. Servers can be accessed at any time of day, anywhere in the world, with no per-minute communication charges.

There are many kinds of servers on the Internet, including mail servers, file servers, Web servers, and commerce servers. Each of these types is discussed.

Types of Servers

Mail servers act as electronic mailboxes that hold incoming electronic mail until the user's client program requests it. They also serve as relay stations for outgoing mail, holding it until the intended recipient's mail server is able to receive it (Figure 3.2). The most common type of mail server on the Internet uses the POP protocol, and for this reason it is often referred to as a POP server. Most POP servers are accessed by clients with an account name and password. The server hands over any new incoming mail to the client and then picks up outgoing mail.

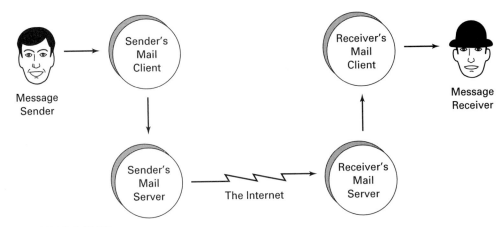

FIGURE 3.2 Mail Server.

Electronic mail (e-mail) messages are normally addressed according to the following form: username@domain_name. For example, one might use the address President@Whitehouse.Gov. The last three letters of the domain name provide information regarding the type of organization to which the message is being sent. "Gov" obviously refers to the government. Similarly, "Mil" refers to the military, "Com" refers to a commercial enterprise, and "Edu" refers to an educational institution. Various other suffixes also exist.

A second type of server is a file server. File servers exist mainly as repositories of files. That is, **file servers** allow authorized clients to retrieve files from libraries of files that exist on remote computers. For example, a company might use a file server to make copies of its annual report available over the Internet to the public. File servers can also receive files. For example, sales persons throughout the United States might prepare daily sales reports and then transfer them to headquarters through the company's file server.

The most common protocol for file servers is called FTP, and a file server that uses this protocol is called an **FTP server.** Because many client programs have the FTP protocol built into them, the actual use of the protocol may be transparent to the user.

A third type of server is called a Web server, and this type of server is by far the one that is used most often on the Internet. A **Web server** is a server that allows a user (client) to access documents and run computer programs that reside on remote computers. Web servers are the engines that run the **World Wide Web,** which consists of all the documents, files, and software on the Internet that are available through Web servers. The clients that access Web servers are called Web browsers. Microsoft Internal Explorer and Netscape Navigator are examples of Web browsers.

As with many other things on the Internet, there exists a protocol that specifies the format of documents on the World Wide Web, namely **HTML** (hypertext markup language). All Web clients automatically read and interpret HTML and convert the remote documents into a format that is easily readable by the user.

One thing that makes HTML especially important is that it provides for the embedding of hyperlinks in Web documents. **Hyperlinks** are pointers to other documents that may be either on the same Web server or any other Web server on the Internet (Figure 3.3). With most Web clients, pointing the mouse at a hyperlink causes the related document to be displayed on the computer screen.

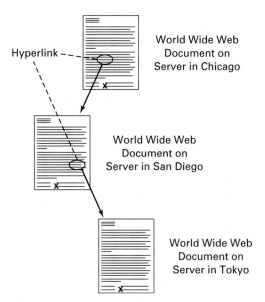

FIGURE 3.3 Hyperlinked Documents on the World Wide Web.

And, of course, the related document may also contain additional hyperlinks of its own.

A Web document is normally located by a combination of the domain name associated with the server and the document file name. For example, a document with the file name index.html on the server with domain name www.bodhop.ais.com might be located with the name http://www.bodhop.ais.com/index.html. This name for a Web document's location is called the **URL** (uniform resource locator).

A **Web site** is a collection of related documents, files, and programs that falls under the control of one individual, the **Web Master.** A given Web server is therefore capable of hosting many different Web sites, with each individual Web site being managed by its own Web master. Similarly, one FTP server is capable of hosting more than one FTP site. But many Web servers have FTP capabilities, and separate Web and FTP servers are often unnecessary.

Commerce servers are specialized types of Web servers with various commerce-related features (Figure 3.4). Such special features may include:

1. Support for the **Secure Electronic Transaction (SET)** protocol. This protocol involves encrypting all communications between the client and the server, thus ensuring that transactions are private and free from outside manipulation.

2. Support for specialized types of client and server authentication, such as digital certificates, which positively assures both the client and the server of each other's identity.

3. Support for interfacing with "external" programs. This type of support makes it possible for the client to use exchange information with accounting programs and databases that may reside on the server's computer. Examples of external program support include the **CGI** (Common Gateway Interface), **JAVA**™, and **ActiveX**™ languages. CGI is a means for the client to run programs on the server system. On the other hand, JAVA is more sophisticated and allows the server to pass programs to the client for execution on the client machine.

4. Enhanced security features such as multilevel security access and detailed transaction logging.

5. On-line credit card or bank verification.

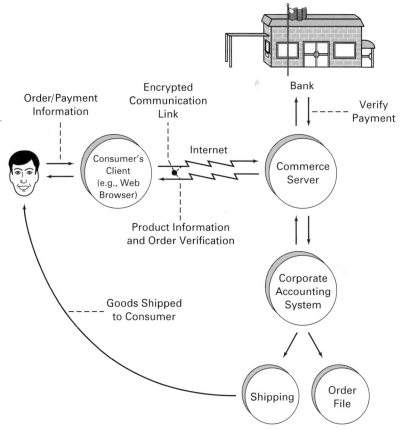

FIGURE 3.4 Commerce Server.

Electronic Payment Systems

The Internet has created demand for specialized types of payment systems. Several of these are discussed.

Traditional Electronic Bill Payment Systems.   In these types of systems, the payer sends electronic instructions to his or her bank. The instructions detail who is to be paid, when the payment is to be made, and the amount of the payment. The bank then makes the payment either electronically or by mail.

Traditional Credit Card Systems.   In these types of systems, the payer transmits a credit card number to a secure server. (A **secure server** is one in which the communications link between the client and server is protected by encryption.) The payee then presents the credit card information to a bank for collection, probably through a secure credit card network.

Secure Electronic Transaction (SET) Systems.   SET is a protocol established by MasterCard and Visa for consumer-based electronic payments on the Internet. The MasterCard/Visa system works in conjunction with an Internet Web browser and an electronic wallet. The electronic wallet contains encrypted credit card information and a digital certificate. (**Digital certificates,** the electronic counterparts to driver licenses, passports, and membership cards, serve as proof of identity. They are discussed in detail later.)

The consumer then makes an SET purchase by presenting the digital certificate and encrypted credit card to the merchant, who then forwards it to a participating bank for approval. Interestingly, the merchant never learns the credit card number, since it is encrypted. The entire process, including obtaining the bank's approval, may only take a second or two. The process is also simple, since SET is integrated into most Web browsers which automatically handle all the details. SET is a broad standard that can be used in a wide range of electronic payment systems.

Virtual Cash Systems.   There is a wide range of virtual cash systems. These are discussed later in a separate section.

SECURITY FOR ELECTRONIC TRANSACTIONS

Introduction

Encryption technology is essential for electronic commerce. **Encryption** involves using a **password** or **digital key** to scramble a readable **(plaintext)** message into an unreadable **(ciphertext)** message. The intended recipient of the message then uses the same or another digital key (depending on the encryption method) to convert the ciphertext message back into plaintext.

Consider, for example, how it might be possible to encrypt the plaintext word *ACE*. Assume that each letter of the alphabet is associated with a number, so that *A* is associated with 1, *B* with 2, *C* with 3, and so on. Then in numerical terms *ACE* would be 135. Now assume that this number is to be encrypted using a key value of 2. One simple way to do this would be to add the number 2 to each digit in the number 135. This would produce the new number 357, which when converted back to the alphabet yields the ciphertext word *CEG*. This process could easily be reversed by anyone who knows the secret key.

Types of Encryption Systems

Secret-Key Encryption

The preceding encryption example demonstrates the use of secret-key encryption. With **secret-key encryption** (Figure 3.5), the same key is used for both encrypting and decrypting a message. The obvious difficulty with this method is that the secret key must be communicated to the receiver of an encrypted message. This means that the secret key may be vulnerable to interception.

Public-Key Encryption

The most commonly used encryption method is public-key encryption. **Public-key encryption** uses two keys in association with each encrypted message, one key to encrypt the message and another key to decrypt it. Either key can decrypt what the other key encrypts. But the key that encrypts the message *cannot* be used to decrypt it. Only the other key can decrypt the message.

In practice, the sender of a message keeps one key private and makes the other public. Hence, one key is called the public key and the other the private key. The advantage of public-key encryption is that the sender of a message only

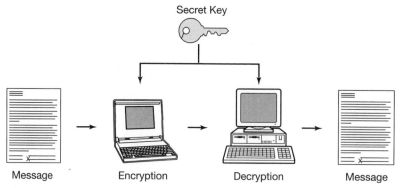

FIGURE 3.5 Secret-Key Encryption.

needs to know the recipient's public key. Neither the sender nor the receiver needs to know the other's private key.

To send someone a secret message (Figure 3.6), all one has to do is to encrypt the message with the recipient's public key. The recipient then decrypts the message with his or her private key. So if Company A wants to send Company B a secure message, then Company A uses Company B's public key to encrypt the message. Company B then uses its private key to decrypt the message.

What happens if someone intercepts the encrypted message? Can the person intercepting the message decrypt it? The answer is no; only Company B's private key can do that. The public key is worthless in decrypting the message, even though it is used to encrypt it.

Hybrid Systems and Digital Envelopes

In general, secret-key encryption requires fewer computations than public-key encryption. Thus, for large messages secret-key encryption may be considerably faster.

Digital envelopes involve using both public-key and secret-key encryption (Figure 3.7 and 3.8). This is accomplished through the following procedure:

1. The sender of the message generates a single random key.
2. The sender of the message uses this secret key to encrypt the message, using a fast secret-key encryption system.

FIGURE 3.6 Public-Key Encryption.

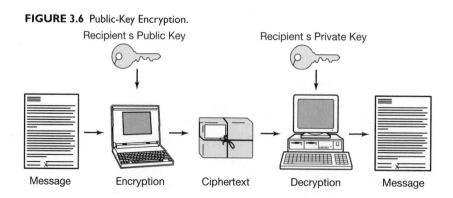

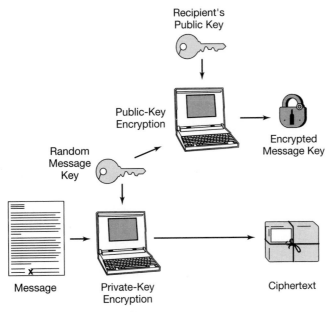

FIGURE 3.7 Double-Key Encryption.

3. The sender uses the recipient's public key to encrypt the randomly generated secret key. This encryption is done using a public-key encryption system.

4. The sender transmits both the encrypted key and the encrypted message. Together, these two items constitute a digital envelope.

5. The recipient uses his or her private key to decrypt the randomly generated secret key.

6. The recipient uses the secret key to decrypt the message.

FIGURE 3.8 Double-Key Decryption.

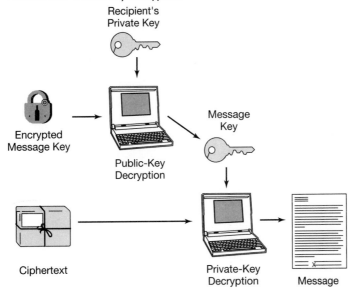

The method behind digital envelopes is sometimes referred to as double-key encryption.

Digital Signatures

Public-key encryption can also be put to another very interesting use. Consider what would happen if Company A uses its private key to encrypt a message. Then anyone, anywhere with the related public key can decrypt it. This is important because anyone can test the message to see if Company A's public key will successfully decrypt it. If Company A's public key successfully decrypts the message, then one can be certain that the message was written and encrypted by Company A. The result is that the message can be said to be digitally signed by Company A, for no one else could have encrypted the message except Company A. A **digital signature** occurs when someone encrypts a message with his or her own private key (Figure 3.9). Anyone can then use that person's public key to verify that it was in fact encrypted by that person (Figure 3.10).

There are many cases in which the sender of a message does not want to encrypt the message but does want to attach a digital signature to it. One obvious way to accomplish this is for the sender of the message to transmit both a plaintext copy and a ciphertext copy of the same message, with the encryption being based on the sender's private key. This way, anyone wanting to verify the digital signature needs only to use the sender's public key to decrypt the ciphertext message. This decrypted message is compared to the plaintext message and, if the two match, the sender's identity is certain. The only drawback to this approach is that two full copies of the message must be transmitted, both the plaintext and ciphertext versions.

An alternative approach exists in which it is not necessary to send two full copies of the message. This is accomplished by using a hashing function to create a digest of the message to be digitally signed. The **message digest** is much shorter than the message itself, and it is the digest that is encrypted with the sender's pri-

FIGURE 3.9 Digital Signature Creation.

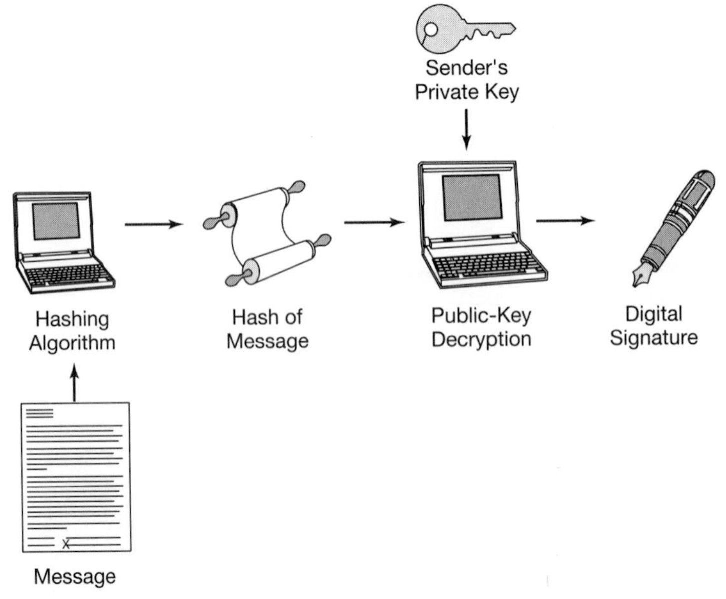

Hashing Algorithm

Hash of Message

Public-Key Decryption

Digital Signature

Sender's Private Key

Message

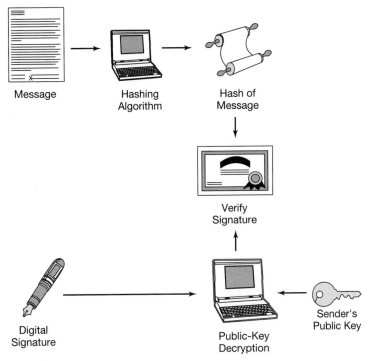

FIGURE 3.10 Verification of Digital Signature.

vate key and attached to the plaintext message as a signature. To verify the signature, one uses the sender's public key to decrypt the digital signature. Next, one applies the same hashing function to the plaintext message to produce a message digest. Finally, one compares the resulting digest to what was obtained from decrypting the digital signature with the sender's public key.

There are many standard hashing functions available. A **hashing function** takes a long variable-length string of characters and converts it into a short fixed-length string. For example, the preceding paragraph might be hashed into a message digest that might look something like "%^&ae#a5O2Ht." Similarly, the entire chapter you are now reading might be hashed into the following message digest: "TSCH4(&&!te0)." Note that both these digests are the same length (i.e., 12 characters), and each represents a unique (or nearly unique) digital fingerprint for the text being digested.

Digital signatures can be broken by either attacking the encryption or the hashing function. In practice, however, hashing functions that produce long digests are difficult to break. As a rule, it's desirable to use a digest function that produces message digests that are about the same length as the user's public and private keys. Using a longer message digest produces no additional security because an attacker can be expected to attack the public-key encryption if it is the weakest link.

Many believe that digital signatures are more secure than conventional handwritten signatures. Whereas handwritten signatures are relatively easy to forge, digital signatures are next to impossible to forge. Furthermore, digital signatures prove not only the identity of the message's signer but also that the signed message has not been altered in any way. This is because if a digitally signed message is altered its digest will no longer match the decrypted signature.

Digital signatures have many interesting applications. For example, a university could issue a digitally signed diploma showing the name of the graduate, the graduate's major, the date of the degree, and so on. Anyone could readily verify the authenticity of the diploma simply by using the university's public key to decrypt the signature and compare the result to a digital digest of the diploma.

Similarly, a company could transmit a digitally signed purchase order over the Internet. The receiving company could then readily verify the authenticity of the purchase order. Another company might want to issue employees digital credentials (such as identification cards) with digital signatures.

The Legality of Digital Signatures.   The question arises as to whether or not digital signatures are legally binding. This issue in law is still at the formative stage, and some companies sidestep any problems by entering into a conventional written contract with others, with all parties agreeing to be bound by their digital signatures.

Digital Time-Stamping.   In order to ensure the validity of electronic documents over time, there needs to be some way to attach trusted dates to them. This can be accomplished by a **digital time-stamping service (DTS),** an organization that adds digital time-stamps to documents.

The message to be digitally time-stamped is digested, and the digest is sent to a DTS (Figure 3.11). The DTS attaches a time-stamp to the digest, and then adds its digital signature to the two. Anyone can verify the date by decrypting the digital signature of the DTS using its public key (Figure 3.12). Note that with this method the DTS time-stamps the message without learning its contents.

FIGURE 3.11 Digital Time-Stamp Procedure.

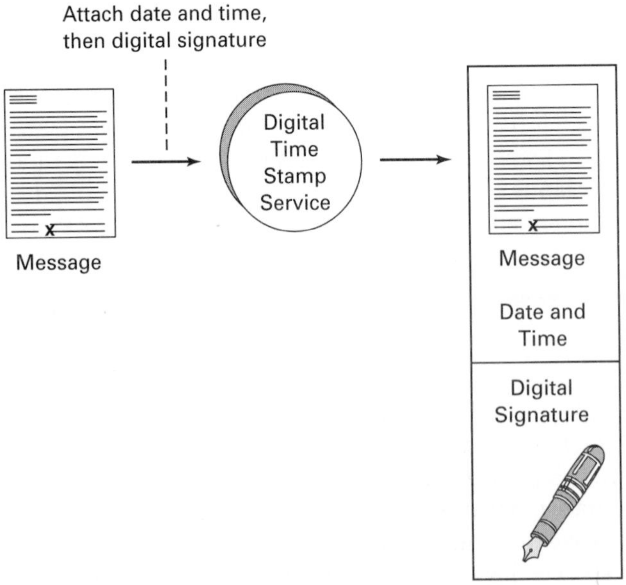

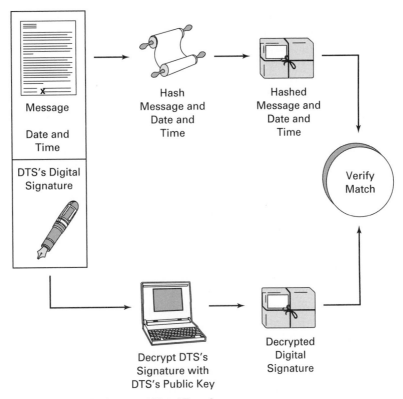

FIGURE 3.12 Verification of Digital Time-Stamp.

SECURITY ISSUES FOR PUBLIC-KEY ENCRYPTION SYSTEMS

As with any encryption system, public-key encryption is potentially vulnerable to various types of attacks. These include cryptanalysis attacks and factoring attacks.

Cryptanalysis Attacks

Cryptanalysis involves various techniques for analyzing encrypted messages for purposes of decoding them without legitimate access to the keys. The simplest possible attack on a message encrypted with public-key encryption is the **guessed plaintext attack.** This works if the attacker can guess the contents of a message. For example, the attacker might intercept an encrypted message and guess that it consists of the words "Secret project approved." To see if this guess is correct, the attacker would use the recipient's public key to encrypt "Secret project approved." The resulting encrypted message would be compared to the encrypted message that was intercepted. If these two encrypted messages match, then the attacker's guess is correct. This attack can be defeated by simply adding some random numbers to the end of the message.

Other more sophisticated cryptanalysis attacks exist, but most of them seem unlikely to prevail against a sufficiently long key. Furthermore, since any attack takes time, the risk against attack can be minimized by frequently changing keys. In some cases, new public and private keys may be generated for each financial transaction.

Obviously, it would be very difficult for an attacker to guess a private key that is used only long enough to transmit a single financial transaction over the Internet. In that case, the attacker would have to guess the key in 1 or 2 seconds. Furthermore, the decoded key wouldn't be useful in attacking other transactions.

Factoring Attacks

In practice, the public key is typically based on the product of two large prime numbers. Prime numbers are numbers that are only divisible by themselves or by 1. For example, the numbers 3, 5, 7, and 11 are all prime numbers. Therefore, 35 would be the product of two prime numbers, for its two factors are 5 and 7.

The problem is that the private key can be obtained from factoring what is essentially the public key. Thus, the whole security of public-key encryption depends on the assumption that an attacker cannot factor the product of two large prime numbers.

Fortunately, factoring such long products of prime numbers is next to impossible, even with the help of the fastest computers. For example, with a supercomputer it might take hundreds or even thousands of years to factor a product of two prime numbers that is 1,000 bits long.

How difficult it would be to simply guess prime number factors can be seen from the prime number theorem. According to this theorem, the number of prime numbers having a length of 512 bits or more exceeds the number of atoms in the universe!

Still, even though products of prime numbers are difficult to factor, mathematicians have not conclusively proved that no fast shortcuts exist for such factoring. But on the other hand, mathematicians do not believe that any such shortcuts will ever be discovered, at least in the foreseeable future.

Key Management

Most attacks against public-key systems are likely to be made at the key-management level. Specifically, attackers are likely to attempt to break into the locations where private keys are stored. Once an attacker obtains the private key, he or she can easily decrypt any messages encrypted with the related public key. For this reason, any well-designed control system must place considerable emphasis on protecting private keys.

Creating and Distributing Keys

Each user should create his or her own public and private keys. Using a central office or authority to create and distribute keys is not recommended because any key distribution system is subject to attack and simply adds an unnecessary layer of vulnerability to the system.

Personal computers that contain sensitive keys should be protected by three methods. First, possible physical access to such machines should be limited through locked doors, security guards, and so on. Second, such machines should be set to require password access at boot-up time. Third, the keys themselves should be protected by passwords.

The longer the life of the key and the more critical it is, the more the security that must be applied to protect it. For example, assume a company uses one public/private pair of keys for all its financial transactions. Further assume that this pair of keys has a life of, say, two years. In this case, extreme caution must be exercised because any attacker who obtains the private key would be able to wreak havoc on all the company's financial transactions.

Verification of Public Keys Through Digital Certificates

Digital certificates (or **digital IDs**) are digital documents that attest to the fact that a particular public key belongs to a particular individual or organization. For all practical purposes, digital certificates serve as electronic proof of identity.

Digital certificates are issued by some **certifying authority** (CA). For example, an employer might issue digital certificates to its employees, a bank to its customers, or a club to its members. The certificates could be stored on individuals' computers for use over the Internet. They could also be encoded onto machine-readable identification cards that could be used for various types of access privileges.

The CA creates a digital certificate by digitally signing a document that includes the name of the person being certified, and the expiration data of the certificate. Other information such as a serial number might also be included (Figure 3.13). Anyone can verify the certificate by checking the digital signature to make sure it belongs to the certifying authority.

For a digital certificate to be useful, every relevant person must recognize and know the public key of the CA. For this reason the public keys of CAs are often widely published over the Internet and are available from many sources. They are so widely published that they become common knowledge, and there is never any question as to whom they belong to.

A digital certificate allows some trusted organization (the CA) to in effect vouch for the ownership of the public key listed in the certificate. This works because one knows and trusts the CA's digital signature. In many situations the exchange of digital certificates might only be necessary the first time two individuals do business with each other. After that time both parties may be certain of each other's public keys.

Certificate Revocation List (CRLs).   A **certificate revocation list (CRL)** is a list of public keys that have been revoked before their expiration dates. Keys might be revoked because they have been compromised or because they are no

FIGURE 3.13 Digital Certificate.

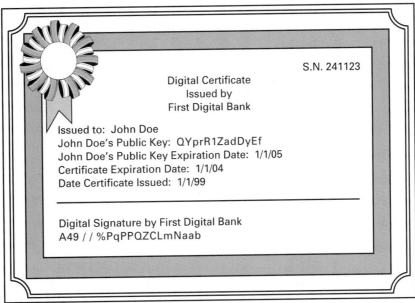

longer applicable. For example, Jane Doe's key might be stolen. Or maybe she is fired and no longer works for XYZ Company, in which case the ABC division would revoke her certificate. The keys of fired employees should immediately be placed on the appropriate CRL associated with the CA that originally issued it.

Certificate Chains.   In some cases digital certificates can be linked together in chains (Figure 3.14). For example, a well-known CA company, say The Good Key Company, might issue a digital certificate for XYZ Company. XYZ Company

FIGURE 3.14 Certificate Chains.

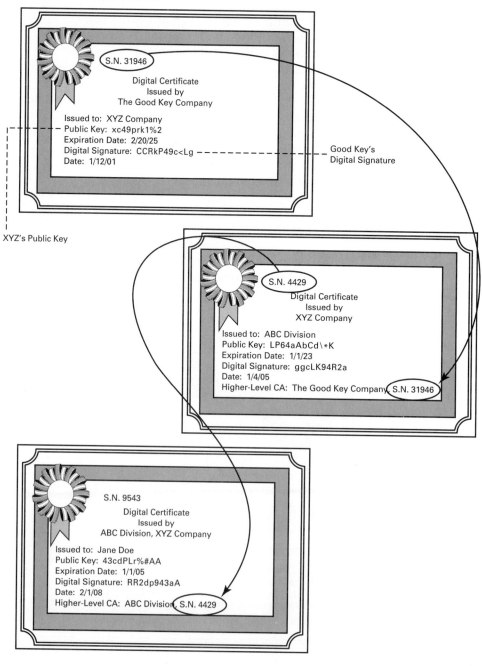

might then in turn issue another digital certificate for one of its divisions, say the ABC division. The ABC division might then issue still another certificate to one of its employees, say Jane Doe.

Someone interested in verifying Jane Doe's public key and her association with XYZ Company would first check the digital certificate issued by the division. This certificate would contain a reference to the certificate issued by XYZ Company, and so that certificate would be checked next. The certificate issued by XYZ Company would in turn include a reference to the one issued by The Good Key Company, which would then be checked.

Certificate-Signing Units.   The private keys of CAs deserve the highest possible level of security. This because an attacker gaining access to the CA's private key could produce an unlimited number of forged digital certificates, and the corresponding results could be disastrous. For this reason, it is important that the CA's private keys be stored in a completely secure manner.

One approach to securely storing keys is by placing them in a **certificate-signing unit (CSU).** A CSU is a tamperproof box for storing private keys. It should be shielded from all outside electromagnetic radiation, and should be such that its contents will automatically be destroyed in the event of tampering. Moreover, it should be built around secret-sharing technology so that the private keys of several employees are required to open it. Finally, there should be a method for authorized employees to use the stored private key without knowing what it actually is.

Various CSUs are available on the market. For example, RSA Data Security sells a full-fledged certificate-issuing system based on a CSU developed by Bolt, Baranek, and Newman. The important thing is that some secure system be adopted for protecting important private keys.

Key Expirations

In general, all keys should have an associated expiration date. First, the longer a key is in the public domain the more time that possible attackers have to perform cryptanalysis and factoring attacks. Furthermore, the power of computers increases over time, making factoring attacks more possible for keys with long lives.

Of course, keys with longer lives should be correspondingly long. For example, a key that is 128 bits long might be perfectly adequate for use in a single transaction that takes place over a 1-minute time span. But a key over 1,000 bits long might be desirable if it is to be used for years. It is widely believed that 1,000-bit keys will not be vulnerable for many years. Still, it is best to change keys regularly.

When keys expire it is sometimes desirable to replace them with new, longer keys. Doing so compensates for any increased vulnerability due to increases in the speed of computers. But if the length of a key is still considered acceptable when it expires, the same key might be recertified by the issuance of a new digital certificate.

APPLICATIONS OF ELECTRONIC COMMERCE AND ENCRYPTION TECHNOLOGY

This section discusses various applications of the concepts discussed thus far in the chapter.

Virtual Cash Systems

Digital Cash

Cryptographic techniques have given rise to whole new payment systems based on digital cash. **Digital cash** (or e-cash or electronic money) is typically created when a bank attaches its digital signature to a note promising to pay the bearer some amount of money (Figure 3.15). For example, the Electronic Bank of America might digitally sign a message that contains the following information.

1. The bank's name and address
2. The dollar value of the bank note being created
3. A unique serial number
4. The date the note is created
5. A possible expiration date

Furthermore, a digital certificate from some large CA might be attached.

Anyone can verify the authenticity of the digital cash by verifying the bank's digital signature. The only problem, however, is the possibility that the note might have already been spent once before. This is because, unlike real currency, digital cash can be easily copied.

A typical way to prevent double spending is to verify with the bank that the digital cash has not already been spent. This can be done by electronically transmitting the digital cash's serial number to the bank. If the serial number has not previously been presented, then the bank verifies the validity of the transaction. It then records the note as having been spent.

In practice, banks will use a different digital signature for each denomination. For example, one digital signature might be used for a $1 note, another for a $2 note, and so on. Digital signatures can also be issued for coins, thus allowing for the making of small change.

Note that anyone can issue his or her own digital notes. Such notes could be accepted and processed in the same way that paper checks now are.

Privacy Issues

Privacy is a major issue in electronic transactions. Most electronic transactions are traceable, and this may be true even with encryption. For example, assume that the ABC Soft Drink Company manufactures a soft drink based on a secret formula. Further assume that ABC deals with its vendors electronically using the best encryption available.

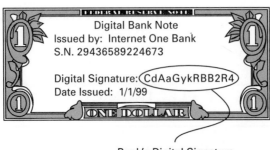

Bank's Digital Signature
Normally Used for $1 Notes   **FIGURE 3.15** Digital Cash.

An attacker interested in discovering ABC's secret formula might monitor the flow of ABC's incoming and outgoing messages over the Internet. This might in turn lead the attacker to discover that ABC frequently communicates with XYZ Company, which specializes in the sale of rare coffees. The result is that the hacker deduces that the secret ingredient is a rare coffee sold by XYZ Company.

There are presently no good defenses to attacks of this sort. Therefore, the Internet should not be used for communications if the IP address of one of the parties in a transaction needs to remain fully anonymous.

Another risk may come from a company using the same public key for many of its transactions. In this case, each transaction would leave a digital record, and at some point in time it would be possible to link all the company's transactions together to form a dossier on all the company's activities. This may especially be a problem with digital cash because, when the bank verifies the serial number on the digital note, it immediately discovers to whom it originally issued the note. So the bank knows both the payer and the payee in the transaction.

Blinded Digital Cash

The technique of **blinding** permits a bank to issue digital cash so that it is unable to link the payer to the payee. This is accomplished by the bank signing the note with a **blinded digital signature,** which works as follows, assuming that Alice is the payer and that she wishes to create a $1 digital note (see Figure 3.16):

1. Alice creates a digital note that contains only a unique serial number.
2. Alice in essence multiplies the serial number by another number called the blinding factor.
3. Alice digitally signs the note.
4. Alice sends the note (with the multiplied serial number) to the bank and requests that the bank digitally sign it with the digital signature it uses exclusively for its $1 notes.
5. The bank deducts $1 from Alice's account and digitally signs the note.
6. Alice uses a special technique to remove the blinding factor from the note's serial number without affecting the validity of the bank's digital signature.
7. Alice gives the note to Joe for payment of goods.
8. Joe presents the note to the bank. The bank doesn't recognize the note number because it originally signed the note in its blinded form, but it recognizes its digital signature for $1 and therefore credits Joe accordingly.
9. The bank keeps a list of note numbers on deposits received so that it doesn't pay the same note twice.

In this case, the bank is unable to link Alice and Joe together. When it receives the note from Joe, it has no way of knowing that it was the same note that it had issued to Alice.

Computer Software and Computer Card Systems

The cryptographic techniques are such that virtual cash payments can be made either on a PC or a stand-alone electronic wallet-sized (smart) card. Both approaches are discussed.

Virtual Cash on the PC

Most electronic cash systems on personal computers are based on the concept of an electronic wallet. An **electronic wallet** is essentially a computer program that keeps track of the various keys, digital certificates, and items of infor-

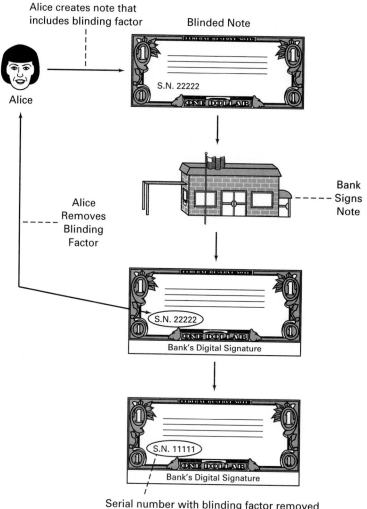

FIGURE 3.16 Blinded Digital Signature.

mation associated with electronic money. The user acquires digital cash (from a financial institution), which is then stored in the electronic wallet. Money is then received or spent by transferring it in or out of the wallet.

Virtual Cash in Electronic Cards

Smart cards are hand-held electronic cards that are used for payments. There are four types of cards: memory cards, shared-key cards, signature-transporting cards, and signature-creating cards. Each type of card is discussed.

Memory cards contain microchips that are only capable of storing information. They also contain the hardware that provides PIN (personal identification number) access to the card's contents. Memory cards possess very weak security and should be used only for the simplest applications where the amount of money is small and security is not of much concern.

An example of a memory card might be a card that allows a small number of employees to purchase lunch in the company cafeteria. Employees would use the cards by inserting them in the cash register at the end of the cafeteria line, followed by PIN verification. The register would deduct the balance of cash stored in the cards according to the employee purchases.

A memory card can easily be defeated by inserting a small computer between it and the cash register the first time the card is used. The small computer would record all the information exchanged between the card and the cash register. The cash register could then be defeated by simply replaying the same information back for all future transactions.

ATM cards are a form of memory card, but they aren't really smart cards since they are only used for identification rather than payment per se. The user inserts the ATM card, enters the PIN, and then requests money from the bank. All the money balances are stored in the bank's computer.

Shared-key cards overcome the weakness of memory cards by using encryption for all communications between the card and the cash register (or other point-of-payment device). Thus, it is useless for an attacker to intercept and record communications between the card and the cash register.

The encryption is carried out with both the card and the cash register using (sharing) the same secret key. For this to work securely, both the card and the register must contain tamperproof modules that will protect the keys from hardware hackers.

The biggest weakness of shared-key cards is that massive fraud is possible if an attacker manages to discover the secret key. Another problem is that the cash register must maintain a list of keys for use with every vendor with which it communicates. This can become complicated and cumbersome.

Signature-transporting cards carry essentially the same hardware as shared-key cards. The main difference is the software: Signature-transporting cards allow the user to spend digital cash notes. These notes are transferred to the cash register upon payment. The cash register can immediately (or later) verify the notes via an on-line link to the bank. In the case of immediate verification, no tamperproof module is required. Alternatively, the card can contain a tamperproof module that prevents the notes from being spent twice, thus avoiding the need for on-line verification.

Finally, **signature-creating cards** are similar to signature-transporting cards but are capable of generating their own digital signatures. This type of card might be used to write electronic "checks" that bear the digital signature of the cardholder. Of the four card types, the signature-transporting card shows the most promise for wide-scale use in retail transactions in the foreseeable future.

SUMMARY

Today many business transactions are conducted over electronic networks, that is, over groups of computers linked together electronically. Networks can be classified according to the distance they span. Hence, networks can be classified as local, metropolitan, or wide area. The Internet is the largest wide area network available today.

The Internet allows many different computers to communicate via the TCP/IP protocols. Each computer on the Internet is assigned a unique address called the IP number. IP numbers can be either dynamic or fixed. Dynamic addresses are normally assigned for temporary use, that is, for a single communications session. Fixed addresses are assigned for permanent use.

Intranets are basically in-house miniature versions of the Internet. They are typically protected from the outside world by firewalls, which restrict access to authorized individuals and are used for authorized business. Proxy servers, on the other hand, limit the outgoing access to the Internet.

Client-server technology serves as the basic technology for many types of business communications on the Internet. Servers are robot-type programs that automate various kinds of information exchanges. Clients are programs that communicate with servers. Major types of servers include mail servers, file servers, FTP servers, Web servers, and commerce servers. Commerce servers typically communicate with clients for the purposes of engaging in secure financial transactions.

Various types of electronic payment systems exist on the Internet. These include traditional bill payment systems, traditional credit card systems, Secure Electronic Transaction (SET) systems, and virtual cash systems.

On the Internet, information security is achieved in part through encryption technology. Secret-key encryption is sometimes used to encrypt messages, but it does not provide a way for the secret key to be sent from the sender of a message to the receiver. Public-key encryption, however, allows messages to be sent using only public keys. The recipient's public key is used to encrypt a message. That person's private key is then used for decryption.

Digital signatures are a means of positively guaranteeing the identity of the sender of a message without requiring that the message be encrypted. To create a digital signature the sender of the message uses a hash function to create a digest of the message. The sender then encrypts the digest with his or her private key. The result is the digital signature, which is attached to the original message. Any recipient of the message can verify the signature by using the sender's public key to decrypt the signature. This would then be compared to a digest of the message created by the recipient, using the same digest function used by the sender.

Digital signatures might not be legal in some situations, but they may sometimes be made legal by all parties agreeing to honor them through a traditional written contract. The dates on digitally signed documents can be established by a digital time-stamping service.

Public-key encryption schemes are subject to cryptanalysis and factoring attacks. The best way to prevent both these attacks is to use very long keys. In practice, public-key encryption systems are most likely to be attacked at the key-management level. Users should create and manage their own keys. The central distribution of keys simply adds an additional layer of vulnerability. Access to keys must be strictly limited.

Individuals' public keys can be verified through the use of digital certificates, which are digital documents that associate a particular person or organization with a given public key, and are signed with the private key of some trusted certifying authority.

Critical private keys must be assigned the highest level of protection. One approach to protecting private keys is the certificates-signing unit. This device is a tamperproof box for storing private keys. Authorized individuals should be able to use the protected keys without being able to see them. Finally, keys should have expiration dates, and it may be desirable to replace them with new, longer keys upon their expiration. The longer keys may compensate for any improvements in hacker technology that may have occurred during the keys' lifetime.

Digital cash is an important application of encryption technology. It is created when a bank (or other institution) digitally signs a financial note. Banks typically use a different digital signature for each denomination.

One privacy-related limitation of digital cash is that it may be traceable, so that the bank can match up the payer and payee. One way to solve this problem is through the use of blinded digital signatures. Blinded digital signatures make it impossible for the bank to link the payer and the payee.

In practice, digital cash is implemented on both PCs and smart cards. On PCs the digital wallet is used to receive and pay money. On smart cards, however, the money value may be stored on wallet-sized electronic cards. Digital cash can also be integrated into a wide range of programs.

Four types of smart cards exist: memory cards, shared-key cards, signature-transporting cards, and signature-creating cards. Memory cards are the least secure. Shared-key cards are more secure, but they use secret keys that may be subject to attack, and catastrophic losses may occur if a secret key is breached. On the other hand, signature-transporting cards carry digital cash that is based on public-key encryption, thus making them less vulnerable. Finally, smart cards actually create their own digital signatures. One of their uses might be to carry the digital signature of the card's owner. This would allow the cardholder to digitally sign transactions.

Glossary

access control list: for a proxy server, the list of IP addresses authorized to access the server.

Active X™: Microsoft's alternative to JAVA.

blinded digital signature: a digital signature and related digital cash that have been issued with blinding.

blinding: a technique in which a bank issues digital cash in such a way that it is unable to link the payer to the payee.

certificate revocation list: a list of public keys that have been revoked before their expiration dates.

certificate-signing unit: a tamperproof box for storing private keys.

certifying authority: individual or organization that issues digital certificates.

CGI: Common Gateway Interface, software that helps Web clients communicate with programs (such as accounting to database programs) linked to the server.

client: a program that accesses and exchanges information with a server.

commerce server: a specialized type of Web server with various commerce-related features.

cryptanalysis: various techniques for analyzing encrypted messages for purposes of decoding them without legitimate authorization.

digital cash: money created when a bank attaches its digital signature to a note promising to pay the bearer some amount of money.

digital certificate: a digitally signed document issued by a certification authority that attests to the ownership of a public key by a particular individual or organization.

digital envelope: an encryption method in which the message is encrypted with a secret key, and the secret key is encrypted with the recipient's public key.

digital time-stamping service (DTS): an organization that adds digital time-stamps to documents.

domain name: an alias name that can be used in place of the IP address.

domain name server: electronic phone book that associates domain names with IP addresses.

electronic networks: groups of computers that are connected together electronically.

electronic wallet: a computer program that keeps track of the various keys and items of information associated with digital money.

encryption: uses a password or digital key to scramble a readable (plaintext) message into an unreadable (ciphertext) message. The intended recipient of the message then uses the same or another digital key (depending on the encryption method) to convert the ciphertext message back into plaintext.

file server: allows authorized clients to retrieve files from libraries of files.

firewall: limits access to information on the company's servers from the rest of the world.

fixed IP address: an IP address that is permanently assigned to an individual, client, or server.

FTP server: a file server that uses the FTP protocol, the most commonly used protocol for file servers.

guessed plaintext attack: the simplest possible attack on a message encrypted with public-key encryption.

HTML: hypertext markup language, a protocol that specifies the format of documents on the World Wide Web.

hyperlinks: pointers to other documents that may be either on the same Web server or any other Web server.

Internet: an electronic highway, consisting of various standards and protocols, which allows computers everywhere to communicate with each other.

intranet: a self-contained, in-house internet.

IP: an addressing protocol that assigns a unique address to each computer on the Internet.

IP address (or IP number): address for an individual computer, client, or server on the Internet.

JAVA: software that extends the functionality of Web clients by allowing the server to transfer software to the client for execution on the client computer.

local area networks: networks that span a single site, such as a building or a group of buildings that are in close proximity to one another.

mail server: acts as an electronic mailbox that holds incoming electronic mail until the user's client program requests it.

memory card: a type of smart card that contains microchips only capable of storing information.

message digest: used with digital signatures, a meaningless fixed-length hash of a message that is much shorter than the message itself.

metropolitan area networks: networks that span a single city or metropolitan area.

proxy servers: typically used on the inside of the company's firewall and serve as filters for all outgoing requests for information.

public-key encryption: an encryption method that uses two keys in association with each encrypted message, one key to encrypt the message and another key to decrypt it.

secret-key encryption: an encryption method in which the same key is used for both encrypting and decrypting a message.

Secure Electronic Transactions (SET) protocol: a protocol that involves encrypting all communications between the client and the server, thus assuring that transactions are private and free from outside manipulation.

secure server: a server in which the communications link between the client and server is protected by encryption.

server: a robot-type program that constantly runs on some computer and exchanges information with clients.

shared-key card: a type of smart card that uses encryption for all communications between the card and the cash register (or other point-of-payment device).

signature-creating card: a type of smart card that is capable of generating its own digital signatures.

signature-transporting card: a type of smart card that stores digital cash.

smart card: a wallet-sized electronic card that is used for payments.

spoof: a type of hacker attack in which the attacker assumes a false identity such as a false IP address.

URL: uniform resource locator, the name for a Web document's location.

Web server: a server that allows a user (client) to access documents and run computer programs that reside on remote computers.

wide area networks: networks of computers that span at least two metropolitan areas.

Chapter Quiz

Answers to the Chapter Quiz appear on page 105.

1. Which of the following best describes the Internet?
   (a) developed by Microsoft and IBM.
   (b) highly centralized.
   (c) highly decentralized.
   (d) none of the above.

2. Which of the following is true?
   (a) the Internet is faster than most local area networks.
   (b) most metropolitan networks are faster than the Internet.
   (c) the speed of the Internet is usually critical in processing single accounting transactions.
   (d) none of the above.

3. TCP/IP is _____.
   (a) an approach to networking developed by the RAND Corporation.
   (b) the standard for virtually all long-distance Internet communications.
   (c) the standard protocol for the formatting of Web documents.
   (d) none of the above.

4. Spoofing would be most applicable to _____.
   (a) a hacker attack.
   (b) a failure in a proxy server.
   (c) the elimination of an access control list.
   (d) none of the above.

5. An FTP server is an example of a _____.
   (a) Web server.
   (b) mail server.
   (c) commerce server.
   (d) none of the above.

6. The SET protocol would be most applicable to _____.
   (a) a commerce server.
   (b) a Web server.
   (c) a mail server.
   (d) an FTP server.

7. Which approach to encryption is the most secure for a server that deals with many unknown clients?
   (a) public-key encryption.
   (b) secret-key encryption.
   (c) anonymous encryption.
   (d) none of the above.

8. Which of the following statements is true regarding digital signatures?
   (a) they require the related message to be encrypted.
   (b) they do not require the related message to be encrypted.
   (c) they require the use of message digests.
   (d) none of the above.

9. Encryption keys should be created and distributed at the _____.
   (a) workstation level.
   (b) department level.
   (c) organization level.
   (d) security office level.

10. Which of the following is used to store digital cash on a personal computer?
    (a) electronic digest.
    (b) digital-signing unit.
    (c) virtual cash transporting system.
    (d) none of the above.

Review Questions

1. Describe the different types of electronic networks and contrast the differences between them.
2. Summarize the development of the Internet.
3. Explain the security risks inherent in any intranet.

4. Explain how addressing works on the Internet.
5. Summarize any differences between firewalls and proxy servers. In what situations would both be used?
6. How might EDI (electronic data interchange) be implemented on a commerce server?
7. Define and describe several different types of servers used in electronic commerce.
8. Discuss one or two different types of hacker attacks that might be made against a commerce server.
9. If two companies did electronic business with each other on a regular basis, would they need to exchange digital certificates with each new transaction? Why or why not?
10. Summarize any advantages of public-key encryption over secret-key encryption.
11. What would a hacker have to do to forge a digital signature? How can such an attack be prevented?
12. Why do message digests normally have a fixed length?
13. Why might the message digesting function be the target of an attack for a hacker?
14. Discuss the relative advantages and disadvantages of digital signatures versus traditional signatures.
15. What security issues might exist in maintaining a certificate revocation list?

Discussion Questions and Problems

16. The Boat Company in Chicago manages several divisions around the United States, including the Arco Division. Arco produces sailboats and spans a 100-acre site near the Port of Miami, in Miami, Florida. All of Arco's personal computers are presently linked together over a local area network. Specifically, sales records are kept on a personal computer at the dockside warehouse, and all other records are kept in the main building, where most of top management is also located. The only exception is payroll, which is kept on a personal computer in the maintenance building.

    Arco has recently hired Betty Brill, a new information systems manager. At her first staff meeting Betty informed Brad Wilson, the controller, that she wanted to develop an intranet-type network to link all the company's computers together.

    Brad's initial response was negative. He said the following:

    > Our present systems works fine. As it now stands the sales and payroll departments are translating their accounting files into ASCII text and sending them over the local area network to the main building. When the text files arrive in the main building, we then run a program that converts them into a format compatible with our main computer system.

    Betty interrupted:

    > Brad, that's an archaic system. We're using all kinds of incompatible formats, and on top of that we're wasting a lot of effort by expressing mailing disks of our payroll files to Chicago every week so that they can handle the taxes and write the paychecks. What we really need is our own intranet with an outside link to the Internet. That will help us make the transition to compatible file formats. We can also set up a server so that the people in Chicago can access any of the accounting data any time they need them. There will be no need to send them disks all the time.

    Brad responded:

    > That's really dumb, Betty. Our present system works fine. But your plan will probably cost a lost of money, generate a lot of hassle, and it will even open us to potential hackers. The results could be a major disaster.

Betty concluded her argument:

> Brad, I don't appreciate your calling my ideas dumb. Yours are even dumber. You need to go back to school and learn about today's technology. Everyone is switching to intranets and wiring up to the Internet. We don't even have our own Web site. When you get right down to it, we don't have any choice but to keep up with the times.

Required

1. Select one side of the argument and defend your position.
2. Assume that Arco has decided to implement Betty's plan. What would be some important considerations relevant to the implementation?

17. The ABC Company operates in Boston, where it designs and manufactures its own line of specialized women's clothing. The company is linked to the Internet and recently started accepting orders through a commerce server that it developed in-house. The problem is that the commerce server stores incoming orders in a format that is not consistent with the format used by the accounting system. In fact, the problem is so bad that all incoming data require a considerable amount of manual editing in a word processor before they can be read into the accounting system.

Required
Sketch out a general solution to ABC's problem.

18. Comway Corporation is a medium-sized shoe wholesaler whose sales territory includes Illinois, Michigan, and Indiana. Every day the sales managers for these states collect orders from retail stores. They then use local Internet service providers to connect to the Internet and enter the order information. In each case the sales manager uses a Web-browser client to enter the information into a Web server dedicated to collecting orders.

A problem has arisen recently with deliveries to some of Comway's retail customers. For example, one customer, Brown Shoe Store, complained that it never received delivery of a $6,000 order that it had recently made. In order to investigate the matter, Sandra Hill, Comway's controller, looked at the order files and concluded that the shoes were in fact shipped to a warehouse several blocks from Brown Shoe Store. Brown, however, said that it had never authorized a shipment to anywhere but directly to its store.

Puzzled, Sandra Hill checked with Brown's sales manager, who immediately produced a printed copy of the order. The sales manager had printed out the contents of the computer screen at the time he had entered the order, and sure enough he had set the shipment up for normal delivery right at Brown's store.

To further investigate, Sandra Hill checks the logs of the Web server used to collect orders from the sales managers. However, everything seemed in order, and it appeared the sales manager had used his proper password to access the Web server.

Required
Analyze the problem and make suggestions as to its possible cause. What additional information would you need to complete Sandra Hill's investigation? What additional security measure should be taken, if any?

19. ACE Company is a small start-up company that intends to publish electronic documents on the World Wide Web. It does not intend to engage in publishing any printed materials.

Janet Thompson, the president of ACE, has decided that a Web commerce server will be set up to take all orders. The server will also be required to take payments and distribute documents to customers.

Required
Design and specify the requirements for the desired commerce server. Your design should include all relevant considerations, including the following:

1. Information collected by the server.
2. Means for organizing electronic documents. (Assume that ACE's catalog will consist of approximately 2,000 documents.)
3. Security issues.
4. Payment methods.
5. The overall structure of ACE's Web site, and any necessary and related hyperlinks.

20. For each of the following electronic payment systems, give an example of a company for which it might be applicable:

    1. Traditional electronic bill payment system.
    2. Traditional credit card system.
    3. Secure Electronic Transaction system.
    4. Virtual cash system.

21. Tireco is a medium-sized firm that manufactures and distributes specialty tires. The company has good separation of duties, and at the top of the organization chart is the president, controller, vice president of manufacturing, vice president of marketing, and the finance officer. Under the vice president of manufacturing are four departments.

    The company has decided to do all its business over the Internet using a whole array of commerce servers, each with a JAVA or CGI interface to the central accounting system. The commerce servers are set up to process secure EDI-based orders with customers and vendors.

    The president, a recent accounting graduate, has insisted that the company use digital certificates in all its transactions. Furthermore, the company has informed all its vendors that it will not be responsible for the payment of any invoices, electronic or paper, that are not supported by a digital certificate issued by Tireco.

    Required
    Assuming that Tireco elects to use public-key encryption, design a system for managing the company's keys and digital certificates. Your design should consider at least the following:

    1. the number of keys that will be needed, and the number of departments that will need them.
    2. who will issue keys
    3. the expiration dates to be used for keys
    4. who will have the authority to issue digital certificates
    5. the structure of the company's certificate chains
    6. the security measures that will need to be adopted.

22. XYZ Company is a large manufacturer of kitchen cabinets. In all, the company has seven divisions spread out across the country. Furthermore, the company has adopted a policy of issuing digital certificates for all company transactions, and it has even decided to issue digital credentials for all key employees. The typical employee's credentials contain the employee's social security number, name, position in the company, public key, and any special authorizations to act on the company's behalf. For example, the purchasing officers all contain credentials that contain the words "Authorized Purchasing Officer." All credentials are digitally signed using the company's general private key.

    A dispute has arisen between management, accounting, and finance regarding the proper procedures for issuing the digital credentials. Accounting argues that a major control issue is at stake, and that it should process all credentials. Management sees no need for accounting's involvement and argues that it alone should do the processing. Finance, on the other hand, argues that digital credentials are like the keys to the safety deposit box, or to the signature-signing machine. Therefore, finance feels that it should assume sole responsibility for processing the digital credentials.

Required

1. Which function (accounting, finance, or management) should process the digital credentials? In formulating your answer, keep in mind at least the following considerations:
   (a) segregation of duties.
   (b) the types of credentialing that might be done.
   (c) the ability of the function to handle the type of work required.
2. What procedures should be followed in issuing the digital credentials?

23. Given the information in the previous question, analyze and criticize the information that is issued with the purchasing officer's credentials.

24. GGG Company has entered into a contract with its financial institution that would allow it to issue its own digital cash. GGG would create sequenced notes that would be digitally signed with one of several private keys. The exact keys used would depend on the denominations of the individual notes.

    GGG would then electronically transmit the signed notes to its suppliers, who in turn would either use them somewhere else as cash or present them to GGG's bank for collection.

    Required
    How well would GGG's payment system work? What problems might arise?

25. Ramco Company sells gift items and flowers through its Internet store. In the past it has accepted traditional credit card payments through its secure commerce server. However, the company has recently decided to accept digital cash.

    The company's head of finance feels that digital cash would save the company a considerable amount of money in bank processing fees, as compared to credit card transactions. The only problem is that if digital cash is accepted, many customers may elect to pay with blinded digital notes.

    Ramco's vice president of marketing is against accepting blinded digital cash because it will allow customers to order and pay with pseudonyms, that is, fake names designed to protect the customers' identities. The result is that the marketing department will not be able to build its usual database of information for customers paying with the blinded notes. That in turn will prevent marketing from soliciting those customers for repeat business.

    John Carlos, Ramco's controller, is more concerned about the potential for fraud. Specifically, he is concerned that the company may end up accepting counterfeit digital money. Furthermore, due to cost considerations Ramco does not have the resources for on-line verification of each note of digital cash. He estimates that in most cases approximately two days will elapse before a note can be determined to be counterfeit. The problem is that flowers are normally shipped the same day the order is taken.

    Required
    Present the arguments for and against implementing the acceptance of digital cash. What changes might be made to make the system more workable?

26. Roadco Company has been hired to collect tolls for the Blue Ocean toll road. Robert Asphalt, the controller of Roadco, has been analyzing the situation and has come up with the following pieces of information:

    1. During rush hour commuters must presently wait in line for approximately 40 minutes at the main exit from the toll road.
    2. Estimates show that during the rush hour 95% of all cars on the toll road are driven by regular commuters.
    3. The technology is available for the inexpensive creation of electronic smart cards that are capable of radio-controlled communications directly with the toll booths.

Required

Design a smart card for collecting tolls from regular commuters. Your design should include the following:

1. procedures for issuing and accounting for cards
2. procedures for accounting for card usage
3. security measures
4. specifications for the types of smart cards to be used
5. procedures for communicating between the toll booth and the central office

---

Discussion Questions and Problems from the Appendix

27. What is the binary (base 2) representation of the following base 10 (decimal) values?
    (a)   7
    (b)   13
    (c)   28
    (d)   71
    (e)   93
    (f) 428

28. Compute the decimal (base 10) equivalents of the following binary (base 2) numbers:
    (a) 111000
    (b) 101010
    (c) 100111

29. Discuss whether or not computer output microfilming (COM) would be appropriate in the following situations:
    (a) filing name and address changes on a customer mailing list
    (b) storing canceled checks and bank statements
    (c) storing charge sales slips

30. A disk has 200 cylinders. There are ten recording surfaces per disk pack and each track can hold 7,200 bytes.
    (a) What is the maximum capacity of each cylinder? Of the entire disk pack?
    (b) Assume that a file has 1,200 records, each 600 bytes long. Calculate the following:
        (1) records per track.
        (2) number of tracks required
        (3) number of cylinders required for the file.

31. Suveys have indicated that about 60% of all computer-related fraud in the government might be attributed to the input of fraudulent data for computer processing. What does this suggest concerning the design of computer-based accounting information systems?

32. Inventory records will be stored on magnetic tape. The tapes that will be used are 2,400 feet long with a density of 1,600 bytes per inch. The interblock gap is 0.6 inch. The inventory records are a fixed length of 400 bytes each.
    (a) How many records can be stored on a reel of tape if four records are combined as a block?
    (b) How many records can be stored on a single reel if the blocking factor is increased to eight records per block?
    (c) By storing the inventory records in packed decimal format, 60% of the data in each record could be stored at two characters per byte of storage. If the blocking factor is kept at four records per block, how many records can be stored on a reel of tape?

33. Which method of input would you recommend for the following activities? Explain your choice.
    (a) entering grades for courses
    (b) entering data from bank checks

      (c) entering data for payroll calculations

      (d) entering data from questionnaires

      (e) entering data for sales transactions

      (f) entering data for customer payments on account

      (g) entering computer programs for processing

34. Distinguish between a mainframe computer, a minicomputer, and a PC. Do you think minicomputers are obsolete? Explain your answer.

35. Operating systems such as OS/2 and Windows have caused terms such as *multitasking, multiuser,* and *concurrent processing* to be applied to PCs. Explain what these capabilities provide to PC users.

36. Take a field trip to a computer store and evaluate several PC systems that are sold there. Prepare a report comparing the key features and prices of several of the systems. Include such characteristics as CPU word size (e.g., 16- or 32-bit), size of main memory, type of disk drives and storage capacity, type of monitors, processing speeds, and availability of printers. How would you choose between these different PC systems if you were going to buy one?

37. Take a field trip to a computer store and evaluate several business-oriented PC software packages that are sold there, such as spreadsheet software and database software. Prepare a report comparing the key features and prices of several of the PC software packages.

38. Take a field trip to the central computer facility at your university. Diagram the hardware configuration of the university's computer system. Include such items as the number of CPUs, disk drive units, tape drive units, printers, data terminals, and communication devices.

39. Prepare a hardware configuration diagram for each of the following computer systems.

      (a) A PC system used by an accountant to prepare tax returns and other types of financial reports. The system has a color monitor, a laser printer, two external disk drives, and a 600-Mb internal hard drive.

      (b) A minicomputer system used by a medium-sized consumer appliance retail store. The unit has two disk drive units, one tape drive unit, and one high-speed line printer. In addition to the operator's console video terminal, the minicomputer is attached via communication lines to four terminals in the retail area for data entry and one terminal in the receiving room.

      (c) A large mainframe system at the central office of a manufacturing firm. The system has two CPUs, 16 disk drive units, eight tape units, three high-speed line printers, one page printer, and a COM unit. In addition to the operator's console video terminal, the computer is attached via communication lines to 48 data entry terminals in the central office and 4 minicomputer systems located in different manufacturing plants. A front-end processor is used for communications control at the central office. Each of the distributed minicomputer systems has two disk drives, a high-speed line printer, and four to eight video terminals for data entry.

40. Ibex Insurance Corporation has over 2,000 PCs networked locally in its regional offices that are connected over leased telephone lines to mainframe computers in the company's central offices. Ibex originally chose the PCs to function as stand-alone workstations for its employees, but in considering the problems associated with transferring data to and from the company's mainframe computers, it was decided to link the workstations to the company's mainframe computers in a data communications system.

      The PCs function as intelligent workstations. Each office has a specially designed minicomputer that acts as the controller in the network. Each PC is linked to the minicomputer, which handles the communication links between the PCs and the mainframe. The minicomputer collects and concentrates data and then sends them to the company's mainframe computers for processing. The communications occur over voice-grade telephone lines between each regional office and the central office.

Required

Identify basic components of communications network architecture in the Ibex network. What are the functions of each component?

41. Arthur Yangly is a serious accounting student who has done very well in most of his accounting and business courses. Recently, however, Arthur received a dismal grade on an examination in his accounting information systems course. Arthur had taken the course as an elective on the advice of his academic advisor, who had said that the course would increase Arthur's computer literacy. The examination on which Arthur received his dismal grade was on computer hardware concepts.

Arthur was quite perturbed when he met with the instructor to discuss his grade on the examination. As Arthur explained to the instructor:

I took this course to increase my computer literacy as a future accountant. To me this means the ability to recognize situations in which using a computer is appropriate and the ability to use the computer for those applications. This exam had nothing to do with computer literacy as it relates to a future accountant. It was full of bits and bytes and other such nonsense that only engineers need to understand. I don't care how computer hardware works. You don't need to know how the engine of a car works in order to drive one.

The instructor disagreed with Arthur's definition of computer literacy, arguing that his definition was incomplete. While she agreed that computer literacy includes an ability to recognize situations in which using a computer is appropriate, she argued that computer literacy also includes a reasonable understanding of how computers actually work. This includes knowledge of topics such as hardware design and operation, file storage structures, and file processing techniques, in addition to some experience with writing computer programs.

Required

(a) What is your definition of computer literacy? Do you agree more with Arthur's definition or with his instructor's definition?

(b) Is computer literacy different for different majors (e.g., accounting versus marketing)?

42. The ABC Company has utilized computer data processing for many years. All the company's operations are computerized, and every manager receives a wide variety of printed reports and detailed listings concerning his or her area of operations. The company operates a mainframe computer with four high-speed impact printers and a full-page printer and has just ordered a laser printer in order to keep up with the volume of printed output.

Recently, several managers met with Bill Hill, the director of computer processing at ABC, to complain about the mountains of printed-paper reports and listings they receive from the computer department. The comments of Henry Rice, the vice president of sales at ABC, were typical:

Bill, I'm drowning in a sea of paper. At first the reports and listings about sales that I received from computer operations seemed very useful. Maybe it was the sharp contrast to the almost total lack of sales information I had to contend with before we computerized sales reporting. But as the years have gone by, I find that more and more often I don't even have time to look at one report before another is on my desk. And your programmers have been very busy over the last couple of years designing new sales reports. I get so many different reports that I almost don't know which one to look in to find the data I'm interested in. Moreover, as our sales volume has grown, so has the size of both the reports and listings. The listings are now so voluminous that I often can't find what I'm looking for. I know it's in there, in some report or listing, but where? And I haven't yet mentioned the problem of storing all this paper in a way that lets me find something later. Do you have any idea what it's like trying to find a particular item in an old report when you have a big stack of old reports in a small room next to your office? Isn't there something we can do to get control of this printed output?

Required

(a) Indicate steps that might be taken at ABC Company to gain control of this situation. What devices might be used to cut down on the excessive volume of paper?

(b) Is a different hardware configuration for output the only relevant consideration in cutting down the excessive volume of paper facing Henry Rice? Explain.

Answers to Chapter Quiz

1. C	4. A	7. A	10. D
2. B	5. D	8. B	
3. B	6. A	9. A	

APPENDIX

An Introduction to Computer Technology

A **computer system** is an integrated combination of hardware, software, communications, human resources, information resources, and processing procedures. Any one of these components is by itself of little value in satisfying computing needs. For example, a personal computer cannot process payroll without an appropriate software program. Computer **software,** or computer programs, contain the instructions required for the physical machine (the **hardware**) to complete the desired tasks, which in the case of payroll would include calculating the total pay and the withholdings for each employee.

Computer hardware are the pieces of equipment that are collectively referred to as the computer. These pieces include the central processor unit, its support processors, secondary storage, input devices, and output devices (Figure 3.17). The basic components of a computer are the same regardless of its physical size. Still, the size of the computer will affect its overall processing capabilities. There are four classes of computers that vary according to both their physical sizes and processing capabilities: supercomputers, mainframe computers, minicomputers, and personal computers.

Supercomputers are the fastest computers. They are sometimes cooled by special liquids that allow faster operation of their circuits. For this reason, the Cray supercomputers have the nickname of Bubbles, attributable to their bubbling liquids. The speed of supercomputers is also enhanced by manufacturing them in cylindrical shapes, thus shortening the distances that their internal signals must travel, thereby minimizing even small electrical delays. The primary advantage of supercomputers over other machines is their lightning-fast processing speed, which allows them to process hundreds of billions of instructions per second. Supercomputers have been used extensively for special numerically or graphically intensive applications such as weather simulations. They are not normally used for ordinary processing in corporate information systems.

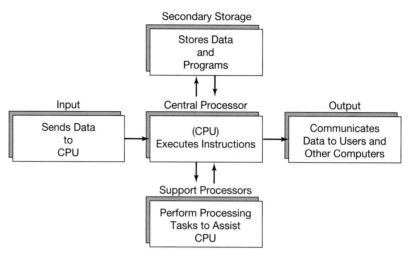

FIGURE 3.17 The Components of a Computer.

Mainframe computers are used by many large corporations and government institutions for centralized data processing. The size and performance of the machines vary greatly, but the larger ones can process hundreds of millions of instructions per second.

Midrange, sometimes called **minicomputers,** are slower than mainframes. However, the distinction between large midrange computers and small mainframes is somewhat blurred because many computers in these two classes of machines are of comparable size and processing capabilities. Midrange computers, like mainframes, are used by many corporations and government institutions.

Personal computers are distinguishable by being small enough to fit onto someone's desktop or under a desk, and by being inexpensive enough to be owned by one person. Individually, their processing speed is measured in millions of operations per second. But linked together in networks, their collective processing power can exceed that of the largest mainframes. Still, mainframes are faster at processing centralized tasks. Nevertheless, many businesses sometimes find it advantageous to replace their minicomputers or mainframes with a network of personal computers. This approach, called **downsizing,** has in many cases reduced costs by a factor of as much as 20 while maintaining the same overall processing capabilities.

Some personal computers use **RISC** (reduced instruction set computing) technology. These machines run faster than other machines by using fewer internal machine instructions to complete numerical and local operations. The trend is toward incorporating RISC technology into all personal computers.

Personal computers come in all sizes and shapes. There are laptop computers, notebook computers, subnotebook computers, hand-held computers, palmtop computers, pocket computers, and even computers on a single microchip.

COMPUTER HARDWARE

Machine Language

Computer hardware "thinks" in a language of its own called **machine language.** Surprisingly, this language is very simple, for at the most basic level all computers can understand only two things: on and off. This is because electrical circuits, like light bulbs, typically have only two states: on and off. In a computer, an on state represents the number 1, and an off state represents the number 0. By using the **binary number system,** it is possible to represent any number (or by extension any character) with an appropriate set of 0's and 1's.

In the binary number system, each 0 or 1 is called a **bit,** a shortened term for binary digit. Here is how to count to ten using binary numbers:

- 0001,
- 0010,
- 0011,
- 0100,
- 0101,
- 0110,
- 0111,
- 1000,
- 1001,
- 1010.

Can you guess what the next number, 11, is? It is 1011. The pattern can be made clearer by examining powers of 2 under this system. That is, $2^0, 2^1, 2^2, 2^3, 2^4, 2^5$, and so on. In binary, these numbers are

- 000001,
- 000010,
- 000100,
- 001000,
- 010000,
- 100000.

General rule →

Stated differently, in binary, one can represent any power of 2 (i.e., 1, 2, 4, 8, 16, 32, and so on) by simply placing a 1 in the appropriate position and 0's elsewhere. This is a simple rule to learn and remember. Furthermore, it is really the only rule needed to convert any "normal" number to binary. You do not need to worry about rules for numbers other than 1, 2, 4, 8, 16, 32, and so on, because you can convert any other number by combining two of these numbers. For example, the number 3 is 2 + 1, which in binary is 10 + 01, or binary 11. A 7 is 4 + 2 + 1, or 100 + 010 + 001, which equals 111. Similarly, a 6 is 4 + 2, or 100 + 010, which equals 110. This method can be used to convert any number to binary. Of course, doing this would require more work for a large number like 452,393, but the principle is the same.

Binary numbers can all be written as sums of powers of 2, so the system of binary numbers is sometimes called the **base-2 number system.** We are normally accustomed to the **base-10,** or decimal, number system, in which any number can be represented as the sum of powers of 10. For example, the number 4,921 really means

$$(4 \times 10^3) + (9 \times 10^2) + (2 \times 10^1) + (1 \times 10^0)$$

In binary this would be

$$(1 \times 2^{12}) + (0 \times 2^{11}) + (0 \times 2^{10}) + (1 \times 2^9) + (1 \times 2^8) + (0 \times 2^7) + (0 \times 2^6) +$$
$$(1 \times 2^5) + (1 \times 2^4) + (1 \times 2^3) + (0 \times 2^2) + (0 \times 2^1) + (1 \times 2^0)$$

or

$$(1 \times 2^{12}) + (1 \times 2^9) + (1 \times 2^8) + (1 \times 2^5) + (1 \times 2^4) + (1 \times 2^3) + (1 \times 2^0)$$

or simply

$$4096 + 512 + 256 + 32 + 16 + 8 + 1,$$

which follows the rule just set forth.

Character data such as the letters of the alphabet must also be represented in binary. This is accomplished through the use of bytes. A **byte** is a collection of bits used to represent a single character or special symbol such as & or $, as well as single numerical digits such as 2 or 7. The terms byte and **character** are used interchangeably. There is a variety of systems for arranging groups of bits to represent characters. These systems are called **coding schemes,** the most common of which are as follows:

- **ASCII.** American Standard Code for Information Interchange, an 8-bit coding scheme (i.e., each byte is made up of 8 bits).
- **BCD.** Binary Coded Decimal. A 6-bit coding scheme.
- **EBCDIC.** Extended Binary Coded Decimal Interchange Code, an 8-bit coding scheme.
- **Packed Decimal.** A 4-bit scheme for numbers. Two single-digit numbers can be "packed" into an 8-bit byte that could otherwise hold one alphanumeric character.

ASCII is sometimes called a **universal character code,** and it is often used to facilitate the transfer of data from one computer to another. Examples of ASCII codes are 1100001, 1100010, 1100011, which represents the letters *a, b,* and *c,* respectively. Uppercase letters have their own codes. The ASCII codes 1110, 1111, 10000 represent the digits 0, 1, and 2, respectively. Note that those are different than the binary equivalents of the numbers 0, 1, and 2, which would be 00, 01, and 10, respectively.

A third way to represent computer data is through a word. Like a byte, a **word** is also a collection of bits. A word, however, differs from a byte in that it is mainly used internally in the computer to represent numbers in binary. Recall that all data and instructions must be converted into binary before processing. The normal procedure, therefore, is to translate numbers into words before processing. For example, the number 4921 (which is four bytes) would be translated into a single binary word, that is, 1001100111001. So bytes represent characters, and words represent whole numbers. Numbers are normally stored externally as collections of bytes, which are translated into words for internal processing.

There are several types of words, and these include floating-point decimal numbers, **integers,** and character words. An example was already given of integers in the previous paragraph. **Floating-point decimal numbers** are numbers with decimal points in them, such as 123.456. The usual procedure is to store such numbers without the decimal point, using a variation of scientific notation. For example, 123.456 could be represented as 123456×10^{-3}, and 435 represented as 4.35×10^2. So, if these numbers are stored in 32-bit words, the **exponents** (i.e., -3 and 2) could be stored in, say, the first 7 bits of the words, the **mantissas** (i.e., 123456, and 435) could be stored in 23 bits, and the signs of both the numbers (both positive) and their exponents could be stored in 1 additional bit each.

Characters are also converted into words. A 32-bit word, for example, would hold 8 ASCII characters. **Character words,** unlike numerical words, usually have no inherent meaning. For example, a person's last name might be externally stored in 16 bytes. When converted into machine language, it would simply be divided into two words.

The Central Processor Unit

 The **central processor unit (CPU)** is the internal part of the computer that executes the instructions given to it by computer programs. The CPU consists of three components: the control unit, the arithmetic logic unit, and the primary memory. In a personal computer, the control unit and arithmetic logic unit normally exist on a single microchip.

Internal Clock

The operation of the CPU is electronically governed by an **internal clock.** Loosely speaking, each time the clock ticks, a pulse of electricity passes through the microcircuits, allowing the CPU time to perform a single operation. **Clock rates** are often measured in a megahertz (MHz), or millions of cycles per second. For example, a CPU with a clock rate of 400 MHz would operate at 400 million clock cycles per second. Practically speaking, as is discussed in what follows, arithmetic operations often require more than one instruction to complete, but, everything else being equal, the clock rate determines how long it takes the CPU to perform a single operation such as an integer addition. The number of instructions that the CPU is capable of executing in 1 second is typically measured in **MIPS,** or millions of instructions per second. For example, a processor rated at 50 MIPS is capable of performing 50 million instructions per second. Some mainframe computers operate at rates of hundreds of MIPS, whereas some very small computers may operate at a rate of less than one MIPS.

Control Unit

The **control unit** directs the entire computer system in carrying out its functions. It is very much like an orchestra director, for its primary function is to direct rather than participate in the activity.

Arithmetic Logic Unit (ALU)

The ALU is that part of the CPU that actually does the computational and logical work. Essentially, all work done by the computer passes through the ALU. As fast as it is, however, the ALU can only execute one instruction at a time. Furthermore, the ALU is physically preprogrammed with **microcode** to execute only a small set of elementary instructions such as add, multiply, compare, fetch, and store. The ALU can also subtract and divide, but in binary arithmetic these operations can be easily accomplished by addition and multiplication.

The ALU uses **registers** to temporarily store data while it performs its operations. For example, the normal procedure to add two numbers involves executing a series of instructions like those that follows:

1. Fetch the first number from primary memory (i.e., memory in the CPU) and store it in **computational register** number 1.
2. Fetch the second number from primary memory and store it in computational register number 2.
3. Add the two numbers together and store the results in a **storage register.**
4. Store the results of the register in primary memory.

Most CPUs contain only a handful of registers, which include computational registers, storage registers, address registers, and general-purpose registers. **Address registers** tell the ALU where in primary memory to find a given instruction or piece of data. **General-purpose registers** can be used for all the preceding functions.

Remember that the ALU processes only binary numbers. And no matter how complicated a task is, it must be broken down into the simple operations performed by the ALU.

Each of the main arithmetic registers is typically capable of storing one 32-bit or 64-bit word. A computer with such registers is called a 32-bit or 64-bit computer.

Primary Memory

The ALU normally retrieves from and stores instructions in **primary** or **central memory.** This type of memory has two important characteristics.

- It is normally **volatile,** meaning that data stored in it are lost if the computer's power is interrupted.
- It is **random-access memory (RAM),** meaning that given the appropriate **memory address,** the ALU can directly access any piece of data (normally a CPU word) in memory without having to search for it.

An example of memory addresses is given in Figure 3.18.

Read-only memory (ROM) is similar to RAM, the only differences being that data stored in ROM are nonvolatile and cannot be altered.

The ALUs in some CPUs contain a **processor cache,** which contains memory that can be more quickly accessed than primary memory. Processor or CPU caches are useful for storing instructions and data when the ALU demands instructions and data faster than they can be retrieved from primary memory. A CPU that outpaces primary memory must be programmed with **wait states,** which force it to slow down and wait for data. Loading data into a processor cache can avoid wait states.

System Bus

The CPU communicates with primary memory and various external devices through the **system bus,** which is simply the network of electrical pathways that connects all the internal components of a computer together. In some cases, external devices can also communicate directly with each other through the system bus.

Multiprocessor Computer Systems

Multiprocessor computer systems use multiple processors for their processing functions. Three approaches to multiprocessing are discussed: support processors, coupled processors, and parallel processors.

Support Processors

One approach to multiprocessing uses **support processors,** auxiliary CPUs or processors that are dedicated to performing special functions. Examples of special functions include communications, video, input/output, and audio processing. The main function of support processors is to take the workload off the main CPU, thus speeding up the computer's overall rate of operation.

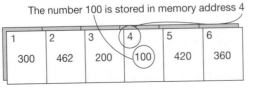

The number 100 is stored in memory address 4

1	2	3	4	5	6
300	462	200	100	420	360

FIGURE 3.18 Example of Memory Addresses.

Support processors operate by receiving instructions from the CPU. For example, in a video game, the main processor will send a few bytes of data to the audio processor, instructing it to play a note of music. The CPU will then continue about its business, without waiting for the audio processor to complete its task.

Most personal computers have **adapter slots** in which can be inserted **adapter cards** containing support processors and extra primary memory. Such adapter cards typically provide support for video graphics, communications, external storage devices (e.g., tapes and disks), and so on.

Coupled Processors

Some systems use **coupled processors**—multiple CPUs that share the same primary storage unit. One application of coupled processing is **fault tolerance,** which means that one CPU can fail or make an error without adversely impacting the performance of the overall system. A second application of coupled processing is **vector processing,** in which mathematical operations are broken down into components that are simultaneously executed on more than one processor.

Parallel Processors

Parallel processor systems use clusters or networks of possibly millions of interconnected processors (with some of them possibly coupled) that simultaneously operate on the same problem. Such systems are widely considered to be the key to providing artificial intelligence capabilities in future generations of computer systems.

Secondary Storage

Secondary storage is any means of storing data outside of the CPU. In this section we discuss several external storage devices, but first we define three additional data storage concepts: fields, records, and files.

A **field** or **data item** is an organized collection of bytes. Examples of fields include an employee social security number, a customer account number, a vendor name, and a customer account balance.

An organized collection of fields is called a **logical record** or **record.** For example, a customer record might consist of several fields, including customer account number, customer address, customer name, and account balance. Normally, the fields in a record pertain to some individual or object such as an employee, vendor, inventory part, or product.

A **physical record** or **block** is a collection of bytes separated from other physical records by blank space on an external storage device. Although the term *physical record* looks a lot like the term *logical record,* these two terms have no relationship to one another. Yet, because the two are so similar, there is sometimes confusion between them. This problem is compounded because often only the term **record** is used. To avoid confusion, we will use *record* and *logical record* interchangeably, but only *physical record* will be used to refer to physical records. Physical records are more thoroughly defined and discussed in what follows.

A **file** is a collection of related logical records. The typical accounting information system has all kinds of files—payroll files, inventory files, customer account files, sales order files, and so on. Finally, the term **database** is used to refer to an organized collection of files.

Figure 3.19 depicts the relationships between the various logical storage concepts pertaining to secondary storage. Machine words are not included in this hierarchy because they pertain only to the CPU, and physical records are not included because they relate primarily to physical (hardware) rather than logical storage concepts.

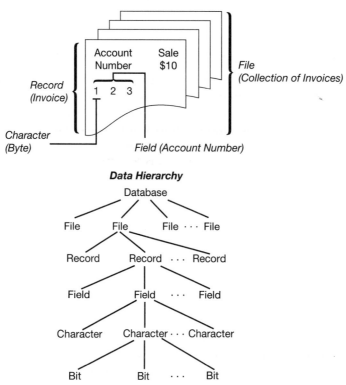

FIGURE 3.19 Relationship between Data Storage Concepts.

Magnetic Tape

There are two primary types of magnetic tapes used for storing data. The first type is the 10½-inch diameter reel of ½-inch-wide Mylar tape. The second type is the magnetic data cartridge, which comes in all sizes and shapes. Both types, however, use the same basic scheme for storing data: The tape is divided into rows called **tracks** or **channels** and columns called **frames.** Figure 3.20 gives an example of these concepts, using nine tracks to spell the word SYSTEMS in ASCII code. Each frame contains 1 byte of information stored in 9 bits or tracks. Note that the ninth track (i.e., the bottom one) is not part of the ASCII code. This track is used for error checking and contains the **parity bit.** In this example the parity bit is such that the total number of one bits in each frame, including the parity bit, adds up to an even number. This scheme is called **even parity.** If the parity bit is such that all the one bits in the frame, including the parity bit, add up to an odd number, the error-checking scheme is called **odd parity.** The computer utilizes this scheme by issuing a warning to the user whenever the total number of bits in a particular frame does not add up to the right number.

The capacity of a reel of tape in characters or bytes depends on how the data are recorded on the tape. To operate properly, the tape must pass under the read/write mechanism of the tape drive at a certain speed, otherwise pickup is distorted. In order for the tape to accelerate and come to a stop without bypassing data, blank sections of tape called interblock gaps (IBGs) must be left between physical records on the tape. A typical recording density is 6,250 BPI (bytes per inch). One logical record, for example, might contain 80 bytes of data. A ¾-inch gap is typical of that required by most tape drive units to stop and start again. If these records were placed on tape one by one with separating gaps, the tape would have the following format:

¾-inch gap, 0.0128-inch data, ¾-inch data, 0.0128-inch data, . . .

Using this scheme, over 98% of the tape would be blank. In order to increase the amount of data stored on the tape, several logical records are combined or **blocked** and written and read from the tape as a single physical record without separating gaps. The number of logical records that are grouped together as one physical record is called the **blocking factor.** In some cases, the user may select the blocking factor; in other cases, this will be done automatically by the software. Storing data on magnetic tape is depicted in Figures 3.21 and 3.22.

Magnetic tapes are very popular as a backup media. They carry the following benefits:

- **Portability.** Magnetic tapes can easily be carried from place to place.
- **Low cost.** Magnetic tapes are one of the least expensive ways to store data.
- **Reliability.** If stored under the right environmental conditions, magnetic tapes can retain data for many years.
- **High capacity.** Depending on the recording format, one magnetic tape can store billions of bytes of information.
- **Reusability.** Tapes can be written to, erased, and reused many times.

The major disadvantage of tape is that it is inherently a sequential-access medium. That is, in order to access a record or file that is on the end of a tape, one must first read the entire tape. On some systems, it can take as long as 10 minutes to retrieve a single piece of information from the end of the tape.

FIGURE 3.20 How Bytes Are Stored on Magnetic Tapes. The Bytes on This Section of Tape Spell the Word SYSTEMS in ASCII.

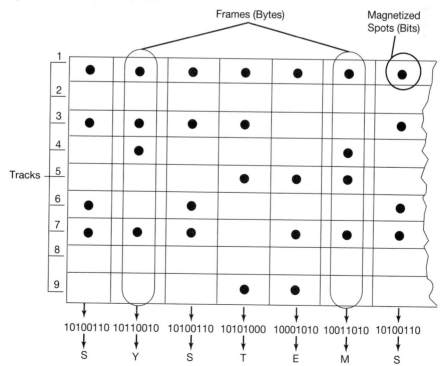

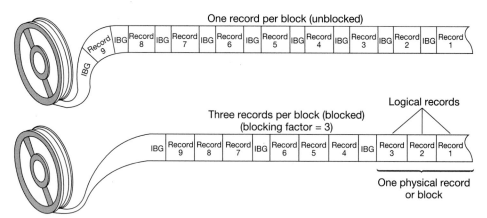

FIGURE 3.21 How Logical Records Are Blocked on Magnetic Tape.

Most cartridge tape systems are designed for backing up whole files. Individual files are arbitrarily broken up into blocks and copied to tape, and users do not need to be concerned about blocking. Furthermore, many of these systems use a different encoding scheme than that used by reel type tapes, and store all the data for one file on a single track. This allows the tape measurement software to store on the tape a master index that allows **quick file access** to any file on the tape. When the user requests that a particular file be restored, the program consults that master index to find out what track the desired file is stored on. The software then searches the indicated track. When used with a large number of tracks, this system can substantially reduce the time to restore a single file.

Direct-Access Storage Devices

A **direct-access storage device (DASD)** provides almost instant access to any physical record. Specifically, any physical record can be directly retrieved from the storage device without having to process unwanted data, as is the case with magnetic tape. The three major types of DASDs are magnetic disks, optical disks, and semiconductor memory. Each of these is discussed.

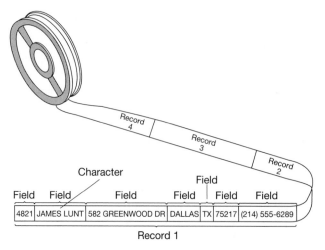

FIGURE 3.22 How Records Are Stored on Magnetic Tape.

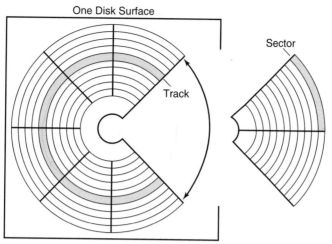

FIGURE 3.23 Looking Down a Disk Surface for a Personal Computer Diskette.

✓ **Magnetic Disks.**   In many ways, magnetic disks are similar to magnetic tapes. Data on disk are also stored in physical records called **sectors.** On a magnetic disk however, the physical records are stored in concentric circles called **tracks** (not to be confused with tracks on tapes), as is shown in Figure 3.23. The disk surface rotates at a high speed, allowing the drive unit's read/write heads to move in and out and quickly access any sector on the disk.

A diskette for a personal computer normally has two disk surfaces, which are stored inside a plastic casing. Diskettes, however, store only a relatively small amount of data, as compared to larger disk systems that contain many surfaces stacked on top of one another, with space in between them for read/write heads to pass. In multisurface disk systems, an additional storage concept is used, that of a cylinder. A **cylinder** consists of the set of tracks formed by including the same track number from each surface. For example, the outermost tracks on all surfaces would collectively form one cylinder. Cylinders are important because the drive unit can access any sector on a given cylinder without moving the read/write head. This means that access time can sometimes be improved by placing related records on the same cylinder.

✓ **Optical Disks.**   One of the most recent forms of disk storage is the **optical disk.** Optical disks work much like magnetic disks, except bits are encoded with laser beams rather than magnetic read/write heads. Optical disks are sometimes preferred to magnetic disks because data on them are normally stored more compactly than on magnetic disks. For example, a 3½-inch magnetic diskette might store a few megabytes of data, as compared to 600 or more megabytes on an optical disk that is about the same size.

Optical disks are often used for distributing copies of large databases such as encyclopedias, customer lists, maps of countries, and so on. In some cases optical disks might be used for backing up files, but magnetic tape is usually the preferred medium for this task. One reason for this is that many types of optical disks are not considered reliable for long-term storage.

Optical disks come in all sizes. **CD-ROM** (compact disk–read-only memory) disks are often used to distribute copies of databases to personal computer users. These disks cannot be altered. Another type of optical disk is the **rewritable** disk, which is capable of being written to and erased many times.

Semiconductor Storage.   Another method used for storage contains no moving parts: nonvolatile semiconductor memory. Random-access memory (RAM) is an example of semiconductor memory; only RAM is volatile, meaning its data are lost when the power is turned off or interrupted. One example of nonvolatile semiconductor memory used for secondary storage is **bubble memory.** There is also **battery-backed, low-power-consumption RAM,** which is volatile memory, but behaves like nonvolatile RAM because batteries provide a continuous power supply that may last for years.

Disadvantage   Semiconductor storage is more expensive than disk and tape, so it is mainly used for special applications, such as hand-held computers, that benefit from its light weight. Some predict, however, that semiconductor or other solid-state storage will eventually replace disks.

INPUT DEVICES

The Keyboard

The primary input device is the **keyboard.** The most common type of keyboard is the **QWERTY keyboard,** whose name represents the order of the keys across the top row of letters. A second type of keyboard is the **DVORAK,** which orders the keys in a more efficient manner that speeds up typing. Although most experts agree that the layout of keys on the DVORAK keyboard is more efficient than on the QWERTY keyboard, it has not become generally popular.

Many systems use custom keyboards, with special keys to ease data entry. McDonald's fast-food franchise, for example, uses one special key for hamburgers, another for small french fries, and so on. Many companies employ clerks and data entry operators, whose primary job is to key in (i.e., type) data into the computer system.

Pointing Devices

There are many devices that allow users to point to objects on the computer screen. One such device is the **mouse,** which is commonly used with graphically oriented computer programs to allow users to point to and select objects on the screen. Some programs allow users to point to **icons,** pictorial symbols of computer-related objects such as files or programs. For example, one can point to an icon of a trash can to discard (erase) an unwanted file.

Another pointing device is the **touch screen,** which is normally used to allow the user to select items from simple lists or menus. Touch screens are often used in applications that are oriented toward people with no previous computer experience.

There are many other kinds of pointing devices, including **joysticks** and **trackballs** (often seen in video arcades); there is even a **foot mouse** that attaches to one's foot, leaving both hands free. A **joystick** works like a mouse, except the user moves a short "stick" or vertical shaft back and forth to point. This device was popularized with video games.

Pen input is becoming increasingly popular. **Pen-based systems** allow users to write on the video display with something that looks like an ordinary ball-point pen. The pen can be used either as a pointing device like a mouse or to actually input handwriting into computer files such as word processing documents. Another form of pen input is the **light pen,** which uses a photoelectric circuit to enable the computer to determine the exact location of the pen on the video display.

A **digitizing tablet** is a pad or tablet on which the user draws images that are stored on the computer and displayed on the video display. This device allows the user the convenience of writing on a large surface in a natural manner.

Source Data Automation Devices

Source data automation refers to the use of special equipment to collect data at their source and directly input them into the computer. The purpose is to increase the productivity and efficiency of data entry by completely eliminating the need for human intervention. Devices used in source data automation include magnetic-ink character recognition, optical character recognition, and voice input.

Magnetic-Ink Character Recognition

Abbreviated MICR and pronounced "miker," **magnetic-ink character recognition** is commonly used by banks to read the numbers at the bottom of most checks. These numbers contain the bank routing number and the check owner's account number. Some telephone companies also use MICR to read the portions of customers' telephone bills returned with their monthly payments.

One advantage of MICR is that it can be used on ordinary paper. Characters are printed in ordinary-appearing but special magnetized ink, using a **MICR inscriber.** This provides the additional benefit of making the characters readable by both people and machines.

Optical Recognition Devices

All optical recognition devices somehow use the properties of light to scan and input data.

Optical Mark Recognition

scantron tests

One type of optical recognition method familiar to most students is **optical mark recognition (OMR).** This method is commonly used when students mark their answers with a number 2 pencil on answer sheets. Students place marks in small circles or boxes that correspond to the correct answers. This method has the advantage of working with ordinary paper, and individuals can make marks without special computer equipment or computer training.

Optical Character Recognition

There are many types of **optical character recognition (OCR)** devices. One of the most common is the **bar code reader,** which typically reads universal product codes with light reflected from projecting a laser or other beam onto the object to be scanned. **Universal product codes (UPCs)** are patterns of vertical lines (or bars) that uniquely identify almost all retail products sold in the United States.

Bar code readers are very often used at **point-of-sale (POS) terminals,** which collect the scanned pricing and product information for either immediate or delayed processing by the company's computer network. When such information is processed immediately, it provides the company with up-to-the-moment access to its inventory levels.

Another type of optical recognition device is the **wand reader.** This device reads a special kind of typeface called **OCR-A,** which consists of boxy-looking characters imprinted in ordinary ink. Like MICR characters, OCR-A has the advantage of being readable by both people and machines. This device is used mostly in retail stores, libraries, and hospitals.

There is also the graphics-oriented **optical scanner.** This device might be either a hand-held or flatbed scanner that is used to scan text and graphics images from sources such as photographs, books, newspapers, and so on. **OCR software** is required to convert images of scanned text into actual text that can be used by various computer applications. However, this process of converting images to text suffers from errors and is therefore often too unreliable to use for critical applications of source data automation.

In general, there are almost an unlimited number of ways to input data into the computer. For example, in weather analysis, devices exist to measure and digitize rainfall. In medicine, cardiologists use electrodes to connect their patients to computers and measure pulse, blood pressure, and so on. In publishing, cameras are plugged directly into the personal computer to transfer images directly into documents.

Voice Input Devices

In many applications there is a need for someone to input data into the computer without using his or her hands. For example, someone inspecting items on the assembly line might not have a free hand to note that a particular item failed inspection. At present, **voice input** is accomplished with **speech recognition,** a combination of hardware and software that converts speech first into digital data and then into words or characters. Many speech-recognition systems must be trained to recognize specific words for a specific user's voice. Furthermore, most of these systems require individuals to pause between spoken words. Despite their limited abilities, however, these systems can be very useful in applications where the input is limited to a reasonably small number of words.

OUTPUT DEVICES

Video Display

The **video display monitor,** or **monitor,** is the most common output device relating to the user's direct interaction with the computer. Video images are composed of a large number of small dots called **pixels.**

Printers

One of the fastest and most versatile types of printer is the **laser printer.** This type of printer looks and acts very much like a photocopying machine. It prints a whole page at a time and is quiet, fast, and capable of printing graphics. The most expensive laser printers are capable of printing hundreds of pages per minute.

Ink-jet printers literally spray ink onto the paper. They have most of the advantages of laser printers, except they are often not as fast.

Voice Output

Voice output can be achieved by using prerecorded sounds or words, or by speech synthesis. **Speech synthesis** is often accomplished by an auxiliary processor and special-purpose software. Computer-based text is converted into various **phonemes,** the sounds that make up all words. It is also possible to digitally record and store various words on, say, disk. Computer programs are commercially available that will convert computer text into voice output.

Computer Output on Microfilm (COM)

Computer output on microfilm (COM) equipment outputs computer data on microfilm in human-readable form. There are two techniques for generating COM from computer data. One method first displays information on the computer screen. The microfilm record is then produced by photographing the displayed information. Another method imprints the data directly onto the film without photographing the display.

A COM device can output upward of 32,000 lines per minute. Furthermore, space reductions of 90% to 95% (as compared to paper output) are typically realized through the use of COM, thus resulting in a space-saving way to output data.

Graphics Output Devices

Some output devices are dedicated primarily to generating **graphics output.** These include plotters, overhead transparency makers, and 35-mm slide makers.

Plotters

Sometimes it is desirable to output graphics such as charts, maps, and drawings onto paper much larger than normally used by graphics printers. This can be accomplished by a **pen plotter,** a device with a small mechanical arm that moves an ink pen across the paper and draws the desired graphic objects. Some pen plotters hold a carousel containing an assortment of different pens, thus allowing the user's software to change pens repeatedly as the plot is being generated. For relatively small and simple drawings, a pen plotter might not be necessary, and a graphics printer should suffice.

Overhead Transparency Makers

Many graphics printers (especially laser printers) and plotters are capable of printing on sheets of acetate, as well as sheets of paper. This allows the generation of overhead transparencies.

35-mm Slide Makers

The Polaroid Pallet is an example of a device that plugs into the personal computer and produces instant slides, no developing required. Another method to making slides and photographs of computer graphics is to first display the image of interest on the video display, and then take its picture using an ordinary camera. Some manufacturers sell conelike devices that fit over the front of both the display and camera lens, thus keeping external light from affecting the photograph.

There are many more input and output devices not discussed here. New devices are coming to the market all the time. Those discussed here should be thought of as important examples.

COMPUTER SOFTWARE

Software is perhaps the most important part of the computer system, next to the user. In fact, the best way to buy a computer is to first select the software and then select the computer. No matter how state-of-the-art the computer is, it is of little value without the right software. The discussion that follows divides software into three broad categories: operating systems and their extensions, user application programs, and computer languages (translators).

Operating System

The **operating system** is a set of computer programs that is part of the software interface between the user and the hardware (Figure 3.24). It serves three primary functions: accounting and security, management and allocation of computer system resources, and software services to user application programs. The extent to which these three functions are provided depends on the particular operating system. For example, some operating systems have extensive layers of security, but others (such as those used on single-user personal computers) have little or no security at all.

Accounting and Security

Most **multiuser operating systems** such as those used in networks and large computer systems provides extensive security that limits access to the system and its resources, protects files, and protects memory. Accounting and security are partly accomplished by assigning computer accounts to all users.

All access to the computer is controlled through the user account. The **user account,** created by systems personnel, allows the user to **log on** (access) the computer by entering an appropriate **user account number** (or **user ID**) and **log-on password.** Once logged on, the user's activities and utilization of computer system resources are constantly monitored, recorded, and limited by the operating system.

The operating system associates with each user account a set of predefined **user limits,** established by systems personnel. These limits specify the resources available to the user, stated in terms of maximums such as those that follow:

- The maximum amount of disk storage the user can utilize.
- The maximum number of files the user can create.
- The maximum number of lines or pages the user can print.
- The maximum amount of CPU time the user can use.
- The maximum amount of primary memory available to the user.

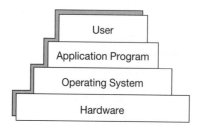

FIGURE 3.24 Conceptual Diagram for the Operating System.

There are also access limits that may or may not give the user permission to do other things, including the following:

- Access magnetic tape drives.
- Access particular files or programs.

Some operating systems allow the assigning of **security levels** to users. For example, if the highest level of security is 1 and the lowest level is 10, then an individual with a security level of 4 could do anything that someone with a security level of 5 could do. But the individual with level-4 security would have privileges not available to the individual with security level 5.

Many operating systems allow systems personnel to specify complicated formulas for charging users for their **computer usage.** In such systems, the user account limits will contain the maximum number of dollars that a user can use. Once a user reaches that dollar limit, he or she can no longer log onto the system. Furthermore, users' charges can be a basis of allocating or charging the costs of operating the computer system to individual users, departments, or divisions.

Most operating systems also provide security by providing each user with a private file catalog. Within this area, the user can create, modify, and erase files. Furthermore, each user can assign to each file his or her own **file permissions** such as the following:

- Public: any user on the system could access the file
- Private: no one else can access the file
- Semiprivate: any user with the correct password can access the file

The user can also designate whether others can or cannot modify or erase each of his or her public or semiprivate files.

Allocation and Management of Systems Resources

All multiuser computer operating systems must deal with **resource contention,** the simultaneous demand by more than one user for the use of a particular component of the computer. For example, if at the same time two users both attempt to use the CPU, the operating system must ensure that both users' needs are met in an orderly and secure manner. **Multiprogramming** is a general-operating-system-related technique that allows two or more programs to execute concurrently on the same computer. The operating system achieves such **concurrent processing** by having the CPU swap its attention back and forth between the different programs. Normally, the **swapping** is done so fast that each concurrently executing program appears to have that CPU all to itself.

Applications of Multiprogramming.   One application of multiprogramming is **time sharing,** a technique that allows more than one user to concurrently interact with or execute programs on the computer. The operating system often accomplishes time sharing by allocating the CPU in small **time slices** (amounts of time) to users in a **round-robin** fashion: Each user in turn receives the attention of the CPU. This technique often works well because individual users normally do not need to use the CPU while their programs are inputting data, or while they are idle or merely typing at a **computer terminal** (a keyboard and video display attached to the computer). Such tasks are often managed by support processes. If all users really need the CPU at the same time, and there are too many users at once, then the overall **response time** of the system will be degraded. That is, the computer will seem inordinately slow to all users.

A second application of multiprogramming is **multitasking,** which is the concurrent execution of more than one program by the same individual. In some operating systems and their extensions, users are allowed to concurrently run several programs, with each program appearing on a portion of the video display called a **window.** When several programs are executing concurrently, but only one program appears on the screen, it is called the **foreground task.** The executing programs not visible on the screen are called **background tasks.** It is sometimes desirable to allocate larger time slices to foreground tasks.

[handwritten margin note: several programs running at the same time.]

In multiprogramming, it is desirable to have more than one user's program residing in memory at the same time. If all the concurrent programs are collectively too large to fit into primary memory at the same time, then one or more of them will be swapped to disk when it is not executing, and then swapped back to primary memory when necessary. Having more than one program in memory at the same time, however, makes it possible for one program to destroy or modify another. This is prevented by **memory protection,** which in some CPUs is implemented at the hardware level, with the CPU running in **protected mode.**

Other Resource Allocation Techniques.   In some systems it is possible to execute a program that is too large to fit into memory. This is accomplished by virtual memory, which means that at any one point in time, only part of the program is in primary memory and the rest is on disk. The part on disk is said to be in **virtual memory,** and the part in primary memory is said to be in **real memory.** The system swaps the parts of the program in and out of real memory as needed. Running some programs in virtual memory, however, may require excessive swapping, called **thrashing.** A program that thrashes too much might not complete its work in a reasonable length of time, because it is being slowed down by too many disk operations.

What if more than one user wants to print a file or document at the same time? This problem is solved by a technique called **spooling,** in which the files or documents to be printed are copied to a special storage area and placed in a **queue** where each job is printed according to its turn or priority. Spooling may also be used for other purposes besides printing.

Software Services

Operating system software service includes software libraries, program loading and linking, and a control language.

✓ **Software Libraries.**   Many operating systems provide a library of programs that can be accessed by user programs. An example of such programs includes **input/output routines.** For example, when a user's program wants to read data from a disk, it will make an appropriate request to the operating system routine for reading disk drives. This routine will then request the data from the disk controller (the support processor controlling the disk), which will return the needed data to the operating system. The operating system will then relay the data to the user's program.

Why such a complicated, multilevel method of retrieving data? The answer is that with this method the user program does not need to know the commands to operate the disk controller, which would be difficult to learn because there are many types of controllers on the market, and because these commands vary from controller to controller. Further, if the user's program directly accesses the controller, it might no longer work if the controller were replaced by a newer model.

The operating software programs that control access to the disk controller and other input/output devices are called **device drivers.** Relying on device drivers helps make the user's application program **device independent.** A program is device independent if it will work with any device supported by the operating system under which it is developed, or with any device supported by any other operating system that supports the same device drivers.

Program Loading and Linking.   Another software service provided to user programs by the operating system is program loading and linking. **Program loading** or **loading** refers to loading (i.e., copying) a machine language program from a secondary storage device into central memory for execution. **Program linking** or **linking** refers to the process of connecting together more than one related program before loading.

Operating System Control Language.   Many operating systems provide users with a wide variety of utility programs that are executed in response to users' commands. The **operating system control language,** also called **operating system (OS) commands** or **job control language (JCL),** is the set of commands or control statements that the operating system accepts from users. Simple OS commands might do things like erasing files, copying files, printing files, or loading programs.

In most sophisticated systems, OS commands can be entered either in immediate mode or batch mode. In **immediate** or **interactive mode,** the operating system executes commands as the user enters them. For example, a user might enter the command ERASE JONES.DAT and receive an immediate response "JONES.DAT erased."

When executing OS commands run in batch mode, the user places many OS control statements in files, which the operating system executes in sequence. Such a file of OS commands is called a **batch** or **procedure file.** Batch files are useful for carrying out routine tasks, because they obviate the need to repeatedly type the same commands.

In many systems, the user does not need to learn the operating system control language but rather issues commands through a shell program. A **shell** is a user-friendly program, typically a **graphical user interface (GUI),** that allows users to execute OS commands without having to learn them. Microsoft Windows and Microsoft NT are good examples of GUI type operating environments, and these operating environments allow users to run programs, erase files, print files, and so on, by simply pointing and clicking a mouse. Another example is OS/2 Presentation Manager, which runs on most IBM-compatible personal computers.

Standardized Operating Systems

The majority of operating systems are designed to run on a particular group of computers with similar processors. In the IBM mainframe environment, many computers use CMS and TSO. DEC computers often use VMS. IBM-compatible personal computers use Microsoft's MS-DOS, Windows, OS/2, or sometimes UNIX, a multiuser, time-sharing operating system. Apple computers use their own operating system. Many in the scientific community and the federal government have advocated UNIX as a "standard" operating system. UNIX was popularized in the late 1970s, before the personal computer revolution, when its developer, AT&T's Bell Laboratories, gave it away to many colleges and universities. Today, UNIX still remains so popular that it runs on every type of computer from the Cray supercomputer to personal computers. It is doubtful, however, that any one operating system will become a universal standard adopted by all users.

User Application Programs

User application programs, or **user applications,** are programs developed to meet particular user needs. Such programs can be either internally developed or purchased from an outside vendor.

✓ Computer Languages

Computer languages can be classified according to generations. **First-generation programs** are written in machine language, sometimes called **object code,** which consists of simple binary instructions. Almost no one writes programs in machine language anymore. **Second-generation programs** are written in **assembly language,** which is almost identical to machine language, except the binary instructions are replaced by **mnemonics** (names) like ADD, FETCH, and so on. Programs written in assembly language must be converted or **translated** into binary by an **assembler** program, which mainly substitutes the binary codes for the mnemonics. Very few people write programs in assembly language. Nevertheless, some programmers prefer to use assembly language because it allows them to work closely with the hardware, which very often results in relatively fast-running program code. **Third-generation programs** are written in **high-level languages** such as BASIC, COBOL, Fortran, or C. Such languages greatly simplify the task of programming, because they allow the programmer to accomplish in a single program statement what would take many assembly-language or machine-language statements.

Each high-level programming language has its unique advantages. Some examples follow.

- **BASIC** (Beginners All-purpose Symbolic Instruction Code) was developed for teaching programming skills to college students.
- **C** (which evolved from earlier versions of the same language called A and B) was developed for systems programmers to develop operating systems.
- **C++** was developed to be an **object-oriented language,** which allows programmers to manipulate "objects," or classes, that are related to each other through a property called **inheritance.** An object inherits all the properties of its class. Object-oriented programming is becoming increasingly popular.
- **COBOL** (COmmon Business-Oriented Language) was developed for business applications and introduced by a consortium called **CODASYL (COnference of DAta SYstem Languages).**
- **FORTH** was originally designed for controlling physical devices (such as telescopes) and is sometimes used in graphics applications.
- **Fortran** (short for formula translator) was developed for scientific and engineering applications.

Third-generation programs, like assembler programs, must also be translated into machine language. This is accomplished with a compiler program. The **compiler program** converts the **source code** (a generic name for program statements) into object code. **Fourth-generation languages,** sometimes called **very-high-level languages,** require even fewer programming statements to accomplish a given task than do third-generation languages. Languages in this generation tend to allow the programmer to focus on *what* he or she wants to accomplish rather than *how* he or she wants to accomplish it. A good example of a language from this generation is dBase. This database language allows the programmer to define an entire database with a single program statement. Fourth-generation programs must also be converted into machine language.

Fifth-generation languages include natural languages that allow the "programmer" or user to converse with the computer without any training in programming or experience in computing. Some of the higher-end database programs contain natural-language interfaces. A true natural language, however, would be ordinary English.

Programs can be compiled, or interpreted, into machine language for execution. A compiler takes an entire computer program and converts it into machine language. An interpreter, on the other hand, converts program statements to binary and executes them individually as they are interactively entered into the computer. Many computer languages work as either interpreters or compilers. Compiled code runs much faster than interpreted code.

COMMUNICATIONS NETWORKS

A computer network, or **network,** exists when one computer communicates with another computer. (We use the term *computer* loosely to include computer terminals, personal computers, mainframes, and so on.) Recall that networks are sometimes classified according to the geographical area they cover. **Wide area networks (WANs)** typically cover more than one metropolitan area. **Metropolitan area networks (MANs)** cover a single metropolitan area, and local **area networks (LANs)** cover a small area such as a single building or group of buildings that are near each other.

All networks can be characterized by their **architecture,** which consists of the physical layout, or **topology,** and a set of communication protocols. **Communication protocols** consists of both the physical equipment and the software services required for one computer device to communicate with another. Protocols are necessary to ensure an orderly flow of data through the network.

Managing Networks

A network is managed by a **network administrator.** Even for a small network, the responsibilities of a network administrator are important. Some of the administrator's problems include adding and deleting users from the network, assessing and managing network throughput and response time, diagnosing hardware and software problems, developing and distributing documentation, file and document management, security, and providing consulting to users. For a large enough network, the administrator might manage hundreds or even thousands of employees. The important point is that all networks, even small ones, require some administration, and someone has to be in charge.

Appendix Glossary

ADSL: a high-speed communications protocol capable of carrying full-motion video over standard copper telephone wires.

ARCHIE: a software product that searches anonymous FTP sites for files.

arithmetic logic unit (ALU): part of the CPU that actually does the computational and logical work.

ASCII: American Standard Code for Information Interchange, an 8-bit coding scheme.

assembler program: software that converts assembly language source code into object code.

assembly language: binary machine instructions are replaced by mnemonic codes.

BCD: Binary coded decimal, a 6-bit data coding scheme.

bit: binary digit.

block: several logical records that are separated from other physical records by blank space on an external storage device.

blocked records: several logical records are combined and written and read from magnetic tape as a single physical record without separating gaps.

broadcast: WAN topology where a given message is received at more than one destination.

byte: a collection of bits used to represent a single character of data.

CD-ROM: compact (optical) disk–read-only memory.

central processor unit (CPU): the internal part of the computer that executes the instructions given to it by computer programs.

communication protocols: the physical equipment and the software services required for one computer device to communicate with another.

compiler program: software that converts high-level language source code into object code.

computer output on microfilm (COM): equipment that outputs computer data on microfilm in human-readable form.

computer system: an integrated combination of hardware, software, communications, human resources, information resources, and processing procedures.

coupled processors: multiple CPUs that share the same primary storage unit.

cylinder: the set of tracks formed by including the same track number from each surface of a magnetic disk.

database: an organized collection of files.

data highway: the emerging worldwide communications network.

data item: synonym for field.

desktop publishing: the capability to produce typeset-quality formatting and printing on a personal computer.

device drivers: operating software programs that control access to the disk controller and other input/output devices.

domain name: the last part of an Internet address.

dot-matrix printers: print characters as tightly grouped sets of very small dots.

downsizing: replacing minicomputers or mainframes with a network of personal computers.

EBCDIC: Extended Binary Coded Decimal Interchange Code, an 8-bit data coding scheme.

Ethernet: a popular and relatively inexpensive LAN technology.

fault tolerance: use of coupled processors such that one CPU can fail or make an error without adversely impacting system performance.

field: an organized collection of bytes.

fifth-generation languages: natural languages that allow the "programmer" or user to converse with the computer without any training in programming or experience in computing.

file: a collection of related logical records.

first-generation program: written in machine language, which consists of simple binary instructions.

floating-point decimal numbers: numbers with decimal points in them.

fonts: character sets used in graphics printers.

fourth-generation program: written in languages that require even fewer programming statements to accomplish a given task than do third-generation languages.

front-end processors: support processors used as communications processors.

FTP: an Internet-related program that allows one to send and receive files from a catalog on a remote computer.

GOPHER: an Internet-related program that allows one to use menus to access files on a particular remote computer.

hardware: physical computer equipment.

high-level languages: languages that simplify the task of programming by allowing the programmer to accomplish in a single program statement what would take many assembly-language or machine-language statements.

icons: pictorial symbols of computer-related objects such as files or programs.

Internet: a large public network that comprises hundreds of smaller, connected, public and private networks.

Internet address: the unique address that allows one to access a remote computer on Internet.

Internet Service Mediator: a program that provides simplified, menu-oriented access to Internet-related programs such as ARCHIE, VERONICA, and HYTELNET.

ISDN: an all-digital telephone network.

job control language (JCL): synonym for operating system (OS) commands.

laser printers: fast and versatile type of printer that operates much like a photocopying machine.

leased lines: full-time dedicated lines that can be leased from the major telephone companies.

local area network (LAN): covers a small area such as a single building or a group of buildings that are near each other.

logical record: synonym for record.

log on: to access a computer by entering an appropriate user account number and password.

machine language: binary instructions that are directly executable by computers.

magnetic-ink character recognition (MICR): an input method commonly used by banks to read the numbers at the bottom of checks.

mainframe computers: large computers used by corporations and government institutions for centralized data processing.

metropolitan area network (MAN): covers a single metropolitan area.

MIPS: millions of instructions per second.

modem: device that converts digital computer signals into the analog signals used by telephone companies (for outgoing data), and converts analog signals into digital signals (for incoming data).

multiplexing: type of medium-access control where devices on a network take turns using the medium, with each device using the medium for only a fraction of a second at a time.

multiprogramming: a general operating-system-related technique that allows two or more programs to execute concurrently on the same computer.

multitasking: the concurrent execution of more than one program by the same individual.

network: technology that allows one computer to communicate with another computer.

network administrator: person responsible for network management.

object code: synonym for machine language.

OCR-A: a typeface used in OCR.

open systems interconnection (OSI) model: seven-layer model (set of protocols) for network communications sponsored by the International Standards Organization (ISO).

operating system: a set of computer programs that is part of the software interface between the user and computer hardware.

operating system control language: the set of commands or control statements that the operating system accepts from users.

optical character recognition (OCR): source data automation devices used to recognize character input.

parity bit: a bit used for error checking.

PBX: private telephone branch exchange that provides digital lines.

personal computer: one inexpensive enough to be owned by one person.

physical record: synonym for block.

point to point: WAN topology where a given message is received at only one destination.

processor cache: contains memory that can be more quickly accessed than primary memory.

random-access memory (RAM): directly accessible memory that can be both written to and read from.

read-only memory (ROM): nonvolatile memory that is read only, as it cannot be altered.

record: an organized collection of fields.

registers: used by the ALU to temporarily store data while it performs its operations.

RISC: reduced instruction set computing technology. Fewer internal machine instructions are used to complete numerical and logical operations.

secondary storage: any means of storing data outside of the CPU.

second-generation program: written in assembly language.

shell: a user-friendly program that allows users to execute OS commands without having to learn them.

software: computer programs that contain the instructions required for a computer to complete a task.

source code: a generic name for user-prepared program statements that is applicable to all generations of languages.

source data automation (SDA): the use of special equipment to collect data at its source and directly input it into the computer.

supercomputers: the fastest computers.

support processors: auxilliary CPUs or processors that are dedicated to performing special functions.

system bus: means by which the CPU communicates with primary memory and various external devices.

TELNET: an Internet-related program that allows one to log onto an account on a remote computer.

third-generation program: written in high-level language.

time sharing: a technique that allows more than one user to concurrently interact or execute programs on the computer.

token passing: a special message (token) is needed to access the communication medium in a LAN.

vector processing: mathematical operations are broken down into components that are simultaneously executed on more than one processor.

very-high-level languages: synonym for fourth-level language.

virtual memory: operating system technique that makes it possible to execute a program that is too large to fit into primary memory.

wide area network (WAN): typically covers more than one metropolitan area.

word: a collection of bits used internally in the computer to represent numbers in binary.

WORM: write once, read many form of optical disk.

WWW (World Wide Web): a browsable world-wide virtual library in which documents on different computers are connected to each other by key words.

CHAPTER 4

Introduction to Transaction Processing

LEARNING OBJECTIVES

Careful study of this chapter will enable you to:

- Provide an overview description of the flow of transaction data in a manufacturing firm.

- Discuss the basic components of transaction processing systems.

- Describe the process by which a double-entry accounting system would be designed and implemented.

- Depict common coding systems that are used in transaction processing, with particular emphasis on coding an organization's chart of accounts.

- Discuss forms design and records retention requirements, including federal electronic tax-records retention requirements.

TRANSACTION FLOWS: AN OVERVIEW

The term **transaction processing** encompasses the variety of activities an organization must undertake to support its day-to-day operations. Figure 4.1 is a logical data flow diagram of the transaction flows of a manufacturing firm. Each square in Figure 4.1 represents an entity—a customer, a vendor, or an employee. The processes represent closely related processing activities that are commonly organized as **application systems.** As defined in Chapter 1, an application system processes logically related transactions. Each arrow in Figure 4.1 indicates a transaction flow from one entity/application system to another entity/application system. The following discussion is keyed to the numbers on the arrows shown in Figure 4.1. These flows occur in both manual and computerized systems.

Transaction Flows in a Manufacturing Firm

1. Customers place orders for items with the sales order application system. Orders may be placed by customers themselves or through salespeople. Orders may be written or telephoned. The sales order system must convert the order into the data necessary to support further processing of the order by other related application systems.

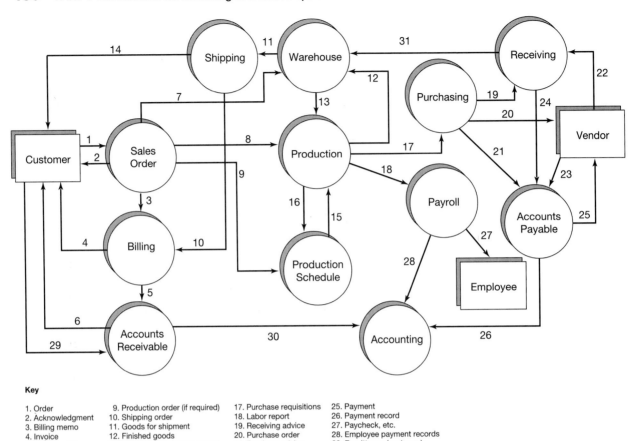

Key

1. Order
2. Acknowledgment
3. Billing memo
4. Invoice
5. Invoice advice
6. Statement
7. Shipping order
8. Production order
9. Production order (if required)
10. Shipping order
11. Goods for shipment
12. Finished goods
13. Production order (if required)
14. Goods to customer
15. Production schedule
16. Production status
17. Purchase requisitions
18. Labor report
19. Receiving advice
20. Purchase order
21. Purchase advice
22. Merchandise
23. Invoice
24. Receiving voucher
25. Payment
26. Payment record
27. Paycheck, etc.
28. Employee payment records
29. Remittance (customer)
30. Cash receipts
31. Purchased goods

FIGURE 4.1 Transaction Flows in a Manufacturing Firm.

2. The sales order application will often send the customer an acknowledgment form to inform the customer that the order was received and is in processing.

3. The sales order application sends a billing memo to the billing application system. This memo provides data that will be necessary in preparing the customer's invoice for the items that were ordered.

4. The billing application system sends an invoice (bill) to the customer for payment. Frequently, the bill is not prepared until a shipping advice (flow 10) has been received from shipping.

5. Billing sends an invoice advice to the accounts receivable application system. Accounts receivable is responsible for maintaining the customer database and must update this to reflect this transaction.

6. Periodically, the accounts receivable application system sends customers a statement that specifies the total amount each customer owes the firm. Generally, these statements show more than one single customer order/transaction.

7. The sales order application system sends a shipping order to the warehouse. This document specifies what a customer has ordered as well as when and where the shipment should be sent.

8. A customer order might require that a production order be sent to the production facilities if the goods ordered are either a custom, nonstock order or if the goods ordered are temporarily out-of-stock.

9. Alternatively, depending on how the production application systems are organized, production orders placed by the sales order application may be sent to production scheduling.

10. After shipping items to customers, shipping sends a copy of the shipping order to the billing system to document actual shipments and to permit accurate completion of the billing process.

11. Items to be shipped to customers are sent from the warehouse to the shipping function.

12. Finished goods are sent from the production system to the warehouse for storage.

13. Depending on the way in which application systems are organized, out-of-stock conditions may be noted in the warehouse. In this case a production order is sent to production (or possibly production scheduling) to replace the stock.

14. Goods are sent or delivered to the customer.

15. The production scheduling application sends a production schedule to the production system. This schedule authorizes and controls the production system.

16. A production status report is sent to the production scheduling system so that production schedules can be reviewed and revised.

17. The production system sends a purchase requisition to the purchasing application system. Raw materials must be ordered for production. The purchasing application system is responsible for placing orders with vendors.

18. Production sends a labor report to the payroll system so that employees can be paid and production costs accumulated.

19. Purchasing sends a receiving advice to the receiving application. This document authorizes the receiving function to accept shipments from vendors.

20. Purchasing sends purchase orders to vendors to order goods.

21. A purchase advice is sent to the accounts payable application system to initiate the payment process.

22. Merchandise is received from vendors.

23. Vendors send invoices to the firm for payment. These invoices must be approved by the accounts payable application system.

24. Receiving notifies accounts payable that goods that have been ordered have been received.

25. Accounts payable authorizes payment to the vendor.

26. Payment records are forwarded to the accounting application system for processing.

27. Employees receive paychecks and other documents from the payroll system.

28. Employee payment records are forwarded to the accounting application system for processing.

29. Customers remit payments on their account to the firm.

30. Cash receipts records are processed by the accounting application system.

31. Purchased goods are sent from receiving to the warehouse for storage.

Transaction Cycles and Application Systems

The previous discussion illustrates the complexity of transaction flows in a typical organization. Even though no two organizations process transactional data in exactly the same manner, most organizations experience and process similar transaction flows. The transaction processing cycle concept, introduced in Chapter 1, suggests that operational transaction flows can be grouped according to four common cycles of business activity:

1/26/99

- Revenue cycle. Events related to the distribution of goods and services to other entities and the collection of related payments.
- Expenditure cycle. Events related to the acquisition of goods and services from other entities and the settlement of related obligations.
- Production cycle. Events related to the transformation of resources into goods and services.
- Finance cycle. Events related to the acquisition and management of capital funds, including cash.

Transaction cycles provide a framework for discussing transaction processing systems. For example, the 31 transaction flows just discussed might be classified as illustrated in Table 4.1.

This classification should be viewed as illustrative only. Every organization is unique and, accordingly, has its own perception of which transaction flows could be classified into each cycle. Even though every organization is unique, the application systems shown in Figure 4.1 are common to the vast majority of organizations. Most organizations have a sales order application, a billing application, an accounts receivable application, and all of the other application systems mentioned in the discussion of Figure 4.1.

Why is this so? There are two factors that contribute to this commonality. The first is specialization of function. For example, as more and more bills need to be prepared, it makes sense to have a separate bill-preparing function—a billing application system. This is true for purchase orders, paychecks, and any other document that must routinely be generated. Thus, purchasing application systems and payroll application systems are common in organizations.

The second factor is the nature of internal control, which was introduced in Chapter 1. As indicated there, a common control principle is to maintain a separation of function between operational activities and the record keeping for those activities. One common example of this principle is the separation of the billing function—an operational activity—from the accounts receivable function—the related record-keeping function.

Internal control also exerts a major influence on the design of application systems. Principles of internal control are discussed in depth in Chapter 5.

* A process designed to provide reasonable assurance regarding the achievement of objectives in:
a) reliability in financial reporting
b) effectiveness & efficiency of operations
c) compliance w/ applicable laws & regulations.

TABLE 4-1   Classification of the Transaction Flows in Figure 4.1 by Transaction Cycle

| | Cycle | | |
Revenue	Expenditure	Production	Finance
1	17	8	25
2	19	9	29
3	20	12	30
4	21	13	
5	22	15	
6	23	16	
7	24	18	
10	26		
11	27		
14	28		
	31		

Chapters 7 and 8 discuss in-depth principles of internal control as these principles are implemented in revenue, expenditure, production, and finance application systems.

1/26/99

COMPONENTS OF THE TRANSACTION PROCESSING SYSTEM

4

The principal components of a transaction processing system include inputs, processing, storage, and outputs. These components or elements are part of both manual and computerized systems.

① Inputs

Source documents, such as customer orders, sales slips, invoices, purchase orders, and employee time cards, are the physical evidence of inputs into the transaction processing system. They serve several purposes:

- Capture data
- Facilitate operations by communicating data and authorizing another operation in the process
- Standardize operations by indicating what data require recording and what actions need to be taken
- Provide a permanent file for future analysis, if the documents are retained

Source documents are typically forms carefully designed for ease of use and accurate data capture.

② Processing

Processing involves the use of journals and registers to provide a permanent and chronological record of inputs. The entries are done either by hand in simple manual systems (journalized) or by a data entry operator using a PC. Journals are used to record financial accounting transactions, and **registers** are used to record other types of data not directly related to accounting.

Journals are used to provide a chronological record of financial transactions. It is theoretically possible, but not often practicable, to use the two-column general journal as the only book of original entry. However, to effect a division and saving of labor, special journals with special analysis columns are used to record similar and recurring transactions. Some of the more common special journals that may be kept are as follows:

- **sales journal:** used to summarize sales made on account
- **purchase journal:** used to summarize purchases made on account
- **cash receipts journal:** used to summarize receipts of cash
- **cash disbursements journal:** used to summarize disbursements of cash

These four types of journals are often used in conjunction with a separate general journal to provide a complete bookkeeping system (see Figure 4.2). Special columns can be used in these books of original entry to facilitate recording transactions or for classification of data.

The design of special-purpose journals is one of the most important steps in

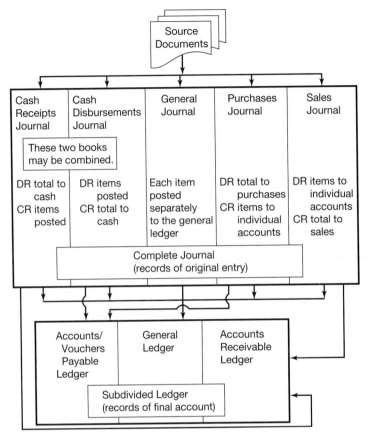

FIGURE 4.2 Five-Journal Bookkeeping System.

the design of an accounting system. Journals must be carefully designed if they are truly to economize clerical effort and at the same time function as true posting media in routing debits and credits to the ledger. Properly designed special journals eliminate numerous postings and at the same time enable one to obtain quickly the totals for all major transactions.

Storage

Ledgers and files provide storage of data in both manual and computerized systems. The general ledger, the accounts/vouchers payable ledger, and the accounts receivable ledger are the records of final account. They provide summaries of a firm's financial accounting transactions. All accounting transactions must be reflected in the general ledger. A debit–credit entry is input for every transaction. Traditionally, this process has been called **posting.** The general ledger generates a trial balance to test the accuracy of all the prior record keeping.

A **file** is an organized collection of data. There are several types of files. A **transaction file** is a collection of transaction input data. Transaction files usually contain data that are of temporary rather than permanent interest. By contrast, a **master file** contains data that are of a more permanent or continuing interest. To illustrate this difference, consider the posting of sales on account to the accounts receivable ledger. Because a sales journal is a chronological record of sales-on-account transactions, it may be called a transaction file. The transaction file consists of raw data concerning sales to customers. Although there may be several sales to the same customer, this will not be known until the transaction data are processed. The process of posting sales to the accounts receivable ledger summarizes sales to an individual customer. Processing converts data into information. Management is more interested in summary data such as total sales and total account balance than in the details of a particular sales transaction. Management thus has a permanent interest in the information that is contained in the accounts receivable master file. In contrast, management's interest in transaction files is temporary. Once the data have been processed to update master files, they are no longer of direct interest to management. Transaction files must be saved, of course, to maintain an audit trail.

A **reference** or **table file** contains data that are necessary to support data processing. Common examples of reference files used in data processing are payroll tax tables and master price lists.

④ Outputs

There is a wide variety of outputs from a transaction processing system. Any document generated in the system is an output. Some documents are both output and input (e.g., a customer invoice is an output from the order-entry application system and also an input document to the customer). Other common outputs of a transaction processing system are the trial balance, financial reports, operational reports, paychecks, bills of lading, and voucher checks (payments to vendors).

The trial balance lists the balances of all the accounts in the general ledger and tests the accuracy of the record keeping. Thus, it is fundamental to financial control and preparation of financial statements.

Financial reports summarize the results of transaction processing and express these results in accordance with the principles of financial reporting. Two common financial reports are the balance sheet and the income statement. In addition to these two reports, a wide variety of financial reports can be prepared to suit the needs of management and others. Operational reports summarize the results of transaction processing in a statistical or comparative format. Reports summarizing goods received, goods ordered, customer orders received, and other such activities are essential to the operation of a firm. The nature and content of such reports depend on the nature of a firm and its transaction processing activities.

DESIGNING DOUBLE-ENTRY SYSTEMS

This section provides an overview of the steps in the design and implementation of double-entry systems. These steps are essential regardless of whether the resultant data processing system is manual or computerized. The complexity of these steps increases as one moves from a manual to a computer-based system.

A Systems Approach

An accounting system must "fit" a particular organization. A variety of factors—the nature and purpose of the organization, its structural and functional characteristics, its physical layout, products, and services, the existing accounting system, and the personnel who operate the system—are all relevant considerations. A suggested design model is drawn from systems theory. This model is structured systems analysis, which is characterized by top-down design with successive re-

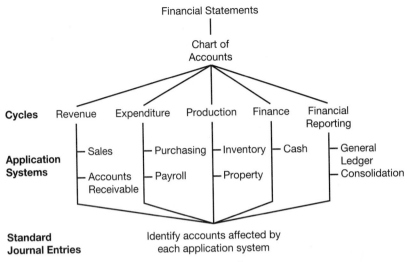

FIGURE 4.3 Hierarchical Model of an Accounting System.

finement. The model is illustrated in Figure 4.3. The figure illustrates a hierarchical structure for the logical design of a double-entry accounting system. The process begins with a determination of the desired outputs of the accounting system, that is, an at-the-top or broadest view of the system to be designed. The basic objective of an accounting system is to record, process, and report financial information. This objective is best expressed by an organization's financial statements and other reports. Accordingly, financial statements and other reports are the logical place to begin the overall design of an accounting system. The four steps in this process are generally the following:

1. Design a rough classification of accounts, or chart of accounts, and related financial statements and reports.
2. Review this with management and operating personnel.
3. Finalize statements, chart of accounts, and other reports.
4. Prepare a plan of journalizing and design the necessary business papers and procedures to implement and operate the system.

The **chart of accounts** is used to achieve an organization's objectives for financial reporting and control. The accounts in the general ledger provide a separate record for each of the company's assets, liabilities, capital fund balances, revenues, and expenses in which all transactions pertaining to that account are recorded. There are many sources of basic chart of account guidelines and models. The chart of accounts will be discussed in detail in a subsequent section of this chapter.

Once the chart of accounts and related statements have been finalized, a plan for journalizing and posting transactions must be formulated. This is accomplished through a step-down process of successive refinement. The first step is to analyze the nature of activities within the four basic transaction cycles. The chart of accounts is then factored, with each account being assigned to one of the firm's transaction cycles.

As discussed in Chapter 1, it is common to identify a fifth major transaction cycle to group accounts that are not directly affected by transactional activity. The fifth transaction cycle is called the financial reporting cycle. The financial reporting cycle—unlike the revenue, expenditure, finance, and production cycles—does not process transactions involving external parties. The financial reporting cycle obtains accounting and operating data from the other cycles and processes these data so that financial statements can be prepared in accordance with generally accepted accounting standards. Common activities within a financial reporting cycle are maintaining the general ledger, adjusting and closing entries, reclassifying entries for financial statement purposes, consolidating entries, depreciation, and other such valuation entries.

Once activities within each major transaction cycle have been identified, they are grouped into application systems. An application system processes a logically related set of transactions. The nature of application systems depends on the nature of the organization and its operation.

Once application systems have been identified, a complete set of standard or recurring journal entries can be designed to facilitate, document, and complete the system design. The operating activities of each application system should be logically summarized in the form of a standard journal entry. Thus, the linkage from the operating activities of an organization to the chart of accounts and subsequent financial statements is completed. The development of a complete set of standard journal entries completes the system design.

Standard Journal Entries

Standard journal entries are pro forma or hypothetical entries that are expected to occur in the normal operation of the system. Properly prepared, they provide a concise guide through the bookkeeping cycle. They formalize the closing process. In large organizations, standard journal entries allow the closing process to be parceled out (subdivided) to the various responsible organizational subunits, such as divisions or departments. In this case, a file of standard journal entries is accumulated and verified prior to the closing process. A standard journal entry should indicate three items:

1. The accounts affected by the entry.
2. The source (that is, journal, department, computer run, etc.) of the entry.
3. The date or period of the entry (weekly, monthly).

In providing a detailed set of standard journal entries, the operation of the accounting system under normal circumstances is described. Not all transactions can be foreseen; accordingly, standard journal entries do not or cannot provide for the recording of every transaction. However, an analysis of recurring transactions can indicate ways to streamline the accounting function. Standard journal entries are the source for designing special journals. Figure 4.4 shows a hypothetical standard journal entry to record sales on account in a retail firm and a model sales journal designed to facilitate this entry in a manual system. Note the correspondence between the entry and the number of special columnar classifications in the journal form. In computer systems, standard journal entries specify the desired outputs from specific applications, such as the payroll system, and indicate how these outputs enter the general ledger (master file).

Recurring adjusting and closing entries should also be included in the set of standard journal entries. Figure 4.5 illustrates an adjusting entry to record commissions earned at month's end and the use of a standard journal to facilitate the recording of this transaction from month to month in a manual system. As Figure 4.5 illustrates, a standard journal is a section or a subdivision of the general jour-

Sales Journal					Page 1		
		Debits		Credits			
		Accounts Receivable		Sales			
Date	Reference Number	Customers 120	Other 121	Class 1 511	Class 2 512	Services 520	Tax 550

Standard Journal Entry	
No. 15	Monthly
DR. 120	Accounts Receivable–Customers
DR. 121	Accounts Receivable–Others
CR. 511	Sales–Class 1
CR. 512	Sales–Class 2
CR. 520	Sales–Services
CR. 550	Sales–Tax

FIGURE 4.4 Journal and Journal-Entry Relationship.

nal in which recurring standard journal entries are recorded in a columnar format to eliminate the need to transcribe the account titles affected by the entry.

To implement a double-entry accounting system, forms and business papers must be designed, a technology must be selected, and operating procedures must be designed with due care for internal control considerations. Each of these aspects is important. However, these aspects should not affect the overall logical design of a double-entry accounting system. One should decide what a system is supposed to do before trying to decide how it will do it. Forms, technology, and operating procedures are "how" considerations concerning physical implementation. Considering these aspects too early can cause one to be "prematurely physical" in the design of an accounting system. That is, considering specific documents, procedures, or techniques too early commits the systems analyst to specific alternatives that may subsequently limit or encroach upon a full understanding of the logical requirements of the system. In systems terms, the concept of equifinality suggests that there are a variety of paths to a systems goal. You should not start to choose paths until you know where you are going.

Modes of Transaction Processing

In a traditional manual accounting system, source documents are recorded in journals to provide a chronological record of transactions. Journals are subsequently posted to ledgers to summarize financial data. Ledgers are processed to

Standard Journal						
				Page 1		
	Date: 1/31/xx			Date:		
Particulars	Account Number	DRs	CRs	Account Number	DRs	CRs
Commissions	610	1560				
Wages Payable	320		1400			
Accrued Taxes	322		120			
Withholding Tax	325		40			

FIGURE 4.5 Recurring Adjusting Entry in a Standard Journal.

generate financial statements. The flow of processing in such a system is from source documents to journals, journals to ledgers, and from ledgers to financial statements. Variations on this traditional flow are possible even in manual accounting systems.

Multiple Transcription Techniques

Multiple transcription techniques become essential as the volume of transactions grows. Journalizing and posting both involve copying data from one place to another; often this information is almost identical for both journalizing and posting. Numerous **one-write systems** have been designed to reduce the clerical functions of journalizing and posting in manual systems. Figure 4.6 illustrates a **writing board,** which is often used in manual systems. A writing board is designed to allow simultaneous recording on several documents ingeniously arranged and held on a special board. In preparing a payroll, for example, one must prepare a current earnings statement and check for each employee, a payroll register, and update a cumulative earnings record for each employee. Through the use of a writing board it is possible to prepare all three items, which contain identical data, in one writing. The payroll register is placed over pegs on the writing board first and is covered with carbon paper. Next, a group of paychecks and earnings statements is placed on the pegs over the carbon paper and payroll register. The appropriate earnings record for the first employee is selected and inserted between the first check and the payroll register. When the payroll clerk fills in the earnings statement, the data, because of the appropriate placement of the carbon, are simultaneously recorded on the earnings record and the payroll register. This one-writing technique eliminates the need to transcribe the same data into two additional records. The one-writing technique can be used wherever it is operationally feasible to do so. Other possibilities include invoicing, accounts payable, cash receipts, and cash disbursements. Another advantage of one-write systems is that they ensure consistent information; for example, because what appears on the check has been proofread, it is not necessary to proof the comparable lines on the other media.

Ledgerless Bookkeeping

Ledgerless bookkeeping systems are a form of data processing in which source documents are filed rather than transcribed ("posted") to other media. The file of source documents serves as (and therefore physically replaces) a separate ledger. Accounts receivable and accounts payable systems are typically best suited for ledgerless bookkeeping applications. In a strict sense, ledgerless bookkeeping involves no posting. This is possible only under rather restricted conditions. No posting means that statements of account will not be periodically mailed

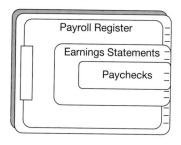

FIGURE 4.6 Writing Board.

to customers. Thus, ledgerless systems are better suited for situations where the industry practice is to pay on receipt of an invoice rather than a monthly statement. A further restriction concerns payments on account: If payments are made in the exact amount of invoices, ledgerless systems may be very cost-effective because a minimum of clerical effort is required. (See Figure 4.7 for a diagram of this ideal situation.) If partial payments on account are common, or sales returns and allowances and other invoice adjustments are common, ledgerless bookkeeping will require significant modifications and postings and will differ very little from a normal system. For example, if partial payments are made, the payment must either be posted to the relevant invoice or a special partial payment slip must be prepared and placed in the invoice file. In addition, some note has to be made in the "paid" file. A situation where ledgerless bookkeeping has traditionally worked very efficiently is one where there are periodic billings for small fixed amounts. This situation is common to monthly magazines and periodicals, which bill small fixed amounts on a regular basis.

Ledgerless bookkeeping systems have less redundancy, and therefore less inherent control, than normal posting systems. Numerical control of documents, prelisting and batch controls, and subdivision of the file to keep batch sizes reasonable are essential steps to compensate for the lack of a second (redundant) record of transactions. If an invoice is lost, misfiled, or posted incorrectly, there exists no second record to assist in locating the error. Careful design of document flow is essential for sound control. To illustrate, note that in Figure 4.7 the cash receipt tape and corresponding advices are filed by date. If a customer complains that a payment was not credited to his or her account, one may take the customer's alleged payment date and search the file efficiently for evidence of the transaction. If advices were not filed by date, this situation would become much more tedious. Of course, filing by both date and customer account is desirable, but this involves some form of transcription, which is precisely what ledgerless systems try to avoid.

Computer Processing

When computers are used to process transactions, two different modes of processing accounting transactions are possible. These modes are **batch processing** and **direct processing.** Batch processing is conceptually very similar to a traditional manual accounting system. Batches of transactions are accumulated as a transaction file. This transaction file is the computer equivalent of a journal in a manual system in that it is a collection of similar transactions. Transaction files are usually printed to provide documentation of inputs to the accounting system. Transaction files are subsequently posted to ledgers by computer programs. The ledgers are then periodically processed to generate financial statements. The flow of processing in a batch processing computer system is essentially the same as in a traditional manual system—source documents to journals (transaction files), journals to ledgers, and ledgers to financial statements.

In direct processing, individual transactions are posted directly to ledgers rather than being batched to build a transaction file. A ledger may periodically be processed to generate a listing of transactions that have been posted to it over some period of time. But this transaction file (the equivalent of a journal) is created as a by-product of posting the ledger. Ledgers are periodically processed to generate financial statements.

The essential difference between batch and direct processing is that in direct

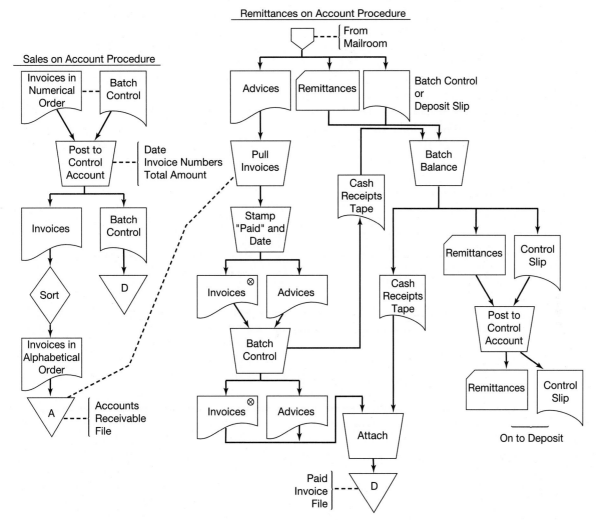

FIGURE 4.7 Ledgerless Bookkeeping.

processing individual transactions rather than batches of transactions are posted to ledgers. The need for separate journals prior to posting to a ledger is eliminated.

Data Validation

Data validation is the process of reviewing transaction details for accuracy and completeness during the input stage of computer processing. The accuracy of financial reports depends on the accuracy of inputs to the accounting system. This point becomes very important when computers are used to process accounting data. In a manual system, the accountant may recognize incorrect or invalid transactions and correct them prior to processing. When computers are used to process data, incorrect or invalid transactions might be inadvertently processed unless they are detected and corrected during input.

Many types of errors can occur when recording transactions. For example, consider the input of a sales invoice to a PC accounting application. An important data element, such as the customer's account number, could be omitted. The customer's account number could be input incorrectly. In either event it would not be possible to post the invoice to the customer's account. Other possible errors could include an incorrect date, incorrect invoice amount, or invalid credit terms. Each data element on a source document should be validated if that field is an important factor in subsequent processing.

The need for data validation is an important aspect of using computers in accounting. The accuracy of financial reports depends on the accuracy of inputs to the accounting system. The benefits of using computers in accounting can be negated if incorrect data are routinely input into the system for processing.

Need for a Chart of Accounts

In order to design financial statements and other reports, a *chart of accounts* has to be designed. In any accounting system there are separate accounts for storing recorded monetary information from transactions. Each account is assigned a number from the organization chart of accounts, which is a numbering system designed to classify and organize the accounts. In order to classify, a coding system is necessary. Coding will be discussed in the next section of this chapter.

Conceptually, an account is a place where data relevant to a particular activity or object are recorded and/or summarized. An account can take a variety of physical forms. In manual systems it might be a standardized business form. In computer systems it might be a card or a location on a magnetic disk. Data can be classified in different ways; the question of what is a relevant classification is best addressed by focusing on the intended or mandatory use of data.

The basic double-entry accounting model contains just three accounts: assets, liabilities, and equity. Each of these accounts is generally subdivided into numerous subclassifications. Assets are classified as current or noncurrent, and further subdivided into cash, inventory, and the like. Equity is subdivided to contain revenue and expense accounts, among others. Sales revenues are classified as "sales," and increase owners' equity as a result of the closing process. Why not post sales revenues directly to the owners' equity account? The reason is that "sales revenue" is a classification of information that is useful to management and others interested in a particular organization. If sales were posted directly to owners' equity, this information would be combined with other transactions that affect equity, such as additional investments or withdrawals. Obtaining sales information would consequently be tedious because this information would either have to be extracted from the equity accounts or prepared separately. Now consider an organization with several distinct sales outlets. To monitor the operations of individual outlets, management is likely to require sales information by outlet. To post all sales information to one account, "sales," might create a situation similar to the one discussed before. Accordingly, the organization would likely subdivide its sales account into several subaccounts, one for each outlet. Now consider salespersons: Should there be a separate account for each? Perhaps. If this information is relevant, such data will have to be accumulated at some point in the data processing cycle. There are many alternatives, of which a separate general ledger account is only one.

Certain accounts may be required by law. Tax laws require an accounting for payroll taxes and related payments; state laws often dictate the accounting for equity components, and many regulated industries must follow a chart of accounts promulgated by the relevant regulatory agency. Public utilities must use a chart of accounts promulgated by the Federal Power Commission.

Designing a Chart of Accounts

A chart of accounts must be responsive to both the external reporting requirements and internal information needs of an organization. As Figure 4.8 illustrates, one way to organize a chart of accounts is to group asset, liability, equity, revenue, and expense accounts in that order, setting aside a "block" or group of sequential account numbers for each major group of accounts. This organization technique is called **block coding.** Although there are similarities among all charts of accounts, specific differences abound in different situations. Accounting for a meat-packing plant is similar to, but also certainly different from, accounting for a radio station. Uniform classifications of accounts have been developed, published, and promoted by trade associations and numerous other groups to encourage good accounting practice. These publications are practical models for the design of a chart of accounts in the same manner that an internal control questionnaire provides a model or guideline for a review of internal control. Figure 4.9 illustrates a section of a uniform account classification for radio stations published by the Na-

Current Assets (100–199)
101   Cash in Bank
102   Petty Cash
110   Inventory
120   Accounts Receivable
150   Supplies
155   Prepaid Rent

Plant and Equipment (200–250)
201   Land
230   Office Machines

Intangible Assets (280–299)
281   Organizational Costs

Liabilities and Equity (300–499)
310   Accounts Payable
330   Notes Payable
400   Bonds Payable
450   Capital Stock
460   Retained Earnings

Revenues (500–599)
501   Sales Territory A
503   Sales Territory B

Expenses (600–799)
610   Salaries
620   Power
630   Supplies
640   Rent

Summary Accounts (900–999)
910   Income Summary

FIGURE 4.8 Chart of Accounts.

Direct Expenses (400–499)
40   Agency commissions and other direct expenses
401 Agency commissions—national sales
402 Agency commissions—local sales
403 Other direct expenses

Technical Expenses (500–599)
50   Compensation
501 Salaries—supervisory
502 Salaries and wages—nonsupervisory
508 Payroll taxes
511 Transmitter tubes expense
512 Other tubes expense
513 Transmitter line charges
514 Outside engineering expense
515 Power and light
516 Maintenance and repair of technical equipment
517 Equipment parts and supplies
518 Depreciation
549 Other technical expenses

FIGURE 4.9 Portion of a Chart of Accounts for a Typical Radio Station.

tional Association of Broadcasters.[1] Many associations that promote a uniform chart of accounts also collect and publish comparative statistics for their industry. Such statistics can be very helpful to an organization; the uniformity among the industry's charts of accounts strengthens the validity of comparing one's own organization to published data. Such comparisons can provide helpful insights into an organization's operations and management policies.

The journal–ledger relationship is fundamental to double-entry accounting. The journal supports the ledger and vice versa. Ledgers and journals should be tailored to a specific organization's needs. Although several relevant factors such as the size and shape of the organization and the detail of posting desired (e.g., each sale or total sales) can be identified, there are no hard and fast rules for deciding on a particular configuration. Basic questions in ledger design concern the amount of detail to be posted (i.e., detail or totals only) and subdivisions of the ledger to include subsidiary ledgers. If a ledger contains accounts (which may be controlling accounts rather than detailed accounts) for all the assets, liabilities, and equity, including revenues and expenses, it is called a **general ledger.** It summarizes the chart of accounts for the entire organization. Supporting ledgers, called **subsidiary ledgers,** are used to tabulate and centralize information pertaining to specific accounts such as accounts receivable, fixed assets, and accounts payable. In some cases, where the detail is not voluminous, the general ledger will include the subsidiary detail as well as the control account.

As an organization grows, its general ledger (i.e., number of accounts) will expand, creating a need for an organizational structure within the ledger system itself. At one extreme, there may be only a general ledger, which is posted from journals. At some point subsidiary ledgers are required for convenience. Subsidiary ledgers may be kept by the individual in charge of the general ledger or by another individual. In a large system, subsidiary ledgers are kept by departments.

---

[1]*Accounting Manual for Radio Stations.* Washington, D.C.: National Association of Broadcasters, 1975.

Ledgers can be further subdivided for groups of related accounts. Accounts receivable, for example, can be further subdivided by sales district or by alphabet or customer number (as in cycle or rotated billing systems). The result is a hierarchical relationship of subsidiary ledgers and control accounts. The general ledger, through the use of numerous subsidiary ledgers, can consist almost entirely of control accounts.

Documentation

Ordinarily, it is desirable to have an account manual with explanations of what should be included in particular accounts. This need increases as an organization grows in size. An account manual is a form of procedural documentation. Ideally, any question concerning an accounting system could be resolved by consulting the accounting system's documentation. Complete documentation of the organization and procedures of an accounting system would include a detailed description of job titles and related duties, the chart of accounts, and complete specification of standard journal entries and related procedures. If charges and credits to accounts are not carefully defined and controlled, different operating units and/or bookkeepers may record similar transactions in different ways. Manuals also help formalize internal control procedures.

CODING SYSTEMS FOR TRANSACTION PROCESSING

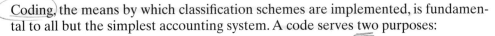

Coding, the means by which classification schemes are implemented, is fundamental to all but the simplest accounting system. A code serves two purposes:

1. It provides a brief identification.
2. It gives meaning to data in subsequent processing.

The first purpose, brief identification, is a practical consideration. It is more convenient to enter "M" or "F" on a document than "male" or "female"; moreover, the data have been compressed. Using "M" rather than "male" saves three characters and in doing so facilitates both processing and storage, especially in automated systems. This example fails to highlight the basic dilemma in coding systems (and classification schemes in general); the more detailed (i.e., longer) the code, the better the accuracy of the description; on the other hand, the more detailed the code, the more cumbersome the processing of that code. Lengthy codes provide more accurate descriptions of data, but they also require more storage (at a cost) and are more subject to transcription or other conversion errors in usage. To illustrate the second purpose, once an employee has been coded by sex, age, or education, these data can be combined with similar data, sorted, summarized, and processed to yield information such as a personnel report.

Types of Codes

A coding system consists of a **character set;** that is, a set of admissible, predefined symbols that are used to identify the object of interest. Numeric codes use digits exclusively (normally the character set 0, 1, 2, . . . , 9). They are used extensively in automated data processing. Alphanumeric codes use numbers, letters of the alphabet, and other special symbols such as *, (, and +. Finally, special machine-readable codes exist, such as bar codes. The familiar

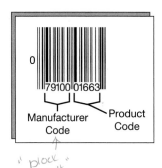

FIGURE 4.10 Universal Product Code.

universal product code (Figure 4.10) is an example of a bar code. This code contains two five-digit fields; the first field is for the manufacturer, and the second is for product number.

The basic building block in a coding system is the individual character. Rules specify the manner in which characters are interpreted; rules specify the meaning given to the value and position of characters. Probably the most common and simplest rule is to assign documents consecutive numbers. For example, checks are usually numbered in sequence. Numbers can be consecutively assigned in either ascending or descending order, with ascending order most common. This scheme is called **sequential coding.** Sequential codes are simple to administer, and they organize data on the basis of position. A strict sequential code, however, contains no information about the element identified other than its position in a list. Frequently, more descriptive codes are desired. To attain this end, more complex rules are needed.

A **block code** is used to classify objects into certain groups. Characters are assigned sequentially (without any particular meaning other than sequence) within each block. In a block code, the position of a character or group of characters has a special meaning; by contrast, a character in a pure sequential code has no meaning other than relative position (e.g., 9 is greater than 8). The universal product code is a block code. In Figure 4.10, the first five digits specify, or "block out," a particular manufacturer; the next five digits identify or block out a specific product for a particular manufacturer. In a strict block code there is no classification scheme inherent in each block. Numbers are assigned to elements with no regard to meaning other than to uniquely identify each element in a block. Manufacturers in Figure 4.10 are identified only by sequential coding. It is not possible with this code to identify directly the type of manufacturer. The universal product code does not classify manufacturers; it merely identifies them.

It is common to give meaning to the value as well as the position of a character. Such schemes are interchangeably called **group** or **hierarchical codes.** Group or hierarchical codes implement several subclassifications within each major block of data. Certain characters are reserved for each classification desired. Such codes generally consist of several blocks, called fields; usually the leftmost field is of greatest significance, as is the case in the zip codes used by the U.S. Postal Service.

The zip code system is a hierarchical coding scheme in which both the value and position of a character (restricted to decimal digits) have meaning. Characters assigned within each zip code field designate a particular classification within that field. The value 2 in the first zip code field indicates a particular major region of the country. All addresses within this major mailing region begin with a 2 to indicate a common geographical location.

A special variation of hierarchical codes is the **decimal code.** A decimal code differs from a typical block code in that a decimal code allows for unlimited expansion to the right of a decimal point. The decimal point itself is included in the character set. Major classifications are represented by fields to the left of the decimal point, whereas digits to the right of the point are not standardized and are used to provide subclassifications. Many libraries use the Dewey decimal classification. This system divides all knowledge into ten major classifications and provides subclassifications by utilizing extra digits. For example, 610.736 is "special nursing," subcategorized in the major classification "applied science" (600–699). The major advantage of decimal codes is the capacity for unlimited, easy expansion; this capacity is also the major disadvantage of decimal codes. The lack of complete standardization allows and promotes uneven code lengths; these are a disadvantage in machine processing, and perhaps dangerous even in a manual system. Consider the code 610.73. Is this the complete code? Sometimes yes, sometimes no. Questions of this type complicate the use of coding systems that are not completely specified as to length. Their use should be carefully considered by the analyst.

Considerations in Designing Codes

Several observations can be made concerning the use of codes. Clearly, a code must yield the desired classification. A code should also be flexible. In this context it is important to realize that systems are not static. A decimal code is flexible, but the lack of standardization that yields this quality also complicates machine processing. Block codes are usually organized as follows:

- The character position has significance.
- It has a predetermined number of characters.
- All codes are the same length.

Flexibility is built into a typical block coding system by leaving gaps or spaces in the original classification. This allows room for future additions without extensive system modification.

Another consideration concerns the integration of data files. A sales order, for example, ultimately affects sales, accounts receivable, and inventory. Cross-linking poses system maintenance and system security considerations. An individual's social security number is a unique identifier that might be used to cross-link several related data files.

Numerous standardization procedures can facilitate data processing. Most of these relate to converting alphanumeric data to numeric data through the use of appropriate codes. Days and weeks can be numbered 1 to 7 and 1 to 52, respectively, and dates put into a condensed "year–month–day" numeric format. For example, September 18, 1990, can be coded as 900918. A 24-hour clock avoids A.M.–P.M. confusion.

Many accounting applications require the use and manipulation of calendar dates, such as the determination of due dates for vouchers payable. Calendar dating procedures can be standardized through the sequential assignment of dates. This is called **Julian dating.** In Julian dating, all days are numbered sequentially from an arbitrary date, and months and years are not directly identified as such. December 31, 1989, might be Julian coded 286050. January 1, 1990, would then be the Julian date 286051. The condensed Gregorian calendar code for these same two dates would be 891231 and 900101, respectively. Julian calendar dating is more convenient for arithmetic manipulation than the Gregorian system. In Julian calendar dating, the number of days difference between two dates can be determined by simple subtraction. In the Gregorian system one has to convert a month to days or a year to months to complete the same subtraction. (Consider the previous December 31, 1989, example.)

PC spreadsheet packages utilize Julian dating. Lotus 1-2-3, for example, stores dates that are used in date functions as serial numbers representing the number of days since December 31, 1899. This is to say that Lotus 1-2-3 uses a Julian calendar that has January 1, 1900, as day number 1. All dates are numbered sequentially from January 1, 1900. The serial date number for January 1, 1990, is 32873.

One type of code not yet mentioned is the **mnemonic code.** A mnemonic code utilizes an alphanumeric character set; letters (and numbers) are combined to form shortened or abbreviated codes that are similar to the pronunciation or spelling of the object of interest. SJ for "sales journal," PA for "Pennsylvania," and HQ for "headquarters" are examples of mnemonic codes. Such codes are amenable to human processing and often facilitate human processing of codes to the extent that one can recall more readily "PA" as Pennsylvania, as compared to an arbitrary two-digit numerical code for the same state.

A final point concerns the length of codes. Empirical studies have unveiled a bell-shaped curve phenomenon related to human use of codes. Most people can readily work with codes containing seven plus or minus two digits. Although larger codes are being used increasingly, the analyst should be aware of human limitations when devising such coding schemes. Blocks or fields may be subdivided, if necessary, to make them more amenable to human processing.

Coding Examples in Accounting Systems

Codes are widely used in accounting systems. This section provides two common examples. The first relates to customer coding, which is an example of activity coding, closely related to the accounting function of distribution. Accountants use the term **distribution** to denote the process of extracting and accumulating detailed information from transactional data. Posting invoices to a subsidiary ledger or posting payroll data to an expense ledger are examples of distribution functions in an accounting system. The second example relates to the chart of accounts.

Many organizations have implemented large coding systems to enable them to analyze activity relating to their customers. A typical customer coding scheme is presented by example: Consider the code 12340019333103; the first five digits (12340) (the first field) might represent an account number; the next two digits (01) a geographical code; the next two digits (93) a trade classification; the next five digits (33103) sales territory (331) and salesperson (03); and so on. Such codes might appear cumbersome, but computers manipulate lengthy codes quite readily. The longer the code the better the description.

The chart of accounts is a hierarchical coding system. Once the accounts have been selected, they must be organized into a manageable framework. This is typically done by assigning each account a multidigit code in which each digit denotes a particular classification. A typical account coding structure is

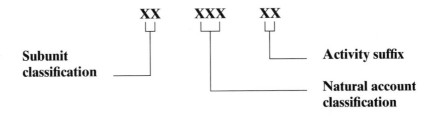

The first two digits of the seven-digit code are used to identify a division, department, profit, or cost center accounted for separately. These subunits can be numbered 01 through 99. Examples include:

01   Electronics Division
02   Research Division
07   Production Department
08   Marketing Department

Note that several digits are skipped to provide for future expansion. The next three digits represent specific categories:

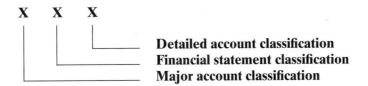

Major account classifications can be numbered 100 through 900 (in hundreds):

100   Assets
300   Liabilities
400   Stockholders' equity
500   Sales
600   Cost of sales
700   Expenses
800   Other income

Financial statement classifications are the account titles used on a company's financial statements. These accounts can be numbered 10 through 90 (in tens):

Account 110

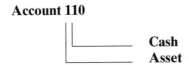

Detailed account classifications are the transaction-level accounts into which information is posted. These accounts can be numbered 1 through 9:

Account 111

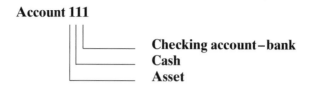

Checking account – bank
Cash
Asset

The rightmost two digits (the activity suffix) can be used to denote a company's products or activities within subunits:

01   Product one
02   Product two

The total expense recorded in the natural expense accounts must equal the total expense recorded in the activity (e.g., product-line) accounts. The purpose of the activity suffix accounts is simply to show the organization's expenses in a different context. Natural expense classifications organize expenses by type (e.g., office supplies and telephone), whereas activity classifications organize the same expenses by the purpose for which they were expended.

The example just presented is just one of numerous ways in which accounts can be coded. The point to keep in mind is that a code should facilitate the desired presentation of information. The desired outputs (reports) must be identified before a chart of accounts is constructed; otherwise, the coding scheme can prevent economical presentation of information desired by management.

FORM DESIGN AND RECORDS RETENTION CONSIDERATIONS

Many accounting application systems are built around a single form: The production and handling of the form is the major function of the system. The function of a billing system is to process invoices; a sales system processes customer orders. Forms are used to collect information and also to provide evidence that an operation (a specific stage in a system) has been performed. A receiving report provides evidence that goods have been received and verified prior to actual payment. Procedures and forms must be designed as a single integrated system. Forms are used to standardize the inputs and outputs of a data processing application. Forms themselves can be paper documents or formats displayed on computer input/output devices such as video display terminals. A completed form is called a record in data processing systems.

Accounting-related forms and papers serve several functions. First, they serve as a physical medium to store and transmit data. This function is necessary both to determine the results of operations and to keep track of (to control) assets. Simply recording transactions and keeping a record of assets (e.g., inventory stock cards or a fixed asset register) is basic to the concept of accounting control. Accurate records provide a check or control on the use or misuse of assets. Accounting media also facilitate operations. In an organizational context, forms transmit authority and responsibility. For example, a petty cash slip authorizes the custodian to release cash and transmits responsibility for the use of this asset to the receiver. Literally, the receiver is now accountable for the cash, as evidenced by the petty cash slip. Accounting media also standardize operations. Repetitive processes, such as recording sales, must generally be standardized to ensure uniformity and completeness. Forms also assist inexperienced (as well as experienced) employees by indicating what data should be recorded and the format or layout for them. Such considerations increase in importance as the level of automation in a system increases.

Form Design Considerations

The fundamental consideration in form design is the user. If the user does not understand a form, or cannot use it, the result is evident. Clear instructions on how the forms should be filled out, adequate spacing for entries, and shaded or blocked areas to indicate sections that are not to be used are examples of details that should be considered in the design of a form. Coordination of data items on a form or set of related forms is usually desirable. For example, a form that will eventually be keyed into the computer (i.e., coded for computer processing) should have its data items arranged in the order in which they will be keyed. If multiple-color paper forms are used, the same color should be used for the same department in all multiple forms used in the organization. Color itself, however, should not be relied upon exclusively because color blindness is more common than most people realize.

Concerning paper forms, optional design features such as multiple colors, prenumbering, and rigid specifications for size and quality of the paper stock are often desirable, but they adversely affect the cost of printing the form itself. These extra-cost features should be related to the intended use of the form. There are several basic considerations: (1) the number of times the form will be handled; (2) storage time or active use; (3) the type of handling—machine or manual; (4) the quantity used; and (5) whether all copies in a multiple-copy form will be identical with respect to preprinted information and quality of paper stock. From a systems design viewpoint, the most fundamental choices are the number of copies of a form, its destinations, and whether the first copy is the same as all other copies. In all of these decisions, the analyst must consider that forms preparation and handling costs are usually far in excess of the cost of printing the form itself. If an extra-cost feature such as prenumbering or having another copy can save a procedural step at another point in the system, the extra cost of printing the form will be recovered many times over.

Form design and control is essential to systems work. The printed form on a clerk's desk, in a typewriter, or displayed on a monitor is often a more eloquent device for directing the flow of work than the written procedure that is filed away in the supervisor's bookcase. Large organizations have found it expedient to create media or form control units, perhaps as large as a department, to standardize and thereby reduce the cost of using forms. A typical form control unit has authority and responsibility to review and approve all requests for forms. Most units also have responsibility for technical aspects of form design; in this respect they function much like a purchasing department, offering design assistance to users and interfacing between the user and the printer. Form control units are usually also responsible for inventory control, dealing with supplies (running out versus being overstocked), and organization (form numbering systems).

Records Retention Considerations

Records retention requirements must be considered in the design of an accounting system. Various government and tax regulations set specific guidelines and legal requirements over records retention. Records retention must also be considered from the internal viewpoint of information storage and usage. Nonessential outdated forms occupy space and can hinder effective access to more current information.

Keeping current with federal and, in particular, Internal Revenue Service requirements is the responsibility of the systems analyst. There are several basic reference sources. *A Guide to Record Retention Requirements* is published periodically in the *Federal Register*; the latest guide is available through the office of the Superintendent of Documents, U.S. Government Printing Office, Washington D.C. 20402. The *Guide* is a digest to the provisions of federal laws and regulations relating to the keeping of records by the public. It indicates what records must be kept, by whom, and for how long. Basic tax-related records retention requirements can be found in the current volumes of specialized tax-reporting services, the Commerce Clearing House (CCH) and Prentice Hall tax guides.

Electronic Tax-Record Retention Requirements

Revenue Procedure 91-59, effective for tax years beginning after December 31, 1991, specifies the basic requirements that the Internal Revenue Service considers essential in cases where taxpayers maintain their records on automatic data processing equipment. 91-59 takes into consideration that automatic data processing continues to evolve rapidly, with new methods and techniques being constantly developed. 91-59 is intended to ensure that all machine-sensible records generated by a taxpayer's system will be retained as long as they may be or become material in the administration of any Internal Revenue law.

All machine-sensible data must be retained by the taxpayer if it is or may become material to the administration of the Code. The retained records should be in a retrievable format that provides information necessary to determine the correct tax liability. Furthermore, documentation that provides a complete description of the accounting system, including all subsystems, shall be retained and made available upon request.

The taxpayer must be able to process the retained records at time of examination. If a system conversion occurs that creates incompatible formats, the taxpayer shall convert records to a format compatible with the new system. The taxpayer shall provide the Service the necessary resources to process the retained records at the time of the examination.

91-59 states that, except as otherwise provided, it does not relieve the taxpayer of retaining hard-copy records and documentation. However, hard-copy records generated at the time of the transaction (e.g., credit card receipts) need not be retained if all details relating to the transaction are subsequently received by the taxpayer in an EDI transaction and these records are retained in accordance with this procedure. If hard-copy records are not produced or received in the ordinary course of transacting business (as in EDI), hard-copy printouts need not be created unless requested. Printouts that are made for validation, control, or other temporary purposes need not be retained.

SUMMARY

Transaction processing includes a variety of activities an organization must undertake to support its day-to-day operational activities. The extent and diversity of transaction flows in an organization were illustrated in the context of a manufacturing firm. Even though every organization is unique, most organizations have application systems that are similar to those illustrated at the beginning of this chapter. Subsequent chapters will study these common application systems in depth.

The terminology associated with the basic elements of transaction processing procedures was defined and illustrated. This discussion included all of the basic components of a double-entry accounting system—source documents, journals, ledgers, and the chart of accounts. As discussed, these basic elements can take a variety of forms depending on the nature of the technology used for transaction processing.

A systems approach to the design of a double-entry accounting system suggests that the design proceed from the top down, that is to say, from the desired financial statements down to the transactional data that will be necessary to produce these statements. Standard journal entries are used to document the design of a double-entry accounting system. The design principles that were illustrated are equally relevant to both manual and computer-based accounting systems.

Coding systems are fundamental to all but the simplest data processing systems. Different methods of coding data were discussed and illustrated. Two common examples of the use of codes in accounting systems include customer/activity coding and the chart of accounts.

Principles of forms design were discussed. Forms often appear on monitors rather than on paper. The user of a form should always be a major consideration in the design of any form. The chapter provided an overview of records retention considerations, emphasizing those related to federal requirements. Revenue Procedure 91-59 legally extends the concept of internal accounting controls to federal electronic tax-records retention requirements. No longer is it sufficient for a taxpayer to simply provide for the retention of electronic tax-related records. Such records must now be maintained by a taxpayer.

Glossary

batch processing: a form of processing in which batches of transactions are accumulated and processed as a group.

block code: characters in a code are grouped together (i.e., "blocked") to classify objects into certain groups.

chart of accounts: a listing of all asset, liability, revenue, expense, and equity accounts used in an accounting system.

data validation: the process of reviewing transaction details for accuracy and completeness during input.

decimal code: a code that allows for unlimited expansion to the right of a decimal point in the code.

direct processing: a form of processing in which individual transactions are processed separately.

distribution: the process of extracting and accumulating details from transactional data.

file: an organized collection of data.

general ledger: a ledger that contains and/or summarizes all of the accounts in an accounting system.

group code: a block code in which subclassifications are implemented within each block of the code.

hierarchical code: synonym for group code.

journal: a chronological listing of transactions.

Julian dating: the assignment of sequential numbers to dates.

ledgerless bookkeeping: a form of processing in which source documents are sorted and filed rather than posted to ledgers.

master file: a collection of summarized data pertaining to transactions.

mnemonic code: a code that is similar to the pronunciation of the object that is coded.

one-write system: a device that both posts a transaction and journalizes it in the same operation.

reference file: contains reference data that are useful in processing transactional data.

register: similar to a journal, but used to record data not directly relating to accounting.

sequential code: consecutive numbers are assigned to objects.

standard journal entries: pro forma entries that are used to document the plan of journalizing recurring transactions.

subsidiary ledger: used to tabulate and centralize information pertaining to a specific account.

table file: a synonym for reference file.

transaction file: a collection of data pertaining to transactions.

transaction processing: the variety of activities an organization must undertake to support day-to-day activities.

writing board: synonym for a one-write system.

Chapter Quiz

Answers to the Chapter Quiz appear on page 163.

1. The universal product code (bar code) that is commonplace on consumer products is a
   (a) sequential code.
   (b) block code.
   (c) group or hierarchical code.
   (d) decimal code.

2. A journal is
   (a) a chronological listing of transactions.
   (b) similar to a transaction file.
   (c) similar to a reference file.
   (d) a and b.

3. Payroll tax tables would be found in a(n) _____ file.
   (a) master
   (b) open data
   (c) reference
   (d) transaction

4. Which type of file has only temporary significance to management?
   (a) master
   (b) open data
   (c) reference
   (d) transaction

5. What sequence of events is pertinent in designing an accounting information system?
   (a) design inputs, processes, and then outputs
   (b) design chart of accounts, inputs, and then processes
   (c) design reports, inputs, and then chart of accounts
   (d) design reports, chart of accounts, and inputs

6. Which type of coding scheme allows for the most flexibility?
   (a) block
   (b) sequence
   (c) group
   (d) decimal

7. Many data processing systems standardize calendar dating procedures by assigning sequential numbers to dates. This procedure is known as
   (a) decimal dating.
   (b) Julian dating.
   (c) mnemonic dating.
   (d) Gregorian dating.

8. The fundamental consideration(s) in forms design is (are)
   (a) prenumbering, forms control sequence numbers, revision codes, spacing, color, and data layout.
   (b) the number of times a form will be handled, storage time, activity, type of handling, number of copies, and quantity used.

    (c) users.
    (d) internal control.

9. Standard journal entries are used to
    (a) document the plan of journalizing recurring transactions.
    (b) document the chart of accounts.
    (c) eliminate the need for adjusting entries.
    (d) eliminate the need for subsidiary ledgers.

10. A writing board system is used to prepare checks for the payment of invoices. The one-writing operation prepares the check and
    (a) posts the transaction.
    (b) journalizes the transaction.
    (c) both a and b.
    (d) neither a nor b.

Review Problem

Universal Floor Covering is a manufacturer and distributor of carpet and vinyl floor coverings. The home office is based in Charlotte, North Carolina. Carpet mills are located in Dalton, Georgia, and Greenville, South Carolina; a floor covering manufacturing plant is in High Point, North Carolina. Total sales last year were just over $250 million.

The company manufactures over 200 different varieties of carpet. The carpet is classified as being for commercial or residential purposes and is sold under five brand names with up to five lines under each brand. The lines indicate the different grades of quality; grades are measured by type of tuft and number of tufts per square inch. Each line of carpet can have up to 15 different color styles.

Just under 200 varieties of vinyl floor covering are manufactured. The floor covering is also classified as being for commercial or residential use. There are four separate brand names (largely distinguished by the type of finish), up to eight different patterns for each brand, and up to eight color styles for each pattern.

Ten different grades of padding are manufactured. The padding is usually differentiated by intended use (commercial or residential) in addition to thickness and composition of materials.

Universal serves over 2,000 regular wholesale customers. Retail showrooms are the primary customers. Many major corporations are direct buyers of Universal's products. Large construction companies have contracts with Universal to purchase carpet and floor covering at reduced rates for use in newly constructed homes and commercial buildings. In addition, Universal produces a line of residential carpet for a large national retail chain. Sales to these customers range from $10,000 to $1 million annually.

There is a company-owned retail outlet at each plant. The outlets carry overruns, seconds, and discontinued items. This is Universal's only retail sales function.

The company has divided the sales market into seven territories, with the majority of concentration on the East Coast. The market segments are New England, New York, Mid-Atlantic, Carolinas, South, Midwest, and West. Each sales territory is divided into five to ten districts, with a salesperson assigned to each district.

The current accounting system has been adequate for monitoring the sales by product. However, there are limitations to the system because specific information is sometimes unavailable. A detailed analysis of operations is necessary for planning and control purposes and would be valuable for decision-making purposes. The accounting systems department has been asked to design a sales analysis code. The code should permit Universal to prepare a sales analysis that would reflect the characteristics of the company's business.

Required

(a) Account coding systems are based on various coding concepts. Briefly define and give an example of the following coding concepts:
(1) sequence coding
(2) block coding
(3) group coding

(b) Identify and describe factors that must be considered before a coding system can be designed and implemented for an organization.

(c) Develop a coding system for Universal Floor Covering that would assign sales analysis codes to sales transactions. For each portion of the code,
(1) explain the meaning and purpose of the position.
(2) identify and justify the number of digits required.

(CMA)

Solution to Review Problem

(a) (1) Sequence coding is the assignment of numbers or letters in some designated consecutive order, that is, 1, 2, 3, 4, . . . or A, B, C, D, ... The next incident or increment is assigned the next higher sequential designation. Examples include check numbers, calendar years, purchase orders, and so on.

(2) Block coding assigns specific groups of numbers for designated purposes. Address numbers in cities, for example, 100–199, are referred to as the 100 block. Accounting systems commonly use blocks of numbers to specify classes of accounts, 100–199 for assets, 200–299 for liabilities, and so on.

(3) Group coding consists of two or more subgroups or digits or letters combined in a field to designate several classifications. Each subgroup specifies a data classification in a series. The series is generally a left-to-right arrangement with the positions or blocks of designators becoming more specific the farther to the right they are in the series. Postal zip codes are an example of group coding, with each successive digit indicating an ever more precise geographic location.

(b) A chart of accounts coding system must satisfy specific requirements. These requirements will dictate the nature and type of coding used. Among these factors are the following:

Organizational Considerations. The company's organizational factors need to be considered, that is, the type and complexity of business structure: number of divisions, plants, departments, number of product lines, and so on.

Type of Information Requirements. A system user must be able to access information for retrieval by addressing major groups of data. The composition of the account numbers must allow for easy identification and use.

Growth. The coding must allow for growth in the number of items that will be included in the system. A one-position field in a strictly numeric system can specify no more than ten items or classes: if alphanumeric, no more than 36. If the items or classes to be identified by the field have the potential to exceed these limits the field should be expanded.

Cost Effectiveness. The longer the code designation, the more costly it is to maintain and process the associated data. If the coding system will be used in a mechanical or electronic data processing system, numeric codes are more efficient. In all systems shorter codes are preferable.

(c) A group coding system would provide the best approach to a sales analysis coding system for Universal Floor Coverings. The sales analysis code would include the following positions:

Item Identification	Digit	Explanation
Type of use	1	Only two types of use—commercial and residential
Product	1	Only three product lines now—carpet, vinyl floor covering, padding
Brand*	1	One digit should be sufficient because this is a subcode: Carpet—five brands each Vinyl—four brands
Line/pattern*	1	One digit should be sufficient because this again is a subgroup: Carpet—five lines maximum per brand Vinyl—eight patterns per brand
Color	1 or 2	There are a maximum of 15 color styles for the carpet. This would require two numeric digits or one alphabetic or alphanumeric digit.
Type of sale	1	One digit would be sufficient to identify wholesale, retail showroom, corporations, contractors, retail chain, and outlet.
Territory	1	There are currently seven territories: One digit is sufficient unless the company plans to expand the number of territories.
District	1 or 2	Currently, there are ten districts in some territories. This means that one digit is sufficient now, but another position or an alpha coding might be used for expansion.
Specific customer identification	4	If sales analysis by customer is desired, then a four-digit numeric code should be used to provide adequate expansion.

A digit is not needed for salespeople because only one salesperson is assigned to each district. If this is due to change in the near future, then a digit should be added now.

*The type of pad could be identified under brand or line/pattern.

All of these codes would be numeric except as indicated before.

Review Questions

1. How does an organization identify the specific accounts it needs in its chart of accounts?
2. Why are control accounts commonly found in the general ledger of an organization?
3. What functions are served by accounting forms and papers in an organization?
4. What are the uses of standard journal entries?
5. What are the basic objectives of coding systems?
6. Define and give an example of the following types of codes:
   (a) sequential
   (b) block
   (c) group
   (d) decimal
7. What is the major disadvantage of a decimal code?
8. Identify several standardization procedures pertinent to the coding of calendar data.
9. Distinguish between Julian and Gregorian calendar dating. Which is more advantageous in data processing environments?
10. What is a mnemonic code?
11. Are forms always paper documents? Explain.
12. Identify several basic considerations in form design.

13. Identify a fundamental principle of form design that pertains to the features that appear on the form itself.

14. What are the functions of a form control unit? Why is forms control important in large organizations?

15. Why are records retention requirements an important consideration in systems design?

16. Identify several sources that list federal records retention requirements.

17. What is the major difference between computer batch processing and direct processing of transactions?

18. Describe how a writing board is used to process transactions.

19. Why is data validation important when computers are used to process transactions?

Discussion Questions and Problems

20. Discuss the importance of an accounting systems manual to
    (a) the training of new personnel.
    (b) the uniformity and consistency of reports.
    (c) an external audit.
    (d) the revision of an accounting procedure.

21. Figure 4.11 contains a schematic diagram of a one-write system. Identify the probable uses of forms A, B, and C if the system is used for the following functions:
    (a) accounts payable
    (b) accounts receivable
    (c) payroll

22. Modify Figure 4.7 to illustrate ledgerless bookkeeping when partial payments are made.

23. A form should permit the right thing to be done at the right time. What form would you want as proper authorization to perform the tasks that follows?
    (a) Assemble the items ordered by a customer and prepare them for delivery.
    (b) Arrange for the purchase of goods for your company at the best price.
    (c) Write a check, except for signature, in payment of a company bill.
    (d) Assign work to factory operators in your department.
    (e) Issue materials and supplies to employees for use in their work.
    (f) Post charges (debits) to customers' accounts.
    (g) Make out the payroll summary each week.
    (h) Disburse petty cash.
    (i) Repair equipment that is not functioning properly.
    (j) Release operators of cash registers at the end of their shift.

24. The purchasing agent of the Hirz Company has approved the design of the purchase requisition in Figure 4.12. Criticize the design of the purchase requisition, limiting your comments to the original copy that is illustrated.

25. Olivia Mace has recently been appointed controller of a family-owned manufacturing enterprise. The firm, S. Dilley & Company, was founded by Mr. Dilley about 20 years ago, is 78% owned by Mr. Dilley, and has served the major automotive companies as a

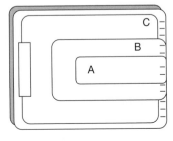

FIGURE 4.11 Schematic Diagram for a One-Write System.

Hirz Company
Washington, D.C.

To: Purchasing Agent No. ______

Quantity Required	Description	Amount

FIGURE 4.12 Purchase Requisition.

parts supplier. The firm's major operating divisions are heat treating, extruding, small parts stamping, and specialized machining. Sales last year from the several divisions ranged from $150,000 to over $3 million. The divisions are physically and managerially independent except for Mr. Dilley's constant surveillance. The accounting system for each division has evolved according to the division's own needs and to the abilities of individual accountants or bookkeepers. Ms. Mace is the first controller in the firm's history to have responsibility for overall financial management. Mr. Dilley expects to retire within six years and has hired Ms. Mace to improve the firm's financial system.

Ms. Mace soon decides that she will need to design a new financial reporting system that will do the following:

(a) Give managers uniform, timely, and accurate reports on business activity. Monthly divisional reports should be uniform and available by the tenth of the following month. Companywide financial reports also should be prepared by the tenth.
(b) Provide a basis for measuring return on investment by division. Divisional reports should show assets assigned each division and revenue and expense measurement in each division.
(c) Generate meaningful budget data for planning and decision-making purposes. The accounting system should provide for the preparation of budgets that recognize managerial responsibility, controllability of costs, and major product groups.
(d) Allow for a uniform basis of evaluating performance and quick access to underlying data. Cost center variances should be measured and reported for operating and nonoperating units, including headquarters. Also questions about levels of specific cost factors or product costs should be answerable quickly.

A new chart of accounts, as it appears to Ms. Mace, is essential to getting started on other critical financial problems. The present account codes used by divisions are not standard.

Ms. Mace sees a need to divide asset accounts into six major categories, that is, current assets, plant and equipment, and so on. Within each of these categories, she sees a need for no more than ten control accounts. On the basis of her observations to date, 100 subsidiary accounts are more than adequate for each control account.

No division now has more than five major product groups. The maximum number of cost centers Ms. Mace foresees within any product group is six, including operating and nonoperating groups. She views general divisional costs as a nonrevenue-producing product group. Altogether, Ms. Mace estimates that about 44 natural expense accounts and about 12 specific variance accounts would be adequate.

Ms. Mace is planning to implement the new chart of accounts in an environment that at present includes manual records systems and one division that is using an EDP system. She expects that in the near future most accounting and reporting for all units will be automated. Therefore, the chart of accounts should facilitate the processing of transactions manually or by machine. Efforts should be made, she believes, to restrict the length of the code for economy in processing and convenience in use.

Required

(a) Design a chart of accounts coding system that will meet Ms. Mace's requirements. Your answer should begin with a digital layout of the coding system. You should explain the coding method you have chosen and the reason for the size of your code elements. Explain your code as it would apply to *asset* and *expense* accounts.

(b) Use your chart of accounts coding system to illustrate the code needed for the following data:

(1) In the small parts stamping division, $100 was spent by foreman Bill Shaw in the polishing department of the Door Lever Group on cleaning supplies. Code the expense item, using the code you developed before.

(2) A new motorized sweeper has been purchased for the maintenance department of the extruding division for $3,450. Code this asset item using the code you developed before.

(CMA)

26. Forward Corporation is a progressive and fast-growing company. The company's executive committee consists of the president and the four vice presidents who report to the president—marketing, manufacturing, finance, and systems.

The company has ordered a new computer to use in processing its financial information. Because the computer acquisition required a substantial investment, the president wants to make certain that the computer is employed effectively.

The new computer will enable Forward to revise its financial information system so that the several departments will get more useful information. This should be helpful especially in marketing because its personnel are distributed widely throughout the country.

The marketing department is organized into 9 territories and 25 sales offices. The vice president of marketing wants the monthly reports to reflect those items for which the department is responsible and can control. The marketing department also wants information that identifies the most profitable products; this information is used to establish a discount policy that will enable the company to meet competition effectively. Monthly reports showing performance by territory and sales office also would be useful.

The vice president of finance has recommended that the accounting system be revised so that reports would be prepared on a contribution margin basis. Furthermore, only those cost items that are controlled by the respective departments would appear on their reports. The monthly report for the manufacturing department would compare actual production costs with a budget containing the standard costs for the actual volume of production. The marketing department would be provided with the standard variable manufacturing cost for each product so it could calculate the variable contribution margin of each product. The monthly reports to the marketing department would reflect the variable contribution approach; the reports would present the net contribution of the department calculated by deducting standard variable manufacturing costs and marketing expenses (both variable and fixed) from sales.

A portion of Forward Corporation's chart of accounts follows:

Account Number	Description
2000	Sales
2500	Cost of sales
3000	Manufacturing expenses
4000	Engineering expenses
5000	Marketing expenses
6000	Administrative expenses

The company wants to retain the basic structure of the chart of accounts to minimize the number of changes in the system. However, the numbering system will have to be expanded in order to provide the additional information that is desired.

Required

The coding structure now in effect must be modified to satisfy the needs of Forward's management. Using the marketing areas as an example, devise an account number coding system that will permit the preparation of the contribution reports for the marketing department. In the presentation of the account number coding system:

(a) add additional accounts to the chart of accounts as needed.

(b) provide flexibility in the coding structure so that it would not have to be revised completely should Forward expand or restructure its sales area.

(c) explain and justify the coding structure presented.

(CMA)

27. The campus bookstore has recently come under new ownership. The owner has asked you to design an accounting system to support her new method of operating the store. The store occupies rented space under a lease that covers heat and water but not electricity or telephone expenses. Assets include miscellaneous office furniture, store fixtures, and machinery such as cash registers, typewriters, and adding machines, in addition to an inventory of books and supplies.

The major changes made by the new owner concern the type of merchandise carried and the terms of sale. In an effort to improve profitability, only cash sales will be made, and several types of merchandise previously carried will be dropped. The store will carry four major classes of merchandise:

(a) textbooks

(b) other books

(c) paper and printing supplies

(d) miscellaneous desk/office furnishings

The staff includes the owner/manager, two office employees who handle the accounting/office paperwork, three full-time sales clerks, a part-time janitor, and several part-time sales clerks. The office employees and full-time clerks are paid on the first and fifteenth of each month, and the janitor and part-time clerks are paid weekly. Deductions are made for withholding tax and social security tax. The owner has a drawing account: The store is organized as a sole proprietorship. Sales clerks receive commissions on all sales merchandise in previous class d. The commissions are calculated monthly and paid a few days after the end of each month.

The store will purchase all merchandise on account and sell only for cash. There are three programmable cash registers, which will be used to record sales. These registers have been programmed to accumulate sales totals for four different classes of sales and also to accumulate total sales tax. Cash payments ("paid outs") will be made from one of the three registers. This register has a separate "paid out" key and accumulator for such items. A paid out slip will be written for each such payment and kept in the drawer of the register until the cash is balanced at the end of the day. Each register will be provided with a $100 change fund. The store maintains a checking account at a local bank. Gross cash receipts less paid outs will be deposited intact daily. Payroll checks as well as checks for merchandise and supplies will be drawn on this account.

Textbooks will be ordered from publishers under certain return privileges. Other merchandise will be bought subject to terms of 2/10, n/30. There will be about 150 merchandise suppliers. Physical inventories will be taken at midyear and at year-end. The store will use a periodic inventory system.

The owner asks you to design a system that will give her proper and timely financial and operating information and a set of books in which to collect the necessary information.

Your assignment should include the following:

- A complete chart of accounts
- A draft set of financial statements in outline form
- A set of standard journal entries
- A set of journals in draft outline to record the store's transactions

The store will operate a manual system. Statements will be prepared twice yearly. Be sure to indicate the timing of each of your journal entries. You need not discuss or provide formal closing entries.

28. Four days of sales data for the campus bookstore are listed below. Design a cash sales journal and use your journal to record these data. If possible, use a PC spreadsheet package for this assignment.

What advantages are (or would be) gained by using a PC spreadsheet package rather than paper for a sales journal such as this?

DAY 1

Cash	$4,687.52
Postage expense	$50.12
Sales returns	$200.88
Sales tax payable	$212.52
Sales—textbooks	$2,020.32
Sales—other books	$1,089.99
Sales—paper and printing	$715.67
Sales—miscellaneous	$900.02

DAY 2

Cash	$4,023.44
Drawing—owner	$300.11
Sales returns	$50.09
Sales tax payable	$188.06
Sales—textbooks	$1,570.21
Sales—other books	$615.02
Sales—paper and printing	$1,220.27
Sales—miscellaneous	$780.08

DAY 3

Cash	$4,808.95
Store expense	$215.23
Sales returns	$445.55
Sales tax payable	$235.77
Sales—textbooks	$2,845.12
Sales—other books	$810.03
Sales—paper and printing	$890.01
Sales—miscellaneous	$688.80

DAY 4

Cash	$4,533.86
Freight-in expense	$65.01
Sales returns	$100.87
Sales tax payable	$202.12

Sales—textbooks	$1,460.67
Sales—other books	$900.92
Sales—paper and printing	$1,020.78
Sales—miscellaneous	$1,115.25

Answers to Chapter Quiz

1. B   4. D   7. B   10. C
2. D   5. D   8. C
3. C   6. D   9. A

CHAPTER 5

Transaction Processing and the Internal Control Process

LEARNING OBJECTIVES

Careful study of this chapter will enable you to:

- Understand the nature of control exposures.

- Discuss the concept of the internal control process.

- Identify general and application processing controls.

- Discuss the behavioral assumptions inherent in traditional internal control practices.

- Describe the techniques used to analyze internal control systems.

THE NECESSITY FOR CONTROLS

Controls and Exposures

Controls are needed to reduce **exposures.** An organization is subject to a variety of exposures that can have an adverse effect on its operations or even its very existence as a viable going concern. An exposure consists of the potential financial effect of an event multiplied by its probability of occurrence. The term *risk* is synonymous with *probability of occurrence.* Thus, an exposure is a risk times its financial consequences.

Undesirable events such as floods or thefts are not themselves exposures. An organization's exposure to these types of events is the organization's potential financial loss times the probability of the occurrence of these events. Exposures do not arise simply due to a lack of controls. Controls tend to reduce exposures, but controls rarely affect the causes of exposures. Exposures are inherent in the operation of any organization and may result from a variety of causes (Figure 5.1).

Common Exposures

✓ Excessive Costs

Excessive costs reduce profits. Every expenditure made by an organization is potentially excessive. Prices paid for goods purchased for use in the organization may be excessive. Paychecks may be distributed for work that was ineffective, in-

FIGURE 5.1 Common Business Exposures.

efficient, or both. Production may be inefficient, causing the purchase and use of excessive materials and labor. Excessive assets may be purchased. Excessive expenses for advertising and travel expense may be incurred. Bills or taxes may be paid late, causing penalty fees and interest expense to be incurred.

Deficient Revenues

Deficient revenues reduce profits. Bad debt expense on credit sales may be excessive. Sales may be shipped to customers but not recorded and thus not collected. Customers may be incorrectly billed for smaller amounts than they should. Bills may be lost or incorrectly summarized as receivables. Sales may be returned or canceled due to late shipment of orders, shipment of unacceptable quality, or incorrect shipment of items ordered. Excessive sales allowances may be incurred for similar reasons.

Loss of Assets

Assets may be lost due to theft, acts of violence, or natural disaster. An organization has custody of a large quantity of assets, all of which are subject to loss. Assets may be lost unintentionally. Cash, materials, or equipment may be accidentally misplaced or damaged by careless employees or even careful employees. Cash, materials, or equipment may also be intentionally misplaced or damaged by employees, including management.

Inaccurate Accounting

Accounting policies and procedures may be error-prone, inappropriate, or significantly different than those that are considered to be generally acceptable. Errors may include valuation, timing, or classification of transactions. Errors in record keeping may be unintentional or intentional. Errors can result in inaccurate information for management decisions and materially misleading financial statements.

Business Interruption

Business interruption may consist of a temporary suspension of operations or ultimately the termination of operations and end of the organization. Business interruption may result from excessive operating exposures, from physical acts of violence, or from natural disaster.

Statutory Sanctions

Statutory sanctions include any penalties that may arise from judicial or regulatory authorities who have jurisdiction over an organization and its operations. An organization must ensure that its activities are in compliance with a variety of laws and regulations. Interruption of normal business operations might result as a penalty imposed by regulatory agencies when corporate crime has been committed.

Competitive Disadvantage

Competitive disadvantage is the inability of an organization to remain viable in the marketplace. Competitive disadvantage might result from any combination of the previous exposures, and also might result from ineffective management decisions.

Fraud and Embezzlement

Fraud is the intentional perversion of truth in order to induce another to part with something of value or to surrender a legal right. Embezzlement occurs when assets are fraudulently appropriated to one's own use. Fraud and embezzlement may be perpetrated by outsiders against an organization or by insiders within the organization. Excessive costs, deficient revenues, loss of assets, inaccurate accounting, business interruption, statutory sanctions, and competitive disadvantage may all result from fraud and embezzlement.

Fraud and White-Collar Crime

The term **white-collar crime** describes a grouping of illegal activities that are differentiated from other illegal activities in that they occur as part of the occupation of the offender. White-collar crime occurs when assets are deceitfully diverted from proper use or deceitfully misrepresented by an act or series of acts that are nonviolent in nature. White-collar crime often involves the entry of fictitious (i.e., fraudulent) transactions into an accounting system.

Three basic forms of theft occur in white-collar crime. Employee theft involves diversion of assets by an employee for personal gain. Employee–outsider theft involves diversion of assets by an employee in collusion with an outsider (i.e., nonemployee) for personal gain. Management fraud concerns diversion of assets or misrepresentation of assets by management. **Management fraud** may involve diversion or misrepresentation of assets from either employees, or third-party outsiders, or both. Management is responsible for the establishment of controls in an organization, and is thus not subject to these controls to the extent that other employees are. Irregularities by management are less likely to be detected than are irregularities committed by other employees.

White-collar crime may result in fraudulent financial reporting. **Fraudulent financial reporting** is intentional or reckless conduct, whether by purposeful act or omission, that results in materially misleading financial statements. Employees at any level of the organization might be involved. Fraudulent financial reporting might involve fictitious transactions processed by an accounting system, falsified valuation of assets such as inventories, or misapplication of accounting principles. No organization of any size is immune from the possibility that fraudulent financial reporting might occur.

Corporate crime is white-collar crime that benefits a company or organization rather than the individuals who perpetrate the fraud. Such individuals may benefit indirectly. Examples of corporate crime include defense contract cost overages charged to the federal government by defense contractors, publicized charges for reimbursement for noncontract-related expenses by universities, and bidding improprieties at auctions for government securities by major brokerage firms.

The fascinating aspect of white-collar crime is that it often seems to be victimless. Crimes such as embezzlement, tax fraud, fraudulent financial statements, unemployment insurance fraud, and the like require some sort of procedural analysis (a physical examination and analysis of transaction records, documentation, inventories, and so on) as a prerequisite to discovering and proving that a crime has been committed. In one publicized case of corporate crime, a major brokerage firm was convicted of mail and wire fraud concerning bank deposits that it processed. During the investigation, most of the banks that had been victims of the fraud were surprised to learn that they had in fact been robbed. They were unaware of this until they were contacted by investigators, which was well after the crimes had occurred.

Forensic Accounting

Forensic accounting is concerned with the prevention and detection of fraud and white-collar crime. **Forensic accounting** is one of several terms that is used to describe the activities of persons who are concerned with preventing and detecting fraud. The terms *fraud examiner, fraud auditor,* and *loss-prevention professional* are also descriptive of this type of activity.

The National Association of Certified Fraud Examiners (NACFE) is a professional organization that was established as a response to the increased concern for fraud in business and government. The mission of NACFE is to reduce the incidence of fraud and white-collar crime, and to assist its membership in its detection and deterrence. NACFE provides bona fide qualifications for Certified Fraud Examiners (CFE) through administration of the Uniform CFE Examination. Certified Fraud Examiners have expertise to resolve allegations of fraud, obtain evidence, take statements and write reports, testify to findings, and assist in the prevention and detection of fraud and white-collar crime. Typical CFEs include fraud auditors and investigators, forensic accountants, public accountants, law enforcement personnel, loss-prevention professionals, and academicians. All CFEs must exemplify high moral and ethical standards, and must abide by a Code of Professional Ethics.

Fraud examination draws on the fields of accounting, law, and criminology. A knowledge of accounting is necessary to understand the nature of fraudulent transactions. There are many legal aspects involved in fraud examination, thus an understanding of related law is essential. The basics of criminology are essential to understand the behavior of criminals. Principles of legal investigation are also central to fraud examination. Fraud examiners must know how to legally gather evidence related to fraud—how to obtain documentation, interview witnesses, take lawful statements, and write unbiased reports. Fraud examination has to adhere to investigation standards acceptable to a court of law.

Seriousness of Fraud

Fraud is a serious problem. KPMG Peat Marwick conducted a survey of 2,000 of the largest companies in the United States.[1] Companies were asked questions pertaining to overall awareness of fraud, perceptions of fraud in American business, specific instances with fraud, procedures to prevent fraud, and vulnerability to fraud. More than half of the 330 respondents had gross revenue/assets between $1–$4.9 billion.

The survey results leave no doubt that fraud is a significant problem for business. More than 75% of the 330 respondents experienced fraud during the past year, with 23% reporting losses of $1 million or more. More than half of these respondents (58%) experienced up to five incidents of fraud; 25% observed more than 21 cases of fraud. The three most expensive types of fraud were patent infringement, credit card fraud, and false financial statements, each totaling more than $1 million per company involved. The most frequent type of fraud was misappropriation of funds—accounting for 20% of all acts of fraud reported. This was followed by check forgery (19%), credit card fraud (15%), false invoices (15%), and theft (12%). Other types of fraud reported include accounts receivable manipulation, false financial statements, diversion of service, phantom vendors, purchase for personal use, diversion of sales, unnecessary purchases, vandalism, and sabotage.

Internal controls were cited most frequently as the reason frauds are discovered (59% of respondents). Internal auditor review and specific investigation by management were the next two most frequently mentioned methods of discovering fraud. Poor internal controls were identified as the most frequent reason that frauds occurred (56% of respondents). Collusion between employees and third parties was an important factor in 44% of reported cases. Management overrode existing controls in 40% of the cases. Forty-eight percent of respondents indicated that there were "red flags"—such as changes in an employee's lifestyle or spending habits—that pointed to the possibility of fraud(s), but these red flags were either ignored or not acted upon quickly enough by personnel or management.

Computer Processing and Exposures

Many aspects of computer processing tend to significantly increase an organization's exposure to undesirable events. Some aspects of computer processing increase either the risk and/or potential dollar loss of exposures that would exist in an organization regardless of whether or not computer processing was employed. Other aspects of computer processing create their own types of exposures.

Mechanical processing of data, mechanical data storage, and complexity of processing are aspects of computer processing that can increase either the risk and/or potential dollar loss of exposures that would exist in an organization regardless of whether computer processing was employed. Concentrated processing, concentrated data storage, and the data processing assets themselves are aspects of computer processing that create their own types of exposures.

---

[1]*Fraud Survey Results 1993.* KPMG Peat Marwick, 1993.

Data Processing Assets

The data processing assets must be protected, as must any other asset in the organization. Mainframe computer equipment can be quite expensive, and often requires a special environment for efficient operation. Restricted access is a major consideration. There should be few entrances to the computer system location. Only individuals with proper validation should be permitted to enter. There are a number of approaches to restricting access. These include programmable locks (which can be programmed to reject particular keys), security guards, and closed-circuit television monitors.

Control Objectives and Transaction Cycles

Controls act to reduce exposures. The analysis of exposures in an organization is often related to the transaction cycle concept. Although no two organizations are identical, most organizations experience the same types of economic events. These events generate transactions that may be grouped according to four common cycles of business activity:

- **Revenue Cycle:** events related to the distribution of goods and services to other entities and the collection of related payments
- **Expenditure Cycle:** events related to the acquisition of goods and services from other entities and the settlement of related obligations
- **Production Cycle:** events related to the transformation of resources into goods and services
- **Finance Cycle:** events related to the acquisition and management of capital funds, including cash

Each transaction cycle will have exposures. Management should develop detailed control objectives for each transaction cycle. These control objectives provide a basis for analysis. Once control objectives have been stated, management may collect information to determine the extent to which control objectives are being achieved in each of the organization's transaction cycles.

Figure 5.2 lists of representative control objectives for each transaction cycle. Control objectives such as those illustrated are drawn from the concept of an internal control structure. Management must first develop an internal control structure. This structure can then be applied to transaction cycles by developing specific control objectives for each cycle.

COMPONENTS OF THE INTERNAL CONTROL PROCESS

Internal control is a process—affected by an entity's board of directors, management, and other personnel—designed to provide reasonable assurance regarding the achievement of objectives in the following categories: (a) reliability of financial reporting, (b) effectiveness and efficiency of operations, and (c) compliance with applicable laws and regulations.[1]

An organization's internal control process consists of five elements: the control environment, risk assessment, control activities, information and communication, and monitoring (Figure 5.3). The concept of internal control is based on two major premises: responsibility and reasonable assurance.

Representative Control Objectives	
Revenue Cycle	Customers should be authorized in accordance with management's criteria.
	The prices and terms of goods and services provided should be authorized in accordance with management's criteria.
	All shipments of goods and services provided should result in a billing to the customer.
	Billings to customers should be accurately and promptly classified, summarized, and reported.
Expenditure Cycle	Vendors should be authorized in accordance with management's criteria.
	Employees should be hired in accordance with management's criteria.
	Access to personnel, payroll, and disbursement records should be permitted only in accordance with management's criteria.
	Compensation rates and payroll deductions should be authorized in accordance with management's criteria.
	Amounts due to vendors should be accurately and promptly classified, summarized, and reported.
Production Cycle	The production plan should be authorized in accordance with management's criteria.
	Cost of goods manufactured should be accurately and promptly classified, summarized, and reported.
Finance Cycle	The amounts and timing of debt transactions should be authorized in accordance with management's criteria.
	Access to cash and securities should be permitted only in accordance with management's criteria.

FIGURE 5.2 Representative Control Objectives.

The first premise, **responsibility,** has to do with management and the board of directors being responsible for establishing and maintaining the internal control process. While specific responsibilities for controls may be delegated to subordinates, final responsibility remains with management and the board of directors. External auditors, internal auditors, and other parties may be directly concerned with an organization's internal control process, but the ultimate responsibility for the control remains with management and the board of directors.

The second premise, **reasonable assurance,** has to do with the relative costs and benefits of controls. Prudent management should not spend more on controls than the benefits to be received from the controls. For example, suppose that purchasing a credit check report for new customers costs $35. The credit check would tend to reduce bad debt expense for new customers (i.e., reduce the probability or risk of its occurring), and thus would reduce the organization's exposure in this area. But if

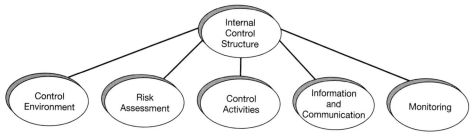

FIGURE 5.3 Internal Control Structure.

sales to new customers average only $25, then the cost of this control would exceed its expected benefits. It would not be rational to implement this control.

Quite often management's consideration of the relative costs and benefits of controls will necessarily be subjective in nature. It is often difficult to measure costs and benefits when intangible factors such as the reputation of the company or the morale effects of controls on employees are major considerations. Management must exercise its judgment to attain reasonable assurance that its control objectives are being met.

External Influences Concerning an Entity and Internal Control

Many organizations are subject to specific statutory requirements which are issued by judicial or regulatory authorities. An organization must ensure that its activities are in compliance with laws and regulations issued by those who have jurisdiction over an organization and its operations. The Securities and Exchange Commission (SEC) is active in the area of financial accounting, as is the Financial Accounting Standards Board (FASB). Laws, regulations, and pronouncements from such agencies are a major factor in an organization's internal control process.

The Federal Foreign Corrupt Practices Act of 1977 (FCPA) is a specific legal requirement that concerns many organizations. Failure to comply with this law could result in fines and imprisonment.

Section 102 of the FCPA requires all companies who are subject to the Securities Exchange Act of 1934 to

A. make and keep books, records, and accounts, which, in reasonable detail, accurately and fairly reflect the transactions and dispositions of the assets of the issuer;

B. devise and maintain a system of internal accounting controls sufficient to provide reasonable assurances that

1. transactions are executed in accordance with management's general or specific authorization;

2. transactions are recorded as necessary (i) to permit preparation of financial statements in conformity with generally accepted accounting principles or any other criteria applicable to such statements and (ii) to maintain accountability for assets;

3. access to assets is permitted only in accordance with management's general or specific authorization;

4. the recorded accountability for assets is compared with the existing assets at reasonable intervals and appropriate action is taken with respect to any differences.

Noncompliance with these provisions could result in fines up to $10,000 for both the corporation and its officials along with five years imprisonment for those executives involved.

A section of the Omnibus Trade and Competitiveness Act of 1988 (OTCA) amends both the accounting and antibribery provisions of the FCPA. The FCPA requires registrants to keep records in "reasonable detail" and to maintain systems of internal accounting control that provide "reasonable assurances" that specified goals are met. As originally passed, the act did not contain definitions of either "reasonable detail" or "reasonable assurances." A new subsection added by the OTCA defines the terms *reasonable detail* and *reasonable assurances* to mean a level that would satisfy prudent officials in the conduct of their own affairs. Another amendment to the accounting provisions limits criminal liability to intentional actions taken to circumvent the internal accounting control systems or to falsify company records. The OTCA also includes several amendments that clarify or modify the antibribery provisions of the FCPA and increase penalties for violation of the antibribery provisions.

The Impact of the Business Environment on Internal Control

Another important consideration is that an entity's internal control process will vary depending on the context of its size, organizational structure, ownership characteristics, methods of transmitting, processing, maintaining and assessing information, legal and regulatory requirements, and the diversity and complexity of its operations.

For example, in small organizations there may not be a large enough number of employees to achieve the same degree of separation of duties that might be expected in a large company. This situation can often be dealt with by involving the owner in various aspects of transactions, such as signing checks, approving invoices, and record keeping. Furthermore, procedure manuals, policy manuals, organization charts, and many other types of documentation, as well as policies and procedures, may prove infeasible for the small organization.

Control Environment

An organization's control environment, the first of the five components of internal control, is the foundation of all other components of the control system. The **control environment** is the collective effect of various factors on establishing, enhancing, or mitigating the effectiveness of specific policies and procedures. In other words, the control environment sets the overall tone of the organization and influences the control consciousness of the employees.

Factors included in the control environment are as follows:

- integrity and ethical values
- commitment to competence
- management philosophy and operating style
- organizational structure
- attention and direction provided by the board of directors and its committees
- manner of assigning authority and responsibility
- human resource policies and procedures

Corporate Ethics Breaches
Marketing executives of Anheuser-Busch were accused of taking kickbacks from a supplier, Hanely Wordwide, Inc. It was alleged that this supplier contributed $13,500 toward the purchase of a Porsche automobile by Anheuser-Busch's director of promotions.
Chrysler Corporation was charged in a 16-count indictment. The allegations stated executives of the company drove Chrysler automobiles with their odometers disconnected. The automobiles were then allegedly sold as new.
General Dynamics, a large defense contractor, was suspended from doing business for defrauding the Pentagon. Investigators alleged that General Dynamics was guilty of fraudulently billing the government.
General Electric and Rockwell were found guilty of fraudulently billing the federal government.
E. F. Hutton & Company pleaded guilty to 2,000 counts of mail and wire fraud.

FIGURE 5.4 Corporate Ethics Breaches.

Integrity and Ethical Values

Potential ethical violations present a significant loss exposure for the corporation (Figure 5.4). Such exposures include the possibility of large fines or criminal prosecution against both the company and its executives. For example, E. F. Hutton was fined $12 million when it pleaded guilty to allegations relating to wire and mail fraud. In another case Film Recovery Systems, which used cyanide to extract silver from film, was accused of knowingly creating a dangerous work environment that led to the death of an employee. Three of the company's executives were charged and convicted of murder. They were subsequently sentenced to 25 years in prison. In another case, Manville Corporation was driven into bankruptcy by problems relating to health hazards associated with asbestos, its primary product. Court testimony indicated that for years the company knew and intentionally overlooked severe damage to the health of company employees by asbestos.

Ethics and Corporate Culture   Many companies have adopted **ethics codes of conduct** that specify guidelines for conducting business in an ethical manner. Similarly, many professional organizations, such as the AICPA, have adopted codes of conduct. The code of conduct is often written in legal-style language that focuses on laws that might be broken. Accordingly, such codes have been sometimes criticized as being devoid of general ethical values such as "diligently looking out for the safety of employees" or "always telling the truth when dealing with customers."

Many have argued that every corporation has its own corporate culture, and that it is this **corporate culture** that either promotes or hinders ethical behavior. The corporate culture pertains to the general beliefs, practices, and attitudes of employees. It doesn't matter how good a code of conduct is if there are significant problems in the corporate culture. For example, some companies have an excessively inward focus. A company that focuses too much internally and not enough on the outside world is more likely to get into trouble. Examples of excessive internal focus would include overemphasis on sales quotas, making unreasonable deadlines, pleasing the boss, and so on. For example, if construction employees were told to either complete a building by a certain date or be fired, they might be tempted to cut corners and compromise safety. An excessive short-run focus may also be a problem. A company that focuses too much on the short run might be more inclined not to worry about the long-term consequences of its actions. In the case of Manville Company, the long-run health hazards of asbestos were overlooked to the point that the company was destroyed. Morale can be a problem. Unhappy employees can be dangerous. One such case involved a disgruntled employee of a company that produced an accounting software package. The employee made changes to the software that scrambled up the records of those companies who used the accounting system. Some companies have an excessively autocratic organizational structure. Highly autocratic managers are relatively unlikely to accept criticism, and the employees of such managers may fear pointing out ethics problems.

Producing a corporate culture supportive of ethical behavior can be difficult and certainly cannot be accomplished without education, training, and compliance. Some companies use seminars to educate and train their employees. Compliance is achieved by giving ethics a formal place in the organization chart. Each division should have an ethics director. The ethics director should be readily available to employees for consultations. All employees should be trained in how and when to contact the ethics director. Employees should be advised of penalties for ethics violations. The ethics director should be contacted whenever an employee observes an ethics violation, is ordered to commit an ethics violation, or whenever an employee needs advice on any problem involving ethics. Employees should be able to anonymously report problems. Some companies have "squeal systems" that reward employees for reporting ethical violations.

For any ethics program to work, the company should have a **cultural audit** of its culture and ethical behavior. Ethical problems can exist in many areas. Some of the areas that must be dealt with relate to safety, equal opportunity employment, sexual harassment, product and service quality, privacy, honesty in business dealings, conflicts of interest, and respect for intellectual property.

Ethical Considerations in Job Design   Consider the following job description:

> The person who accepts the treasurer's position shall be entirely responsible for the company's securities transactions. The position entails keeping the supporting records, exclusive control over the safe deposit box, and complete discretion over buying and selling of securities.

Would you accept this job?

Many readers will recognize several violations of conventional internal control principles in the preceding job description. Is this job offering an invitation to fraud? That is, does the lack of conventional controls over the treasurer's duties constitute the equivalent of an invitation to steal? What is an organization's responsibility for the integrity of its employees?

These questions raise issues that should be considered in the design of business systems. The need for an adequate system of internal control can be viewed ethically as well as from the view of efficient management. The following quotation is representative of this often expressed view:

I can recall a sizable industrial concern which was headed by a president who was perhaps more interested in his avocation of preaching than in running his business. Attempts to improve internal control in his corporation were constantly rebuffed because he believed that people were fundamentally honest, that his employees could be trusted and, therefore, there was no need for any system of checks and balances. The accountant became increasingly concerned with the company's exposure of its assets to possible defalcation. Finally, he went to the company president and said, "As a good Christian, you have a moral obligation to remove temptation from your employees!" This ethical appeal succeeded where an appeal to good business judgment alone failed, and the company's system of internal control was improved after all.[2]

Organizations should have sufficient controls to deter fraudulent actions, if only through reducing temptation by the threat of being caught. On the other hand, overly rigid controls hamper the actions and decisions of individuals, artificially limiting an employee's response to the variety of her or his task. Accountability and pressures for performance may boomerang. Rigid control systems may create or stimulate the types of action that the controls were designed to prevent.

Commitment to Competence

Competence in employees is essential to the proper functioning of any process of internal control. In the final analysis, it is the quality and competence of the employees that ensure the ability to carry out the control process. No control process can function adequately without competent employees.

Management Philosophy and Operating Style

Effective control in an organization begins with and ultimately rests with management philosophy. If management believes that controls are important, then it will see to it that effective control policies and procedures are implemented.

This control-conscious attitude will be communicated to subordinates through management's operating style. If, on the other hand, management pays only "lip service" to the need for controls, it is very likely that subordinates will sense management's true attitude and control objectives will not be achieved.

Organizational Structure

An organization's structure is defined by the patterns of authority and responsibility that exist within the organization. The formal organization structure is often denoted by an organization chart, such as Figure 5.5. As shown, the billing function is directly responsible to the accounting manager. At the next higher level in the chart, the accounting manager is responsible to the controller. And the controller is in turn responsible to the president.

An organization chart indicates the formal communication patterns within an organization. In Figure 5.5, for example, one would not normally expect the billing function to communicate the results of its operations to the vice president of production. As indicated in the chart, billing is not directly responsible to the vice president of production. An informal organization structure exists when regular communication patterns do not follow the lines indicated by the formal organization structure.

---

[2]"Business Ethics." *Review.* New York: Price Waterhouse, 1977.

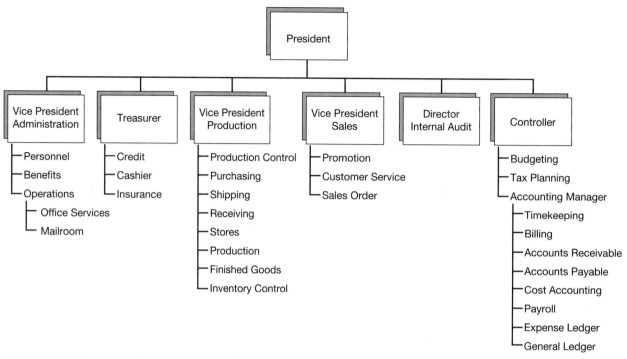

FIGURE 5.5 Organization Chart.

Functions of the Board of Directors and Its Committees

An organization's board of directors is the interface between the stockholders who own the organization and the organization's operating management. Stockholders exercise control over management through the functions of the board of directors and its committees. If the board consists entirely of members of management, or if the board meets infrequently, then stockholder control over operating management is likely to be weak or nonexistent.

Audit Committee. Typically a board of directors delegates specific functions to various operating committees. All public companies whose stock is traded on the New York Stock Exchange are required to have an audit committee composed of outside directors. Many other companies also have audit committees.

The audit committee should be independent of an organization's management, composed primarily of outside members of the board of directors (Figure 5.6). The audit committee is usually charged with overall responsibility for the organization's financial reports, including compliance with existing laws and regulations. The audit committee nominates public accountants, discusses the scope and nature of audits with public accountants, and reviews and evaluates reports prepared by the organization's public accountants. Audit committees should be charged with reviewing management's reaction to public accountants' reports on the organization's internal control process.

To be effective, the audit committee must maintain communication with an organization's internal audit function as well as with the organization's external auditors (i.e., public accountants). As shown in Figure 5.6, internal audit should report to the audit committee of the board of directors to maintain independence of internal auditing from other functions.

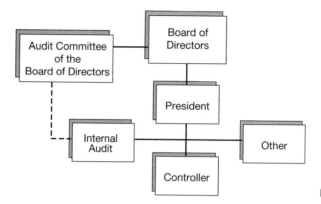

FIGURE 5.6 Audit Committee.

Manner of Assigning Authority and Responsibility

The methods of assigning authority and responsibility within an organization are indicative of management's philosophy and operating style. If only verbal or informal methods exist, control is likely to be weak or nonexistent.

A formal organization chart, a written document, is often used to indicate the overall assignment of authority and responsibility in an organization. The organization chart is often accompanied by formal job descriptions and statements of work assignments. Written memoranda, policy manuals, and procedure manuals are other common means used to formally assign authority and responsibility within an organization.

Budgeting.   Budgeting is the process of preparing budgets. Budgeting is a major management activity. Budgets are generally set for the entire organization as well as for each subunit. The budget for the entire organization is usually called the *master budget.* The master budget is often presented as a set of pro forma financial statements. Pro forma financial statements are forecasted statements—such as a balance sheet and income statement—that represent the predicted financial results of management's plan of operation for the coming budget period. The master budget is the accumulated result of all of the detailed budgets that are prepared for the organizational subunits. Detailed operating budgets are prepared for subunits to evidence management's plan concerning operation of each subunit and to serve as the device by which management's plans are communicated to subunits. In addition to operating budgets, other types of budgets may be prepared as necessary to help management plan and control the activities of the firm. A common example is the capital expenditure budget, which is used to plan capital expenditures. Budgets are generally prepared on both a monthly and a yearly basis; frequently, a five- or ten-year long-term budget is prepared as well.

Budgeting data are used to plan and control the activities within a firm. Control is established by comparing the results of activity to the budget for each activity. A budget is a control that sets forth a financial plan and/or an authorized amount of resources that may be utilized by a subunit in performing its functions. Budgets are set in advance of organizational activity and serve as the control by which management authorizes the transactional activity that the organization will undertake.

Human Resource Policies and Practices

Personnel should be competent and have capabilities and/or training commensurate with their duties. In the final analysis, personnel are the key components in any control system. The qualifications established for each job position in a company should reflect the degree of responsibility associated with the position. Qualifications may include experience, intelligence, character, dedication, and leadership ability. Fidelity bonding is common for employees who are directly responsible for the custody of assets. A **fidelity bond** is a contract with an insurance company that provides a financial guarantee of the honesty of the individual who is named in the bond contract. The insurance company will usually investigate the background of a person who is to be bonded. Thus, fidelity bonding helps ensure that an organization is hiring reliable personnel.

Segregation of Duties.   Responsibility for specific tasks in an organization should be clearly designated by manuals, job descriptions, or other documentation. Effective segregation of duties depends to a considerable extent on the precise and detailed planning of all procedures and the careful assignment of functions to various people in the organization. The details of the procedures should be set forth in memoranda that also show explicit assignment of duties to individual departments or employees. Written procedures, instructions, and assignments of duties will prevent duplication of work, overlapping of functions, omission of important functions, misunderstandings, and other situations that might weaken the internal accounting controls. Such notes typically form the basis for a formal manual on procedures and policy.

Supervision.   Supervision is the direct monitoring of personnel performance by an employee who is so charged. In addition to properly selecting and adequately training employees, proper supervision is necessary to ensure that duties are being carried out as assigned. Supervision becomes very important in a small firm or in other situations where segregation of duties is not possible.

Job Rotation and Forced Vacations.   Job rotation and forced vacations allow employees to check or verify the operations of other employees by performing their duties for a period of time. Several advantages may be gained by these techniques.

Irregularities that may have been committed by an employee may be disclosed while the employee is on vacation and her or his duties are assumed by another employee. Job rotation allows more than one employee to become familiar with certain duties and procedures so that the replacement of employees in cases of emergency is less difficult. Job rotation frequently serves as a general check on the efficiency of the employee on vacation or who has been rotated to another job. Finally, job rotation broadens the training of the personnel in general.

Dual Control.   Closely related to direct supervision is the concept of **dual control**—the assignment of two individuals to perform the same work task in unison. The intent of dual control is not work reduction but work redundancy. Each individual is assumed to check the work of the other constantly. Responsibility for the custody of high-valued securities, for example, is frequently delegated to two or more people working in unison. Multiple control involves three or more people in unison. Dual or multiple control differs from supervision in that a supervisor is expected to supervise several people or operations simultaneously and, therefore, may effectively supervise a particular operation or employee less than 100% of the time. Dual control is essentially "dedicated" supervision; that is, one employee constantly checks the work of another, and vice versa.

Risk Assessment

Risk assessment, the second of the five components of internal control, is the process of identifying, analyzing, and managing risks that affect the company's objectives. Probably the most critical step in risk assessment is identifying internal and external changing conditions and related actions that may be necessary. Examples of risks relevant to the financial reporting process include changes in the organization's operating environment, changes in personnel, changes in the information system, new technology, major industry changes, new product lines, new rules, laws, or accounting pronouncements.

Control Activities

Control activities, comprising the third component of internal control, are the policies and procedures established to help ensure that management directives are carried out. There are many potential control activities that may be utilized by organizations. These include accounting controls designed to provide reasonable assurance that the following specific control objectives are met for every significant application system within an organization:

- The plan of organization includes segregation of duties to reduce opportunities to allow any person to be in a position to both perpetrate and conceal errors or irregularities in the normal course of his or her duties.
- Procedures include the design and use of adequate documents and records to help ensure the proper recording of transactions and events.
- Access to assets is permitted only in accordance with management's authorization.
- Independent checks and reviews are made on the accountability of assets and performance.
- Information processing controls are applied to check the proper authorization, accuracy, and completeness of individual transactions.

Each of these specific control objectives is discussed in turn.

Segregation of Duties

Segregation of duties is necessary to reduce opportunities to allow any person to be in a position to both perpetrate and conceal errors or irregularities in the normal course of his or her duties. Segregation of duties is implemented by assigning to different people the responsibilities of authorizing transactions, recording transactions, and maintaining custody of assets. To achieve segregation of duties, the responsibilities of authorizing transactions, recording transactions, and maintaining custody of assets should be performed by independent functions.

Segregation of Authorization from Recording of Transactions.   Segregation of authorization of transactions from recording of transactions reduces opportunities for errors and irregularities by establishing independent accountability for authorization functions. If each function in an organization kept its own records, there would be no accountability. There would be no basis for an independent reconciliation and analysis of a function's activities as there are no assurances that all transactions have been recorded. In order to ensure unbiased information, record-keeping functions are usually centralized in a separate function headed by the controller.

For example, in a sales order application the sales manager authorizes credit sales. A copy of the sales order form is sent to the warehouse to authorize the shipment of goods. If notice of the shipment is subsequently sent only to the sales manager, then the sales manager is accountable for his or her own performance. The sales manager is thus in a position to perpetrate errors and irregularities in the normal course of his or her duties. Perhaps he or she has authorized a shipment to a relative or friend. When notice of the shipment is received, the sales manager may simply destroy it, or ignore it, rather than forward it to billing for collection.

Segregation of Authorization from Custody of Assets. Segregation of authorization of transactions from custody of assets reduces opportunities for errors and irregularities by establishing independent accountability for the use (custody) of assets. Authorization of activities is communicated to those who have custody of assets, and simultaneously communicated to the record-keeping function (i.e., accounting). Those charged with the custody of assets subsequently communicate the results of activity (i.e., transactions) to the record-keeping function. Reconciliation of these data to the authorizations that were received from an independent function provides accountability for both the authorization and the subsequent use of assets.

For example, in a sales order application the sales manager authorizes credit sales. A copy of the sales order form is sent to the warehouse to authorize the shipment of goods. Another copy of the sales order form is sent to accounting. Notice of the shipment is subsequently sent to accounting. Reconciliation of shipment data to the authorizations which were received from an independent function provides accountability for both the authorization and the subsequent use of assets. Notice of shipment without a matching authorization indicates unauthorized shipments. Notice of authorization without subsequent shipment indicates ineffectiveness or inefficiency in completing sales transactions.

Segregation of Recording Transactions from Custody of Assets. Segregation of recording transactions from custody of assets reduces opportunities for errors and irregularities by establishing independent accountability for the use of assets. Authorization of activities is communicated to those who have custody of assets, and simultaneously communicated to the record-keeping function (i.e., accounting). Those charged with the custody of assets subsequently communicate the results of activity (i.e., transactions) to the record-keeping function. Reconciliation of these data to the authorizations which were received from an independent function provides accountability for both the authorization and the subsequent use of assets.

If there is no segregation of duties between recording transactions from custody of assets, then those charged with the custody of assets are accountable for their own performance. There would be no basis for an independent reconciliation and analysis of a function's activities as there are no assurances that all transactions have been recorded. The persons charged with the custody of assets are in a position to perpetrate errors and irregularities in the normal course of their duties by omitting records or falsifying entries into the records. In the preceding sales example, goods may be shipped by those who have custody of assets without authorization and without recording the shipment, as there is no independent accountability for shipments.

Adequate Documents and Records

Procedures should include the design and use of adequate documents and records to help ensure the proper recording of transactions and events. Documents and records are the physical media used to store information. They may take many different forms, ranging from common paper documents such as sales orders and purchase orders to magnetic and optical storage media such as magnetic tape and optical disk.

Certain control practices are relevant to any type of documents and records. Items should be prenumbered in sequential order to facilitate accountability. Items should be easy to use and clearly understood by those who use them. Forms should provide specific space for the indication of necessary authorizations and approvals. Principles of forms design and use were detailed in Chapter 4.

Restricted Access to Assets

Access to assets should be permitted only in accordance with management's authorization. This requires adequate physical controls and safeguards over access to and use of assets and records, such as secured facilities and authorization for access to computer programs and data files.

It is well documented that physical theft and embezzlement are substantial threats to the solvency of business organizations. Physical controls are directed at reducing the opportunities for theft and embezzlement. Safeguarding of assets such as cash, securities, and inventory is accomplished by close supervision, physical protection devices, and segregation of duties. Common examples of physical controls include the following:

- Cash registers and lock boxes
- Locks, vaults, and limited-access areas
- Security forces
- Closed-circuit TV monitors
- Alarm systems

No physical control or safeguard in and of itself can protect assets; it is the procedures surrounding the use of physical controls that dictate whether or not the controls are effective. For example, every lock has a key; therefore, a lock is only as effective as is access to the key. TV monitors are effective only if they are constantly being watched or, alternatively, if personnel believe they are being watched. Limited-access areas are effective only if access is truly limited. The effectiveness of physical controls depends largely on the measures surrounding their use, not the mere existence of the devices.

Independent Accountability Checks and Reviews of Performance

The recorded accountability for assets should be compared with the existing assets at reasonable intervals and appropriate action taken with respect to any difference. This reconciliation function should be performed by someone who is independent of authorization, record keeping, and custody of the assets in question. Examples of independent checks on performance and proper valuation of recorded amounts include clerical checks, reconciliations, comparison of assets with recorded accountability, computer-programmed controls, management review of reports that summarize the detail of account balances (e.g., an aged trial balance of accounts receivable), and user review of computer-generated reports.

Budgets and general performance reviews are also an important means for assessing performance. These reviews are accomplished by comparing actual results to budgets, forecasts, standards, and prior-period performance.

Information Processing Controls

Information processing controls ensure the proper authorization, accuracy, and completeness of individual transactions.

Authorization limits the initiation of a transaction or performance of an activity to selected individuals. Authorization prevents unauthorized transactions and unauthorized activities. Proper authorization of transactions and activities is necessary if management is to obtain reasonable assurance that its control objectives are achieved.

Management's authorization may be general or specific in nature. Specific authorization pertains to individual transactions. Setting automatic reorder points for inventory items is an example of general authorization as no specific transaction is involved. Approval of a construction budget for a (specific) warehouse is an example of specific authorization. Establishment of general requirements to be met in determining customers' credit limits is an example of general authorization as no specific transaction (i.e., customer) is involved. Establishment of sales prices for products to be sold to any customer is another example of general authorization.

Approval is the acceptance of a transaction for processing after it is initiated. Approval comes after authorization and is used to detect unauthorized transactions and unauthorized activities. Approval is necessary to ensure that employees are operating within the realm of their authority.

Completeness and accuracy ensure the integrity of the data and information in the accounting system. Both completeness and accuracy are necessary to ensure a system whose information can be relied upon. There is a wide range of transaction controls that enhance completeness and reliability. Transaction controls are discussed later in a separate section.

Information and Communication

Information and communication comprise the fourth component of internal control. *Information* refers to the organization's **accounting system,** which consists of the methods and records established to identify, assemble, analyze, classify, record, and report the organization's transactions and to maintain accountability for the related assets and liabilities. The accounting system of an organization may be simple, or it may be complex. Many organizations have systems that are able to process huge numbers of various types of transactions. Information systems are designed and installed not only to produce the ledger balances from which financial statements are prepared but also to produce management control and operational information. Thus, accounting systems and operational control are closely related in an organization.

Documentation of the Accounting System

Documentation of the accounting system is essential. Accounting procedures should be set forth in accounting procedure manuals so that policies and instructions may be explicitly known and uniformly applied. Well-designed forms should be used to report transactions. Subsidiary ledgers should be used to accumulate detailed information which is summarized in the general ledger. A chart of accounts containing detailed descriptions of the meaning and uses of accounts in the general ledger should be maintained and revised as necessary. A chart of accounts will aid in the consistent application of accounting policies, ensure proper recording of transactions, and facilitate the preparation of financial statements. Control accounts should be used extensively as they are a proof of accuracy between the account balances of duly segregated employees in a double-entry system of accounting.

Double-Entry System of Accounting

An accounting system should contain features that readily confirm or question the reliability of recorded data. Double-entry systems of accounting should not be underestimated as a device that will produce a balanced set of records. To conceal an irregularity under a double-entry system, it is necessary to omit from the accounts both sides of the transaction or to record entries offsetting the amount of the irregularity. Errors can be made under a double-entry system, however; the system alone will not prove omission, incorrect entry, or dishonesty.

Audit Trail.   The term *audit trail* originates with the concept of an external auditor who is asked to express an opinion on the financial statements of an organization. An **audit trail** exists if a financial total that appears in a general ledger account can be supported by evidence concerning all the individual transactions that comprise that total and vice versa. If an audit trail exists, the auditor can be confident that the accounting information system and related financial statements are very reliable; that is, the system and its outputs are accurate. If an audit trail does not exist, then the reliability of the accounting information system must be suspect.

The audit trail concept is basic to the design and audit of an accounting information system and is relevant to internal auditors, management, systems analysts, and other parties involved in the operation of an accounting information system. An audit trail is comprised of the documentary evidence of the various control techniques that a transaction was subject to during its processing. Each transaction should be subjected to a set of control techniques that in total provide a sufficient degree of assurance that the transaction was accurately and reliably processed. The nature of the documentary evidence that comprises the audit trail will depend on the technology of the system and also on the design of the system. Audit trails do not have an independent existence—they are a consideration that must be included in the design of an accounting information system. That is particularly true in computer-based systems.

Communication

Communication relates to providing a clear understanding regarding all policies and procedures relating to controls. Good communication requires effective oral communication, adequate procedure manuals, policy manuals, and other types of documentation.

Effective communication also requires an adequate upstream flow of information in the organization. Such information is used for performance reviews, exception reports, and so on.

Monitoring

Monitoring, the fifth component of internal control, involves the ongoing process of assessing the quality of internal controls over time and taking corrective actions when necessary. The quality of controls might be adversely affected in various ways, including a lack of compliance, changing conditions, or even misunderstandings.

Monitoring is accomplished through ongoing activities, separate evaluations, or some combination of the two. Ongoing activities would include management supervisory activities and other actions that personnel might take to assure an ongoing effective internal control process.

An internal audit function is common in large organizations to monitor and evaluate controls on an ongoing basis. The expanded span of control and the growth in the volume of transactions associated with large organizations were factors in the emergence of the internal audit function. The increased reliance on accounting data that is necessary in management of a large organization, coupled with the increased possibilities of defalcations and improperly maintained accounting records in a large organization, have created the need for continuous auditing. The objective of the internal audit function is to serve management by furnishing management with the results of analysis and appraisals of such activities and systems as:

- the organization's information systems
- the organization's internal control structure
- the extent of compliance to operating policies, procedures, and plans
- the quality of performance by company personnel

As indicated, the scope of auditing activity undertaken by a modern internal audit function is broader than just the financial activities of the organization. The terms **management audit** and **operational audit** describe internal audit services to management that extend beyond the financial activities of the organization. The existence of an effective internal audit function does not substitute for the external auditor, although internal audit may be of assistance to the external auditor in arranging and accumulating audit evidence.

The internal audit function has no less of a need for independence than the external auditor. But the nature of independence is different. The external auditor must be independent of the organization, for his or her opinion is given to third parties (e.g., banks, stockholders, etc.). The internal auditor cannot be independent of the organization but he or she must be independent from the management of the activities being reviewed. This can be accomplished by having the internal audit function report to the organization's audit committee.

External auditors may participate in monitoring controls. For example, it is common practice for external auditors to provide lists of specific recommendations for management to improve internal control.

TRANSACTION PROCESSING CONTROLS

Transaction processing controls are procedures designed to ensure that elements of an organization's internal control process are implemented in the specific applications systems contained within each of an organization's transaction cycles. Transaction processing controls consist of general controls and application controls. **General controls** affect all transaction processing. **Application controls** are specific to individual applications.

General Controls

General controls concern the overall environment of transaction processing. General controls comprise the following:

- The plan of data processing organization
- General operating procedures
- Equipment control features
- Equipment and data-access controls

General controls are not a substitute for application controls. It is possible to have relatively strong general controls with relatively weak or nonexistent application controls. General controls may thus be seen as necessary but not sufficient for adequate control of transaction processing.

A plan of organization for data processing includes provision for segregation of duties within data processing and the organizational segregation of data processing from other operations. General operating procedures include written manuals and other documentation that specify procedures to be followed. Equipment control features are those that are installed in computers to identify incorrect data handling or erroneous operation of the equipment. Equipment and data-access controls involve procedures related to physical access to the computer system and data. There should be adequate procedures to protect equipment and data files from damage or theft.

The Plan of Data Processing Organization and Operation

Segregation of Duties. Responsibility for authorization, custody, and record keeping for handling and processing of transactions are separated.

> Example: The computer librarian function maintains a depository of computer programs and documentation, but does not have access to or authority to operate the computer processing equipment.

Segregation of Duties in Data Processing. Computer data processing functions should be centralized. Computer data processing should have neither custody nor authority over any assets other than the data processing assets.

> Example: Departments that are responsible for the custody of inventories should not report to the vice president of computer data processing.

It is also desirable to segregate the following personnel functions associated with computer processing within the data processing department.

- *Systems Analysts.* Systems analysts are responsible for the development of the general design of computer system applications. Systems analysts work with users to define their specific information requirements.
- *Programmers.* Computer programmers develop the programs that produce computer output. They design and code newly developed computer programs based on specifications provided by systems analysts.
- *Computer Operators.* Computer operators operate the mainframe computer equipment. They should not have access to detailed program listings in order to maintain a segregation of functions between programming and operations.

- *Librarian.* The librarian function maintains a depository of computer programs and documentation. This function is responsible for the custody of information assets.
- *Data Control Clerks.* Data control clerks establish control over jobs and input data for processing. This includes consideration of the quality of input, the completeness of processing, and the reasonableness of output.

General Operating Procedures

DEFINITION OF RESPONSIBILITIES: Descriptions of tasks for each job function within a transaction processing system. Beginning and termination points for each job function should be clearly indicated, as should the relationship of job functions to each other.

EXAMPLE: The computer operator has restricted access to programs and data files.

RELIABILITY OF PERSONNEL: Personnel performing the processing may be relied on to function in a consistent manner.

EXAMPLE: The supervisor of computer operations has a good attendance record and a good performance record.

TRAINING OF PERSONNEL: Personnel are provided explicit instructions and tested on their understanding before being assigned new duties.

EXAMPLE: All new programmers attend a five-day training seminar before beginning duties.

COMPETENCE OF PERSONNEL: Persons assigned to processing or supervisory roles in transaction processing systems have the technical knowledge necessary to perform their functions.

EXAMPLE: The director of data processing is an MBA.

ROTATION OF DUTIES: Jobs assigned to people are rotated periodically at irregularly scheduled times, if possible, for key processing functions.

EXAMPLE: Responsibility for the destruction of sensitive data is rotated among clerical personnel.

FORMS DESIGN: Forms are constructed to be self-explanatory, understandable, and concise and to gather all necessary information with a minimum of effort.

EXAMPLE: The form to authorize a purchase has clear and concise instructions for each field in which data are to be entered.

PRENUMBERED FORMS: Sequential numbers on individual forms are printed in advance to allow subsequent detection of loss or misplacement.

EXAMPLE: Checks are prenumbered.

PREPRINTED FORMS: Fixed elements of information are entered on forms in advance and sometimes in a format that permits direct machine processing to prevent errors in entry of repetitive data.

EXAMPLE: MICR account encoding on checks and deposit tickets.

SIMULTANEOUS PREPARATION: The one-time recording of a transaction for all further processing, using multiple copies, as appropriate, to prevent transcription errors.

EXAMPLE: A one-write system is used to prepare a receiving report form and receiving register simultaneously.

TURNAROUND DOCUMENT: A computer-produced document that is intended for resubmission into the system.

EXAMPLE: The part of a utility bill that the customer returns with payment.

DOCUMENTATION: Written records for the purpose of providing communication.

EXAMPLE: Standard journal entries communicate the accounting data to be supplied by various operating departments.

LABELING: The identification of transactions, files, or other items for control purposes.

EXAMPLE: All computer files have an external label.

Equipment Control Features

BACKUP AND RECOVERY: Backup consists of file equipment, and procedures that are available if the originals are destroyed or out of service. Recovery is the ability to re-create master files using prior files and transactions.

EXAMPLE: Master files and transaction files are maintained after the creation of an updated master file in case the current master file is corrupted.

TRANSACTION TRAIL: The availability of a manual or machine-readable means for tracing the status and contents of an individual transaction record backward or forward and between output, processing, and source.

EXAMPLE: A list of changes to on-line computer files is stored on magnetic tape to provide a transaction trail.

ERROR-SOURCE STATISTICS: Accumulation of information on the type of error and origin. This is used to determine the nature of remedial efforts needed to reduce the number of errors.

EXAMPLE: The data input supervisor collects and reviews statistics on input errors made by clerks.

Equipment and Data-Access Controls

SECURE CUSTODY: Information assets are provided security similar to tangible assets such as cash, negotiable securities, and the like.

EXAMPLE: The general ledger master file is locked in a safe each night.

DUAL ACCESS/DUAL CONTROL: Two independent, simultaneous actions or conditions are required before processing is permitted.

EXAMPLE: A safe deposit box for sensitive computer files requires two keys to open it.

2/2/99 ## Application Controls

Application controls are specific to individual applications. Application controls are categorized into input, processing, and output controls. These categories correspond to the basic steps in the data processing cycle.

✓ Input Controls

Input controls are designed to prevent or detect errors in the input stage of data processing. When computers are used for processing, the input stage involves the conversion of transaction data into a machine-readable format. Typical input controls include the following items.

AUTHORIZATION: Limits the initiation of a transaction or performance of a process to selected individuals.

EXAMPLE: Only the timekeeper may submit payroll hours data for processing.

APPROVAL: The acceptance of a transaction for processing after it is initiated.

EXAMPLE: An officer of the company approves the payroll before it is distributed to employees.

FORMATTED INPUT: Automatic spacing and format shifting of data fields during data input to a recording device.

EXAMPLE: The computer automatically inserts commas into the numbers that are input by clerks using data terminals.

ENDORSEMENT: The marking of a form or document to direct or restrict its further processing.

EXAMPLE: Checks are restrictively endorsed "Pay only to the order of ABC Company" immediately upon receipt.

CANCELLATION: Identifies transaction documents in order to prevent their further or repeated use after they have performed their function.

EXAMPLE: Marking bills as "paid" to prevent duplicate payment.

EXCEPTION INPUT: Processing proceeds in a predefined manner unless specific input transactions are received that indicate special processing with different values or in a different sequence.

PASSWORDS: The authorization to allow access to data or processing by providing a code or signal known only by authorized individuals.

ANTICIPATION: The expectation of a given transaction or event at a particular time.

TRANSMITTAL DOCUMENT (BATCH CONTROL TICKET): The medium for communicating control totals over movement of data, particularly from source to processing point or between processing points.

BATCH SERIAL NUMBERS (BATCH SEQUENCE): Batches of transaction documents are numbered consecutively and accounted for.

CONTROL REGISTER (BATCH CONTROL LOG): A log or register indicating the disposition and control values of batches of transactions.

AMOUNT CONTROL TOTAL: Totals of homogeneous amounts for a group of transactions or records, usually dollars or quantities.

DOCUMENT CONTROL TOTAL: A count of the number of individual documents.

LINE CONTROL COUNT: A count of the number of lines of data on one or more documents.

√ **HASH TOTAL:** A meaningless total that is useful for control purposes only.

BATCH CONTROL (BATCH TOTALS): Any type of control total or count applied to a specific number of transaction documents or to the transaction documents that arrive within a specific period of time.

VISUAL VERIFICATION: The visual scanning of documents for general reasonableness and propriety.

SEQUENCE CHECKING: A verification of the alphanumeric sequence of the "key" field in items to be processed.

OVERFLOW CHECKS: A limit check on the capacity of a field, file, or device.

FORMAT CHECK: Determination that data are entered in proper mode—numeric or alphabetic—in fields.

EXAMPLE: Overtime hours are input on special forms.

EXAMPLE: An automatic bank terminal requires that a user enter his or her password before processing is initiated.

EXAMPLE: Daily cash deposits are always made at 3:00 P.M.

EXAMPLE: Daily cash deposits are accompanied by a deposit slip that indicates the total amount of the deposit.

EXAMPLE: Sales tickets are batched daily, numbered, and filed by date.

EXAMPLE: A register is used to record the time and batch control number of express mail that is picked up by courier services.

EXAMPLE: Total net pay is an amount control total for a payroll processing application.

EXAMPLE: A count of the number of time cards is a document control total for a payroll application.

EXAMPLE: A count of the number of individual products sold (i.e., a line) on invoices is a line control count for a sales order application.

EXAMPLE: Total department number of all paychecks processed is a meaningless total that is useful for control purposes only.

EXAMPLE: Total sales dollars is a batch control total for a billing application.

EXAMPLE: Clerks visually scan each invoice before submitting the document for further processing.

EXAMPLE: Prenumbered checks are sorted in sequence for further processing.

EXAMPLE: The number 12345 cannot be entered into a four-digit, numeric field.

EXAMPLE: Vendor number is checked to ensure that all characters in the field are numeric.

COMPLETENESS CHECK: A test that ensures that fields cannot be processed in a blank state.

EXAMPLE: A voucher will not be processed if the "vendor number" field is blank.

CHECK DIGIT: A digit that is a function of the other digits within a record or number used for testing an accurate transcription.

EXAMPLE: An account number contains a check digit that is validated during processing.

REASONABLENESS TEST: Tests applied to various fields of data through comparison with other information available within the transaction or master records.

EXAMPLE: A male patient should not be billed for services by the gynecology department of a hospital.

LIMIT CHECK: A test to ensure that only data within predetermined limits will be entered into and accepted by the system.

EXAMPLE: A test ensures that rate per hour cannot be lower than the minimum set by law or higher than the maximum set by union contract.

VALIDITY CHECK: The characters in a coded field are either matched to an acceptable set of values in a table or examined for a defined pattern of format, legitimate subcodes, or character values, using logic and arithmetic other than tables.

EXAMPLE: All social security numbers should have nine numeric digits.

READBACK: Immediate return of input information to the sender for comparison and approval.

EXAMPLE: A computer echos messages received from a data terminal back to the terminal for visual verification.

DATING: The recording of calendar dates for purposes of later comparison or expiration testing.

EXAMPLE: Customer remittances are stamped with the date received.

EXPIRATION: A limit check based on a comparison of current date with the date recorded on a transaction, record, or file.

EXAMPLE: Checks to vendors are dated and marked "void after 60 days."

KEY VERIFICATION: Reentry of transaction data with machine comparison of the initial entry to the second entry to detect errors.

EXAMPLE: A second clerk keys payroll into a computer. The computer compares this input, character by character (i.e., key by key) to the initial input of the data by the first clerk and reports differences.

Processing Controls

Processing controls are designed to provide assurances that processing has occurred according to intended specifications and that no transactions have been lost or incorrectly inserted into the processing stream. Typical processing controls include the following items.

MECHANIZATION: Consistency is provided by mechanical or electronic processing.

EXAMPLE: Cash deposits are totaled by adding machine.

STANDARDIZATION: Uniform, structured, and consistent procedures are developed for all processing.

EXAMPLE: A chart of accounts documents the normal debits and credits to each account.

DEFAULT OPTION: The automatic utilization of a predefined value in situations where input transactions have certain values left blank.

EXAMPLE: Salaried employees receive pay for 40 hours each week.

BATCH BALANCING: A comparison of the items or documents actually processed against a predetermined control total.

EXAMPLE: The cashier batch balances deposit tickets to control totals of cash remittances.

RUN-TO-RUN TOTALS: The utilization of output control totals resulting from one process as input control totals over subsequent processing. The control totals are used as links in a chain to tie one process to another in a sequence of processes over a period of time.

EXAMPLE: Beginning accounts payable balance less payments plus net purchases should equal ending accounts payable balance.

BALANCING: A test for equality between the values of two equivalent sets of items or one set of items and a control total. Any difference indicates an error.

EXAMPLE: The balance of the accounts receivable subsidiary ledger should equal the balance of the general ledger control account.

MATCHING: Matching items with other items received from independent sources to control the processing of transactions.

EXAMPLE: The accounts payable clerk matches vendor invoices to purchase orders and receiving reports.

CLEARING ACCOUNT: An amount that results from the processing of independent items of equivalent value. Net control value should equal zero.

EXAMPLE: The imprest payroll checking account has a zero balance after all paychecks have been cashed.

TICKLER FILE: A control file consisting of items sequenced by age for processing or follow-up purposes.

EXAMPLE: Invoices are filed by due date.

REDUNDANT PROCESSING: A repetition of processing and an accompanying comparison of individual results for equality.

EXAMPLE: A second payroll clerk computes the gross and net pay of each employee for comparison purposes.

SUMMARY PROCESSING: A redundant process using a summarized amount. This is compared for equality with a control total from the processing of the detailed items.

EXAMPLE: Total overhead applied to production is recomputed by applying the overhead rate to the total amount of direct labor cost charged for all jobs.

TRAILER LABEL: A record providing a control total for comparison with accumulated counts or values of records processed.

EXAMPLE: The last record of an inventory file contains a record count of the number of records in the file.

AUTOMATED ERROR CORRECTION: Automatic error correction of transactions or records that violate a detective control.

EXAMPLE: A credit memo is automatically generated when customers overpay their account balances.

Output Controls

Output controls are designed to check that input and processing resulted in valid output and that outputs are properly distributed. Typical output controls include the following items.

RECONCILIATION: An identification and analysis of differences between the values contained in two substantially identical files or between a detail file and a control total. Errors are identified according to the nature of the reconciling items rather than the existence of a difference between the balances.

EXAMPLE: The bank reconciliation identifies service charges and fees on the monthly bank statement that have not yet been recorded in the company's accounts.

AGING: Identification of unprocessed or retained items in files according to their date, usually the transaction date. The aging classifies items according to various ranges of duties.

EXAMPLE: The aging of accounts receivable balances to identify delinquent accounts.

SUSPENSE FILE: A file containing unprocessed or partially processed items awaiting further action.

EXAMPLE: A file of back-ordered items awaiting shipment to customers.

SUSPENSE ACCOUNT: A control total for items awaiting further processing.

EXAMPLE: The total of the accounts receivable subsidiary ledger should equal the balance of the general ledger control account.

PERIODIC AUDIT: Periodic verification of a file or process to detect control problems.

EXAMPLE: All customers are mailed monthly statements of account to confirm their balances.

DISCREPANCY REPORTS: A listing of items that have violated some detective control and require further investigation.

EXAMPLE: A list of customer accounts that have exceeded their credit limit is sent to the credit manager for review.

UPSTREAM RESUBMISSION: The resubmission of corrected error transactions backwards (i.e., upstream) in the flow of transaction processing so that they pass through all or more of the detective controls that are exercised over normal transactions.

EXAMPLE: Rejected transactions are resubmitted as a special batch as if they were new transactions.

Preventative, Detective, and Corrective Controls

Transaction processing controls may also be classified as being primarily preventive, detective, or corrective in nature. **Preventative controls** act to prevent errors and fraud before they happen. **Detective controls** act to uncover errors and fraud after they have occurred. **Corrective controls** act to correct errors.

Many detective controls apply to both the input and processing stages of transaction processing. An example is the batch control total procedures used in an insurance company. Each day's incoming premium payments (checks) are grouped into batches of 50 checks; a clerk totals and records the dollar amount of the 50 checks. Then the batches of checks are given to a data conversion operator, who keys the check data into the computer, by batch. A printout of the batch totals from the computer is then compared to the totals recorded by the clerk. Discrepancies are immediately uncovered and traced back, usually to mistakes by either the clerk or operator, or both. This control procedure affects both the input and processing steps and is illustrated in a manual system in Figure 5.7.

The general ledger clerk compares the totals at point A in the figure with the totals at point B. Notice how the concept of segregation of duties is employed. An output detective control is simply a procedure to compare output totals with the control totals generated at the input and processing steps.

Classification of the general and application controls discussed here as preventative, detective, or corrective in nature is shown in the applications control matrix, Figure 5.9.

Communicating the Objectives of Internal Control

Internal control must be seen not as a process unto itself but as part of a larger process. It must fit in or it may be totally ineffective or perhaps even harmful. One must not lose sight of what the purpose of internal control is.

People are an essential element in every internal control process. People are not perfect; they commit errors of omission and commission. If people were perfect, internal control would be an unnecessary waste of resources. Internal control is people. An internal control process consists of people checking the work of other people. The principal function of internal control is to influence the behavior of people in a business system.

There is a paradox inherent in a system of internal control. Controls such as

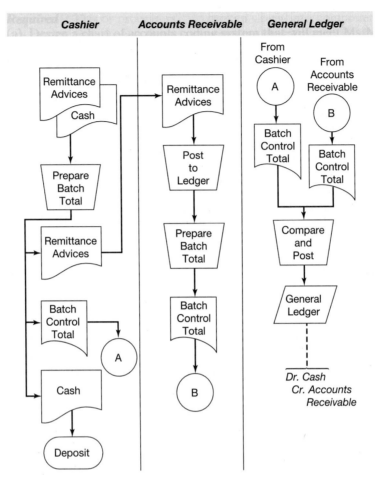

FIGURE 5.7 Batch Control Total Illustration.

rules and procedures are imposed on people who ideally, from a more humanistic view, should be responsible for their own self-control and self-direction. This inconsistency must be dealt with in every organizational control system.

Management's job is to ensure the efficiency of operations. Thus, behaviors and activities need to be organized and controlled so that the organization's goals are attained. A system of internal control does interfere to some extent with an individual's self-control. But by promoting the interests and safeguarding the assets of the overall organization, a system of internal control is really protecting the interest and integrity of each individual employee who is a part of that organization.

The objectives of internal control must be seen as relevant to the individuals who will comprise the control system. The system must be designed such that each employee is convinced that controls are meant to prevent difficulties or crises in the operation of the organization that could otherwise affect him or her very personally.

Goals and Behavior Patterns

An information system has several goals; chief among them is productivity. Reliability of information and the safeguarding of assets are also important goals. These goals are at times contradictory. Productivity in an information system is often constrained by the consideration of reliability. Controls are redundant. They constrain productivity but increase the reliability of resulting outputs. This conflict between internal controls and productivity must be acknowledged and carefully considered by the analyst because it may influence the behavior of people in a control system.

A common behavior caused by this goal conflict is the omission of an internal control duty (such as counting documents) in the interest of increasing production. Consider a clerk manually posting invoices. If the clerk double-checks each posting, the number of postings is approximately 50% of what would have been performed without double-checking. If the clerk's performance is evaluated by postings per time period, there will be a temptation to omit the double-checking for at least some items if the clerk falls behind schedule. Internal control duties typically require a trade-off with production. The basic motivational problem is that productivity is usually measurable and forms the basis for performance evaluation, whereas reliability and degree of internal control are not as easily measured or incorporated into performance reviews. The systems analyst should keep this in mind in designing and evaluating internal controls.

The goals of an internal control system are achieved through the actions of the people in the system. The reliance on a formal plan of organization and related methods and measures to attain these goals entails important assumptions concerning collusion, reporting of irregularities, power relationships, and other behavior patterns within the organization. Organizational independence and segregation of duties are consistent with good internal control only if the probability of collusion between two or more duly segregated employees is low.

Collusion is agreement or conspiracy among two or more people to commit fraud. In a purchase procedure, control over acquisitions is obtained when duly segregated personnel from both receiving and stores acknowledge that the materials have been received by stores. Both must sign for the material, and neither could deceive the other without collusion or fraud. Of course, errors of omission are possible, such as both parties miscounting quantities. In fact the same error (a shortage) could occur unintentionally as well as intentionally. However, if unintentional, the error would not be covered up and other controls would probably uncover the discrepancy.

Justification for the assumption that the probability of collusion between two or more people will be low is found in the formal plan of organization. For one individual to suggest an irregularity to another person and be rejected would entail prohibitive costs to the first individual. He or she will be turned in by the second individual and hence lose his or her job or incur another punishment. This entails a related assumption that employees will always report irregularities to those higher up in the organization. This assumption in turn requires several others. One is that the formal plan of organization as denoted in procedures manuals and the like solely determines power relations in a system. A related assumption is that actions not specified by a system are dysfunctional or "wrong"; that is, deviations suggest irregularities that should be reported to those higher up.

Numerous factors influence an individual's behavior in a control system. One important influence is the formal plan of organization and the related methods and measures employed by an organization. Other factors do exist, however. Groups and other sources of informal pressure bear upon an individual's behavior and may at times mitigate the desired, formally planned relationships between people in the system. For example, an individual with lengthy service may convince a young co-worker that the omission of a control step is okay and need not be reported, because "it's been done that way in the past."

A receiving clerk transferring goods to inventory may convince the inventory clerk just to sign and not waste time counting the items she or he is receiving. A clerk performing a bank reconciliation may not examine several checks in detail as it is near quitting time.

What might be called "people failure" is the source of all theft and fraud in a system and is a prime contributor to serious errors of the production type and other ineffectiveness and inefficiency. In cases of defalcations, "the procedures did not fail, the people did." The variety and complexity of human behavior and the value constraints (principles of just, humane, compassionate conduct) we work within combine to make the production of "people-proof" procedures infeasible. As long as people have access to valuables there will be the possibility of theft, sabotage, and serious error. These possibilities are minimized when employees fully understand, accept, and internalize the objectives of the internal control system of which they are the essential element.

ANALYSIS OF INTERNAL CONTROL PROCESSES

The analysis of an internal control process requires an understanding of the process both as it is designed and as it actually operates. The actual process may or may not conform to expectations. Documentation may be outdated, and the structure may be operating under new procedures. Procedures may have changed informally to adapt to circumstances not foreseen when the original system was designed and documented.

Internal control processes routinely collect information concerning fulfillment of duties, transfer of authority, approval, and verification. This documentation of internal control duties must be examined to evaluate the reliability of the system's operation.

Reliability is dependent on the people who administer internal control procedures. Designing an internal control process is only the first part of the problem; it is essential that internal control duties are actually performed as prescribed. There are several reasons why internal control duties may not be administered. New employees, or perhaps even experienced employees, may not understand their duties. More common is the omission of an internal control duty (such as counting documents) in order to increase production.

Analytical Techniques

The **internal control questionnaire** is a common analytical technique used in internal control analysis. Internal control questionnaires have traditionally been a central element in an audit program; accordingly, questionnaires are a standard form in public accounting firms, internal audit departments, and other organizations that are regularly involved in reviews of internal controls. Questionnaires are available for the review of specific application areas as well as for special reviews such as computer center audits. At times the analyst may design a questionnaire specifically for a particular audit, or she or he may modify a standard questionnaire to better suit the needs or nature of a particular audit. Questionnaires are usually designed so that an affirmative answer to a question indicates an adequate degree of internal control, and a negative answer indicates the need for further information or a potential weakness in the structure.

However, a negative answer does not always indicate a weakness because other controls may compensate for the omission identified by the negative response. Questionnaires are essentially checklists to ensure that a review does not omit an area of major importance. Figure 5.8 illustrates a portion of a questionnaire for sales and shipping procedures.

Questionnaires are only tools; the manner in which they are used is extremely important. The questionnaire should be filled in on the basis of actual observations and inquiries. But filling in the questionnaire is not the essence of the review. The essence of a review is the analyst's analysis of his or her findings. Questionnaires do serve as documentation that a review was undertaken; however, questionnaires are necessarily standardized and therefore are not equally applicable in all circumstances. Their use must often be supplemented with other forms of analysis, such as write-ups, flowcharts, or other charting techniques.

Sales and Shipping

1. Are sales orders adequately controlled?
2. Are all orders approved by the credit manager or department before shipment?
3. Is the credit department entirely independent of the sales department?
4. Are sales prices and credit terms based on approved standard price lists?
5. If so, are any deviations from standard approved
    a. by an officer?
    b. by another? Explain.
6. If not, are all sales prices and credit terms approved by the sales manager or in the sales department?
7. Are prenumbered shipping advices prepared for all goods shipped?
8. Are the quantities shown on the shipping advices double-checked in the shipping department?
9. Does the billing clerk or some other designated employee receive the shipping advices directly from the shipping department? (If so, identify this employee.)
10. Does this employee check the numerical sequence of shipping advices to assure that all are accounted for?
11. Are sales invoices checked
    a. as to prices?
    b. as to quantities?
    c. as to credit terms?
    d. as to extensions and footings?
    e. against customers' orders?
    f. against shipping advices?
    (Identify the department or individual responsible for the above.)
12. Are sales invoices prenumbered?
13. Is there a check on the arithmetical accuracy of total sales by means of a statistical or product analysis?
14. Are total sales for the respective accounting periods (e.g., monthly) reported directly to the general ledger bookkeeper independently of the work of the accounts receivable bookkeepers?
15. Are there adequate safeguards against understatement of sales through the suppression of sales invoices or shipping advices?
16. Are returned sales cleared through the receiving department (i.e., the department receiving incoming purchased materials and supplies)?
17. Are credit memos for returned sales supported by adequate data from the receiving department as to quantity, description, and condition?
18. Are the following classes of sales accounted for in substantially the same manner as regular credit sales of merchandise:
    a. Sales to employees?
    b. C.O.D. sales?
    c. Sales of property and equipment?
    d. Cash sales of merchandise?
    e. Scrap and waste?
    (If the answers are negative in any case, amplify by a concise description of the procedures.)
19. Is there an adequate check on freight allowances
    a. by reference to terms of sale?
    b. by checking against freight bills or established and up-to-date schedule of freight rates?
    c. Other? (If any, explain.)
    Comment on adequacy of internal control.

FIGURE 5.8 Portion of an Internal Control Questionnaire.

Analytic flowcharts might be used in internal control analysis, particularly if the analysis involves a computer system application. Flowcharting itself is not a form of structured analysis but rather a technique to organize data for analysis. An **application controls matrix** provides a structured form of analysis that is particularly relevant to internal control reviews of information systems. The rows of the matrix consist of various control techniques. The columns of the matrix consist of activities or data values in the system under review. The matrix organization provides a structured method for the systematic evaluation of each activity or data item with respect to each type of control activity listed in the rows. Figure 5.9 illustrates an application controls matrix that is preprinted with a comprehensive list of controls. An application controls matrix can be designed as needed in any specific situation by providing one's own list of controls as the rows of the matrix.

To use the matrix, the analyst identifies the activities or data items that should be subject to control and lists them as the columns of the matrix. A matrix can be used systematically to evaluate an analytic or other type of flowchart by listing the sequence of operations shown in the chart as the columns of the matrix. Each row/column contribution of control/activity or control/data items can then be evaluated systematically. The analyst might enter an "X" or other symbol in each row/column box where a control existed and/or was performed, leaving blank those combinations that were absent. Another technique would be to rate the strength or relative reliability of each present control/activity combination by assigning numbers or letters to indicate relative strength or reliability. A "1" might indicate highly reliable, a "3" reliable, a "5" functioning but not reliable, and so on.

Illustration of an Internal Control Analysis

Many professional examinations, such as the Certificate in Public Accounting (CPA) examination and the Certified Internal Auditor (CIA) examination, test a candidate's knowledge of internal controls by requiring the candidate to evaluate potential control structure weaknesses that are evident in a narrative or graphic (flowchart) description of an application system. The candidate is usually required to do the control analysis solely on the basis of analytic reasoning. That is, questionnaires or other analytical aids, such as the applications controls matrix discussed previously, are not provided for the candidate's use. In such a case the candidate must carefully evaluate the described system and, with the professional definition of internal control structures as a reference, identify potential control weaknesses through analytical reasoning.

As an illustration, following is a CPA examination question in which one is expected to evaluate internal controls in the manner just described. The published unofficial answer immediately follows the question.

> The Art Appreciation Society operates a museum for the benefit and enjoyment of the community. During hours when the museum is open to the public, two clerks who are positioned at the entrance collect a five dollar admission fee from each nonmember patron. Members of the Art Appreciation Society are permitted to enter free of charge upon presentation of their membership cards.
>
> At the end of each day one of the clerks delivers the proceeds to the treasurer. The treasurer counts the cash in the presence of the clerk and places it in a safe. Each Friday afternoon the treasurer and one of the clerks deliver all cash held in the safe to the bank, and receive an authenticated deposit slip which provides the basis for the weekly entry in the cash receipts journal.
>
> The Board of Directors of the Art Appreciation Society has identified a need to improve their system of internal control over cash admission fees. The Board

	Transaction/Process
Control Feature	

PREVENTIVE CONTROLS

Characteristics that Constitute Controls

		Check digits
Reliability of personnel		Reasonableness
Segregation of duties		Limit check
Definition of responsibilities		Validity check
Rotation of duties		Read back
Training of personnel		Dating
Competence of personnel		Expiration
Secure custody		Keystroke verification
Dual access/dual controls		Approval
Standardization		Exception input
Mechanization		Default option
Forms design		Labeling
Prenumbered forms		**Completeness of Processing**
Precoded forms		Run to run totals
Authorization		Balancing
Endorsement		Reconciliation
Cancellation		Aging
Simultaneous preparation		Suspense file
Documentation		Suspense account
Formatted input		Matching
DETECTIVE CONTROLS		Clearing account
Accountability of Input		Tickler file
Anticipation		Periodic audit
Transmittal documents		Activity log
Batch serial numbers		**Correctness of Processing**
Control register		Redundant processing
Completeness of Input		Summary processing
Amount control total		Sequence checking
Document control total		Overflow checks
Line control count		Scan before distribution
Hash total		Trailer label
Batch totals		**CORRECTIVE CONTROLS**
Batch balancing		Discrepancy reports
Visual verification		Transaction trail
Turnaround document		Error source statistics
Passwords		Automatic error correction
Correctness of Input		Upstream resubmission
Format		Backup and recovery
Completeness check		

FIGURE 5.9 Application Controls Matrix.

had determined that the cost of installing turnstiles, sales booths, or otherwise altering the physical layout of the museum will greatly exceed any benefits that may be derived. However, the Board has agreed that the sale of admission tickets must be an integral part of its improvement efforts.

Smith has been asked by the Board of Directors of the Art Appreciation Society to review the internal control over cash admission fees and provide suggestions for improvement.

Required. Indicate weaknesses in the existing system of internal control over cash admission fees, which Smith should identify, and recommend one improvement for each of the weaknesses identified.

Organize the answer as indicated in the following illustrative example:

Weaknesses	*Recommended Improvements*
1. There is no basis for establishing the documentation of the number of paying patrons.	1. Prenumbered admission tickets should be issued upon payment of the admission fee.

Unofficial Answer

Weaknesses	*Recommended Improvements*
1. There is no segregation of duties between persons responsible for collecting admission fees and persons responsible for authorizing admission.	1. One clerk (hereafter referred to as the collection clerk) should collect admission fees and issue prenumbered tickets. The other clerk (hereafter referred to as the admission clerk) should authorize admission upon receipt of the ticket or proof of membership.
2. An independent count of paying patrons is not made.	2. The admission clerk should retain a portion of the prenumbered admission ticket (admission ticket stub).
3. There is no proof of amounts collected by the clerks.	3. Admission ticket stubs should be reconciled with cash collected by the treasurer each day.
4. Cash receipts records are not promptly prepared.	4. The cash collections should be recorded by the collection clerk daily on a permanent record that will serve as the first record of accountability.
5. Cash receipts are not promptly deposited. Cash should not be left undeposited for a week.	5. Cash should be deposited at least once each day.
6. There is no proof of accuracy of amounts deposited.	6. Authenticated deposit slips should be compared with daily cash collection records. Discrepancies should be promptly investigated and resolved. In addition, the treasurer should establish a policy that includes an analytical review of cash collections.
7. There is no record of the internal accountability for cash.	7. The treasurer should issue a signed receipt for all proceeds received from the collection clerk. These receipts should be maintained and periodically checked against cash collection and deposit records.

(CPA)

SUMMARY

Controls are needed to reduce exposures. An organization is subject to a variety of exposures that can have an adverse effect on its operations or even its very existence as a viable going concern. Many aspects of computer processing tend to significantly increase an organization's exposure to undesirable events. The analysis of exposures in an organization is often related to the transaction cycle concept. Management should develop detailed control objectives for each transaction cycle.

An entity's internal control process consists of the policies and procedures established to provide reasonable assurance that the following entity objectives will be achieved: (a) reliability of financial reporting, (b) effectiveness and efficiency of operations, and (c) compliance with applicable laws and regulations. An internal control process consists of five components: the control environment, risk assessment, control activities, information and communication, and monitoring. Controls can be classified as either general controls or application controls. A standard method of classifying application controls is by considering whether a given control applies to inputs, processing, or outputs. This chapter discussed and illustrated a variety of common control practices.

Ethical considerations must be addressed in the design of an internal control structure. People are an essential element in every internal control structure. It is important that the objectives of internal control be communicated and understood. The objectives of internal control must be seen as relevant to the individuals who will comprise the control system.

The analysis of an internal control structure requires an understanding of the structure both as it is designed and as it actually operates. The most common analytical technique used in internal control analysis is the internal control questionnaire. Analytic flowcharts are also useful in internal control analysis.

Glossary

accounting system: the methods and records established to identify, assemble, analyze, classify, record, and report the organization's transactions and to maintain accountability for the related assets and liabilities.

aging: identification of unprocessed or retained items in files according to their date, usually the transaction date.

amount control total: totals of homogeneous amounts for a group of transactions or records, usually dollars or quantities.

anticipation: the expectation of a given transaction or event at a particular time.

application controls: specific to individual applications.

application controls matrix: a structured form of analysis that utilizes a matrix of application controls.

approval: the acceptance of a transaction for processing after it is initiated.

audit committee: subcommittee of the board of directors that is charged with overall responsibility for the organization's financial reports.

audit trail: financial totals that appear in a general ledger account can be supported by evidence concerning all the individual transactions that comprise that total and vice versa.

authorization: limits the initiation of a transaction or performance of an activity to selected individuals.

batch control: any type of control total or count applied to a specific number of transaction documents or to the transaction documents that arrive within a specific period of time.

batch control log: synonym for control register.

batch control ticket: synonym for transmittal document.

batch sequence: synonym for batch serial numbers.

batch serial numbers: batches of transaction documents are numbered consecutively and accounted.

batch totals: synonym for batch control.

cancellation: identification of transaction documents in order to prevent their further or repeated use after they have performed their function.

clearing account: an amount that results from the processing of independent items of equivalent value. Net control value should equal zero.

collusion: agreement or conspiracy among two or more people to commit fraud.

control environment: the collective effect of various factors on establishing, enhancing, or mitigating the effectiveness of specific policies and procedures.

control procedures: the policies and procedures in addition to the control environment and accounting system that management has established to provide reasonable assurance that specific entity objectives will be achieved.

control register: a log or register indicating the disposition and control values of batches or transactions.

corporate crime: white-collar crime that benefits a company or organization, rather than the individuals who perpetrate the fraud.

corrective controls: act to correct errors.

detective controls: act to uncover errors and fraud after they have occurred.

document control total: a count of the number of individual documents.

dual control: the assignment of two individuals to perform the same work task in unison.

endorsement: the marking of a form or document so as to direct or restrict its further processing.

exposure: the potential financial effect of an event multiplied by its probability of occurrence.

fidelity bond: a contract with an insurance company that provides a financial guarantee of the honesty of the individual who is named in the bond contract.

forensic accounting: an activity concerned with preventing and detecting fraud.

fraudulent financial reporting: intentional or reckless conduct, whether by purposeful act or omission, that results in materially misleading financial statements.

general controls: affect all transaction processing.

hash total: a meaningless total that is useful for control purposes only.

input controls: designed to prevent or detect errors in the input stage of data processing.

internal accounting control: the plan of organization and the procedures and records that are concerned with the safeguarding of assets and reliability of financial statements.

internal control questionnaire: a set of questions pertaining to internal controls in an application area.

internal control process: the policies and procedures established to provide reasonable assurance that the following entity objectives will be achieved: (a) effectiveness and efficiency of operations, (b) reliability of financial reporting, and (c) compliance with applicable laws and regulations.

line control count: a count of the number of lines of data on one or more documents.

management audit: internal audit services to management that extend beyond the financial activities of the organization.

management fraud: diversion of assets or misrepresentation of assets by management.

operational audit: synonym for management audit.

output controls: designed to check that input and processing resulted in valid output and that outputs are properly distributed.

preventative controls: act to prevent errors and fraud before they happen.

processing controls: designed to provide assurances that processing has occurred according to intended specifications and that no transactions have been lost or incorrectly inserted into the processing stream.

reasonable assurance: principle that the costs of controls should not exceed their benefits.

responsibility: management and the board of directors are responsible for the internal control process.

risk: the probability of occurrence of an event.

run-to-run totals: the utilization of output control totals resulting from one process as input control totals over subsequent processing.

segregation of duties: responsibilities for authorization, custody, and record keeping for handling and processing of transactions are separated.

supervision: the direct monitoring of personnel performance by an employee who is so charged.

suspense account: a control total for items awaiting further processing.

suspense file: a file containing unprocessed or partially processed items awaiting further action.

tickler file: a control file consisting of items sequenced by age for processing or follow-up purposes.

transmittal document: the medium for communicating control totals over movement of data, particularly from source to processing point or between processing points.

upstream resubmission: the resubmission of corrected error transactions backward (i.e., upstream) in the flow of transaction processing so that they pass through all or more of the detective controls that are exercised over normal transactions.

white-collar crime: deceitful diversion of assets from proper use or deceitful misrepresentation of assets by an act or series of acts that are nonviolent in nature.

Chapter Quiz

Answers to the chapter quiz appear on page 214.

1. The potential negative financial effect of an event multiplied by its probability of occurrence is a(n)
   (a) control.
   (b) exposure.
   (c) hazard.
   (d) risk.

2. Fraud that benefits a company or organization, rather than the individual(s) who perpetrate the fraud, is known as
   (a) white-collar crime.
   (b) corporate crime.
   (c) management fraud.
   (d) fradulent financial reporting.

3. The responsibility for establishing and maintaining an internal control structure rests with
   (a) internal auditing.
   (b) the treasurer.
   (c) management.
   (d) the controller.

4. Which of the following is an element of an internal control process?
   (a) information and communication
   (b) reasonable assurance
   (c) internal audit function
   (d) management control methods

5. Which of the following limits the initiation of a transaction or performance of an activity to selected individuals?
   (a) authorization
   (b) approval
   (c) fidelity bond
   (d) audit trail

6. Computer master files and transaction files are maintained after the creation of an updated master file in case the current master file is corrupted. This is an example of
   (a) labeling procedures.
   (b) recovery procedures.
   (c) documentation procedures.
   (d) secure custody.

7. Marking bills as "paid" to prevent duplicate payment is an example of
   (a) cancellation.
   (b) backup.
   (c) approval.
   (d) endorsement.

8. A meaningless total that is useful for control purposes only is called a(n)
   (a) line control count.
   (b) hash total.
   (c) document control total.
   (d) amount control total.

9. An imprest payroll checking account has a zero balance after all paychecks have been cashed. This type of control practice is an example of a(n)
   (a) tickler file.
   (b) upstream resubmission.
   (c) redundant processing.
   (d) clearing account.

10. Agreement or conspiracy among two or more people to commit fraud is known as
    (a) dual control.
    (b) complicity.
    (c) intrigue.
    (d) collusion.

Review Problem

The Fox Company, a client of your firm, has come to you with the following problem. It has three clerical employees who must perform the following functions:

  a. maintain general ledger
  b. maintain accounts payable ledger
  c. maintain accounts receivable ledger
  d. prepare checks for signature
  e. maintain cash disbursements journal
  f. issue credit memos on returns and allowances
  g. reconcile the bank account
  h. handle and deposit cash receipts

Assuming there is no problem as to the ability of any of the employees, the company requests that you assign these functions to the three employees to achieve the highest degree of internal control. Assume that these employees will perform no other accounting functions than the ones listed and that any accounting functions not listed will be performed by people other than these three employees.

  a. State how you would distribute these functions among the three employees. Assume that, with the exception of the nominal jobs of the bank reconciliation and the issuance of credits on returns and allowances, all functions require an equal amount of time.

  b. List four possible unsatisfactory pairings of the listed functions.

(CPA)

Solution to Review Problem

UNDESIRABLE COMBINATIONS ARE AS FOLLOWS:

1. Cash receipts and accounts receivable
2. Cash receipts and credit memos on sales returns and allowances
3. Cash disbursements and accounts payable
4. Cash receipts and bank reconciliation
5. Cash disbursements and bank reconciliation
6. Cash receipts and general ledger
7. Accounts receivable and credit memos on sales returns and allowances

ASSIGNMENT OF FUNCTIONS:

Employee No. 1:
   a. maintain general ledger
   f. issue credit memos on returns and allowances
   g. reconcile bank account

Employee No. 2:
   e. maintain cash disbursements journal
   d. prepare checks for signature
   h. handle and deposit cash receipts

Employee No. 3:
   b. maintain accounts payable ledger
   c. maintain accounts receivable ledger

Review Questions

1. Distinguish between risks and exposures.
2. Identify several common business exposures.
3. What is corporate crime?
4. What is management fraud?
5. Does computer processing increase an organization's exposure to undesirable events?
6. List the basic elements of an internal control process.
7. Distinguish between general controls and applications controls.
8. Why are written procedures manuals control tools?
9. Differentiate preventative, detective, and corrective controls. Give an example of each.
10. What is the purpose of a forced vacation policy?
11. What is batch control?
12. Why is collusion a problem in internal control design?
13. Why is it important that the purpose and nature of internal control be communicated to employees within an organization?
14. Discuss the statement "The procedures did not fail; the people did."
15. What role do physical security devices have in a system of internal control?
16. Why has the importance of the internal audit function continued to grow?
17. What are the functions of an audit committee?

18. Discuss the advantages and disadvantages of using a questionnaire or checklist in evaluating an internal control system.

19. Does filling out a questionnaire constitute an evaluation of internal controls?

20. What is an analytic flowchart? What is an applications control matrix?

Discussion Questions and Problems

21. Internal accounting controls are not designed to provide reasonable assurance that
    (a) transactions are executed in accordance with management's authorization.
    (b) irregularities will be eliminated.
    (c) access to assets is permitted only in accordance with management's authorization.
    (d) the recorded accountability for assets is compared with the existing assets at reasonable intervals.
    (CPA)

22. Internal control is a function of management, and effective control is based on the concept of charge and discharge of responsibility and duty. Which of the following is one of the overriding principles of internal control?
    (a) Responsibility for accounting and financial duties should be assigned to one responsible officer.
    (b) Responsibility for the performance of each duty must be fixed.
    (c) Responsibility for the accounting duties must be borne by the audit committee of the company.
    (d) Responsibility for accounting activities and duties must be assigned only to employees who are bonded.
    (CPA)

23. Effective internal control requires organizational independence of departments. Organizational independence would be impaired in which of the following situations?
    (a) The internal auditors report to the audit committee of the board of directors.
    (b) The controller reports to the vice president of production.
    (c) The payroll accounting department reports to the chief accountant.
    (d) The cashier reports to the treasurer.
    (CPA)

24. Transaction authorization within an organization may be either specific or general. An example of specific transaction authorization is the
    (a) setting of automatic reorder points for material or merchandise.
    (b) approval of a detailed construction budget for a warehouse.
    (c) establishment of requirements to be met in determining a customer's credit limits.
    (d) establishment of sales prices for products to be sold to any customer.
    (CPA)

25. A system of internal accounting control normally would include procedures that are designed to provide reasonable assurance that
    (a) employees act with integrity when performing their assigned tasks.
    (b) transactions are executed in accordance with management's general or specific authorization.
    (c) decision processes leading to management's authorization of transactions are sound.
    (d) collusive activities would be detected by segregation of employee duties.
    (CPA)

26. When considering internal control, an auditor must be aware of the concept of reasonable assurance that recognizes that
    (a) the employment of competent personnel provides assurance that the objectives of internal control will be achieved.

(b) the establishment and maintenance of a system of internal control is an important responsibility of management, not of the auditor.

(c) the cost of internal control should not exceed the benefits expected to be derived from internal control.

(d) the segregation of incompatible functions is necessary to obtain assurance that the internal control is effective.

(CPA)

27. Which of the following elements of an entity's internal control structure includes the development of personnel manuals documenting employee promotion and training policies?
    (a) control procedures
    (b) control environment
    (c) information and communication
    (d) quality control system

(CPA adapted)

28. Which of the following statements about internal control structure is correct?
    (a) A properly maintained internal control process reasonably ensures that collusion among employees cannot occur.
    (b) The establishment and maintenance of the internal control structure is an important responsibility of the internal auditor.
    (c) An exceptionally strong internal control structure is enough for the auditor to eliminate substantive tests on a significant account balance.
    (d) The cost–benefit relationship is a primary criterion that should be considered in designing an internal control structure.

(CPA adapted)

29. Which of the following is not an element of an entity's internal control process?
    (a) control risk
    (b) control activities
    (c) information and communication
    (d) the control environment

(CPA adapted)

30. Employers bond employees who handle cash receipts because fidelity bonds reduce the possibility of employing dishonest individuals and
    (a) protect employees who make unintentional errors from possible monetary damages resulting from their errors.
    (b) deter dishonesty by making employees aware that insurance companies may investigate and prosecute dishonest acts.
    (c) facilitate an independent monitoring of the receiving and depositing of cash receipts.
    (d) force employees in positions of trust to take periodic vacations and rotate their assigned duties.

(CPA)

31. Proper segregation of functional responsibilities calls for separation of the
    (a) authorization, approval, and execution functions.
    (b) authorization, execution, and payment functions.
    (c) receiving, shipping, and custodial functions.
    (d) authorization, recording, and custodial functions.

(CPA)

32. A company holds bearer bonds as a short-term investment. Custody of these bonds and submission of coupons for interest payments normally is the responsibility of the
    (a) treasury function.
    (b) legal counsel.
    (c) general-accounting function.
    (d) internal-audit function.

(CPA)

33. Operating control of the check-signing machine normally should be the responsibility of the
    (a) general-accounting function.
    (b) treasury function.
    (c) legal counsel.
    (d) internal-audit function.

(CPA)

34. Internal control over cash receipts is weakened when an employee who receives customer mail receipts also
    (a) prepares initial cash receipts records.
    (b) records credits to individual accounts receivable.
    (c) prepares bank deposit slips for all mail receipts.
    (d) maintains a petty cash fund.

(CPA)

35. For good internal control, the monthly bank statements should be reconciled by someone under the direction of the
    (a) credit manager.
    (b) controller.
    (c) cashier.
    (d) treasurer.

(CPA)

36. For good internal control, the person who should sign checks is the
    (a) person preparing the checks.
    (b) purchasing agent.
    (c) accounts payable clerk.
    (d) treasurer.

(CPA)

37. For good internal control, the credit manager should be responsible to the
    (a) sales manager.
    (b) customer service manager.
    (c) controller.
    (d) treasurer.

(CPA)

38. The authorization for write-off of accounts receivable should be the responsibility of the
    (a) credit manager.
    (b) controller.
    (c) accounts receivable clerk.
    (d) treasurer.

(CPA)

39. In general, material irregularities perpetrated by which of the following are **most** difficult to detect?
    (a) cashier
    (b) controller
    (c) internal auditor
    (d) data entry clerk

(CPA)

40. A well-designed system of internal control that is functioning effectively is most likely to detect an irregularity arising from
    (a) the fraudulent action of several employees.
    (b) the fraudulent action of an individual employee.
    (c) informal deviations from the official organization chart.
    (d) management fraud.

(CPA)

41. To provide for the greatest degree of independence in performing internal auditing functions, an internal auditor most likely should report to the
    (a) financial vice president.
    (b) corporate controller.
    (c) board of directors.
    (d) corporate stockholders.
    (CPA)

42. The use of fidelity bonds may indemnify a company from embezzlement losses. The use also
    (a) reduces the company's need to obtain expensive business interruption insurance.
    (b) protects employees who made unintentional errors from possible monetary damages resulting from such errors.
    (c) allows the company to substitute the fidelity bonds for various parts of internal accounting control.
    (d) reduces the possibility of employing people with dubious records in positions of trust.
    (CPA)

43. For good internal control, which of the following functions should **not** be the responsibility of the treasurer's department?
    (a) data processing
    (b) handling of cash
    (c) custody of securities
    (d) establishment of credit policies
    (CPA)

44. Which of the following sets of duties would ordinarily be considered basically incompatible in terms of good internal control?
    (a) preparation of monthly statements to customers and maintenance of the accounts receivable subsidiary ledger
    (b) posting to the general ledger and approval of additions and terminations relating to the payroll
    (c) custody of unmailed signed checks and maintenance of expense subsidiary ledgers
    (d) collection of receipts on account and maintaining accounts receivable records.
    (CPA)

45. The Foreign Corrupt Practices Act requires that
    (a) auditors engaged to examine the financial statements of publicly held companies report all illegal payments to the SEC.
    (b) publicly held companies establish independent audit committees to monitor the effectiveness of their system of internal control.
    (c) U.S. firms doing business abroad report sizable payments to non-U.S. citizens to the Justice Department.
    (d) publicly held companies devise and maintain an adequate system of internal accounting control.
    (CPA)

46. Establishing and maintaining a system of internal accounting control is the primary responsibility of
    (a) management and the board of directors.
    (b) the internal auditor.
    (c) the external auditor.
    (d) a financial analyst.
    (e) the data processing manager.
    (CMA adapted)

47. A certain business receives all payments of account by check. Checks are always received, so an analyst wants to use the checks themselves as posting media to the accounts receivable ledger rather than have to prepare and process remittance advices. Discuss the conflict between productivity and reliability that is inherent here.

48. What duties should not normally be performed by the same individual in each of the following procedures?
    (a) bad debt write-off
    (b) payroll preparation
    (c) sales returns
    (d) inventory purchases

49. The internal auditing department was told that two employees were terminated for falsifying their time records. The two employees had altered overtime hours on their time cards after their supervisors had approved the hours actually worked.

    Several years ago, the company discontinued the use of time clocks. Since then, the plant supervisors have been responsible for manually posting the time cards and approving the hours for which their employees should be paid. The postings are usually entered in pencil by the supervisors or their secretaries. After the postings for the week are complete, the time cards are approved and placed in the mail racks outside the supervisors' offices for pickup by the timekeepers. Sometimes the timekeepers do not pick up the time cards promptly.

    Required
    Assuming the company does not wish to return to using time clocks, give **three** recommendations to prevent recurrence of the situation described. For each recommendation, indicate how it will deter fraudulent reporting of hours worked.

    (IIA)

50. Discuss the purpose of the following questions that appear on an internal control questionnaire.
    (a) Does the company have an organization chart?
    (b) Are the duties of the principle accounting officer segregated from those of the treasurer?
    (c) Are employees in positions of trust bonded?
    (d) Are bank accounts reconciled regularly by the company?
    (e) Does the company maintain a ledger of its fixed assets?
    (f) Are journal entries approved by a responsible official?
    (g) Are aging schedules of accounts receivable prepared periodically and reviewed by a responsible person?
    (h) Does the company compare budgeted amounts with actual expenditures?
    (i) Are trial balances of the accounts receivable ledgers prepared and reconciled regularly?
    (j) Do the employees who maintain inventory records have physical access to the inventory?
    (k) Are the inventory records adjusted to physical counts at least once a year?
    (l) Are remittance advices that accompany receipts separated and given to the accounting department?
    (m) Are costs and expenses under budgetary control?
    (n) Is a postage meter used?
    (o) Are monthly statements of account mailed to all customers?
    (p) In reconciling bank accounts do employees examine endorsements?
    (q) Has the bank (or banks) been instructed not to cash checks payable to the company?

51. Mary's mother was dismayed. Her daughter had just been brought home by a city detective. Mary has been arrested at the bank where she had been working for three months.

    Mary's job had been in the cash receipts/payment processing operation. Mary's job was to operate a machine that would magnetically encode the amount of a customer's payment on the customer's remittance advice. Mary did not have access to the customer's payment. The amount that she was to encode was handwritten on each remittance advice. The magnetic encoding allowed the remittance advices to be processed by a computer.

"I was only trying to help us, Mom," Mary explained. "With Dad laid off from the mill and all, I just figured that no one would notice if I took our utility bills in to work, encoded them with amounts as if payment had been made, and then inserted them with the other remittances I was working on. I didn't realize that my work was being checked. I guess I should have known better."

Required

Should Mary have known better? Does an organization, such as the bank where Mary worked, have any obligation to explain the control environment of a job to an employee?

52. Identify an internal accounting control or procedure that would detect the following errors or omissions in a transaction processing system.

(a) A nonprofit organization regularly receives unsolicited cash donations in the mail. Clerks opening the mail routinely steal a sizable percentage of the cash sent as donations.

(b) Employees in the mailroom routinely mail their own — as well as their friends' — letters at the company's expense.

(c) A clerk accidentally posts a customer payment of $35 as $53 to the customer's account in the receivables ledger.

(d) A clerk purposefully posts a payment of $35 received from a close friend as $53 to the friend's account in the receivables ledger.

(e) A customer receives a bill for an item that was ordered but never shipped.

(f) A vendor sends a company a bill for 50 copies of a report when only 25 copies of the report were ordered and received.

(g) A clerk sends a check to a vendor to pay an invoice. The same invoice was paid by a check drawn last week by a different clerk.

(h) Certain workers in a factory routinely request more materials than are needed for a job, taking the excess materials home for personal use.

(i) A customer orders an item, which is requisitioned and shipped. The customer is never billed for the shipment.

(j) A shipment received from a vendor is accepted by an employee in the receiving department. The employee forwards a receiving report to payables so that the vendor will receive payment. The shipment, however, is taken home for personal use.

53. The internal auditor of a manufacturer is reviewing order-entry and shipping procedures. Figure 5.10 represents the procedures in place. All documents used in the procedure are prenumbered. There are many undershipments on customers' orders, but goods not shipped are **not** automatically back-ordered.

Required

(a) Identify deficiencies and/or omissions in the control system for the order-entry and shipping functions.

(b) Suggest improvements in the control system to remove the deficiencies you noted.

Use the following format in responding to this question:

    a. Deficiency and/or omission   b. Improvements suggested

(IIA)

54. Listed are 12 internal control procedures and requirements for the expenditure cycle (purchasing, payroll, accounts payable, and cash disbursements) for a manufacturing enterprise. Next to the list of controls is a list of reasons for the various controls.

Required

List the numbers 1 through 12 and then match each procedure or requirement with the most appropriate reason for implementing the control. Each reason can be used only once.

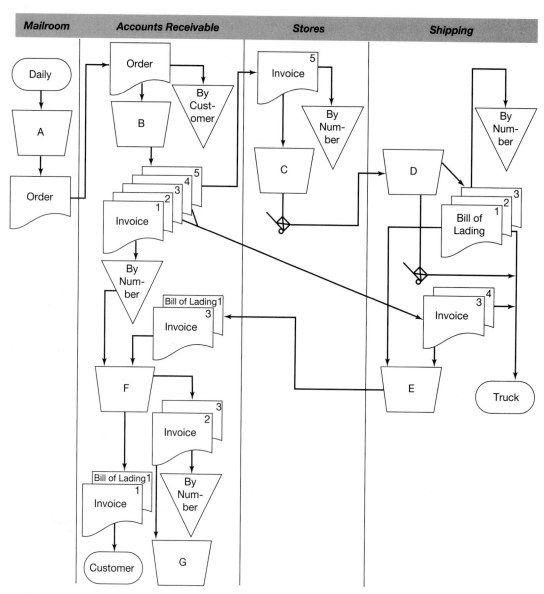

Explanatory Notes
A = Open Mail
B = Prepare Invoice from Customer Order and Distribute
C = Pick Goods to Extent Available and Forward to Shipping
D = Prepare Bill of Lading and Label Cartons for Shipment
E = Note Undershipments on Invoice #3 after Goods are Shipped
F = Complete Invoice Extensions Based on Actual Quantities Shipped
G = Post to Ledger and Prepare Daily Sales Journal
= Handtruck–Goods Movement

FIGURE 5.10 Flowchart for Problem 53.

Procedures and Requirements	Reasons for Controls
1. Duties between the cash payments and cash receipts functions are segregated.	a. Prevents people from processing phony payables and diverting the signed checks to themselves.
2. Signature plates are kept under lock and key.	b. Prevents payroll checks for excessive amounts from being cashed.
3. The accounting department matches invoices to receiving reports or special authorizations prior to payment.	c. Ensures that people writing checks cannot cover a temporary "borrowing" of cash.
4. All checks are mailed by someone other than the person making out the check.	d. Prevents the abstraction of cash receipts from being concealed by the recording of fictitious payments.
5. The accounting department matches invoices to copies of purchase orders.	e. Helps guard against checks being forged.
6. The blank stock of checks is kept under lock and key.	f. Prevents the fraudulent use of properly signed checks.
7. Imprest accounts are used for payroll.	g. Helps prevent temporary "borrowing" from established cash funds.
8. Bank reconciliations are to be accomplished by someone other than the one who writes checks and handles cash.	h. Helps prevent unauthorized changes to very important documents.
9. A check protector is used.	i. Prevents payment for goods and services not actually received.
10. Surprise counts of cash funds are conducted periodically.	j. Prevents payments for purchases that have not been properly authorized.
11. Orders can be placed with approved vendors only.	k. Assures that purchases are "arm's-length" transactions.
12. All purchases must be made by the purchasing department.	l. Prevents inappropriate purchases by unauthorized people.

(IIA)

55. The cashier of the Easy Company intercepted Customer A's check payable to the company in the amount of $500 and deposited it in a bank account that was part of the company petty cash fund, of which he was custodian. He then drew a $500 check on the petty cash fund bank account payable to himself, signed it, and cashed it. At the end of the month while processing the monthly statements to customers, he changed the statement to Customer A so it showed that A had received credit for the $500 check that had been intercepted. Ten days later he made an entry in the cash received book that purported to record receipt of a remittance of $500 from Customer A, thus restoring A's account to its proper balance but overstating the cash in the bank. He covered the overstatement by omitting from the list of outstanding checks in the bank reconcilement two checks, the aggregate amount of which was $500.

   List what you regard as five important deficiencies in the system of internal control in this situation and state the proper remedy for each deficiency.

(CPA)

56. As the internal auditor for a large company, you have been asked to consult with the operating management of a new division that consists of a chain of video game arcades. Specifically, management wants advice on the nature of accounting risks posed by the new operation and on the internal controls needed to reduce those risks. In reviewing the proposed video game arcade operation, you learn the following information.

   The chain will consist of 40 locations, the most distant location being only 200 miles from the corporate offices. The 40 locations will be divided into two regions, each having a regional manager. Each location will contain an average of 35 machines, with some locations having as many as 60 machines and others having as few as 10 machines. Access to the game counter and coins in each machine will be by use of a master key.

To minimize cost, management insists on minimizing the number of operating and accounting personnel. However, management has agreed to hire sufficient maintenance personnel in-house to minimize downtime. Management has also agreed to provide a local manager for each operating location because of the cash nature of the business.

Management insists on daily collection and deposit of coins in a local bank by the resident manager. Validated deposit slips are to be mailed to the corporate offices. Bank statements will be mailed directly by the banks to corporate offices.

Required

The definition of internal accounting control addresses aspects of transaction execution, transaction recording, access to assets, and periodic comparisons of accountability. Based on these aspects and using the format that follows:
(a) Identify the risks for the major activities listed.
(b) Suggest internal accounting controls for the risks identified.
The required answer format is as shown:

Activity	Risk	Control
Transaction execution		
Transaction recording		
Access to assets		
Periodic comparisons of accountability		

57. The Carle & Ham division of the GHB Corporation publishes college textbooks. Carle & Ham employs about 20 senior editors, each of whom manages the production of several different textbooks.

In the production of a textbook, editors usually request several manuscript reviews from different college professors, with each professor being paid a fee for their services. Each senior editor is given a yearly budget that is to be spent for manuscript reviews.

Senior editors select professors whom they think will provide useful reviews. Requests for manuscript reviews are made by sending a letter that specifies the general terms and the fee to be paid. If the professor agrees to perform a review, a signed copy of the letter is returned to the editor. The editor then forwards the manuscript to the professor for review.

When the professor's review is received, the editor sends a memo to accounts payable indicating the account number charge, the professor's name and address, and the amount to be paid. Accounts payable prepares a check for the amount indicated and forwards it to the editor for delivery to the professor.

Required

(a) Identify deficiencies and/or weaknesses in the procedures described.
(b) Suggest an improvement to remove each weakness/deficiency you noted in part a.
Use the following format to answer this question.

    a. Deficiency/weakness   b. Improvement suggested

58. You were recently appointed the internal auditor for a private college. Your first assignment is to appraise the adequacy and effectiveness of the student registration procedures. You have completed your preliminary survey. Based on your interviews and a walk-through of the student registration operation, you prepared an informal flowchart.

Required

Examine the following informal flowchart and list five internal control weaknesses (such as omission of certain steps or measures) in the student registration procedures.

Admission—Processing of Registrations

(a) **Mailroom**

Opens all mail, prepares remittance advices and remittance listings.

Sends copies of advices and listings to

1. cashier (with cash and checks).
2. accounts receivable clerk.
3. general bookkeeper.

Destroys other copies of advices and listings.

(b) **Registration clerk**

Receives three copies of completed registration forms from students.

Checks for counselor's or similar approval.

Records appropriate fee from official class catalog.

If completed properly, approves forms and sends student with registration forms to cashier.

If not completed properly, returns forms to student for follow-up and reapplication.

(c) **Cashier**

Collects funds or forwards two copies of registration forms to billing clerk.

Records cash receipts in daily receipts record.

Prepares and makes daily deposits.

Forwards duplicate receipted deposit slips and daily receipt records to general bookkeeper.

Destroys copies of daily receipts records.

(d) **Billing clerk**

Receives two copies of registration form, prepares bill, and makes entries in registration (sales) journal.

Forwards copies of billings and registration forms to accounts receivable clerk and forwards copies of bill to general bookkeeper.

(e) **Accounts receivable clerk**

Posts accounts receivable subsidiary ledger detailed accounts from remittance listings. Matches billings and registration forms and posts accounts receivable subsidiary ledger detailed accounts.

(f) **General bookkeeper**

Journalizes and posts cash receipts and applicable registrations to general ledger.

Enters registration (sales) journal data in general ledger.

(IIA)

59. Collateral Deposit (Part 2)[3]

(This is a continuation of Problem 27 in Chapter 2.)

Required

Part 1 Prepare an analytic flowchart and cross-reference it to the list of procedures that accompanies Problem 27 in Chapter 2.

Part 2 Prepare an application controls matrix for the process, using the form shown in Figure 5.9. Cross-reference the controls to the matrix using the appropriate numbers from the list of procedures.

Identify any apparent weaknesses noted in the description of the collateral receipt process.

[3]Problems 59 and 60 were prepared by Frederick L. Neumann, Richard J. Boland, and Jeffrey Johnson; funded by The Touche Ross Foundation Aid to Accounting Education Program.

60. Collateral Withdrawal

Dan Matt drew up a flowchart for the depositing of collateral (Problem 59) and turned it over to his senior. The senior inquired if collateral was only deposited and never withdrawn. Dan realized he had not followed the collateral process through to its completion. He still had to investigate the withdrawal of collateral that resulted when the loan was paid.

Dan found that the customer initiates the withdrawal of collateral by presenting the pink receipt copy to the loan officer. The loan officer forwards the customer's request for return of the collateral to the collateral clerk, who prepares a prenumbered, four-part withdrawal form. Each copy of the form is a different color to facilitate its distribution. The original (pink) of the request is sent back to the loan officer, the second (blue) copy is sent to the vault custodian, and the third (white) copy is filed by the collateral clerk with the deposit form. Again, the yellow or fourth copy is discarded. The vault custodian takes the blue copy of the request to the vault attendant, and together they remove the collateral and match it against the request. If they match, both the vault custodian and the vault attendant sign the blue copy of the request. If they are not in agreement, the vault custodian contacts the loan officer to iron out the discrepancy. The signed blue copy is sent back to the loan officer, accompanied by the collateral. The loan officer verifies that everything is proper and then signs the blue copy and turns over the collateral to the customer. The customer, after verifying that the collateral is correct, signs the pink copy of the request, which had been on file with the loan officer. Then both the blue and the pink copies are returned to the collateral clerk. The collateral clerk matches the two copies of the request to the white copy in his file. If they are all in agreement, he records the return of the collateral in his log, staples the copies together, and files them in the completed file by number.

Required

(a) Prepare an analytic flowchart of the collateral withdrawal process using the description given in the case.

(b) Prepare the application control matrix for the process, using the form shown in Figure 5.9.

(c) List any apparent weaknesses in the collateral withdrawal process as described.

Answers to Chapter Quiz

1. B	4. A	7. A	10. D
2. B	5. A	8. B	
3. C	6. B	9. D	

CHAPTER 6

Computer and Information Systems Security

LEARNING OBJECTIVES

Careful study of this chapter will enable you to:

■ Describe general approaches to analyzing vulnerabilities and threats in computer systems.

■ Identify active and passive threats to computer systems.

■ Identify key aspects of a computer security system.

■ Discuss contingency planning and other disaster risk management practices.

AN OVERVIEW OF COMPUTER SECURITY

The **computer security system** is the subsystem of the organization that controls the special risks associated with computer-based information systems. The computer security system has the basic elements of any information system, such as hardware, databases, procedures, and reports. For example, data concerning software usage and security violations might be collected in real time, stored in databases, and used to generate reports.

The Computer Security System Life Cycle

The computer security system is an information system, so its development requires application of the life-cycle approach. Computer security systems are developed by applying the established methods of systems analysis; design; implementation; and operation, evaluation, and control. The objective of each of these life-cycle phases is as follows:

LIFE-CYCLE PHASE	OBJECTIVE
Systems analysis	Analyze system vulnerabilities in terms of relevant threats and their associated loss exposures.
Systems design	Design security measures and contingency plans to control the identified loss exposures.

Systems implementation	Implement the security measures as designed.
Systems operation, evaluation, and control	Operate the system and assess its effectiveness and efficiency. Make changes as circumstances require.

The objective of the first phase of the computer security system life cycle is to produce a **vulnerability and threat analysis report.** The objective of the second phase is to design a comprehensive set of risk-control measures, including both **security measures** to prevent losses and **contingency plans** to deal with losses should they occur. Collectively, all four phases are referred to as computer system risk management. **Computer system risk management** is the process of assessing and controlling computer system risks.

The Computer Security System in the Organization

If the computer security system is to be effective, it must be managed by a chief security officer (CSO). This individual should report directly to the board of directors so as to maintain complete independence. A primary duty of the CSO should be to present reports to the board of directors for approval. These reports should cover each phase of the life cycle:

LIFE-CYCLE PHASE	REPORT TO THE BOARD OF DIRECTORS
Systems analysis	A summary of all relevant loss exposures.
Systems design	Detailed plans for controlling and managing losses, including a complete computer security system budget.
Systems implementation, systems operation, evaluation, and control	Specifics on computer security system performance, including an itemization of losses and security breaches, an analysis of compliance, and costs of operating the security system.

Analyzing Vulnerabilities and Threats

There are two basic approaches to analyzing system vulnerabilities and threats. In the **quantitative approach to risk assessment,** each loss exposure is computed as the product of the cost of an individual loss times the likelihood of its occurrence. For example, assume that the likelihood of a loss can be represented by a risk factor between 0 and 1. Then a threat analysis report might look something like the one in Figure 6.1. In this example, data theft is the largest loss exposure, immediately followed by fraud and virus attacks (i.e., attacks that result from computer programs designed to sabotage important files). A significant benefit of an analysis such as this is that it often shows that the most likely threat to occur is not the threat with the largest loss exposure. For example, in Figure 6.1, the threat most likely to occur is equipment theft, but this threat represents one of the smallest loss exposures.

There are several difficulties in applying the quantitative approach to assessing loss exposures. First, identifying the relevant costs per loss and the associated likelihoods can be difficult. The relevant cost of a loss is the decrease in the company's profitability as a result of the loss's occurrence. But this cost can be difficult to estimate because it might involve estimating unpredictable business interrup-

THREAT ANALYSIS REPORT			
	Potential Loss ($)	Risk	Loss Exposure ($)
Data Theft	700,000,000	0.050	35,000,000
Fraud and Virus Attacks	1,200,000,000	0.025	30,000,000
Sabotage	2,500,000,000	0.010	25,000,000
File Alteration	400,000,000	0.050	20,000,000
Program Alteration	80,000,000	0.020	1,600,000
Equipment Theft	15,000,000	0.100	1,500,000
Natural Disaster	100,000,000	0.008	800,000

FIGURE 6.1 Threat Analysis Report.

tion costs, or estimating the replacement cost of a computer that can only be replaced by a noncomparable, newer model. Second, estimating the likelihood of a given failure requires predicting the future, which is particularly difficult in a rapidly changing technological environment. For example, many managers fail to foresee problems with computer viruses. Furthermore, in assessing the likelihood of intentional attacks on the system, one must estimate the costs and benefits of such attacks to potential perpetrators. This estimate, however, requires assumptions about perpetrators' risk preferences. For example, one perpetrator might be willing to undergo substantially larger risks than another for the same dollar gain. An extremely **risk-seeking perpetrator** will take very large risks for a small reward.

A second method of risk assessment for computer security is the **qualitative approach.** This approach simply lists out the system's vulnerabilities and threats, subjectively ranking them in order of their contribution to the company's total loss exposures. Both the qualitative and quantitative approaches are used in practice, and many companies mix the two methods. Regardless of the method used, any analysis must include loss exposures for at least the following areas:

- business interruption
- loss of software
- loss of data
- loss of hardware
- loss of facilities
- loss of service and personnel

If the quantitative approach is used, costs might be estimated using one of many methods, including replacement cost, service denial, third-party liability (resulting from the company's inability to meet contracts), and business interruption.

VULNERABILITIES AND THREATS

A **vulnerability** is a weakness in a system, and a **threat** is a potential exploitation of a vulnerability. There are two categories of threats: active and passive. **Active threats** include computer fraud and computer sabotage, and **passive threats** include system faults, as well as natural disasters, such as earthquakes, floods, fires, and hurricanes. **System faults** represent component equipment failures such as disk failures, power outages, and so on.

The Seriousness of Computer Fraud

Computer-based crimes are part of the general problem of white-collar crime. The problem of white-collar crime is serious. Statistics have shown that corporate losses due to fraud and embezzlement exceed total losses due to bribery, burglary, and shoplifting by a wide margin. This might seem surprising because we seldom read about crimes such as embezzlement in the newspaper. This is because, in the vast majority of cases, detected frauds are never brought to the attention of law enforcement people because this would lead to public disclosure of internal control weaknesses. Managers tend to shy away from the adverse negative publicity that would result from public prosecution.

Computer security is an international problem. Accordingly, many countries have laws directed at computer security (see Figure 6.2). In the United States, various laws, regulations, and pronouncements address the problem of computer crime. Most states have enacted specific criminal statutes directed against computer crimes. The **Computer Fraud and Abuse Act of 1986** makes it a federal crime to knowingly and with intent fraudulently gain unauthorized access to data stored in the computers of financial institutions, computers owned or used by the federal government, or computers operating in interstate commerce. Trafficking

INTERNATIONAL COMPUTER SECURITY LAWS	
 Canada	Criminal Code 301.2(1), Unauthorized Use of Computers, sets criminal penalties of up to 10 years for fraudulent use of computer service or interception of computer signals or functions.
 Denmark	Criminal Code Section 263, Access to Another Person's Information, sets criminal penalties of up to 2 years for unlawful access to another person's data processing information or programs.
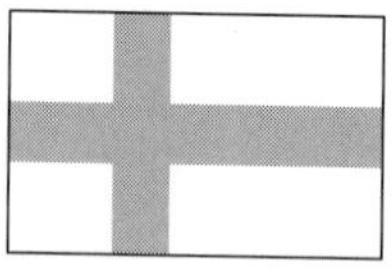 Finland	Penal Provisions of the Personal Registers Act, 1987, Section 45, Personal Register Trespass, sets criminal penalties of up to 6 months for use of another individual's user code or fraudulent means to access personal data maintained with automated data processing.
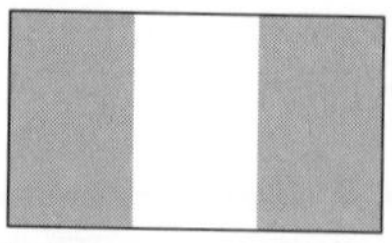 France	Law Number 88-19, Criminal Code, Chapter III, Article 462-2 through 9, sets criminal penalties of up to 3 years for unauthorized access to, falsification, modification, or deletion of data, or the use of such data from an automated data processing system.
 Switzerland	Criminal Code Section 147, Fraudulent Misuse of a Data Processing System, sets criminal penalties of up to 10 years for intentionally adding or deleting a data processing record for the intent of enrichment.

FIGURE 6.2 International Computer Security Laws.

in computer access passwords is also prohibited. Felonies are determined by damage to $1000 or more of software, the theft of actual goods, services, or money, or unauthorized access or alteration of medical records. Fines could range up to $250,000, or twice the value of stolen data, and first offenders could be sentenced to one to five years in prison.

The National Commission on Fraudulent Financial Reporting (Treadway Commission) linked management fraud to computer crime. **Management fraud** is deliberate fraud committed by managers with the intent of deceiving investors and creditors using materially misleading financial reports. This type of fraud is committed by those who are high enough in an organization to override accounting controls. Management might commit other types of errors or omissions that could potentially defraud employees or investors, but the term *management fraud* generally refers to financial statement manipulations.

The Treadway Commission defined fraudulent financial reporting as intentional or reckless conduct, whether by act or omission, that results in materially misleading financial statements. The commission studied 456 lawsuits brought against auditors. Management fraud was found to be present in about half of these cases. The commission noted that computer-based information systems multiply the potential for misusing or manipulating information, thus increasing the risk of fraudulent financial reporting.

Individuals Posing a Threat to the Computer System

A successful attack on a computer system requires access to hardware, sensitive data files, or critical programs. Three groups of individuals—computer systems personnel, users, and intruders—differ in their normal ability to access these things. Computer systems personnel often pose a potential threat because they are often given wide-ranging access privileges to sensitive data and programs. Users, on the other hand, are given much narrower access, but they still find ways to commit fraud. Intruders are given no access at all, but they are often highly determined individuals who are capable of inflicting great losses on the company.

Computer Systems Personnel

Computer systems personnel include computer maintenance persons, programmers, computer operators, computer and information systems administrative personnel, and data control clerks.

Computer Maintenance Persons.   Computer maintenance persons install hardware and software, repair hardware, and correct minor errors in software. In many cases, these individuals must have high-level security access to do their jobs. For example, an individual installing a new version of an accounting program is often given complete access to the file catalog containing the accounting system and its related data files. In some cases such an individual might not even work for the company but rather for the vendor from whom the company bought the accounting software. In any case, maintenance persons typically possess the ability to illegally browse through and alter data and program files. Some maintenance persons may even be in the position to make undesirable modifications to the security portion of the operating system.

Programmers.   Systems programmers often write programs to modify and extend the network operating system. Such individuals are typically given accounts with universal access to all the company's files. Application programmers might make undesirable modifications to existing programs, or write new programs that do undesirable things.

Network Operators.   Those individuals who oversee and monitor the immediate operation of the computer and communications network are called computer and network operators. In some systems, the computer operator monitors operations from a **system console**, a workstation dedicated solely to the operator's use. Typically, the operator's console is assigned a high level of security clearance, thus allowing the operator to secretly monitor all network communications (including individual users entering passwords), as well as access any file on the system.

Computer and Information Systems Administrative Personnel.   The systems supervisor is in a position of great trust. This person normally has access to security secrets, files, programs, and so on. Account administrators have the ability to create fictitious accounts, or to give away passwords to existing accounts.

Data Control Clerks.   Those responsible for the manual and automated inputting of data into the computer system are called data control clerks. These individuals are in the position to fraudulently manipulate the input data.

Users

Users are composed of heterogeneous groups of people and can be distinguished from the others because their functional area does not lie in data processing or computing. Many users have access to sensitive data that they can disclose to competitors. In some cases, users may control important computer inputs such as credit memos, account credits, and so on.

Intruders

Anyone who accesses equipment, computer data, or files without proper authorization is an **intruder.** Intruders who attack computer systems for fun and challenge are known as **hackers.** Other types of intruders include unnoticed intruders, wiretappers, piggybackers, impersonating intruders, and eavesdroppers.

Unnoticed Intruders.   A customer might walk into an unguarded area and view sensitive data on an unattended personal computer.

Wiretappers.   A large portion of the information processed by the company's computers travels over wires and cables. Some information is transmitted only from one room to the next, and other information may be transmitted across the country. These lines are vulnerable to wiretapping, which may be done with inexpensive devices (e.g., a simple tape recorder and a short piece of wire) that are capable of performing the task without giving any clues that the wire is being tapped.

Piggybackers.   The most sophisticated type of wire tapping is called **piggybacking**. With this method, the penetrator intercepts legitimate information and substitutes fraudulent information in its place.

Impersonating Intruders.   Impersonating intruders are individuals who pose as someone else in order to defraud the company. One type of intruder uses an illegally obtained user ID and password to access the company's computer resources. Many companies are very lax about security over user IDs and pass-

---

**"Crackers" force universities
to shut down computer systems
and change their passwords**

Computer administrators around the world were racing last week to change users' passwords in the wake of a warning that hackers had stealthily collected computer passwords and were using them to infiltrate computers connected to the Internet. . . .

One site affected by the security breach was Rice University, where administrators had brought back their systems to near-normal last week after an attack by hackers forced the institution to cut off its links with the Internet and shut down a campus network used by students. . . .

The shutdown at Rice was necessary because the "crackers" — a name given to mean-spirited hackers who attempt to destroy data, pirate software, or obtain information for financial gain — were roaming the system virtually unchecked and setting up numerous entry points that they planned to exploit in the event their initial point of entry was sealed.

Excerpts From *The Chronicle of Higher Education,* February 9, 1994.
Posted on ACADEME THIS WEEK

FIGURE 6.3 Hacker Attack on the Internet.

words. In some cases, an individual can obtain a user ID and password simply by calling the computer center on the telephone. Another type of intruder is the hacker (Figure 6.3), who may gain access through remote communications by guessing someone's password. Guessing passwords is not as difficult as it might seem because hackers know that many individuals use the name of a close relative or pet for a password. A third type of intruder is the professional industrial spy, who, for example, typically enters through a rear door wearing a service or repair uniform. This individual knows from experience that many companies have a rear door that employees often use for cigarette breaks. This door is often blocked open so that the employees can easily reenter. It can be identified by the cigarette butts around it on the ground.

Eavesdroppers. Standard cathode ray tubes (CRTs) used in common video display units emit electromagnetic interference (EMI) on a frequency capable of being picked up by an ordinary television set. Wim Van Eck, a Dutch electronics researcher, proved to a number of banks that it was possible to read the information on their CRTs almost a mile away, using an ordinary television, a directional antenna, and an external sync generator. Anyone with this equipment can monitor sensitive information as it appears on the company's CRTs. Any information that passes through any public communication network is vulnerable to eavesdropping and piggybacking. For example, simply removing one wire from a Tandy (Radio Shack™) scanner will allow one to monitor cellular telephone communications. There are clubs of individuals who make a regular habit of recording telephone conversations involving celebrities and public figures.

Active Threats to Computer Systems

We discuss six methods that an individual might use to perpetrate a computer fraud. These methods are input manipulation, program alteration, direct file alteration, data theft, sabotage, and misappropriation or theft of computer resources.

Input Manipulation

In most cases of computer fraud, manipulation of input is the method used. This method requires the least amount of technical skill. One can alter input with almost no knowledge of how a computer system operates.

- A teller employed by Union Dime Bank was discovered skimming money from bank accounts. This was accomplished by inputting fraudulent entries for computer processing. The crime was uncovered after police raided a bookie the teller was frequenting and discovered that the teller was betting over $30,000 per week. The bank lost more than $1 million.

- The bank Morgan Guaranty accepted a fraudulent telex from the Central Bank of Nigeria. Twenty million dollars in funds were to be electronically transferred to three different banks. However, when an attempt was made to transfer funds to a recently opened $50 account in Santa Ana, California, the transfer was refused. This led to the discovery of the fraud, with no loss to Morgan Guaranty.

- In one case, four men who were involved in a complicated bank fraud scheme stole $1.3 million through manipulating deposit memos.

- In another case, not only did a woman steal $200 a month for ten years by altering the input documents, she also paid herself an extra salary.

- The systems analyst in a department store purchased some items on his personal account, intercepted the documents, and lowered the prices.

- A data processing operator put flaws in some of the checks that were being processed. As a result of the errors, the checks were rejected by the computer and had to be processed manually. He then converted the checks to his own use.

Program Alteration

Program alteration is perhaps the least common method used to commit computer fraud. This is because it requires programming skills that are possessed only by a limited number of people. Also there are program testing methods available in most large companies that can be used to detect an altered program.

- Managers of Equity Funding Life Insurance Company created a program that generated over $100 million in fictitious insurance policies. The bogus policies were sold to other insurance companies, and the company's billing program was then altered to omit the billing of these policies. This was done by assigning fictitious policies to department 99. When the computer came to a department 99 policy, it would ignore the billing process.

- A programmer programmed the computer to ignore overdrafts in his account. He was caught when the computer broke down and the records had to be processed manually.

- The data processing manager of a brokerage firm stole $81,000 over several years, based on a scheme relying on unauthorized program changes. He drew checks on his firm and then sent them to false accounts he had constructed.

A **trapdoor** is a portion of a computer program that allows someone to access the program while bypassing its normal security. Sometimes program developers place a trapdoor in a program to ensure that they will always have access to it. Trapdoors can exist in accounting systems, database programs, operating systems, and so on.

Direct File Alteration

In some cases, individuals find ways to bypass the normal process for inputting data into computer programs. When this happens, the results can be disastrous.

- An employee of Waltson, one of the top ten brokerage houses on Wall Street, allegedly stole $278,000 by transferring some of the firm's revenues to his personal account. The district attorney admitted that if the accused had not confessed, the prosecution would have had no evidence.

- One defrauder substituted his own version of a master file of accounts receivables for the real one.
- An operations officer at Wells Fargo used the bank's computerized interbranch account settlement process to withdraw funds from a different branch. Fraudulent credits were created to cover the withdrawals. The bank lost more than $20 million over a three-year period.

Data Theft

Theft of important data is a serious problem in business today. In many highly competitive industries, both quantitative and qualitative information about one's competitors is constantly being sought.

The courts have long upheld that data stored in a company's computer are private and cannot be used without the company's permission. For example, in California, data theft can lead to conviction of violating a trade secret, punishable by a ten-year prison sentence. Similar trade secret laws apply in other states.

A considerable amount of information is transmitted between companies by public networks, long-distance lines, and satellite links. This information is vulnerable to theft while en route. It may be intercepted or tapped.

It may also be possible to steal an optical disk or diskette by smuggling it out of the firm in a pocket or briefcase. Bulkier items such as thick reports can be smuggled out in the trash.

- The Encyclopaedia Britannica Company allegedly accused the computer operators on its night shift of copying nearly three million names from the computer file containing the company's most valued customer list. Employees were accused of selling the list to a direct mail advertiser. Encyclopaedia Britannica claimed that the list was worth $3 million.
- A California man was accused of dialing his competitor's computer, bypassing the computer security system, and copying information as needed.

There are many other cases on record of an individual dialing into a company's computer and accessing privileged information.

Sabotage

Computer sabotage poses a very serious danger to any computer installation. The destruction of a computer or software can result in the bankruptcy of a firm. Disgruntled employees, especially fired ones, are common perpetrators of sabotage to the computer system.

In some cases, a defrauder may use sabotage to create confusion to cover up fraud. For example, an individual might alter the master file and later try to cover up by sabotaging the computer disk or other media.

There are many ways to cause serious damage to the computer installation. Magnets can be used to erase magnetic tapes and magnetic disks by simply placing the magnet (a common magnet will suffice) near the media. A tape does not even need to be removed from its container. A radar beam can have a similar effect if it is pointed at a building containing magnetic media.

- The head of a computer department of a leading credit card company, angry at top management, erased computer files containing hundreds of thousands of dollars worth of accounts receivable.
- A Cleveland manufacturer was put out of business when a disgruntled employee, left alone a few minutes in a data storage vault, erased many data files with a simple hand magnet.

- A Dow Chemical Company employee aided a group of radicals in erasing a thousand of the company's computer files.
- An editor who had been fired from Encyclopaedia Britannica Company sabotaged some of the company's computer files by rewriting history and substituting the names of Britannica employees for those of various historical figures.
- Some IRS employees destroyed 27,000 tax returns and approximately 80,000 inquiry letters from taxpayers simply to avoid processing them.

Sometimes computer programs are used to commit acts of sabotage. One of the oldest methods for committing such acts is the logic bomb. A **logic bomb** involves a dormant piece of code placed in a program for later activation by a specific event.

- A programmer for USPA, a Fort Worth–based insurance company, was fired for alleged misconduct. Two days later, a logic bomb allegedly activated itself and erased approximately 160,000 vital records from the company's computers. Investigators concluded that the programmer had planted the logic bomb two years before he was fired.

A **trojan horse** is a destructive program masquerading as a legitimate one.

- A Macintosh program called the Sexy Ladies HyperCard stack lured victims with the promise of erotic pictures. Although it delivered on its unsavory promise, it also erased data on the computers that loaded it.
- Thousands of computer users received a professional-looking disk marked "AIDS Information, Introductory Diskette, Version 2.0." Users who loaded this program eventually found their hard disks locked, with its files encrypted. The program printed a message on the screen saying "The lease for a key software package has expired." Users were told to pay a "leasing fee" to unlock their hard disks by mailing a considerable amount of money to a post office box in Panama.

A **virus program** is similar to a trojan horse but can spread itself to other programs, "infecting" them with the same virus. Viruses have become so prevalent that the majority of all companies now experience at least one virus attack per year.

- The Ambulance virus causes the image of an ambulance to move across the bottom of the display.
- The Ogre virus causes a sudden reformatting of the hard disk.
- The Ping-Pong virus causes images of Ping-Pong balls to bounce around the screen, erasing characters from the display.
- The Falling Letter virus causes letters in words to suddenly fall to the bottom of the display.
- The Yankee Doodle virus treats its victim to a daily playing of the tune "Yankee Doodle," right before 5:00 P.M. on the system clock.

Viruses can quickly spread through a company's computers, wreaking havoc.

- In one hospital, a virus destroyed nearly 40% of the patient records.

University computer laboratories have been especially vulnerable to viruses. In many cases, student and faculty computers have been almost shut down by runaway infections.

A **worm** is a type of virus that spreads itself over a computer network. Because all the computers in a network are connected together, a worm actually grows in size as it infects more and more computers. The term *worm* arises from the different infected computers in the network being thought of as connected segments that resemble the buglike creature.

- Robert Morris, Jr., a 22-year-old graduate student at Cornell University, developed a computer virus program that entered the Internet. The worm spread through the network very rapidly, temporarily disabling the operation of thousands of computers across the United States.

The word *virus* is sometimes used loosely to include all malicious programs, including logic bombs, trojan horses, and worms. Some programs contain the essential features of more than one of these programs.

Misappropriation or Theft of Computer Resources

One type of misappropriation of computer resources exists when employees use company computers resources for their own business:

- Five employees were accused of using their employer's mainframe computer during slack hours to operate their own data processing firm. The employees used the computer so heavily that their employer almost inadvertently upgraded the system to keep up with their demand.

The extent of this problem, like other types of computer fraud, is not well known. However, it is very likely that this problem occurs to some degree in many companies.

- Several employees stole their company's mainframe computer over a period of days, smuggling it out the back door a piece at a time!

THE COMPUTER SECURITY SYSTEM

Controlling threats is accomplished by implementing security measures and contingency plans. Security measures focus on preventing and detecting threats; contingency plans focus on correcting the effects of threats. It is well-accepted doctrine in computer security that some active threats cannot be prevented without making the system so secure that it is unusable. Furthermore, no security system is of much value without a general atmosphere of honesty and security consciousness.

It should be emphasized that all controls discussed in the previous chapter need to be applied as part of the computer security system. The computer security system must be part of the company's overall internal control structure. This means that the basic elements of internal control (adequate supervision, job rotation, batch control totals, validity checks, and so on) are all important to the computer security system. Computer security is simply a particular application of established internal control principles to particular problems in the computer system.

The Control Environment

The control environment is basic to effectiveness of the overall control system. Establishing a good control environment depends on eight factors. Each of these factors is discussed as it pertains to the computer security system.

Management Philosophy and Operating Style

The first and most important activity in computer security is creating high morale and an atmosphere conducive to security. No matter how sophisticated a system is, there is always a way around it. Therefore, the primary line of defense should be an overall atmosphere of security consciousness. This can be accomplished in many ways.

All employees should receive education in security. The objective of security education is to obtain security by consent. Security should be taken seriously. All violations should result in immediate apprehension of the guilty. Those in charge should set a good example.

Security rules should be monitored. Otherwise, the system will soon be forgotten. Good relations must be kept with employees. Low morale may result in a higher probability of fraud. Good communication with employees may mitigate problems. For example, files should contain a statement to the effect that they are the property of the company and that their inappropriate use may constitute a criminal offense or a cause for dismissal.

Organizational Structure

In many organizations, accounting, computing, and data processing are all organized under one chief information officer (CIO). Such a division, therefore, performs not only the traditional record-keeping functions of accounting, but also various computing functions. This poses various problems for establishing and maintaining clearly defined patterns of authority and responsibility. For example, systems analysts and computer programmers may be called on to design, program, and implement an accounts receivable system. An accountant might be called on to make programming changes to an accounting package. The important thing is that clear organizational lines be drawn to designate who is responsible for making the decision directly pertaining to accounting software and accounting procedures. And, as was discussed, one individual must be in charge of the computer security system.

Board of Directors and Its Committees

The board of directors must appoint an audit committee. The audit committee must in turn appoint or approve the appointment of an internal auditor. Ideally, the internal auditor should have a good background in computer security and serve as the chief computer security officer. In any case, this individual should periodically report to the audit committee on all phases of the computer security system. The audit committee should periodically consult with the external auditors and top management as to the performance of the chief security officer and the computer security system.

Methods of Assigning Authority and Responsibility. The responsibilities of all positions should be carefully documented using organization charts, policy manuals, job descriptions, and so on.

Management Control Activities

It is important to establish controls relating to the use and accountability of all resources relating to the computer and information system. Budgets should be established for the acquisition of equipment and software, for operating costs, and for usage. In all three categories, actual costs should be compared to budgeted amounts, and significant discrepancies should be investigated.

Budgetary control is especially important in the computer environment because there is often a tendency for companies to either overspend on information technology or spend on the wrong things. Employees often demand computing hardware, software, and services they really do not need. Buying the most recent model of a personal computer or the latest software package can be emotionally satisfying without producing any benefit to the company.

Internal Audit Function

The computer security system must be constantly audited and then modified to meet changing needs. The chief security officer should establish security policies relevant to the existing system and changes to the system. All modifications to the system, either hardware, software, or personnel, should be implemented in accordance with the established security policies.

Security policies and procedures should be tested for both compliance and effectiveness. Some companies actually hire computer hackers to look for security system vulnerabilities. In more than one case, a hacker's arrest and conviction have turned out to be good credentials in applying for a security job.

The system should periodically be "challenged" with hypothetical test transactions. Furthermore, changes to master files should be traced back to the relevant source documents. Such tracing is one way to detect unauthorized direct changes to master files. Another way to detect some such unauthorized changes is through batch control totals.

Personnel Policies and Practices

Segregated duties, adequate supervision, job rotation, forced vacations, and double checks are all important personnel practices. Probably the most important rule is that the duties of computer users and computer systems personnel should be separated. This stems from the need to separate custody and record-keeping responsibilities. Users often have physical access to the company's assets, and computer systems personnel often have access to the data files containing the accounting records. Putting these two types of access privileges together is an invitation to commit fraud.

There should also be, if possible, a separation of duties regarding access to key accounting files. In many computer environments, having access to a file for an asset account might be very close to having access to the asset itself. For example, it might be possible to transfer cash out of a cash account using electronic transfer, if the cash account is linked directly to an account in a financial institution.

Job rotation and mandatory vacations should apply to all computer-related personnel who have access to sensitive files. Many fraudulent schemes, even in a computer environment, require continued attention from the perpetrator. For example, an individual with access to both the cash and accounts receivable files might engage in electronic lapping. Such an activity would be very likely to be discovered by someone taking over the position either temporarily or permanently.

Personnel practices concerning hiring and firing are also important. Prospective employees should be carefully screened for the types of problems that might lead to fraud. Such problems include credit difficulties, various addictions (e.g., drugs, alcohol, and gambling), as well as previous employment problems. The more sensitive the position, the more extensive the background investigation should be. Remember, one deviant individual in a critical position might completely destroy the entire company.

Employees should be laid off and fired with the greatest care because terminated employees account for a significant portion of all sabotage incidents. When key employees are fired, all of their access privileges to critical hardware, software, and data files should be immediately revoked.

External Influences

The company's information systems must be in compliance with all federal, state, and local laws and regulations. Among other things, these laws and regulations govern the security and privacy of many types of data, including those relating to customer and client credit, customer and client history, personnel, and government-classified records. They also govern the exportation of certain information to other countries. Failure to provide adequate security in any one of these areas could be a criminal offense.

It is also important to implement a well-documented internal policy to prevent **software piracy,** the illegal copying and distributing of copyrighted software. A company without such a policy might be subject to a variety of legal attacks.

Controls for Active Threats

The primary way to prevent active threats concerning fraud and sabotage is to implement successive layers of access controls. If all general organizational and data processing controls are in place and working, the primary consideration then becomes limiting unauthorized access to sensitive data and equipment. Just as it is impossible to start a fire without access to heat, it is impossible to commit computer fraud without access to sensitive data or equipment. Access controls separate the perpetrator from his or her potential target.

The philosophy behind the **layered approach to access control** involves erecting multiple layers of controls that separate the would-be perpetrator from his or her potential targets. Three such layers are: site-access controls, system-access controls, and file-access controls.

The first step in establishing access controls is to classify all data and equipment according to their importance and vulnerability. Mission-critical equipment and data should be given the strictest controls. Of course, all controls must be applied on a cost–benefit basis within permissible legal constraints. Each group of controls is discussed.

Site-Access Controls

The objective of **site-access controls** is to physically separate unauthorized individuals from computer resources. This physical separation must especially be applied to hardware, data entry areas, data output areas, data libraries, and communications wiring.

All users should be required to wear security identification badges (with photographs). All rooms containing computer devices or sensitive data should have locked doors. Preferably, the locks should be programmable so that they can reject the keys of those who have been transferred or fired. Many companies use card-key systems. **Biometric hardware authentication** systems are also readily available. These systems automatically identify individuals based on their fingerprints, hand sizes, retina patterns, voice patterns, and so on. Guards should patrol the premises. Operations should be monitored by closed-circuit television.

Data processing complexes should be located in isolated buildings surrounded by fences with gate access. No one except authorized employees should be permitted to enter the gate without having a prior appointment that is verified by security.

All concentrations of computer data (e.g., data libraries, network printers, data entry, and data output sites) and equipment should be located in hard to find places, behind doors with programmable locks. There should be no signs on how to find them, and their location should be kept as secret as possible, for there are many cases of highly visible mainframe computers having been bombed.

Attacks on the disk and tape library and other mission-critical rooms can be minimized by a very strict entry system. One such system involves a double-door

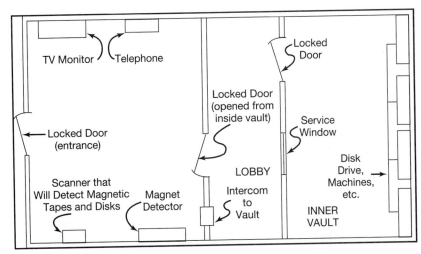

FIGURE 6.4 Data Storage Vault.

setup for a computer data storage vault, as shown in Figure 6.4. The person desiring admittance to the room must pass through two doors to gain entrance. The individual first uses the programmable lock to enter the outer door, and then enters a small room where the intercom must be used to gain admittance to the vault. The vault may then call security, which checks the individual by way of the television monitor and informs the vault whether or not to admit the person. The room can also contain a magnet detector.

Centralized data entry centers should be highly protected areas and strictly off limits to all nonessential persons. Network printers or other central printers, plotters, and facsimile machines, as well as their output, must also be protected. Highly sensitive output can be printed on hooded printers. The distribution of output should be controlled by a formal, secure delivery system.

Individual personal computers, terminals, disks, and tapes must also be protected. All these objects are subject to theft, malicious tampering, and destruction. Keeping everything under lock and key is the best protection. Personal computers should be locked to avoid internal tampering, should boot only from internal or network devices, and should only be accessible by password. Point-of-sale terminals should be locked when not in use. Finally, when possible, all computer devices should be located behind locked doors, and the walls should be shielded to prevent intrusions of undesirable electromagnetic radiation. Shielding, however, might not be sufficient to prevent EMI eavesdropping. This is best avoided by not displaying passwords and other critical information on CRT displays. LED and gas plasma displays give off minimal EMI emissions and are relatively safe.

No software should be installed on any computer without prior approval of security. This is a difficult problem, because viruses can enter the computer so many ways. Nevertheless, the guard at the front gate should check for the entry of unauthorized software. All software purchases should be required to pass through central purchasing and receiving. Any access to outside communication networks should be limited to those who can be trusted to not accept programs from outside without approval. Any programs received in the mail or on the network from unsolicited sources should be immediately destroyed, erased, or referred to security for inspection.

There are other ways to physically limit the intrusion of viruses. One is to assign employees diskless workstations (i.e., that use network disks for storage). All software and data are stored on central file servers. This approach has the advantage of centralizing the installation of all software, as well as file backups. A second way to physically inhibit the intrusion of viruses is to use ROM-based operating systems on all personal computers. Many viruses alter key operating system files and routines. Putting the operating system in ROM therefore will provide some protection from virus threats.

Finally, all physical wiring should be unobtrusive, both indoors and outdoors. In some areas it might be advisable to add air-shielding to the wiring that will sound an alarm if broken. Fiber-optic cable is generally considered reasonably safe from tapping, and might be used. Wiring centers and communication devices should be located behind locked doors.

System-Access Controls

System-access controls are software-oriented controls designed to keep unauthorized users from using the system. The objective of **system-access controls** is to authenticate users by using such means as user IDs, passwords, and hardware devices.

Each user can be assigned a user ID number and password at nine levels: at the level of the workstation or personal computer, the network, the host computer, the file server, the file catalog, the program, the data file or database, the record, and the data field. Each of these levels provides a successive layer of protection, separating a would-be intruder from sensitive data. At the top level, the workstation level, the user must enter the correct identifying information before even being able to request access to the communications network. Then, after accessing the network, the user must enter more identifying information before accessing a host computer or file server. After that, additional identification is required before accessing a particular file catalog. This process of identification can continue on down to the individual data field in the database. The operating system(s) should automatically record the time, date, and user number associated with all accesses. This information can be used to investigate any illegal accesses after they occur.

All entries to master files and critical databases should automatically include the user's identification credentials and the time of the transaction entry. This makes it possible to audit all of an individual's transactions.

Passwords should be carefully controlled by a password management system. The system should initially assign passwords to users and then reassign them periodically. The most secure procedure is not to allow users to change their passwords. The reason for this procedure is that user-selected passwords are often very easy to guess because most users will select the name of a relative or pet, or one of many well-known passwords such as ABC, HELLO, APPLE, BANANA, IBM, PASSWORD, or TEST.

The ideal password should consist of uppercase and lowercase letters, special symbols, and numbers. Connecting two unrelated words together with a special symbol is a good compromise between simplicity and security. An example of such a password would be DOG&SKY.

An additional layer of security can be introduced by using a sign–countersign system. The user first enters a user identification number. The system then responds with a sign (i.e., a codeword). The user is then given a few seconds to enter the correct countersign. The strength of this system is that the same sign–countersign pair is never used twice. The user is periodically issued a list of the words to be used for this procedure.

Some systems allow users to select their own passwords subject to constraints. The passwords must be at least a minimum number of characters long, must not be certain easy-to-guess words, and must be changed periodically. By using this approach, passwords have expiration dates. Users who do not change their passwords by their expiration dates cannot access the system again until their accounts are reset by security.

Under some operating systems, the account limits for user accounts can be assigned a maximum number of attempted security violations within a given time interval. After this limit is exceeded, the account must be reset by security before it can be used again. Under such systems, entering a wrong password may be considered a security violation. A related operating system feature is the ability to automatically disconnect any remote communication device from which several consecutively wrong passwords are received.

Personnel should immediately notify security of any pending or actual termination or transfer of employees. Account numbers for these individuals should be immediately canceled. Programmable locks should also be reprogrammed accordingly.

No password system is of much value unless the passwords themselves are protected. There are many reported cases of intruders finding passwords in the trash or obtaining them from the computer department over the telephone. All employees need to be educated in the proper handling of passwords.

Hardware can also be combined with software to authenticate individuals requesting access to some part of the system. The biometric devices mentioned before can be used. An additional precaution is to authenticate the communication device requesting access. Some data terminals and network adapters in personal computers contain unique codes in ROM that are automatically transmitted to the host computer. The operating system or communication software can be programmed to analyze these codes and reject unrecognized devices.

Another device for using both hardware and software to limit access is the **call-back modem.** This device works for users dialing into the company's communication network. When the call-back modem answers a user's call, it requests a user number and password. If this information is entered correctly, the modem then calls the user back by dialing a preauthorized phone number. Therefore, in following this procedure, the modem physically authenticates the phone number of the incoming call.

Firewalls (which are typically based on both hardware and software) can be programmed to reject any incoming packets of data that do not originate from preapproved IP addresses on the Internet. Still, a determined hacker can spoof a valid IP address, and for this reason firewalls represent more of a deterrent than a total solution. A stronger solution combines the use of firewalls with encryption techniques. Outsiders may be required to present digital certificates to identify themselves, and then all exchanges of information can be made over encrypted channels.

File-Access Controls

The final layer of access controls is applied at the file level. **File-access controls** prevent unauthorized access to both data and program files.

The most fundamental file-access control is the establishment of authorization guidelines and procedures for accessing and altering files. Special restrictions should be placed on programmers who have the specific knowledge to make program changes. They should not be permitted access to any of the company's computer files without written approval. Operators and supervisors should be told not to take instructions from programmers without written approval. And not even authorized program changes should be made without written approval. Programmers should make all properly authorized changes to a duplicate copy of the original program, not the original program itself, and the duplicate copy should be inspected before being substituted for the original.

All important programs should be kept in **locked files.** This means that the program can be run but not looked at or altered. Only security should know the code (password) to unlock the file. Security should keep a library of programs that are in operation. They should periodically check the programs in operation to determine if they are bit-for-bit identical to authorized versions in the library.

Programs can also be digitally signed (as discussed in Chapter 3) in the same way that electronic messages are signed, and verification of the digital signature can both positively authenticate the identity of the source of the program and verify that it has not been altered. For example, the XYZ Company might purchase a program for analyzing accounts receivables. To protect itself, XYZ would require the program to carry the digital signature of the vendor/developer. Furthermore, if XYZ does not know and trust the vendor/developer's public key, then XYZ can also require that the vendor/developer's public key be certified by a recognized certification authority.

It is possible to install resident programs that constantly run as background tasks and check for signs of viruses or altered files. Unfortunately, there are almost too many viruses in circulation to count, and there are new ones all the time that may outsmart existing virus detection programs. To give you an idea of the problem, consider what happened to an early version of one antivirus program. Someone distributed an unauthorized and bogus version of this program that contained a trojan horse! Some virus detection programs such as Microsoft's Anti-Virus (Figure 6.5) also eradicate recognizable viruses from infected systems. The best way to avoid problems with viruses is to control the addition of new files to the system.

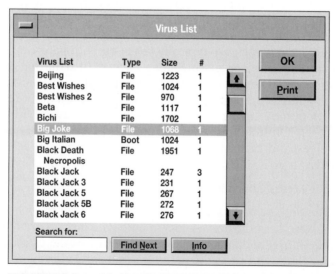

FIGURE 6.5 Part of the Virus List in Microsoft Anti-Virus for Windows.

Controls for Passive Threats

Passive threats include problems like power and hardware failures. Controls for such threats can be either preventive or corrective.

Fault-Tolerant Systems

Most methods of dealing with system component failures rely on monitoring and redundancy. If one part of the system fails, a redundant part immediately takes over, and the system continues operating with little or no interruption. Such systems are called **fault-tolerant systems.** Fault tolerance can be applied at five levels: to network communications, CPU processors, DASDs, to the power supply, and to individual transactions. Many companies have a high degree of fault tolerance in their systems because computer failures can corrupt data and completely disrupt operations. Some companies could not survive a few days without a high degree of operational capability in their computers.

Networks can be made fault-tolerant by introducing duplicate communication paths and communications processors. There are two main approaches to redundant CPU processing. Systems with **consensus-based protocols** contain an odd number of processors; if one processor disagrees with the others, it is thereafter ignored. Other systems use a second **watchdog processor** that takes over processing if something happens to the first processor.

DASDs are made fault-tolerant by several methods, including read-after-write checks, bad-sector lockouts, and disk mirroring. With **read-after-write checks,** the disk drive rereads a sector after writing it to disk, confirming that it was written without error. If the confirmation fails, the offending sector on the disk can be **flagged** and locked out so that it will not be used again. The data can then be written to a good sector. If the software program does not support bad-sector error recovery, it will abort the write process and return an error message. A utility program can then be used to lockout the offending sector, and the application program can be tried again. **Disk mirroring** or **disk shadowing** involves writing all data in parallel to two disks. If one disk fails, the application program can automatically continue, using the good disk. There are also software programs helpful in recovering data from damaged files or disks.

Fault tolerance for power failures can be achieved with an uninterruptable power supply. If the power fails, the backup system, sometimes battery powered, takes over so fast that no loss of continuity in the processing activities occurs. Then there is plenty of time to either switch the system to a generator or shut it down in an orderly manner. In brief power outages, the power is restored before either of these measures is necessary. Finally, some devices smooth out voltage drops and surges, which can cause severe damage to some electronic components.

Fault tolerance applied at the transaction level involves **rollback processing** and **database shadowing.** With rollback processing, transactions are never written to disk until they are complete. If the power fails or another fault occurs while a transaction is being written, at its first opportunity, the database program automatically rolls itself back to its prefault state. Database shadowing is similar to disk shadowing, except a duplicate of all transactions is made, and possibly sent via communications to a remote location.

Correcting Faults: File Backups

Some studies have suggested that over 50% of personal computer owners do not properly back up their files. For this reason, a system that centralizes the backing up of files is essential. Such systems are commonly used to back up critical disks. For example, Prudential Bache's system calls for files to be backed up every 2 to 5 minutes.

There are three types of backups: full backups, incremental backups, and differential backups. A **full backup** backs up all files on a given disk. In most systems, each file contains an **archive bit** that is set to 0 during the backup process. The operating system automatically sets this bit to 1 whenever a file is altered. An **incremental backup** backs up all files whose archive bit is set to 1. Each file's archive bit is then reset to 0 during the backup process. An incremental backup, therefore, backs up only those files that have been modified since the last full or incremental backup. Finally, a **differential backup** is the same as an incremental backup, only the archive bits are not reset to 0 during the backup process.

The simplest backup scheme is to periodically make full backups. After such backups the backup sets (e.g., tapes or optical disks) should immediately be removed to an off-site storage area. ideally, all full backups should be made in duplicate as an extra precautionary measure.

In many cases, if not most, taking continual backups of the entire disk or computer system throughout the business day is not practical. Many such systems do incremental or differential backups between full backups, only backing up the altered files. This procedure can save both time and storage media costs, and is useful in many situations. In general, incremental backups require less storage media and are faster than differential backups. One problem, however, comes in restoring incremental backups. The procedure to restore incremental backups involves first restoring the last full backup set and then restoring all incremental backup sets, one after the other, in chronological order. The problem with this procedure is that it can result in files being restored that were erased from the system sometime between the full backup and the last incremental backup. Of course, this is only a problem if files are erased. The differential backup, on the other hand, avoids this problem altogether.

Backing up files is not the same as archiving them. This is because the media used for backup might not be reliable for long-term storage. For example, some optical disks are said to have an archival life of ten years or less.

DISASTER RISK MANAGEMENT

Disasters happen. The bombing of the World Trade Center in New York City is just one example of an unexpected disaster that quickly and seriously interrupted normal business activity. Many organizations are critically dependent on computer systems to support daily operations. Consequently, if computer systems processing is delayed or interrupted, the organization may incur significant losses. Disaster risk management is essential to ensure continuity of operations in the event of a catastrophe.

Disaster risk management concerns prevention and contingency planning. In some cases, insurance might help control risks, but most insurers are reluctant to underwrite the costs of business interruptions for large companies, especially for those companies without disaster recovery plans. Both prevention and contingency planning are discussed in what follows.

Preventing Disasters

Disaster prevention is the first step in managing disaster risk. Studies have shown the following frequencies of disaster causes:

Natural disaster	30%
Deliberate actions	45%
Human error	25%

These data imply that a large percentage of disasters can be mitigated or avoided by good overall security policy.

Many disasters resulting from sabotage and errors can be prevented by good security policy and planning. Careful consideration should be given to natural-disaster risks associated with prospective building sites. Concentrations of computer equipment and data should be located in parts of buildings least exposed to storms, earthquakes, floods, and fire, as well as deliberate acts of sabotage.

Adequate electronic and mechanical systems for fire, flood, and intrusion are important. Water-based sprinkler systems can be harmful to electronic components. Many companies use fire-extinguishing systems that rely on something besides water, such as gas, foam, or powder.

Contingency Planning for Disasters

A **disaster recovery plan** must be implemented at the highest levels in the company. Ideally, it should be approved by a committee of the board of directors as part of the general computer security plan.

The first steps in developing a disaster recovery plan should be obtaining the support of senior management and setting up a planning committee. When completed, the disaster recovery plan should be thoroughly documented and approved by these same individuals. Overall, a life-cycle approach should be used to design, implement, operate, and evaluate the plan. Estimates suggest that the initial costs of implementing a disaster recovery plan can range from 2% to 10% of the overall information systems budget. The design of the plan should include three major components: an evaluation of the company's needs, a list of priorities for recovering based on these needs, and a set of recovery strategies and procedures.

Assess the Company's Critical Needs

All mission-critical resources should be identified. These include hardware, software, power and maintenance requirements, building space, vital records, and human resources.

List Priorities for Recovery

Even with a good plan, fully recovering from a major disaster can take a long time. Priorities should therefore be established that correspond to the company's critical needs. The priority list might indicate that certain mission-critical activities and services are to be reestablished within minutes or hours after the disaster. On the other hand, the plan might indicate that other activities and services are to be reestablished days, weeks, or months later.

Recovery Strategies and Procedures

A complete set of recovery strategies and procedures is essential. The plan should include such detail so that when disaster strikes, the company immediately knows what to do, who should do it, how to do it, and how long it should take. These considerations are discussed in detail in what follows.

Emergency Response Center. When disaster strikes, all authority for data processing and computer operations is transferred to the **emergency response team,** headed by the **emergency operations director.** These individuals direct the execution of the recovery plan from the **emergency operations center,** a predesignated site.

Escalation Procedures. The **escalation procedures** state the conditions under which a disaster should be declared, who should declare it, and who that person should notify when executing the declaration.

Alternate Processing Arrangements. The most important part of a disaster recovery plan is the specification of a backup site to be used if the primary computing site is destroyed or unusable. Three types of backup sites are possible: cold sites, hot sites, and flying-start sites. A **cold site** is an alternate computing site that contains the wiring for computers but no equipment. A **hot site** is an alternate site that contains the wiring, and the equipment as well. A **flying-start site** is an alternate site that contains the wiring, the equipment, and also very up-to-date backup data and software. A cold site is capable of assuming full operation in a matter of days, a hot site in a matter of hours, and a flying-start site in a matter of seconds or minutes. In practice, the type of backup site used must be determined for each company on a cost–benefit basis, although few companies find justifiable the high cost of owning a flying-start site.

One way to maintain up-to-date data at a flying-start site is to mirror all transactions at the primary site, and then immediately transmit them via communications to the backup site. Such data could be transmitted at high speed through the use of fiber-optic channel extenders. In some cases, a nearby backup site might be acceptable.

There are, however, alternatives besides actually purchasing an alternate site. Three such alternatives involve contracting with a computing service bureau, a commercial vendor of disaster services, or with another ordinary company, one possibly in the same industry.

A **service bureau** specializes in providing data processing services to companies who choose not to process their own data. In some cases, it may be useful to establish a contingency plan based on a contract with a service bureau. This option may be viable for relatively small companies with simple data processing needs. However, the service bureau is unlikely to be a workable solution for a company with complex computing needs. The computing needs of most large companies are too complex to be satisfied by the limited data processing services offered by typical service bureaus. Further, most service bureaus will not put computers on employees' desks, something that might be needed.

Several vendors provide disaster recovery services, including Comdisco, IBM, and Sungard. Comdisco, for example, specializes in leasing hot sites for a monthly fee. This company supports an international disaster recovery network of hot sites linked together by satellite.

The third type of arrangement is a contract with another ordinary company. Some companies have enough excess computing power to temporarily assume the needs of others. A **shared contingency agreement** or **reciprocal disaster agreement** is an agreement between two companies in which each company agrees to help the other if the need arises. In a variation on this agreement, the two companies share a common hot site through joint ownership.

The Personnel Relocation Plan. Contingency plans need to be made for the possibility of having to suddenly relocate employees to a backup site. Careful planning is needed in this regard, because many employees might have difficulty in relocating on short notice.

The Personnel Replacement Plan. The possibility of losing employees to the disaster must be considered. Replacing highly skilled employees can be difficult, and the replacement employees may require extensive training.

The Salvage Plan. In some disasters, it is possible to recover equipment and valuable records if quick action is taken. For example, a building that loses its roof in a hurricane will be exposed to rain. Losses in such a situation might be minimized if salvage efforts get underway immediately.

The Plan for Testing and Maintaining the System. Companies' computing needs often change rapidly. For this reason, any disaster recovery plan should be tested every six months. Outdated or untested plans might not work in a crisis.

SUMMARY

The computer security system is the subsystem of the organization that controls the special risks associated with computerized information systems. Computer security systems are developed by applying the traditional life-cycle approach of systems analysis, design, implementation and operation, evaluation, and control.

There are two major approaches to analyzing system vulnerabilities and threats in computer security planning. In the quantitative approach to risk assessment, each loss exposure is computed as the product of the cost of an individual loss times the likelihood of its occurrence. In the qualitative approach to risk assessment, the system's vulnerabilities and threats are listed and subjectively ranked in order of their contribution to the company's total loss exposures.

A vulnerability is a weakness in a computer system, and a threat is a potential exploitation of a vulnerability. Various laws, regulations, and pronouncements address the problem of computer crime. A successful attack on a computer system requires some sort of access to the hardware, sensitive data files, or critical programs. Anyone who accesses equipment, computer data, or files without proper authorization is an intruder. There are many types of intruders, such as unnoticed intruders, impersonating intruders, wiretappers, piggybackers, and eavesdroppers. There are at least six different methods that an individual might use to perpetrate a computer fraud. These are input manipulation, program alteration, direct file alternation, data theft, sabotage, and misappropriation or theft of computer resources.

Computer sabotage poses a very serious danger to any computer installation. There are many ways to cause serious damage to the computer installation. Computer programs might be used to commit acts of sabotage. Potential problems include logic bombs, trojan horses, virus programs, and worms. Controlling threats is accomplished by implementing security measures and contingency plans. Security measures focus on preventing and detecting threats; contingency plans focus on correcting the effects of threats. The organization's control environment is basic to effectiveness of the overall control system.

The primary way to prevent fraud and sabotage is to implement successive layers of access controls. A layered approach to access control involves erecting multiple layers of control that separate the would-be perpetrator from potential targets. Three such layers are site-access controls, system-access controls, and file-access controls.

Most methods of dealing with system component failures rely on monitoring and redundancy. If one part of the system fails, a redundant part immediately takes over, and the system continues operating with little or no interruption. Such systems are called fault-tolerant systems. Fault tolerance can be applied at five levels: to network communications, CPU processors, DASDs, the power supply, and to individual transactions. Many companies have a high degree of fault tolerance in their systems because computer failures can corrupt data and completely disrupt operations.

Disaster risk management includes prevention and contingency planning. Disaster prevention is the first step in managing disaster risk. A disaster recovery plan must be implemented at the highest level in the company. It should be approved by a committee of the board of directors as part of the general computer security plan.

Glossary

active threats: computer fraud and computer sabotage.

archive bit: a bit used to determine whether or not a file has been altered.

biometric hardware authentication: systems that automatically identify individuals based on their fingerprints, hand sizes, retina patterns, voice patterns, and other personal features.

call-back modem: when a user's call is answered, the device requests a user number and password. If this information is entered correctly, the modem then calls the user back by dialing a preauthorized phone number.

chief security officer (CSO): individual charged with management of the computer security system.

cold site: an alternate computing site that contains the wiring for computers but no equipment.

Computer Fraud and Abuse Act: makes it a federal crime to knowingly and with intent fraudulently gain unauthorized access to data stored in the computers of financial institutions, the federal government, or computers operating in interstate or foreign commerce.

computer security: the practice of controlling the special risks associated with computerized information systems.

computer security system: the subsystem of the organization that controls these risks.

consensus-based protocols: systems that contain an odd number of CPU processors; if one processor disagrees with the others, it is thereafter ignored.

database shadowing: a duplicate of all transactions is automatically recorded.

differential backup: an incremental backup in which the file archive bits are not reset to 0 during the backup process.

disaster recovery plan: a contingency plan for recovering from disasters.

disk mirroring: fault-tolerant processing control that involves writing all data in parallel to two disks.

disk shadowing: synonym for disk mirroring.

emergency operations center: a predesignated site designed to assist in disaster recovery.

emergency response team: individuals who direct the execution of a disaster recovery plan.

encryption: the transformation of input data—referred to as plaintext or cleartext—to ciphertext using a cryptographic technique.

escalation procedures: state the conditions under which a disaster should be declared, who should declare it, and who that person should notify when executing the declaration.

fault-tolerant systems: use of redundant components such that if one part of the system fails, a redundant part immediately takes over, and the system continues operating with little or no interruption.

file-access controls: prevent unauthorized access to both data and program files.

flagging: marking and locking out a disk or DASD sector so that it will not be used again after it has been found to be unreliable.

flying-start site: an alternate processing site that contains the necessary wiring and equipment, and also up-to-date backup data and software.

full backup: all files on a given disk are backed up.

hackers: individuals who attack computer systems for fun and challenge.

hot site: an alternate computer processing site that contains the wiring and the equipment as well.

incremental backup: all files whose archive bit is set to 1 are backed up.

information systems security: synonym for computer security.

intruders: anyone who accesses computer equipment, data, or files without proper authorization.

layered approach to access control: erecting multiple layers of access control that separate a would-be perpetrator from potential targets.

locked files: a program can be run but not looked at or altered.

logic bomb: a dormant piece of code placed in a computer program for later activation by a specific event.

passive threats: system faults and natural disasters.

piggybacking: the interception of legitimate information and substitution of fraudulent information in its place.

public-key encryption: an encryption method that allows secure messages to be communicated without any concern about someone intercepting the key.

qualitative approach to risk assessment: a system's vulnerabilities and threats are listed and subjectively ranked in order of their contribution to the company's total loss exposures.

quantitative approach to risk assessment: each loss exposure is computed as the product of the cost of an individual loss times the likelihood of its occurrence.

read-after-write checks: a DASD (e.g., disk drive) rereads a sector after writing it to disk, confirming that it was written without error.

reciprocal disaster agreement: synonym for shared contingency agreement.

risk management: the process of assessing and controlling computer system risks.

risk-seeking perpetrator: one who will take very big risks for a small reward.

rollback processing: transactions are not written to disk until they are complete so that if power fails or another fault occurs while a transaction is being written, the database program may automatically roll itself back to its prefault state.

service bureau: provides data processing services to companies who choose not to process their own data.

shared contingency agreement: an agreement between two companies in which each company agrees to help the other with disaster recovery should the need arise.

site-access controls: controls that physically separate unauthorized individuals from computer resources.

software piracy: the copying and distributing of copyrighted software without permission.

system-access controls: software-oriented controls designed to keep unauthorized users from using the system by such means as account numbers, passwords, and hardware devices.

system console: a workstation or terminal dedicated solely to the computer operator's use.

system faults: system component failures, such as disk failures or power outages.

threat: a potential exploitation of a system vulnerability.

trapdoor: a portion of a computer program that allows someone to access the program while bypassing its normal security.

trojan horse: a destructive program masquerading as a legitimate one.

virus program: similar to a trojan horse but can spread itself to other programs, "infecting" them with the same virus.

vulnerability: a weakness in a system.

watchdog processor: a second CPU processor that takes over processing if something happens to the first CPU processor.

worm: a type of virus program that spreads itself over a computer network.

Chapter Quiz

Answers to the chapter quiz appear on page 252.

1. Collusion appears to be (_____) in a computerized versus manual system.
   (a) less likely
   (b) more likely
   (c) equally likely

2. Which of the following is an active threat to computer security?
   (a) computer sabotage
   (b) earthquake
   (c) equipment failures
   (d) power outages

3. Individuals who attack computer systems for fun and challenge are sometimes called
   (a) duffers.
   (b) geeks.
   (c) hackers.
   (d) flaggers.

4. The interception of legitimate information and substitution of fraudulent information in its place is called
   (a) EMI eavesdropping.
   (b) flagging.
   (c) hacking.
   (d) piggybacking.

5. In most cases of computer fraud, (_____) is the method used.
   (a) program alteration
   (b) input manipulation
   (c) direct file alteration
   (d) misappropriation or theft of computer resources

6. A destructive computer program masquerading as a legitimate one is called a
   (a) trapdoor.
   (b) logic bomb.
   (c) trojan horse.
   (d) worm.

7. Five employees were accused of using their employer's mainframe computer during slack hours to operate their own data processing firm. This is an example of
   (a) program alteration.
   (b) input manipulation.
   (c) direct file alteration.
   (d) misappropriation or theft of computer resources.

8. An alternate computer processing site that contains the necessary wiring and computer equipment for operation, but not data files, is called a
   (a) hot site.
   (b) cold site.
   (c) flying-start site.
   (d) fault-tolerant site.

9. Marking and locking out a disk or DASD sector so that it will not be used again after it has been found to be unreliable is called
   (a) hacking.
   (b) flagging.
   (c) disk shadowing.
   (d) disk mirroring.

10. A dormant piece of code placed in a computer program for later activation by a specific event is a
    (a) trapdoor.
    (b) logic bomb.
    (c) trojan horse.
    (d) worm.

Review Problem

Hart Manufacturing has a large computer department. Barbara May is in charge of the internal audit staff. A routine investigation revealed that several customer accounts are phony and that several accounts with balances in excess of $1,000 each could not be traced to the names and addresses listed on the accounts. For example, one account was listed as belonging to an individual named John Day. When she tried to contact this individual, she found that the address was that of her local cemetery. In addition, the telephone number was not a working number. Furthermore, there was no individual in the telephone directory listed as John Day. Additional investigations revealed that there was no credit application on file for this individual.

To make things more complicated, it was found that all of these accounts were 12 months overdue. For some reason that had not yet been ascertained, none of these accounts appeared on the accounts receivable aging reports.

Required
What type of fraud has probably been committed here? Which individuals are the ones most likely to have been involved?

Solution to Review Problem

Program alteration is the most likely cause of this problem:

A. It is very likely that someone has altered the accounts receivables program to allow transactions by individuals not on the approved credit list. This individual has covered up by fixing the aging program to omit these accounts. There is also the possibility of collusion between a programmer and someone in the credit department. This would explain the fact that there was not adequate supporting documentation on file supporting credit approval. Of course, the programmer might have put a trapdoor in the program that would allow credit to certain individuals, even though they were not in the approved customers database. This could have been done without the help of someone in the credit department.
   (1) It should be noted that the program alteration might have been done by a system operator. System operators sometimes have access to all files on the computer system. The operator might have replaced the legitimate version of the accounts receivables program with an altered one.
B. The solution to this type of problem is to have a formal system for installing and maintaining software.
   (1) All changes to software should be supported by documentation, including complete review and approval.
   (2) Programmers should not have access to the working versions of software. They should be restricted to making changes, on an approved basis, to copies of working software. The modified copies should be reviewed before formal installation.
   (3) Master copies of software should be kept in a secure place. These master copies should be periodically compared, using readily available file comparison utilities, to the operating versions.

Review Questions

1. Identify several unique problems and risks associated with computerized information networks.
2. What elements are included in a computer security system?
3. Does the development of a computer security system require application of the life-cycle approach? Discuss.
4. What is risk management?
5. Distinguish between the qualitative and the quantitative approaches to analyzing system vulnerabilities and threats.
6. Identify some of the general types of threats that affect computer systems.
7. Is it possible to rigorously identify characteristics of the white-collar criminal?
8. What types of individuals pose a threat to a computer system?
9. Identify several different types of intruders.
10. Identify and discuss six different methods that an individual might use to perpetrate a computer fraud.
11. How might computer programs be used to commit acts of sabotage?
12. What is a virus program? Give several examples.
13. What role does an organization's control environment play in information system security? Give several specific examples.
14. Describe the layered approach to access control. What specific layers of access control might be implemented?
15. What are fault-tolerant systems? Illustrate the application of fault tolerance to the following areas:
    (a) network communications
    (b) CPU processors
    (c) DASDs
    (d) power supply
    (e) individual transactions
16. Distinguish between full backups, incremental backups, and differential backups of files.
17. What steps should be taken in the development of a disaster recovery plan?
18. Identify several recovery strategies and procedures that might be included in a disaster recovery plan.
19. Identify several alternate processing arrangements that might be included in a disaster recovery plan.

Discussion Questions and Problems

20. ABC Hardware Retailing Company runs a batch system for accounts receivable. On the first Monday of each month, the operations specialist runs an accounts receivable update. The procedure is as follows: the accountant prepares a list of all updates on a disk file; this disk file is then transferred to the account of a systems specialist; the operations specialist then carefully edits the data and then generates the batch job.

    Required
    Evaluate this procedure from a control standpoint.

21. The Wales Company is a medium-sized toy manufacturer. The information services division of this company is composed of user services, systems programming, and systems maintenance. In addition, the company has a batch-oriented accounts receivable system. All the databases related to accounts receivable are maintained by the systems programmer. Recently, a minor bug was detected in the accounts receivable program. The procedure to correct the bug was as follows: first, it was reported to the sys-

tems programmer by a member of the accounting staff; next, the systems programmer discussed the problem with the head of systems programming and agreed to an appropriate change; then the individual who reported the problem was notified that appropriate corrective action was being taken.

Required
Evaluate the procedures used in the Wales Company for program modification.

22. Deborah Hills is a high-ranking officer in the Air Force. She has recently been placed in charge of computer-assisted design and manufacturing for a highly classified project relating to a new high-technology aircraft. The project is so secret that she has been assigned to develop it in an abandoned base high in the mountains of California. Project resources included are a mainframe computer, 100 military personnel (including programmers, operations specialists, and so on) and 50 nonmilitary support staff. Most of the support staff do not have security clearances. The problem is that their skills lie primarily in programming, computer operations, and hardware maintenance.

Required
Develop an overall security system that maintains appropriate security regarding outsiders and effectively utilizes the nonmilitary support staff without violating security.

23. Clark Manufacturing has had a problem with unauthorized access to its accounts receivable database. The chief accountant suspects that one of the systems operators is somehow making changes to the accounts receivable database in an unauthorized manner. The accountant, however, is uncertain about the methods being used. It is possible that an operator has made changes to the accounting program. Another possibility is that the operator is accessing the accounting program without proper authorization.

Required
Discuss appropriate methods for resolving this problem.

24. Rauls Retailing has a high turnover rate among its employees. It maintains a very large computer system that supports approximately 200 terminals in a time-sharing mode. It addition, there are 64 dial-up ports available for the sales staff's use. The company maintains fairly extensive databases regarding its customers. These include customer profiles, past purchasing patterns, and prices charged.

Recently, the company has been having major problems with competitors. It appears that one competitor seems to be very effective at taking away Rauls' customers. Most of the company's customers have been visited by this competitor and identical products have been offered at lower prices in every case.

Required
What is the possible security problem? What can be done about it?

25. Brown Manufacturing maintains a large computer systems division. The company has recently faced a major problem with its software. It seems that ever since one of the computer programmers has been fired, disk files are mysteriously being erased. The chief analyst suspects that the fired programmer had placed a logic bomb in the operating system somewhere so that disk files would be erased in the event that his social security number was no longer in the accounting database.

Required
Discuss the methods for the detection of this logic bomb. What methods could be used to prevent this type of problem?

26. Acts Merchandising specializes in purchasing bankrupt firms and disposing of their assets by direct mail. It maintains about 30 sales offices around the United States. Each of these sales offices does the actual direct mail work within its own region. The central office in Atlanta maintains the customer database, and customers' names are transferred from this office to the individual sales offices on a weekly basis. The transfer is presently being done through one of the major public packet-switched networks.

It is suspected that customers' names are somehow leaking out to competitors as a result of their being transmitted through the public network.

Required
Discuss at least two alternatives that might be used to ensure greater security.

27. Hart Manufacturing Company is relatively small, with approximately 100 employees. The company's minicomputer is run by two individuals. One individual is responsible for the physical operation of the computer. This includes maintaining the company's magnetic tape library. At present, the tape library includes master files for most of the important accounting systems databases. Although the company has plenty of disk space, the accounting master files are maintained on tapes. The system is primarily batch oriented, and updates are run only once a month. Currently, the tape library is adjacent to the computer room and can be entered either through the computer room or another outside door. Because this individual is very busy, most employees enter the tape room and log their tapes in and out as needed.

Required
Given the limited resources of this company, discuss an appropriate security system for the tape library.

28. Bundy Retailing sells building supply materials. It is located in a medium-sized midwestern town and has four sales offices there. Each sales office has its own computer terminal that is hardwired to the company's main computer through a dedicated line. These terminals are used to authorize sales transactions. Given that an appropriate credit check has been made, the salesperson simply types in the sales order on one of the computer terminals, and authorization to release the goods is immediately printed out at the company's central warehouse. Recently, however, the company has detected a security problem. There are several salespeople working in each office and sharing the same terminal. It appears that one of the salespeople has been entering sales transactions and charging them to Brown Contracting Company. The problem is that Brown Contracting has never received any of these goods. In fact, all of the goods have been released to an impostor. This is a very serious problem because the total amount of goods released cost the company approximately $20,000. The chief of security is perplexed, because she does not know which salesperson is responsible. There is even some discussion about the possibility that an unauthorized intruder may have accessed the terminal.

Required
Discuss appropriate security measures that could have been taken to prevent this problem from occurring.

29. Waldo Company has had a problem with one of its employees using the computer network to play games. In the past, the company has not been very strict about controlling the use of the company's network, because employees often have slack time during the off-season. Recently, however, a serious problem has occurred. It appears that one of the game programs run on the network contained a virus. The virus is a special type of computer program that can cause considerable damage to a network when run with other computer programs in the system concurrently. The virus "looks around" the network and checks to see if other computer programs in the network are infected with the virus. If not, the virus program will then infect them. Part of the infection process involves making certain random changes to the other programs. These random changes are such that the infected program will produce unpredictable or invalid results at some specified date subsequent to the infection. For example, an accounting program might be modified so that it will scramble all the accounting databases exactly six months after its infection. The nature of the virus is particularly bad, because a program, once infected, has the ability to spread the infection to other programs. Therefore, once a virus is introduced into a computer network, all programs in the network might be infected in a matter of a couple of weeks. To make things worse, the infection process may carry to all of the company's backup copies as well. This is

particularly true if the virus program lies dormant for a long period of time before producing its disastrous results.

On June 15, this company went into a major state of disaster. The virus had evidently invaded all major portions of the computer network. The network database manager looked with great horror to find that all the databases were completely scrambled. To make things worse, backup copies were scrambled as well. Inspection of the backup copies of databases revealed that they were completely worthless. As a result, the company was unable to do its accounts receivable billing. Two months later it filed for a Chapter 11 bankruptcy.

Required

Discuss the means by which this problem should have been prevented.

30. The Morgan Department Store has approximately 1,000 customer accounts. Each month, a special clerk opens the mail and prepares a remittance list of all monies received on account. The checks are then sent to a cashier for further processing. In addition, copies of the remittances are sent to accounting and computer services. At the computer services office, an operator keys the remittances directly onto a disk file. The disk file is then used to update the accounts receivable master file.

The computer operator has devised an interesting scheme for defrauding the company. The operator keys in approximately a $100 credit to a friend's account each month. The operator and the friend agree in advance about the amount to be keyed in. The friend will then make purchases exactly in this amount. Normally, the error entered into the system by this procedure would be detected by the batch control totals; however, the operator decreases the amount credited to a number of other accounts. In each case, the amount of the decrease is only $1 or $2. Because the error is very small, most customers let it go unnoticed. However, in a relatively small number of cases where they do detect the error, corrections are made on an authorized basis without further comment. For example, in the previous month, a total of $10 worth of corrections were made because of the complaints. However, these corrections were all processed semiautomatically by the system, and no one realized that it was part of a cover-up.

Required

What can be done to detect and prevent this problem relating to input manipulation?

31. The Mid City Sales Company manages a discount store that sells most department store items at a discount. The entire accounting system is computerized. Barbara West is in charge of computer operations and oversees a medium-sized minicomputer with ten support personnel. The present system is based on on-line input and on-line accounting processing. All accounting updates are keyed directly into the system and processed immediately.

The company's accounts payable program works as follows. Customer invoices are matched with purchase orders and receiving reports. Assuming that these documents are in order, the chief accountant enters the appropriate information into the accounts payable program. Entering this information results in a computer-generated check (to pay the supplier) and updates the accounts payable. The check is processed by the finance manager, who signs it and then mails it out. To ensure against unauthorized access to the system, both an identification number and a password are required before the accountant can request the computer to make a payment on an account.

The company's computer system is such that the operator can access any account from the operator's console. Over a period of several months, the operator has been accessing the accounts payable system and ordering the computer to make payments to fictitious vendors.

Required

What security measures can be taken to prevent and detect this type of problem?

32. A programmer in the Ace Bottle Company installs a patch in one of the computer's billing routines that skips over the billing of a friend's account. The program allows

the account balance to increase without bounds. Another patch was put into the program to ensure that the friend's account balance never appeared in an aging report.

Required
Discuss the appropriate security measures that could detect and prevent this problem.

33. West Manufacturing's computer division is quite large, consisting of over 200 employees. Relations among the employees within the company are quite good. Although the accounting department is a separate group, the accountants and computer people eat lunch together and socialize regularly. This has led to some problems. Recently, two accountants, a systems programmer, systems analyst, and computer operator worked together to divert the deposit of funds from the company's bank account to their individual personal accounts. The defalcation involved the forging of source documents by the accountants and cover-up by the systems programmers and operators. The systems analyst designed the entire scheme. The whole thing was discovered by accident when the accountant was forced to take time off from work for a surgical operation. The replacement accountant suspected that something was wrong when she noticed that a number of deposit slips were missing.

As it turns out, the total loss to the company was only a couple of thousand dollars. However, if it had not been for the accidental discovery by the temporary accountant, the fraud could have grown to the extent that it could have bankrupted the company.

Required
What could have been done to prevent the problem that occurred?

34. Manchester Sales Company is a medium-sized retail operation with a computer staff of ten employees. The computer staff effectively maintains all accounting functions as well as computer operations. The overall internal control and security system is quite good. However, there are a number of problems. First, all of the computer employees know the passwords to each others' accounts. Although this is a breach of the security system, most employees feel that the other employees are basically honest and that there is no need to worry. Second, employees are lax about document distribution procedures. Almost anybody can come into the computer room and pick up a printout without an entry being logged into the records. Security has repeatedly complained to these employees about the problem, but to no avail.

Required
Discuss the problem of lax security in this company. What are its implications? What can be done about it?

35. Beard Manufacturing is extremely security conscious, especially in the area of its computer. Because of this, the director of the computer center has installed a sophisticated computer security system costing the company over $1 million. The system is so sophisticated that all communications terminals require positive voice identification. In addition, each user is assigned a security-level clearance by the operating system. All systems application and data files require specific levels of security for access. For example, individuals running accounting reports are assigned a low-level classification that will allow them to access the data files that they need, but will not allow them to make any changes to these files. In addition, a large number of other measures are part of the system, including security guards and closed-circuit television.

In spite of this sophisticated system, a very intelligent systems programmer managed to break through the company's security and alter the accounts receivable files. He managed to find a trapdoor in the operating system that allowed him to operate with a Level 8 security clearance. In addition, he was able to access the system update log to instruct the computer to completely forget that he accessed the data files. In other words, he was able to make changes to the data files without any trace being left of the transaction.

In this case, the company was very lucky because the systems programmer was honest and took his scheme to the director of computer security. Needless to say, the director of security was flabbergasted. As a result of what the programmer did, the director of security is considering replacing the entire security system with a more sophisticated $2 million system.

Required

What response should the director of security make regarding the systems programmer? What measures could have been taken to prevent the problem from occurring? Is a more expensive security system a good idea?

36. Equity Financing Life Insurance Company is headquartered in Miami, Florida. The company is very large, so it operates an enormous mainframe computer system. Recently, a group of political radicals threw a small bomb through the window (breaking the glass) in the main computer room. Because this happened late at night, there were no human injuries. However, the damage was extensive, and the central processing unit and three major disk drives were completely destroyed.

Required

Is what happened in any way the company's fault? Why or why not?

37. Eagle Airlines is headquartered in Chicago. The corporate administrative offices consist of ten buildings in a complex that spreads over four square miles. The main computer system is centrally located. All of the buildings in the complex contain computer users and, therefore, are connected to the main computer center by way of telephone cables.

Recently, the company's computer system was violated by the following scheme. A couple of college students from a nearby university purchased an inexpensive magnetic cassette tape recorder with a plug-in microphone and line-powered modem. The modem does not require any power supply because it derives its power needs directly from the telephone line to which it is connected. Using this equipment and a PC, the two students removed the microphone and connected the bare wires directly to one of the telephone lines coming out of the computer center. They then proceeded to record onto cassette everything that came across the telephone line. After trying this procedure a couple of times, they found that the cassette player was unnecessary and learned to capture the communications information directly onto the PC's disks. Later, they connected the PC to a printer and printed the contents of the disk.

To their amazement, the listings included the sign-on procedures and passwords for access to all of the company's major databases, including accounts payable and accounts receivable. To exploit this information, it was necessary for the students to obtain access to the company's computer through a data terminal. This posed a problem, however, because most of the company's data terminals were carefully guarded. To get around this, one of the students suggested that the company might have a dial-up port into the company's computer. The biggest problem, however, was finding the correct telephone number of the computer. They reasoned that the company's computer dial-up telephone number was probably very similar to the telephone number for the administrative offices. Therefore, they wrote a computer program that simply dialed one telephone number after another looking for a computer modem carrier signal. The program was set to try all numbers that matched administrative telephone numbers in the first four digits. Therefore, the program was set to test 999 different telephone numbers. This procedure worked out very well, and the company's computer was discovered on about the twentieth try. As it turned out, the computer's number differed from the administrative number in only the last two digits.

Once into the company's computer, it then became necessary to try a scheme to try to defraud the company. After much discussion, they finally decided to order the computer's accounts payable program to issue checks to a post office box registered under a fictitious name. Finally, the illegally obtained checks were deposited to the bank account registered to the fictitious name.

The students might have gotten away with their scheme if they had not gotten greedy. They had requested a large number of small checks totaling $100,000. This would have gone unnoticed; however, the checks requested bounced because there was not enough money in the company's bank account to pay them. Once the checks bounced, the accountant immediately figured out that the checks were not supported by adequate documentation. The authorities were notified, and the students were caught while checking their post office box for mail.

Required

Discuss the specific security measures that could have been taken to prevent this scheme.

38. The Base Level National Bank of Washington, D.C., has utilized computers to process cash deposits made by its customers for more than 20 years. The bank's computer system for customer deposit accounting is a batch processing system. Customers fill out a deposit slip when they deposit cash. The cashier validates the deposit slip, collects the cash, and then issues a dated receipt to the customer to evidence the deposit. The batches of deposit slips are processed overnight in a computer batch processing run to update the customer account records.

Two different types of deposit slips might be used by a customer. One type is a blank-form deposit slip that the customer obtains at the bank. Typically, large quantities of blank-form deposit slips are left on counters in the bank's lobby for the customers' convenience. A blank-form deposit slip does not contain any preentered data. In particular, the customer or the cashier must manually enter the customer's account number on this form. The other type of deposit slip is contained in a customer's checkbook. In the case of a checkbook deposit slip, the customer's account number has already been entered on the form in computer-readable form. Each checkbook deposit slip contains the customer's account number in magnetic-ink character recognition (MICR) format to facilitate computer processing.

The two types of deposit slips look similar but are distinguishable. When batches of deposit slips are processed in the computer department, one of the first steps is to enter, using a special machine, both the customer's account number and the amount of the deposit in MICR format at the bottom of each deposit slip. MICR input is used because of the large volume of transactions. Because each checkbook type deposit slip already has the customer's account number in MICR, it is only necessary to MICR-encode the amount of the deposit. Both the customer's account number and the amount of the deposit must be MICR-encoded on the blank-form deposit slips.

Several months ago Base Level National Bank was the victim of a clever fraud. It seems that some person entered the busy bank and left a stack of fraudulent blank deposit slips on one of the bank's counters. These deposit slips were exact duplicates of those normally placed on the counters, with one important difference. Each fraudulent blank deposit slip had been MICR-encoded with the account number of a checking account that apparently had been opened under a false name. Recall that MICR-encoded account numbers are normally entered on the blank-form deposit slips after the deposit has been accepted by a cashier. During the day, the fraudulent deposit slips were used by many people making deposits at the bank. Most or all of these deposits were incorrectly credited to the fraudulent checking account in the overnight computer batch processing run of the day's deposit slips. Within a few minutes of opening the next morning, this person returned to the bank, inquired as to his checking account balance, and withdrew 90% of the balance in cash. To date the identity of the person is unknown, and the cash, more than $150,000, has not been recovered.

Required

(a) What factors contributed to the success of this clever fraud? What role did Base Level's computer system play in the perpetration of this fraud?

(b) Suggest control procedures that could prevent the occurrence of this type of fraud.

39. Grand Bank Corporation (GBC)—Case A

Grand Bank Corporation (GBC) operates a communications network that supports data processing for its subsidiary banks and their branches. The corporate database is centralized at the GBC Network Communication Command Center (NCCC). About 100,000 transactions are processed against the database each day.

GBC's NCCC consists of two coupled mainframe processors, 16 magnetic disk drive units, 12 tape drives, and other equipment. The communication network uses dedicated lines leased from a PBX. The system supports processing for demand deposit (checking), savings, commercial and personal loans, and general ledger.

Processing Controls

Control procedures exist to prevent unauthorized access to the communication network and unauthorized use of files. Transactions are entered by tellers using intelligent data terminals. In the case of communication interruptions, the terminals can do limited off-line processing. At the end of each day, the terminals print transaction totals for balancing the cash drawer. A log of all transactions received during the day is reprocessed off-line that evening and reconciled to the day's on-line processing. These totals along with an updated general ledger are transmitted to the network members each morning.

Each terminal's identification code is hard-wired. Each transaction is identified by the terminal identification code, along with the employee identification code and time of day. The central computers recognize only authorized terminal identifications and requests to use the system.

Software controls are used to ensure that users access only their own data files and the application programs authorized for them. All files and programs are protected by frequently changed codes and passwords.

Access Controls

All visitors sign in and out in a log indicating the time of day, whom they represent, and whom they are visiting. Visitors are issued badges and are required to wear them in plain view while on the premises.

Access to the data processing area is restricted to authorized management and operating personnel. Access is controlled by doors activated with magnetic card readers attached on-line to a separate computer security system. Codes in the magnetic cards issued to each authorized employee designate which doors are available for access. A log is maintained of the card number and all access attempts.

Access to the computer room is restricted to the operations staff and equipment vendors only. A building security guard is on duty at all times.

Environmental Controls

An electronic heat, fire, and smoke detection alarm system has been installed at NCCC. A halon gas fire extinguishing system is incorporated into the system to put out any fire in the computer area. The fire alarm system is connected to an automatic power-off trip switch and to the building's manned engineer console.

Portable carbon dioxide fire extinguishers are readily accessible in and around the computer facility. These are periodically weighed and kept charged, and computer operators are trained to use them. All electrical equipment is approved by Underwriters' Laboratories (UL).

Flammable material in or around the data processing center is removed daily to avoid potential fire hazards. Waste containers are designed to retain and smother fires. Paper and other combustible supplies are not stored in the computer room. The computer room construction material is noncombustible. Exterior computer room walls have a 2-hour fire rating. A no-smoking rule is enforced in the computer room.

There are several independently controlled air conditioning modules distributed between two independently fused power panels. The failure of any module can be compensated for by the other modules. All air conditioning modules are inspected monthly when filters are changed. There is a backup system for pumping water to the air conditioning system. If one motor fails, that motor will be bypassed and pumping capacity maintained by a second motor and pump. The water softening system utilizes a dual filter to prevent clogging of water intake systems. A separate electrical power supply for the air conditioning systems is maintained.

Maintenance Procedures

Proper maintenance procedures concerning hardware help NCCC prevent failures. The maintenance technicians perform preventive maintenance on the equipment daily, and on every Sunday, they thoroughly check the mainframe processors.

The operations manager, in order to locate problems, reviews the engineer's weekly report of preventive and remedial maintenance. The operations manager also closely supervises the work being done to ensure a prompt and proper solution.

File Security

The library of data files is physically controlled by a librarian who maintains the file usage records. Periodically, file media are checked and their operating condition certified. The librarian is the only person authorized to erase file media.

The librarian controls all files in the library and in the off-site storage location. Each file has retention instructions printed on it. All file media that are necessary for recovery and restart are stored in a heat resistant, fireproof, locked vault.

The locked computer center vault holds the first-generation backup files, which can be used for immediate backup. The files in the vault include program object files, transaction backup files, and account master files. Operating system backup is ensured by periodically copying the object code and related data files from the system residence device directly to cartridge tape. A copy of the source code for each application is also kept on cartridge tape.

Each day, two copies of the daily transactions are prepared and put on cartridge tape. One tape is placed in the computer room vault and the other one is sent to an off-site storage location. On-line and off-line month-end master files, month-to-date history, and object and source programs are sent to off-site storage twice a week and after each end-of-month processing.

Hardware Controls

Either of the two coupled processors can be used individually for running all on-line and off-line processing. If hardware problems should develop in one machine, the other is available for backup.

All peripheral equipment, which includes tape drives, disk drives, printers, and communication equipment, can be switched to either computer.

Backup telephone lines connect the telephone center to the computer room. If a restart is needed, the on-line system files from the beginning of the day can be processed against the network transactions entered during the day.

Recovery and Restart

Procedures that are necessary for computer operators to restart and recover from a business interruption are fully documented. The run manual documents all necessary recovery and restart procedures for the network communications system together with their priorities.

The tape library retains all necessary system files and transaction files so that the network communications processing for any of the last 30 days can be re-created.

In the event of the destruction of files at NCCC, the present system provides the capability to be operational with up-to-date files in 24 hours. To achieve this type of recovery, files would be removed from off-site storage and the most recent master files would be processed off-line with the 1 to 3 days of daily transactions required to re-create current master files.

There is a 20-page set of detailed procedures and guidelines to be followed in the case of a disaster. These procedures indicate who is to be notified, what tasks they are to perform, and in what order.

NCCC has letters of support from suppliers of the center's equipment and related elements that indicate that in case of a disaster, support will be offered on a timely basis. These letters are from the suppliers of business forms, the air conditioning company, the computer manufacturer, the suppliers of the peripheral equipment, and the PBX company.

Required

1. Identify major areas that should be considered in a security review to determine the potential for loss of data or the ability to process it. Identify some controls in each of these areas.

2. Evaluate the general security and recovery procedures as described at NCCC. What other areas might warrant consideration in a review of security and recovery procedures?

40. Grand Bank Corporation (GBC)—Case B

Management of GBC commissioned a security review task force to review compliance with corporate security policies and procedures at NCCC. The following observations were made during several on-site visits to NCCC and the off-site file backup storage location.

(1) Frequent visitors, such as equipment technicians or important management personnel, often do not have to sign the visitor's log.

(2) The computer room door is often left unlocked by employees who are "running out for something and will be right back."

(3) The back door to the computer room is sometimes opened on very hot days to help reduce the load placed on the air conditioners.

(4) Several holiday banners were noticed hanging from a fire detector and a halon gas register.

(5) Several computer programmers were observed playing video games on the data terminals at their desks.

(6) Several unlabeled data files were observed in the computer room. Several files that should have been destroyed several days previous were found in the library.

(7) Several persons have "extra" keys to the file storage vault.

(8) An outside vendor provides cleaning services on Sundays during off-hours. Often no NCCC employees are at the center during this weekly cleaning.

(9) The company that picks up and transports data files to the remote storage location is often late picking up the files for off-site storage.

(10) Several programmers were observed walking directly into the file library and picking up data files for usage.

(11) The off-site file storage location, a very old warehouse building, lacks adequate temperature and humidity controls, and also has inadequate fire detection and prevention systems.

(12) Records maintained at the off-site storage location—which is used by several different companies as well as GBC—were inadequate and not up-to-date. The physical storage of the backup files was in locked closets labeled only by numbers.

(13) Letters sent to confirm the backup support promised to NCCC in letters obtained before equipment was actually purchased received lukewarm and sometimes contradictory responses from vendors. In several cases, the claim was made

that existing NCCC equipment is quite different and somewhat incompatible with the products now offered and supported by the vendor.

Required

1. Discuss the security problems indicated by the items noted.
2. What do these data suggest about the evaluation of general security and recovery procedures such as those in effect at GBC's NCCC?

Answers to Chapter Quiz

1. B	4. D	7. D	10. B
2. A	5. B	8. A	
3. C	6. C	9. B	

CHAPTER 7

Revenue- and Expenditure-Cycle Applications

LEARNING OBJECTIVES

Careful study of this chapter will enable you to:

■ Describe the major features and operations in a sales order application system.

■ Describe the major features and operations in an accounts receivable application system.

■ Describe the major features and operations in a purchasing application system.

■ Describe the major features and operations in a payroll application system.

Revenue, expenditure, production, and finance activities are common to business organizations. Chapters 7 and 8 provide an overview of transaction processing applications in each of these major cycles of business activity. Chapter 7 discusses common revenue- and expenditure-cycle application systems. These systems include sales order processing, accounts receivable, purchasing, and payroll. Chapter 8 discusses common production and finance application systems, including production and inventory control, property accounting, cash receipts, and cash disbursements.

The application systems discussed in this chapter and the next illustrate and emphasize the concept of **organizational independence** (separation of functions) in the design of application systems. Organizational independence requires that the custody of an asset be under a separate authority from record-keeping functions related to that asset and that both custody and record-keeping functions be under separate authority from any operating functions that utilize the asset. The applications presented are not intended to serve as blueprints to be duplicated without regard to the specific situation at hand. They are, however, a checklist. They provide a frame of reference against which an analyst may contrast a proposed or existing system.

The data flow diagrams and document flowcharts presented in Chapters 7 and 8 focus on the logical necessities of an application system rather than on physical features. The information represented by the document symbol in these diagrams may be a paper form, a telephone call, a computer or satellite data transmission, or any other physical form. Technological considerations (equipment and devices) are not specifically addressed because, although technology may alter the operating configuration of an application system, the same ends should be accomplished regardless of technology.

REVENUE-CYCLE APPLICATIONS

An organization's revenue cycle includes the functions required to exchange its products or services with customers. Common functions include credit granting, order taking and processing, shipment of goods, billing, and accounts receivable. This section discusses two revenue-cycle application systems: sale order processing and accounts receivable. Cash receipts are discussed in Chapter 8 as a finance-cycle application.

Sales Order Processing

Figure 7.1 illustrates a data flow diagram of a sales order application system. A sales order application system comprises the procedures involved in accepting

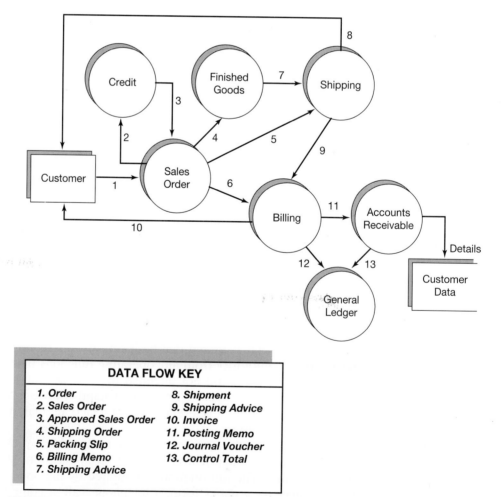

DATA FLOW KEY

1. Order
2. Sales Order
3. Approved Sales Order
4. Shipping Order
5. Packing Slip
6. Billing Memo
7. Shipping Advice
8. Shipment
9. Shipping Advice
10. Invoice
11. Posting Memo
12. Journal Voucher
13. Control Total

FIGURE 7.1 Data Flow Diagram: Sales Order Application System.

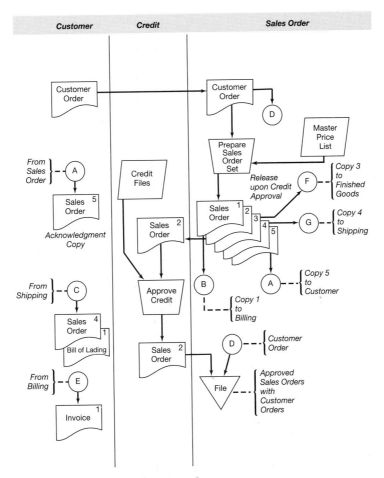

FIGURE 7.2 Sales Order Application System.

and shipping customer orders and in preparing invoices that describe products, services, and assessments. Figure 7.2 illustrates an analytic flowchart of a model sales order application system. The chart illustrates a **separate order and billing** system in which customer orders are filled from an inventory of finished goods. The **sales order** (Figure 7.3) is the interface between the various functions necessary to process a customer order. As shown in Figure 7.2 and discussed in what follows, these functions are sales order, credit, finished goods, shipping, billing, accounts receivable, and general ledger.

Sales Order

The sales order function initiates the processing of customer orders with the preparation of a sales order. The sale order contains descriptions of products ordered, their prices, and descriptive data concerning the customer, such as name, shipping address, and, if necessary, billing address. At this point, the actual quantities shipped and freight charges (if any) are not known. The invoice will be prepared after the goods have been shipped and notice of this event is forwarded to billing. Because the invoice is prepared after shipment, separate order and billing is also called **postbilling.**

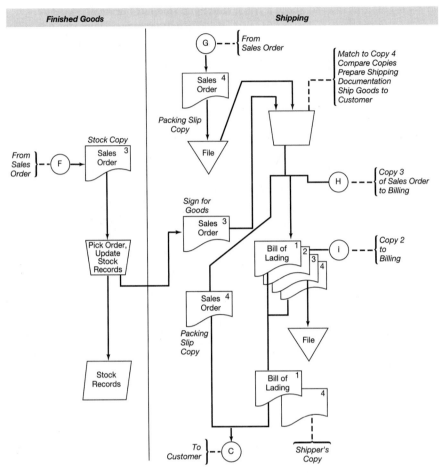

FIGURE 7.2 (continued)

Credit

A customer's credit standing should be verified prior to the shipment of goods. For regular customers, the credit check involves determining that the total amount of credit granted does not exceed management's general or specific authorization. For new customers, a credit check is necessary to establish the terms of sale to the customer. As Figure 7.2 illustrates, the sales order function should be subject to the control of an independent credit function to maintain the separation of duties.

Once credit has been approved, the sales order function distributes the sales order set, as shown in Figure 7.2. One copy of each sales order is forwarded to billing. These are filed as open orders, allowing the billing function to anticipate the receipt of matching shipping advices from the shipping function. One copy—usually called the *packing slip copy*—is forwarded to shipping. This copy authorizes shipping to receive goods from finished goods for shipping. Another copy—usually called the *stock copy*—is forwarded to finished goods. This copy authorizes finished goods to release goods from its custody for shipment to customers.

In some cases, a customer's order may require that a production order be issued to produce the goods, because the goods are not in stock. Such situations arise when the order is for a special nonstock item. They also may arise as standard company practice due to either the customized nature of the product or a

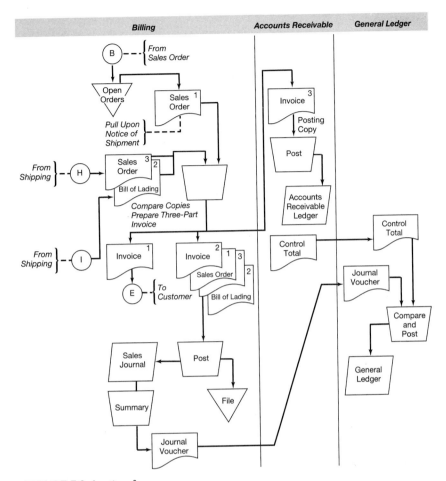

FIGURE 7.2 (continued)

short production cycle that alleviates the need for an inventory of finished goods. Such situations also occur when items are out-of-stock and must be back ordered. If the time between receiving an order and actual shipment of the order is significant, an *acknowledgment copy* of the sales order may be sent to the customer to inform the customer that the order has been received and is being processed.

Finished Goods

Finished goods picks the order as described on the stock copy of the sales order (copy 3). Stock records are updated to reflect the actual quantities to be forwarded to shipping. Actual quantities are noted on the stock copy of the sales order, which is then forwarded along with the goods to shipping. As noted in Figure 7.2, shipping should sign the stock copy to acknowledge receipt of the quantities noted thereon from finished goods.

Shipping

Shipping accepts the order for shipment after matching the packing slip copy to the stock copy of the sales order. Shipping documentation is prepared according to the situation. Frequently, this requires the preparation of a **bill of lading** (see Figure 7.4). A bill of lading is the documentation exchanged between a shipper and a

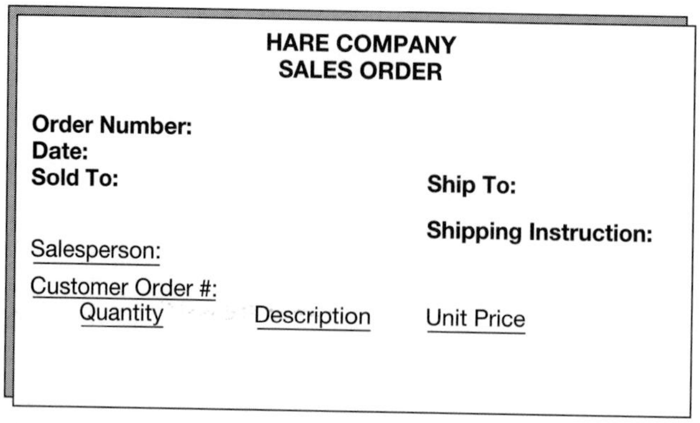

HARE COMPANY
SALES ORDER

Order Number:
Date:
Sold To: Ship To:

                                  Shipping Instruction:

Salesperson:

Customer Order #:
    Quantity   Description   Unit Price

FIGURE 7.3 Sales Order.

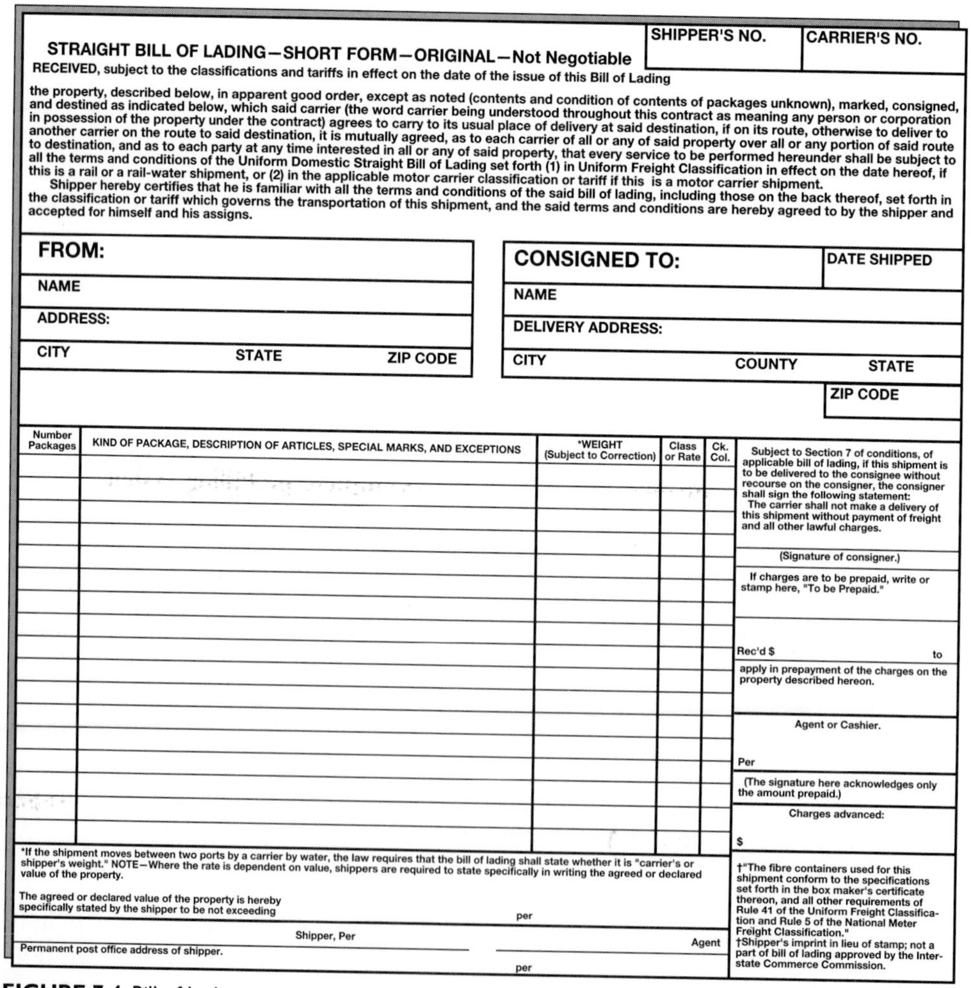

STRAIGHT BILL OF LADING—SHORT FORM—ORIGINAL—Not Negotiable

| | SHIPPER'S NO. | CARRIER'S NO. |

RECEIVED, subject to the classifications and tariffs in effect on the date of the issue of this Bill of Lading

the property, described below, in apparent good order, except as noted (contents and condition of contents of packages unknown), marked, consigned, and destined as indicated below, which said carrier (the word carrier being understood throughout this contract as meaning any person or corporation in possession of the property under the contract) agrees to carry to its usual place of delivery at said destination, if on its route, otherwise to deliver to another carrier on the route to said destination, it is mutually agreed, as to each carrier of all or any of said property over all or any portion of said route to destination, and as to each party at any time interested in all or any of said property, that every service to be performed hereunder shall be subject to all the terms and conditions of the Uniform Domestic Straight Bill of Lading set forth (1) in Uniform Freight Classification in effect on the date hereof, if this is a rail or a rail-water shipment, or (2) in the applicable motor carrier classification or tariff if this is a motor carrier shipment.
    Shipper hereby certifies that he is familiar with all the terms and conditions of the said bill of lading, including those on the back thereof, set forth in the classification or tariff which governs the transportation of this shipment, and the said terms and conditions are hereby agreed to by the shipper and accepted for himself and his assigns.

FROM:

NAME

ADDRESS:

CITY   STATE   ZIP CODE

CONSIGNED TO: DATE SHIPPED

NAME

DELIVERY ADDRESS:

CITY   COUNTY   STATE

ZIP CODE

Number Packages	KIND OF PACKAGE, DESCRIPTION OF ARTICLES, SPECIAL MARKS, AND EXCEPTIONS	*WEIGHT (Subject to Correction)	Class or Rate	Ck. Col.	

Subject to Section 7 of conditions, of applicable bill of lading, if this shipment is to be delivered to the consignee without recourse on the consignor, the consignor shall sign the following statement:
    The carrier shall not make a delivery of this shipment without payment of freight and all other lawful charges.

(Signature of consignor.)

If charges are to be prepaid, write or stamp here, "To be Prepaid."

Rec'd $ to apply in prepayment of the charges on the property described hereon.

Agent or Cashier.

Per

(The signature here acknowledges only the amount prepaid.)

Charges advanced:

$

*If the shipment moves between two ports by a carrier by water, the law requires that the bill of lading shall state whether it is "carrier's or shipper's weight." NOTE—Where the rate is dependent on value, shippers are required to state specifically in writing the agreed or declared value of the property.

The agreed or declared value of the property is hereby specifically stated by the shipper to be not exceeding

    per

Shipper, Per

Permanent post office address of shipper.

    Agent

    per

†*The fibre containers used for this shipment conform to the specifications set forth in the box maker's certificate thereon, and all other requirements of Rule 41 of the Uniform Freight Classification and Rule 5 of the National Meter Freight Classification."
†Shipper's imprint in lieu of stamp; not a part of bill of lading approved by the Interstate Commerce Commission.

FIGURE 7.4 Bill of Lading.

carrier such as a trucking company. The bill of lading documents freight charges and the transfer of goods from the shipping company to the transportation company. Frequently, freight charges are paid by the shipper but billed to the customer on the sales invoice. The packing slip copy of the sales order is usually included with the customer's order when it is shipped, as shown in Figure 7.2.

Billing

Shipping forwards documentation of the shipment to the billing function. This documentation is termed the **shipping advice** and is usually the stock copy of the sales order and a copy of the bill of lading. Billing pulls the related open order documentation, verifies the order, then prepares the invoice by extending the charges for actual quantities shipped, freight charges (if any), and taxes (if any). Invoices are mailed to customers. Invoices are recorded in the sales journal and posting copies are sent to accounts receivable. Periodically, a journal voucher is prepared and forwarded to the general ledger function for posting to the general ledger.

Accounts Receivable and General Ledger

The distinction between billing and accounts receivable is important to maintain separation of functions. Billing is responsible for invoicing individual sales transactions, and accounts receivable maintains customer-accounts information and sends periodic statements of account to customers. Billing does not have access to the financial records (the receivables ledger), and the financial records are independent of the invoicing operation. Note in Figure 7.2 that the control total of postings to the accounts receivable ledger that is sent to the general ledger by accounts receivable is compared to the journal voucher sent from billing to validate postings to the general ledger. In the same fashion, the distinction between shipping and finished goods is important to the establishment of accountability for the release of finished goods from inventory.

Types of Sales Order Systems

Various relationships between the order, billing, and shipping functions are feasible, depending on the circumstances. The major consideration is the preparation of the **invoice** (Figure 7.5). In a **complete prebilling system,** the complete invoice is prepared at the same time as the shipping order. In this case, the shipping order is usually a copy of the invoice. This system minimizes paperwork. The invoice is released after the goods are shipped. A complete prebilling system requires that all invoicing information be known prior to the preparation of the invoice/shipping order set. This requires few back-orders or other inventory problems. Also, freight and other charges must be either absorbed by the seller or standardized (e.g., "add 50 cents for postage"). Any change between the customer order as prewritten and as actually shipped requires a new invoice and the destruction of the original invoice. If such situations are common, complete prebilling is very inefficient.

As indicated previously, Figure 7.2 illustrates a **separate order and billing system.** The shipping order in this type of system is prepared separately from the invoice. The invoice is prepared after the goods have been prepared for shipment. A separate order and billing system is necessary when there is a significant difference between the information on the shipping order (internal to the seller) and the invoice. For example, technical specifications in the shipping order may not be required or desired on the invoice. Excessive back-order and out-of-stock condi-

SOLD TO:	CITRUS SUPPLY CO. 1467 CLAY STREET PETERSBURG, WISCONSIN 44444				INVOICE **Burroughs** Ⓑ			
SHIP TO:	CITRUS SUPPLY CO. 1467 CLAY STREET PETERSBURG, WISCONSIN 44444							

TERMS	ORDER NO.	CUSTOMER NO.	SOLD BY	SHIP VIA	DATE	INVOICE NO.
2-10 NET 30	P87654	102,912	7	OUR TRUCK	NOV. 15	12,347

CODE	QUANTITY	DESCRIPTION	PRICE	UNIT	GROSS	DISCOUNT	NET
13414522	10	CUTTING TIP TT-3	2.80	EA	28.00	.00	28.00
12415710	10	SCREWDRIVER 6"	1.90	EA	19.00	.38	18.62
15611410	5	WELDING GLOVE #10	1.50	PR	7.50	.15	7.35
12488806	10	DSK	1.00	EA	10.00	.00	10.00
							63.97
					TAX	5.0%	3.20
					HANDLING		25.00
							92.17

FIGURE 7.5 Invoice.

tions also warrant this approach, because the final content of the invoice cannot be determined until the goods are ready for shipment. In many industries, alterations or substitution of goods ordered are allowed by customary trade practices. In retailing, for example, different styles or colors may be substituted in an order for clothing. The changed specifications from the customer's order must be shown on the invoice. In other instances, several shipments are made to the same customer over a specific time period under a single **blanket order.** In this case, there is no one-to-one correspondence between the customer order and the subsequent invoices. Typically, one blanket order requires several separate invoices—one for each shipment made under the blanket order.

Incomplete prebilling is a third type of sales order system. The incomplete prebilling system is very similar to a separate order and billing system. The only difference is that an invoice is originally prepared by the sales order department rather than a sales order. The invoice is completed to the extent possible, but because actual quantities shipped and freight charges (if any) cannot be known with certainty until shipment, the invoice is incomplete (i.e., only partially finished). This invoice is then distributed in the same fashion as the sales order in a separate order and billing system—with copies to finished goods, shipping, and billing—except that multiple copies of the invoice are sent to billing. When billing receives notification of shipment, it pulls its copies of the invoice and completes them. In separate order and billing, billing prepares the original copy of the invoice when it receives notification of shipment.

Both separate order and billing and incomplete billing are postbilling systems. Incomplete billing is commonly used in manual systems, as only one document (an invoice) rather than two documents (a sales order and an invoice) must be prepared. This reduces transcription of information and thus is often more efficient in a manual system.

Note that the sales order is primarily an internal document. The invoice, on the other hand, is the customer's formal notification of the amount due for the shipment. Note also that the terms *invoice* and *bill* can be used interchangeably. A bill of lading is an invoice for freight charges. Separate order and billing might also be called separate order and invoicing.

Accounts Receivable System

Accounts receivable represents the money owed by customers for merchandise sold or services rendered. Because approximately 90% of U.S. business is done on credit, accounts receivable often represents the majority of an organization's working capital. Accounts receivable also maintains customer credit and payment history information, which is useful in the overall administration of company credit policies.

Conceptually, the accounts receivable procedure is straightforward. A subsidiary ledger of individual accounts is maintained, with a control account in the general ledger. Remittance advices are routed from the cash receipts function; credit memos and other invoice adjustments are routed to the accounts receivable department from the billing department. Debits and credits are posted to the individual accounts; periodically, statements are prepared and sent to customers. Aging schedules are prepared as a by-product of sending statements. Special credit reports may also be prepared.

There are two basic approaches to an accounts receivable application: open-item and balance-forward processing. In **open-item processing,** a separate record is maintained in the accounts receivable system for each of the customer's unpaid invoices. As customer remittances are received, they are matched to the unpaid invoices. In **balance-forward processing,** a customer's remittances are applied against a customer's total outstanding balance rather than against a customer's individual invoices.

Data processing of accounts receivable can be tedious because of the volume of transactions and number of accounts that may exist. A large insurance company or bank may have close to a million separate accounts. Even with computer processing, mailing all statements at month's end may be impossible. Many businesses use a **cycle billing plan,** in which the accounts receivable file is subdivided by alphabet or account number. The idea is to distribute the preparation of statements over the working days of the month; for example, accounts A to H may be billed on the 10th, I to P on the 20th, and so on. These plans often have a beneficial effect on a company's cash flow, because consumers generally pay bills shortly after receiving them.

Ledgerless bookkeeping may be used to streamline receivable procedures in certain situations. An important procedural question is whether copies of sales slips are to be included with the monthly statement. This practice is increasingly uncommon. Usually, individual transactions are itemized on the statement, with supporting documents references by either code or invoice number. A company is obligated to produce supporting documents at the customer's request; this demands careful attention to the details of filing source documents. Owing to the preceding procedural aspects, some companies sell their accounts receivable at a discount to collection agencies. This process, called **factoring,** avoids record-keeping costs. This alternative should be considered by the analyst, but he or she must also carefully consider the potential negative effects of factoring on customer relations.

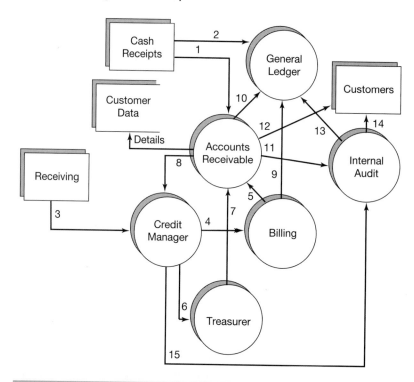

DATA FLOW KEY

1. *Remittance Advices*
2. *Control Total*
3. *Sales Return Memo*
4. *Sales Return Advice*
5. *Credit Memo*
6. *Write-Off Memo*
7. *Write-Off Advice*
8. *Aged Trial Balance*
9. *Journal Voucher*
10. *Control Total*
11. *Worthless Account List*
12. *Statements*
13. *Total Write-Offs*
14. *Write-Off Confirmation*
15. *Write-Off Memo*

FIGURE 7.6 Data Flow Diagram: Accounts Receivable System.

Transaction Flows in an Accounts Receivable System

Figure 7.6 illustrates a data flow diagram of an accounts receivable application system. Figure 7.7 illustrates a document flowchart of the flow of transactions in an accounts receivable application system. The main feature in each of these illustrations is the separation of the following functions.

Cash Receipts

Customer remittance slips are forwarded to accounts receivable for posting from cash receipts. Accounts receivable does not have access to the cash or checks that accompany customer remittances.

Billing

Invoices, credit memos, and other invoice adjustments are routed to accounts receivable for posting to the customer accounts. This maintains a separation of functions. Billing does not have direct access to the accounts receivable records.

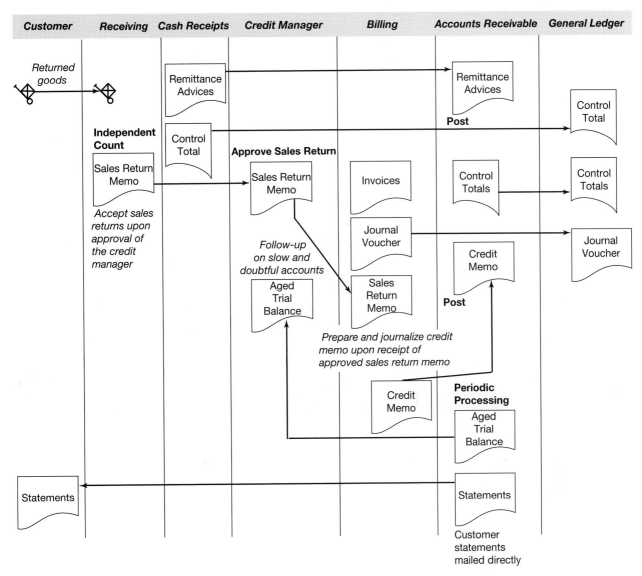

FIGURE 7.7 Accounts Receivable Application System.

Accounts Receivable

Accounts receivable is responsible for maintaining the subsidiary accounts receivable ledger. A control account is maintained in the general ledger department. Debits and credits are posted to the customer accounts from the posting media—remittance advices, invoices, and so on—received from billing and cash receipts. This maintains separation of functions. Periodically, customer statements are mailed directly to customers by the accounts receivable department. Periodic processing also includes the preparation of an aged trial balance of the accounts receivable subsidiary ledger for review by the credit department. Other types of customer credit reports may be prepared based on the needs of the company. Such reports are often prepared as a by-product of the processing required to send customers their statements.

Credit

Credit department functions in an accounts receivable application system include the approval of sales returns and allowances and other adjustments to customer accounts, the review and approval of the aged trial balance to ascertain customer's creditworthiness, and the initiation of write-off memos to charge accounts to bad-debt expense. These functions are discussed in what follows.

General Ledger

General ledger maintains the accounts receivable control account. Debits and credits are posted to the accounts receivable control account from the journal vouchers/control totals received from billing and cash receipts. These amounts are reconciled to the control totals sent to the general ledger directly from accounts receivable. This reconciliation is an important control in the accounts receivable application system.

Sales Returns and Allowances

Sales returns and allowances typically require careful control. Allowances occur when, because of damaged merchandise, shortages, clerical errors, or the like, the customer and the seller agree to reduce the amount owed by the customer. Generally, the merchandise is retained or destroyed by the customer. The amount of an allowance is negotiated between the customer and the sales order department (or salesperson). The allowance should be reviewed and approved by an independent party (usually the credit department); when authorized, billing issues a **credit memorandum** to document the reduction to the customer's account. As Figure 7.7 illustrates, sales return procedures (i.e., for goods actually returned, usually for full credit) are typically initiated by the receiving department. Once goods are received and returned to inventory for proper control (this would be evidenced by documentation), the credit manager authorizes billing to issue a credit memorandum. Note that for both returns and allowances, two independent parties are required to approve the transaction, and a third party maintains the records. This is another example of organizational independence in the design of application systems.

Write-Off of Accounts Receivable

The principle of organizational independence also applies in the write-off of accounts receivable procedure. The central feature in a write-off procedure is an analysis of past due accounts, usually done with an aged trial balance. Numerous techniques are available to collect past due accounts (e.g., follow-up letters, collection agencies), but some accounts are ultimately worthless. In this case (as Figure 7.8 shows), the credit manager initiates a write-off, which is approved by the treasurer. On approval, accounts receivable is authorized to write off the account. A copy of the authorization is also sent to an independent third party (internal audit in Figure 7.8) for purposes of record keeping. This is necessary because after the write-off, accounts receivable no longer has an active record of the account. Figure 7.8 details the role of the independent third party. Note that internal audit confirms write-offs directly with the customer to ensure that no collections have been made on written-off accounts. An employee might intercept a customer's payment on account and then arrange for the account to be written off, so that the customer does not continue to be billed for the amount.

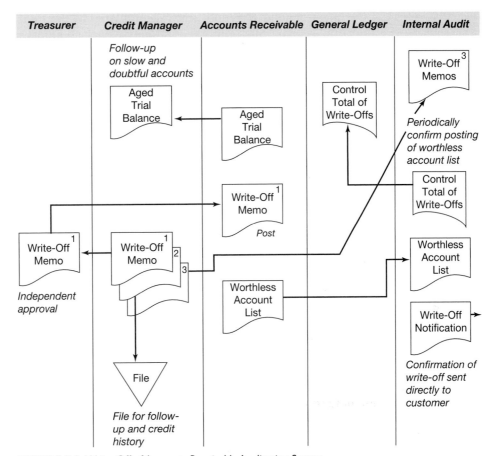

FIGURE 7.8 Write-Off of Accounts Receivable Application System.

Other Revenue-Cycle Application Systems

Every organization defines its own unique application systems. A large organization probably has several specialized application subsystems within its overall sales and accounts receivable application systems. For example, a sales or order-entry application system might include a separate pricing or quotation subsystem—a set of files, documents, and procedures used to price complex products such as electrical generating equipment. Another special subsystem might maintain a firm's product or service catalog. The shipping application might include a warehouse subsystem concerned with converting an order into the exact storage locations that need to be picked. An automated warehouse system might also generate an optimal path for pickers to take through the warehouse to minimize travel distance in picking the order. The shipping application might include a shipper-ordering subsystem concerned with selecting shippers, grouping individual shipments to minimize freight costs, and controlling all shipments. The finished goods function would maintain several inventory files, and billing would need its own files and procedures.

Basic transaction processing systems are the source of important tactical and strategic control information. Data for sales analyses such as product sales by territory, product sales by salesperson, sales forecasting, customer credit analysis, and other such summarized reports are accumulated by the transaction processing application systems. Such reports and analyses are common and routine in a computerized accounting system. It is important to realize that these types of upper-level management reports cannot be more accurate or reliable than the data on which they are based. The application systems presented in this chapter and in Chapter 8 illustrate the types of controls necessary to provide reliable and accurate data.

EXPENDITURE-CYCLE APPLICATIONS

An organization's expenditure cycle includes the functions required to acquire goods and services that are utilized by the organization in conducting its operations. The expenditure cycle includes the acquisition of goods for resale or use in production, the acquisition of personnel services, and the acquisition of property and equipment. Common functions include vendor selection, requisitioning, purchasing, receiving, accounts payable, and payroll accounting.

This section discusses two important expenditure-cycle applications: purchasing and payroll. Cash disbursements and accounts payable are discussed in Chapter 8.

Purchasing

In some companies, all purchases of goods and services are channeled through and controlled by a centralized purchasing department. In others, the authority to place orders with vendors is dispersed throughout the company—a decentralized approach. Centralized purchasing may yield increased quantity discounts, a stronger market position, better inventory control, buyer specialization, and the like. Decentralized purchasing may yield similar benefits because of the increased responsibilities placed on the ultimate user. For example, decentralized buyers may have greater knowledge of the use and specifications of the desired goods and thereby maintain optimal inventory levels. As in any organizational decision, the choice is largely one of management style and philosophy.

A purchase application system includes five basic functions:

1. Someone outside the purchasing department determines that materials are needed; a requisition is prepared and approved.

2. Bids are requested, a vendor selected, and a purchase order issued by the purchasing department.

3. When the materials are received, a receiving report is prepared by the receiving department. In many cases, only a person with technical ability can adequately inspect the materials and give assurance to the requisitioning or using department. In unusual cases, it may be desirable to have the quality of materials received tested before payment is made. An inspection function may be established for this purpose, either as a part of the receiving department or as a separate department.

4. Details of the invoice submitted by the vendor are compared to the purchased order and to the receiving report. The invoice is checked for mathematical accuracy. If everything is in order, the invoice is approved for payment.

5. A check is prepared and sent to the vendor, and all the previous documents are canceled to avoid the possibility of duplicate payments.

Figure 7.9 illustrates a data flow diagram of a purchase application system. Figure 7.10 illustrates an analytic flowchart of the flow of transactions in a pur-

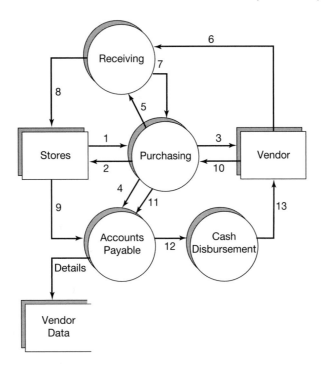

DATA FLOW KEY

1. Requisition	*8. Receiving Report*
2. Acknowledgment	*9. Notice of Receipt*
3. Purchase Order	*10. Invoice*
4. Purchase Advice	*11. Approved Invoice*
5. Receiving Advice	*12. Voucher Package*
6. Shipment	*13. Payment*
7. Receiving Advice	

FIGURE 7.9 Data Flow Diagram: Purchase Application System.

chasing application system. The main feature in each of these illustrations is the separation of the following functions.

Requisitioning (Stores)

Requests for purchases originate outside the purchasing department. In Figure 7.10, **purchasing requisitions** originate in the stores department. Purchase requisitions might also originate in other departments within the firm. Purchase requisitions should be approved in the originating department.

Purchasing

Regardless of where purchase requisitions originate, it is the function of the purchasing department to select a vendor and arrange for terms and delivery. How this is done will depend on the relative degree of centralization in the company's purchasing function. Purchasing may at times override a purchase requisition due to insufficient budget, lack of authorization, or some other reason. Purchase requisitions might also be altered or returned to the originating department for modification.

Purchasing selects a vendor, then prepares and distributes a **purchase order** (Figure 7.11) for the requisition. Copies are distributed to the vendor, accounts

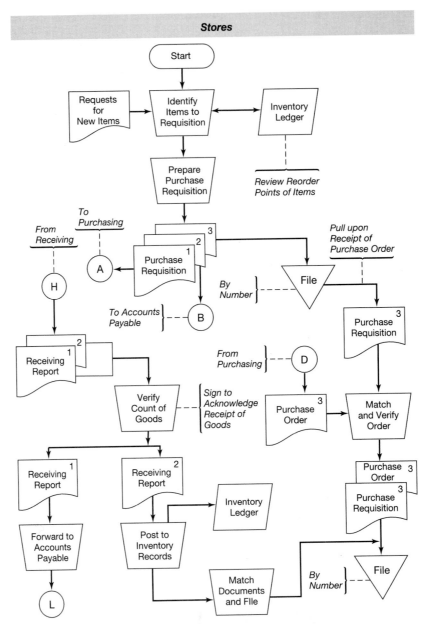

FIGURE 7.10 Purchase Application System.

payable, the originating/requesting department (stores), and receiving. As indicated in Figure 7.10, the vendor may return a copy of the purchase order to the customer to acknowledge receipt of the order. The copy of the purchase order that is sent to the originating/requesting department should be reviewed there to verify the appropriateness of the purchase order for satisfying the needs identified in the purchase requisition.

Receiving

Receiving is separate and independent of the stores function. The copy of the purchase order sent to receiving authorizes the receiving department to ac-

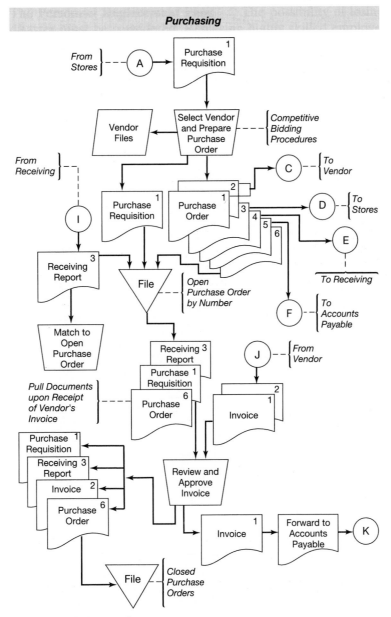

FIGURE 7.10 (*continued*)

cept the shipment from the vendor when it is delivered. Receiving procedures should call for an independent count of the shipment and for the preparation of a receiving report.

An independent or **blind count** of a shipment may be obtained by not allowing the counters to have access to the quantities shown on the purchase order. A supervisor compares the quantities received with those shown on the purchase order and then prepares a **receiving report** for the quantities received. A copy of the receiving report should accompany the transfer of goods to stores, as shown in Figure 7.10.

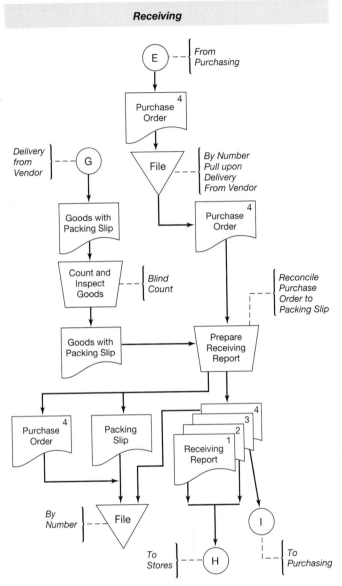

FIGURE 7.10 (continued)

Stores

The stores department acknowledges receipt of the goods from receiving by signing the receiving report and then forwarding the receiving report to accounts payable. If goods are delivered directly to the requisitioning department rather than to stores, a supervisor in the requesting department should acknowledge receipt on the receiving report and then send the receiving report to payables. This independent verification of receipt of the purchase is a central feature of the purchasing application system illustrated in Figure 7.10.

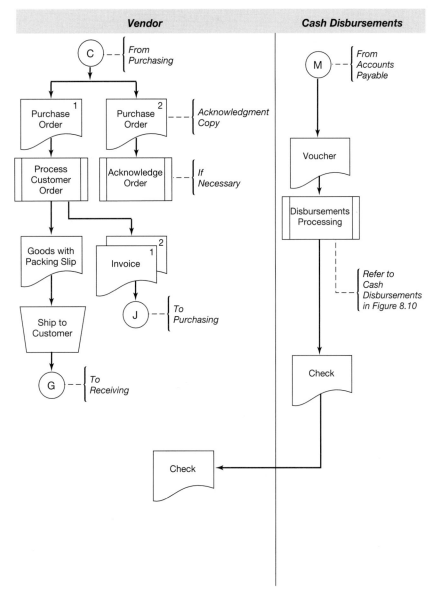

FIGURE 7.10 (*continued*)

Accounts Payable

Accounts payable is responsible for initiating payments to vendors. Four forms—purchase requisition, purchase order, receiving report, and invoice—are required to document a purchase transaction. A major control over purchasing activity is obtained through the use of a voucher system. A voucher system is essentially a review technique to ensure that all appropriate documentation is assembled, verified, and reviewed prior to actual payment. This review of documentation is called the **matching process** and assumes that documentation evidences the execution of the procedural steps illustrated in Figure 7.10.

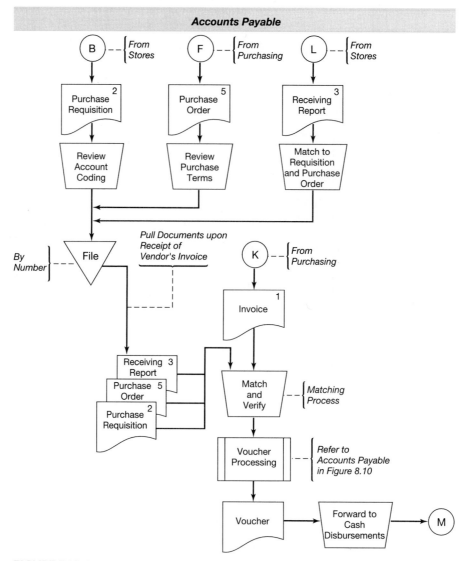

FIGURE 7.10 (*continued*)

Approved vouchers are forwarded to cash disbursements for payment. Voucher systems are discussed in detail in the discussion of the cash disbursements application system in Chapter 8.

Several other features to note in Figure 7.10 include the following:

- Purchasing does not control the actual goods nor does purchasing have complete control over the documentation that is required for payment.

- Receiving is separate from final custody of goods. Acknowledgment from both receiving and custody is required before payment is authorized.

- Accounts payable handles only documents and is not able to obtain merchandise or cash independently.

- Purchase requisitions should be independently reviewed outside of purchasing. This is done by accounts payable in Figure 7.10. This review could verify the accounting charges shown on the requisition and also ensures that requisitions do not originate in purchasing.

FROM:	DATE_____ 19____
	FOR _____
	HOW SHIP_____
	TERMS_____
	☐ TAXABLE ☐ RESALE — PERMIT No.
TO _____	SHIP TO _____
ADDRESS _____	ADDRESS _____
	DATE REQUIRED

QUANTITY	DESCRIPTION	UNIT PRICE	AMOUNT

IMPORTANT
PLEASE NOTIFY US IMMEDIATELY IF YOU ARE UNABLE TO SHIP
COMPLETE ORDER BY DATE SPECIFIED

PURCHASING AGENT

FIGURE 7.11 Purchase Order.

- Invoices should be routed to purchasing for review and approval prior to being sent to accounts payable. This is particularly important if purchasing expertise is necessary to evaluate the propriety of the invoice.
- Purchase terms should be reviewed for propriety outside the purchasing department. This is done by accounts payable in Figure 7.10.
- Inventory records should be updated to reflect the receipt of goods.

Integrity of the Purchasing Application System

Purchase documentation simply ensures that individual orders are received as expected. Purchase orders, receiving reports, and the like control individual purchases, but not the purchasing application itself. Control of the purchasing application centers on the integrity of the buyer–vendor relationship. Bribery, kickbacks, and conflicts of interest (such as buying from a relative or friend) are examples of improper buyer–vendor relationships that the purchase order application system must address. Buyer–vendor relationships are more a matter of policy than procedure. Most companies have found it desirable and often necessary to have formal written policy and procedure manuals covering the purchasing function. Purchasing policies may require competitive bidding, usually implemented through use of request-for-quotation forms.

Buyers must request competitive bids through **request-for-quotation** forms. Copies of these forms are filed and reviewed by purchasing management. Selecting the lowest-cost bid is not always an acceptable basis for selecting a vendor. Methods of evaluating and selecting bids based on vendor attributes (vendor rating plans) may be formalized, with decisions subject to review by a higher authority. A policy of rotating a buyer's responsibilities weakens buyer–vendor relationships but reduces possibilities for buyer specialization. **Approved vendor lists,** prepared by an independent function, may be used to restrict a buyer's options to those vendors who have been found reliable, financially sound, and free of conflicts of interest. These examples are not exhaustive, but they indicate the types of controls that may be used to ensure the integrity of purchasing personnel.

The Attribute Rating Approach to Vendor Selection

The **attribute rating** approach to vendor selection is appropriate whenever an objective evaluation of the opinions of several independent evaluators is desired: that is, an amalgamation of evaluations of the same system. The following steps are involved:

- Identify and list the attributes to be included in the evaluation.
- Assign a weight to each attribute, based on relative importance and objectivity.
- Have individual evaluators rank each vendor on each attribute, giving a numerical score on a range of 1 to 10 or some other scale.
- Total the individual evaluations by multiplying each attribute's numerical ranking by its weight; then total all evaluations by adding the scores together.

Given that the relevant costs, such as a vendor's prices or a system's cost, have been identified, a benefit–cost ratio can be computed for comparisons. Although this method appears to be objective, both assignment of weights and numerical ranking are very subjective processes. Accordingly, attribute evaluation techniques are most useful for screening proposals, and identifying those vendors or systems that should be subject to final considerations.

Payroll

A payroll/personnel system involves all phases of payroll processing and personnel reporting. The system provides a means of promptly and accurately paying employees, generating the necessary payroll reports, and supplying management with the required employee skills information. The processing should include a deduction for withholding taxes, specialized deductions, government reporting, and internal personnel requirements. An efficient system is necessary to establish and maintain good employer–employee relationships.

Payroll processing is extremely complex. In a large organization, it is often the most complex procedure in operation. This is because of the social significance payrolls have assumed over the last few decades. All levels of government impose payroll taxes of one sort or another; regulations and rates are constantly changed, with the result that a payroll system usually has a relatively short life. The strategy here is to provide an overview of a typical payroll procedure and discuss factors influencing the actual calculation of payroll. No attempt is made to provide current rates: tax laws are arbitrary and change quite rapidly. Payroll processing is one area in which the law imposes not only a fine but a jail sentence for willful negligence in maintaining adequate records. As with any law, ignorance is no excuse. The responsibility is on the systems analyst to keep current in this area.

Figure 7.12 illustrates a data flow's diagram of a payroll application system. Figure 7.13 illustrates a document flowchart of the flow of transactions in a payroll application system. The main feature in each of these illustrations is the separation of the following functions.

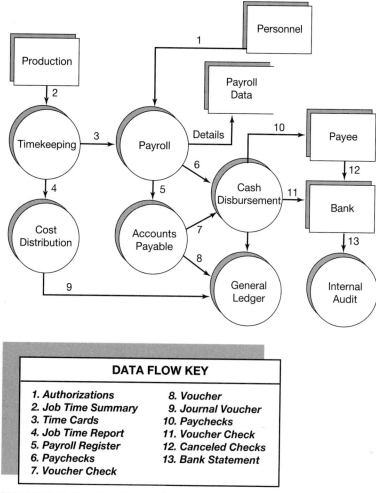

FIGURE 7.12 Data Flow Diagram: Payroll Application System.

Personnel

The personnel (employment) office is responsible for placing people on the company's payroll, specifying rates of pay, and authorizing all deductions from pay. All changes, such as adding or deleting employees, changing pay rates, or changing levels of deductions from pay, must be authorized by the personnel office. The personnel function is distinct from timekeeping and from the payroll preparation function.

Timekeeping

The timekeeping function is responsible for the preparation and control of time reports and job time tickets. In a manufacturing firm, an hourly employee typically clocks on and off of the job. At the end of a pay period, the employee's time card (or time report) indicates the amount of time that the employee was on the job and the time that he or she expects to receive pay for. Timekeeping is responsible for collecting and maintaining time cards or time reports, and reconcil-

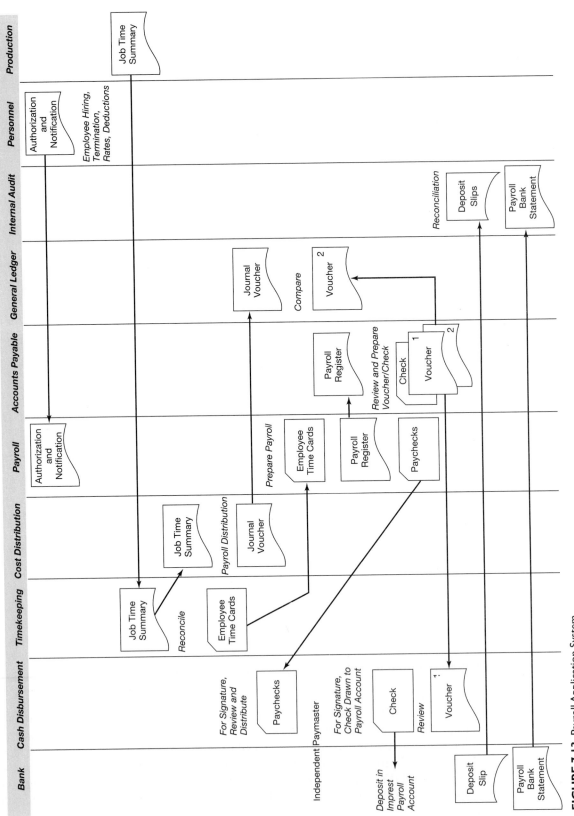

FIGURE 7.13 Payroll Application System.

ing these data to job time summary reports that are received from production. Job time summary reports indicate the jobs that employees were assigned to in production. Timekeeping reconciles time reports to the related job time summary report received from production and then forwards time cards to the payroll department.

Salaried employees typically do not clock on and off the job in the same manner as hourly employees. If no accounting for time is required, a supervisor's approval is usually required to initiate payroll processing. If salaried employees are required to submit time reports, the analogy to Figure 7.13 is straightforward.

Payroll

The payroll department is responsible for the actual computation and preparation of payroll. Note that preparing payroll is independent of the preparation of the input data on which pay is based, the time reports and personnel data. Personnel data are received from the personnel office; time reports are received from timekeeping. The payroll register details the computation of net pay (gross pay less deductions from pay). Paychecks are sent to cash disbursements for signature, review, and distribution. A copy of the payroll register is sent to accounts payable to initiate the recording of a voucher for the payroll.

Several other features to note in Figure 7.13 include the following:

- The use of a separate imprest payroll account for paychecks to facilitate reconciliations
- An independent reconciliation of the payroll account bank statement
- The use of an **independent paymaster.** The person who distributes the pay is independent of personnel, timekeeping, and payroll preparation. Neither the personnel office, the timekeeping department, nor the payroll department has access to the paychecks once they have been drawn.

Payroll Processing Requirements

Numerous files must be maintained in a payroll system. Basic employee information, such as name, address, rate of pay, and deductions, is necessary to prepare a payroll. A payroll register or journal must be maintained to document actual payments. Files pertaining to government reports, tax tables used in processing, pensions plans, hospitalization plans, and similar plans are examples of information required to support a payroll procedure.

Social security and other tax legislation impose four taxes based on payrolls:

1. Federal old-age, survivors', disability, and hospital insurance (F.I.C.A.)
2. Federal unemployment insurance
3. State unemployment insurance
4. Income taxes withheld

The Federal Insurance Contributions Act (F.I.C.A.) provides that employees contribute equally to funds for old age, survivors', disability, and hospital insurance benefits for certain individuals and members of their families. The contribution is based on a tax rate applied to gross wages.

The employer is required to deduct the amount of F.I.C.A. tax from each employee's pay each pay period. The employer is then required to match these deductions and deposit the entire amount in a government depository. A penalty is levied for failure, without reasonable cause, to make required deposits when due. Taxpayers who willfully claim credit on the record of federal tax deposits for deposits not made are subject to fine and/or other criminal penalties. The employer is responsible for the full amount of the tax even when he or she fails to withhold contributions from employees.

The Federal Social Security Act and the Federal Unemployment Tax Act provide for the establishment of unemployment insurance plans. Employers with covered workers employed in each of 20 weeks during a calendar years are affected. Payment to the federal government is required quarterly. Unemployment benefits are provided by the systems created by the individual states. Revenues of the federal government under the acts are used to meet the cost of administering state and federal unemployment plans as well as to provide supplemental unemployment benefits.

Unemployment compensation laws are not the same in all states, but all states participate in the federal–state unemployment insurance program. In most states, laws provide for taxes only on employers. The federal legislation applies to all employers of one or more employees. Tax payment is generally required on or before the last day of the month following each calendar quarter. Most states have a merit-rating plan that permits a reduction in the tax rate for employers who establish a record of stable employment.

Federal income taxes on wages of an individual are collected in the period in which the wages are paid. Our "pay-as-you-go" system requires employers to withhold a portion of the earnings of their employees. The amount withheld depends on the amount of the earnings and on the number of exemptions allowed the employee. A withholding exemption certificate must be prepared by each employee. The certificate states the number of exemptions to which the employee is entitled. This certificate is given to the employer so that she or he will be able to compute the proper amount of tax to be withheld.

Current regulations provide a graduated system of withholding designed to make the amount of tax withheld closely approximate the rates used in computing the individual's tax liability at the end of the year.

Employers engaged in interstate commerce are required by the Federal Fair Labor Standards Act (also known as the Wages and Hours Law) to pay overtime at a minimum rate of one and one-half times the regular rate for hours worked in excess of 40 per week. Many companies also pay overtime premium rates for night shifts and for work on Sundays and holidays.

Employers must take care to deduct payroll taxes from all employees. A distinction is drawn between employees and independent contractors. Public accountants, architects, attorneys, and other people who render services to a business for a fee but are not controlled or directed by the client are not employees but independent contractors, and the amounts paid to them are not subject to payroll taxes.

At the close of each quarter an employer is required to file a quarterly return of Form 941 or 941E and pay the balance of undeposited taxes. If the taxes were deposited in full, 10 additional days are allowed. This return covers income tax withheld and F.I.C.A. tax for all employees.

On or before January 31, each employer is required to give each employee a completed Form W-2 Wage and Tax Statement. The employer is required to forward a copy of these W-2 forms with a Form W-3 on or before February 28 to the government. Also on or before January 31, employers must file Form 940, Employer's Annual Federal Unemployment Tax Return.

The basic information about what the U.S. government requires with respect to payroll is outlined in the Department of Treasury Internal Revenues Service publication *Circular E Employers Tax Guide*. This publication contains all the lat-

TABLE 7-1 Sample Payroll Events Timetable

Date	Event
January 31	Form W-2 (Wage and Tax Statement) to be furnished to employees
January 31	Form 941 (Employer's Quarterly Federal Tax Return) due for 4th quarter of preceding calendar year
January 31	Form 1099-Misc. (U.S. Information Return for Recipients of Miscellaneous Income) to be furnished to consultants paid directly
February 28	Form W-3 (Transmittal of Wage and Tax Statements) due with Copy A of each Form W-2; Form 1096 (Transmittal) with each 1099-Misc.
February 28	Duplicate of Form 1096 due with State Copy of Form 1099-Misc.
March 15	File Form 1120 or 1120-S (Federal Corporate Income Tax Return for calendar year)
April 30	Form 941 due for 1st quarter
July 31	Form 941 due for 2nd quarter
October 31	Form 941 due for 3rd quarter

est information on new laws and detailed information for employers. It tells how to fill out all the forms and reports required, how to compute employment taxes, how and when to make deposits and payments, and lists the invaluable tax tables. If an employer does not have this publication or access to the information contained in it, she or he will sooner or later make an error in payroll procedure that will cost a penalty.

Table 7.1 contains a schedule of payroll-related deadlines that illustrates some of the processing and information that a typical payroll system must provide.

Other Expenditure-Cycle Application Systems

A large organization will have many specialized application subsystems in its expenditure cycle. Each of these subsystems processes data against files, uses forms and other documentation, and requires segregation of duties and other controls to ensure reliable operation. Examples of expenditure-cycle subsystems that are specialized in most organizations include the following:

Requisitioning	Monitors and consolidates user requests for purchases.
Vendor selection	Accepts, evaluates, selects, and reviews the firm's approved vendor list.
Receiving	Identifies goods received and conducts inspection procedures.
Project accounting	Oversees capital budgeting systems, major maintenance accounting, research and development accounting, and computer system project accounting.
Job requirements	Maintains an organized listing of all job positions available in a firm.
Employee profile	Maintains job and skill information on employees.
Fringe benefits administration	Maintains the required files to administer employee benefit plans.
Insurance and/or accident claims	Processes data relevant to such claims.

Each of these subsystems provides data relevant to the strategic and tactical management of the firm. The discussion of the purchasing and payroll application systems has been directed at basic internal control considerations. Such considerations must be included in any expenditure-cycle subsystem to ensure that data provided to upper-level management and outsiders are accurate and reliable.

SUMMARY

Sales order processing is a common revenue-cycle application system. A sales order application system comprises the procedures involved in accepting and shipping customer orders and in preparing invoices that describe products, services, and assessments. A model sales order application system includes a separation of the following functions: sales order processing, credit authorizations, custody of finished goods, shipping, billing, accounts receivable, and the general ledger.

Accounts receivable processing is another common revenue-cycle application system. An accounts receivable application system is conceptually straightforward. Debits and credits are posted to customer accounts; statements are periodically prepared and mailed to customers. A model accounts receivable application system includes a separation of the following functions: cash receipts, credit authorizations, billing, accounts receivable, and the general ledger. Procedures that handle sales returns and allowances and procedures used to write off accounts receivable require careful design and control.

Purchasing is a common expenditure-cycle application system. A purchasing application system comprises the procedures involved in vendor selection, requisitioning, purchasing, receiving, and authorizing payment to vendors. A model purchasing application system includes a separation of the following functions: requisitioning, purchasing, receiving, stores, accounts payable, and the general ledger. Adequate vendor selection procedures are an important factor in the overall integrity of a purchasing application system.

Payroll is another common expenditure-cycle application system. A payroll/personnel application system comprises the procedures involved in promptly and accurately paying employees, generating the necessary payroll reports, and supplying management with the required employee skills information. A model payroll/personnel application system includes a separation of the following functions: personnel (employment), timekeeping, payroll accounting, and the general ledger. An independent bank reconciliation is an important control in a payroll/personnel application system, as it is in any expenditure-cycle application system.

Glossary

approved vendor list: a list of vendors approved for use by the purchasing function.

attribute rating: an approach to vendor selection that identifies, lists, and evaluates several different aspects concerning a vendor.

balance-forward processing: a customer's remittances are applied against a customer's outstanding balance rather than against individual invoices.

bill: a synonym for invoice.

bill of lading: the invoice received from a carrier for shipments.

blanket order: a single order that calls for several shipments to the same customer over a specific time period.

blind count: counters in receiving do not have access to quantities shown on purchase orders.

complete prebilling: the complete invoice is prepared at the same time as the shipping order.

credit memorandum: a form used to document reductions to a customer's account due to sales returns or sales allowances.

cycle billing: the processing of accounts receivable is subdivided by alphabet or account number in order to distribute the preparation of statements over the working days of the month.

factoring: the selling of accounts receivable at a discount to a collection agency.

incomplete prebilling: the invoice is not completed until the goods are ready for shipment.

independent paymaster: the person who distributes pay is independent of the payroll preparation process.

invoice: the document that informs a customer of charges for goods or services rendered.

matching process: the review of purchasing documentation prior to authorizing payment to vendors.

open-item processing: a customer's remittances are applied against individual invoices rather than a customer's outstanding balance.

organizational independence: the separation of functions in the design of application systems.

partial billing: synonym for incomplete billing.

postbilling: the invoice is prepared or completed after shipment.

purchase order: form issued to a vendor to initiate a purchase.

purchase requisition: form used to document a request for a purchase.

receiving report: a form prepared to document the receipt of shipments from vendors.

request-for-quotation: forms used to request competitive bids from vendors.

sales order: a document prepared to initiate the shipment of goods to a customer.

separate order and billing: both a sales order and an invoice are used in a sales order application system.

shipping advice: documentation that is forwarded to the billing function to evidence a shipment to a customer.

Chapter Quiz

Answers to the chapter quiz appear on page 300.

1. Which of the following documents is used to post sales on account to customers in the accounts receivable ledger?
   (a) purchase orders
   (b) invoices
   (c) remittance advices
   (d) bills of lading

2. Which of the following departments should match shipping documents with open sales orders and prepare daily sales summaries?
   (a) billing
   (b) sales order
   (c) accounts receivable
   (d) shipping

3. In an incomplete prebilling sales order system, the invoice is
   (a) completed when payment is received from the customer.
   (b) completed when the goods have been shipped.
   (c) completed when the sales order is approved by the credit manager.
   (d) completed when the customer has acknowledged receipt of the shipment.

4. The billing function should normally report to which of the following?
   (a) controller
   (b) treasurer
   (c) director of internal auditing
   (d) vice president of sales

5. Which of the following departments should normally be responsible for the preparation and journalizing of credit memos upon the receipt of approved sales return memos to authorize a reduction in customer account balances because of returned goods?
   (a) receiving
   (b) accounts receivable
   (c) credit
   (d) billing

6. In a purchase application system, which of the following departments should normally be responsible for the preparation of purchase requisitions?
   (a) cash disbursements
   (b) purchasing
   (c) receiving
   (d) stores

7. In a purchase application system, which of the following departments should normally be responsible for the preparation of purchase orders?
   (a) cash disbursements
   (b) purchasing
   (c) accounts payable
   (d) stores

8. In order to provide accountability for purchasing, copies of purchase requisitions should be sent to
   (a) the vendor.
   (b) cash disbursements.
   (c) accounts payable.
   (d) receiving.

9. In a payroll application system, which of the following should be responsible for the preparation of the payroll register?
   (a) personnel department
   (b) payroll department
   (c) cash disbursements department
   (d) timekeeping department

10. In a payroll application system, which of the following should be responsible for the authorization of pay rates for employees?
    (a) personnel department
    (b) payroll department
    (c) cash disbursements department
    (d) timekeeping department

Review Problem

You have been engaged by the management of Alden, Inc. to review its internal control over the purchase, receipt, storage, and issue of raw materials. You have prepared the following comments that describe Alden's procedures.

Raw materials, which consist mainly of high-cost electronic components, are kept in a locked storeroom. Storeroom personnel include a supervisor and four clerks. All are well trained, competent, and adequately bonded. Raw materials are removed from the storeroom only upon written or oral authorization of one of the production foremen.

No perpetual inventory records are kept; hence, the storeroom clerks do not keep records of goods received or issued. To compensate for the lack of perpetual records, a physical inventory count is taken monthly by the storeroom clerks, who are well supervised. Appropriate procedures are followed in taking the inventory count.

After the physical count, the storeroom supervisor matches quantities counted against a predetermined reorder level. If the count for a given part is below the reorder level, the supervisor enters the part number on a materials requisition list and sends this list to the accounts payable clerk. The accounts payable clerk prepares a purchase order for a predetermined reorder quantity for each part and mails the purchase order to the vendor from whom the part was last purchased.

When ordered materials arrive at Alden, they are received by the storeroom clerks. The clerks count the merchandise and agree the counts to the shipper's bill of lading. All vendor's bills of lading are initialed, dated, and filed in the storeroom to serve as receiving reports.

Required
(a) Prepare a logical data flow diagram.
(b) Prepare an analytic flowchart.
(c) Describe the weaknesses in internal control and recommend improvements of Alden's procedures for the purchase, receipt, storage, and issue of raw materials.

(CPA adapted)

Solution to Review Problem

(a) See Figure 7.14.
(b) See Figure 7.14.
(c) As follows:

Weaknesses	*Recommended Improvements*
1. Raw materials may be removed from the storeroom upon oral authorization from one of the production foremen.	1. Raw materials should be removed from the storeroom only upon written authorization from an authorized production foreman. The authorization forms should be prenumbered and accounted for, with quantities and job or production numbers listed, and they should be signed and dated.
2. Alden's practice of monthly physical inventory counts does not compensate for the lack of a perpetual inventory. Quantities on hand at the end of one month may not be sufficient to the last until the next month's count. If the company has taken this into account in establishing reorder levels, then it is carrying too large an investment in inventory.	2. A perpetual inventory system should be established under the control of someone other than the storekeepers. The system should include quantities and values for each item of raw material. Total inventory value per the perpetual records should be compared to the general ledger at reasonable intervals. When physical counts are taken, they should be compared to the perpetual records. Where differences occur they should be investigated, and if the perpetual records are in error, they should be adjusted. Also, controls should be established over obsolescence of stored materials.
3. Raw materials are purchased at a predetermined reorder level and in predetermined quantities. Because production levels may often vary during the year, quantities ordered may be either too small or too great for the current production demands.	3. Requests for purchases of raw materials should come from the production department management and be based on production schedules and quantities on hand per the perpetual records.

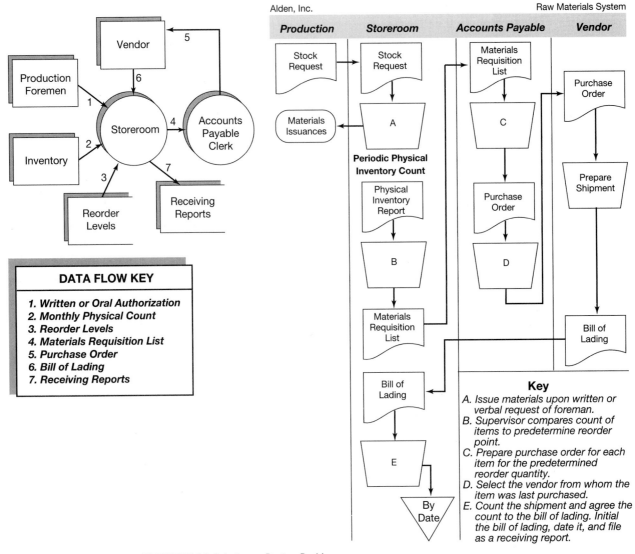

FIGURE 7.14 Solution to Review Problem.

4. The accounts payable clerk handles both the purchasing function and payment of invoices. This is not a satisfactory separation of duties.

4. The purchasing function should be centralized in a separate department. Prenumbered purchase orders should originate from and be controlled by this department. A copy of the purchase order should be sent to the accounting and receiving departments. Consideration should be given to whether the receiving copy should show quantities.

5. Raw materials are always purchased from the same vendor.

5. The purchasing department should be required to obtain competitive bids on all purchases over a specified amount.

6. There is no receiving department or receiving report. For proper separation of duties, the individuals responsible for receiving should be separate from the storeroom clerks.

6. A receiving department should be established. Personnel in this department should count or weigh all goods received and prepare a prenumbered receiving report. These reports should be signed,

7. There is no inspection department. Because high-cost electronic components are usually required to meet certain specifications, they should be tested for these requirements when received.

dated, and controlled. A copy should be sent to the accounting department, purchasing department, and storeroom.

7. An inspection department should be established to inspect goods as they are received. Prenumbered inspection reports should be prepared and accounted for. A copy of these reports should be sent to the accounting department.

Review Questions

1. What are several factors that make internal control an important consideration in the design of business procedures?
2. In what circumstances might a customer order require the use of a production order prior to a shipping order?
3. Distinguish between the billing and accounts receivable functions in a sales order procedure.
4. Briefly describe and contrast the following types of sales order procedures:
   (a) separate order and billing
   (b) incomplete prebilling
   (c) complete prebilling
5. What accounting journal entry or entries summarize the activities of a sales order procedure?
6. What is cycle billing? State two advantages of using cycle billing.
7. When is it desirable to use an acknowledgment copy of a sales order?
8. Outline the major features of internal control in a sales return and allowance procedure.
9. What functions are served by periodic statements of account?
10. Identify the two major aspects of a purchasing application system.
11. What accounting entry, if any, is necessitated by the issuance of a purchase order?
12. Define and indicate the purpose of the following forms:
   (a) requisition
   (b) purchase order
   (c) invoice
   (d) receiving report
13. What is the matching process?
14. Identify several controls directed at ensuring the integrity of the procurement function.
15. How might budgetary control be exercised over the purchasing function? Give specific examples.
16. What factors or qualifications might be considered in the implementation of an approved vendors' list?
17. What are the objectives of a payroll system?
18. What is the basic source of information concerning federal requirements with respect to payroll processing?
19. Identify the major controls in a payroll procedure.
20. Identify each of the following forms:
   (a) Form 941
   (b) Form W-2
   (c) Form W-3
   (d) Form 1099-Misc.
   (e) Earnings statement

Discussion Questions and Problems

21. The internal auditor is reviewing shipping procedures of a manufacturing company. The auditor should be greatly concerned when
    (a) merchandise is shipped without an approved customer's order.
    (b) invoiced prices on merchandise are not checked before orders are shipped.
    (c) the sales department is not promptly notified when merchandise is shipped.
    (d) only one quotation on transportation costs is obtained.
    (e) transportation tariffs are not checked before merchandise is shipped.
    (IIA)

22. Which of the following is an effective internal accounting control over accounts receivable?
    (a) Only people who handle cash receipts should be responsible for preparing documents that reduce accounts receivable balances.
    (b) Responsibility for approval of the write-off of uncollectable accounts receivable should be assigned to the cashier.
    (c) Balances in the subsidiary accounts receivable ledger should be reconciled to the general ledger control account once a year, preferably at year-end.
    (d) The billing function should be assigned to people other than those responsible for maintaining accounts receivable subsidiary records.
    (CPA)

23. Which of the following would be the *best* protection for a company that wishes to prevent the "lapping" of trade accounts receivable?
    (a) Segregate duties so that the bookkeeper in charge of the general ledger has *no* access to incoming mail.
    (b) Segregate duties so that *no* employee has access to both checks from customers and currency from daily cash receipts.
    (c) Have customers send payments directly to the company's depository bank.
    (d) Request that customers' payment checks be made payable to the company and addressed to the treasurer.
    (CPA)

24. Matching the supplier's invoice, the purchase order, and the receiving report normally should be the responsibility of the
    (a) warehouse receiving function.
    (b) purchasing function.
    (c) general-accounting function.
    (d) treasury function.
    (CPA)

25. To avoid potential errors and irregularities, a well-designed system of internal accounting control in the accounts payable area should include a separation of which of the following functions?
    (a) cash disbursements and vendor invoice verification
    (b) vendor invoice verification and merchandise ordering
    (c) physical handling of merchandise received and preparation of receiving reports
    (d) check signing and cancellation of payment documentation
    (CPA)

26. It would be appropriate for the payroll accounting department to be responsible for which of the following functions?
    (a) approving employee time records
    (b) maintaining records of employment, discharges, and pay increases
    (c) preparing periodic government reports as to employees' earnings and withholding taxes
    (d) temporarily retaining unclaimed employee paychecks
    (CPA)

27. Jackson, the purchasing agent of Judd Hardware Wholesalers, has a relative who owns a retail hardware store. Jackson arranged for hardware to be delivered by manufacturers to the retail store on a C.O.D. basis, thereby enabling this relative to buy at Judd's wholesale prices. Jackson was probably able to accomplish this because of Judd's poor internal control over
    (a) purchase orders.
    (b) purchase requisitions.
    (c) cash receipts.
    (d) perpetual inventory records.
    (CPA)

28. To determine whether the system of internal accounting control operated effectively to minimize errors of failure to invoice a shipment, the auditor would select a sample of transactions from the population represented by the
    (a) customer order file.
    (b) bill of lading file.
    (c) open invoice file.
    (d) sales invoice file.
    (CPA)

29. For effective internal accounting control, employees maintaining the accounts receivable subsidiary ledger should *not* also approve
    (a) employee overtime wages.
    (b) credit granted to customers.
    (c) write-offs of customer accounts.
    (d) cash disbursements.
    (CPA)

30. Which of the following departments should have the responsibility for authorizing payroll rate changes?
    (a) personnel
    (b) payroll
    (c) treasurer
    (d) timekeeping
    (CPA)

31. Which of the following control procedures may prevent the failure to bill customers for some shipments?
    (a) Each shipment should be supported by a prenumbered sales invoice that is accounted for.
    (b) Each sales order should be approved by authorized personnel.
    (c) Sales journal entries should be reconciled to daily sales summaries.
    (d) Each sales invoice should be supported by a shipping document.
    (CPA)

32. To achieve good internal accounting control, which department should perform the activities of matching shipping documents with sales orders and preparing daily sales summaries?
    (a) billing
    (b) shipping
    (c) credit
    (d) sales order
    (CPA)

33. Which of the following constitutes the most significant risk within the purchasing cycle?
    (a) Receiving department personnel sign receiving documents without inspecting or counting the goods.
    (b) Large quantities of relatively inexpensive parts are stored in open areas near workstations to reduce production slowdowns.

(c) Poor records of transfers between warehouses often result in unnecessary purchases and excess inventories.

(d) Warehouse personnel do not compare quantities received to quantities shown on transfer tickets.

(IIA)

34. Upon receipt of a requisition, the stores manager initiates a three-part purchase order. Two copies go to the vendor and one copy stays in the stores file. Upon receipt of goods, the stores manager matches the purchase order with the invoice and forwards them to accounts payable for payment. Which of the following statements best describes the internal control over purchasing?
    (a) Adequate internal control exists.
    (b) Inadequate separation of duties exists.
    (c) Inadequate control over accounts payable exists.
    (d) Inadequate control over the requisition process exists.

(IIA)

35. Shipping documents should be compared with sales records or invoices to
    (a) determine whether or not payments are properly applied to customer accounts.
    (b) assure that shipments are billed to customers.
    (c) determine whether or not unit prices billed are in accordance with sales contracts.
    (d) ascertain whether or not all sales are supported by shipping documents.

(IIA)

36. An appropriate compliance test to confirm that only valid employees are on the payroll is to ensure that
    (a) separate personnel folders are originated for each new employee.
    (b) payroll checks are delivered directly to each supervisor by the payroll clerk.
    (c) personnel places names on payroll only on the basis of written, prenumbered authorizations.
    (d) payroll bank accounts are reconciled monthly to appropriate personnel.

(IIA)

37. Which of the following would be the most appropriate test to determine whether purchase orders are being processed on a timely basis?
    (a) Determine the dates of unpaid accounts payable invoices.
    (b) Compare dates of selected purchase orders with those of purchase requisitions.
    (c) Select a block of used purchase order numbers and account for all numbers in the block.
    (d) Discuss processing procedures with operating personnel and observe actual processing of purchases.

(IIA)

38. As payments are received, one mailroom employee is assigned the responsibility of prelisting receipts and preparing the deposit slip prior to forwarding the receipts, deposit slip, and remittance advices to accounts receivable for posting. Accounts receivable personnel refoot the deposit slip, stamp a restrictive endorsement on the back of each check, and then forward the receipts and deposit slip to the treasury department. Evaluate the internal control of the described process. Which of the following is a reasonable assessment of internal control in this process?
    (a) Adequate internal control.
    (b) Inadequate internal control because mailroom employees should *not* have access to cash.
    (c) Inadequate internal control because treasury employees should prepare the deposit slip.
    (d) Inadequate internal control because of a lack of segregation of duties.

(IIA)

39. Which of the following procedures, noted by an auditor during a preliminary survey of the payroll function, indicates inadequate control?
    (a) All changes to payroll data are documented by the personnel department on authorized change forms.
    (b) Prior to distribution, payroll checks are verified to a computer-produced payroll register.
    (c) A separate payroll bank account is used and payroll checks are signed by the treasurer and distributed by personnel from the treasurer's office.
    (d) All unclaimed payroll checks are returned to the payroll clerk for disposition.

    (IIA)

40. Which of the following internal control procedures will *most* likely prevent the concealment of a cash shortage resulting from the improper write-off of a trade accounts receivable?
    (a) Write-offs must be approved by a responsible officer after review of credit department recommendations and supporting evidence.
    (b) Write-offs must be supported by an aging schedule showing that only receivables overdue several months have been written off.
    (c) Write-offs must be approved by the cashier who is in a position to know if the receivables have, in fact, been collected.
    (d) Write-offs must be authorized by company field sales employees who are in a position to determine the financial standing of the customers.

    (CPA)

41. For the purpose of proper accounting control, postdated checks remitted by customers should be
    (a) restrictively endorsed.
    (b) returned to the customer
    (c) recorded as a cash sale.
    (d) placed in the joint custody of two officers.

    (CPA)

42. Proper internal control over the cash payroll function would mandate which of the following?
    (a) The payroll clerk should fill the envelopes with cash and a computation of the net wages.
    (b) Unclaimed pay envelopes should be retained by the paymaster.
    (c) Each employee should be asked to sign a receipt.
    (d) A separate checking account for payroll should be maintained.

    (CPA)

43. A company policy should clearly indicate that defective merchandise returned by customers is to be delivered to the
    (a) sales clerk.
    (b) receiving clerk.
    (c) inventory control clerk.
    (d) accounts receivable clerk.

    (CPA)

44. A CPA reviews a client's payroll procedures. The CPA would consider internal control to be less than effective if a payroll department supervisor was assigned the responsibility for
    (a) reviewing and approving time reports for subordinate employees.
    (b) distributing payroll checks to employees.
    (c) hiring subordinate employees.
    (d) initiating requests for salary adjustments for subordinate employees.

    (CPA)

45. To conceal defalcations involving receivables, the auditor would expect an experienced bookkeeper to charge which of the following accounts?
    (a) miscellaneous income
    (b) petty cash
    (c) miscellaneous expense
    (d) sales returns

(CPA)

46. The most likely result of ineffective internal control policies and procedures in the revenue cycle is that
    (a) irregularities in recording transactions in the subsidiary accounts could result in a delay in goods shipped.
    (b) omission of shipping documents could go undetected, causing an understatement of inventory.
    (c) final authorization of credit memos by personnel in the sale department could permit an employee defalcation scheme.
    (d) fictitious transactions could be recorded, causing an understatement of revenues and overstatement of receivables.

(CPA)

47. Proper authorization procedures in the revenue cycle usually provide for the approval of bad-debt write-offs by an employee in which of the following departments?
    (a) treasurer
    (b) sales
    (c) billing
    (d) accounts receivable

(CPA)

48. Internal accounting control is strengthened when the quantity of merchandise ordered is omitted from the copy of the purchase order sent to the
    (a) department that initiated the requisition.
    (b) receiving department.
    (c) purchasing agent.
    (d) accounts payable department.

(CPA)

49. Which of the following controls would be most effective in assuring that recorded purchases are free of material errors?
    (a) The receiving department compares the quantity ordered on purchase orders with the quantity received on receiving reports.
    (b) Vendors' invoices are compared with purchase orders by an employee who is independent of the receiving department.
    (c) Receiving reports require the signature of the individual who authorized the purchase.
    (d) Purchase orders, receiving reports, and vendors' invoices are independently matched in preparing vouchers.

(CPA)

50. The purpose of segregating the duties of hiring personnel and distributing payroll checks is to separate the
    (a) administrative controls from the internal accounting controls.
    (b) human resources function from the controllership function.
    (c) operational responsibility from the record-keeping responsibility.
    (d) authorization of transactions from the custody of related assets.

(CPA)

51. When goods are received, the receiving clerk should match the goods with the
    (a) purchase order and the requisition form.
    (b) vendor's invoice and the receiving report.
    (c) vendor's shipping document and the purchase order.
    (d) receiving report and the vendor's shipping document.

(CPA)

52. Tracing bills of lading to sales invoices provides evidence that
    (a) shipments to customers were invoiced.
    (b) shipments to customers were recorded as sales.
    (c) recorded sales were shipped.
    (d) invoiced sales were shipped.

53. Effective internal control procedures over the payroll function may include
    (a) reconciliation of totals on job time tickets with job reports by employees responsible for those specific jobs.
    (b) verification of agreement of job time tickets with employee clock card hours by a payroll department employee.
    (c) preparation of payroll transaction journal entries by an employee who reports to the supervisor of the personnel department.
    (d) custody of rate authorization records by the supervisor of the payroll department.
    (CPA)

54. For internal control purposes, which of the following individuals should preferably be responsible for the distribution of payroll checks?
    (a) bookkeeper
    (b) payroll clerk
    (c) cashier
    (d) receptionist
    (CPA)

55. A sales clerk at Schackne Company correctly prepared a sale invoice for $5,200, but the invoice was entered as $2,500 in the sales journal and similarly posted to the general ledger and accounts receivable ledger. The customer remitted only $2,500, the amount on his/her monthly statement. The most effective procedure for preventing this type of error is to
    (a) use predetermined totals to control posting routines.
    (b) have an independent check of sales invoice serial numbers, prices, discounts, extensions, and footings.
    (c) have the bookkeeper prepare monthly statements that are verified and mailed by a responsible person other than the bookkeeper.
    (d) have a responsible person who is independent of the accounts receivable department promptly investigate unauthorized remittance deductions made by customers or others matters in dispute.
    (CPA)

56. For good internal control, the billing department should be under the direction of the
    (a) controller.
    (b) credit manager.
    (c) sale manager.
    (d) treasurer.
    (CPA)

57. The authority to accept incoming goods in receiving should be based on a(n)
    (a) vendor's invoice.
    (b) materials requisition.
    (c) bill of lading.
    (d) approved purchase order.
    (CPA)

58. Which of the following controls most likely would be effective in offsetting the tendency of sales personnel to maximize sales volume at the expense of high bad-debt write-offs?
    (a) Employees responsible for authorizing sales and bad-debt write-offs are denied access to cash.
    (b) Shipping documents and sales invoices are matched by an employee who does **not** have authority to write off bad debts.

(c) Employees involved in the credit-granting function are separated from the sales function.

(d) Subsidiary accounts receivable records are reconciled to the control account by an employee independent of the authorization of credit.

(CPA)

59. Which of the following controls most likely would help ensure that all credit sales transactions of an entity are recorded?

(a) The billing department supervisor sends copies of approved sales orders to the credit department for comparison to authorized credit limits and current customer account balances.

(b) The accounting department supervisor independently reconciles the accounts receivable subsidiary ledger to the accounts receivable control account monthly.

(c) The accounting department supervisor controls the mailing of monthly statements to customers and investigates any differences reported by customers.

(d) The billing department supervisor matches prenumbered shipping documents with entries in the sales journal.

(CPA)

60. Which of the following procedures most likely would be considered a weakness in an entity's internal controls over payroll?

(a) A voucher for the amount of the payroll is prepared in the general accounting department based on the payroll department's payroll summary?

(b) Payroll checks are prepared by the payroll department and signed by the treasurer.

(c) The employee who distributes payroll checks returns unclaimed payroll checks to the payroll department.

(d) The personnel department sends employees' termination notices to the payroll department.

(CPA)

61. Discuss the objectives of the following control procedures:

(a) purchasing policy manual

(b) approved vendors' list

(c) request-for-quotations form

(d) vendor rating plans (attribute evaluation)

(e) rotation of buyers

62. Identify the objective of distributing copies of a purchase order to the

(a) requisitioning department.

(b) receiving department.

(c) accounting department.

63. What are the differences between approving vendor invoices covering services rendered and those for physical goods sent to an organization? Illustrate with several examples.

64. You have completed an audit of activities within the purchasing department of your company. The department employs 30 buyers, seven supervisors, a manager, and clerical personnel. Purchases total about $500 million a year. Your audit disclosed the following conditions:

(a) The company has no formal rules on conflicts of interest. Your analysis produced evidence that one of the 30 buyers in the department owns a substantial interest in a major supplier and that she procures supplies averaging $50,000 a year from that supplier. The prices charged by the supplier are competitive.

(b) Buyers select proposed sources without submitting the lists of bidders for review. Your tests disclosed no evidence that higher costs were incurred as a result of that practice.

(c) Buyers who originate written requests for quotations from suppliers receive the suppliers' bids directly from the mailroom. In your test of 100 purchases based on competitive bids, you found that, in 75 of the 100 cases, the low bidders were awarded the purchase orders.

(d) Requests to purchase (requisitions) received in the purchasing department from other departments in the company must be signed by persons authorized to do so. Your examination of 200 such requests disclosed that three, all for small amounts, were not properly signed. The buyer who had issued all three orders honored the requests because he misunderstood the applicable procedure. The clerical personnel charged with reviewing such requests had given them to the buyer in error.

Required

For each of the four conditions, state

(a) the risk, if any, incurred if each condition described is permitted to continue.

(b) the control, if any, you would recommend to prevent continuation of the condition described.

(IIA)

65. The customer billing and collection functions of the Robinson Company, a small paint manufacturer, are attended to by a receptionist, an accounts receivable clerk, and a cashier who also serves as a secretary. The company's paint products are sold to wholesalers and retail stores.

The following describes *all* the procedures performed by the employees of the Robinson Company pertaining to customer billings and collections:

(a) The mail is opened by the receptionist, who gives the customers' purchase orders to the accounts receivable clerk. Fifteen to twenty orders are received each day. Under instructions to expedite the shipment of orders, the accounts receivable clerk at once prepares a five-copy sales invoice form, which is distributed as follows:

(1) Copy 1 is the customer billing copy and is held by the accounts receivable clerk until notice of shipment is received.

(2) Copy 2 is the accounts receivable department copy and is held for ultimate posting of the accounts receivable records.

(3) Copies 3 and 4 are sent to the shipping department.

(4) Copy 5 is sent to the storeroom as authority for release of the goods to the shipping department.

(b) After the paint order has been moved from the storeroom to the shipping department, the shipping department prepares the bill of lading and labels the cartons. Sales invoice copy 4 is inserted in the carton as a packing slip. After the trucker has picked up the shipment, the customer's copy of the bill of lading and copy 3, on which any undershipments are noted, are returned to the accounts receivable clerk. The company does not back order in the event of undershipments; customers are expected to reorder the merchandise. The Robinson Company's copy of the bill of lading is filed by the shipping department.

(c) When copy 3 and the customer's copy of the bill of lading are received by the accounts receivable clerk, copies 1 and 2 are completed by numbering them and inserting quantities shipped, unit prices, extensions, discounts, and totals. The accounts receivable clerk then mails copy 1 and the copy of the bill of lading to the customer. Copies 2 and 3 are stapled together.

(d) The individual accounts receivable ledger cards are posted by the accounts receivable clerk using a one-write system whereby the sales register is prepared as a carbon copy of the postings. Postings are made from copy 2, which is then filed, along with staple-attached copy 3, in numerical order. Monthly, the general ledger clerk summarizes the sales register for posting to the general ledger accounts.

(e) Because the Robinson Company is short of cash, the deposit of receipts is also expedited. The receptionist turns over all mail receipts and related correspondence to the accounts receivable clerk, who examines the checks and determines that the accompanying vouchers or correspondence contain enough detail to permit posting of the accounts. The accounts receivable clerk then endorses the checks and gives them to the cashier, who prepares the daily deposit. No currency is received in the mail, and no paint is sold over the counter at the factory.

(f) The accounts receivable clerk uses the vouchers or correspondence that accompanied the checks to post the accounts receivable ledger cards. The one-write system prepares a cash receipts register as a carbon copy of the postings. Monthly, the general ledger clerk summarizes the cash receipts register for posting to the general ledger accounts. The accounts receivable clerk also corresponds with customers about unauthorized deductions for discounts, freight or advertising allowances, returns, and so on, and prepares the appropriate credit memos. Disputed items of large amounts are turned over to the sales manager for settlement. Each month, the accounts receivable clerk prepares a trial balance of the open accounts receivable and compares the resultant total with the general ledger control account for accounts receivable.

Required
(a) Prepare a logical data flow diagram of the previous procedures.
(b) Discuss the internal control weaknesses in the Robinson Company's procedures related to customer billings and remittances and the accounting for these transactions. In your discussion, in addition to identifying the weaknesses, explain what could happen as a result of each weakness.

(CPA)

66. Antonia Cardini, CPA, prepared the flowchart in Figure 7.15, which portrays the raw materials purchasing function of one of Antonia's clients, a medium-sized manufacturing company, from preparing initial documents through vouching for invoices for payment in accounts payable. The flowchart was a portion of the work performed on the audit engagement to evaluate internal control.

Required
Identify and explain the systems and control weakness evident from the flowchart. Include the internal control weaknesses resulting from activities performed or not performed. All documents are prenumbered.

(CPA)

67. After a shipment is prepared, the shipping department prepares a shipping order form in three copies. The first copy is included with the goods sent to the customer as a packing slip. The second copy is forwarded to the billing department. The third copy is sent to the accountant. When the billing department receives the second copy of the shipping order, it uses the information thereon to prepare a two-part sales invoice. The second copy of the shipping order is then filed in the billing department. The first copy of the sales invoice is sent to the customer. The second copy of the sales invoice is forwarded to the accountant. Periodically, the accountant matches the copy of the shipping order with the copy of the sales invoice and files them alphabetically by customer name. Before doing so, however, the accountant uses the copy of the sales invoice to post the sales entry in the subsidiary accounts receivable ledger.

Requires
(a) For use in appraising internal control, prepare a flowchart covering the flow of documents reflected in the preceding situation.
(b) List those deficiencies and/or omissions revealed by the flowchart that lead you to question the internal control.

(IIA)

68. The Kowal Manufacturing Company employs about 50 production workers and has the following payroll procedures.

The factory foreman interviews applicants and on the basis of the interview either hires or rejects the applicants. When the applicant is hired, he or she prepares a

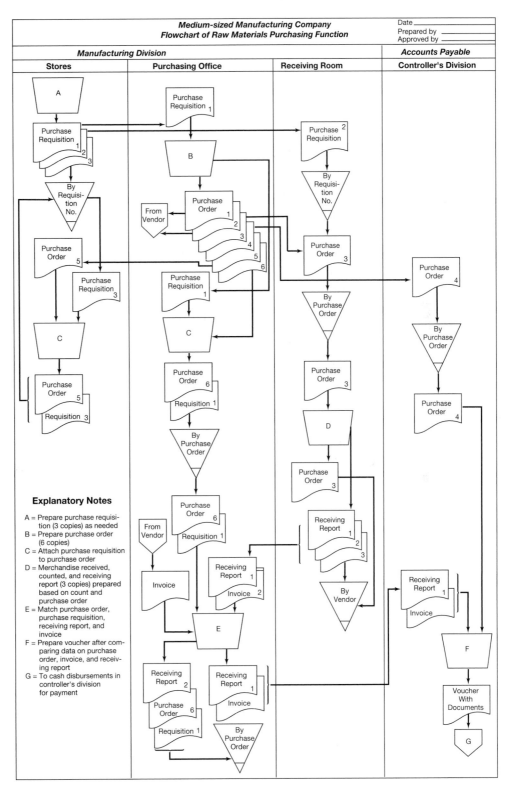

FIGURE 7.15 Flowchart for Problem 66.

W-4 form (Employee's Withholding Exemption Certificate) and gives it to the foreman. The foreman writes the hourly rate of pay for the new employee in the corner of the W-4 form and then gives the form to a payroll clerk as notice that the worker has been employed. The foreman verbally advises the payroll department of rate adjustments.

A supply of blank time cards is kept in a box near the entrance to the factory. Each worker takes a time card on Monday morning, fills in his or her name, and notes in pencil on the time card his or her daily arrival and departure times. At the end of the week, the workers drop the time cards in a box near the door to the factory.

The completed time cards are taken from the box on Monday morning by a payroll clerk. Two payroll clerks divide the cards alphabetically between them, one taking the A to L section of the payroll and the other taking the M to Z section. Each clerk is fully responsible for his or her section of the payroll. He or she computes the gross pay, deductions, and net pay, posts the details to the employee's earnings records, and prepares and numbers the payroll checks. Employees are automatically removed from the payroll when they fail to turn in a time card.

Payroll checks are manually signed by the chief accountant and given to the foreman. The foreman distributes the checks to the workers in the factory and arranges for the delivery of the checks to the workers who are absent. The payroll bank account is reconciled by the chief accountant, who also prepares the various quarterly and annual payroll tax reports.

Required
(a) Flowchart the preceding procedures.
(b) List your suggestions for improving the Kowal Manufacturing Company's system of internal control for the factory hiring practices and payroll procedures.

(CPA)

69. In a large manufacturing organization supplying goods and services, several departments may be involved in the processing of customer complaints and the issuance of any resulting credit memos. Following is a list of such departments:
(a) receiving
(b) sales
(c) production
(d) customer service
(e) accounts receivable

Required
Explain briefly the control function each department performs when processing complaints and issuing credit memos.

(IIA)

70. A CPA's audit working papers contain a narrative description of a segment of the Croyden Factory, Inc. payroll system and an accompanying flowchart as follows:

Narrative

The internal control system with respect to the personnel department is well-functioned and is *not* included in the accompanying flowchart.

At the beginning of each work week, payroll clerk no. 1 reviews the payroll department files to determine the employment status of factory employees and then prepares time cards and distributes them as each individual arrives at work. This payroll clerk, who is also responsible for custody of the signature stamp machine, verifies the identity of each payee before delivering signed checks to the foreman.

At the end of each work week, the foreman distributes payroll checks for the preceding work week. Concurrent with this activity, the foreman reviews the current week's employee time cards, notes the regular and overtime hours worked on a summary form, and initials the aforementioned time cards. The foreman then delivers all time cards and unclaimed payroll checks to payroll clerk no. 2.

Required

(a) Based on the narrative and Figure 7.16, what are the weaknesses in the system of internal control?

(b) Based on the narrative and Figure 7.16, what inquiries should be made with respect to clarifying the existence of *possible additional weaknesses* in the system of internal control?

(*Note:* Do not discuss the internal control system of the personnel department.)

(CPA)

71. Wooster Company is a beauty and barber supplies and equipment distributorship servicing a five-state area. Management generally has been pleased with the overall operations of the company to date. However, the present purchasing system has evolved through practice rather than having been formally designed. Consequently, it is inadequate and needs to be redesigned.

A description of the present purchasing system is as follows. Whenever the quantity of an item is low, the inventory supervisor phones the purchasing department with the item description and quantity to be ordered. A purchase order is prepared in duplicate in the purchasing department. The original is sent to the vendor, and a copy is retained in the purchasing department filed in numerical order. When the shipment arrives, the inventory supervisor sees that each item received is checked off on the packing slip that accompanies the shipment. The packing slip is then forwarded to the accounts payable department. When the invoice arrives, the packing slip is compared with the invoice in the accounts payable department. Once any differences between the packing slip and the invoice are reconciled, a check is drawn for the appropriate amount and is mailed to the vendor with a copy of the invoice. The packing slip is attached to the invoice and filed alphabetically in the paid invoice file.

Required

Wooster Company intends to redesign its purchasing system from the point in time when an item needs to be ordered until payment is made. The system should be designed to ensure that all of the proper controls are incorporated into the system.

(a) Identify the internally and externally generated documents that would be required to satisfy the minimum requirements of a basic system and indicate the number of copies of each document that would be needed.

(b) Explain how all of these documents should interrelate and flow among Wooster's various departments, including the final destination or file for each copy.

(CMA)

72. Beccan Company is a discount tire dealer that operates 25 retail stores in a metropolitan area. Both private-brand and name-brand tires are sold by Beccan. The company operates a centralized purchasing and warehousing facility and employs a perpetual inventory system. All purchases of tires and related supplies are placed through the company's central purchasing department to take advantage of quantity discounts. The tires and supplies are received at the central warehouse and distributed to the retail stores as needed. The perpetual inventory system at the central facility maintains current inventory records, designated reorder points, optimum order quantities, and continuous stocktakings for each type and size of tire and other related supplies.

The documents employed by Beccan in their inventory control system and their use follow:

Retail Stores Requisition

This document is submitted by the retail stores to the central warehouse whenever tires or supplies are needed at the stores. The shipping clerks in the warehouse department fill the orders from inventory and have them delivered to the stores.

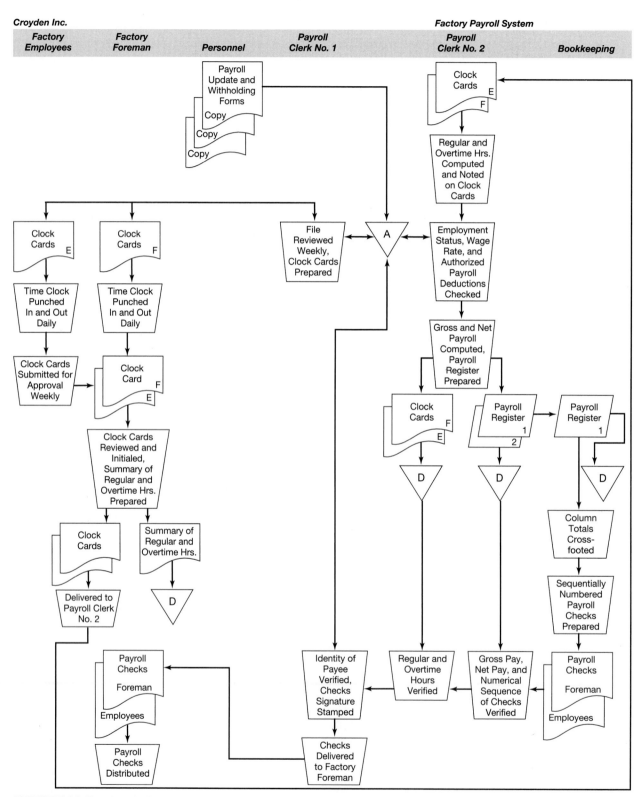

FIGURE 7.16 Flowchart for Problem 70.

Purchase Requisition

The inventory control clerk in the inventory control department prepares the document when the quantity on hand for an item falls below the designated reorder point. The document is forwarded to the purchasing department.

Purchase Order

The purchasing department prepares this document when items need to be ordered. The document is submitted to an authorized vendor.

Receiving Report

The warehouse department prepares this document when ordered items are received from vendors. The receiving clerk completes the document by indicating the vendor's name, the date the shipment is received, and the quantity of each item received.

Invoice

An invoice is received from vendors specifying the amounts owed by Beccan.

The departments involved in Beccan's inventory control system are as follows:

Inventory Control Department

This department is responsible for maintaining all perpetual inventory records for all items carried in inventory. This includes current quantity on hand, reorder point, optimum order quantity, and quantity on order for each item carried.

Warehouse Department

This department maintains the physical inventory of all items carried in inventory. All orders from vendors are received (receiving clerk) and all distributions to retail stores are filled (shipping clerks) in this department.

Purchasing Department

The purchasing department places all orders for items needed by the company.

Accounts Payable Department

Accounts payable maintains all open accounts with vendors and other creditors. All payments are processed in this department.

Required

Prepare a flow diagram to show how these documents should be coordinated and used among the departments at the central facility of Beccan Company to provide adequate internal control over the receipt, issuance, replenishment, and payment of tires and supplies. Assume that the documents have a sufficient number of copies to assure that the perpetual inventory system has the necessary basic internal controls.

(CMA)

73. The flowchart in Figure 7.17 depicts the activities relating to the shipping, billing, and collecting processes used by Smallco Lumber, Inc.

Required

Identify weaknesses in the system of internal accounting control relating to the activities of the
(a) warehouse clerk.
(b) bookkeeper no. 1.
(c) bookkeeper no. 2.
(d) collection clerk.

(CPA)

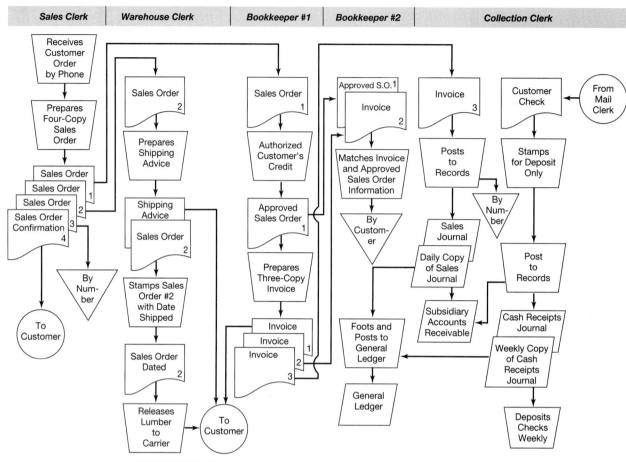

FIGURE 7.17 Flowchart for Problem 73.

CHAPTER 8

Production- and Finance-Cycle Applications

LEARNING OBJECTIVES

Careful study of this chapter will enable you to:

- Describe the major features of a production control system.

- Describe the major features of a property accounting application system.

- Describe the major features and controls in a cash receipts application system.

- Describe the major features and controls in a cash disbursements application system.

This chapter discusses accounting application systems found in an organization's production and finance cycles. The central feature of the illustrated applications is the segregation of duties to achieve organizational independence.

PRODUCTION-CYCLE APPLICATIONS

Production control, inventory control, cost accounting, and property accounting are typical functions in the production cycle of manufacturing firms. Few if any production-cycle activities exist as separate functions in nonmanufacturing firms, but to some extent, most organizations hold some inventories and manage some type of productive activity, such as selling goods or services. Thus, the principles of production control are relevant to most organizations.

This section provides an overview of the transaction flows necessary to support the functions of production control, inventory control, and cost accounting within a manufacturing firm. The discussion of production-cycle applications also includes an overview of the basic factors relevant to property accounting application systems.

Production Control

Cost accounting systems focus on the management of manufacturing inventories: materials, work-in-process (WIP), and finished goods. **Job costing** is a procedure in which costs are distributed to particular jobs or production orders. It requires a production order control system.

In **process costing,** costs are compiled in process or department accounts by periods (day, week, or month). At the end of each period, the cost of each process is divided by the units produced to determine the average cost per unit. Process costing is used where it is not possible or desirable to identify successive jobs or production lots. A classification of processes or departments may be set up for both cost distribution and production reporting purposes. This classification serves the purposes of process cost accounting and repetitive order production control. Costs in either job or process costing may be actual costs or predetermined (i.e., standard) costs.

Figure 8.1 is a data flow diagram of a production control application system. Figure 8.2 is a document flowchart of the transaction flows essential to a manufacturing company. Cost accounting systems encompass both production and inventory control; both are closely related to order-entry, billing, payroll, shipping, and purchasing procedures.

Internal control over inventories and production is based on separation of functions and basic records and documentation, such as production orders, material requisition forms, and labor time cards. Protection of inventories from physical theft involves security and access provisions as well as periodic physical counts and tests against independent records.

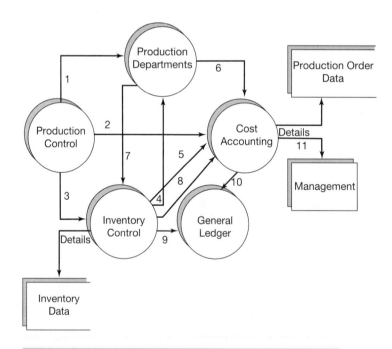

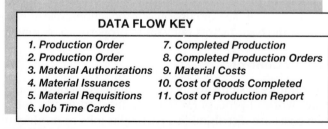

DATA FLOW KEY

1. Production Order	*7. Completed Production*
2. Production Order	*8. Completed Production Orders*
3. Material Authorizations	*9. Material Costs*
4. Material Issuances	*10. Cost of Goods Completed*
5. Material Requisitions	*11. Cost of Production Report*
6. Job Time Cards	

FIGURE 8.1 Data Flow Diagram: Production Control Application.

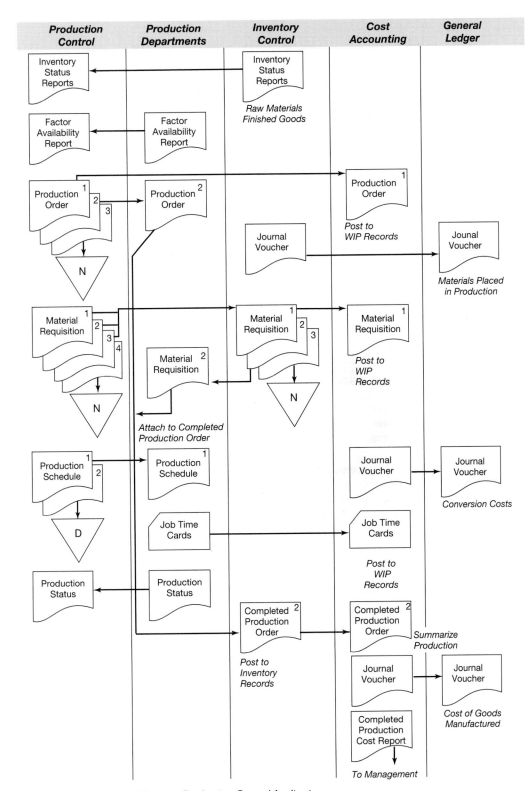

FIGURE 8.2 Transaction Flow in a Production Control Application.

Files and Reports

Production control involves planning which products to produce and scheduling production to make optimal use of resources. Basic production requirements are provided by the **bill of materials** and **master operations list.** Detailed material specifications for a product are recorded on the bill of materials. The bill of materials lists all required parts and their descriptions in subassembly order. The bill can be used as a ready reference for replacement parts, as an aid in troubleshooting subassemblies, or as a parts list for the end user. By distributing copies of bills to all affected departments, management can ensure uniform access to accurate, up-to-date information at every operational level. A master operations list is similar to a bill of materials. Detailed labor operations, their sequencing, and their related machine requirements are specified in the master operations list for a product. The bill of materials and the master operations list are used extensively in the production control function. In a standard cost system, the standard material and labor costs might be included on the bill of materials and master operations list.

Determining what products to manufacture requires an integration of the demand for a product, the product requirements, and the production resources available to the firm. Resources available for production are communicated to the production control function through **inventory status reports** and **factor availability reports.** A few material status report details the material resources in inventory that are available for production. A factor availability report communicates the availability of labor and machine resources. Demand requirements for a product depend on whether it is custom-manufactured per customer order or routinely manufactured for inventory. If the product is manufactured for inventory, production requirements depend on a sales forecast, which may be sent to production control from the sales or marketing department. Sales forecasts must be related to the amount of a product held in inventory. This information is provided in a finished goods status report, which lists the quantities of products in inventory. The integration of all these factors results in a production plan for the organization. The production plan is embodied in a production schedule and production order(s). These documents originate the flow of production data processing.

Transaction Flows

The **production order** serves as authorization for the production departments to make certain products. **Materials requisitions** are issued for each production order to authorize the inventory department to release materials to the production departments. The items and quantities shown on a materials requisition are determined from the specifications in the product's bill of materials. Note the flow of the materials requisition and production order in Figure 8.2. The cost accounting function receives a copy of the production order directly from production control and also from the production departments when the production order is complete. In similar fashion, cost accounting receives copies of materials requisitions from both the inventory control function and the production departments. This distribution of documents implements an adequate segregation of duties and provides accountability for the production departments.

Labor operations are recorded on **job time cards.** These cards are posted to production orders and forwarded to the cost accounting department. The periodic reconciliation of time cards to production labor reports is an important internal control function. This function was detailed in the discussion of payroll processing in Chapter 7.

Production status reports are periodically sent from the production department to the production control function. A production status report details the work completed on individual production orders as they move through the production process. It is used to monitor the status of open production orders and to revise the departmental production schedules as necessary.

The central document in the foregoing process is the production order. A copy of the production order is sent to the cost accounting function to establish a WIP record for each job.

Cost Accounting

The cost accounting department is responsible for maintaining a file of WIP cost records. New records are added to this file upon receipt of new production orders, initiated by production control. Materials costs are posted to this file from copies of materials requisitions. Direct labor costs are posted from job time tickets. Overhead costs are often applied on the basis of direct labor hours or direct labor costs and, therefore, are posted at the same time as labor costs. Cost accounting initiates a journal voucher reflecting each batch of job time tickets posted that contains a debit to WIP and credits to payroll and manufacturing overhead. This journal voucher is transmitted and posted to the general ledger.

As production orders are completed and goods are transferred to inventory, several documents must be updated. Production control removes the production order from its file of open production orders. Cost accounting closes the related WIP record, summarizes this activity, and communicates a completed production cost summary to various managers. The finished goods inventory records are updated to reflect the availability of the product.

Control of production efficiency requires comparisons of actual production with scheduled production and an analysis of related variances. Production control also requires a comparison and analysis of other factors, including budgeted cost versus actual cost for individual production orders and/or departments, and facility usage versus facility availability by department. The control of inventory loss and the maintenance of optimal inventory levels are also important to overall production control.

Inventory Control

The control of inventories is accomplished through a series of inventory records and reports that provide such information as inventory use, inventory balances, and minimum and maximum levels of stock. Reorder points and procedures are established. A **reorder point** is the level of inventory at which it is desirable to order or produce additional items to avoid an out-of-stock condition. The development of reorder points requires an analysis of product demand, ordering or production setup costs, vendor or production lead time, inventory holding costs, and the costs associated with an out-of-stock condition such as lost sales or inefficient use of production facilities.

Because inventory control aims at minimizing total inventory costs, an important decision to be made is the size of each purchase order quantity, that is, the most **economic order quantity (EOQ).** The reorder quantity must balance two systems costs—total carrying costs and total ordering costs. A formula for calculating the EOQ is

$$EOQ = \sqrt{\frac{2 \times R \times S}{P \times I}}$$

where

EOQ = economic order quantity (units)
R = requirements for the item this period (units)
S = purchasing cost per order
P = unit cost
I = inventory carrying cost per period, expressed as a percentage of the period inventory value

Once the EOQ has been calculated, the timing of the order must be decided; that is, the reorder point must be determined. If the order lead time and the inventory usage rate are known, determining the reorder point is straightforward. **Lead time** is the time between placing an order and the receipt of the goods. The **inventory usage rate** is the quantity of the goods used over a period of time. The reorder point should be where the inventory level reaches the number of units that would be consumed during the lead time. In a formula:

$$\text{Reorder point} = \text{lead time} \times \text{average inventory usage rate}$$

Perpetual inventory records are the best source of the inventory information necessary to calculate the EOQ. The units in the beginning inventory, on order, receipts, issues, and balance on hand, should be included in these records. Appropriate control over inventories requires periodic verification of items on hand. This can be done on a rotating basis when perpetual inventory records exist, or it can be done with a periodic physical count.

An important part of inventory control is the evaluation of inventory turnover to determine the age, condition, and status of stock. Special controls should be established to write down obsolete and slow-moving inventory items and to compare the balance to an appropriately established inventory level. A stock status report showing detailed use by period is especially helpful in maintaining the inventory at a proper level and controlling slow-moving items.

Control over inventory includes methods of storing and handling. Items need to be classified and properly identified so that they can be located appropriately and so that proper verification and reporting are possible. The storage and handling of items must provide security against embezzlement, protection against damage or spoilage, avoidance of obsolescence, and assurance of proper control.

Inventory is a substantial investment. An inventory control system should provide status reports on each active product so that the company can reasonably meet customer demands. Because of the large number of inventory items and the variety of transactions affecting them, it is difficult to keep inventory and production information up-to-date with manual systems. A computerized inventory control system can result in a substantial reduction in inventory investment. These savings include a reduction in inventory without a corresponding decrease in service, determination of economic order quantities and order points, establishment of adequate safety stocks, and forecasts of future demand based on current and past information. Usage records, turnover and obsolescence analyses, reorder points and quantities, and other statistics relevant to inventory control are difficult to generate in purely manual systems.

Just-in-Time (JIT) Production

Just-in-time (JIT) production is a term used to describe a production system in which parts are produced only as they are required in subsequent operations. JIT systems differ from conventional production systems in that inventories of work-

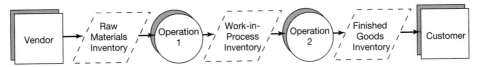

FIGURE 8.3 Just-in-Time (JIT) Production.

in-process, raw materials, and finished goods are minimized or totally eliminated. The JIT concept is illustrated in Figure 8.3. The raw materials inventory, work-in-process inventory, and finished goods inventory are shown within dashed-line boxes to indicate that they are eliminated to the extent possible in JIT production. The terms **minimum inventory production system (MIPS), material as needed (MAN),** and **zero inventory production system (ZIPS)** also describe this concept of minimizing inventories.

Inventories serve as a buffer between different operations. Inventories are eliminated by carefully analyzing operations to yield a constant production rate that will balance input and output at the various stages of production. JIT production also emphasizes quality control. Because inventories are minimized, defective production has to be corrected immediately if the constant flow of production is to be sustained. Vendors guarantee timely delivery of defect-free parts that may be placed immediately into production rather than first being placed into raw materials inventory.

The financial benefits of JIT production stem primarily from the overall reduction in inventory levels. This reduces a firm's total investment in inventories. Costs such as handling and storing materials, obsolescence, storage space, and financing charges on total inventory cost are reduced, perhaps significantly. Other benefits include possible lower labor costs as operations are redesigned for constant-flow production, quantity discounts from vendors who in return receive long-term contracts, and increased emphasis on quality production and the corresponding reduction in the cost of waste and spoilage.

Property Accounting Applications

Property accounting applications concern an organization's fixed assets and investments. An important element of effective internal control is the accurate and timely processing of information relating to fixed assets and investments. Such processing is accomplished through the use of special accounting applications that provide for accounting, operational, and management information needs (see Figure 8.4).

Fixed Assets

There are four objectives of fixed asset of investment accounting applications:

1. Maintain adequate records that identify assets with description, cost, and physical location.
2. Provide for appropriate depreciation and/or amortization calculations for book and tax purposes.
3. Provide for reevaluation for insurance and replacement cost purposes.
4. Provide management with reports for planning and controlling the individual asset items.

Fixed assets are tangible properties such as land, buildings, machinery, equipment, and furniture that are used in the normal conduct of a business. These

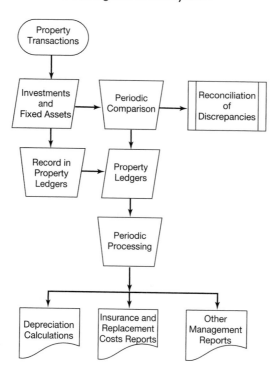

FIGURE 8.4 Property Accounting Application System.

items are relatively permanent and often represent a company's largest investment. Transactions that change the amount of investment in fixed assets tend to occur infrequently and usually involve relatively large amounts of money.

A company accumulates many assets over the life of the business, disposes of assets (by retirement, sale, or other means), moves assets from one location to another, and matches the costs (other than land) to revenues by means of periodic depreciation charges over the estimated useful life of the asset. To accomplish these tasks efficiently and to provide adequate control, an automated system is frequently required.

Every organization, including those on a cash basis, should keep a ledger of fixed assets as an aid to effective control. A **fixed-asset register** is a systematic listing of an organization's fixed assets. A separate section of the fixed-asset register is usually kept for each major category of asset. This categorization should be consistent with the general ledger account descriptions. For example, an organization may have separate ledger accounts for buildings, furniture and fixtures, and automobiles. There would be a separate section for each of these categories. Assets themselves should be labeled with identifiers linked to the fixed-asset register.

When each asset is acquired, it should be tagged and entered in the fixed-asset register. The total dollar amount shown in the register should agree with the general ledger control accounts. For this reason, entries must be made in the fixed-asset register not only to record additions but also to record asset sales or other dispositions.

Several entries must be made when an asset is disposed of. The first records the date of disposal. The second entry removes the original cost of the asset in the current period. A third entry removes the accumulated depreciation taken to date. A fixed-asset register functions as a subsidiary ledger to the corresponding general ledger control accounts.

Investments

Investments, like fixed assets, require separate records; typically, an investment register is used to provide accounting control over investments. As with all other assets, custody of investments should be separate and distinct from record keeping. The **investment register** should contain all relevant information, such as certificate numbers and the par value of securities, to facilitate identification and control. All investment transactions should be duly authorized and documented. A common control practice with respect to the physical handling of investment securities is to require two people to be present when the firm's safe deposit box or other depository is entered.

Internal Accounting Control Practices

The following questions suggest the internal accounting control procedures that would be expected in a property application system.

A. Do procedures require authorization by an official or committee for expenditures (possibly over certain amounts) for
   1. capital assets?
   2. repairs and maintenance?

B. Are actual expenditures compared to budgets and additional approvals required if budget authorization is exceeded?

C. Do written procedures exist that provide for distinguishing between capital additions and repair and maintenance?

D. Do procedures require formal authorization for the sale, retirement, or scrapping of capital assets?

E. Are property and equipment accounts supported by adequate detailed records?

F. Are these records maintained by people other than those who are responsible for the property?

G. Are the detailed records balanced at least annually with the general ledger controls?

H. Are physical inventories of property taken periodically under the supervision of employees who are not responsible for the custody or recording of such properties?

I. Are periodic appraisals of property made for insurance purposes?

J. Are significant discrepancies between book records and physical inventories reported to management?

K. With regard to small tools:
   1. Are these physically safeguarded and is responsibility for them clearly defined?
   2. Are they issued only upon written authorization?

FINANCE-CYCLE APPLICATIONS

Finance-cycle applications concern the acquisition and use of capital funds. Capital funds include working capital (cash and other liquid resources) as well as long-term funds such as bonds, investments, and capital stock. This section discusses cash receipt and cash disbursement applications because these applications are common to all organizations.

Cash Receipts: Basic Considerations

Cash, the most liquid of all assets, has historically been subject to rigid controls. Cash includes currency and negotiable papers such as checks. In most businesses, checks constitute the bulk of cash volume. Cash transactions may be totally electronic, involving neither currency nor checks.

The basic objective in any cash receipt application is to minimize exposure to loss. Procedures such as immediate deposit of receipts intact, centralization of cash handling, maintenance of minimal cash balances, and immediate recording of cash transactions are fundamental control techniques. Physical safeguards such as cash registers, vaults, immediate endorsement of checks, and limited access to cash areas are generally necessary as well.

The most critical phase of cash receipts is the initial documentation evidencing a receipt. Once a record has been prepared, cash is subject to accounting control. Prior to this record, misappropriations are not easily discovered. Consider a cash sale in a retail store. What guarantees are there that this sale will be recorded? It is possible that the clerk simply pockets the cash and releases the goods to the customer. The transaction is never recorded. Inventory analysis may uncover a cash shortage at some later point; however, this is not direct evidence of misappropriation.

Several techniques and devices are useful in establishing an initial record. **Customer audit** is a general term used to describe procedures in which the customer acts as a control over the initial documentation of a transaction. Pricing items at 99 cents rather than $1.00 is a customer audit technique as well as a marketing technique. This forces the recording of a sale, because the customer generally expects change. Techniques relating to sales invoices, such as awarding a customer a free gallon of ice cream if his or her receipt has a red star or other symbol, are intended to have the customer audit the recording of the sale. The possibility of receiving a prize increases the customer's interest in the invoice. Many cash registers sound a bell or buzzer when opened; it is hoped that the customer's attention is drawn to the amount actually being rung on the register. Sending monthly statements of account (to have the customer audit his or her own account) and providing customers with remittance advices (which they should return with their payments) are common examples of customer audit techniques.

Supervision includes direct supervision over clerical work, as in a mailroom where cash receipts are opened. It also includes the use of **professional shoppers,** people hired to purchase goods in a retail environment for the expressed purpose of observing the recording of transactions. Supervision also includes the use of test packages. For example, a precounted amount of cash may be given to a teller or cash counter (with or without that person's knowledge) to ascertain the validity of error rate of the person's work.

Imprest techniques are used to control cash receipts in the same manner (but usually with less accuracy) that they are used to control petty cash disbursements. A clerk is given a precounted number of tickets and must account for either their retail value or the tickets themselves. Retail jobbers must account for the retail value of goods in their possession. Inventory control over sales (gross profit or retail sales analysis) is essentially an imprest technique. Although such controls cannot be effective enough to remove possibilities of manipulation completely, they can limit the size of potential defalcations.

Figure 8.5 illustrates a data flow diagram of a cash receipts application system. The chart includes both cash sales and customer remittances sent on account. The major features of the system are the separation of functions and the generation of initial documentation. Separation of functions ensures that no one person has complete control over a cash receipts transaction. The generation of initial

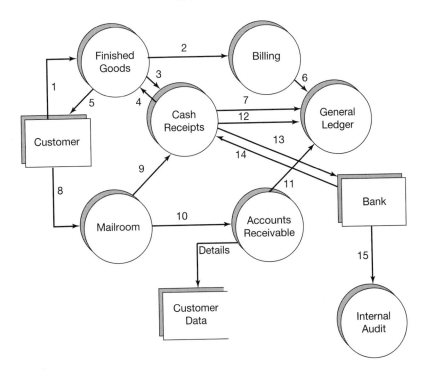

DATA FLOW KEY

1. Cash Sale
2. Sales Slip
3. Sales Slip
4. Sales Receipt
5. Goods Released
6. Journal Voucher
7. Control Total-Cash Sales
8. Mail Receipts
9. Checks
10. Remittance Advices
11. Control Total-Mail Receipts
12. Journal Voucher
13. Deposit
14. Deposit Slip
15. Bank Statement

FIGURE 8.5 Data Flow Diagram: Cash Receipts Application System.

documentation is controlled by supervision or one of the other methods previously discussed.

Cash-Received-on-Account Application System

A cash-received-on-account system is used when there is an established customer account balance. Cash received on account typically comes into a business through the mail or is paid in person to a central cashier or cash window. In either instance the customer should have the payment acknowledged. He or she should receive a receipt and a monthly statement showing amounts paid. This customer audit is a significant control in a cash-received-on-account application system. The recorded receivable that exists on the books prior to payment enhances control over payments received. In the event that a customer's payment is not acknowledged on his or her next statement, the customer will likely notify the company and inquire as to the reason.

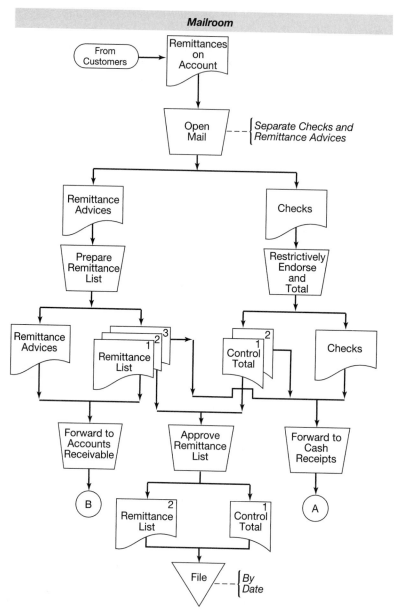

FIGURE 8.6 Cash-Received-on-Account Application System (*continued on pages* *313–315*).

Figure 8.6 is an analytic flowchart of a cash-received-on-account application system. The major feature of the system is the separation of the following functions.

Mailroom

Customer remittances on account are received in the mailroom. The mail is opened and the checks and remittance advices are separated. Checks are restrictively endorsed and totaled. A **remittance list** that documents the payments received is prepared. The remittance list is balanced to the total of the checks received, and the agreement of these amounts is approved. A copy of the remit-

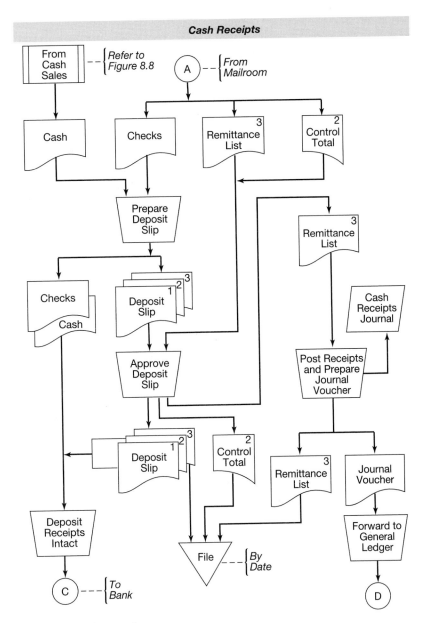

FIGURE 8.6 (*continued*)

tance list and the remittance advices are forwarded to accounts receivable. The checks and a control total are forwarded to cash receipts for deposit. A copy of the remittance list and the control total are filed by date.

Cash Receipts

Checks received from the mailroom are combined with cash receipts, and a deposit slip is prepared in three copies. The remittance list and control total received from the mailroom are balanced to the deposit slip, and the agreement of these amounts is approved. The remittance list is then used to post the amount of the payments received from the mailroom into the cash receipts journal. A journal voucher is prepared and forwarded to the general ledger. The remittance list,

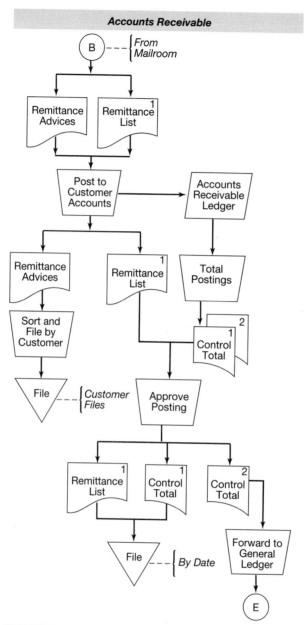

FIGURE 8.6 (continued)

control total, and a copy of the deposit slip are filed by date. The deposit is forwarded intact to the bank.

Accounts Receivable

The remittance advices are posted to the accounts receivable ledger. The postings to the ledger are totaled. The control total is balanced to the remittance list. The agreement of these amounts is approved. The remittance advices are sorted and filed by customer. The remittance list and a copy of the control total of postings are filed by date. A copy of the control total is forwarded to the general ledger.

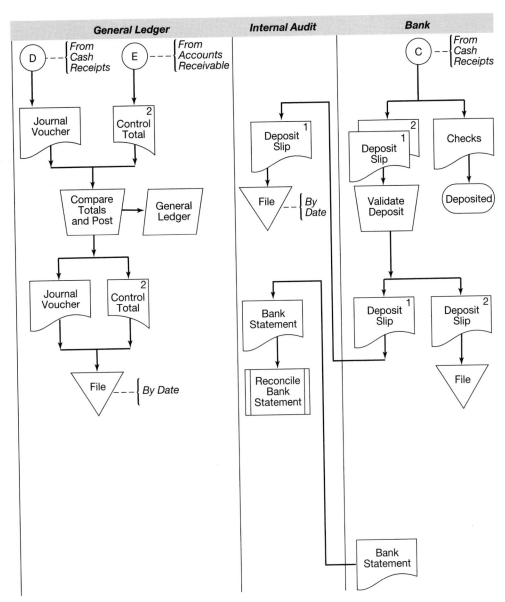

FIGURE 8.6 (continued)

General Ledger

The journal voucher from cash receipts and the control total received from accounts receivable are compared. The amounts are then posted to the general ledger. The source of posting the general ledger is the cashier's journal voucher notification of the amount of the deposit of the payments received. This amount must agree with the total of items posted to the accounts receivable ledger. The journal voucher and the control total are filed by date.

Bank

The bank accepts the deposit and validates a copy of the deposit slip. The validated copy of the deposit slip is returned to internal audit. The validated deposit slip is filed by date.

Internal Audit

Internal audit receives the periodic bank statement. An independent bank reconciliation is a significant control in a cash-received-on-account application system.

To control incoming cash received through the mail, it is important that no one in the mailroom (where the correspondence is opened), in the cashier's office (where the money is summarized and a deposit prepared), or in the accounts receivable section (where the asset reduction is recorded) has complete control over the transaction. In many systems, the invoice or statement that is sent to a customer is prepared in such a way that the portion with the name and address of the customer is returned with the payment. This is common with telephone, utility, and department store invoices, and provides good documentation for the payment (Figure 8.7).

The source of posting the general ledger is the journal voucher notification issued by the cashier indicating the amount of the deposit of cash receipts. This amount must agree with the accumulated total of the items posted to the subsidiary receivable file. Validated copies of the deposit slip go to the internal auditor, who uses them when reconciling the bank account. The control of actual cash (as opposed to checks) received by mail relies largely on direct supervision.

Lock-Box Collection Systems

In collecting accounts receivable, time is money. Even if a firm cannot persuade its customers to pay their accounts more rapidly, using a **lock-box deposit system** can usually reduce **float**—the time between the signing of the payment check by the customer and the moment the firm has use of the funds. A lock-box system reduces the float that usually occurs because the bank does not allow the firm to have use of out-of-state checks until they have been cleared through the customer's bank. This process can take up to a week. A lock-box system reduces the float by having the checks deposited to a firm's account before the firm processes them. A firm in Los Angeles might have its eastern U.S. customers forward their payments to a lock-box in a post office in New York City and arrange with a New

---

Circle Utility Company

NOV 28, 1999   123 _____ _____

PLEASE MAIL THIS ADVICE WITH YOUR PAYMENT
BRING ENTIRE BILL FOR RECEIPT IF PAYING IN PERSON   _____

CUSTOMER NAME

CUSTOMER ADDRESS

CIRCLE UTILITY COMPANY
BOX 1000
ANYWHERE, USA

MAKE CHECKS PAYABLE TO "CIRCLE UTILITY"   402517000005476

TOTAL AMOUNT DUE   54.76

FIGURE 8.7 Remittance Advice.

York City bank to pick up these checks, credit them to the firm's account, and advise the firm as to the names of customers, check amounts, and other payment details. Payments can then be processed after the checks are on their way through the clearing process. Savings of lost interest can be considerable, especially when interest rates are high. A bank will usually require a fee plus a compensating deposit—one on which the firm cannot draw—to provide lock-box services. But the value of net funds freed by float reduction and additional benefits, such as learning of dishonored checks sooner, will generally justify one or more lock-box regional collection systems for a firm whose customers are geographically widespread. An illustrative calculation follows assuming average daily collections of $500,000, seven days' float without a regional lock-box, and two days' float in a regional lock-box collection system.

Float in central system	$3,500,000
Less: Float in regional system	$1,000,000
Gross funds freed	$2,500,000
Less: Required compensating balance	$ 500,000
Net funds freed	$2,000,000

$$\text{Fees and expenses} = \$150,000$$

$$\text{Cost of net funds freed} = \frac{\$150,000}{\$2,000,000} = 7.5\%$$

Cash Sales Application System

The significant difference between a cash sales application system and a cash-received-on-account application system is that there is no previous asset record (customer account balance) in a cash sales system. The generation of initial documentation is thus the focal point of the control system. Once a record has been prepared, cash sales are subject to accounting control. Figure 8.8 is an analytic flowchart of a cash sales application system. The major feature of this system is the separation of the following functions:

Finished Goods

The finished goods department has custody of the assets that are available for sale to customers. Sales to customers are documented on **sales orders.** A sales order indicates the amount due for the purchase as well as the inventory control numbers of the items being sold.

Cash Receipts

The customer takes a copy of the sales order to cash receipts. The cash receipts department records the sale in a cash register or other secure device, accepts the customer's payment, and issues a sales receipt (two copies) to the customer. The sales order is filed by number. At the end of the day, the daily cash summary is generated and includes a control total of the day's cash sales. One copy of this total is forwarded to the general ledger; the other copy is filed by date.

Billing

Sales orders are reviewed by reasonableness and posted to the sales journal. Any inventory control information contained on sales orders could be processed at this point. A journal voucher is prepared to summarize cash sales. The sales orders are filed by date. The journal voucher is forwarded to general ledger.

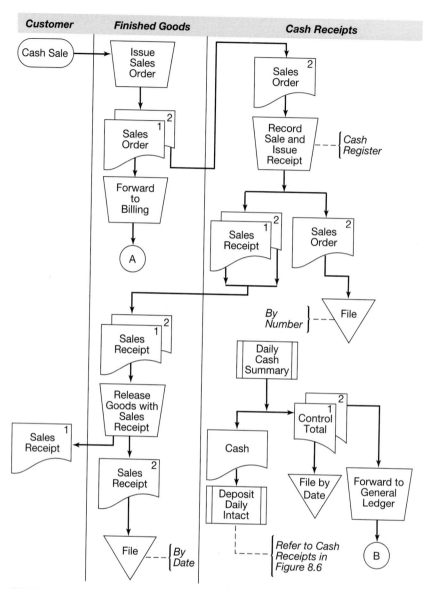

FIGURE 8.8 Cash Sales Application System (*continued on page 319*). (*continued on page 319*)

General Ledger

The journal voucher from the billing department and the control total received from the cash receipts department are compared. The amounts are then posted to the general ledger. Note that the source of posting the general ledger is the journal voucher notification by billing indicating the amount of sales orders received. This amount must agree with the total of the cash received from customers by cash receipts. Goods are not released by finished goods until the customer returns from the cash receipts department with a sales receipt. The goods are released with the sales receipt. A copy of the sales receipt is filed in the finished goods department.

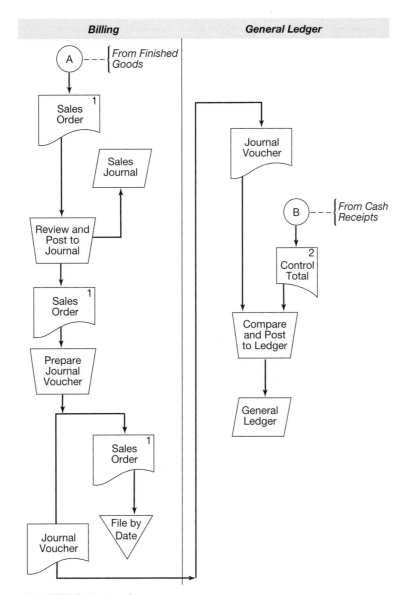

FIGURE 8.8 (continued)

Cash Disbursements Application System

Figure 8.9 illustrates a data flow diagram of a cash disbursements application system. Cash disbursement systems are designed to control check disbursements as well as actual cash disbursement. Typically, checks are used for the majority of disbursements, with currency disbursements restricted to small amounts drawn from and accountable to a petty cash imprest fund. The main concern of this section is with check disbursements; imprest funds will be discussed briefly but not illustrated.

The imprest fund concept is not restricted to petty cash control; imprest payroll funds and imprest charge or expense funds are common in systems design. An

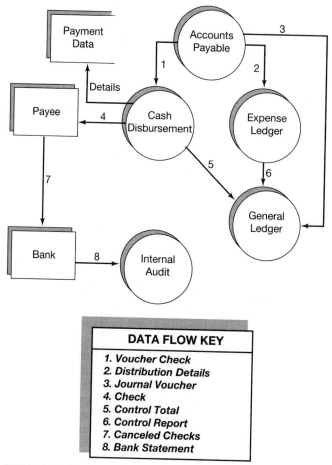

DATA FLOW KEY

1. *Voucher Check*
2. *Distribution Details*
3. *Journal Voucher*
4. *Check*
5. *Control Total*
6. *Control Report*
7. *Canceled Checks*
8. *Bank Statement*

FIGURE 8.9 Data Flow Diagram: Cash Disbursements Application System.

imprest fund is a fund maintained at a specified, predetermined amount. At all times, the amount of cash on hand plus documented expenditures should equal the specified amount of the fund. Periodically, an imprest fund is replenished; documented expenditures (petty cash vouchers) are reviewed and approved, and a check is drawn to the fund or custodian of the fund for the amount necessary to bring the fund back to its specified amount. Separate checking accounts may be maintained for payroll and other expense categories, such as dividend payments.

Figure 8.10 illustrates an analytic flowchart of a cash disbursements application system. The major features of the system are the use of a voucher system to support the drawing of checks, the separation of approval from actual payment, and an independent bank reconciliation. These items are included in the following discussion.

Accounts Payable

The accounts payable department receives copies of the purchase requisition, purchase order, receiving report, and vendor invoice. These documents are reviewed, certified as to completeness, and assembled in a **voucher package.** The voucher package is filed by date.

Periodically, the voucher package file is reviewed and voucher packages that are due are pulled for payment. Accounts payable performs payment process-

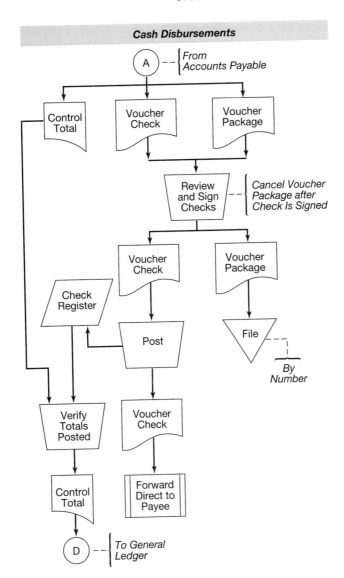

FIGURE 8.10 Cash Disbursements Application System (*continued on pages 322–324*).

ing—calculating the amount due, discount (if any), and other such items. A voucher check is prepared for each voucher. Voucher checks are posted to the voucher register. A total of these postings is prepared. Voucher packages are posted to the accounts payable ledger. This posting is summarized on a journal voucher and a distribution voucher. The voucher checks, voucher packages, and control total are approved and forwarded to the cash disbursements department. The journal voucher is forwarded to general ledger. The distribution voucher is forwarded to the department managing the expense ledger.

Cash Disbursements

After the voucher checks and voucher packages are reviewed, the checks are signed and the voucher packages are canceled and filed by number. The voucher checks are then posted to a check register. This posting is totaled and reconciled to the control total received from accounts payable. Voucher checks are forwarded directly to the payees. The control total is forwarded to general ledger.

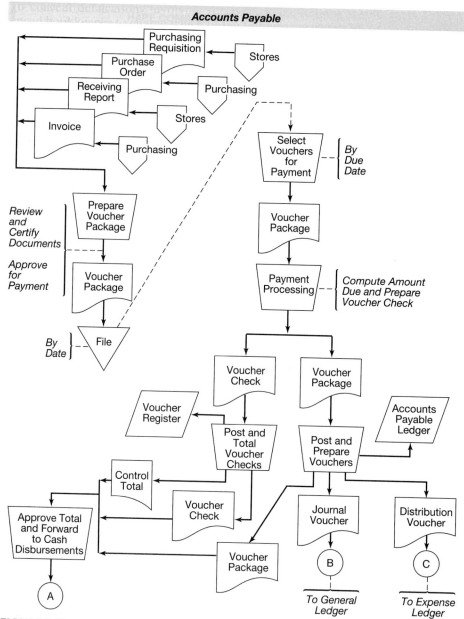

FIGURE 8.10 (continued)

Expense Ledger

The distribution voucher is posted to the expense ledger and/or inventory ledger as appropriate. A distribution summary is prepared, reconciled to the distribution voucher, and approved. The distribution voucher and a copy of the distribution report are filed by date. A copy of the distribution summary is forwarded to general ledger.

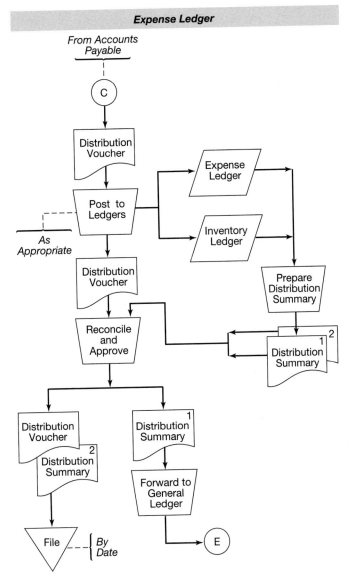

FIGURE 8.10 (continued)

General Ledger

The distribution summary received from the expense ledger, the journal voucher received from accounts payable, and the control total from cash disbursements are reconciled, and the totals are posted to the general ledger. The distribution summary received from the expense ledger, the journal voucher received from the accounts payable department, and the control total from the cash disbursements department are filed by date.

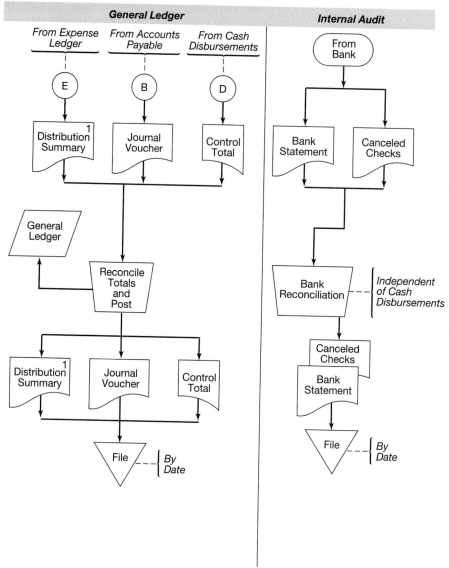

FIGURE 8.10 (continued)

Internal Audit

The canceled checks are received from the bank along with the bank statement. An independent bank reconciliation is an important control in a cash disbursements application system.

Voucher Systems

A **voucher system** is essentially a review technique. The real control over disbursements is a final review of documents evidencing the entire transaction prior to the authorization of payment. Authorization may take the form of physically signing off on a voucher package or preparing (or signing) a form to authorize an entry in the voucher register. This review process evidences that a procedure or operation has been duly authorized and completed according to system specifications. It is the review process, not the actual signing of checks, that is the control. This is particularly evident in computer applications where checks are "signed" with a signature imprinter at the rate of hundreds of checks per minute.

An accounts payable system typically maintains a subsidiary ledger of creditor's accounts, posting invoices and payments on account to each individual creditor's account. Accounts payable generally refers to trade accounts, whereas a voucher payable system encompasses *all* expenditures, including trade accounts, payroll, capital expenditures, and so on. In a strict voucher payable system, individual accounts for creditors need not be kept. A voucher system maintains a voucher register or, alternatively, files of voucher packages in numerical or other order. Several vouchers may relate to the same creditor, as opposed to a single account in an accounts payable system. If information on individual creditors is desired, copies of vouchers may be used to generate this information. Numerous voucher payable files are maintained in most systems because payable information is essential to short-run financial planning.

A voucher system centers around **vouchers,** which can take several forms, ranging from a simple form or envelope to a voucher-check combination (Figure 8.11). A voucher shows, among other things, the name and address of the vendor, a description of the invoice, total or net amount due, and the accounts to be charged (distribution). In a computer application, most of the items in the matching process are coded and processed by the computer. At times, a voucher system may be implemented by rubber-stamping an invoice or purchase order with a voucher stamp and documenting the matching process on this original document. The form of the voucher itself is not significant; a voucher system may operate

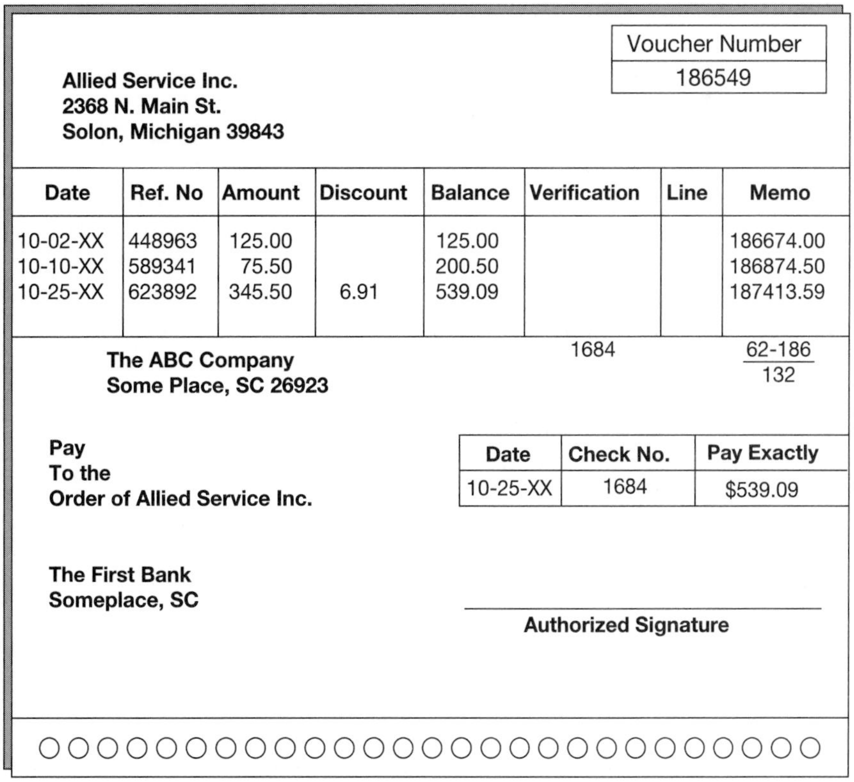

Voucher Number
186549

Allied Service Inc.
2368 N. Main St.
Solon, Michigan 39843

Date	Ref. No	Amount	Discount	Balance	Verification	Line	Memo
10-02-XX	448963	125.00		125.00			186674.00
10-10-XX	589341	75.50		200.50			186874.50
10-25-XX	623892	345.50	6.91	539.09			187413.59

The ABC Company
Some Place, SC 26923

1684

62-186
───
132

Pay
To the
Order of Allied Service Inc.

Date	Check No.	Pay Exactly
10-25-XX	1684	$539.09

The First Bank
Someplace, SC

_____
Authorized Signature

○○○

FIGURE 8.11 Voucher Check.

without a human-readable voucher. In this case, the "voucher" is an approved entry in the voucher register, typically a file on a computer disk. References to documents rather than the documents themselves are provided in the register, and voucher entries are under strict numerical control.

Posting of Payables

A basic question in the design of a voucher system concerns when invoices are to be posted to vouchers payable. Specifically, when are liabilities "booked" (excluding end-of-period accruals)? After invoices have been approved for payment, they may be held until the due date and formally posted at that time; alternatively, they may be booked at the time of approval (which is generally different from the due date). Because most firms attempt to pay invoices on the due date to maximize working capital, this question relates to whether there is a formal record of amounts owed to creditors. If invoices are booked on the due date, there is no formal record of unpaid invoices, because the liability is immediately canceled by payment. If invoices are booked on the date of approval, a formal record of liabilities exist. This advantage is gained at a cost. The voucher register (or file of vouchers) now must be searched or sorted by due date to facilitate payments. Typically, a voucher register is used for numerical control when invoices are booked at the time of approval. This is the only feasible alternative in a large organization.

Preparing vouchers for individual invoices when several invoices refer to the same vendor in the same time period would result in the drawing of several checks to the same vendor in the same month. This is generally inefficient. Most firms attempt to accumulate several invoices from the same vendor and pay these invoices with a single check. Such procedures are called **built-up voucher** procedures.

A built-up voucher system functions essentially as an accounts payable system. After invoices are approved, they are sorted and accumulated by vendor or voucher number. Payments are made at month end or due date. A built-up voucher procedure as just described is a full accrual system; vouchers payable replace accounts payable in the general ledger.

Three files are necessary to maintain useful information: (1) a file of approved but unpaid invoices, with access to due date for payment; (2) a file of paid invoices, usually in numerical order; and (3) a vendor file showing both paid and unpaid amounts, ordered by vendor ID. In a manual system, these files are obtained by filing carbon copies of vouchers. In a computer system, separate files may be maintained, or complex processing methods may yield the same results without having three separate files.

The voucher concept is helpful in the disbursement procedure of any organization when a basic record is desired and proper authorization and control over disbursements are important. Requiring signatures before disbursement documents knowledge and approval of the disbursement. Paid vouchers can be filed in strict numerical sequence to provide documentation for every amount paid. Such a procedure provides orderly records and good documentation and is advantageous in establishing good stewardship of cash.

Other Finance-Cycle Applications

In addition to cash receipts and cash disbursements, a typical finance cycle includes applications dealing with accrual and payment of interest on debt and dividends on capital stock, general financial institution and investor relations—such as stock registration and credit line agreements—and management of foreign currencies. The finance cycle provides important inputs to upper-level financial planning models that are concerned with cash planning and forecasting, operational budgeting, and capital budgeting. Many organizations use sophisticated models that include computer and/or mathematical techniques to forecast and manage the firm's cash position. The output of such models cannot be more accurate or reliable than the basic data inputs the model uses.

SUMMARY

Production control, inventory control, and property accounting are typical production-cycle applications in manufacturing firms. A production control application system plans and schedules production, and issues production orders to authorize production activities. Materials requisition forms and job time cards are used to trace production costs to individual production orders. A model production control application system includes a separation of the following functions: production control, the production departments, inventory control, cost accounting, and the general ledger.

Inventory control is accomplished through a series of records and reports that provide information concerning inventory use and inventory balances. Perpetual inventory records are the best source of inventory information. The storage and handling of inventory items must provide assurance of adequate control.

Property accounting applications concern an organization's fixed assets and investments. Property accounting applications maintain records that identify an organization's fixed assets and investments, provide for appropriate depreciation and/or amortization for book and tax purposes, provide information for insurance purposes, and provide information to management concerning use and availability of an organization's fixed assets and investments.

Finance-cycle applications concern the acquisition and use of capital funds. Capital funds include working capital as well as long-term funds. Cash receipts and cash disbursements are two common finance-cycle application systems.

The basic objective in any cash receipts application system is to minimize exposure to loss. Supervision, customer audit procedures, and imprest fund techniques are common controls in a cash receipts application system. A model cash receipts application system includes a separation of the following functions: mailroom, cash receipts, accounts receivable, and the general ledger. An independent bank reconciliation is an important control in a cash receipts application system.

Cash disbursement application systems are designed to control check disbursements as well as actual cash disbursements. Major controls include the use of a voucher system to support the drawing of checks, the separation of approval from actual payment, and an independent bank reconciliation. A model cash disbursement application system includes a separation of the following functions: cash disbursements, accounts payable, the expense ledger, and the general ledger.

Glossary

bill of materials: lists the raw materials that are necessary to produce a product.

built-up voucher: the accumulation of several invoices from the same voucher and the payment of these invoices with a single check.

customer audit: procedure in which the customer acts as a control over the initial documentation of a transaction.

economic order quantity (EOQ): the order quantity that minimizes total inventory cost.

factor availability report: a report that communicates the availability of labor and machine resources.

fixed-asset register: a systematic list of fixed assets maintained for control purposes.

float: the time between the signing of the payment check by the customer and the moment the firm has use of the funds.

imprest techniques: a control technique in which an item is held accountable to a specified total amount.

inventory status reports: reports that detail the resources available in inventory.

investment register: a systematic list of investments maintained for control purposes.

job: synonym for production order.

job costing: production costs are assigned to production orders.

job time cards: used to document the amount of labor time that is spent working on each production order (job).

just-in-time (JIT) production: a system in which items are produced only as they are required in subsequent operations.

lock-box deposit system: customer remittances are sent directly to a bank and are credited to a company's account before they are posted to customer accounts.

master operations list: identifies and specifies the sequencing of all labor operations and/or machine operations that are necessary to produce a product.

material requisition: document that authorizes the release of raw materials to the production departments.

process costing: production costs are compiled by department rather than by job.

production order: document that authorizes the production departments to make certain products.

professional shoppers: people hired to purchase goods in a retail environment for the express purpose of observing the recording of transactions.

remittance list: a listing of customer remittances that is prepared for control purposes.

reorder point: the level of inventory at which it is desirable to order or produce additional items to avoid an out-of-stock condition.

voucher: synonym for voucher package.

voucher package: a collection of documents that are reviewed and approved to authorize a disbursement.

voucher system: a system in which every organizational expenditure must be documented with an approved voucher.

Chapter Quiz

Answers to the chapter quiz appear on page 346.

1. In a production control application system, which of the following documents serves as authorization to release raw materials to the production department?
   (a) production order
   (b) job time card
   (c) journal voucher
   (d) material requisition

2. In a production control application system, which of the following departments should receive copies of production orders?

(a) inventory control
(b) cost accounting
(c) purchasing
(d) general ledger

3. In a production control application system, which of the following documents serves as authorization to the production departments to make certain products?
(a) production order
(b) job time card
(c) material requisition
(d) journal voucher

4. Which of the following is a characteristic associated with just-in-time (JIT) production?
(a) parts are produced only as they are required in subsequent operations
(b) a constant-flow production rate
(c) both a and b
(d) neither a nor b

5. For adequate internal control, the department responsible for preparing checks for signature should be
(a) the department that signs the checks.
(b) the accounts payable department.
(c) the purchasing department.
(d) the treasury department.

6. In a cash receipts application system, the remittance list prepared in the mailroom should be directly forwarded to
(a) finished goods.
(b) billing.
(c) accounts receivable.
(d) general ledger.

7. In a cash disbursements application system, the voucher package should be canceled by
(a) cash disbursements.
(b) accounts payable.
(c) expense ledger distribution.
(d) general ledger.

8. In a cash receipts application system, the cash remittances received in the mailroom should be directly forwarded to
(a) cash receipts.
(b) billing.
(c) accounts receivable.
(d) general ledger.

9. Which of the following documents should normally be included in a voucher package?
(a) vendor invoice
(b) purchase order
(c) both a and b
(d) neither a nor b

10. Which of the following departments should directly forward to accounts payable the copy of the receiving report that is included in the voucher package?
(a) purchasing
(b) receiving
(c) cash disbursements
(d) stores

Review Problem

You are auditing the Alaska branch of Far Distributing Company. This branch has substantial annual sales, which are billed and collected locally. As a part of your audit, you find that the procedures for handling cash receipts are as follows:

Cash collections on over-the-counter sales and C.O.D. sales are received from the customer or delivery service by the cashier. Upon receipt of cash, the cashier stamps the sales ticket "paid" and files a copy for future reference. The only record of C.O.D. sales is a copy of the sales ticket, which is given to the cashier to hold until the cash is received from the delivery service.

Mail is opened by the secretary to the credit manager and remittances are given to the credit manager for his review. The credit manager then places the remittances in a tray on the cashier's desk. At the daily deposit cutoff time, the cashier delivers the checks and cash on hand to the assistant credit manager, who prepares remittance lists and makes up the bank deposit, which she also takes to the bank. The assistant credit manager also posts remittances to the accounts receivable ledger and verifies the cash discount allowable.

You also ascertain that the credit manager obtains approval from the executive officer at Far Distributing, located in Chicago, to write off uncollectable accounts, and that he has retained in his custody as of the end of the fiscal year some remittances that were received on various days during the last month.

Required

(a) Describe the irregularities that might occur under the procedures now in effect for handling cash collections and remittances.

(b) Give procedures that you would recommend to strengthen internal control over cash collections and remittances.

(CPA)

Solution to Review Problem

(a.) 1. The cashier could destroy cash or C.O.D. sales tickets and pocket the proceeds if sales tickets are not prenumbered or if accountability is not maintained for all sales ticket numbers.

2. Lapping might occur. This involves the withholding of cash receipts without an entry being made on the books. At a later date, cash is collected and an entry is made for the first cash collected. The latest collection is held and used by the dishonest person. In the situation described, any of the four Alaska employees could lap the collections of accounts receivable.

3. Since the assistant credit manager had been told of doubtful accounts previously written off as uncollectable, she could appropriate cash collections to the extent of the remittances received on accounts previously written off.

4. The credit department personnel could enter discounts not taken by the customer or enter discounts on remittances made after the discount date. Those entries could cover the appropriation of an equivalent amount of cash for personal use.

5. Because no record is made of mail receipts until they have been handled by four people, any of the four could abstract funds without any covering action. Upon discovery of the theft there would be no records to identify the thief.

6. The assistant credit manager could cover abstractions of cash by adding or destroying accounts receivable ledger records, by falsifying subsidiary ledger trial balances, by sending statements that differ from the accounts, and so on.

(b.) The following procedures should be put into effect at the Alaska office to strengthen the internal control over cash receipts.

1. All sales tickets should be prenumbered and all sales ticket numbers should be accounted for daily. All sales tickets stamped "paid" should be reconciled to the duplicate deposit slip receipted by the bank. This should be done by a responsible employee other than the cashier or a member of the credit department.

2. An employee other than the cashier or a member of the credit department should open the incoming mail and prepare daily a list in triplicate of remittances received that day. The original of the list should accompany the checks (and cash, if any) turned over directly to the cashier; one copy of the list of remittances should be routed to the responsible employee mentioned in the preceding number 1; one copy should be routed to the person responsible for posting to the accounts receivable ledger.

3. The responsible employee who received the copy of the list of remittances should compare the remittances shown thereon with the duplicate deposit ticket at the same time the cash sales tickets are reconciled to the deposit ticket. Any checks or cash not deposited the day received should be investigated.

4. Different forms (or colors) of sales tickets for cash, C.O.D., and credit sales would facilitate the daily accounting for sales tickets used.

5. The cashier, who should have no duties connected with accounts receivable, should prepare bank deposits and forward the deposits to the bank. A responsible employee other than the cashier or a member of the credit department should establish agreement of the list of remittances and daily collections with the daily deposit ticket.

6. Remittances should not be held; those for each day or for each batch of mail, whichever is more practical, should be deposited intact. The credit department may make whatever record it needs for further follow-up on the remittances that are not in the correct amount.

7. The duty of posting remittances to the accounts receivable ledger may be left with the credit department. This operation should normally be performed subsequent to the receipt and control of cash; therefore internal control over cash will not be weakened if credit department personnel perform the posting duty, providing they have no access to the cash represented by the remittance advices.

Review Questions

1. Distinguish between job order costing and process costing.
2. Identify the accounting journal entries that summarize the activities involved in a manufacturing operation.
3. What is a bill of material? A reorder point? A reorder quantity? A master operations list?
4. Identify the main features of control over inventories and production.
5. What information might be included on a production order? Identify the source(s) of this information. To whom should copies of production orders be distributed?
6. Identify the major features of just-in-time (JIT) production.
7. What are the objectives of a fixed asset or investment accounting system?
8. Identify several controls relevant to fixed assets and investments.
9. What accounting entries are required when fixed assets are disposed of?
10. What is the basic objective in any cash receipts application?
11. What is the most critical phase of a cash receipts procedure? Identify several techniques that may be used to control this phase.
12. What is a remittance advice? What function do remittance advices play in a cash receipts procedure?
13. Identify the major features of control in a cash receipt procedure.
14. Criticize the following statement: "The major control over cash disbursements is the actual signing of the checks."

15. Identify the major control features in a cash disbursement system.

16. What is a voucher system?

17. Identify several files that might be kept in a voucher system to provide useful information.

18. What is the major difference between booking invoices on date of approval and booking them on date of payment?

Discussion Questions and Problems

19. For several years, a client's physical inventory count has been lower than what was shown on the books at the time of the count requiring downward adjustments to the inventory account. Contributing to the inventory problem could be weaknesses in internal control that led to the failure to record some
    (a) purchases returned to vendors.
    (b) sales returns received.
    (c) sales discounts allowed.
    (d) cash purchases.
    (CPA)

20. Ball Company, which has no perpetual inventory records, takes a monthly physical inventory and reorders any item that is less than its reorder point. On February 5, 19XX, Ball ordered 5,000 units of item A. On February 6, 19XX, Ball received 5,000 units of item A, which had been ordered on January 3, 19XX. To prevent this excess ordering, Ball should
    (a) keep an adequate record of open purchase orders and review it before ordering.
    (b) use perpetual inventory records that indicate goods received, issued, and amounts on hand.
    (c) use prenumbered purchase orders.
    (d) prepare purchase orders only on the basis of purchase requisitions.
    (CPA)

21. Sanbor Corporation has an inventory of parts consisting of thousands of different items of small value individually, but significant in total. Sanbor could establish effective internal accounting control over the parts by requiring
    (a) approval of requisitions for inventory parts by a company officer.
    (b) maintenance of inventory records for all parts included in the inventory.
    (c) physical counts of the parts on a cycle basis rather than at year end.
    (d) separation of the store-keeping function from the production and inventory record-keeping functions.
    (CPA)

22. To achieve effective internal accounting control over fixed-asset additions, a company should establish procedures that require
    (a) capitalization of the cost of fixed-asset additions in excess of a specific dollar amount.
    (b) performance of recurring fixed-asset maintenance work solely by maintenance department employees.
    (c) classifying as investments those fixed-asset additions that are not used in the business.
    (d) authorization and approval of major fixed-asset additions.
    (CPA)

23. Which of the following is the most important internal control over acquisitions of property, plant, and equipment?
    (a) Establishing a written company policy distinguishing between capital and revenue expenditures.
    (b) Using a budget to forecast and control acquisitions and retirements.
    (c) Analyzing monthly variances between authorized expenditures and actual costs.
    (d) Requiring acquisitions to be made by user departments.
    (CPA)

24. Which of the following procedures provides substantial assurance that invoices are paid for merchandise actually ordered and received in satisfactory condition?
    (a) The purchasing department sends copies of the purchase requisition to the accounts payable department and the supplier.
    (b) The receiving department counts all merchandise received.
    (c) The accounts payable department sends purchase requisitions to the purchasing department and the stores department.
    (d) The accounts payable department matches the purchase requisition, purchase order, receiving report, and invoice.
    (e) The stores department sends copies of the invoices to the receiving department and the insurance department.

    (IIA)

25. An entity with a large volume of customer remittances by mail could most likely reduce the risk of employee misappropriation of cash by using
    (a) employee fidelity bonds.
    (b) independently prepared mailroom prelists.
    (c) daily check summaries.
    (d) a bank lock-box system.

    (CPA)

26. Which of the following would the auditor consider to be an incompatible operation if the cashier receives remittances from the mailroom?
    (a) The cashier prepares the daily deposit.
    (b) The cashier makes the daily deposit at a local bank.
    (c) The cashier posts the receipts to the accounts receivable subsidiary ledger cards.
    (d) The cashier endorses the checks.

    (CPA)

27. Which of the following is an internal control procedure that would prevent a paid disbursement voucher from being presented for payment a second time?
    (a) Vouchers should be prepared by individuals who are responsible for signing disbursement checks.
    (b) Disbursement vouchers should be approved by at least two responsible management officials.
    (c) The date on a disbursement voucher should be within a few days of the date the voucher is presented for payment.
    (d) The official signing the check should compare the check with the voucher and should deface the voucher documents.

    (CPA)

28. An effective internal accounting control measure that protects against the preparation of improper or inaccurate disbursements would be to require that all checks be
    (a) signed by an officer after necessary supporting evidence has been examined.
    (b) reviewed by the treasurer before mailing.
    (c) sequentially numbered and accounted for by internal auditors.
    (d) perforated or otherwise effectively canceled when they are returned with the bank statement.

    (CPA)

29. Which of the following is an internal accounting control weakness related to factory equipment?
    (a) Checks issued in payment of purchases of equipment are *not* signed by the controller.
    (b) All purchases of factory equipment are required to be made by the department in need of the equipment.
    (c) Factory equipment replacements are generally made when estimated useful lives, as indicated in depreciation schedules, have expired.
    (d) Proceeds from sales of fully depreciated equipment are credited to other income.

    (CPA)

30. Which of the following is an effective internal accounting control over cash payments?
    (a) Signed checks should be mailed under the supervision of the check signer.
    (b) Spoiled checks that have been voided should be disposed of immediately.
    (c) Checks should be prepared only by people responsible for cash receipts and cash disbursements.
    (d) A check-signing machine with two signatures should be used.

    (CPA)

31. In a properly designed accounts payable system, a voucher is prepared after the invoice, purchase order, requisition, and receiving report are verified. The next step in the system is to
    (a) cancel the supporting documents.
    (b) enter the check amount in the check register.
    (c) approve the voucher for payment.
    (d) post the voucher amount to the expense ledger.

    (CPA)

32. For the most effective internal accounting control, monthly bank statements should be received directly from the banks and reviewed by the
    (a) controller.
    (b) cash receipts accountant.
    (c) cash disbursements accountant.
    (d) internal auditor.

    (CPA)

33. Which of the following internal accounting control procedures could best prevent direct labor from being charged to manufacturing overhead?
    (a) Reconciliation of work-in-process inventory with cost records.
    (b) Comparison of daily journal entries with factory labor summary.
    (c) Comparison of periodic cost budgets and time cards.
    (d) Reconciliation of unfinished job summary and production cost records.

    (CPA)

34. In a properly designed internal accounting control system, the same employee may be permitted to
    (a) receive and deposit checks, and also approve write-offs of customer accounts.
    (b) approve vouchers for payment, and also sign checks.
    (c) reconcile the bank statements, and also receive and deposit cash.
    (d) sign checks, and also cancel supporting documents.

    (CPA)

35. Which of the following is a question the auditor would expect to find on the production cycle section of an internal accounting control questionnaire?
    (a) Are vendor's invoices for raw materials approved for payment by an employee who is independent of the cash disbursements function?
    (b) Are signed checks for the purchase of raw materials mailed directly after signing without being returned to the person who authorized the invoice processing?
    (c) Are all releases by storekeepers of raw materials from storage based on approved requisition documents?
    (d) Are details of individual disbursements for raw materials balanced with the total to be posted to the appropriate general ledger account?

    (CPA)

36. The most effective way to prevent an employee from misappropriating cash and then altering the accounting records to conceal the shortage is to
    (a) perform bank reconciliations on a timely basis.
    (b) deposit promptly all cash receipts in the company's bank account.
    (c) prenumber all cash receipts documents.
    (d) enforce a segregation of duties between employees who have custody of cash receipts and those who account for them.

    (IIA)

37. Which of the following is the most important element of internal control relating to the raw materials inventory of a manufacturing company?
    (a) The physical inventory count should be made by personnel independent of the inventory custodians.
    (b) Materials from vendors should be received directly by the production department that will be using the materials.
    (c) Shortages in shipments from vendors should be immediately reported to the production department that will be using the materials.
    (d) Issues from inventory should be supported by sales invoices.
    (IIA)

38. A well-functioning system of internal control over the inventory/production functions would provide that finished goods are to be accepted for stock only after presentation of a completed production order and a(n)
    (a) shipping order.
    (b) material requisition.
    (c) bill of lading.
    (d) inspection report.
    (CPA)

39. If preparation of a periodic scrap report is essential in order to maintain adequate control over the manufacturing process, the data for this report should be accumulated in the
    (a) accounting department.
    (b) production department.
    (c) warehousing department.
    (d) budget department.
    (CPA)

40. In a properly designed internal accounting control system, the same employee should *not* be permitted to
    (a) sign checks and cancel supporting documents.
    (b) receive merchandise and prepare a receiving report.
    (c) prepare disbursement vouchers and sign checks.
    (d) initiate a request to order merchandise and approve merchandise received.
    (CPA)

41. Which of the following is *not* a universal rule for achieving strong internal control over cash?
    (a) Separate the cash handling and record-keeping functions.
    (b) Decentralize the receiving of cash as much as possible.
    (c) Deposit each day's cash receipts by the end of the day.
    (d) Have bank reconciliations performed by employees independent with respect to handling cash.
    (CPA)

42. Cash receipts from sales on account have been misappropriated. Which of the following acts would conceal this defalcation and be *least* likely to be detected by an auditor?
    (a) Understating the sales journal.
    (b) Overstating the accounts receivable control account.
    (c) Overstating the accounts receivable subsidiary ledger.
    (d) Understating the cash receipts journal.
    (CPA)

43. For effective internal accounting control, the accounts payable department should compare the information on each vendor's invoice with the
    (a) receiving report and the purchase order.
    (b) receiving report and the voucher.
    (c) vendor's packing slip and the purchase order.
    (d) vendor's packing slip and the voucher.
    (CPA)

44. Which of the following is the most effective control procedure to detect vouchers that were prepared for the payment of goods that were *not* received?
    (a) Count goods upon receipt in storeroom.
    (b) Match purchase order, receiving report, and vendor's invoice for each voucher in accounts payable department.
    (c) Compare goods received with goods requisitioned in receiving department.
    (d) Verify vouchers for accuracy and approval in internal audit department.
                                                                              (CPA)

45. Which of the following control procedures would most likely be used to maintain accurate perpetual inventory records?
    (a) Independent storeroom count of goods received.
    (b) Periodic independent reconciliation of control and subsidiary records.
    (c) Periodic independent comparison of records with goods on hand.
    (d) Independent matching of purchase orders, receiving reports, and vendor's invoices.
                                                                              (CPA)

46. Which of the following procedures is most likely to prevent the improper disposition of equipment?
    (a) A separation of duties between those authorized to dispose of equipment and those authorized to approve removal work orders.
    (b) The use of serial numbers to identify equipment that could be sold.
    (c) Periodic comparison of removal work orders to authorizing documentation.
    (d) A periodic analysis of the scrap sales and the repair and maintenance accounts.
                                                                              (CPA)

47. Which of the following controls would be most effective in assuring that the proper custody of assets in the investing cycle is maintained?
    (a) Direct access to securities in the safety deposit box is limited to only one corporate officer.
    (b) Personnel who post investment transactions to the general ledger are **not** permitted to update the investment subsidiary ledger.
    (c) The purchase and sale of investments are executed on the specific authorization of the board of directors.
    (d) The recorded balances in the investment subsidiary ledger are periodically compared with the contents of the safety deposit box by independent personnel.
                                                                              (CPA)

48. The objectives of the internal control structure for a production cycle are to provide assurance that transactions are properly executed and recorded, and that
    (a) independent internal verification of activity reports is established.
    (b) transfers to finished goods are documented by a completed production report and a quality control report.
    (c) production orders are prenumbered and signed by a supervisor.
    (d) custody of work in process and of finished goods is properly maintained.
                                                                              (CPA)

49. The mailing of disbursement checks and remittance advices should be controlled by the employee who
    (a) signed the checks last.
    (b) approved the vouchers for payment.
    (c) matched the receiving reports, purchase, orders, and vendor's invoices.
    (d) verified the mathematical accuracy of the vouchers and remittance advices.
                                                                              (CPA)

50. To determine whether or not accounts payable are complete, an auditor performs a test to verify that all merchandise received is recorded. The population of documents for this test consists of all
    (a) vendor's invoices.
    (b) purchase orders.

(c) receiving reports.
(d) canceled checks.

(CPA)

51. Which of the following control procedures is **not** usually performed in the vouchers payable department?
    (a) Determining the mathematical accuracy of the vendor's invoice.
    (b) Having an authorized person approve the voucher.
    (c) Controlling the mailing of the check and remittance advice.
    (d) Matching the receiving report with the purchase order.

(CPA)

52. For effective internal control purposes, the vouchers payable department generally should
    (a) stamp, perforate, or otherwise cancel supporting documentation after payment is mailed.
    (b) ascertain that each requisition is approved as to price, quantity, and quality of an authorized employee.
    (c) obliterate the quantity ordered on the receiving department copy of the purchase order.
    (d) establish the agreement of the vendor's invoice with the receiving report and purchase order.

(CPA)

53. Which of the following procedures in the cash disbursements cycle should **not** be performed by the accounts payable department?
    (a) Comparing the vendor's invoice with the receiving report.
    (b) Canceling supporting documentation after payment.
    (c) Verifying the mathematical accuracy of the vendor's invoice.
    (d) Signing the voucher for payment by an authorized person.

(CPA)

54. Independent internal verification of inventory occurs when employees who
    (a) issue raw materials obtain material requisitions for each issue and prepare daily totals of materials issued.
    (b) compare records of goods on hand with physical quantities do **not** maintain the records or have custody of the inventory.
    (c) obtain receipts for the transfer of completed work to finished goods prepare a completed production report.
    (d) are independent of issuing production orders update records from completed job cost sheets and production cost reports on a timely basis.

(CPA)

55. Mailing disbursement checks and remittance advices should be controlled by the employee who
    (a) approves the vouchers for payment.
    (b) matches the receiving reports, purchase orders, and vendor's invoices.
    (c) maintains possession of the mechanical check-signing device.
    (d) signs the checks last.

(CPA)

56. Indicate the objective of each of the following controls:
    (a) Canceling paid vouchers by perforating them at the time of payment.
    (b) Simultaneously reconciling all bank accounts.
    (c) Using prenumbered checks and carefully accounting for used and unused checks.
    (d) Maintaining a record of numbers of all stock certificates and bonds.
    (e) Making surprise counts of imprest funds.
    (f) Having registers read and cleared by internal auditors rather than cashiers.
    (g) Comparing totals of mail receipts with duplicate bank deposit records (daily).
    (h) Periodically comparing personnel department rosters with payroll registers.

(i) Having checks mailed by people other than those causing them to be drawn.

(j) Providing multidrawer cash registers.

(k) Offering bonuses to customers for "red stars" or other special symbols on sales tickets.

57. The C. P. Bliss Manufacturing Company, Buffalo, New York, is considering using a lock-box system for its customers in California. At present, its credit sales to that area amount to about $21,600,000. Establishing a lock-box in San Francisco would enable the company to reduce its collection float from eight days to two days. The bank in San Francisco will expect the company to maintain a minimum balance of $70,000. The net additional annual cost of adopting the system will be $1,200. Base calculations on a 360-day year.

(a) What is the net amount of cash that will be freed for use elsewhere in the business?

(b) What is the annual percentage cost of the funds released from the float?

58. Indicate the objective of the following questions taken from an internal control checklist:

(a) Are all disbursements, except petty cash, made by check?

(b) Are voided checks properly mutilated and held available for subsequent inspection?

(c) Is the sequence of check numbers accounted for when reconciling bank accounts?

(d) Are payroll checks drawn against a separate payroll bank account?

(e) Are the names of employees hired reported in writing by the personnel office to the payroll department?

(f) Are payroll checks distributed to employees by someone other than the supervisor?

(g) Are salary payrolls approved by a responsible official prior to payment?

(h) Are bank debit advices (such as NSF checks) delivered directly to a responsible employee (other than the cashier) for investigation?

59. A treasurer insists that invoices be stamped "paid" prior to his actually signing the checks for payment. Discuss the merits of this policy.

60. Indicate the objective(s) of the following questions on an internal control checklist:

(a) Are all securities registered in the name of the organization?

(b) Are securities periodically inspected and agreed with records kept by internal auditors or other designated employees?

(c) Is the credit department entirely independent of the sales department?

(d) Are detailed plant ledgers maintained for the various units of property?

(e) Is the approval of a designated officer required for the retirement or dismantling of plant items?

(f) Does the company record accruals of recurring income from rents, royalties, or other such items in advance of collection?

(g) Are requests for petty cash signed by the person who receives the cash?

61. The following is a description of purchasing and accounts payable procedures in effect at the Northwest Manufacturing Company.

Using departments submit purchase requisitions on prenumbered requisition forms. Each requisition is approved by the using department head, who also indicates the accounting distribution on the requisition form. Two copies are forwarded to the purchasing department and one copy is filed numerically.

Purchasing accounts for the numerical sequence of requisition forms upon receipt. Prenumbered purchase orders are prepared, approved, and distributed: one copy each to the requesting, receiving, and accounts payable departments. Two copies of the purchase order are sent to the vendor, and one copy is filed numerically with the requisition form attached to it. A copy of the requisition is also forwarded to accounts payable.

In the receiving department, counters inspect shipments and record their counts on tally sheets. The counters do not have access to purchase orders. The tally sheets are forwarded to the head of the receiving department. She compares the tally sheets to the purchase orders and prepares a prenumbered receiving report. This report indicates the actual quantity received. Items that are returned to the vendor are indicated on the receiving report, and separate prenumbered debit memos are prepared. The department head accounts for the numerical sequence of receiving reports and debit memos. Goods are transferred to the stores department. Copies of receiving reports and debit memos are sent to the requesting, accounts payable, purchasing, and stores department. Each of these departments files its copy numerically.

Invoices are routed from the mailroom to the accounts payable department. Clerks compare invoice details to those shown on the purchase order, requisition form, and receiving report, and check for mathematical errors. The clerks also account for the numerical sequence of purchase orders and receiving reports.

The clerks withhold invoices until all these documents are received and the matching process is complete. Upon completion, the clerks assemble the invoice, purchase order, receiving report, and any related debit memos into a voucher package, initial the package, and forward the package to the accounts payable supervisor. The supervisor reviews the package, initials it to indicate approval for payment, indicates the date payment should be made, and forwards the package to the cash disbursements clerk, who then forwards it to data processing. After processing for input, the voucher packages are returned to the accounts payable department.

Checks prepared by data processing are returned to accounts payable, attached to the corresponding voucher package, and submitted to the accounts payable supervisor for a final review before submission to the controller for signature. The controller reviews each voucher package and manually signs the checks. The checks and voucher packages are then sent to the treasurer, who also manually signs the checks. Two signatures are required on all checks. The treasurer's secretary cancels all supporting documents and returns the canceled documents and the checks to the accounts payable supervisor. The voucher packages are filed by a clerk, who also prepares a data processing input sheet showing payee, check number, amount, and so on. The input sheets are processed to produce the cash disbursements records. The accounts payable supervisor forwards the signed checks to the mailroom.

Freight invoices, which are substantial in total amount, are routed from the mailroom to a clerk, who checks their mathematical accuracy. The freight invoices are then forwarded to the accounts payable supervisor for approval. The supervisor indicates the date payment should be made and then forwards the invoices for check preparation by data processing. At month's end, the cash disbursements book is totaled and a journal entry is prepared by the cash disbursements clerk. It is approved by the accounts payable supervisor and given to the general ledger clerk for posting. The general ledger clerk is independent of all accounts payable and disbursement functions. Monthly bank statements are sent directly to the accounts payable supervisor, who performs the reconciliation.

Required
(a) Flowchart the present system.
(b) Identify potential internal control weaknesses in the present procedures. Exclude the data processing department's operations in your review. Suggest modifications to present procedures to support your recommendations concerning potential weaknesses.

62. Hermit Company manufacturers a line of walnut office products. Hermit executives estimate the demand for the double walnut letter tray, one of the company's products, at 6,000 units. The letter tray sells for $80 per unit. The costs relating to the letter tray are estimated to be as follows for 19XX:
(a) Standard manufacturing cost per letter tray unit—$50.
(b) Costs to initiate production run—$300.
(c) Annual cost of carrying the letter tray in inventory—20% of standard manufacturing cost.

In prior years, Hermit Company has scheduled the production for the letter tray in two equal production runs. The company is aware that the economic order quantity (EOQ) model can be employed to determine optimum size for production runs. The

EOQ formula as it applies to inventories for determining the optimum order quantity is as follows:

$$\text{EOQ} = \sqrt{\frac{2 \, (\text{annual demand}) \, (\text{cost per order})}{(\text{cost per unit}) \, (\text{carrying cost})}}$$

Required

Calculate the expected annual cost savings Hermit Company could experience if it employed the economic order quantity model to determine the number of production runs that should be initiated during the year for the manufacture of the double walnut letter trays.

(CMA)

63. State why each of the following changes would affect (1) reorder point and (2) economic order quantity, and state whether the effect would be an increase or a decrease in quantity.
    (a) Increase in demand for an inventory stock item.
    (b) Decrease in the cost of capital to the firm holding the inventory.
    (c) Increase in salaries in the purchasing and receiving departments.

(IIA)

64. Valpaige Company is an industrial machinery and equipment manufacturer with several production departments. The company employs automated and heavy equipment in its production departments. Consequently, Valpaige has a large repair and maintenance (R & M) department for servicing this equipment.

The operating efficiency of R & M has deteriorated over the past two years. Furthermore, repair and maintenance costs seem to be climbing more rapidly than other department costs. The assistant controller has reviewed the operations of R & M and has concluded that the administrative procedures used since the early days of the department are outmoded, due in part to the growth of the company. The two major causes for the deterioration, in the opinion of the assistant controller, are an antiquated scheduling system for repair and maintenance work and the actual cost system to distribute R & M's costs to the production departments. The actual costs of R & M are allocated monthly to the production departments on the basis of the number of service calls made during each month.

The assistant controller has proposed that a formal work order system be implemented for R & M. The production departments would submit a service request to R & M for the repairs and/or maintenance to be completed, including a suggested time for having the work done. The supervisor of R & M would prepare a cost estimate on the service request for the work required (labor and materials) and indicate a suggested time for completing the work on the service request. R & M's supervisor would return the request to the production department that initiated the request. Once the production department okays the work by returning a copy of the service request, R & M's supervisor would prepare a repair and maintenance work order and schedule the job. This work order provides the repair worker with the details of the work to be done and is used to record the actual repair/maintenance hours worked and the materials and supplies used.

Producing departments would be charged for actual labor hours worked at a predetermined standard rate for the type of work required. The parts and supplies used would be charged to the production departments at cost.

The assistant controller believes that only two documents would be required in this new system—a repair/maintenance service request initiated by the production departments and the repair/maintenance work order initiated by R & M.

Required

(a) For the repair/maintenance work order document:
    1. Identify the data items that would be important to R & M and the production departments that should be incorporated into the work order.

2. Indicate how many copies of the work order would be required and explain how each copy would be distributed.

(b) Prepare a document flow diagram to show how the repair/maintenance service request and the repair/maintenance work order should be coordinated and used among the departments of Valpaige to request and complete the repair and maintenance work, to provide the basis for charging the production departments for the cost of the completed work, and to evaluate the performance of R & M. Provide explanations to the flow diagram as appropriate.

(CMA)

65. The accounting and internal control procedures relating to purchases of materials by the Branden Company, a medium-sized company that manufactures special machinery to order, have been described by your junior accountant in the following terms.

After approval by manufacturing department supervisors, materials purchase requisitions are forwarded to the purchasing department supervisor, who distributes such requisitions to the several employees under her control. These employees prepare prenumbered purchase orders in triplicate, account for all numbers, and send the original purchase order to the vendor. One copy of the purchase order is sent to the receiving department, where it is used as a receiving report. The other copy is filed in the purchasing department.

When the materials are received, they are moved directly to the storeroom and issued to the supervisors on informal requests. The receiving department sends a receiving report (with its copy of the purchase order attached) to the purchasing department and forwards copies of the receiving report to the storeroom and to the accounting department.

Vendors' invoices for material purchases, received in duplicate in the mailroom, are sent to the purchasing department and directed to the employee who placed the related order. The employee then compares the invoice with the copy of the purchase order on file in the purchasing department for price and terms and compares the invoice quantity received as reported by the shipping and receiving department on its copy of the purchase order. The purchasing department employees also check discounts, footings, and extensions, after which they initial the invoice to indicate approval for payment. The invoice is then submitted to the voucher section of the accounting department, where it is coded for account distribution, assigned a voucher number, entered in the voucher register, and filed according to payment due date.

On payment dates, prenumbered checks are requisitioned by the voucher section from the cashier and prepared except for signature. After the checks are prepared, they are returned to the cashier, who puts them through a check-signing machine, accounts for the sequence of numbers, and passes them to the cash disbursements bookkeeper for entry in the cash disbursements book. The cash disbursements bookkeeper then returns the checks to the voucher section, which then notes payment dates in the voucher register, places the checks in envelopes, and sends them to the mailroom. The vouchers are then filed in numerical sequence. At the end of each month, one of the voucher clerks prepares an adding machine tape of unpaid items in the voucher register and compares the total thereof with the general ledger balance and investigates any difference disclosed by such comparison.

Required

Discuss the weaknesses, if any, in the internal control of Branden's purchasing and subsequent procedures and suggest supplementary or revised procedures for remedying each weakness with regard to

(a) requisition of materials.
(b) receipt and storage of materials.
(c) functions of the purchasing department.
(d) functions of the accounting department.

(CPA)

66. Charting, Inc., a new audit client of yours, processes its sales and cash receipts documents in the following manner:

   (a) *Cash receipts.* The mail is opened each morning by a mail clerk in the sales department. The mail clerk prepares a remittance advice (showing customer and amount paid) if one is not received. The checks and remittance advices are then forwarded to the sales department supervisor, who reviews each check and forwards the checks and remittance advices to the accounting department supervisor. The accounting department supervisor, who also functions as the credit manager, reviews all checks for payments of past-due accounts and then forwards the checks and remittance advices to the account receivable clerk, who arranges the advices in alphabetical order. The remittance advices are posted directly to the accounts receivable ledger. The checks are endorsed by stamp and totaled. The total is posted to the cash receipts journal. The remittance advices are filed chronologically.

   After receiving the cash from the preceding day's cash sales, the accounts receivable clerk prepares the daily deposit slip in triplicate. The third copy of the deposit slip is filed by date, and the second copy and the original accompany the bank deposit.

   (b) *Sales.* Salesclerks prepare the sales invoices in triplicate. The original and the second copy are presented to the cashier. The third copy is retained by the salesclerk in the sales book. When the sale is for cash, the customer pays the salesclerk, who presents the money to the cashier with the invoice copies.

   A credit sale is approved by the cashier from an approved credit list after the salesclerk prepares the three-part invoice. After receiving the cash or approved invoice, the cashier validates the original copy of the sales invoice and gives it to the customer. At the end of each day, the cashier recaps the sales and cash received and forwards the cash and the second copy of all sales invoices to the accounts receivable clerk. The accounts receivable clerk balances the cash received with cash sales invoices and prepares a daily sales summary. The credit sales invoices are posted to the accounts receivable ledger, and then all invoices are sent to the inventory control clerk in the sales department for posting to the inventory control ledger. After posting, the inventory control clerk files all invoices numerically. The accounts receivable clerk posts the daily sales summary to the cash receipts journal and sales journal and files the sales summaries by date.

   The cash from cash sales is combined with the cash received on account, and this constitutes the daily bank deposit.

   (c) *Bank deposits.* The bank validates the deposit slip and returns the second copy to the accounting department, where it is filed by date by the accounts receivable clerk.

   Monthly bank statements are reconciled promptly by the accounting department supervisor and filed by date.

   Required
   (a) Flowchart the sales and cash receipts application of Charting.
   (b) Identify potential internal control weaknesses in Charting's procedures.

(CPA)

67. The town of Commuter Park operates a private parking lot near the railroad station for the benefit of town residents. The guard on duty issues annual prenumbered parking stickers to residents who submit an application form and show evidence of residency. The sticker is affixed to the auto and allows the resident to park anywhere in the lot for 12 hours if four quarters are placed in the parking meter. Applications are maintained in the guard office at the lot. The guard checks to see that only residents are using the lot and that no resident has parked without paying the required meter fee.

   Once a week, the guard on duty, who has a master key for all meters, takes the coins from the meters and places them in a locked steel box. The guard delivers the box to the town storage building, where it is opened and the coins manually counted by a storage department clerk who records the total cash counted on a weekly cash report. This report is sent to the town accounting department. The storage department clerk puts the cash in a safe, and on the following day, the cash is picked up by the town's treasurer, who manually recounts the cash, prepares the bank deposit slip, and delivers the deposit to the bank. The deposit slip, authenticated by the bank teller, is sent to the accounting department, where it is filed with the weekly cash report.

Required

Describe weaknesses in the existing system and recommend one or more improvements for each of the weaknesses to strengthen the internal control over the parking lot cash receipts.

Organize your answer sheet as follows:

Weakness	*Recommended Improvement*

(CPA)

68. The mail is opened by an accounting clerk. Vendor invoices are stamped with a voucher stamp and forwarded to the purchasing agent. The purchasing agent matches the receiving report, purchase order, and vendor invoices. He then forwards the combined voucher set to the controller, who reviews the documents, approves them, and records the account coding within the voucher stamp. She then forwards the voucher set to the accounts payable clerk.

The accounts payable clerk records the approved invoices onto an accounts payable vendor card and a purchases journal, using a one-write system. The clerk then initials the invoice and files it alphabetically by vendor. At month's end, the clerk prepares an accounts payable aging report and totals the columns in the purchases journal, which is used by the controller for preparing a monthly journal voucher.

The controller uses the accounts payable aging report to indicate those vendors to be paid. In addition, the accounts payable clerk files invoices that contain cash discount terms in a calendar according to due date. The accounts payable clerk manually writes the checks, posts the amounts to the vendor cards, and records the amount in the cash disbursements journal, using a one-write system. The clerk then runs the checks through a check protector and forwards them to the check signers.

Two signatures are required. Normally, the controller signs the checks first, followed by the office manager. The checks are occasionally signed in advance by the office manager. Normally, the supporting invoice vouchers are not given to the check signers. The checks are then returned to the accounts payable clerk, who mails them along with any requested remittance advices to the vendors. The clerk then files the vouchers alphabetically in a paid bills file.

Each month, the accounts payable clerk receives the bank statement and canceled checks. Using the cash disbursements journal, the clerk prepares the bank reconciliation and forwards it to the controller for her review and approval.

Required

(a) Prepare a logical data flow diagram of the preceding procedures.
(b) Prepare an analytic flowchart of the preceding procedures.
(c) Identify potential internal control weaknesses in the preceding procedures.

69. ConSport Corporation is a regional wholesaler of sporting goods. The systems flowchart in Figure 8.12 and the following description present ConSport's cash distribution system.
    (a) The accounts payable department approves payment of all invoices (I) for the purchase of inventory. Invoices are matched with the purchase requisitions (PR), purchase orders (PO), and receiving reports (RR). The accounts payable clerks focus on vendor name and skim the documents when they are combined.
    (b) When all the documents for an invoice are assembled, a two-copy disbursement voucher (DV) is prepared and the transaction is recorded in the voucher register (VR). The DV and supporting documents and then filed alphabetically by vendor.
    (c) A two-copy journal voucher (JV) that summarizes each day's entries in the VR is prepared daily. The first copy is sent to the general ledger department, and the second copy is filed in the accounts payable department by date.
    (d) The vendor file is searched daily for the DVs of invoices that are due to be paid. Both copies of DVs that are due to be paid are sent to the treasury department along with the supporting documents. The cashier prepares a check for each vendor, signs the check, and records it in the check register (CR). Copy 1 of the DV is attached to the check copy and filed in check number order in the treasury department. Copy 2 and the supporting documents are returned to the accounts payable department and filed alphabetically by vendor.
    (e) A two-copy JV that summarizes each day's checks is prepared. Copy 1 is sent to the general ledger department and copy 2 is filed in the treasury department by date.
    (f) The cashier receives the monthly bank statement with canceled checks and prepares the bank reconciliation (BR). If an adjustment is required as a consequence of the BR, a two-copy JV is prepared. Copy 1 is sent to the general ledger department. Copy 2 is attached to copy 1 of the BR and filed by month in the treasury department. Copy 2 of the BR is sent to the internal audit department.

Required

ConSport's cash disbursement system has some weaknesses. Review the cash disbursement system, and for each weakness in the system:
(a) Identify where the weakness exists by using the reference number that appears to the left of each symbol in Figure 8.12.
(b) Describe the nature of the weakness.
(c) Make a recommendation on how to correct the weakness.
Use the following format in preparing your answer:

Reference Number	Nature of Weakness	Recommendation to Correct Weakness

(CMA)

70. In 19XX, XY Company purchased over $10 million of office equipment under its "special" ordering system, with individual orders ranging from $5,000 to $30,000. Special orders entail low-volume items that have been included in an authorized user's budget. Department heads include in their annual budget requests the types of equipment and their estimated cost. The budget, which limits the types and dollar amounts of office equipment a department head can requisition, is approved at the beginning of the year by the board of directors. Department heads prepare a purchase requisi-

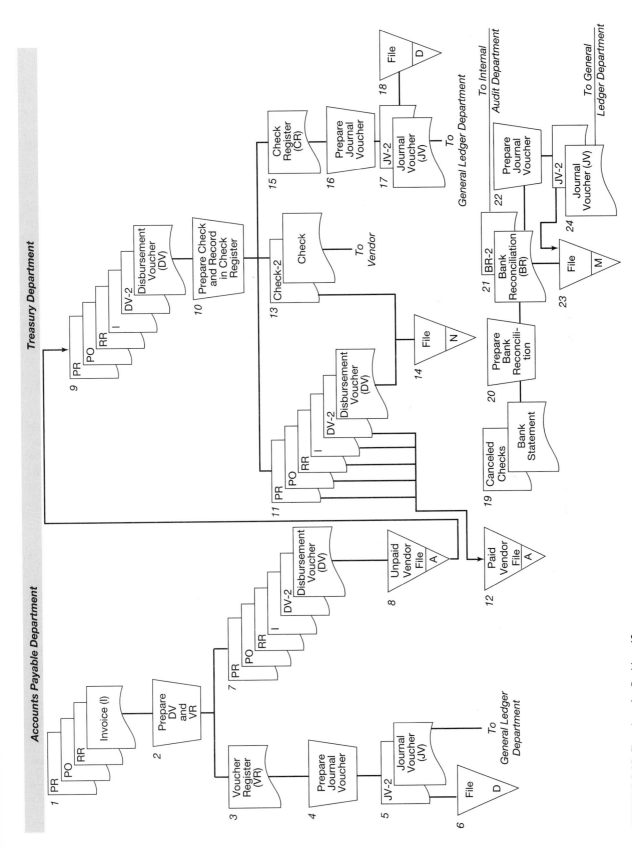

FIGURE 8.12 Flowchart for Problem 69.

tion form for equipment and forward the requisition to the purchasing department. XY's special ordering system functions as follows:

Purchasing

Upon receiving a purchase requisition, one of five buyers verifies that the person requesting the equipment is a department head. The buyer then selects the appropriate vendor by searching the various vendor catalogs on file. The buyer then phones the vendor, requesting a price quotation, and gives the vendor a verbal order. A prenumbered purchase order is then processed, with the original sent to the vendor, a copy to the department head, a copy to receiving, a copy to accounts payable, and a copy filed in the open requisition file. When the buyer is orally informed by the receiving department that the item has been received, the buyer transfers the purchase order from the unfilled file to the filled file. Once a month, the buyer reviews the unfilled file to follow up and expedite open orders.

Receiving

The receiving department receives a copy of the purchase order. When equipment is received, the receiving clerk stamps the purchase order with the date received and, if applicable, in red pen prints any differences between quantity on the purchase order and quantity received. The receiving clerk forwards the stamped purchase order and equipment to the requisitioning department head and orally notifies the purchasing department.

Accounts Payable

Upon receipt of a purchase order, the accounts payable clerk files the purchase order in the open purchase order file. When a vendor invoice is received, the invoice is matched with the applicable purchase order, and a payable is set up by debiting the equipment account of the department requesting the items. Unpaid invoices are filed by due date and, at due date, a check is prepared. The invoice and purchase order are filed by purchase order number in a paid invoice file, and then the check is forwarded to the treasurer for signature.

Treasurer

Checks received daily from the accounts payable department are sorted into two groups: those over $10,000 and those $10,000 and less. Checks for $10,000 and less are machine signed. The cashier maintains the key and signature plate to the check-signing machine and maintains a record of usage of the check-signing machine. All checks over $10,000 are signed by the treasurer or the controller.

Required
Describe the internal accounting control weaknesses relating to purchases and payments of "special" orders of XY Company for each of the following functions:
(a) purchasing
(b) receiving
(c) accounts payable
(d) treasurer

(CPA)

Answers to Chapter Quiz

1. D	4. C	7. A	10. D
2. B	5. B	8. A	
3. A	6. C	9. C	

CHAPTER 9

Systems Development: A Survey

LEARNING OBJECTIVES

Careful study of this chapter will enable you to:

■ Describe the systems development life-cycle concept.

■ Discuss systems documentation standards.

■ Describe systems development technologies and practices.

■ Understand how to plan and control a systems project.

THE SYSTEMS DEVELOPMENT LIFE CYCLE

Systems development is the process of modifying or replacing a portion or all of an information system. This process requires a substantial commitment of time and resources and is an ongoing activity in many organizations.

Organizational Context of Systems Development

Figure 9.1 illustrates the organizational context of systems development. In information systems terminology, a *user or end user* is an organizational function other than the information system function that requires computer data processing. The sales or marketing function is a user that requires computer data processing for sales reports, market analyses, sales projections, sales budgets, and so forth. The accounting function is an end user that requires computer data processing support for posting of journals and preparation of reports. Note that the information system function is separate from user functions. Also, the information system function itself is not a user.

Figure 9.1 shows three subfunctions within the information system function. Each of these subfunctions, systems analysis, systems design, and operations, along with the user function are involved in the process of systems development.

Systems Analysis

Systems analysis is responsible for the development of the general design of system applications. Systems analysis works with users to define their specific information requirements. These requirements are then communicated to the systems design function.

There are four general phases or steps in systems analysis. The first phase is the survey of any existing system. It is important that the analyst understand the

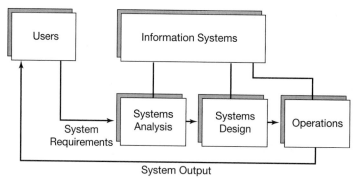

FIGURE 9.1 Systems Development Context.

existing system before changes or modifications are proposed. Also, it is important that the analyst establish a working relationship with users, as ultimate success depends on user acceptance of the new system.

The second general phase in systems analysis is to identify the information needs of users. The analyst must study the decisions that are made by users in terms of their information needs. This phase of systems analysis is often the most difficult because users are often unsure as to what their information requirements actually are.

The third general phase in systems analysis is to identify the system requirements that are necessary to satisfy the information needs of users. Such requirements are usually specified in terms of inputs and outputs. Processing considerations will be determined during systems design. The fourth and final general phase in systems analysis is the preparation of a systems analysis report. This report should document the user specifications for the proposed system and the overall conceptual design of the proposed system. The systems analysis report will be reviewed by management to determine if work on the proposed system should proceed to the systems design phase of development.

System Design

Systems design is the formulation of the detailed specifications for the proposed system. There are three general phases or steps in systems design. The first phase is the evaluation of alternative designs for the proposed system. Alternative designs should be enumerated, described, and evaluated using a cost–benefit criterion.

The second phase of systems design is the preparation of detailed design specifications. The designer should work backwards from the desired outputs to the required inputs. Specific report formats, data structures, and processing steps must be identified. The third and final phase of systems design is the preparation of the systems design report. This report should include everything that is necessary to actually implement the proposed system.

Operations

The operations subfunction of information systems actually operates the computer equipment. **Implementation** occurs when newly developed systems are actually up and running on the computer equipment. Output is then made available to the user, completing the systems development process.

The steps in implementation will vary from system to system. Employee training may be required. Perhaps new equipment is to be purchased and installed. Often the new system requires a conversion or cutover in operations from the old system. The use of project management technique is essential to control implementation activities. Once the system has been implemented, there should be a formal follow-up and evaluation of the new system. This follow-up should include user comments.

The Systems Development Life Cycle

Systems development projects normally are undertaken by a project team composed of system analysts, programmers, accountants, and other people in the organization who are knowledgeable about or affected by the project. Every systems development project goes through essentially the same **systems development life cycle:** planning and analysis, design, and implementation (Figure 9.2). Neglecting any portion of the life cycle may have serious consequences. The life-cycle concept provides a framework for planning and controlling the detailed developmental activities.

This definition of the systems development life cycle is quite general. In practice, the phases in the life cycle are specified in more detail. Table 9.1 lists the detailed phases of the systems development life cycle. Note that analysis, design, and implementation are factored into several subphases. In practice, each of these subphases can be factored further into detailed activities that are relevant to the particular project being developed. Although there are many different ways to factor analysis, design, and implementation into subphases, most discussions of the life-cycle concept use three general phases (perhaps with different names) in their overall scheme. In such cases, the completion of each major phase in the life cycle is often a major management control point, with formal management approval being required to proceed to the next phase.

The life-cycle concept implies that each systems development project should be factored into a number of distinct phases with formal management control points placed between the phases. The basic control principle is that each phase should generate documentation to be formally reviewed and approved prior to entering the next phase of a project's life cycle. The accumulated documentation from the phases is the documentation for the completed project. The amount and

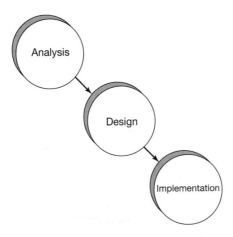

FIGURE 9.2 Systems Development Life Cycle.

TABLE 9-1 A Systems Development Life Cycle

General Phases	Detailed Phases
Analysis	Feasibility assessment
	Information analysis
Design	System design
	Program development
	Procedure development
Implementation	Conversion
	Operation and maintenance
	Audit and review

type of documentation generated during each phase will depend on the nature of the project, with larger projects requiring more extensive documentation. However, the basic principle is always the same: Each phase generates documentation.

Developing a computer-based information system is a creative and demanding task that can and should produce economic benefits for an organization. On the other hand, the systems development process can produce a disaster, with labor and financial resources being expended with no observable return and perhaps even a system that cannot be completed. In practice, the systems development process has often produced both of these results. The history of computer systems development suggests that positive results are more frequently obtained if the systems development process is formally structured, documented, and subject to management control techniques. One of the most important control techniques is to actively involve the ultimate user in the development of information systems.

Some Conventional Wisdom on the Systems Development Life Cycle

The nature of the problems that have historically plagued systems development is humorously summarized in Figure 9.3. This shows the phases in a "real" systems development life cycle. The cycle begins with "wild enthusiasm" in the analysis phase, when all things seem possible and "all systems are go." Disillusionment and total confusion set in during the design phase, as serious problems develop as the project group tries to design unrealistic or hopelessly vague requirements specified during the analysis phase. The result is a system that does not work technically, or operationally, in the sense of doing what it was supposed to do, or economically, in the sense of its return on costs, or some combination of these possibilities. Accordingly, the major phases of implementation consist of the search for the guilty, punishment of the innocent, and promotion of nonparticipants.

Although perhaps a lesson in "how to survive life in a systems group," the figure is, more importantly, a demonstration of the likely outcome of an inadequately structured systems development effort. Management abdication of its responsibilities for the control of systems development is frequently cited as a major reason for such system failures in the past. The need for active involvement of all levels of management in systems development is widely and generally recognized as a major deterrent to the type of system failure just discussed. The best way to ensure this involvement is through the use of the life-cycle concept.

FIGURE 9.3 "Real" Systems Life Cycle.

Another type of problem that has plagued systems development concerns the quality of communication between the many parties in a systems development project. This problem can cause even a well-controlled project to generate a system that fails in the sense that the final user does not actually use it. The system "works," is well documented, and is within budget and time controls, but fails

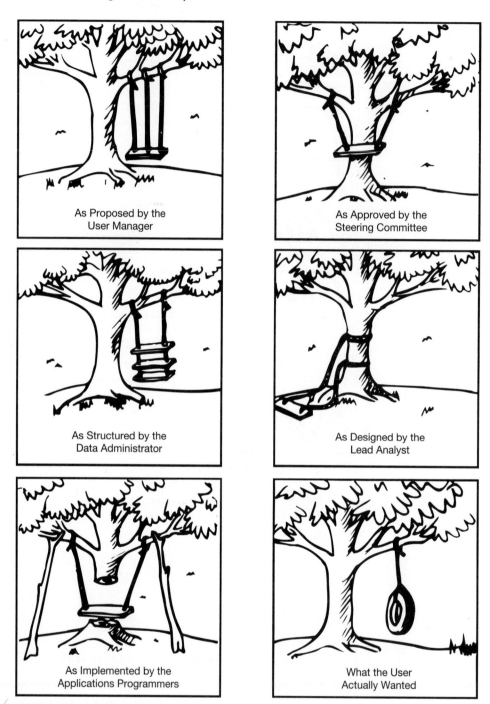

FIGURE 9.4 Communication Problems in Systems Development.

to provide the user with what he or she desires. This situation is pictorially shown in Figure 9.4, which illustrates a lack of communication between the many parties in the systems development process. Each party—user manager, steering committee, and so on—holds a different view of what was to be done. The lesson is that each party's perception of a system to be designed is influenced by his or her own functional specialty. Each functional specialty will see the project from its own viewpoint, preconceiving or assuming things based on its own knowledge. Great care must be taken to ensure that the chain of communication required in a project is effective and complete. Vagueness in communication leads to situations like that shown in Figure 9.4. The solution to the communication problem is to involve the user actively in systems development.

As discussed in Chapter 1, a user-oriented approach to systems design is a true systems approach because it includes user interactions with the system. These interactions are the goal of the system, so it only makes sense to include them in systems development. Users should be actively involved in designing and testing systems. The objective is to maximize later user acceptance and to minimize changes submitted by users after the project has started. The cost of altering a project for a user increases dramatically over a project's life cycle. A modification is easily made in the initial design of a system. Making the same change in an implemented system is much more difficult and expensive. The problem of user-requested changes is a variant of the communication problem, and a very real problem in practice. Users do change their minds about what they want, and users will always be this way. It might even be that active user involvement increases the frequency of user-requested changes. Some writers suggest that system definition documentation generated in the analysis phase should be formally approved by the user and subsequently viewed as a contract between user and provider, with appropriate sanctions for "breach of contract." Whereas a contractual view might be desirable from the provider's view (systems personnel or external consultants), it is undesirable to the extent that it results in systems that are not used by the user.

Business Reengineering

Business reengineering is a term applied to systems development projects in which an entire business function is completely redesigned from the ground up. Interest in business reengineering has been stimulated by several factors. One factor is the TQP (total quality performance) movement in business. Other factors stem from trends in information services, such as the continued and accelerating trend away from mainframe platforms and the trend toward open systems. Increased management concern about returns on the vast amounts companies have invested in information technology has also stimulated interest in the business reengineering concept. Many companies are "rethinking the computer," and discovering that contemporary information technology affords new opportunities for reengineering the way they conduct business (Figure 9.5).

Doing More With Less

TQP (also called TQM—total quality management) is a philosophy that one should do the right thing right the first time. TQP requires high-quality production, operational efficiency, and continuous improvement in operations—in short, TQP emphasizes "doing more with less." In the extremely competitive environment of the global company, TQP is a strategy for survival.

TQP itself, however, may be inadequate as a strategy. Continuous, incremental improvement and quality initiatives, though essential, will no longer be sufficient in the face of intense business competition. As Thomas Davenport notes:

> Objectives of 5% or 10% improvement in all business processes each year must give way to efforts to achieve 50%, 100%, or even higher improvement levels in a few key processes. Today firms must not seek fractional, but multiplicative levels of improve-

Reengineering Customer Service
Management of Otis Elevator Co. centralized and reengineered its customer service. The customer service database is analyzed to assist in dispatching repairmen. Review of repair call data assists in redesign of elevators and changes in maintenance procedures—leading to dramatic reductions in callbacks and entrapments.
Whirlpool focuses on customer service operations as a key source of marketing, sales, and design data. Whirlpool searches customer-call data to identify faulty parts for early replacement in a product's life. Customer service data also helps sell new appliances and warranty services. If records indicate that a particular part breaks too often, Whirlpool uses its data to renegotiate the supplier's warranty on the part.
A unit of AT&T uses computers to track all service calls to ensure contractual obligations are met. Data gathered from customer-service representatives assists in dispatching maintenance personnel more efficiently.
"The Gold Mine of Data in Customer Service." *Business Week*. March 21, 1994.

FIGURE 9.5 Reengineering Customer Service.

ment—10× rather than 10%. Such radical levels of change require powerful new tools that will facilitate the fundamental redesign of work.[1]

Michael Hammer and James Champy sound a similar theme:

America's corporations—even the most successful and promising among them—must develop new techniques that will allow them to survive in today's increasingly harsh, competitive climate.

The alternative is for corporate America to close its doors and go out of business.

The choice is that simple and that stark.[2]

These quotations suggest that innovation—radical change rather than continuous, incremental improvement—is necessary to business survival. Businesses need "home runs"—innovation—instead of the "singles" provided by continuous, incremental improvement.

Reengineering and Process Innovation

Hammer and Champy define reengineering as "the fundamental rethinking and radical redesign of business processes to achieve dramatic improvements in critical contemporary measures of performance such as cost, quality, service, and speed."[3] The terms *fundamental, radical,* and *dramatic* indicate that business reengineering concerns business reinvention—not improvement, enhancement, or modification. One is concerned with multiplicative rather than marginal improvements in performance. The key word *processes* is, according to Hammer and Champy, the most important word in the definition. A process is a collection of activities that transforms input into output that is valued by a customer. But most

---

[1]Thomas H. Davenport, *Process Engineering: Reengineering Work Through Information Technology*, p. 1. Boston: Harvard Business School Press, 1993.

[2]"The Promise of Reengineering." *Fortune* book excerpt. *Fortune*, May 3, 1993, p. 94.

[3]"The Promise of Reengineering." *Fortune* book excerpt. *Fortune*, May 3, 1993, p. 95.

businesspeople are not process oriented—they focus on tasks, jobs, or structure rather than on processes. This focus on jobs or structure arises from organizations that are built upon the central notion of the division of labor and the consequent fragmentation of work—a concept that has its conceptual roots in Adam Smith's 1776 publication *The Wealth of Nations.*

Thomas Davenport also advocates a process view of business. A process is "a specific ordering of work activities across time and place, with a beginning, an end, and clearly identified inputs and outputs: a structure for action."[4] A process orientation places emphasis on how work is done, in contrast to what work is done. Process structure can be distinguished from the traditional hierarchical structure of organizations—which emphasizes responsibility or reporting relationships. Focusing on processes implies a horizontal view of a business that cuts across its hierarchical structure—which generally means deemphasizing the functional structure of the business. According to Davenport, process innovation combines a process view of business with the application of innovation to key processes. Innovation can be distinguished from improvement—which means a lower level of change.

The Role of Information Technology

Information technology is a powerful enabler of process innovation. However, information technology cannot change processes by itself. Human resource factors must be included. Process innovation cannot occur without careful consideration of both technical and human enablers.

Process design should be enabled, but not driven by, information technology. Davenport offers nine categories of ways in which information technology can support process innovation.[5] Automational support eliminates human labor in a process. This is the most commonly recognized benefit of information technology. Informational support occurs when information technology is used to collect process control information. Sequential support occurs when information technology enables a change in a process sequence. Sequential support might enable parallel operation in order to reduce process-cycle time. Tracking support occurs when information technology enables process tracking, as in the now commonplace bar coding and subsequent computer tracking of packages by express delivery services. Analytical support occurs when information technology enables decision making through the use of expert systems. Geographical support occurs when information technology—specifically communications technology—enables coordination of physically distant operations. Integrative support occurs when information technology enables coordination among tasks and process—a case management approach. In **case management,** one individual completes or manages all aspects of service or product delivery. Case management is facilitated by database technology, which centralizes and makes available information concerning the various aspects of a process. Intellectual support occurs when information technology is used to capture and distribute intellectual assets. For example, a consulting firm might maintain a database of its consulting experiences. Finally, disintermediating support occurs when information technology allows the elimination of intermediaries from a process. Electronic stock brokerages, which eliminate human stockbrokers and other human personnel from the process, are cited as an example.

---

[4]Davenport, p. 5.
[5]Ibid., pp. 50–55.

Advantage of Generic processes

* Whole idea is to make the bus. more productive.

Davenport suggests that there are a variety of generic process applications of information technology. The advantage of generic applications is that they should be readily understandable by process design team members who are not themselves technologists. As such, they provide an understandable way to focus a process team on how information technology can enable innovation. In addition, generic applications are a means of solving business problems, not technology looking for uses. Most of the generic applications that Davenport notes can be categorized as expert decision-making systems, such as systems for automated design, simulation, product choice, and forecasting.[6]

Significant productivity gains are to be found only when information technology enables the reengineering of a business process. Multilevel, top-down, hierarchical command and control structures can be reengineered to redeploy workers in multidisciplinary teams that concentrate on getting the correct products and services to customers. User-friendly software, hand-held scanning and computing devices, open systems network structures, and a myriad of other technological features all enable the movement of critical process information to the front line of business operations—the factory floor, the customer service department, or even the salesperson on call at a customer location. Using information technology to support a case management approach to customer service empowers employees to create greater value in their work. In similar fashion, the use of scanning technology in a factory allows production and operational data to be quickly and accurately input to decision-making processes, which empowers employees to create greater value in their work.

DOCUMENTATION STANDARDS

* Communicate thru Users

New system has to be maintainable

Documentation standards set forth explicit requirements for the documentation to be developed during a project. Most large organizations maintain formal systems development standards covering such issues as methods to be used, documentation, project accounting, progress reporting, and review procedures. The existence of documentation standards governing systems development indicates that a plan of organization and related methods, measures, and records is in place to ensure control.

The basic concept of systems development standards is to define the phases in the systems development life cycle and to specify the documents that should be generated during each phase. The principle is that each phase generates documentation. Using the life cycle defined earlier in this chapter, Table 9.2 indicates the types of documentation that might be generated by each phase. The documents listed in the table are discussed in the next section.

Overview of Systems Development Documentation

The specific format of systems development documentation is usually defined in an organization's systems development documentation standards. Whatever the format, an organization should have backup copies of all documentation for recovery purposes in case the originals are destroyed or purposefully sabotaged. Periodic checks of systems documentation should be made to verify that it is complete, current, and sufficient.

---

[6]Ibid., pp. 55–65.

TABLE 9-2 Documentation in the Systems Development Life Cycle

Phase	Documentation
Systems planning and analysis	Feasibility study Logical flow diagrams Data dictionaries User specifications Conceptual design
Systems design	System design report Flowcharts Decision tables Program description Operating procedures Run manual File description Data entry procedure
Systems implementation, evaluation, and control	Conversion plan Testing plan Operating schedules
Systems audit and review	Audit plan User comments

Feasibility Study

A **feasibility study** is an analysis undertaken to determine whether or not a project is worthy of further consideration. The general objective of the feasibility study is to answer overall questions concerning technical, economic, and operational feasibility. Technical feasibility involves determining whether a proposed system is possible, given current technology. Economic feasibility involves determining whether a proposed system will yield benefits that exceed its costs. Operational feasibility is concerned with whether a proposed system will work when it is installed. Work, in this sense, means more than economic or technical feasibility. It means that the system will be used and accepted by the ultimate users.

The length of time taken and the complexity of the feasibility study will depend on the size of the system considered as well as the number of alternatives considered. There are no hard-and-fast rules. The level of detail considered in the feasibility study will vary according to the application considered. The feasibility study should consider the use of outside EDP services or consultants, as appropriate to the organization's interests.

Logical Flow Diagrams

These diagrams can take many forms. Document flowcharts, logical data flow diagrams, HIPO and/or IPO charts, or similar techniques are used to provide the project team with a clear statement of the operational characteristics of a proposed system.

Data Dictionaries

The **data dictionary** documents the specific contents of a database. Each field is listed and described.

User Specifications

This document should provide a narrative description of a proposed system's operational characteristics. Normally, this narrative would be based on interviews with the ultimate user. The description should be nontechnical and reviewed and approved by the ultimate user.

Conceptual Design

The **conceptual design** report—which may include logical flow diagrams and the user specifications—is the basis for detailed system design. It should contain a narrative system overview in nontechnical terms, a somewhat detailed specification of input and output requirements, the proposed hardware and software requirements, a discussion of cost considerations, and, most important, a development plan and budget. The conceptual design should clearly specify desired system outputs with respect to format, content, timing, and distribution. This is normally done by including pro forma output reports. Input requirements and any necessary forms to capture data must also be clearly specified.

Systems Design Report

The **systems design report** is a translation of the conceptual design report into the detailed system performance and functional specifications necessary to begin the physical design of the system. The following items would normally be included:

- *Input Requirements.* The source documents to be used, the means of preparing and transmitting documents, the frequency of preparation, and the volume of transactions expected should be detailed.
- *Processing Specifications.* The new procedures must be defined. How the inputs will be used to prepare the desired outputs should be indicated. All files and records to be used and maintained should be identified, frequency of file use must be known, and processing volumes (both current and expected) associated with the files should be specified.
- *Output Requirements.* Output specifications should include the form, content, and frequency of reports.
- *Control Provisions.* The steps to be taken to provide the necessary internal control should be specified.
- *Cost Estimates.* Preliminary estimates of conversion costs and annual operating costs using the new system should be developed.

Flowcharts and Decision Tables

These documents, which were discussed in Chapter 2, may be used to illustrate the detailed system design.

Program Description

This document should contain a narrative description of the program(s), a program flowchart, a program source listing, and a clear description of the data formats used in the program and the output that it generates.

Operating Procedures; Run Manual

A **run manual** is an organized collection of documents pertaining to the operating procedures surrounding a particular application. The run manual provides a description of the application system, a detailed program description, and detailed operating instructions. Operating instructions are a guide to the actual running of the program and should define the operator's duties in starting, running, and terminating the program.

File Descriptions; Data Entry Procedures

These self-descriptive items involve the preparation of instructions for users, data entry clerks, computer operating personnel, and any other people who will be involved with the operation of the system. These documents are primarily narrative, and they should be clear and concise.

System implementation, evaluation and Control

Conversion Plan

In the implementation phase, the operating personnel need to be coordinated and possibly retrained, and the physical changes that result from the new system need to be made. Scheduling is a major consideration at this point, and formal scheduling techniques, such as Gantt or PERT charts, are frequently used. The major physical changes involve site preparation and file conversion. Conversion of files is likely to be both time-consuming and expensive and must be carefully controlled.

3 conversion possibilities.

Conversion to a new system involves some form of cutover or duplication in processing activity. Figure 9.6 illustrates three possible conversion strategies. Immediate cutover is risky but sometimes warranted for incompatible or minor changes. It is usually desirable to have a pilot test or parallel operation period during which both the old and new systems operate. This allows a check against the capabilities and performance of the new system and an opportunity to debug any deficiencies that could be potentially disastrous if the new system immediately replaced the old system in daily operation. Phased conversion is a middle road that is helpful when feasible. Phased conversion helps to successively refine systems and lower risk, with the sacrifice of some delay and cost. Phasing can be based on system modules, such as data entry, file conversion, and the like, or on organization units or applications (e.g., payroll first, then accounts payable).

Testing Plan

This document should specify the testing plan, the nature of the test data, and a summary of the test results. Adequate testing is an important phase in the life cycle.

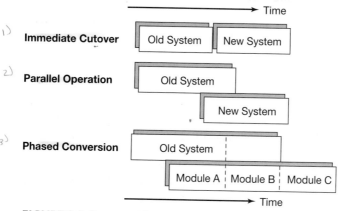

FIGURE 9.6 Conversion Strategies.

Operating and Maintenance Schedules

These documents must correspond to the schedules used in the organization's data processing facility. Maintenance is discussed in detail in a subsequent section of this chapter.

Audit Plan

This document should specify the nature of any audit to be conducted to evaluate the operation of the system.

User Comments

It is desirable to formally solicit and review user comments on the system after it has become operational. This document should specify the plan to accomplish this task and incorporate the results of this process into the system.

Maintenance of Systems Documentation Standards

Maintaining systems documentation standards and using them consistently in systems development are formidable tasks in a large organization. Frequently, a separate function or departmental specialty is created to assume responsibility for these tasks. This group of people monitors and collects the documentation generated by each developmental project but has an essentially passive role in the detail design tasks.

System documentation standards may be developed in-house or purchased from a vendor. Large CPA and management consulting firms generally have their own system documentation standards, which they market or use when they develop systems on a consulting basis. Most major computer vendors, various government agencies, and many large organizations also have system documentation standards that may be obtained by interested parties.

Documentation has many advantages. The process of developing documentation ensures that all relevant considerations and actions have been undertaken during each phase of a project. Documentation provides the medium for effective review of the project by management and all other parties. Documentation is essential to operating and maintaining the system. Documentation is frequently referred to as **deliverables,** the term indicating that documentation is used by the various parties in a systems development project to communicate with each other about the completion of specific tasks and responsibilities.

The only disadvantage of documentation is the work necessary to generate it. This work is frequently repetitive, time-consuming, and seen as an undesirable task by people who would rather be doing more creative things. Frequently, the generation of documentation is planned as the last phase in a project; when the documentation phase is reached, the project is behind schedule. The result is often inadequate documentation. Control over the preparation of documentation is as important as the documentation itself. This is why many firms create special functions to monitor documentation.

The prevalent philosophy toward system documentation is to use structured analysis techniques. These techniques take many forms but are usually tabular or matrixlike and are to be used in a *top-down* fashion with *successive refinement.* The organization inherent in structured analysis techniques makes them self-documenting. When the design is complete, it is evidenced in the documentation that was used to guide and assist the design process.

Thus, an increase in overall productivity might be expected with the use of structured analysis. This increase is amplified if the analysis technique itself is structured with standard forms and procedures or is automated using a computer. A number of automated approaches to system documentation exist. Documentation is automatically generated and maintained by these systems. Automated project management systems also generate and maintain the requisite documentation.

SYSTEMS DEVELOPMENT TECHNOLOGIES AND PRACTICES

Analyst/Programmer Productivity Control

The major portion of total systems development costs is the salaries of analysts and programmers. Increased managerial involvement in systems development has created interest in the factors influencing the production and maintenance of programs. The job of an analyst is not as well defined as that of a programmer. The end product of an analyst is a system design for a program, which is not as concrete as an actual computer program. Because of this, more interest has been directed at the productivity of the programming function. The major control practice directed at the analyst function is explicit documentation of the analyst–user interface. The analyst and user communicate via natural language (e.g., English) and natural language is imprecise and ambiguous for technical communication. Verbal communication (interviewing) is less precise than written communication. Verbal interfaces, therefore, should be documented by the analyst and reviewed and approved by the user. The use of structured analysis, design, and graphic techniques should improve the analyst–user interface and thus increase the overall productivity of the analyst function.

Controls suggested for improving the productivity of programmers concern the way programs are designed and coded and the organization of programming personnel. A major concern is the *maintainability* of the resulting programs as well as productivity during program development. Estimates of the amount of time spent on maintenance as opposed to new development programming by organizations run as high as 80%. Controls directed at increasing the maintainability of programs can provide a significant return on these costs through the subsequent reduction in time needed to maintain a program.

Structured Programming

Structured programming (SP) is a concept concerning general programming style and, in its most abstract form, is a type of symbolic logic concerned with logical proofs of program correctness and design. At a practical level, SP concerns the application of a top-down design and successive refinement philosophy. SP also includes a set of guidelines for programming style that is intended to improve program clarity and, thus, maintainability.

As a systems development practice, SP involves developing program design standards that specify how programmers are to use a programming language, stylistic guidelines, and how programs are to be designed to fit together. The goal of SP is to systematically and inexpensively produce code that works. Systematically means programming via a series of techniques and guidelines. Inexpensive means inexpensive to write, inexpensive to test, and inexpensive to maintain.

Although certain projects are suitable for individual programmers, most business applications require a group or team approach. SP techniques are well-suited to a team approach to systems design. SP techniques are, in essence, a set of systems development standards for the programming phase of the systems development life cycle. All of the considerations relevant to the life-cycle concept, such as documentation and project management, are relevant to the control of programming projects as well.

One major control associated with SP techniques is formal reviews or **walk-throughs** of program code by one or more independent parties, such as the team or project leader. SP techniques facilitate such reviews.

Although SP concepts can be implemented in any programming language, the concept of SP is relatively new in programming circles and, accordingly, many programmers are used to writing programs in their own individual manner. Conventional wisdom concerning programmers holds that they take pride in developing tricky, complex code, which is a testament to their programming skill. SP techniques seek to produce "egoless" code—code that is standardized and simple rather than a testament to the ego of the programmer. The concept and related problems of "private code" are totally eliminated in a highly structured approach to programming that involves the organization of chief programmer teams.

Teams

This approach establishes a team consisting of a lead or chief programmer, assistant programmers as needed, and a programming secretary. The chief and assistant programmers work as a group—all program code is a group rather than individual effort. The programming secretary performs clerical functions for the programmers and is responsible for all program documentation. With group programming, reviews or walk-throughs are incorporated into the process of developing the code rather than left until after code has been developed.

Technical Aids

Programmer productivity may also be increased through technical aids. The use of high-level languages and DBMSs increases productivity. Special software packages called **preprocessors,** and automated documentation systems also increase programmer productivity. The preprocessors are programs that take code submitted by a programmer and modify it in some manner before submitting it for processing to the source statement compiler. Preprocessors can be used in a batch or an on-line processing mode. Preprocessors are used to reduce the clerical effort required of programmers. Common preprocessor functions include expanding abbreviations into full syntax, checking for syntax errors, and reformatting program code into a structured format. Automated documentation is essentially **postprocessing,** relieving the programmer of clerical work related to documentation.

Computer-Aided Software Engineering (CASE)

Computer-aided software engineering (CASE) is the process of using computer software technology that supports an automated engineering discipline for software development and maintenance. The term *CASE* is also used to refer to a particular product or a set of products that automate (at least in part) the process of building and maintaining software. CASE is intended to increase productivity, improve software quality through introduction of rigorous standards and analysis, and decrease the cost of developing, documenting, and maintaining software.

CASE technology is a recent development, and is only beginning to be implemented in many organizations. CASE requires a highly structured approach to analysis, design, coding, testing, and maintenance of software. Traditional software engineering, however, has been a highly iterative process with frequent movement from one task to another. Training programmers to adhere to a rigorous structure is often a challenge. Studies have shown that when a software team switches to CASE methodology, a 10% decrease in productivity is initially experienced. Subsequently, productivity increases approximately 10% to 15%.

There is a great diversity in CASE tools from different vendors. The terms *Upper CASE* and *Front-End CASE* describe tools that are directed at the analysis and design stages. The terms *Lower CASE* and *Back-End CASE* describe tools that are directed at the implementation stage. CASE tools can be further categorized by their orientation toward either the data or process aspects of an information system. Data-oriented CASE tools address the conceptual, logical, and physical levels of database design. Process-oriented CASE tools deal with business function definition, data flow diagrams, program design, and program code. The combination of data and process, together with the combination of upper and lower CASE and the project management support, is called Integrated CASE. When timing and interrupt messages are added to the code in Integrated CASE, it is known as Real-Time CASE. If hardware simulation is then added, it becomes Embedded CASE.

CASE consists of a variety of tools, as shown in Figure 9.7. These tools are described in what follows. Most CASE products include some but not all of these tools. The ideal CASE environment would be one with seamless interfaces between these various tools, even if they were supplied by different vendors. This would represent truly integrated CASE. The establishment of industrywide standards will eventually allow the flow of information between these different tools.

Repository

The repository is central to CASE. In addition to a data dictionary, which contains information pertaining to the data flow, report design, specifications, and the user interface, the repository includes a central directory consisting of code generation and reports. The repository may also contain planning information, such as overall application design information, documentation, and project management data.

Diagramming Tools

Most structured systems analysis techniques use graphics as the medium of communication. Data flow diagrams are a common example. The manual drawing and revision of such diagrams is tedious. CASE diagramming tools provide automated support for drawing data flow diagrams, structure charts, and other such graphics. The advantages that are gained from these tools are similar to those as-

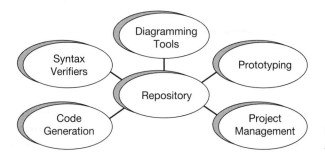

FIGURE 9.7 CASE (Computer-Aided Software Engineering).

sociated with word processing. Overall clarity is improved and revision becomes easier and much less error-prone.

Syntax Verifiers

Structured systems analysis techniques have specific rules associated with their use. In data flow diagrams, for example, each flow line should be labeled. Most CASE products have some ability to verify the proper usage of diagramming techniques. Such products perform consistency checks and other error-checking procedures.

Prototyping

Prototyping tools are used to develop system interfaces—screen displays or printed report formats—with the user prior to the actual development of the system. These tools are often called screen and report "painters." They provide automated support for developing screen displays and printed report formats. They utilize data definitions stored in the repository to specify the input/output fields in a screen or report.

Code Generation

Code generators are computer programs designed to produce other programs. Code generators have been available for many years. Generators allow analysts to automatically develop program code. The analyst supplies input specifications, typically in a high-level language, and the code generator develops modular program code. Typically, the programs that are produced are in a highly structured format. Code generators, especially for COBOL, are quite sophisticated and can often produce more than 75% of the code for a given application. Such tools, when integrated with other CASE tools, can minimize or totally eliminate a distinction between program analysis and design.

handles the user interface

Project Management

Project management tools are used to track progress and manage resources for a project. Standards for project tasks need to be identified and implemented. Project management tools establish and enforce such standards.

Prototyping

Strict application of structured development tools to the development of DSS, ES, and even MIS may be, at times, inappropriate. This is due to the nature of these types of applications. In many applications, user statements of system requirements are accepted as being complete and firm and are to be developed as defined. At the completion of each development stage, there are formal procedures to verify compliance with system requirements. Whenever user requirements are found to be incorrect or inadequate during development, the specifications are revised by the users. Such a process works best if users know *in advance* what they want or need and can clearly specify these data to an analyst *before* the system is actually developed and the user actually has experience with it. This may not be true when a MIS, DSS, or ES is to be developed.

Iterative Design

Prototyping is a different general approach to the process of developing and implementing computer-based application systems. Prototyping is used when user requirements are difficult to specify in advance. The distinguishing feature of the

Distinguishing feature

prototyping approach to systems development is that assurance that systems development requirements are adequate and correct is obtained through actual user experience with the system being developed. Prototyping is based on the notion that users can express their opinions more easily about an actual system (i.e., the prototype) rather than an imagined system.

Prototyping is an iterative process. The initial user requirements are estimated and then implemented in a prototype (i.e., mock) system. The users gain actual experience with the prototype system, and may modify their requirements based on this experience. The prototype is then revised to include these new or modified requirements, and reimplemented. This iterative process continues until the user is satisfied (Figure 9.8).

Potential Disadvantages (2)

Although conceptually appealing, there are several problems with the prototyping approach. One is that unfinished systems may be accepted as final. A user may be satisfied with a system before it is actually finished. Important controls, for example, may have been omitted to speed development of the prototype. Another problem with prototyping is that it is difficult to manage and control a process that invites frequent changes. Users might continue to request minor changes that have no real impact on their use of the system. As an analyst, imagine how you might feel if everything that you do has to be constantly revised. Projects may never be completed. Despite such problems, prototyping is useful when it is difficult to clearly specify user requirements in advance of development. This is often true in DSS and ES. Prototyping allows users to "try out" systems before extensive development costs are incurred.

usefulness

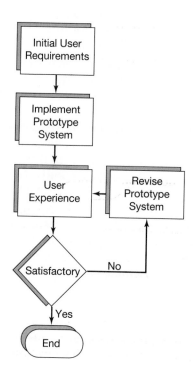

FIGURE 9.8 Prototyping Approach to Systems Development.

programming & database.

Object-Oriented Technology

Object-oriented technology includes object-oriented programming (OOP) and object-oriented databases. These concepts are related, but an object-oriented database could be implemented outside the concept of an OOP environment.

"Objects" are intelligent data items that contain both data and the rules or procedures that determine how objects relate to other objects. An object can be an invoice, purchase order, or any other type of business form, or a physical object such as a product or an employee. Unlike data, objects have the ability to act. Action occurs when an object receives a message and responds to it. The only way to use an object is to send messages to it.

Objects change the traditional relation between programs and data. In data processing, programs process data. Both are separate. In contrast, an object includes programs and data in one unit that fully describe some entity (i.e., object).

Object-Oriented Programming

Object-oriented programming (OOP) is seen as a major conceptual change in the nature of programming computers. Like most concepts, it is difficult to define precisely. OOP concepts are associated with SIMULA language, developed in the late 1960s, and the language Smalltalk, developed in the mid-1970s. Objective C, ADA, Visual Basic, and C++ are considered to be OOP languages.

The goal of OOP is to make software easier to create, simpler to use, and more reliable through reusability. The major advantage of OOP is that objects are reusable. Thus, programs can be built from prefabricated, pretested building blocks in less time than it would take to make them from scratch. Programs can be upgraded simply by adding new objects. Reusability is attained through encapsulation, inheritance, and the use of messages.

Encapsulation. **Encapsulation** is information hiding. The interface to a program is defined in such a way as to hide as much as possible about its inner workings. Encapsulation also separates the user of an object from the author of the object. In OOP, objects contain their own data and procedures. An object knows what messages it can process, which messages it should reject, and which messages it should pass on to other objects. But no object knows the capabilities or inner workings of any other object. This means that an object can be modified with no effect on other objects.

Inheritance. **Inheritance** is the automatic passing of properties or characteristics from a parent or ancestor to a child. Much as children inherit characteristics from their parents, objects inherit characteristics from their "parents." A class is a set of similar objects. In OOP, a class consists of methods and data that summarize common characteristics of a set of objects. An object is an instance of a class. A specific customer's account in an accounts receivable system might be a specific instance of the class "account." Objects (classes) may have subobjects (subclasses).

The ability to abstract common methods and data from a set of objects and store them as a class is central to OOP. Reusable code is stored in a repository rather than expressed repeatedly. Inheritance allows common attributes to be expressed once, and then extended to children. OOP uses inheritance to express commonality. Subobjects (subclasses) are created by changing one or more of the parent object's methods and adding one or more new methods. The actual code for inherited methods remains in the parent. Messages that are not handled by a subobject's unique methods are automatically routed to its parent.

Messages. Objects respond to messages. The set of messages to which an object can respond is called the object's protocol. Messages are the only connection between an object and its environment. Data within an object can only be processed by the procedures contained within the object. These procedures are invoked by messages. In OOP, objects from different classes must be able to respond in their own appropriate manner to common messages. The ability of objects from different classes to respond in their own appropriate manner to common messages is called **polymorphism.** Polymorphism is central to OOP.

Object-Oriented Databases

An object-oriented database stores both data and the procedures that operate on the data as a single unit, that is, as an object. Unlike the record-type data stored in a traditional database, objects are much more varied. An object may be data, a document, or a digitalized image of text, video, or voice data. Objects are stored in a format that allows them to be efficiently accessed and manipulated. Objects in an object-oriented database interact by exchanging messages to perform particular functions. Users are isolated from the details of storage representation. Complex operations may be performed simply by sending messages.

Visual Basic Example

Microsoft Visual Basic is a developmental system especially geared toward the development of graphical applications for use in the Microsoft Windows environment. It includes graphical design tools and a high-level programming language—BASIC. Visual Basic uses two types of objects: forms and controls. Forms appear as "windows" on the user's computer screen. In Visual Basic, you create forms, and on these objects, you draw other objects called controls. Then, using the programming language, you program how forms and control respond to users' actions in an event-driven environment.

Event-Driven Programs. The graphical interface provided by the Windows operating environment differs from the text-based interface supported by DOS in several ways. One important difference is that applications share screen space in the Windows operating environment. Another important difference is that applications share computing time. An application cannot run continually, or if it does, it has to be able to run in the background. A Visual Basic application may run in a group of one or more windows that do not take over the whole of a user's screen. The event-driven approach used by Visual Basic allows applications to share computing time and other resources (such as the Clipboard). An event-driven application consists of objects—forms and controls—that wait for a particular event to happen. An event is an action recognized by a Visual Basic object.

Visual Basic code does not work in the linear fashion of a traditional DOS program—starting at the top, proceeding toward the bottom, and finally stopping. Instead, in event-driven programming, applications use code that remains idle until called upon to respond to specific user-caused or system-caused events. That is, objects in an application respond in their own unique way to messages received from the Windows environment. For example, one might write computer code to program a command button to print the message "Hello" in response to a mouse click. When the command button recognizes that the event has occurred, it invokes the code written for that event and displays the message "Hello" to the user.

While an application is waiting for an event, it remains in the environment (unless the user closes the application). In the meantime, a user can run other applications, resize windows, or customize system settings such as color. But application code is always present, ready to be activated when the user wishes to return to it.

For each type of object that is created for an application, Visual Basic predefines a set of events, that is, messages, that the object can respond to. An application responds to an event by executing program code. Visual Basic makes it very easy to respond to events—forms and controls have the built-in ability to recognize user actions and invoke the code associated with them. The inner workings of this built-in ability to respond to messages are completely hidden, that is, encapsulated, from the developer.

A Menu Application. For illustration, suppose that we want to create a start-up menu for an accounting system that offers a user several choices such as "Sales Journal," "Purchase Journal," and "Exit," among others. The user will select from the menu by clicking the option button associated with the desired choice. Option buttons work as a group; clicking any particular button immediately causes all other buttons in the group to be cleared. We also may wish to have a command button that the user presses with a mouse click to proceed with the selected choice.

Figure 9.9 illustrates the general structure of the menu, and Figure 9.10 illustrates some Visual Basic code to implement this menu. We would begin by defining a form—an object—that will be the window for our menu. On this form, we could draw three controls—a label control for the title "Accounting System," an option button control for the options available to the user, and a command button control.

One of the built-in events recognized by our form is "load"—that is, when the form is first loaded into memory, our object recognizes this event and has the built-in capability to execute any code that we wish at this time. In Visual Basic, all code <u>must be written</u> as subroutines or functions. Sub Form_Load () in Figure 9.10 is executed upon the occurrence of the load event. This is the natural time to do any initialization, such as displaying the title of the form, the option buttons and their related meaning, and the command button (see Figure 9.9). The code segment

- For i = 1 To 5
- Load option1(i)
- option1(i).top = option1(i − 1).top + 400
- Next

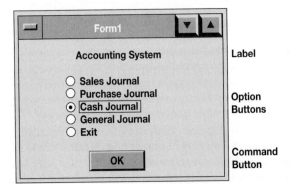

FIGURE 9.9 Menu Form.

```
Sub Form_Load ( )

For i = 1 To 5
Load option1(i)
option1(i).top = option1(i - 1).top + 400
Next

option1(1).caption = "Sales Journal"
option1(2).caption = "Purchase Journal"
        .
        .
        .
option1(5).caption = "Exit"

End Sub

Sub Option1_Click (index As Integer)

Select Case Index

Case 1
' code for selection "Sales Journal"

Case 2
' code for selection "Purchase Journal"
    .
    .
    .
Case 5
' code for selection "Exit"

End Select

End Sub
```

FIGURE 9.10 Visual Basic Program Code.

illustrates several basic features of object-oriented software. This code creates the option buttons for our application. When we design the form, we draw a single option button that has the default name option1. An option button is an object that has more than 20 built-in properties and that has the built-in capability to recognize nine different events. Properties are attributes of the control such as font type, font size, backcolor, and forecolor. Properties concern how the control appears to the user. The Load option1(i) statement creates a new option button for each i. Each option button inherits the property values we selected for the original option button when we drew it on the form. In addition, each option button inherits the built-in capability to recognize and thus respond to the same events as our original option button. For example, if we specified "yellow" as the forecolor of the option button we drew, then each created option button (i.e., index i in the programming statement) inherits yellow as its forecolor. The option1(i).top statement changes the top (i.e., relative vertical location) of each new button, otherwise, they would all be placed in the same place on the screen and thus only one would be visible to the user. Finally, the statement option1(1).caption = "Sales Journal" sets the unique caption—another property of the option button—to its particular value.

One does not have to write code for all of the events to which an object can inherently respond. When you do want an object to respond to an event such as a mouse click, you write code called an event procedure—a procedure that Visual

Basic invokes in response to an event. The procedure is named according to a convention:

objectname_eventname

The name itself establishes the association between the procedure and the event. When an application is running, Visual Basic automatically invokes the appropriate procedure each time an event occurs.

Sub Option1_Click in Figure 9.10 illustrates the general structure of an event procedure. Option1 is the objectname; Click is the eventname. The user will select from the menu by using a mouse to click the option button associated with the desired choice. Option buttons work as a group; clicking any particular button immediately causes all other buttons in the group to be cleared. As indicated by our sample code, responding to this event is quite easy. The inner workings of the object—in this case, a set of option buttons—are encapsulated, that is, completely hidden from the programmer. The working of the option buttons is completely automatic—no code has to be written to recognize the mouse click or to cause the option button group to indicate the currently selected option. The currently selected option is automatically made available to the associated event procedure code as an integer variable named "index." All that one needs to do to respond to a user making a selection from the option-button menu with a mouse click is to use the value of index in code, as indicated by the Select Case index example in Figure 9.10.

The menu application then waits for the next event. To complete our example, the user clicks the command button labeled "OK" to implement his or her selection. As with the option-button object, the command button automatically recognizes this action as a Click event, and Visual Basic then executes the associated event procedure to implement the user's selection.

Visual Basic is illustrative of object-oriented software—the emerging technology for the development of application systems. It provides a good platform for prototyping and developing applications in a GUI environment. It eases transition to event-driven programming, and it encourages a modular programming style. And, as indicated by our example, it provides a powerful and practical tool for the development of GUI-based application systems by end users.

Advantages of Object-Oriented Technology

Developing software in the 1990s is much more complex than it was in the past. Most existing programming languages—including COBOL, which is widely used in business—were developed several decades ago. These languages were developed before the advent of massive on-line computer systems with massive databases. They were developed well before even the concept, much less the reality, of personal computers was envisioned. They were developed before it was common (or even possible) for users to sit at keyboard terminals to directly input data for processing and to observe output on color video monitors. They were developed for use in simple batch processing environments, one where users were entirely isolated from contact with a computer.

In contemporary organizations, many people spend large portions of their working day interacting with computer systems. Users have direct contact with computer systems, directly entering input and directly observing output on video displays. The amount of software necessary to support the direct user interface is enormous. More than 50%, maybe 75%, of current computer system applications is devoted to managing the user interface—things such as pull-down menus, graphic displays, icons, and mouse movements.

This means that a computer application developed in the 1990s requires at least twice as much software, maybe more, than a similar application developed ten or more years ago to do the same function. And there are many more types of applications that should or could be developed in the 1990s than there were previously. In addition to processing of traditional, transactional data records, digitalized voice, text, and image data may be processed. For lack of software, much of the potential of computer hardware is untapped. This is why reusability of existing software has become a major concern.

With OOP, common functions are defined as objects and stored in a repository. Parent objects contain code for common functions. Subobjects need not develop their own code for common functions as they inherit it from their parents. When new children (i.e., objects) need to be developed, they too can inherit, and thus reuse, code stored in their parent objects.

Reengineering

Reengineering is the process of extracting reusable code segments from existing software, and then restructuring this code to enhance its efficiency and reusability. Reengineered code is stored in a repository. New programs can then reuse this code rather than develop their own unique code to perform the same task.

Reusability of existing software has become a major concern in the 1990s. Reengineering is the attempt to make software easier to create, simpler to use, and more reliable through reusability. The major advantage of OOP is that objects are reusable. Reengineering applies to any type of programming system.

Program Change Control

Maintenance of computer programs is inevitable. The need to change a program might arise when an error is discovered or when a change is mandated by external requirements such as government regulations. At other times, changes or enhancements might be requested by users or mandated by changes in the configuration of data files, report formats, and the like.

Program change controls concern the maintenance of application programs. The objective of such controls is to prevent unauthorized and potentially fraudulent changes from being introduced into previously tested and accepted programs. Unfortunately, program maintenance requests often have an emergency or crisis nature, which creates an atmosphere of fixing and patching that is not conducive to effective control. It is tempting to omit testing of changes, for example, in a crisis atmosphere.

Segregation of Duties

Control of program changes involves documentation and review. The objective is to effectively screen all program changes. Documentation centers around the maintenance of a program change register and a program change file. A program change register is used to log and subsequently control all changes. Requests for changes should be written and approved. Requests should be reviewed, sequentially numbered, and entered into the program change register. The person responsible for the program change register notifies programmers of the change request with a written form (typically, a copy of the original request) that serves as authorization for the programmer(s) to obtain a copy of the production program and its related documentation. Changes should not be directly made to production programs, and the custody of production programs should be segregated from programmers.

After the change has been programmed, tested, and the program documentation revised to reflect the change, the change authorization form, the revised program, revised documentation, and testing documentation are returned to the person administering the program change register for review and approval. Appropriate notations are made in the program change register to evidence the process.

Control of Documentation

Program change documentation should be accumulated in a program change file, which provides a cumulative history of program changes for each separate application program. The program changes themselves have to be made to the production programs. It is usually desirable, if possible, to batch several program changes and process them together to minimize overall costs. Documentation and review of adding the changes to the production programs are also necessary in a manner similar to that just discussed, as is segregation of functions in this process. Control and documentation of the actual modification process is simplified if maintenance activities are scheduled and can only occur at specific, preauthorized times. Documentation of the actual modification is provided by the computer's operating system. If maintenance activities are restricted to certain time periods, a review of operating system statistics provides a control over unauthorized changes that might be made during unauthorized time periods.

Management Considerations

From a management viewpoint, maintenance should be considered to be small-scale systems development. As such, maintenance of programs should be subject to systems development controls, although at a level of detail appropriate to the project. It is desirable to attempt to reduce the number of changes that have to be made on an emergency basis, possibly by establishing a schedule to review and solicit user comments for each application on a rotating basis.

Maintenance is frequently made difficult by practices followed by the original programmer(s). Structured programming techniques, adequate program documentation, and the use of high-level, database, and/or object-oriented programming languages all serve to increase the maintainability of programs.

Emergency or crisis exceptions to well-controlled maintenance procedures are probably unavoidable, and each organization handles crisis changes in its own way. Experience has shown that exceptions to documented procedures are major loss exposures. Care must be taken to ensure that emergency maintenance is subsequently reviewed and documented.

Database Administration

The **database administration (DBA) function** is the focal point for design and control of all the elements of data management and database systems. The larger, more integrated the database, the larger the responsibility placed on the DBA. The functions performed by the DBA are not new. These functions, such as data definition and data security, have traditionally been performed separately, perhaps by different individuals, for each separate application program and its related files. As files and access to them are absorbed by the database system, the related data management functions are centralized under the DBA. This centralization of previously separate functions is new, and the result is an opportunity for increased efficiency and control.

A major control activity of the DBA is to establish standards and documentation for the data elements in a database. A data dictionary is often used to accomplish this task. The integration of data into a centralized or distributed database may not be too difficult, technically speaking. However, it may be very difficult as far as organizational or political aspects are concerned. The DBA must assist in resolving incompatibilities and coordination and communication problems between groups sharing a database.

As part of the design process, the DBA must deal with the issues of data security, integrity, data sharing, recovery/backup, and audit trails. Each of these issues is a major control concern. With a database system, resolution of these issues is centralized in the DBA function. The techniques and options that are available to the DBA for addressing these issues are highly dependent on the particular database software system being used.

To achieve organizational independence, the DBA function should not be allowed to operate the computer system or initiate transactions into the database. Documentation of system changes should be the responsibility of an independent control group. Custody of active files and programs also should not be the responsibility of the DBA function.

Auditor Involvement in Systems Development

The auditability of a data processing system is dependent on the underlying system of controls that has been built into the system during its development. This view has been increasingly embraced by management, auditors, and other parties to the systems development process. Internal auditors must participate in the systems development process to ensure that necessary audit and control features are built into computer-based systems.

Traditionally, the audit function maintained a hands-off position toward systems development to preserve independence and objectivity when the audit function is subsequently called to audit the functioning system. However, the nature of control in computer-based systems, the difficulties of establishing controls after a computer application has been implemented, and a general increased concern for financial and operational loss exposures inherent in large-scale computer systems have all contributed to a reversal of the traditional hands-off attitude toward systems development.

Usage of Advanced Techniques

Usage of advanced systems development techniques is highlighted in a survey of North American CIOs conducted by Deloitte & Touche Information Technology Consulting Services.[7] Advanced application development techniques include systems development methodologies, fourth-generation languages, PC-based development, CASE (computer-aided software engineering), prototyping, and object-oriented programming techniques, among several others. Systems development methodologies was the most extensively used technique. Object-oriented programming was the least extensively used technique. Overall, the survey reports only moderate use of advanced application development techniques. However, CIOs expect to increase usage significantly in the future, with object-oriented programming techniques expected to show the greatest increase in usage.

The number of organizations using CASE techniques is reported at slightly more than 50%, just about the same percentage as in the previous year's survey.

---

[7]Deloitte & Touche Information Technology Consulting Services, *Leading Trends in Information Services*, Fifth Annual Survey of North American CIOs—1993, pp. 14–16. Deloitte Touche Tohmatsu International.

CASE is more widely used by companies with large application development staffs. PC-based development techniques were the most broadly used advanced application development technique, closely followed by fourth-generation languages, system development methodologies, and prototyping. The term *broadly used* means that the technique was used for at least one project by the respondent.

PLANNING AND ORGANIZING A SYSTEMS PROJECT

Operationally, project management techniques are the heart of a well-controlled systems development life cycle. The term *project* refers to a specific application that has been approved for development. Once approval has been obtained, project management begins and is concerned with the detailed analysis, design, programming, testing, implementation, operation, and maintenance of the project.

Project Selection

If an organization's resources are limited, project development resources should be allocated to those projects that yield the greatest benefits to the organization. Potential projects may be proposed directly by user departments, proposed by a separate information system or corporate planning function, or arise in response to an immediate problem—such as a change in federal reporting requirements. Typically, proposals arise in all of these ways, and there are more project proposals than can be undertaken by the existing staff. **Project selection** is usually the responsibility of a **steering committee** or other organizationwide unit to assure active user participation in the selection process. Project proposals are submitted to the steering committee in writing. A proposal should provide a statement of the expected benefits and costs if possible. Frequently, costs and benefits can only be subjectively estimated, owing to both the difficulties of costing EDP services and the difficulties of estimating the resources that will be necessary to complete the project. In large organizations, the project selection process may be highly formalized, with the project proposal document providing a detailed analysis of expected costs and benefits, both financial and nonfinancial. Expected return on investment (ROI) is frequently an important selection criterion in such cases. Once a project has been approved for development, a project team must be organized to begin work.

The Project Team

Labor is a basic resource in any systems project. One important task of project management is to assemble a suitable project team. For an applications system project, analysts, programmers, and other technicians are necessary, but representatives of the user department(s) for which the application is being developed should usually be included as well. One member must be selected as the project leader in order to focus control responsibilities for the project. Whether this project leader should come from the user department or the information systems department is a question best answered in the context of the specific project environment. If the project leader comes from a user department, then the user will likely be deeply involved and committed to the project's success. However, the quality of technical leadership may be weaker than if an information systems person is selected as the project leader.

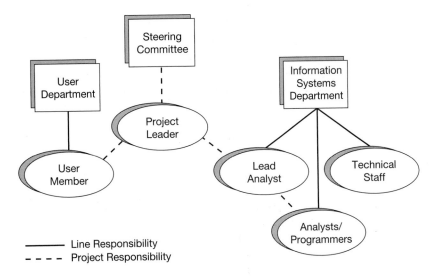

FIGURE 9.11 Project Team Organization.

Project Leader Responsibilities

A diagram of a project team organization appears in Figure 9.11. The project leader has direct responsibility to the steering committee for project progress and completion. A steering committee or other such organizational unit is used to assure a high level of user involvement in the work of the information systems department. The project team consists of the project leader, analysts, and programmers from the information systems department, and one or more user participants from the organizational unit(s) for which the project is being undertaken. Each member of a project team maintains line responsibility to the manager/supervisor of his or her department. However, for project activities, each project team member reports to the project leader. On a large project, one or more lead or chief analysts and/or programmers are assigned to assist the project leader in supervising the technical staff.

The project leader must maintain contact with the principal user department manager who has responsibility for the project. The user manager is typically the person who must formally approve the project at its completion. The project leader must also be in contact with technical specialists such as the database administrator, as required to successfully complete the project. In addition to project team organization, the primary responsibilities of the project leader are planning, scheduling, and controlling the project. These responsibilities are detailed in Figure 9.12. Planning involves the project breakdown and allocation of resources. Scheduling is a successive refinement to the project plan; activities are scheduled chronologically and detailed project responsibilities are assigned to team members. Project scheduling is usually done with the aid of Gantt charts or network charts such as PERT. Project control involves time and progress reporting as well as periodic project status reporting to upper-level management. A project accounting system is the means by which the project leader fulfills her or his project control responsibilities.

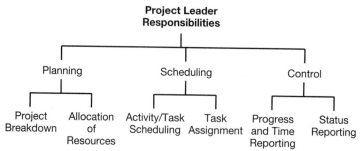

FIGURE 9.12 Project Leader Responsibilities.

Project Uncertainty

The major problem faced by any project team is the uncertainty associated with an application systems project. The technicians have to work with the users to elicit the system's data requirements. Users are often unaware of the problem creating the need for the new project and, in fact, may be unaware of the specific data that they use in their decision-making responsibilities. For these reasons, the user–designer interface is characterized by a high degree of uncertainty. Uncertainty also exists in the development of the system. Once the system design is set, programmers have to interpret the detailed specifications and write the necessary software. Software development—the total time required, whether or not the software is reliable, and whether or not the software conforms to system specifications—is also uncertain. The task of the project team is to reduce all of these uncertainties, coordinate the activities of the diverse parties working on the project, and complete the project within a reasonable time and at a reasonable cost. The selection of an effective project leader is crucial to these tasks.

Project Breakdown into Tasks and Phases

To effectively plan and control a project, the required activities are broken down or factored into a detailed listing of tasks and phases. If a total project is suitably factored into the smaller components of a system life cycle, the project becomes easier to control and understand. There is no standard method for factoring a project into detailed activities, just as there is no standard listing of phases in the systems development life cycle. There are several reasons for this, including different opinions, different commercial project management packages, and different requirements for particular projects. The guiding philosophy is top-down design with successive refinement. The basic operational principle is that each specific task or phase should provide a *deliverable* at its completion, some type of tangible product (i.e., documentation) that can be reviewed and evaluated. The higher the degree of breakdown into specific tasks and phases, the higher the certainty with which each task's or phase's requirements can be predicted. Figure 9.13 illustrates the concept of factoring a project into a set of phases and tasks and the use of a hierarchical (HIPO) chart to document this plan. The numbers assigned to the individual tasks and phases provide a basis for organizing the documentation generated during the course of the project.

The objective of project breakdown is to facilitate assignment and control of labor and other project resources. To the extent possible, tasks should be broken down to a level where task definition is sufficiently clear to enable individual personnel to be assigned to specific tasks. Task assignments should reflect the skills of

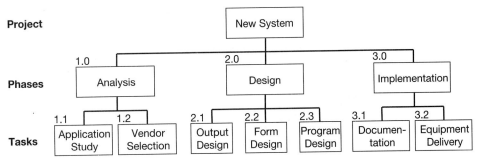

FIGURE 9.13 Factoring a Project into Phases and Tasks.

individual personnel. Estimated time requirements for each specific task must also be included in the project breakdown.

Time Estimates

Estimating accurate task completion times for a systems project is difficult because of the uncertainties inherent in systems development. Poorly estimated task completion times severely limit the effectiveness of project management techniques. Accuracy depends partly on the previous project management experience within an organization. Experience from previous projects should increase the task time estimation skill of project personnel on each new project. But estimates always will be inaccurate to some degree, and this fact must be accepted. Undue pressure to keep to unrealistic schedules may result in an unsatisfactory project outcome. The proper attitude toward time estimates is to accept them for what they are—estimates—and to be prepared to revise them frequently as a project is developed.

Work Measurement Techniques

The simplest approach to estimation is to guess, meaning that no formal calculations are undertaken. The "guesstimate" is based on one's previous experience with similar projects or tasks. More rigorous approaches to estimation are based on the concept of work measurement, as this concept was discussed in Chapter 2. Work measurement involves four basic steps:

1. Identify the tasks to be estimated.
2. For each task, estimate the total size or volume of the task in some suitable manner.
3. Convert the size or volume estimate into a time estimate by multiplying the size or volume estimate by a standard or estimated processing rate.
4. Adjust the estimated processing rate to include circumstantial considerations such as idle time, task complexity, or task newness.

Figure 9.14 illustrates this general approach. Note the adjustment of the initial estimate of 50 standard man-days for the interviews to 65 man-days to reflect the complexity of the task as "somewhat above average." A further refinement involves adjustment of the estimated time for a task as calculated before by experience or competency factors, increasing or decreasing the total estimated time to reflect the relative capabilities of the specific individuals to be assigned to each task. Figure 9.15 illustrates this type of adjustment. Extending the final time estimates by suitable costing or charging rates provides the method for estimating

Standard Man-Days for Interviews

People to Be Interviewed	Number to Be Interviewed	Standard Man-Day Allowance	Total Man-Days
Managers	4	0.5	2
Supervisors	17	1.0	17
Technical Staff	18	1.5	27
Clerical Staff	8	0.5	4
Total	47	—	50

Complexity Factors

Simple	0.50–0.75
Average	1.00–1.50
Complex	2.00–2.50

Complexity judgment for the case in point is "somewhat above average"

Assign a factor of 1.30

Adjusted man-days = standard man-days times complexity factor
= 50 x 1.30
= 65 adjusted man-days

FIGURE 9.14 Sample Work Measurement Calculation.

Personnel Factors

A. Competence and Experience

	Competence Level	
Experience	Low	High
Senior	1.0	0.7
Intermediate	1.8	1.1
Junior	2.8	1.9

B. Knowledge

	Knowledge Required		
Knowledge Available	Little	Average	Much
Much	0.0	0.1	0.3
Average	0.0	0.2	0.7
Little	0.1	0.5	1.0

Actual man-days = adjusted days x (personnel + knowledge)

Assume that a junior analyst of high competence will do the work. Average knowledge is available, and much knowledge is required.

Actual man-days = 65 x (1.9 + 0.7) = 169 man-days

FIGURE 9.15 Competency and Knowledge Adjustments.

the total budgeted project cost. Techniques used to develop cost or charging rates are discussed in Chapter 18.

Although estimation for each different task in a project, such as analysis or programming, requires different basic data to describe its size or volume, the principles of work measurement are the same in each case. Because application development projects are a regular activity in many organizations, standard task times or processing rates can be estimated and refined based on experience. Standards developed in-house are likely to be more effective than standards or estimates available in the project management literature.

Accuracy of Estimates

The literature on project management is a source of estimation techniques as well as of detailed time estimates or standard processing rates for performing various project tasks. There are no commonly accepted standards, largely because there is no general agreement of standard project phases and tasks. However, there is general agreement on several points related to the estimation process. The first point is that estimates are only estimates, no matter how carefully prepared. A second point of agreement is that the accuracy of estimation improves considerably as a project proceeds through its course of activities. That is, estimates of, say, the tenth phase of a project that are made at the completion of, say, the fourth phase are likely to be more accurate than estimates for the tenth phase that were made at the beginning of the project. It is commonly held that estimation errors of 100% are not unreasonable for the latter phases of a project when these estimates are made at a project's conception. This reinforces the importance of frequently revising estimates contained in the project plan to reflect actual project experience. Estimates made during the early phase of a project can be expected to be considerably inaccurate even if carefully prepared. For this reason, "guesstimates" are frequently used in the initial phases of a project rather than detailed calculations. These original estimates are successively revised as the project proceeds through its course of activities. This approach reflects the practical fact that as a project proceeds, it takes shape, meaning that what is left to be done is now based on everything else that has been completed and is now more predictable and hence subject to greater control.

Another area of consensus is that initial estimates are frequently made too low. Estimates that are made by personnel such as computer programmers who are subsequently the ones to perform the tasks for which they are providing time estimates tend to be overly optimistic. In the consulting or contracting businesses, this type of behavior is known as **low-balling**—purposely or inadvertently submitting unreasonably low time or cost estimates to obtain a contract, knowing that once the contract is obtained, the work likely will be completed regardless of the actual amount of time or cost that is required. While low-balling is a possibility for in-house personnel as well, more common reasons for task time underestimation reside in job performance measurement factors such as a natural desire to be perceived as efficient in one's duties by one's superior. Underestimation also occurs when work measurement techniques are used to estimate task times. Often estimates of "productive hours per day," "work-days," or similar work units fail realistically to consider idle or nonproductive time due to sickness, vacations, coffee breaks, washroom breaks, and other such factors. There are also considerable differences in the productive capabilities of different people. One person's day of output might be equivalent to another person's week of output. This is the reason for suggesting in earlier discussions that basic work measurements be adjusted with factors that compensate for the relative capabilities of different people or groups of people (e.g., senior programmers versus junior programmers). There may also be significant variation in the output of a single person over time, even when the same person works on similar tasks. Again, the best strategy is to revise estimates successively based on actual project experience.

Cost overruns are a frequent problem in systems development, but to the extent that costs are higher than predicted by estimates made during the early phases of a project, analysis of the cost overrun should be tempered by the problems of estimation just discussed. This is particularly true because a relatively larger percentage of total systems development costs are incurred during the later phases of a project (design and implementation), and it is these later project phases for which initial estimates are likely to be optimistic. Typically 30% to 40% of total project *time* is spent in the analysis phase of the systems development life cycle, but 75% or more of total project *costs* is incurred during the design and implementation phases. Project resources tend to be spent at an increasing rate as a project proceeds to completion. Thus, control of project costs in the early phases of the systems development life cycle is essential.

Project Accounting

Project control is established by setting measurable goals for each phase and task in the overall project, reporting actual performance against these goals, and evaluating any significant deviations from the project plan. Measurable goal analysis is facilitated by the documentation or deliverable that is required of each phase or task to evidence its completion as well as major milestones or project checkpoints, at which times the overall status of the project to date is subject to review by upper-level management. Well-established, clearly defined responsibilities for project personnel (which is facilitated by a detailed project breakdown) and some form of project accounting system to measure and report actual performance against responsibility are essential elements of a project control system.

Operation of System

A project accounting system is a cost accounting system in which costs are assigned to individual projects as the projects proceed through their development. Regardless of whether project costs are assigned to users in the context of a responsibility accounting system, effective project control requires a project accounting system that can keep track of costs incurred to date on a project and provide a summary cost report at a project's completion. Timely cost data are essential to making rational decisions about resource usage. Historical cost data from previous projects are an important source of information to use in estimating the time and cost components of new projects.

The project accounting system might be manual or automated. A large firm that generally has several projects underway at the same time requires an automated system. Such a system would probably be run once a week. The important consideration is that status reports be prepared on time. A weekly cost report that is available two weeks later is not likely to be effective for control purposes.

Figure 9.16 illustrates the components of a project accounting system. Projects must be numbered for identification purposes. The system operates much like a conventional cost accounting system: materials, labor, and overhead charges are accumulated by project and periodically compared to budgeted costs, and reports are prepared. Materials in the case of application projects consist mostly of computer

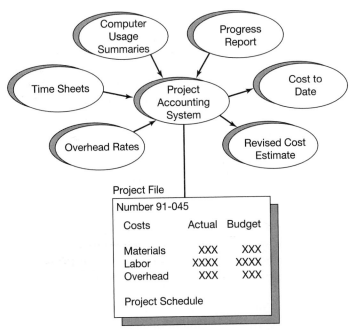

FIGURE 9.16 Project Accounting System.

use charges for program development and testing. Labor costs are obtained from time sheets on which project personnel assign their chargeable hours to work-in-progress. Overhead consists of other charges that are only indirectly attributable to projects, such as the office space of personnel and the cost of running the project accounting system. Overhead charges are usually applied on the basis of an overhead rate. The final input that is needed on a regular basis is a progress report detailing the progress to date on each project. This is necessary if estimates of future costs to complete each project are to be successively revised. Progress is frequently measured in terms of **earned hours**—the equivalent of "standard earned hours" in a standard cost accounting system for manufactured products. Earned hours are used to represent the percentage of completion. For example, if a task time estimate is 40 hours and the task is estimated to be 30% complete, then the progress report would show 12 earned hours on the project task. Charging rates and the project budget are used in conjunction with the progress reports to provide revised cost estimates, project costs to date, and charges to users (if such charges are to be made). Periodically, special summary reports detailing the total cost of projects-in-process are prepared for supervisory management.

Level of Detail

The operation of a project accounting system as just discussed is identical to that of the production control system that was detailed in Chapter 8. As in any control system, if too much detail is required by the project accounting system, then the overhead cost of running the system will be too high and project workers will be antagonized by the data required of them. If too little detail is provided, then the results will be ambiguous. The appropriate level of detail must be determined by project management. In most cases, weekly reports based on earned hours are sufficient for control purposes.

Cost-Overrun Trends

2 reasons

Uncertainty upfront (low ball)

Scope creep

In a survey of North American CIOs (chief information officers) conducted by Deloitte & Touche Information Technology Consulting Services,[8] system development cost overruns were most often attributed to "scope creep"—the project growing larger in scope than originally anticipated. Staff turnover was reported as having the least effect on cost overruns. Other factors contributing to cost overruns—in decreasing importance—include lack of user consensus, inaccurate project plans, lack of user involvement, inaccurate cost projections, lack of qualified personnel, inaccurate processor estimates, and cost of training.

SUMMARY

Systems development is the process of modifying or replacing a portion or all of an information system. The systems life cycle consists of three general phases: planning and analysis, design, and implementation. From the developer's point of view, the entire process needs to function within the auspices of management control. This means that each phase should create sufficient documentation for management review and approval.

Each phase of development generates specific types of documentation. The planning and analysis phase produces feasibility studies, logical data flow diagrams, user specifications, and conceptual designs. The design phase produces a wide range of documents, including a systems design report, flowcharts, decision tables, run manuals, and so on. Finally, implementation involves documents including the conversion plan, operating schedules, and maintenance schedules.

Documentation standards can be maintained by establishing explicit company-wide documentation standards and practices for development. Analyst/programmer productivity can be enhanced by using structured systems development practices. Computer-aided software engineering (CASE) is the process of using computer software technology that supports an automated engineering discipline for software development and maintenance. The goal of object-oriented programming (OOP) is to make software easier to create, simpler to use, and more reliable through reusability. Reusability is attained through encapsulation, inheritance, and the use of messages. In the prototyping approach to systems development, assurance that systems development requirements are adequate and correct is obtained through actual user experience with the system being developed.

Control over program changes should involve formal approval (with documentation) for all program changes. Database administration should involve centralized control over all databases by a database administrator. This individual should ensure that all databases are adequately documented. The data dictionary often meets this objective. Finally, audits of systems operations and development efforts should be regularly undertaken to ascertain their effectiveness.

Key concepts in systems project management include establishing a project team, division of responsibilities (and tasks), dividing the project into phases, establishing time tables, and maintaining an accounting for project costs and compliance with time tables. Collectively, these steps work to ensure that the overall developmental effort produces systems that are cost-effective and meet the needs of the organization.

---

[8] Deloitte & Touche, p. 16.

Glossary

business reengineering: systems development projects in which an entire business function is completely redesigned from the ground up.

case management: a system in which one individual completes or manages all aspects of service or product delivery.

code generation: the use of computer programs designed to produce other programs.

computer-aided software engineering (CASE): the process of using computer software technology that supports an automated engineering discipline for software development and maintenance.

conceptual design: a report that specifies the conceptual design of a proposed system.

conversion plan: a report specifying the events to occur in the implementation of a new system.

data dictionary: documents the specific contents of a database.

database administration (DBA): the organizational function responsible for the establishment of standards and documentation for the data elements in the data base.

deliverable: synonym for documentation.

diagramming tools: an element of computer-aided software engineering (CASE) that provides automated support for drawing data flow diagrams, structure charts, and other such graphics.

encapsulation: interfaces to programs are defined in such a way as to hide as much as possible about their inner workings.

feasibility study: an analysis undertaken to determine whether a systems project is worthy of further consideration.

implementation: the phase of systems development in which newly developed systems are effected into computer operations.

inheritance: the automatic passing of properties or characteristics from a parent or ancestor to a child.

low-balling: purposely or inadvertently submitting unreasonably low time or cost estimates to obtain a contract.

object-oriented programming (OOP): an approach to computer programming based on "objects," which are intelligent data items containing both data and the rules or procedures that determine how objects relate to other objects.

polymorphism: the ability of objects from different classes to respond in their own appropriate manner to common messages.

program change register: used to log and subsequently control all changes to computer programs.

project management: tools used to track progress and manage resources for a systems development project.

prototyping: (1) in computer-aided software engineering (CASE), automated support for developing screen displays or printed report formats; (2) an iterative approach to systems development process in which initial user requirements are estimated and then implemented in a prototype (i.e., mock) system.

reengineering: the process of extracting reusable code segments from existing software, then restructuring this code to enhance its efficiency and reusability.

repository: centralizes information pertaining to computer-aided software engineering (CASE), such as a data dictionary, report design specifications, and the user interface.

structured programming (SP): a set of concepts concerning general programming style and programming conventions.

syntax verifiers: the ability of a computer-aided software engineering (CASE) package to verify proper usage of diagramming techniques.

system documentation standards: explicit requirements for the documentation to be developed during systems development.

systems analysis: the phase of systems development that is responsible for the development of the general design of computer system applications to solve user's problems.

systems design: the phase of systems development concerned with the formulation of the detailed specifications for a proposed system.

systems design report: a detailed specification of systems performance and functional specifications necessary to implement a proposed system.

systems development life cycle: the concept that every systems development project goes through essentially the same process or life cycle of systems analysis, systems design, and implementation.

user specifications: a narrative description of a proposed system's operational characteristics.

walk-through: a formal review of program code by one or more independent parties, usually the team or project leader.

Chapter Quiz

Answers to the chapter quiz appear on page 392.

1. Which of the following functions is *not* a user in the systems development process?
   (a) information systems
   (b) sales
   (c) production
   (d) accounting

2. Which of the following functions works directly with users to identify their specific information requirements?
   (a) operations
   (b) systems design
   (c) systems analysis
   (d) programming

3. An analysis that is undertaken to determine the value of further considering a project is called
   (a) information assessment.
   (b) project acceptability.
   (c) a feasibility study.
   (d) information analysis.

4. The document that provides a narrative description of a proposed system's operational characteristics is called
   (a) user specifications.
   (b) conceptual design.
   (c) an operating schedule.
   (d) a feasibility study.

5. What document is a translation of the conceptual design into the detailed systems performance and functional specifications necessary to begin the physical design of the system?
   (a) logical flow diagram
   (b) user specification
   (c) systems analysis report
   (d) systems design report

6. Which of the following tools is central to the application of CASE (computer-aided software engineering) technology?
   (a) repository
   (b) project management
   (c) diagramming tools
   (d) syntax verifiers

7. The ability of objects from different classes to respond in their own appropriate manner to common messages is called
   (a) encapsulation.
   (b) class action.
   (c) polymorphism.
   (d) inheritance.

8. The process of extracting reusable code segments from existing software and then restructuring this code to enhance its efficiency and reusability is known as
   (a) prototyping.
   (b) reengineering.

(c) polymorphism.
(d) structured programming.

9. The project team leader for a systems development project should have direct responsibility to the
   (a) user department.
   (b) information systems department.
   (c) steering committee.
   (d) project lead analysts.

10. Which of the following is a characteristic of structured programming (SP)?
    (a) modular program code
    (b) polymorphism
    (c) bottom-up design
    (d) multiple entry and exit points

Review Problem

Curtis Company operates in a five-county industrial area. The company employs a manual system for all its record keeping except payroll; the payroll is processed by a local service bureau. Other applications have not been computerized because they could not be cost-justified previously.

The company's sales have grown over the past five years. With this substantial growth rate, a computer-based system seemed more practical. Consequently, Curtis Company engaged the management consulting department of its public accounting firm to conduct a feasibility study for converting their record-keeping systems to a computer-based system. The accounting firm reported that a computer-based system would improve the company's record-keeping system and still provide material cost savings.

Therefore, Curtis Company decided to develop a computer-based system for its records. Curtis hired a person with experience in systems development as manager of systems data processing. Her responsibilities include overseeing the system's operation, with special emphasis on the development of the new system.

Required

Describe the major steps that will be undertaken to develop and implement Curtis Company's new computer-based system.

(CMA)

Solution to Review Problem

There are several distinct functions or steps that Curtis Company must undertake to develop and implement its new computer-based system. Although these steps are more or less conducted in order, some steps overlap considerably and some are conducted throughout the entire development of the system.

The first step to be performed by the systems department in developing its new system would be a systems analysis. The detail required in the systems analysis depends to a great extent on the detail of the previously conducted feasibility study. During the systems analysis phase, the existing system is analyzed. The way the system operates and functions is noted and data regarding the system and information flows are gathered. At the same time, the systems department would attempt to determine the information desires and requirements of the different departments of the company.

Once the systems department becomes familiar with the present system and has a good idea of the future information requirements of the company, the company should identify feasible hardware configurations and then select the optimal computer system that best fulfills the company's needs. At the same time, the company should be planning for an appropriate on-site location for the system that provides for appropriate power, air conditioning, and physical security.

Once the hardware has been selected, the systems design can be started by identifying and developing the new procedures. Specifications regarding inputs, outputs, and files are developed. Control procedures are proposed and developed. The necessary computer programs are identified and written.

The implementation and conversion phase of systems development consists of planning for the implementation and conversion and then actually completing the transition to the new system.

The company should identify new positions required as the result of the system, develop a plan for persons who will be displaced by the new system, and identify the appropriate training for new systems department personnel and for users of the new system. An implementation and testing plan should be established.

The files should be converted, the system tested, and finally, a complete conversion to the new system should be accomplished.

There should be complete documentation throughout this process. This includes a complete record of all activities throughout the system's development and the creation of a complete system's manual and user's manual.

Once the system is operating, the company should conduct a postcompletion audit to evaluate the system and to determine if it is functioning as planned.

Review Questions

1. What is the systems development life cycle?
2. Identify some user-related problems that have historically plagued the development of computer-based information systems.
3. Identify several systems development practices in each of the following areas:
   (a) documentation standards
   (b) analyst/programmer productivity
   (c) maintenance and program change control
   (d) database administration
   (e) audit involvement in systems development
4. What are structured analysis and structured programming?
5. What is CASE (computer-aided software engineering)?
6. Describe the following CASE tools:
   (a) repository
   (b) diagramming tools
   (c) syntax verifiers
   (d) prototyping
   (e) code generation
   (f) project management
7. Describe the following aspects of object-oriented programming:
   (a) objects
   (b) encapsulation
   (c) inheritance
8. What is prototyping?
9. What are some factors that should be considered when selecting a project leader?
10. What is the objective of project breakdown?
11. Identify several types of adjustments that might be made to basic time estimates in a project breakdown.
12. What is low-balling? What are some reasons that make time estimates often overly optimistic?
13. Identify the basic components of a project accounting system.

14. Do project costs always have to be charged to users? If not, why is a project accounting system necessary?

Discussion Questions and Problems

15. The productivity of programmers is typically of concern to project management. Identify some factors that may affect the productivity of a programmer. How would you measure or evaluate the productivity of programmers assigned to a project team? What means might be used to increase the productivity of programmers?

16. A specific project task has been estimated to require 100 work-hours to complete. Using the adjustment factors in Figures 9.14 and 9.15, adjust this estimate to reflect the following:
    (a) The complexity is judged to be quite simple.
    (b) The task is assigned to a "junior" whose competency level is low.
    (c) Average knowledge is available and average knowledge is required.

    Required
    What is the adjusted time estimate? Are adjustments of these types worthwhile?

17. If it is estimated that five programmers can complete a task in 50 work-days, is it likely that 50 programmers can complete the same task—such as coding programs for an application system—in five days? Would you expect diminishing returns in the addition of labor to project tasks? Why?

18. How might a project accounting system assign overhead to individual projects? Does the assignment of overhead to individual projects enhance management control?

19. A data processing department uses the measure *lines of program code* as a means to evaluate the performance of the programming staff in the department. What types of problems might a single measure such as this have in evaluating the performance of programmers? What would happen if the programming staff began to write more of its programs in a database or query language?

20. The success of a computer-based system is affected by the quality of programming and the integrity of the input data.

    Required
    (a) List three procedures that should be followed by a programmer before a program is used in a regular production run.
    (b) List six control procedures that should be followed in the preparation of input data to ensure the integrity of the data.

    (IIA)

21. Identify the types of costs that are likely to be incurred by an organization when it makes a major computer system acquisition. Classify the costs you identify as one-time costs or recurring costs. An example is the one-time costs incurred during the feasibility study.

22. The documentation of data processing applications is an important step in the design and implementation of any computer-based system. Documentation provides a complete record of data processing applications. However, documentation is a phase of systems development that often is neglected. Although documentation can be tedious and time-consuming, the lack of proper documentation can be very costly for an organization.

    Required
    (a) Identify and explain briefly the purposes proper documentation can serve.
    (b) Discuss briefly the basic types of information that should be included in the documentation of a data processing application.
    (c) What policies should be established to regulate access to documentation data for purposes of information or modification for the following four groups of company employees?

(1) computer operators
(2) internal auditors
(3) production planning analysts
(4) systems analysts

(CMA)

23. You are assigned to review the documentation of a data processing function.

Required

(a) List three advantages of adequate documentation for a data processing function.
(b) Following are two lists of information. The first list has six categories of documentation, and the second list has eighteen elements of documentation related to the categories. Match each of the elements of documentation with the category in which it should be found. List letters A through F on your answer sheet. After each letter, list the numbers of the elements that **best** apply to that category. Use every element, but none more than once.

CATEGORIES

A. Systems documentation
B. Program documentation
C. Operations documentation
D. User documentation
E. Library documentation
F. Data entry documentation

ELEMENTS

1. Flowcharts showing the flow of information
2. Procedures needed to balance, reconcile, and maintain overall control
3. Storage instructions
4. Contents and format of data to be captured
5. Constants, codes, and tables
6. Verification procedures
7. Logic diagrams and/or decision tables
8. Report distribution instructions
9. Messages and programmed halts
10. Procedures for backup files
11. Retention cycle
12. Source statement listings
13. Instructions to show proper use of each transaction
14. A complete history from planning through installation
15. Restart and recovery procedures
16. Rules for handling blank spaces
17. Instructions to ensure the proper completion of all input forms
18. List of programs in a system

(IIA)

24. Rayo Corporation: Completion of Systems and Programming Questionnaire.[9]

Mike Kess, a senior auditor for the regional accounting firm Sanders and McDonald, was assigned to audit the Rayo Corporation. He was to conduct a preliminary review of the general controls over systems and programming. He has already identified the current applications and the equipment used in the data processing system (Figure 9.17) and is about to start on system maintenance.

Mike contacted Jim Stram, the manager of systems and programming in the EDP department. A summary of their conversation follows:

---

[9]Prepared by Frederick L. Neumann, Richard J. Boland, and Jeffrey Johnson; funded by the Touche Ross Foundation Aid to Accounting Education Program.

Data Center Organization Chart

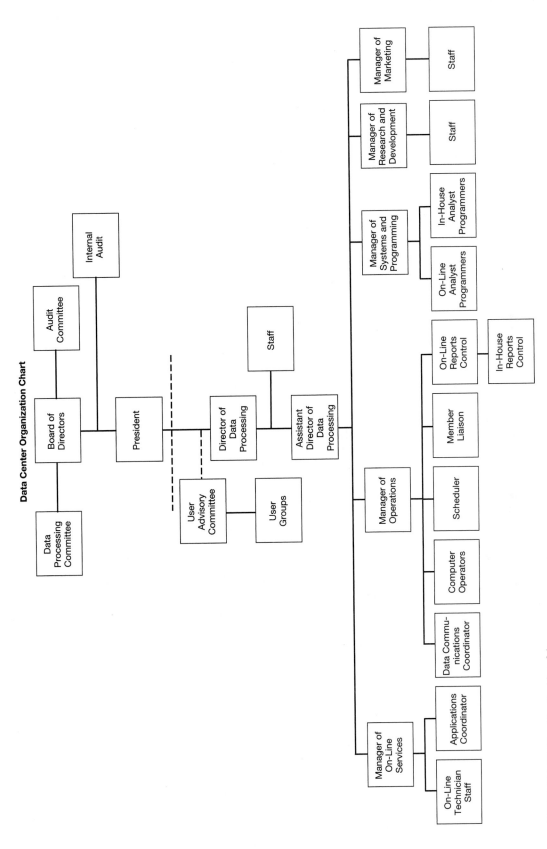

FIGURE 9.17 Chart for Problem 24.

MIKE: How are system maintenance projects initiated and developed?

JIM: All potential projects are sent to a member of my staff, called an applications coordinator, for analysis. We do all our systems and programming work in-house. If a programming change is required for a project, the applications coordinator prepares a revision request form. These revision request forms must be approved by both the manager of operations and myself. The director of data processing and the internal auditor receive copies of each revision request form for information purposes.

MIKE: How does the applications coordinator keep track of the revision request form and any change that might be made to it?

JIM: The revision request forms are numbered in different series depending on the nature of the change requested. The applications coordinator assigns the next number in the sequence and records in a master log each request he prepares. Changes in revision requests, from whatever source, are prepared on request forms just as initial requests are. Each change request is given the same basic number with a suffix indicating it is an amendment, and there is a place for recording amendments in the master log.

MIKE: What is the distribution of an approved request form?

JIM: It goes to one of my systems supervisors for design, programming, and testing. The primary effort is usually performed by a programmer who has responsibility over the area of the application or the specific programs to be changed.

MIKE: But how are projects controlled?

JIM: At the beginning of each programming project, an estimated start and completion date are assigned and entered on the request form and the master log. The system supervisor keeps on top of the projects assigned to him, and the applications coordinator also monitors the open requests. The system supervisor files a written status report with the applications coordinator twice a month, and he briefs me on any problems. However, I'm usually aware of any difficulties long before then.

During the programming and testing phase, I think we have good control over the project. None of the compiles made during this phase changes any production source code for the existing computer programs. Also, all test object programs are identified by a strictly enforced naming convention that clearly distinguishes them from production programs. So far this has been successful in inhibiting their use in processing production. If a programmer has specific questions or problems on a project, his systems supervisor is generally available to give advice.

MIKE: Are there written guidelines to direct this activity? If so, how detailed are they?

JIM: Only informal procedures exist to provide any uniformity to the programs and the coding changes that are made to a program. But, formal standards do exist that define what documentation should be present for a system and for the programs within a system. These apply to program changes as well, and again are strictly enforced. There is a periodic management review to see we comply. We just had one about a month ago and got a clean bill of health.

MIKE: Are adequate tests and reviews made of changes before they are implemented?

JIM: The applications coordinator, the systems supervisor, and the individual programmer informally discuss the necessary tests for a specific project. Sometimes I get involved, too, but our guidelines are pretty good in this area and provide a fairly thorough approach to test design. After the tests have been completed to the systems supervisor's satisfaction, the applications coordinator reviews and approves the test results. This must be done on all revision requests before they are implemented into production. I usually review the programmer's work to see that all authorized changes are made correctly and are adequately tested and documented.

MIKE: How does implementation take place and what controls are exercised over it?

JIM: After the test results for a revision request have been approved by the applications coordinator, it is the responsibility of the programmer to implement the changes into production. In order for a programmer to put a program change into production, he or she must update the source code of the production program version. The programmer is required to provide program name and compile date information for all changed programs to the system supervisor. The programmer also has the responsibility of updating the systems and programming documentation. The system supervisor is supposed to review this and certify completion to the applications coordinator, who then completes the log entry.

MIKE: Are postimplementation reviews undertaken on system maintenance projects?

JIM: Once the project is implemented, the applications coordinator reviews the output from the first few production runs of the changed program. He or she also questions users to see if any problem areas can be identified.

A documented audit trail is provided by a completed project file that is maintained by the applications coordinator for each request number. This file contains all the required documentation, including test results. A copy of the final summary goes to the department that originally submitted the request. A table in the computer is updated to provide listings of the most current compile dates for each set of production object code within the system. Before any program is implemented it is checked against the table.

MIKE: Well, that seems to be it. I think I have all that I need for now, but I'll probably be back to take a look at the files and records. I may have more questions for you then. Thanks very much for your time and thoughtful answers. I really appreciate your help.

JIM: That's quite all right. If I can be of any more help, just let me know.

Required

(a) Keeping in mind that this is part of the preliminary phase of the review, are there any additional questions you would have asked of Jim if you had been in Mike's place?

(b) Complete as much of the page of the questionnaire shown in Figure 9.18 as you can from the information Mike did collect in the interview.

(c) Make a list of weaknesses that you feel should be considered in the preliminary assessment of the internal control in this area.

Client _____ Audit Date _____

Systems and Programming

	Yes	No	N/A
1. Are there systems and programming standards in the following areas:			
a. Applications design?	___	___	___
b. Programming conventions and procedures?	___	___	___
c. Systems and program documentation?	___	___	___
d. Applications control?	___	___	___
e. Project planning and management?	___	___	___
2. Does the normal documentation for an application include the following:			
Application Documentation			
a. Narrative description?			
b. Systems flowchart?	___	___	___
c. Definition of input data and source format?	___	___	___
d. Description of expected output data and format?	___	___	___
e. A listing of all valid transactions and other codes and abbreviations and master file fields affected?	___	___	___
f. File definition or layouts?	___	___	___
g. Instructions for preparing input?	___	___	___
h. Instructions for correcting errors?	___	___	___
i. Backup requirements?	___	___	___
j. Description of test data?	___	___	___
Program Documentation			
a. Program narrative?			
b. Flowchart of each program?	___	___	___
c. Current source listing of each program?	___	___	___
Operations Documentation			
a. Data entry instructions, including verification?			
b. Instructions for control personnel, including batching?	___	___	___
c. Instructions for the tape librarian?	___	___	___
d. Operator's run manual?	___	___	___
e. Reconstruction procedure?	___	___	___
3. Is there a periodic management review of documentation to ensure that it is current and accurate?	___	___	___
If yes, when and by whom was it last performed?_____			
4. Is all systems and programming work done in-house?	___	___	___
If not, is it done:			
a. By computer manufacturer's personnel?	___	___	___
b. By contract programming?	___	___	___
c. Other? Describe_____			
5. Are all changes programmed by persons other than those assigned to computer operations?	___	___	___
6. Are program changes documented in a manner that preserves an accurate chronological record of the applications?			
If yes, describe _____	___	___	___
7. Do the users participate in the development of new applications or modifications of existing applications through frequent reviews of work performed?			
If yes, are the results of reviews documented?	___	___	___
8. Are testing procedures and techniques standardized?	___	___	___
9. Are program revisions tested as stringently as new programs?	___	___	___
10. Are tests designed to uncover weaknesses in the links between programs, as well as within programs?	___	___	___
11. Are users involved in the testing process, i.e., do they use the application as it is intended during the testing process?	___	___	___
12. Do user departments perform the final review and sign off on projects before acceptance?	___	___	___
13. What departments and/or individuals have the authority to authorize an operator to put a new or modified program into production? _____			
14. What supervisory or management approval is necessary for the conversion of files? _____			

FIGURE 9.18 Questionnaire for Problem 24.

Answers to Chapter Quiz

1. A	4. B	7. C	10. A
2. C	5. D	8. B	
3. C	6. A	9. C	

CHAPTER 10

Management Decision Making and Reports

LEARNING OBJECTIVES

Careful study of this chapter will enable you to:

■ Describe in detail the nature of management decisions.

■ Elaborate on the types of decisions that managers make.

■ Describe various reports used for management planning and control.

■ Describe various types of reporting systems.

MANAGERS AND DECISIONS

All organizations face resource allocation problems, which are solved through managerial decision making. The power to make decisions is delegated to managers within an organization. Management is decentralized to the extent that decisions are made on a low organizational level and centralized to the extent that decisions are made at a high organizational level.

Planning and Control

Planning and control are fundamental activities common to all managers. Once management has established a general set of objectives, it will attempt to carry out these objectives in terms of day-to-day decision making. This involves decisions relating to a wide range of activities such as the following:

- Organizing tasks to be completed and delegating the necessary authority to carry out these tasks.
- Acquiring the necessary resources to carry out the desired tasks.
- Allocating the acquired resources to their respective tasks and determining their appropriate use.
- Coordinating and supervising employees as needed in order to carry out the company's objectives.
- Monitoring the activities of a company and the outcome of particular tasks and correcting any deviations from plans.

These activities constitute a substantial portion of what managers do. If you watched a manager work for a day, you would probably see some or all of these activities taking place. Additionally, you would find two overall patterns to these activities: planning and control. For example, top management might decide to develop a new product line. This would involve a substantial amount of planning, such as determining the appropriate tasks that would be carried out in order to successfully complete the project. Some of these tasks might involve such things as marketing research, engineering design, or quality control planning. Top management would have to make decisions regarding the appropriate employees to be in charge of each of these functions. Once such a plan is completely worked out, it has to be implemented. Top management would not be able to perform all the tasks involved personally, so they would have to monitor or control the activities as carried out by middle-level management.

Decision Making

All planning and control activities involve decision making on the part of the manager. In fact, the main contribution a manager makes to a company is that of decision making. Managers make other important contributions, such as leadership and motivation of fellow employees, but decision making is the glue that holds together everything a manager does. It is therefore important to look at the decision-making process in detail.

Decision making is primarily a process. It is not something the manager does in a passing moment, but rather something that often takes a substantial amount of time. For example, a manager might decide to hire ten new employees, a decision that might appear simple but in reality is quite complex, and time-consuming. To clarify this point, assume that the manager is faced with problems in meeting deadlines for delivery of his product to customers. Furthermore, assume that he has extensively analyzed this problem and has considered a number of possible alternative solutions, such as speeding up production by adding new machinery, or changing the production process. After analyzing the situation, the manager concludes that the best solution is to hire ten new employees. The entire process may take several months. For example, he may have to look at a large number of new kinds of machines as part of his considering the purchase of new equipment. Maybe he also has to gather detailed information relating to alternate production processes. This gathering of detailed information might require many hours of work on the part of his subordinates.

There are six systematic steps a manager typically follows when making decisions (see Figure 10.1):

1. Identifying and defining the problem
2. Determining alternative courses of action
3. Evaluating the possible courses of action
4. Selecting the best course of action
5. Carrying out the selected course of action
6. Following up to ensure that the desired results are obtained

Identifying and Defining the Problem

This is often the most difficult part of the decision-making process. One reason for this is that it is often difficult for the manager to distinguish between the problem itself and the symptoms of the problem. For example, consider a

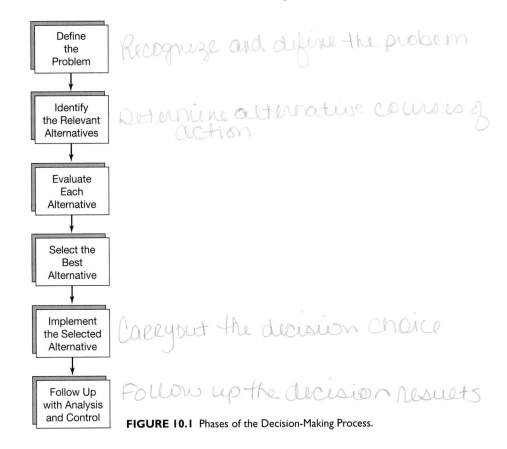

FIGURE 10.1 Phases of the Decision-Making Process.

company that manufactures transistor radios. Assume that the production department is having a problem with labor inefficiency. The production manager has found that, despite her best efforts, the manufacturing process has been taking approximately 20% too much labor time, on the average, to produce a radio. At this point, it would be very easy to define the problem as a labor problem. However, upon thorough investigation, the manager finds that the problem is caused by substandard material attributable to one particular supplier. The manager is able to eliminate the negative variances entirely by switching to a different supplier.

From this example, we can see that it is critical that the problem be carefully defined. Had the manager defined this as a labor problem and dealt with it by reprimanding the production supervisor, a completely different result might have been obtained, and the manager would have lost credibility with subordinates. The successful treatment of the problem came as a result of careful analysis of the situation before making a final decision regarding the cause. This involved the careful collection of information.

Determining Alternative Courses of Action

At the heart of the decision-making process is the manager's choice of a particular choice of action. In order for the manager to properly make this choice, it is very important that each alternative be known. For example, assume that the advertising manager of Castor Manufacturing is trying to decide on the best form of advertising to introduce a new commercial product. In this case, he has no trouble defining the problem, which is to pick the best form of advertising in order to successfully introduce his new product. However, he faces a large number of alternatives: newspaper, direct mail, magazines, radio or television, or combinations of media.

Considering alternatives could become quite complicated. For example, in this case, it might be useful to go with one or more outside advertising agencies. To the inexperienced advertising manager, the number of alternatives is overwhelming. However, one very important function the manager serves here is narrowing the set of alternatives to those that are the most reasonable. For example, an experienced manager might know that a direct-mail campaign is an ineffective method for introducing a new product like the one in question.

In some situations, analyzing alternatives can be very complicated and consume a large amount of the manager's time. For example, assume that the Baby Toy Company is designing a new toy for small children. The company is concerned with safety and product liability considerations. In this case, the company might find it necessary to consider a large number of alternative product designs in order to meet safety requirements. Each design would be evaluated by both attorneys and safety engineers. In addition, each product would be tested extensively, by carefully observing young children using it. The test reports, legal opinions, and other matters would be summarized into reports that would be evaluated by management, who would then narrow down the number of alternative product designs. Economic and other considerations would be used to select the final product design to be implemented.

Evaluating Alternatives

Given that a reasonable number of alternatives have been set forth, the manager must evaluate the relative merits of each alternative. One useful framework for evaluating alternatives is the **cost–benefit approach.** Under this approach, the manager lists the various costs and benefits associated with the selection of each alternative. Often, a manager will consider pro forma statements of profitability associated with various alternatives. For example, assume that top management is considering building a new plant in one of four alternative cities in the United States. Management would most certainly want to see the costs and benefits associated with each possible plant site. For example, some major cities are very heavily unionized. Construction costs at a highly unionized site might be relatively high. Or construction of a plant site near a major sales outlet might result in improved sales due to increased ability to make faster deliveries. As a result of these and other factors, each possible plant site may have a completely different bottom line in terms of projected profit.

Finally, nonmonetary considerations are often important in evaluating decision alternatives, but they are very difficult to quantify. Some of these factors are goodwill and the reputation of the company. In addition, the expected outcome associated with a given alternative is never guaranteed. Essentially, the evaluation of alternatives always involves making projections about the future. Because the future cannot be known with certainty, the manager must factor in the chance element as an integral part of the decision process.

Selecting the Best Alternative

In many cases this is the simplest part of the decision-making process. Consider the following set of facts relating to a hypothetical decision to close a plant:

	Retain Plant	Close Plant
Sales	$ 200,000	—
Variable expenses	(40,000)	—
Fixed expenses	(200,000)	$(200,000)
Net Income	$ (40,000)	$(200,000)

In this case, neither alternative is especially attractive, but the first is obviously preferable. Even though this decision appears simple, the manager must do two things in making the actual selection of the best alternative: (1) define an objective and (2) make a choice in light of this objective. In the present situation, the objective is to maximize the company's net income (or minimize the loss). The manager applies this objective in conjunction with the information given and chooses to keep the plant open.

Many decision problems are much more complicated than this simple example. It is often difficult to quantify each alternative in terms of monetary considerations. Many decisions involve human factors, such as goodwill on the part of customers or employees. For example, in determining the optimal level of inventory, a manager will consider such factors as the cost of recording, storage, insurance, and the cost of lost sales due to stock-outs. Within this framework it is possible to minimize total costs. However, there is an additional major factor to consider— the impact of inventory size on the company's ability to maintain good customer relations by giving prompt deliveries. The company might not fully optimize its inventory costs by maintaining excessively large inventories, but it would keep a strong base of customer loyalty by always having what is needed on hand. It is clear from this example that managers must deal with decision problems that cannot be dealt with on the basis of a single objective. In fact, many decisions involve the use of multiple objectives by managers.

Another factor that complicates most real-world decisions is uncertainty. In the previous plant-closing problem, it was assumed that the manager knew with certainty the outcomes associated with each of the two alternatives. Unfortunately, this is rarely the situation in real-world decision problems. Generally, the manager must forecast what will happen if a given alternative is selected. One common way to deal with uncertainty is **risk analysis,** which involves evaluating each alternative on the basis of both profitability and risk.

Implementing the Selected Alternative

Given that an alternative has been selected, the manager then follows through and implements the choice. This phase can be time-consuming. A decision made in weeks might take years to implement. For example, if the decision is to build a new plant in Dallas, it then becomes necessary to select a site and a building plan. Plans must be developed for hiring and training employees. Necessary funds may have to be obtained by borrowing from banks or issuing securities. The manager has a complicated job to do in implementing a major decision such as this.

Analysis and Control

At this point, it is necessary to ensure that everything has gone according to plan. If the company is opening a new plant in Dallas, it must make sure that construction costs go according to the projections made in earlier phases of the decision process. A good decision could easily turn into a bad decision if costs overrun the budget by 200%.

A common approach to analysis and control of decisions is to rely on **budgetary reporting systems,** in which periodic reports highlight budgeted versus actual expenses and revenues. The exact format and frequency of these reports depend on the specific set of circumstances, but all decisions require analysis and control.

The principle that guides most managers in analysis and control is **management by exception.** This states that management investigates only those deviations from the budget that are considered material. Of course, materiality is often a matter of judgment on the part of the manager.

Useful Information for Planning and Control

Information differs from data in that information is useful to the decision maker, whereas data are not. Data are only the basic raw materials from which information is produced. Consider an automobile versus a large pile of automobile parts. One is useful and the other is not. The same goes for information. If we take the right data and process them by classification, aggregation, and summarization, we might have information. Whether we do or not depends on the usefulness of the data.

How do we know when possible information is useful? The usefulness of information comes from its impact on the manager's beliefs regarding events relevant to the decision process. In regard to planning, information is useful if it aids the manager in predicting future outcomes under various alternative courses of action. Consider the planning problem relating to modernizing plant and equipment. Such a decision requires a prediction of the company's cash flows under two alternatives—with and without modernization. Anything that aids in improving the accuracy of these predictions or increases their certainty will be useful to the manager. The question of accuracy is relatively straightforward. You would be obviously better off with a forecast within 10% of the actual amount as opposed to one within 20% of the actual amount. The question of certainty is more subtle. Consider two forecasts of profitability for the case of plant and equipment renovation. One forecast indicates that the net income will be $10 million without plant renovation. The company is certain that this level will be achieved without modernization. The second forecast is $11 million net income with plant modernization. The second forecast, however, is less certain. Furthermore, the company believes that there is a large probability that profits with modernization might only reach the $5 million level. Based on this information, management might conclude that modernization involves unacceptable levels of risk.

In summary, information's usefulness can be defined in terms of its ability to assist in prediction and risk assessment for planning. However, for control purposes these concepts are not of primary importance. This is because information for control decisions tends to focus on events after they have occurred, even though the controls might be preventive.

Information for control primarily needs to be accurate and timely in order to be useful. Of course, it needs to be relevant or pertinent to the decision at hand, but this usually is not a problem in a budgetary control system because the actual numbers simply correspond to budgeted numbers.

Information Properties and the Degree of Usefulness

All information is not equally useful. As discussed previously, the **timeliness** of a report is important for control purposes. The early detection of a large variance is helpful in eliminating a problem before it gets out of hand. A daily production variance report might reveal that a particular machine is not functioning correctly and, as a result, substantial quantities of materials have been wasted. The problem can then be corrected and the damage limited to what occurred in a single day's production. However, if the report were weekly, the problem would be much more costly.

Information has other properties in addition to timeliness. These are quantifiability, accuracy, conciseness, and relevance. **Quantifiability** refers to the degree of difficulty in representing a given event numerically. Some things, such as employee–employer relations, are difficult to quantify. A company might have an expensive annual party for all its employees. Because the benefits of such an event cannot be expressed in dollars and cents, the event is difficult to quantify. **Accuracy** relates to the degree to which a given information set measures what it purports to measure. One obvious source of inaccuracy is errors in the data used to generate the information. Other less obvious sources of inaccuracy relate to using the wrong data to generate the information. For example, there are various ways of measuring customer satisfaction. One might use the number of customer complaints to measure this variable. However, this measure might produce inaccurate results because many customers might show their dissatisfaction by doing business with someone else. **Conciseness** relates to the degree of detail in the information. In general, a concise report will be brief and to the point. The level of summarization or aggregation will also be high. For example, a sales report could show sales by week, product, and sales division. Alternatively, it could show sales for the whole year, product, and sales division. The latter report would be relatively concise. The concept of **relative conciseness** is important here because a report might be concise for one purpose but not for another. Another property of information is **relevance,** which relates to how well the information relates to a given decision problem. For example, projected cost savings would be relevant to the decision to acquire an internal corporate legal staff. The president's salary would be irrelevant to the same decision.

The Value of Information

Information derives value from its effect on decisions. However, information is obtained at a cost; therefore, if information does not improve or affect a decision, it has negative value.

The quality of information generally improves if the following conditions are met:

- Accuracy—the information is correct in reflecting reality
- Timeliness—the information is current or up-to-date
- Response time—the information is made available quickly
- Completeness—the information contains everything that is needed
- Relevance—the information affects the decision at hand

The perceptive reader will observe that the definitions are circular. Qualitative discussions of information are necessarily ambiguous. For example, information should always be relevant. Who would want or use irrelevant information?

Quantitatively, a model of information value exists in terms of incremental expected payoff from the decision-theory literature. Payoff is the benefit derived from a decision. An incremental increase in payoff is the **value of information** that yields this increase. Payoffs are usually measured monetarily.

Consider an example: A product costs $10 to make and sells for $15. Historically, it is known that the production generates a 10% defective rate. If the product is sold and returned as defective, the producer incurs an additional $8 per unit handling cost, for a total loss on the defective unit of $18 (10 + 8). Figure 10.2 illustrates the payoff matrix for the decision either to scrap or sell an item as it is produced. The expected value of this decision is the sum of its possible payoffs multiplied by their probability of occurrence. The expected profit of selling each item as it is produced can be computed as follows:

$$E \text{ (selling)} = \text{probability (good item) (profit/good item)}$$
$$+ \text{ probability (defect) (cost/defective item)}$$
$$= (0.9)(\$5) + (0.1)(-\$18)$$
$$= \$2.70$$

To reject each item would cost $10 per item.

The **value of perfect information** can be computed as the incremental increase in expected payoff that would result from a decision if perfect information were available. Perfect information would allow the best decision to be made in every instance. In our example, perfect information about individual items would allow the sale of only nondefective production and the scrapping of all defective production. The expected value of perfect information can be computed as

$$E \text{ (perfect information)} = (0.90)(\$5) + (0.10)(-\$10)$$
$$= \$3.50$$

Comparing this to the expected value obtained with no information about individual items, we get

$$\$3.50 - \$2.70 = 80\text{¢/unit}$$

The value of perfect information would be 80 cents per unit, *less* the unit cost of obtaining perfect information.

But the information is rarely perfect. Suppose our manufacturer installed an electronic quality control system to inspect each item prior to its sale. Figure 10.3 illustrates the accuracy characteristics of this imperfect information system. Note that the system catches all the defects but classifies some good items as defective. If this system is used, the expected profit from selling only the items that pass inspection is

$$E \text{ (quality control)} = 0.9[0.94 \ (\$5) + 0.06(-\$10)]$$
$$+ 0.1[0(-\$18) + 1(-\$10)]$$
$$= \$2.69$$

State of Nature

Action		Good Item	Defective Item
	Sell	$5	-$18
	Reject	-$10	-$10

FIGURE 10.2 Hypothetical Payoff Matrix.

State of Nature

		Good Item	Defective Item
Reported Information	Good	0.94	0
	Defective	0.06	1

FIGURE 10.3 Hypothetical Accuracy Characteristics of an Imperfect Information System.

The expected profit is *less* than operating the system with no information on individual items. This information system is therefore useless, regardless of its cost.

The illustration is obviously contrived. However, it shows that it is all too easy to overvalue information. It also illustrates the problem of qualitatively discussing information. The information system in the example is highly accurate and timely, has an instantaneous response time, is obviously relevant, and is 100% complete. However, these qualities are not necessarily of economic value.

Computing the value of information requires the construction of alternatives and payoffs. Generally, these can be only approximated; nevertheless, a careful estimate is desirable. Knowledge concerning outcomes ranges from complete certainty to risk to complete uncertainty. Risk is characterized by some amount of previous information concerning outcomes. The example was a risk situation in which we had prior knowledge of outcomes (10% are defective). As one moves up in the organization hierarchy, uncertainty typically becomes the prevalent state of affairs concerning outcomes.

Software for Decision Making

Computer software has been developed to assist managers in making decisions. Database software assists managers in collecting relevant information for a decision by allowing them to perform structured queries on information in a database. The desired information is extracted from the database by a database software system. Decision support software and expert systems software provide computational support and expert advice on particular management decisions.

Database Software

Database software is available on both mainframes and personal computers. A database is a collection of data that is used by several different applications. Data are stored in a nonredundant fashion and are independent of each application that uses them. Database software provides a common and controlled method by which the data are made available to users. Database software allows managers to perform structured queries to obtain information in the database.

A **query** is a request for information in the database. Data are accessed from the database by performing a structured query. A structured query describes the desired data and the actions (if any) to be taken when the data are located. The query is structured in the particular syntax or format that is supported by the database software system. Actions indicate the desired processing of the data, such as comparing it to decision criteria or calculating totals or averages. Actions also indicate the desired format of any reports to be printed.

Structured queries generally use Englishlike language with a few key words. The following is an example.

Report on Sales of Product B in District 5 for the Month of June

The desired data are sales of product B in district 5 for the month of June, and the desired action is to list these data. The query would be entered from a computer keyboard, processed by the database software, and the response displayed at the manager's video display for immediate use. In addition to preparing lists of desired data, structured queries may also be used to select a subset of desired data by specifying conditions in the query to screen the data. The following is an example of this.

Report on All Expenses for John Doe That Are Greater Than $500 for the Month of May

Because the condition "greater than $500" has been added to this query, the response will list only those expenses that satisfy this condition. The ability to perform these types of data searches quickly and easily with Englishlike structured queries makes database software a valuable tool in managerial decision making.

Decision Support Systems

Decision support systems (DSSs) refer to computer-based information systems that provide support to a decision-making process. A DSS is oriented more toward processing data in a decision context rather than toward retrieving data. In contrast, a database software system is oriented more toward retrieving data than processing them. DSSs respond quickly to the needs of a decision maker and are capable of answering what-if types of questions.

Spreadsheet software is a common example of a DSS. Although a spreadsheet software is not in itself a DSS, it may be used to build a DSS for a wide variety of decisions. To build a DSS, the user enters data and formulas in the cells of the spreadsheet to construct a model of the particular decision that is to be made. For example, in an investment analysis, the user might enter predicted cash inflows and outflows for a proposed investment and then use the present value formulas built in the spreadsheet software to compute the discounted return on investment. The user can easily examine the effects of alternative cash inflow and/or outflow assumptions by altering the data in the cells of the spreadsheet. The spreadsheet software automatically updates all the calculations and presents the revised return on investment. This what-if capability is what makes spreadsheet software useful as a DSS.

Many other types of modeling software are used to build DSSs. Some software is designed specifically to build DSSs, and it is also possible to use conventional programming languages such as BASIC. All types of DSS software support the same types of general features that were illustrated in the context of spreadsheet software, and may also provide additional features such as the ability to retrieve information from a database or to use more sophisticated processing options such as linear programming. Modeling software may also use Englishlike language rather than formulas, and thus be easier to use.

Expert Systems

An **expert system** is a highly developed DSS that utilizes knowledge generally possessed by an expert to solve a problem. An expert system is designed to emulate the knowledge and problem-solving techniques of a human expert. An expert system is capable of storing many decision rules, and it draws conclusions from manipulating these rules. A characteristic of expert systems is the ability to declare or explain the reasoning process that was used to make a decision.

An expert system consists of two parts—a **knowledge base** and an **inference engine.** The knowledge base stores the rules, data, and relationships that are used to solve problems. The inference engine is the program that requests data from the user, manipulates the knowledge base, and provides a decision to the user.

Expert systems are used in well-defined problem areas where judgment and expertise rather than well-defined solution algorithms such as linear programming are required to solve a problem. An expert system is developed by carefully analyzing and then building a knowledge base that models the decision processes that are used by an expert decision maker. This task is both difficult and time-consuming. Once the model is developed, it is tested by comparing its performance in making decisions to that of the human expert it is designed to mimic.

Once built and tested, an expert system may be used for consultation or training. In either use, the expert system interrogates the user to obtain the facts relevant to the problem. In order to determine which of the many rules in the knowledge base apply to the particular problem, the system asks the user various questions to verify the facts and obtain any required additional information. Using the responses to these questions, the expert system determines which rules apply and offers a solution to the user.

Executive Information Systems

An **executive information system (EIS)** is software tailored to the strategic information needs of top management. Much of the information used by top management comes from sources other than the organization's information system. But important information also comes from an organization's information system. An EIS provides top management with easy access to selective information that has been processed by the organization's information system. An EIS is easy to operate and provides output in a graphical or other format that is easy to understand. The many types of reports discussed in the following section might be made available to top management by an EIS.

REPORTING TO MANAGEMENT

Reports provide an important interface between an information system and the users of the system. An information system transforms data into information. Reporting is the formal distribution of this information to the various users within an organization.

Types of Reports

Table 10.1 provides a classification scheme for the various types of reports commonly found in most companies. At the most general level, reports can be categorized according to their purpose. The table shows seven different purposes for reports. **Planning reports** typically take the form of budgets and are useful in helping managers allocate and acquire resources for future operations of the firm. A wide range of planning reports is used at all levels within the organization. Planning reports can be either financial or nonfinancial. A good example of a financial planning report is given in Figure 10.4, which is a sales budget for a typical

TABLE 10-1 Reports Classified

Classification Scheme	Examples
1. Purpose	Planning
	Control
	Operational
	Income taxes
	Stockholder
	Government regulation
2. Time horizon	Long range
	Short range
	Historical
3. Scope	Firmwide
	Divisionwide
	Departmentwide
4. Occurrence	Upon request
	Periodic
	Event-triggered
	One time
5. Organizational function	Production
	Sales
	Finance
	Inventory
6. Report format	Monitor
	Color graphics
	Computer printout
	Narrated
7. Conciseness	Brief
	Testing plan
	Detailed
	Variance report

Charles Manufacturing Company **Sales Budget**					
All Sales Departments **First Quarter**					
Sales Territory	**Steel**	**Copper**	**Wire**	**Electrical**	**Total**
R. Hill	$125,000	$200,000	$	$	$ 325,000
G. Welch		200,000	50,000		250,000
B. Nadir	75,000	25,000	100,000		200,000
T. Marcus	200,000	75,000		100,000	375,000
L. Green			50,000		50,000
L. Wolfe		50,000			50,000
Total	$400,000	$550,000	$200,000	$100,000	$1,250,000

FIGURE 10.4 Typical Sales Budget/Planning Report.

manufacturing company. The sales figures are budgeted for individual sales territories on a product-by-product basis. In addition, the report is both footed and cross-footed so that the manager can note at a glance the total sales budget (in the lower right-hand corner) or the budgeted sales for a given product or sales territory. Most firms have a **master budget** that guides the firm as a whole. The master budget is then supplemented by a number of subsidiary budgets. Examples of subsidiary budgets include budgets for capital expenditures, cash planning, labor utilization, and raw materials acquisition.

Some planning reports are nonfinancial. For example, the plant manager might request a space utilization report in order to determine where to locate new machinery. Such a report might specify a number or alternatives for relocating existing machinery in order to make new space. Other factors in such a report might include flow diagrams that would assist the manager in ensuring that all machines are located in such a manner as to optimize the flow of product and materials through the plant.

A very important characteristic of good planning reports is flexibility. Many planning reports are tied to a specific level of sales activity. Such reports might prove to be completely useless if sales projections turn out to be inaccurate. A **flexible budget** is a budget that specifically allows for varying levels of activity. Figure 10.5 is an example of a flexible cash budget. In this example, the budget projects cash needs at 10,000, 20,000, and 30,000 unit levels of sales. Such a budget would allow the company to adjust its borrowing needs in the event of a change in the sales outlook during the year.

Control reports assist the manager in assuring that operations follow according to plan. All control reports have certain common elements: benchmarks and actual performance results. The benchmarks are compared to the actual perfor-

	June		
	Updike Manufacturing Company **Partial Cash Budget**		
	Projected Sales		
Item	**10,000 units**	**20,000 units**	**30,000 units**
Cash Inflows: Collections	$1,000,000	$2,000,000	$3,000,000
Cash Outflows: Supplies	100,000	200,000	700,000
Labor	700,000	1,725,000	2,750,000
Selling	100,000	140,000	150,000
Administration	200,000	200,000	200,000
Net Cash Flow	(100,000)	(265,000)	(800,000)
Beg. Balance	100,000	100,000	100,000
Min. Balance	200,000	200,000	200,000
To Borrow	$ 200,000	$ 365,000	$ 900,000

Note: Some costs do not vary in proportion to sales due to varying returns to scale.

FIGURE 10.5 Partial (One-Month) Flexible Cash Budget.

Hill Manufacturing Company Excess Materials Requisition Report				
Production Department				Week of August 3–10
Job #	Standard Materials	Material Used	Variance	Explanation
364	100	170	($700)	Bad materials
395	75	100	($250)	Production error
400	100	60	$400	Reworked from 364

Notes: 1. Raw materials standard cost = $10 per unit.
2. Defective raw materials were purchased from Ace Supply.
3. Deviations larger than 10% indicated.

FIGURE 10.6 Typical Exception Report.

mance results, and material deviations are typically highlighted. For example, consider Figure 10.6, which shows an excess materials requisition report. This report shows, on a job-by-job basis, the standard materials allowed versus the actual materials used. In this case, the difference between the actual materials used and standard materials allowed is costed out at $10 per unit and noted in a separate variance column. The manager can quickly scan the variance column and note any irregularities. Note also that in each case an explanation is given. If the manager is satisfied with the explanation as written, no further investigation might be necessary. On the other hand, the manager might request a special report explaining the cause of the problem in more detail.

A technique that is often useful in control reporting is graphical analysis. Figure 10.7 is an example of a process control report graph. In this example, raw material usages are displayed on a day-by-day basis by a solid line. The dotted line represents the standard quantity of materials allowed. Note also that +10% and −10% control limits are included on the graph. These control limits may serve as guidelines with respect to acceptable deviations from the standard. In the present example, the control limits are exceeded on one day only—Thursday. Assuming that negative variances on this chart refer to unfavorable uses of materials, the manager might want to investigate the cause of Thursday's deviation.

Operational reports focus on the current status of operations within the

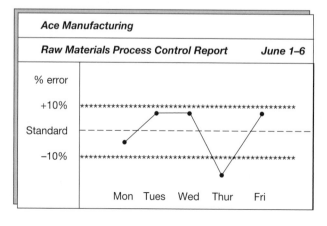

FIGURE 10.7 Process Control Report Graph.

company. Their major purpose is to provide support for individuals in carrying out day-to-day operational activities. For example, a production manager needs specific information relating to work orders in order to schedule a week's production. Therefore, the information system typically gives the production manager an operational report that summarizes new orders. An example of this type of report is given in Figure 10.8.

We also use the term *operational report* to refer to a status report. For a second example, consider a salesperson who might want to see the credit limit of an individual before approving a particular sale. This might be done by displaying the customer credit status on a video display. The salesperson could then immediately assess the current status of the customer's credit. In summary, operational reports tend to reflect the current status of operations.

The reports just discussed relate primarily to the decision-making needs of managers within the organization. Also important are reports that are primarily useful to decision makers outside the organization. These include income tax statements, stockholder reports, and informational forms supplied to government regulators. Income tax reports can be very complex because income tax reporting requires that the information system maintain and produce information that would otherwise not be kept for managers. In some situations, the depreciation or inventory methods used for income tax purposes may differ from those used for financial recording purposes. Stockholder reports primarily include the income statement, the statement of financial position, and the statement of changes in financial position. A third important category of external reports relates to government regulation. In many industries, government regulations require a number of special reports. The pharmaceutical industry, for instance, is required to produce a large number of reports relating to requirements for government approval of new drugs. Other industries produce reports on such diverse things as pollution control and occupational safety. In addition, companies listed on the open stock exchange are required to file various quarterly and annual reports with the SEC.

Reports can also be classified according to their *time horizon*. They are either long range, short range, or historical. Long-range reports are more useful for strategic planning, whereas short-range reports are more useful for either tactical or operational planning. Historical reports can be useful for a wide variety of purposes, including comparing present period results to results of previous years.

The James Company New-Order Report			
June 1			
Customer Name	Date Promised	Estimated # Labor Hours	Estimated # Machine Hours
Jones	6/5	100	60
Charles	6/8	200	50
Bacon	6/8	150	90
Willis	6/9	75	20
Sheldon	6/7	100	70
Wolfe	6/10	300	110

FIGURE 10.8 Typical Operations Report.

A third categorization scheme for reports is *scope*. The scope of a report can be firmwide, divisionwide, departmentwide, or it might even relate to only one individual. Reports of varying scope are necessary because higher-level managers tend to require reports that are wider in scope. Also, it is necessary to continuously evaluate the firm from a wide variety of perspectives. Management must be able to assess performance of entities within the firm at all levels. For example, if the firm's profits are sagging, management must find a reason. To do this, they might investigate to determine which division is causing the problem and, then, within each division, determine which department is causing the problem. There are, of course, other ways to view wider and narrower scopes. For example, a report showing the profitability of all the firm's products combined might be considered very broad in scope, and a report showing the profit for one product out of many might be considered narrow in scope.

The fourth categorization scheme in Table 10.1 is *occurrence*. Very often reports are periodic and are produced at regular intervals. Examples of periodic reports include weekly sales summaries and quarterly income statements. In addition, reports can be made available on a requested basis. For example, a manager might have a one-time decision to make and a special report might be requested. Other reports might be event-triggered. These kinds of reports are usually produced when some predefined event occurs. For example, a plant manager might require a special report any time there is significant downtime on a particular machine. The report could include an explanation of the cause of the downtime and the cost to the company.

The next category in Table 10.1 is *organizational function*. The number of possible reports within an organizational function scheme is practically endless. Every department within an organization performs a particular function. Therefore, a departmental report is considered a functional area report. In addition, there are subfunctions performed within departments. For example, within the production department there might exist several functions, including assembly, painting, and packaging. Functional area reports might also be given for general areas of the company, such as sales, manufacturing, or accounting.

The sixth category, *report format*, refers to the means in which the given report is presented. For example, some reports are presented to the manager on a computer printout, and others might appear on a video display. There are, of course, endless categories of possible report formats. The format of a report can be very important. For example, a simple, concise, easy-to-read report is much more likely to be used effectively by a manager. In some companies, managers might receive hundreds of pages of reports on a regular basis. In situations such as this, managers tend to ignore some of the reporting information. Good reporting formats can minimize this problem. Consider a variance report in which negative variances are shown in red and positive variances are shown in blue. The clarity of this format might result in a report that is well-liked and effectively used by managers.

Finally, reports can be classified as to their *conciseness*. A concise report might be 1 or 2 pages, and a detailed report might be 200 pages. For planning and control purposes, conciseness is usually a good characteristic. A manager, when reviewing operations for a given day's production, would typically prefer a 1- or 2-page report that highlights any difficulties. Psychology has shown that the human mind can process only three or four variables at a time. When more than three or four variables are present, **information overload** can occur. Many things can happen in the case of information overload, but it is very likely that the manager will ignore some or all the information in the report. Therefore, an effective reporting system should be one that presents information in a concise format.

Reporting Systems

It is important to view individual reports within the larger context of the overall information system. According to this view, the report can be considered as part of a subsystem called the **reporting system,** which is an integral component of the overall information system.

For a reporting system to be effective, it must be an integral component of an information system in which all accounts follow a uniform coding scheme. An example of this concept is given in Figure 10.9. The Midwestern sales division has an account code 04 09 10 for sales of eggs. The account code is directly linked to the statement of sales in the bottom half of the figure. This type of uniform coding scheme allows reports that contain varying levels of detail to be generated. This is especially true in a computerized system, in which the computer can easily sort transactions by account code. For example, in Figure 10.9, the first two digits of the account code relate to the region of the country to which the transaction pertains. Note that the Eastern sales account code begins with 05. It would be possible, therefore, to generate reports summarizing all Eastern sales by instructing the computer to select all transactions that begin with 05.

Given an effective coding scheme and an overall information system design that incorporates management decision-making needs, it is possible to devise a number of useful reporting systems. At the most general level, these reporting systems can be classified as either *horizontal* or *vertical.* **Horizontal reporting systems** produce information for planning and control within related operational functions of the organization. **Vertical reporting systems** maintain the upward and downward flow of information particularly important to planning and control.

A good example of a horizontal reporting system can be seen from the relationship between sales (order entry), billing, production, and shipping. When orders are received, information is transmitted to the production department, giving

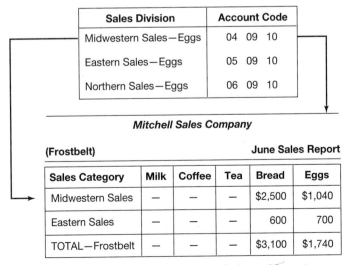

Sales Division	Account Code
Midwestern Sales—Eggs	04 09 10
Eastern Sales—Eggs	05 09 10
Northern Sales—Eggs	06 09 10

Mitchell Sales Company

(Frostbelt)   **June Sales Report**

Sales Category	Milk	Coffee	Tea	Bread	Eggs
Midwestern Sales	—	—	—	$2,500	$1,040
Eastern Sales	—	—	—	600	700
TOTAL—Frostbelt	—	—	—	$3,100	$1,740

FIGURE 10.9 Relationship between Account Coding and Reporting.

specific directions for filling the computer's order. Completed goods must then be transmitted to the shipping dock department for eventual delivery to the customer. The shipping department then notifies the billing department, which in turn invoices the customer. In an effective system, it is possible for a salesperson to check the status of a given order at any time and find out where it is in the system. For example, a salesperson would be able to check and find that a given order has been completed and the goods have been shipped to the customer.

Vertical reporting systems establish an information flow between the various levels of management. Budgets are developed by collecting upward flows of information, such as historical summaries of sales. This information is then assembled and transmitted downward in the form of a final budget. Vertical reporting systems tend to emphasize planning and control, whereas horizontal reporting systems tend to focus on carrying out operational functions.

Both horizontal and vertical reporting systems form an important basis for a number of specialized reporting systems. Some of these specialized systems include the financial accounting reporting system, the cost accounting reporting system, responsibility centers, and profitability centers. Each of these different types of specialized reporting systems is discussed in what follows. It should be emphasized, however, that each individual company has its own reporting needs, and there are a wide variety of specialized reporting systems that might be useful. For example, an asphalt manufacturing company might need a specialized system that accounts for combining different chemicals in the production of asphalt. In this case, managers might need daily reports describing the availability of materials and specific grades of asphalt that come out of the production process. The needs of a construction company may vary considerably from those of a typical manufacturing firm. One very important information need in the construction business is reports on the progress toward completion of a given contract. For example, a company might contract to finish a building within six months. A construction project such as this will involve a large number of factors: plumbing, masonry, steel erection, roofing, carpentry, and electrical work. A delay in one of these areas might delay the entire project. Therefore, a construction company needs reports that relate to critical factors and the impact of these factors on the completion date of the overall project.

The Financial and Cost Reporting Systems

The main objective of the financial accounting system is to produce stewardship reports for the company's owners and creditors. This system focuses on obtaining the traditional reports, namely, the statement of income, statement of financial position, and statement of changes in financial position. Although a large amount of resources may be devoted to the financial accounting reporting system, the information may be of little use to managers. This is not to say that most managers are not interested in the income statement and balance sheet. But these financial accounting reports often include arbitrary cost allocations and depreciation methods that are not very useful for internal decision making.

The cost accounting reporting system often has the objective of providing numbers for cost of goods sold and finished goods to be used in the financial reporting system. As described in Chapter 8, there are two main types of cost accounting systems: job order systems and process costing systems. Job order systems are applicable in industries where customer orders are made on a custom basis. Examples are shipmaking, construction, and custom cabinet making. The main task of the job order system is to collect labor, material, and overhead costs for individual jobs.

In industries where goods are mass-produced, a process costing reporting system is normally used. Process costing systems differ from job order systems in that costs are not collected for individual customer orders but rather for production batches. A good example of a situation in which process costing is more desirable is a paint manufacturing company. A manufacturer of paints will produce hundreds of thousands of gallons that are absolutely identical. In this case, it makes little sense to have separate accounting for each gallon of paint. Therefore, costs are collected around batches of paint. The batches might be determined by the amount of production in a given time period or particular production run.

An effective cost accounting system can be very helpful in producing useful reports for managers. Take, for example, a job order situation in which the company bids on individual jobs. One case in point might be an electronics manufacturer who manufacturers components used in television sets. Assume that the company does not manufacture television sets itself but rather places bids on jobs for major companies that manufacture televisions. In order to place a bid, the company must be able to determine the cost of producing a given number of units. In addition, a good cost accounting system allow this company to produce reports that indicate profitability (or lack thereof) for completed jobs. Such information is vital for a company's survival in a competitive environment.

Responsibility Accounting Reporting Systems

One of the most important concepts in internal reporting is that of the responsibility accounting center. The concept of **responsibility accounting** states that all events that occur within a company's environment can be traced to the responsibility of a particular individual. For example, assume that a manufacturing company has to throw away a large number of units of finished product due to substandard material problems. The concept of responsibility accounting implies that a particular individual should be held responsible for the occurrence of this event. In this case, the problem might be attributable to the manager of materials inspection. Furthermore, responsibility accounting systems are typically able to allocate costs to the relevant responsibility center. In the present case, the system would charge the cost of the thrown-away units to the manager of materials acquisition. These costs would, therefore, appear on this manager's report of budgeted versus actual costs. The manager's supervisor would, of course, allow for a reasonable amount of "throw-away" (spoilage) costs before taking corrective action.

Consider a situation in which several production managers are in charge of manufacturing operations. Furthermore, assume that responsibility accounting is not in effect and that problems with production are not traceable to an individual manager. Next, assume that the company has a recurring problem with delays in production. With a responsibility accounting system in place, the plant manager should be able to determine easily the individual production manager responsible for the problem. However, without this information it may be very difficult or impossible to take any corrective action.

Figure 10.10 provides a graphical conceptualization of the responsibility accounting concept. In this figure, note that the line of authority flows all the way from the president of the organization down to the worker on the assembly line. In each case, individuals are responsible to the person above them in the organizational chart. For example, a problem for a worker at the bottom of the organiza-

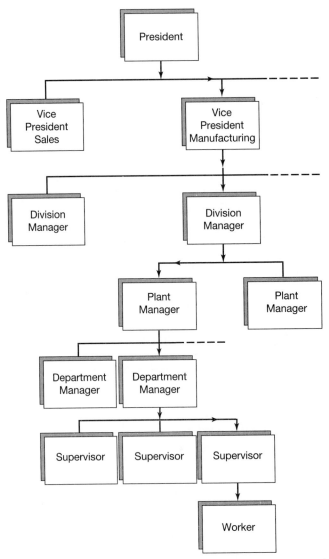

FIGURE 10.10 Responsibility Accounting and the Organizational Span of Authority.

tional chart is also a problem for that worker's supervisor. Furthermore, the supervisor must be held accountable for the performance of the worker to the department manager. The department manager's performance is in turn evaluated by the plant manager. This process moves up the organizational chart, and, in the final analysis, the president is responsible for the individual worker's performance.

A very important application of responsibility accounting is the investment center concept. Consider Figure 10.11, which gives profitability reports for two different divisions. An important aspect of this report is the **contribution margin controllable by division manager.** Note the computation of this number. It involves taking net sales and subtracting costs that are subject to the division manager's control. Note that nonallocatable selling/administrative expenses are not charged to the division. Therefore, the contribution margin and operating income figures in this report are based on cost numbers that are subject to the control of

Hill Manufacturing Company	Total	Division A	Division B
Net Sales	$5,200	$2,000	$3,200
Less Variable Costs:			
Direct labor	1,600	100	1,500
Direct material	300	100	200
Variable overhead	500	200	300
Variable selling and administrative expenses	800	400	400
Total Variable Expenses	3,200	800	2,400
Contribution margin controllable by division manager	2,000	1,200	800
Less Fixed Costs:			
Fixed costs controllable by division manager	900	500	400
Controllable operating income	1,100	700	400
Nonallocatable selling and administrative expenses	500		
Net Income Before Taxes	$ 600		

FIGURE 10.11 Responsibility Reporting: Investment Center Concepts.

the division manager. This differs from traditional financial accounting reporting that allocates central selling/administration expenses to the various divisions. The net result is that the numbers in Figure 10.11 can be used to evaluate the division manager.

The concept of an **investment center** goes one step further. Not only are revenues and expenses considered important when traceable to a particular investment center, but the division manager is also accountable for the use of company assets. Therefore, the operating profits of the two divisions in Figure 10.11 would be compared to their respective asset bases. A number of different techniques are used in practice to relate the income to the asset base. One example is return on investment. Assume that the assets of Division A and Division B in Figure 10.11 are both $10,000. This implies a return on investment of 7% for Division A and 4% for Division B.

In summary, the important concept behind responsibility accounting is that of traceability. All costs should be traced to some responsibility center. Given this, reports can be produced for purposes of evaluating a given responsibility center as an investment. In addition, the individual in charge of the responsibility center can be evaluated as a manger of that investment.

Profitability Reporting Systems

Profitability reporting involves a system of budgets and control reports and spans the various levels of the organization chart. Figure 10.12 gives examples of various types of budgetary reports along with their associated control reports.

The key concept behind profitability reporting is **profit planning.** The organization can be viewed as a group of profit centers. The company's overall prof-

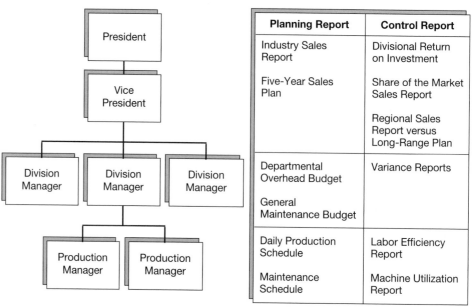

	Planning Report	Control Report
President	Industry Sales Report	Divisional Return on Investment
Vice President	Five-Year Sales Plan	Share of the Market Sales Report
		Regional Sales Report versus Long-Range Plan
Division Manager / Division Manager / Division Manager	Departmental Overhead Budget	Variance Reports
	General Maintenance Budget	
Production Manager / Production Manager	Daily Production Schedule	Labor Efficiency Report
	Maintenance Schedule	Machine Utilization Report

FIGURE 10.12. Planning and Control Reports and Organizational Structure.

itability plan is derived by setting targets for profit in each of the individual profit centers. Major categories for profit centers are various company divisions and products. Consider Figure 10.13, which gives a sales profitability report for three different products. The overall planned profit margin for this hypothetical company is 10%; however, the actual profit margin is only 5%. A quick inspection of the individual product profit margins easily reveals that the overall failure to meet the desired profit margin percentage was largely attributable to product 3, which had a profit margin of 0%. The very low profit margin for this product pulled down the profit margin for the company as a whole.

From this example, we can see that profitability reporting is not only a useful planning tool but also a helpful evaluation aid. In addition, it has the advantage of providing individual managers with a view of how their organizational unit contributes to the overall profits of the company.

ABC Sales Company
Profitability Report

		First Quarter		
			Product	
	Total	1	2	3
Sales	$1,000	$200	$300	$500
Less variable expenses	700	100	200	400
Contribution margin	300	100	100	100
Less fixed expenses	250	75	75	100
Operating margin	50	25	25	0
Actual profit margin	5%	12.5%	8.33%	0%
Planned profit margin	10%	10%	10%	10%

FIGURE 10.13 Example of Profitability Planning.

SUMMARY

Resource allocation problems in organizations are solved through the process of management decision making. All planning and control activities involve decision making. The phases and steps involved in the process of management decision making were defined and illustrated.

Information derives its value from its effect on decisions. The quality of information depends on the properties information possesses, such as timeliness and accuracy. Quantitatively, the value of information might be measured in terms of the incremental expected payoff that would result from the information being made available to the decision maker. As the illustration in the chapter indicated, it is easy to overvalue information. Even though information that is available to a decision maker may possess desirable qualities, such as accuracy and timeliness, such qualities are not necessarily of economic value.

Computer software has been developed to assist managers in making decisions. Database software allows managers to perform structured queries to obtain information in a database. Decision support systems provide support to a decision-making process. Expert systems are designed to emulate the knowledge and problem-solving techniques of a human expert. Executive information systems provide top management easy access to information and reports.

Reports provide an important interface between an information system and the users of the information system. Reports can be either financial or nonfinancial. At the most general level, reports to management can be categorized as to their purpose, such as planning or control. Several other methods of classifying reports were discussed and illustrated to indicate the wide variety of reports that may be prepared by an accounting information system.

An organization's reporting systems are an integral component of the firm's information system. Common reporting systems include the financial accounting reporting system, the cost accounting reporting system, the responsibility accounting reporting system, and the profitability reporting system. It should be emphasized that each organization has its own unique reporting needs that might be satisfied with specialized reporting systems.

Glossary

accuracy: an information property concerned with the degree to which information measures what it purports to measure.

budgetary reporting systems: reporting system in which periodic reports highlight budgeted versus actual expenses and revenues.

conciseness: an information property concerned with the degree of detail in information.

control reports: reports that assist in assuring that operations follow according to plan.

cost–benefit approach: criterion in which the costs associated with a decision alternative should not exceed its expected benefits.

decision support systems (DSSs): computer-based information systems that provide support to a decision-making process.

executive information system (EIS): software tailored to the strategic information needs of top management.

expert system: a highly developed DSS that utilizes knowledge generally possessed by an expert to solve a problem.

flexible budget: a budget that specifically allows for varying levels of activity.

horizontal reporting systems: reporting systems that produce information for planning and control within related operational functions of the organization.

inference engine: in an expert system, the program that requests data from the user, manipulates the knowledge base, and provides a decision to the user.

information overload: a decision maker receives more information than can effectively be processed.

knowledge base: stores the rules, data, and relationships that are used to solve problems in an expert system.

management by exception: the investigation of only those deviations from budget that are material.

master budget: a budget for the entire organization.

operational reports: reports that focus on the current status of operations within a company.

planning reports: reports that assist in acquiring and allocating resources for future operations.

profit planning: reporting system in which a company's overall profitability plan is derived by setting targets for profit in individual profit centers.

profitability reporting: a system of budgets and control reports that assist in profit planning for profit centers within the organization.

quantifiability: an information property concerned with the degree of difficulty in representing a given event numerically.

relevance: an information property concerned with how well information relates to a given decision.

reporting system: the component of an information system concerned with individual reports.

responsibility accounting: a reporting system in which financial information is accumulated and processed by responsibility centers.

timeliness: an information property concerned with being current or up-to-date.

value of information: the incremental increase in expected payoff that results from a decision if the information in question were available.

value of perfect information: the incremental increase in expected payoff that results from a decision if perfect information were available.

vertical reporting systems: reporting systems that maintain the upward and downward flow of information particularly important to planning and control.

Chapter Quiz

Answers to the chapter quiz appear on page 427.

1. Which of the following is an information property concerned with the degree of detail in information?
   (a) accuracy
   (b) conciseness
   (c) relevance
   (d) quantifiability

2. Which of the following is an information property concerned with the degree to which information measures what it purports to measure?
   (a) accuracy
   (b) conciseness
   (c) relevance
   (d) quantifiability

3. Which of the following is an information property concerned with the degree of difficulty in representing a given event numerically?
   (a) accuracy
   (b) conciseness
   (c) relevance
   (d) quantifiability

4. Which of the following is an information property concerned with how well information relates to a given decision?
   (a) accuracy
   (b) conciseness
   (c) relevance
   (d) quantifiability

5. Which of the following is a type of budget that specifically allows for varying levels of activity?
   (a) master budget
   (b) flexible budget ✓
   (c) profit budget
   (d) static budget

6. Which of the following types of reports assist in acquiring and allocating resources for future operations?
   (a) master reports
   (b) control reports
   (c) operational reports
   (d) planning reports ✓

7. Which of the following might be described as *status reports?*
   (a) master reports
   (b) control reports
   (c) operational reports
   (d) planning reports

8. Which of the following terms is used to describe a request for information contained in a database?
   (a) report
   (b) dialog
   (c) query
   (d) seek

9. Microcomputer spreadsheet software is a common example of which of the following?
   (a) expert system
   (b) decision support system
   (c) executive information system
   (d) reporting system

10. Consider the following payoff matrix for a golddigger:

| | | Action | |
State of Nature	Probability	Dig	Do Not Dig
Gold	0.2	$40,000	$0
No Gold	0.8	−$10,000	$0

What is the value of perfect information?
(a) $0
(b) $8,000
(c) $32,000
(d) $40,000

Review Problem

Charles Hill is a production manager at the Hillcrest Toy Manufacturing Company located in Boca Raton, Florida. Hill is responsible for managing approximately 25 employees on an assembly line. These employees work in three areas: assembly, painting, and packaging. Each of the three areas has its own supervisor. Some of the decisions Hill must make are described in the following list:

a. Develop a weekly production schedule. On the first day of each week, Hill receives a report from the sales department describing the orders to be processed. Hill then takes these reports and develops a detailed day-by-day production schedule that summarizes the number of hours spent on each product.

b. Hill discusses the production schedule with the purchasing manager in terms of raw material requirements. If some of the raw materials are not available, the production schedule is modified accordingly.

c. Four times a year, Hill is required to evaluate all employees under his supervision in terms of their job performance.

d. Hill meets with the vice president of production planning annually. They discuss the general production needs for the entire year ahead. Together they develop a budget that is used for obtaining new equipment and hiring employees.

Required

a. Make a general description of the information needs of Charles Hill.

b. For each of the previous decisions, describe the basic information requirements. In each case, give the sources of the information required and state how the information would be used.

c. For each decision, describe specific reports that would be helpful to Hill in his work.

Solution to Review Problem

In order to schedule production effectively, Hill should meet with each of the supervisors, probably on a weekly basis. This, of course, would depend on the exact nature of the manufacturing process, but there should be at least occasional meetings between Hill and the supervisors. One very helpful report might be a list of material requirements versus material availability. This report might be especially helpful in the sales department, where the materials required could be input into the report. The report could then go to the purchasing and inventory control managers, where problems with availability could be noted. In this system, it would be possible to order materials immediately as the sales order is processed.

Also helpful to the production manager would be periodic reports relating to the effectiveness of the production planning process. Specifically, it would be useful to have a description of the planned schedule for each order versus the actual time taken. Any discrepancies might indicate either a deviation from the plan due to a production problem or a problem in the planning process. This type of analysis would have the overall benefit of maintaining better control over production operations as well as maximizing efforts to complete products according to plan. The latter is very important in terms of customer satisfaction (filling orders within the time limits promised). Maintaining adequate availability of raw materials is very important for reasons discussed in the previous paragraph. Another useful report might be a periodic analysis of the delays in manufacturing due to raw material availability. With this, Hill could highlight particular problems of availability that might produce repeating bottlenecks in filling orders on time.

Finally, it might be helpful to have direct contact with the sales department in this regard. This would help Hill coordinate problem orders directly with the sales staff. For example, if Hill found it difficult to produce an order within the time specified, he might reprioritize his production scheduling without harm if he knew the specific priorities to be placed on filling the individual orders. This information could come from the sales department. More specifically, each order could have a priority code on the order itself. Orders with high-priority codes would be given the utmost attention in the production schedule. Orders with low-priority codes could be delayed if necessary.

The problem of performance evaluation is best handled by collecting specific performance data for each employee. The most useful instrument for doing this is the production-variance report. Specific variances should be reported for labor and material. Furthermore, both labor and material variances should be broken down in terms of their respective causes. The causes could be attributable either to price variances in input factors (i.e., labor and material) or efficiency. The efficiency variance would relate for each employee a summary of the actual number of hours required to produce a given amount of output versus the standard or budgeted level of hours allowed. The materials efficiency variance would compare the actual amount of materials used to the standard amount of materials allowed.

The yearly production plan can be an effective technique for dealing with situations in which there is a lot of sales growth. Very often a large growth in sales will require the hiring of additional employees and possible expansion of the amount of floor space or equipment. In such situations, it is very useful to get the opinion of the production manager, because this person will be involved in implementing any expansion in production. In addition, the production manager is in the best position to point out problems that higher-level managers might not be able to see quite so easily.

A report that might be particularly helpful to Hill in terms of long-run planning might be a 12-month-ahead report projecting on a month-by-month basis the expected level of sales and corresponding production demand. This report could be modified on a monthly basis and transmitted to Hill for review.

Review Questions

1. Define each of the following terms:
   (a) phases of the decision process
   (b) operational control
   (c) relevance
   (d) quantifiability
   (e) accuracy
   (f) conciseness
   (g) timeliness
   (h) delay
   (i) frequency
   (j) scope
   (k) variance
   (l) budgetary control system
2. Describe the major activities performed by managers.
3. List and discuss each of the six phases of the decision process.
4. Which phase of the decision process is the most critical? Why?
5. What phase of the decision-making process is the most difficult for the manager?
6. Which phases of the decision-making process primarily involve planning? Which primarily involve control?
7. Distinguish between the following types of software that are used to assist managers in making decisions:
   (a) database software
   (b) decision support systems
   (c) expert systems
   (d) executive information system
8. What is a "structured query"? How do structured queries assist managers in making decisions?
9. Why must information have value? Can the value of information always be measured?
10. Explain the meaning of each of the following terms:
    (a) operational report
    (b) planning report
    (c) control report
    (d) benchmark

(e) horizontal reporting system
(f) vertical reporting system
(g) responsibility accounting
(h) cost accounting system
(i) profitability reporting
(j) controllable cost
(k) information overload

11. Identify several types of reports. For each type of report, give several examples.
12. Contrast and compare planning versus control reports.
13. Discuss several types of reports that a production manager might use.
14. Describe several features that are necessary for a control report to be effective.
15. Describe several examples of operational reports.
16. Explain the use of benchmarks in control reports.
17. Describe flexible budgeting and its importance.
18. Is timeliness more important for control reports or planning reports? Why?
19. How are account codes relevant to reporting systems?
20. What are the key elements of a responsibility accounting system?
21. What are the key elements of a profitability reporting system?
22. How do profitability reporting systems differ from responsibility accounting reporting systems?

Discussion Questions and Problems

23. For each of the following decisions, describe at least two alternative courses of action that might be available to a manager.
    (a) how to hire a new employee
    (b) how to stimulate sales
    (c) how to reduce labor inefficiency
    (d) how to improve customer relations
24. Consider each of the following decision situations. In each case, describe the importance of each phase of the decision process.
    (a) relocating a plant
    (b) redesigning a product to reduce costs
    (c) developing a new product line
    (d) hiring a new company president
25. In each case, discuss the necessary vertical flows of information.
    (a) developing a production budget
    (b) investigating a quality control problem
    (c) investigating reasons for poor profitability for a particular product
    (d) investigating reasons for a low return on investment for a particular division of a company
26. For each of the following types of decisions, describe the usefulness of periodic reporting (e.g., a monthly budget report)
    (a) evaluating the effectiveness of the sales staff
    (b) evaluating the effectiveness of a production supervisor
    (c) degree to which sales targets are met
    (d) effectiveness of employee hiring policies
    (e) problems with delinquent collection of accounts receivable
    (f) problems with excessive use of raw materials in the manufacturing process
27. The chapter contained an illustration in which the value of the information provided by a quality control system was measured using the incremental expected-payoff model of decision theory.

(a) Can relevance be determined qualitatively?

(b) Could the accuracy of the information system be improved to a point where the value of information it provided was economic? What level of accuracy is required?

28. A machine produces either 2%, 10%, or 25% defectives. It costs $600 to check the machine each morning to guarantee that it will produce 2% defectives for that day. If the machine is not checked, the extra cost created by a batch containing 10% defectives is $500, and with a batch containing 25% defectives is $3,000. The probability that the machine will be in a state producing a percentage of defectives of 2%, 10%, or 25% is 0.7, 0.2, and 0.1, respectively. What should the manager decide if her objective is to minimize the expected costs?

What is the expected value of perfect information concerning the true state of nature (2%, 10%, or 25%)?

29. The Argon County Hospital is located in the county seat. Argon County is a well-known summer resort area. The county population doubles during the vacation months (May–August) and hospital activity more than doubles during these months. The hospital is organized into several departments. Although it is a relatively small hospital, its pleasant surroundings have attracted a well-trained and competent medical staff.

An administrator was hired a year ago to improve the business activities of the hospital. Among the new ideas he has introduced is responsibility accounting. This program was announced along with quarterly cost reports supplied to department heads. Previously, cost data were presented to department heads infrequently. Excerpts from the announcement and the report received by the laundry supervisor are presented in what follows.

The hospital has adopted a responsibility accounting system. From now on you will receive quarterly reports comparing the costs of operating your department with budgeted costs. The reports will highlight the differences (variations) so you can zero in on the departure from budgeted costs (this is called management by exception). Responsibility accounting means you are accountable for keeping the costs in your department within the budget. The variations from the budget will help you identify what costs are out of line, and the size of the variation will indicate which ones are the most important. Your first such report accompanies this announcement.

Argon County Hospital Performance Report—Laundry Department July–September 19X3				
	Budget	*Actual*	*(Over) Under Budget*	*Percentage (Over) Under Budget*
Patient days	9,500	11,900	(2,400)	(25)
Pounds processed (laundry)	125,000	156,000	(31,000)	(25)
Costs				
Laundry labor	$ 9,000	$ 12,500	$ (3,500)	(39)
Supplies	1,100	1,875	(775)	(70)
Water, water heating and softening	1,700	2,500	(800)	(47)
Maintenance	1,400	2,200	(800)	(57)
Supervisor's salary	3,150	3,750	(600)	(19)
Allocated administrative costs	4,000	5,000	(1,000)	(25)
Equipment depreciation	1,200	1,250	(50)	(4)
	$ 21,550	$ 29,075	$ (7,525)	(35)

Administrator's comments: Costs are significantly above budget for the quarter. Particular attention needs to be paid to labor, supplies, and maintenance.

The annual budget for 19X3 was constructed by the new administrator. Quarterly budgets were computed as one-fourth of the annual budget. The administrator compiled the budget by analyzing the prior three years' costs. The analysis showed that all costs increased each year, with more rapid increases between the second and third year. He considered establishing the budget at an average of the prior three years' costs, hoping that the installation of the system would reduce costs to this level. However, in view of the rapidly increasing prices, he finally chose 19X2 costs less 3% for the 19X3 budget. The activity level measured by patient days and pounds of laundry processed was set at the 19X3 volume, which was approximately equal to the volume of the past three years.

(a) Comment on the method used to construct the budget.
(b) What information should be communicated by variations from budgets?
(c) Does the report effectively communicate the level of efficiency of this department? Give reasons for your answer.

(CMA)

30. An important concept in management accounting is responsibility accounting.

   Required
   (a) Define the term *responsibility accounting.*
   (b) What conditions must exist for there to be effective responsibility accounting?
   (c) What benefits are said to result from responsibility accounting?
   (d) Listed in what follows are three charges found on the monthly report of a division that manufactures and sells products primarily to outside companies. Division performance is evaluated by the use of return on investment. You are to state which, if any, of the following charges are consistent with the responsibility accounting concept. Support each answer with a brief explanation.
      (1) A charge for general corporation administration at 10% of division sales.
      (2) A charge for the use of the corporate computer facility. The charge is determined by taking actual annual computer department costs and allocating the amount to each user on the ratio of its use to total corporation use.
      (3) A charge for goods purchased from another division. The charge is based on the competitive market price for the goods.

(CMA)

31. In each of the following cases, something is wrong. Indicate what this is.
   (a) A production manager in charge of four employees receives a daily variance report. This report shows a job-by-job summary of all costs incurred.
   (b) A vice president of manufacturing for a large company is given weekly production variance reports. The reports show, on an employee-by-employee basis, the actual labor used for each job and the standard labor allowed.
   (c) A corporate treasurer receives a report once a year relating to the company's cash budget. This report shows projected cash inflows and outflows. Any shortages of cash are noted so that arrangements can be made in advance for borrowing.
   (d) The vice president of manufacturing receives quarterly reports that evaluate each division manager. These reports show division sales minus cost of goods sold. Included in the cost of goods sold computations are fixed and variable manufacturing costs. In addition, selling and administrative expenses are allocated to each division based on the sales of that division.

32. Several decision problems follow. In each case, describe an appropriate report to assist the manager in making a correct decision.
   (a) Determine the cause of poor profitability for a particular product.
   (b) Decide whether to install a new computer system.
   (c) Decide whether to purchase new machinery in order to replace outmoded machinery.
   (d) Decide whether to introduce a new product line.
   (e) Decide whether to move a given plant to a new location.

(f) Decide whether to hire an outside business consultant for purposes of buying a new computer system.

33. The Hall Consulting Firm specializes in developing accounting information systems. In all cases, clients are provided detailed bids specifying the services provided and costs involved. In addition, a general timetable is provided that serves as a guide for the overall development of the project. The project timetable generally gives the length of time for each major aspect of this system's development. A typical timetable might specify something like (a) systems analysis—three months; (b) systems design—five months; and (c) systems implementation—seven months.

   The Hall Consulting Firm is very concerned about the length of time that a particular engagement requires, because time is the major resource of the firm. If a job requires more time than planned, considerable losses can result. As a result, the head partner of the firm, Barbara Hall, needs an information system that emphasizes control over employee time. Moreover, this control system must be integrated with the bidding system, so that the number of hours bid can be reconciled against the actual number of hours billed.

   ### Required

   Describe a reporting system that would be helpful to the Hall Consulting Firm with regard to control over bidding and time spent on individual engagements.

34. The Day Company of North Carolina makes custom-manufactured sofas. Orders are processed in the following manner. First, the customer's order is reviewed and the appropriate materials are selected. (This company uses over 200 possible materials to upholster its sofas.) Next, the appropriate model number is taken from the sales order. This is important because the company manufactures seven different models of sofas. Given this information, the appropriate materials are obtained and the job is assigned to three or four individuals who will assemble and upholster the job. Everything is done by hand, so the process is very expensive.

   The Day Company has always focused on the highest-quality work. This has been a key success factor for many years.

   Recently sales orders have slumped. In order to find the cause of this problem, the vice president of sales contacted a number of furniture stores who act as distributors for the Day Company. Discussions with these individuals revealed that a large number of customers were opting to order sofas from competitors who were selling similar products, but at a cost of about 20% lower. Further examination revealed that the competitors sold very similar products with one key difference. The competitors were substituting a lower-cost prefabricated frame for the Day Company's hand-constructed frame. Many times in the past, the chief executive has considered using prefabricated frames, but this option had always been rejected as being a compromise to quality. The Day Company has always maintained the reputation of being one of the highest-quality companies in the industry, and it was felt that such a change would hurt the company's image.

   ### Required

   (a) Describe the basic decision problem facing the Day Company. Assuming that the sales department expects sales to continue to drop for the reasons stated previously, what corrective action might be taken?
   (b) What information would be required in order for management to evaluate the alternatives suggested in part (a)? Does the Day Company need to revise its strategic plan? If so, how can it go about identifying alternative courses of action?
   (c) Assuming that the company modifies its strategic plan and decides to produce a lower-cost product, what could it then use as a key success factor in order to distinguish itself from its competitors?
   (d) Describe at least one alternative besides redesigning the frames. If this additional alternative was implemented, what information would be required for control?

35. Diamond Dawn owns a small gambling house in Legal Valley. She has just returned from a business trip to Pacific City, where she visited several large modern gambling casinos. Dawn was quite impressed, but also confused by what she learned about the use of computer information systems in the management of casinos.

As Dawn explained:

> I operate a very small house compared to the ones I visited in Pacific City. I'm a sole proprietor and "on the floor" most nights I'm open; the casinos in Pacific City are owned by large corporations and are run by professional managers. But the general nature of operations is quite similar.
>
> Complimentary expenses—free drinks, free lodging, free floor shows, free transportation to and from the casino, and other gratuities—are a major concern in my business. The old saying that "you've gotta spend it to make it" is particularly true for casinos. You have to lavish complimentaries on the high-rollers to get them into your casino and out of someone else's. The problem is to figure out who the high-rollers are. It doesn't do you much good to spend $500 on someone who comes to your tables and loses only $200.
>
> This is where I depend on my pit bosses—the people who actually run the gambling tables. It has been a long-standing tradition in the casino business that the pit bosses set complimentary limits for players. This makes sense. The pit boss is the only person who actually sees how much somebody spends. I might see somebody walk in who has all the appearances of a high-roller—but they may only lose peanuts at the tables. My pit bosses have been in this business for a long time and they have worked at other places besides mine. They know the high-rollers and the high-rollers know them. In fact, high-rollers traditionally follow pit bosses as they move from one casino to another.
>
> It's a crazy business. But I've been in it for a long time. I guess that I trust my pit bosses and never much thought about it any further than that. That is, until my recent trip to Pacific City. The new casinos are taking a "professional information systems" approach to casino management. For example, someone told me that complimentary limits for known players are stored on computer files. Players exchange money for gambling chips at centralized locations rather than at the tables. When a player cashes money for gambling chips, these data are entered into the computer and processed. Pit bosses still set complimentary limits for some new players, but they are given a set of guidelines to use in determining the amount of complimentaries to give to a player. And there are "observers" at many of the gaming tables in addition to the pit bosses. The observers record the gambling behavior of players—how much they bet, lose, and so on. They tell me that these data are also processed by the computer. Finally, they tell me that the slot machines are computer-monitored; coins taken in, money paid out, hit ratios, and things like this are collected and processed for each machine.
>
> All in all, I was very impressed. However, I am not at all sure I really like what I saw. It is best to say that I am very confused. I will summarize my questions as follows:
>
> 1. What kind of management reports would such a system be capable of producing?
>
> 2. Do I need this type of information system to manage my casino? If I don't, then why are they doing this in Pacific City?

Required
Answer Dawn's questions.

36. (Requires microcomputer spreadsheet software.) Harvard Company is considering an investment opportunity. The investment amount is $2 million. The company plans to use a microcomputer spreadsheet package to analyze the projected returns for the investment over a six-year period. The following data have been assembled to evaluate the potential investment.

Harvard Company Analysts						
Assumptions	*Year 1*	*Year 2*	*Year 3*	*Year 4*	*Year 5*	*Year 6*
Market size						
Market share percent						
Unit sales volume						
Unit sales price						

Projected Returns							
	Year 0	*Year 1*	*Year 2*	*Year 3*	*Year 4*	*Year 5*	*Year 6*
Total revenue							
Cost of sales:							
Materials							
Conversion cost							
Total cost of sales							
Gross margin							
Other expenses:							
Marketing							
Distribution							
Administrative							
Total other expenses							
Net operating flows							
Investment							
Total flows							
Internal rate of return							
Net present value @ 12%							

Assumptions for Spreadsheet Analysis

- Total Market Size:
  250,000 units in year 1. Increasing by 10% a year for years 2 through 6.
- Harvard Company's Market Share Percentage:
  Fifty percent in year 1. Increasing by 10% a year for years 2 through 6.
- Unit Sales Price:
  $8.00 in year 1. Increasing by 6% a year for years 2 through 6.
- Material Cost:
  $1.50 per unit each year.
- Conversion Cost:
  $250,000 plus $2.75 per unit produced in excess of 200,000 units. When more than 200,000 units are produced in a year, Harvard Company expects to pay overtime.
- Marketing Cost:
  11% of total revenue each year.
- Distribution Cost:
  $0.75 per unit sold each year.
- Administrative Cost:
  $75,000 in year 1. Increasing by 8% a year for years 2 through 6.

Part 1. Using the preceding data, prepare a spreadsheet in the following format: The following items are computed for years 1 to 6.

- Gross margin is total revenue less total cost of sales.
- Net operating flows are gross margins less total other expenses.

The investment amount should be entered in year 0.

- Total flows are net operating flows less investment. These should be computed for years 0 to 6.
- The internal rate of return should be computed using the total flows range from 0 to year 6. Compare the internal rate of return using the formula(s) provided by your spreadsheet software.
- The net present value @ 12% (discounted at 12%) should be computed using the net operating flows range from years 1 to year 6. Compute the net present value @ 12% using the formula(s) provided by your spreadsheet software.

Part 2. The advantage of grouping assumptions in a separate section of the spreadsheet (as shown in Part 1) is that it is easy to ascertain the effects of changes in basic assumptions. Modify the solution to Part 1 to incorporate the following changes in assumptions. **Treat each change as an independent case.**
(a) Initial market size is 200,000 units.
(b) Harvard Company's initial market share percentage is 40%.
(c) Initial sales price is $9.00.
(d) Total market size increases by 5% a year for years 2 through 6.
(e) Harvard Company's market share percentage increases by 5% a year for years 2 through 6.

Revised Spreadsheet Format to Incorporate Taxes
Net operating flows
Depreciation
Taxable operating flows
Tax
After-tax operating flows (net operating flows – tax)
Investment
Total after-tax flows
Internal rate of return
Net present value @ 12%

Part 3. Modify the solution to Part 1 to incorporate tax considerations. The following changes are necessary.
(a) As shown, add rows for depreciation, taxable operating flows, tax, and after-tax operating flows between net operating flows and investment to your spreadsheet. Change total flows to total after-tax flows.
(b) Compute sum-of-the-years'-digits depreciation for the investment over the six-year period. Assume a useful service life of 15 years, and a $250,000 salvage (residual) value. Sum-of-the-years'-digits depreciation should be computed using the formula provided by your spreadsheet software.
(c) Deduct depreciation from net operating flows to get taxable operating flows.
(d) Compute tax expense as 35% of taxable operating flows.
(e) Compute after-tax operating flows as net operating flows less tax.

(f) The internal rate of return should be computed using the total after-tax flows range from year 0 to year 6.

(g) The net present value @ 12% (discounted at 12%) should be computed using the after-tax operating flows range from year 1 to year 6.

Part 4. Modify Part 3 to use double-declining balance depreciation rather than sum-of-the-years'-digits depreciation. Assume a useful service life of 15 years, and a $250,000 salvage (residual) value. Double-declining balance depreciation should be computed using the formula provided by your spreadsheet software.

Answers to Chapter Quiz

1. B	4. C	7. C	10. B (0.2)
2. A	5. B	8. C	($40,000) — (0.8)
3. D	6. D	9. B	($0) — $0

CHAPTER 11

File Processing and Data Management Concepts

LEARNING OBJECTIVES

Careful study of this chapter will enable you to:

■ Define the basic terms used in database technology.

■ Explain the historical development of database architecture.

■ Identify the three levels of database architecture.

■ Compare and contrast the different logical models of databases.

■ Explain the different methods of accessing files.

■ Explain the benefits of database management systems.

■ Describe the considerations that are appropriate to the design of computer-based files and databases.

INTRODUCTORY TERMINOLOGY

Fields, Data Items, Attributes, and Elements

The terms **field, data item, attribute,** and **element** are used interchangeably to denote the smallest block of data that will be stored and retrieved in the information system. If only some portion of the field is desired by the users, then the field should be split into several data items. A field may be a single character or number, or it may be composed of many characters or numbers. Examples of fields include items such as

- customer name
- employee social security number
- purchase order number
- customer account number

A field is usually logically associated with other fields; logical groupings of fields are called **records.** Records are groups of data items that concern a certain entity such as an employee, a customer, a vendor, an invoice, and so forth. We will denote a record structure as follows:

428

```
RECORD-NAME (FIELD 1, FIELD 2, . . . , FIELD N)
```

RECORD-NAME is the name of the record, such as VENDOR or EMPLOYEE. The entries in parentheses are the names of individual files in the record. The following examples explain:

- CUSTOMER(ACCOUNT_NUMBER, NAME, ADDRESS, ACCOUNT_BALANCE)
- EMPLOYEE(NAME, SSN, AGE)
- PURCHASE_ORDER(PO_#, DATE, AMOUNT, VENDOR, QUANTITY, PRICE)

In the first example, CUSTOMER is the name of the record, and ACCOUNT_NUMBER, NAME, ADDRESS, and ACCOUNT_BALANCE are the names of the fields.

Data Occurrences

A record structure has **occurrences,** also called **instances.** A record occurrence is a specific set of data values for the record. For example, for the record

```
EMPLOYEE(NAME, NUMBER, AGE)
```

we might have the occurrence

```
EMPLOYEE(Brown, 111222333,33),
```

and an occurrence for the CUSTOMER record previously described might be

```
CUSTOMER(12122, ABC Hardware, 222 West Street, $1,050)
```

Fixed- and Variable-Length Records

Records within a file may be of either fixed or variable length. In a **fixed-length record,** both the number of fields and the length (character size) of each field are fixed. Fixed-length records are easier to manipulate in computer applications than variable-length records because the size of fixed-length records is standardized. Most records stored on direct-access storage devices (DASDs) are fixed length.

The drawback of fixed-length records is that each field must be large enough to contain the maximum expected entry into the field. This typically results in wasted space, as in leaving 25 or so spaces for a name, whereas many names have eight characters or fewer. In **variable-length records,** however, the width of the field can be adjusted for each data occurrence. Furthermore, in variable-length records, the actual number of fields can vary from one data occurrence to another.

The end of a variable-length record must be indicated by a special symbol or a record-length field contained in the record itself. Variable-length records efficiently utilize available storage space, but manipulating such records is relatively difficult. Figure 11.1 illustrates several ways to implement variable-length records.

One approach to variable-length records that does not require programming system support for the variable-length structure is to use fixed-length trailer records. A **trailer record** is an extension of a master record. It is separate from the master record and written as required. By using an open-item accounts receivable file, for example, the master records contain information common to all accounts and the number of invoices sufficient for most of the accounts, whereas the trailer record contains more invoices. A master record may have as many trailer records associated with it as required. The trailer records may be written immediately after the associated master record.

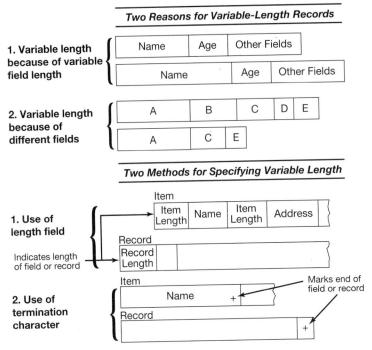

FIGURE 11.1 Variable-Length Records.

Consider a hypothetical manufacturing company, Ace Tools, that maintains a raw materials inventory of hundreds of machine parts. Furthermore, assume that Ace Tools purchases each part from one of several suppliers and then stores it in one of several warehouses. Any part can be purchased from any one or more of the suppliers and then stored in any one or more of the warehouses. The following data fields pertain to the parts inventory:

PART_NO	part number
PNAME	part name
TYPE	type of part
COST	standard cost per unit of the part
PVEND	name of the vendor (supplier) from whom the part is purchased
WARHSE	warehouse where the part is stored
LOC	last two digits of the zip code of the warehouse where the part is stored

Note that it is not possible, in general, to store all information about a particular part in the following fixed-length record:

```
PART(PART_NO, PNAME, TYPE, COST, PVEND, WARHSE, LOC)
```

This is not possible, for example, because there may be more than one supplier for each part, and because the record has room for only one supplier. The two-supplier case would require the following record format (assuming there is only one storage location):

Variable-Length Record		
RECORD NAME	SUPPLIER (Repeated group 1)	LOCATION (Repeated group 2)
PART (PART_NO, PNAME, TYPE, COST,	PVEND # 01, PVEND # 02, PVEND # 03, PVEND # 04, ••• PVEND # 99,	WARHSE # 01, LOC # 01, WARHSE # 02, LOC # 02, WARHSE # 03, LOC # 03, WARHSE # 03, LOC # 03, ••• WARHSE # 99, LOC # 99)

FIGURE 11.2 Repeated Groups as Part of Variable-Length Records.

```
PART(PART_NO, PNAME, TYPE, COST, PVEND#1, WARHSE#1, LOC#1, PVEND#2,
WARHSE#2, LOC#2)
```

where suffix #1 applies to the part supplied by vendor number 1, and suffix #2 to the part supplied by vendor number 2. The record would need to be even longer if there were three suppliers, and in general its length would depend on the number of vendors and storage locations associated with a given part. Such a record would therefore be a variable-length record.

Note that the variable record length arises because both the supplier (PVEND) and the storage locations (WARHSE and LOC) can occur more than once per record. That is, they are repeating (or repeated) groups of fields. (WARHSE and LOC are grouped together because they both relate to the storage location.) **Repeated groups** are related groups of fields that repeat themselves in variable-length records. This is shown in Figure 11.2. The first block shows the SUPPLIER group, and the second block shows the LOCATION group. Both of these repeating groups belong to PART. This relationship is depicted in Figure 11.3 in a diagram that looks like a family tree. PART is shown to be the **parent** of SUPPLIER and LOCATION because each instance of PART may give rise to more than one supplier or location. In general, the highest-level element in a tree diagram is the parent; lower-level elements in the tree diagram that are connected to (i.e., part of) the parent are called **children.**

PART itself might have a "parent." For example, PART might be one of many children belonging to INVENTORY, with the other children being things like SUPPLIES and EQUIPMENT. For this reason, we shall refer to all the nodes in the tree, including PART, as repeated groups. In some cases, we shall simply refer to them as **segments** or groups, or even **nodes.** Thus, the terms *segment, group,* and *node* are shorthand for repeated groups. As we shall see in a subsequent sec-

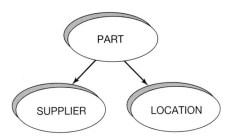

FIGURE 11.3 Tree Diagram for PART, SUPPLIER, and LOCATION.

tion of this chapter, segments are one of the fundamental building blocks used to construct databases.

Segments can be summarized in the same shorthand that is used for records. For example, PART, SUPPLIER, and LOCATION can be written as follows:

```
PART(PART_NO, PNAME, TYPE, COST)
SUPPLIER(PVEND)
LOCATION(WARHSE, LOC)
```

Thus, a record and a segment are in essence the same thing. Both are a collection of fields. In fact, there is nothing wrong with thinking of segments as records as long as it is remembered that segments, unlike simple records, have parents and children.

Record Key and File Sequence

A **key** or **record key** is a data item or combination of data items that uniquely identifies a particular record in a file. Consider a file containing records of the following format:

```
PART(PART_NO, WARHSE),
```

where PART_NO is the part number of the part, and WARHSE is the warehouse number associated with its location. Furthermore, assume that the file contains the following four records.

```
PART(101,1)
PART(102,2)
PART(103,1)
PART(106,1)
```

In this example, PART_NO is an acceptable key because it can be used to uniquely identify any one of the four records. This is not true, however, for WARHSE. For example, specifying a value of 1 for WARHSE does not uniquely identify one particular record; rather, it identifies three records, the first, third, and fourth ones.

In some cases, it might be necessary to combine two fields to produce a key. Assume, for example, that one part can be stored in two warehouses. This would produce records such as

```
PART(101,2)
PART(101,1)
PART(102,1)
PART(103,1)
PART(103,2)
```

In this case, neither PART_NO nor WARHSE would in general uniquely identify an individual record. But both fields together would. Thus, combining the two fields into a single key would permit unique identification. For example, appending the value of WARHSE onto the value of PART_NO would work, giving key values of 1012, 1011, 1021, 1031, and 1032 for each of the five records, respectively.

It is sometimes useful to sort the records in a file so that they are in either ascending or descending order relative to the key. The four records in the first example are in ascending order by PART_NO. The five records in the second example could be ordered by the PART_NO+WARHSE key to produce the following:

```
PART(101,1)
PART(101,2)
PART(102,1)
PART(103,1)
PART(103,2)
```

In such cases, the first field (`PART_NO`) is called the **primary sort key** (or simply the **primary key**), and the second field (`WARHSE`) is called **secondary sort key** (or simply **secondary key**). Any additional fields required to uniquely identify and sort the records would be called **tertiary sort keys.** Therefore, a primary key is a field used to sort the records in a file, and a secondary key is used to determine relative position among a set of records when the primary key has the same value in each record of the set. In terms of the previous example with five records, this means that when two records have the same value for `PART_NO`, the record with the smallest value for `WARHSE` will come first. In other words, the secondary key determines the order for records whose primary key values are all the same.

We shall denote key fields by underlining them. For example, `QUANTITY` is a key field in the following record:

```
PART(PART_NO, WARHSE, QUANTITY)
```

The term **relative random order** applies to a field on which the file is not sorted. Before sorting the previous five records, the file is in random order relative to the `WARHSE` field. In the first record, `WARHSE=2`; in the second record, `WARHSE=1`; and in the fifth record, `WARHSE=2`. Therefore, the file is not ordered by `WARHSE`.

Keys are important because they are necessary to process and locate records in files. These topics are discussed in what follows.

THE EVOLUTION OF DATABASE TECHNOLOGY

Database technology has developed in tandem with computer hardware and software. During the 1960s, the ascendancy of mainframe systems brought to corporate America vast amounts of mass storage and a proliferation of data files. Since that time, the cost per gigabyte or mass storage has continued to drop exponentially, and this trend has been accompanied by larger and larger increases in the amount of data stored on computers.

Networking and communication technology changed the economies of scale for building databases. A good example of this is Prodigy Service, a joint venture of Sears and IBM, which has over a million subscribers throughout the United States. Using a standard telephone line and a personal computer, any subscriber to the service can access the Prodigy computer and its many databases for a low monthly fee. Prodigy Service communication technology has resulted in the costs of databases being spread over a large number of subscribers, as well as advertisers. This has resulted in more total dollars available to invest into databases. The same principle applies to corporate databases that are remotely accessible by employees.

Improvements in technology for inputting data into computers have contributed to the general proliferation of databases. Scanning equipment is one of the most prominent of these improvements. Almost any kind of information, including text, voice, and photographs, can be scanned, digitized, and stored on the computer.

Period	Event	Related Database Technique
1960s	Mainframe environments	File systems
	Database management systems	Database management
	On-line information services	Text management
1970s	Expert systems	Inference and deduction
	Object-oriented programming	Inheritance and abstraction
1980s	Hypertext systems	Association
1990s	Intelligent database systems	Combination of techniques

FIGURE 11.4 Evolution of Database Technology.

Figure 11.4 depicts some of the major developments in database technology. Each phase of development is briefly discussed.

Mainframe Environments

Initially, the main problem was dealing with large numbers of files. The computer was viewed as a simple extension of the file cabinet, and the biggest problem was cataloging and accessing files.

Database Management Systems

Eventually, companies ran into problems with simple file systems. The main difficulties included finding the right file for the information desired, uneconomical duplication of the same data in different files, and a lack of standardization across files. For example, two departments would store the same information on the same computer in two different formats. This was not only uneconomical, but also made it difficult for a third department trying to access the data of the first two departments. These problems resulted in the development of **database management systems (DBMSs)** that standardized the storage, manipulation, and retrieval of data. Under DBMS, data are stored in a standard format using a data definition language (DDL), manipulated and updated using a database manipulation language (DML), and retrieved using a database query language (DQL). In today's business world, DBMSs represent the dominant model for managing information.

-minimize data redundancy
-accessed by one or more programs
-enables users to create, modify & utilize database information efficiently.

On-Line Information Services

One of the largest on-line database services is Dialog, which now contains hundreds of databases and hundreds of million of records. Its databases contain information on almost every conceivable topic, and include the full text and abstracts of many major newspapers, magazines, trade journals, and economic reports, as well as massive amounts of financial, technical, and marketing data pertaining to thousands of corporations throughout the world. Still, Dialog contains only a small portion of the information available through on-line services worldwide.

Many companies collect information from on-line services that has to be systematically incorporated into their information systems. This has given rise to a new need, **text management,** which, along with graphic and voice data, requires technology beyond that provided by traditional database systems. Such **multimedia systems** are becoming increasingly important.

Expert Systems

Expert systems mimic high-level decision making and have been successful in areas such as approving loans, deciding where to dig for minerals, and diagnostic medicine. The typical components of such systems include a database of decision rules; hence, even the logic of decision making has become a database problem.

Object-Oriented Programming

Object-oriented programming involves defining objects from lists or complex sets of information. Almost anything can be an object, such as a list of inventory parts, a group of customers, or even a collection of photographs. Moreover, objects can be related to in special ways called inheritance, making it easier to manipulate them. Recently, some database systems have been developed or extended to have object-oriented features. In such systems, users can define and manipulate objects from the data without having to write computer programs.

Hypertext Systems

Hypertext systems allow users to browse through databases in a somewhat random fashion by selecting key words. A good example is the *Grolier Encyclopedia* on CD-ROM. Assume that on your computer screen you are reading an article in an encyclopedia on internal control. In the middle of the article you see the word *lapping,* and you decide you want to find out more about it. To do this, you simply place the cursor over *lapping* and press the enter key. A window automatically opens and an article on lapping pops up. Next, while you are reading about lapping, you see another unfamiliar word, say, *AICPA*. So you put the cursor on *AICPA,* press enter, and up comes an article on the American Institute of Certified Public Accountants. This process of chaining to new articles can go on indefinitely.

The initial applications of hypermedia in business have related mostly to reference-type materials such as policy and training manuals. But as time passes, it is likely that more and more applications will become involved.

Intelligent Database Systems

Intelligent database systems reflect a trend toward combining all the foregoing technologies, as well as emerging ones, into a single database system. In the future, most geographically separated database systems will have the ability to communicate with others and exchange information. Their enhanced data-acquisition capabilities will be combined with higher levels of artificial intelligence oriented toward structuring and solving the user's problems. The user will simply pose a problem to the system, and the system will decide what data to acquire, where to acquire them from, and how to apply them to solving the user's problem.

DATABASE MANAGEMENT SYSTEMS AND THEIR ARCHITECTURE

As depicted in Figure 11.5, there are three levels of architecture relevant to databases and database management systems: the **conceptual level of architecture,** the **logical level of architecture,** and the **physical level of architecture.** At the conceptual level, databases are collections of various elements of information to be used for assorted purposes. Consider, for example, a sales-order database. Such a database might be defined at the conceptual level in terms of the kinds of information it includes (e.g., sales transactions, cash receipts, and customer information) and the purposes for which it is to be used (e.g., order entry and customer billing).

In order to implement a database defined at the conceptual level, specific data fields and records must be defined. It is also necessary to specify ways in which data records and fields will be viewed or reported, as well as related to each other. For example, it might be desirable to display the customer's account history with his or her open orders. This requires that the records and fields in the database be structured and organized in some logical manner, thus giving rise to **logical data structures.** There are three basic types of logical data structures that can be used to accomplish this objective: **hierarchical, network,** and **relational.** Each of these data structures is discussed in what follows.

The physical level of database architecture deals with specific implementation techniques and issues relating to methods for accessing data. The three most important data-access methods (sequential, indexed sequential, and direct) are discussed in detail.

Conceptual Architecture

There is no one standard approach for developing a conceptual data model of a particular system. The **entity-relationship (E-R)** data model is one popular approach. The E-R model simple depicts the relationships between segments. In the E-R model, however, the term *entity* is used instead of segment, and the term *attribute* is used to refer to individual fields or data items. Graphically, the E-R model uses square boxes for entities, ellipses for attributes, and diamond-shaped boxes for depicting relationships. Figure 11.6 shows an E-R diagram for the segments relating to the example record PART described previously. Note that two

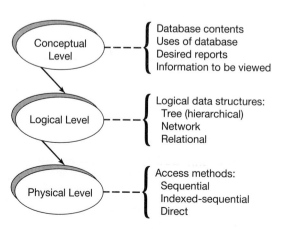

FIGURE 11.5 Database Architecture.

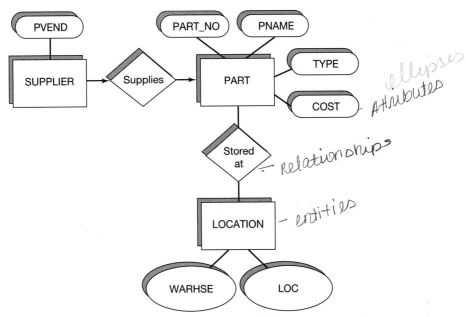

ellipses → Attributes

← Relationships

← entities

FIGURE 11.6 Entity-Relationship Diagram for PART, SUPPLIER, and LOCATION.

relationships are used, one indicating the relationship between the supplier and the part, and the other between the part and its storage location.

Other conceptual methods exist, including the **object-oriented modeling technique (OMT),** originally developed for object-oriented programming and adapted for data modeling by Blaha, Premerlani, and Rumbaugh. This works by viewing the components of the system being modeled as object classes. In this method, an **object class** corresponds to a segment, and an **object** corresponds to a particular instance. Like, the E-R model, OMT defines relationships between segments. The most fundamental of these relationships is called **inheritance.** An inheritance relationship is created when an object class is divided into subclasses. For example, a general or parent class might be plant equipment, which might have subclasses such as hand tools, heavy machinery, repair equipment, and so on. The important thing is that the attributes of the general plant-equipment class are all inherited by each subclass. To further elaborate, we will define an object class as follows:

Stores Objects

Superclass
↓
Classes
↓
Sub-classes

- Programmed instructions are reusable
- Libraries of commonly used objects can be maintained
- Reduce Reprogramming efforts

```
PLANT_EQUIPMENT(ACCOUNT_NO, COST, DEPRECIATION)
```

We also define the following two subclasses:

```
HEAVY_EQUIPMENT(ACCOUNT_NO, COST, DEPRECIATION, MAINTENANCE_FREQ,
DATE_PURCHASED)
```

and

```
HAND_TOOLS(ACCOUNT_NO, COST, DEPRECIATION, USAGE)
```

Note that HAND_TOOLS and HEAVY_EQUIPMENT inherit all the attributes of PLANT_EQUIPMENT (i.e., ACCOUNT_NO, COST, and DEPRECIATION). The two subclasses, however, have their own unique attributes (i.e., USAGE for HAND_TOOLS and MAINTENANCE_FREQ, DATE_PURCHASED for HEAVY_EQUIPMENT).

Characteristics of Objects
Attributes Make Model
Object CAR
Operations Drive Park

Encapsulation:
Stores procedures/
operations called methods

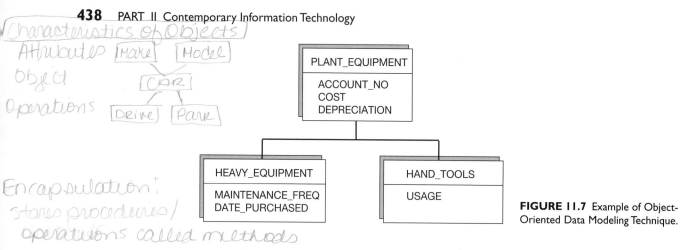

PLANT_EQUIPMENT

ACCOUNT_NO
COST
DEPRECIATION

HEAVY_EQUIPMENT

MAINTENANCE_FREQ
DATE_PURCHASED

HAND_TOOLS

USAGE

FIGURE 11.7 Example of Object-Oriented Data Modeling Technique.

In general, subclasses have all the attributes of their parent class, plus their own attributes. For our example, these relationships are depicted in Figure 11.7.

The subclasses might be further divided. For example, HEAVY_EQUIPMENT might be divided into grinding and cutting equipment, with both of these subclasses having their own unique attributes.

In summary, there are various ways to conceptually model a system. All methods seek to gain a better understanding of the system and document what is learned. Ideally, one would like to derive a logical model from the conceptual model, and then a physical model from the logical model. Conceptual modeling techniques, however, all share two common weaknesses. First, there are many ways to model an enterprise, so evaluating the results of a particular technique may be difficult. Second, there is a risk that the application of a particular technique might result in an incomplete picture of the system being modeled. The E-R model, however, can also lead directly to an implementable database. In fact, commercial software is available that takes the analyst's E-R model and automatically generates a working database system.

The OMT is perhaps the most promising modeling technique. It can be used with additional relationships besides inheritance (such as aggregation and association). Furthermore, it can be implemented in successive levels of detail, leading directly to an implementable database.

Database Architecture at the Logical Level: Logical Data Structures

The major task an analyst faces in designing a database is to identify and design systematic relationships between its segments. The database must be structured so that it is able to provide users with the information they need to make effective decisions. The relationships that exist between the segments in the database are determined by the **logical data structure,** also called the **schema** or **database model.**

Three major models of logical data structures appear in the literature: (1) tree or hierarchical models, (2) network models, and (3) relational models. Some authorities define as many as eight additional models, but the ones discussed in what follows are of special importance to practice.

3 types of structures.

Tree or Hierarchical Structures

Tree structures are a direct representation of the segmenting process described before. In a **tree structure,** each node represents a set of fields (i.e., a segment), and a node is related to another node at the next highest level of the tree.

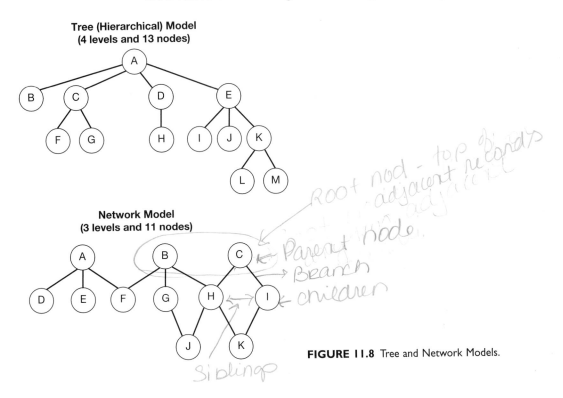

FIGURE 11.8 Tree and Network Models.

The latter is called the **parent** node. Every parent may have one or more **children,** and the connection between the children and parents is called a **branch.** The significant feature of the tree model is that a child node cannot have more than one parent. The tree model corresponds to the data structures supported by COBOL and other widely used programming languages and has been implemented in many commercial DBMSs such as IMS and IDMS. Figure 11.3 is a simple example of a tree structure, and Figure 11.8 depicts both tree and network structures in general.

Network Structures

A **network structure** is one that allows a child segment to have more than one parent. A network, therefore, is a more general data structure than a tree. As Figure 11.9 shows, any network structure can be transformed to one or more tree structures by introducing a redundancy of nodes. Some DBMSs do not directly support network structures, but because any network may be transformed to a tree structure, it is possible to implement network structures in tree-oriented systems. The CODASYL model is a network model.

Both trees and networks are implemented with imbedded **pointer fields,** which cross-link segments, as discussed more thoroughly in what follows. This creates a subtle intermingling of the logical structure of the data with the physical structure of pointers and chaining mechanisms needed to logically connect the segments together. Logical tree and network structure may become unduly complex as the logical description of the data tries to represent a complicated set of relationships between segments as a set of lines, physically representing the pointers in the logical diagram. Critics of tree and network approaches to database design have held that these models cause the analyst to be prematurely physical in database design.

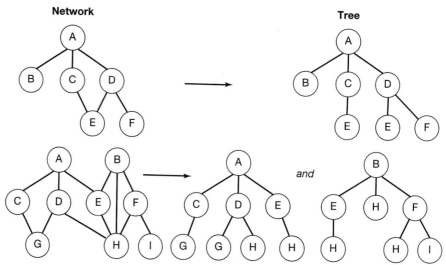

FIGURE 11.9 Transformation of Networks into Trees.

Implementing Tree and Network Structures. The topic of implementing tree and network structures is more a part of the physical architecture of databases than it is of the logical architecture. Still, we discuss physical implementation here because, as discussed immediately before, it is intertwined with the logical structures of the tree and network models.

There are various ways to implement tree and network structures. These include using lists and pointers. In a **list organization,** each record contains one or more pointers (fields) indicating the address of the next logical record with the same attribute(s). An invoice record may contain a field that contain (points to) the key of another invoice from the same vendor. A record may be part of several lists. This list is called **multilist organization.** A customer record, for example, may contain pointers for geographic location and customer type (industrial, etc.). By including a pointer in a record to point to the next logical record, the logical and physical structure can be completely different. Figure 11.10 illustrates a simple **list structure** and a **ring structure.** A ring structure differs from a list in that the last record in the ring list points back to the first record. In addition, all records in a ring may point backward as well as forward through the use and maintenance of additional pointer fields. In a **multiple-ring structure,** several rings pass through individual records.

Designing and maintaining such structures is complicated, and pointers require additional disk space. Furthermore, updating pointers is necessary every time a record is added or deleted. Nevertheless, using pointers in conjunction with hierarchical and tree structures is often a useful approach to data modeling, especially in cases when records are seldom added or deleted.

Two growing areas of application for pointer-based systems are **hypertext** and **semantic data networks.** Both of these data models work similarly to the *Grolier Encyclopedia* example discussed previously. The only difference between the two models is that in semantic networks, the cross-linking of records is limited to text, whereas in hypertext models, the cross-linking can include multimedia objects such as photographs and other graphic forms.

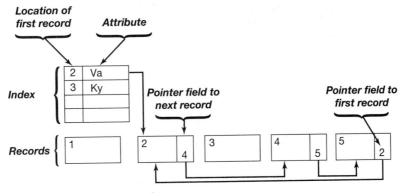

FIGURE 11.10 List and Ring Structures.

Relational Data Structures

The **relational model** views the database as a collection of two-dimensional tables rather than a hierarchical- or network-type structure. Recall the variable-length PART record used in the previous discussion on segments:

```
PART(PART_NO, PNAME, TYPE, COST
                PVEND#1,      WARHSE#1,      LOC#1,
                PVEND#2,      WARHSE#2,      LOC#2
                .             .              .
                .             .              .
                PVEND#n,      WARHSE#n,      LOC#n)
```

This record can be segmented as follows:

```
PART(PART_NO, PNAME, TYPE, COST)
SUPPLIER(PART_NO, PVEND)
LOCATION(PART_NO, WARHSE, LOC)
```

Note that, unlike in the previous example, we now assume that PART_NO, PVEND, and WARHSE are key fields. We have also added PART_NO to the SUPPLIER and LOCATION segments so that it is possible to identify the supplier and the storage location for each product.

① Present data to users as tables only

② Support the relational algebra functions of Restrict [Select], Project & join, without requiring any definitions of access paths to support these operations.

PART						
PART_NO	PNAME	TYPE	COST	(SUPPLIER) PVEND	(LOCATION) WARHSE	LOC
101	wheel	A	1.40	ELFO	1	01
101	wheel	A	1.40	ELFO	2	72
101	wheel	A	1.40	GREEN	1	01
101	wheel	A	1.40	ACE	1	01
101	wheel	A	1.40	ACE	2	72
101	wheel	A	1.40	ACE	3	64
101	wheel	A	1.40	ACE	4	81
102	gear	D	6.60	ELFO	2	72
102	gear	D	6.60	ELFO	3	64
102	gear	D	6.60	ACE	2	72
103	cog	A	1.40	ELFO	2	72
104	wire	A	1.40	ELFO	1	01
105	pin	D	6.60	GREEN	3	64
105	pin	D	6.60	GREEN	4	81

FIGURE 11.11 Partial Listing of Parts Inventory for Ace Tools.

Data (instances) for each of these three segments can be stored in a table, as is shown in Figure 11.11. This is the essence of the relational model—representing segments in tables. The advantage of this logical data structure over trees and networks is immediately obvious. There are no complicated pointers or lists. Furthermore, any information that can be extracted from a tree or network structure can also be extracted from relational tables. For these reasons, (the relational model is the most popular data structure in today's business environment.) However, despite its popularity, it is less efficient than trees and networks when the database is seldom updated and the relationships between nodes can be reasonably defined.

Information (e.g., a financial report) is extracted from tables using **relational algebra,** which can be summarized in three basic operations:

OPERATION	FUNCTION
Selection	Creates a new table from selected rows of existing tables. The rows are selected on the basis of their data values. *only rows*
Join	Creates a new table from the rows of two existing tables. The rows are selected on the basis of their data values.
Projection	Creates a new table by deleting columns from an existing table.

Other operations also exist, but they are not discussed here, since selection, join, and projection represent the essence of the relational algebra. By using the three basic operations, it is possible to create a new table that contains any single occurrence of a data element or combinations of data elements.

Certain rules called **normal forms** govern the creation of tables. The process of applying these rules is called **normalization.** Tables that satisfy these rules are

Normalization is a method of arranging elements in a way that reduces anomalies

data redundancies
inconsistencies
inefficiencies
data base maintenance : info.
updates,

said to be normalized. Tables that do not satisfy these rules are unnormalized. Normalization is important because without it, updating the entries in the tables can cause problems. We will show this with an example.

Normalization is simply the process of converting the record structure from a tree or network format into the appropriate tables. This is not a difficult process, because it is always possible to collapse a tree diagram into a single table, as is demonstrated for PART in Figure 11.11. This table is completely unnormalized, so it will serve as a good example of why normalization is necessary.

Note that part number 101 (as well as its name and cost) appears in each of the first seven rows. This is unnecessary duplication that not only wastes storage space, but makes it possible for the same part to have two different names in different rows. Thus, a primary purpose of normalization is to eliminate unnecessary duplication.

The first step in normalization is to create a separate table for each repeating group. This is accomplished in Figure 11.12. Tables without repeating groups are said to be in **first normal form.** In the first normal form, no repeated groups (variable-length records) are allowed. There are also second and third normal forms, which can be obtained by eliminating redundancies from the tables in first normal form. The first of these additional redundancies can be seen in the LOCATION table. Note that LOC is always 01 when WARHSE is 1, 72 when WARHSE is 2, 64 when WARHSE is 3, and 81 when WARHSE is 4. It is therefore true that the value of WARHSE strictly determines the value of LOC. The value of LOC is therefore re-

KEY — *non-key fields*

Step #1 ⟹ first normal form

PART			
PART_NO	PNAME	TYPE	COST
101	wheel	A	1.40
102	gear	D	6.60
103	cog	A	1.40
104	wire	A	1.40
105	pin	D	6.60

key field — *non-key field*

SUPPLIER	
PROD_NO	PVEND
101	ELFO
101	GREEN
101	ACE
102	ELFO
102	ACE
103	ELFO
104	ELFO
105	GREEN

LOCATION		
PROD_NO	WARHSE	LOC
101	1	01
101	2	72
101	3	64
101	4	81
102	2	72
102	3	64
103	2	72
104	1	01
105	3	64
105	4	81

FIGURE 11.12 PART, SUPPLIER, and LOCATION Depicted as Relational Tables.

dundant. Again, as was the case with the first normal form, the redundancy not only wastes space, but makes it possible for the same warehouse (WARHSE) to have two different zip codes in two different rows. This problem occurs because the value of a key field (WARHSE) strictly determines the value of a nonkey field (LOC). In the **second normal form,** no key is allowed to determine the values of a nonkey field. The LOCATION table can be put in second normal form by dividing it into two tables, putting LOC in its own table away from PROD_NO:

```
LOCATION (PROD_NO, WARHSE)
WAREHOUSE (WARHSE, LOC)
```

In the **third normal form,** no nonkey field can determine the values on another nonkey field. This form is violated in the PART table. Both TYPE and COST are nonkey fields, and TYPE strictly determines COST. Again, this problem can be solved by splitting the table:

```
PART(PROD_NO, PNAME, TYPE)
COSTS(TYPE, COST)
```

In summary, the three normal forms are as follows:

NORMAL FORM	RULE
First normal form	Divide tables to eliminate repeated groups
Second normal form	Divide tables so that no key determines the values of a nonkey field
Third normal form	Divide tables so that no nonkey field determines the values of another nonkey field

Finally, we note that in the terminology of relational databases, the term **relation** is synonymous with **table,** and **tuple** refers to a row in a table.

Database Architecture at the Physical Level

In discussing the physical level of database architecture, we will focus on the three file-access methods: sequential, indexed, and direct. DASDs are capable of supporting all these methods, and the choice of the best one will depend on the particular application.

Sequentially Accessed Files

In a **sequential-access file,** records can only be accessed in their predefined sequence. For example, if there are 100 records in a file, one must access the first 99 records before accessing the last record. The predefined sequence is normally a result of the records having been sorted on some record key. For example, instances of the record PART(PART_NO, PNAME) would be sorted by PART_NO, and the record for part number 101 would appear in the file before the record for part number 102. In general, however, the sorting can be in either ascending and descending order.

Sequential file organization is not a useful means of storing data when only a small number of records needs to be accessed in a file containing a large number of records. For example, accessing the last record in a file containing a million records would require 999,999 records to be accessed before reaching the desired record. This would produce an intolerable delay (perhaps several minutes) on a disk storage unit.

Sequential files are useful in batch processing, which normally accesses all the records in the file. The usual procedure is to first sort both the transaction and master files on the same key. A typical application might be updating customers' accounts receivable (in the master file) to reflect payments received (in the transaction file). First, the program sorts both files in ascending order by account number. Next, the program reads one record from each file. If the account numbers on these two records match each other, then the information on the payment record is used to update the balance field on the accounts receivable record. The updated account record is then written to a new master file. This procedure continues according to the logic in Figure 11.13 until all records in both files are processed.

A careful study of Figure 11.13 will reveal that this sequential updating procedure will not work unless the files are sorted. For example, if the record in the transaction file with the highest key value is placed at the beginning of this file (instead of at the end where it belongs if the file is sorted in ascending order), then the program will find and update the matching record at the end of the master file, and then immediately terminate processing. In other words, the program will process only one transaction and quit. This happens because the program makes only one pass through each file and must go all the way to the end of the master file to find the record matching the first record in the transaction file. After that, there are no records left in the master file to process.

In conclusion, sequential file organization is useful when batch processing is required. Batch processing normally involves sorting and processing all the records in both the transaction and master files. In cases where only a small pro-

FIGURE 11.13 Sequential File Processing Logic.

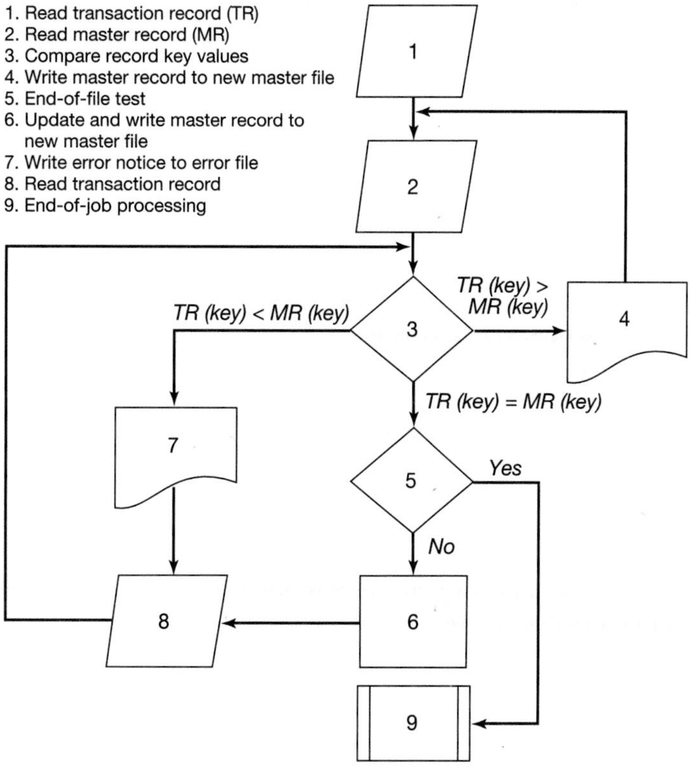

1. Read transaction record (TR)
2. Read master record (MR)
3. Compare record key values
4. Write master record to new master file
5. End-of-file test
6. Update and write master record to new master file
7. Write error notice to error file
8. Read transaction record
9. End-of-job processing

portion of the records need to be accessed, one of the other file-access methods discussed in what follows is more efficient.

Indexed Files

Any attribute can be extracted from the records in a primary file and used to build a new file whose purpose is to provide an index to the original file. Such a file is called an **indexed** or **inverted** file. For example, assume a customer invoice file exists with the following record format:

```
CUSTOMER(ACCOUNT_NO, INVOICE_NO)
```

and the following instances followed by their disk addresses.

RECORD	RECORD'S ADDRESS ON THE DISK (CYLINDER #-SURFACE #-RECORD #)
CUSTOMER(141, 901)	1-2-1
CUSTOMER(164, 902)	9-5-2
CUSTOMER(175, 903)	6-1-6
CUSTOMER(141, 904)	7-4-4
CUSTOMER(182, 905)	2-3-7
CUSTOMER(164, 906)	2-2-8

An index for ACCOUNT_NO is given in Figure 11.14. In this example, the account number 164 is typed into the computer, located in the index along with two related disk addresses, 9-5-2 pointing to invoice number 902, and 2-2-8 pointing to invoice number 906.

This example shows that using the index to locate records on the disk is a two-step process. In the first step, the index is searched for the specified value of an attribute, and the desired disk addresses are retrieved. In the second step, the disk addresses are used to directly retrieve the desired records. This process can be considerably faster than sequentially searching every record in the file, especially when the entire index can be loaded into primary memory before it is searched, for searching in primary memory is fast, relative to searching on a disk. Still, if the index is very long and will not fit into primary memory, it may take an undue length of time to complete the search. This problem can be solved by factoring a long index into subindexes, but even this technique is impractical if the file is large enough.

Of course, it is possible to have more than one index for a given file. A file is said to be **fully inverted** when indexes exist for all its fields. The processing time required to maintain a fully inverted file can be high, because the indexes must be updated whenever records are added, deleted, or modified. Furthermore, each index requires additional disk storage, and the indexes can end up requiring more storage space than the data file itself.

Indexed-Sequential Files. One important type of indexed file is an indexed-sequential file. An **indexed-sequential file** is a sequential file that is stored on a DASD and is both indexed and physically sorted on the same field. Such files are commonly referred to as **ISAM** files, with ISAM being a contraction of the indexed-sequential access method. ISAM is a powerful compromise between sequential and direct-access (discussed below) file organizations, providing the capabilities of both at a reasonable increase in cost.

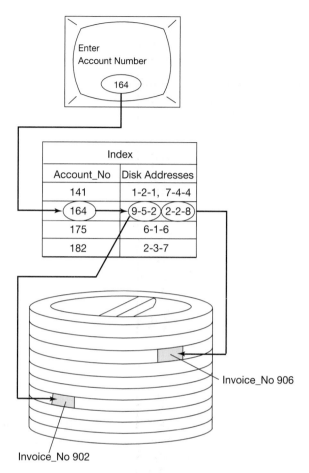

FIGURE 11.14 Example of Using a File Index.

The twin objectives of file usage—processing and inquiry—are both addressed by ISAM organization. The processing of a batch of records may be done sequentially, whereas individual inquiries to the file may be handled using the index. The more detailed the index, the quicker the access; the trade-off occurs in maintaining the index. Consider first, a main file in sequence and an index (list of keys and record locations) to that file. If every record key is represented in the index (not normally necessary), then each time a main file record is added or deleted, the index must be changed. If, as is more likely, only every *n*th record, or the first or last record in a major memory subdivision, is represented in the index, then the index need not be changed so often, but it is always necessary to check to see whether this is the case. Most database programs automatically update the indexes as changes are made to the data file.

Structure of an ISAM File. An ISAM file structurally consists of three distinct areas: the index, the prime area, and the overflow area. The index is a map that relates the key fields of records to their corresponding addresses in the prime area. Each entry in the index gives the range of key fields on a particular track of the disk on which the file is stored. By searching the index, a program can locate the track containing the desired record. Although the track must then be searched sequentially, this search is very rapid.

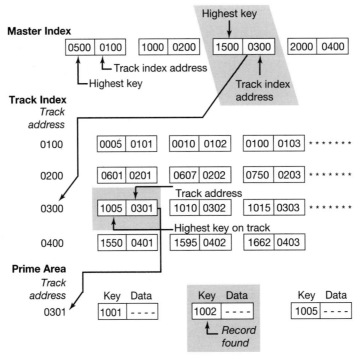

FIGURE 11.15 Structure of an ISAM File.

Figure 11.15 illustrates the process by which a computer would locate a file record whose key is 1002. The computer reads the first record in the master index, which refers to records with key values between 0001 and 0500. Because 1002 is greater than 0500, the computer looks at the next index record; but this refers to file records with key numbers between 0501 and 1000. Then the machine checks the next master index record, which contains information about file record keys 1001 to 1500, and therefore includes 1002, the record key it is searching. The computer reads in the index that the next level of the index associated with this record is on track 0300. The computer goes to track 0300 and starts to read the records on that track. The first record indicates that it has information pertaining to records 1001 to 1005. Because 1002 is within this range, the computer notes that the record being sought is on track 0301 in the prime area. The computer goes to track 0301, searches sequentially until it finds record 1002, and retrieves the record called for. All this takes place in a fraction of a second.

The **prime area** is the portion of the disk on which the actual records are written. The **overflow area** is a separate section of the disk that is allocated to the file to allow additions to be made without extensive processing of the initial file. The overflow area is originally empty. When a new record is to be added to the file, it must be placed in its correct position in the prime area to maintain the sequential organization of the file. Existing records in the prime area must be bumped to make room for the new record. If space is available on the track where the record must be inserted, the record is inserted in position and the other records on the track are moved. Space may be available for the new record because some empty prime space was originally left in the file to facilitate additions or because prime space was made available by the deletion of one or more records. At times, however, the addition of a new record will bump an existing record off the track being updated. In this case, the bumped record is moved to the overflow area. Although records in the overflow area are not physically in key sequence, they can be accessed in key sequence by using the index. As before, the index is used to identify the track on which the record should be located. If the record is not found on the track referenced in the index, the overflow area is automatically checked sequentially until the record is found. Overflow lengthens the time needed to process an ISAM file; accordingly, an ISAM file should be periodically reorganized to make access more efficient. Reorganization consists of merging all the records so that the file is once again in physical sequential order in the prime area.

The index may be factored into a hierarchical set of master and subindexes—usually a cylinder index and a track index—to facilitate retrieval. This is shown in Figure 11.15. At times, a single-level index will be sufficient. Record key fields are listed sequentially in the index. In an ISAM file, it is not normally possible for the record key field (e.g., account number or vendor number) to serve also as the address. The index links the record key to the address.

Directly Accessed Files

Direct-access files allow individual records to be almost instantly retrieved without the use of an index. This is accomplished by assigning each record to a storage location that bears some relationship to the record's key values. Therefore, with the direct-access method, the only thing needed to locate a record is its key value.

There are several addressing methods used to store and locate records in a direct-access file. One method is to have a record's key field correspond directly to the coding scheme used by the computer itself to identify the physical address on a DASD. A related method is to store physical device addresses as a field within a file's records. Neither of these methods requires any conversion of the key prior to access. Neither of these methods is widely used because storage location addresses are rarely suitable as record identifiers, and security and systems management problems are associated with users knowing actual physical storage locations.

Most direct-access file systems convert a key to a storage location address using either an index (table) or a randomizing transformation. This means that it is possible to almost instantly access any record on the disk given its key value. The key value is converted to a disk address, and the record is directly accessed without any searching. This process is depicted in Figure 11.16.

A **randomizing transformation** is a widely used method of storing and locating records in a direct-access file. Figure 11.17 illustrates the use of a randomizing transformation to load a file on a disk. There are four records in the file; in turn, each record key is used in a mathematical calculation (divide by 7, note the remainder, and add a displacement factor). Once the file is loaded, any record may be directly accessed by passing the key through the randomizing calculation to determine its address; the device then directly accesses this particular record, bypassing all other records in the file.

Figure 11.17 illustrates several important concepts relating to direct-access file organization. The first is the use of a randomizing transformation to store and access individual records. Note that dividing by 7 yields seven possible remainders (0 through 6); dividing by a prime number yields remainders that should tend to be uniformly and randomly distributed (thus, the term **random access** is often used synonymously with **direct access**). In addition, it is very likely that several

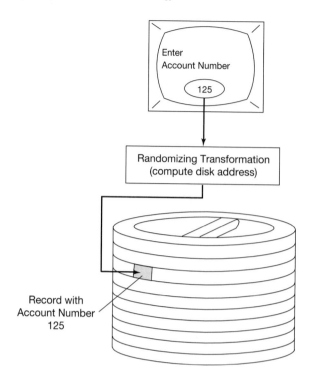

FIGURE 11.16 Example of Using the Direct-Access Method.

different records will randomize **(hash)** to the same physical address. Both of these points are significant. The first point means that the storage space required for the file is largely determined by the range of the transformation results (0 to 7 in the example), even if the file is expected to be smaller than the range of the transformation. The second point is called **overflow,** and means that some method of storing and retrieving overflow must be built into the system. In Figure 11.17, two records are hashed to the same address, requiring that one of them be stored in a different location. Overflow occurs when two or more records (called **synonyms**) yield the same address; in such cases, a special pointer field is used to indicate the addresses of the locations used to store overflow records. Note that overflow considerations require storage space in addition to that required by the randomizing transformation. The overall result is that storage efficiency is typically not high in direct-access files.

The drawbacks of vacant storage and overflow considerations are typically more than offset by the advantages of direct-access file organization. Direct access permits nonsequential updating—there is no need to sort and batch transactions. In fact, in a straight direct-access file update, nothing would be gained by batching and sorting transactions. Another major advantage of direct-access files is the speed of access to individual records. Records are accessed almost instantly. Often such speed is essential—as in an airline reservation system or a stock market quotation system. In addition, direct-access organization permits simultaneous updating of several related files. A sale affects both inventory and receivable files. If the inventory and receivable files are direct access, both may be updated in a single pass of an invoice by noting both inventory number and customer number, using each key to directly access and update the respective records. If both files were sequential, separate passes (and separate sorts) would be needed to accomplish this same task.

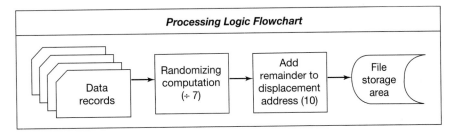

Processing Logic Flowchart

Data records → Randomizing computation (÷ 7) → Add remainder to displacement address (10) → File storage area

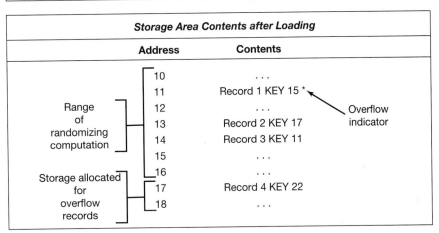

File Loading Illustration

Record	Key	Remainder after division by seven	+	Displacement factor (initial address of file area)	=	Record storage address	
1	15	1		10		11	*
2	17	3		10		13	Overflow
3	11	4		10		14	
4	22	1		10		11	*

Storage Area Contents after Loading

	Address	Contents
	10	. . .
	11	Record 1 KEY 15 *
Range of randomizing computation	12	. . .
	13	Record 2 KEY 17
	14	Record 3 KEY 11
	15	. . .
	16	. . .
Storage allocated for overflow records	17	Record 4 KEY 22
	18	. . .

Overflow indicator

FIGURE 11.17 Use of a Direct-Access File.

There is, however, a major limitation of the direct-access method. A record cannot be located if its key is not known. For example, it would not be possible to conveniently locate all sales transactions for product X with amounts greater than $1,000, because there is no common key to identify such transactions.

Economic Relations Between File Organization Techniques

The file-access techniques just discussed (sequential, indexed, and direct-access) are appropriate in different circumstances. Figure 11.18 summarizes when to use each file organization technique. The basic economics of file processing are largely determined by the **activity ratio** (the number of accessed records divided by the number of records in the file), and the desired response time for processing and inquiries.

Figure 11.19 compares the average cost per transaction processed for these three techniques over a range of activity ratios. Sequential organization is a fixed-cost approach to file processing as contrasted to direct-access organization, which

File Organization Techniques	When Best to Use	Limitations
Sequential	High activity ratio, as in batch processing	Not possible to access quickly a single record
Indexed	Low activity ratio, moderate to large file size	File updates require indexes to be updated
Indexed-Sequential	File needs to be processed both in batch (high activity ratio) and nonbatch (low activity ratio) modes	Same as with indexed and sequential
Direct	Low activity ratio, very large files, networks, and trees	Need keys to locate records

FIGURE 11.18 When to Use Each File Organization Technique.

is a variable-cost approach. In direct access, each record processed costs about the same amount, regardless of the number of records processed. For high activity, this is expensive relative to sequential processing. In sequential processing, the total costs are largely fixed (loading and passing the entire file); as these costs are spread over more and more transactions, the cost per transaction decreases rapidly. ISAM offers a middle ground: for low activity, records may be accessed through the index; for high activity, the index is ignored and the file is processed sequentially. For either low or high activity, ISAM is less attractive than either direct or sequential processing; however, for a file with both low- and high-activity requirements, ISAM offers economic advantages over either of the other two methods.

FIGURE 11.19 Unit Costs and File Activity.

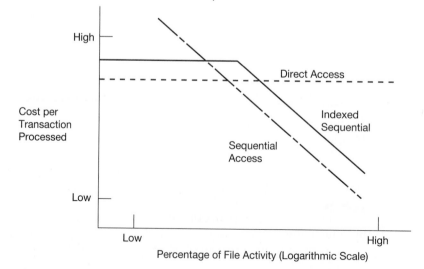

The second economic consideration concerns response time. In relation to databases, **response time** is the length of time the user must wait for the system to complete an operation, such as a query. Direct-access files are necessary for very quick response times; longer response times (hours or more) can be economically handled by sequential files. When long response times can be tolerated, queries or file updates typically can be appended to batch processing runs. For example, a copy of customers' records can be obtained as a by-product of posting invoices to the accounts receivable file. ISAM again offers a middle ground. Short-response-time requests may be processed using the index; longer-response-time requests may be appended to any sequential processing runs against the file. Response times are also affected by hardware considerations, as is discussed in what follows.

Physical Architecture, Hardware, and Response Time

Response time can become a major problem with large databases that might be accessed by hundreds, or even thousands, of users at the same time. If the database system and computer hardware are not suited for the demands placed on them, then users might find themselves waiting a hopelessly long time for responses to their queries. Therefore, the database system must be properly designed for the use it will be put to, and the hardware must be fast enough to get the job done.

On the hardware side, response time is affected by physical access time. This is typically the time required for the CPU to retrieve a single block of data from the disk, called the **disk access time.** One problem is that the CPU operates much faster than the disk does, requiring the CPU to wait while disk input/output operations are being executed. This means that minimizing disk input and output in some cases can result in considerable increases in response time.

Another factor that can affect response time is how data records are physically distributed on the disk. If a group of records is to be accessed in sequence, then the response time will be faster if these records are contiguous (physically next to each other) on the disk. If they are contiguous, the read–write head on the disk drive will need to move only a small distance each time it accesses the next record in the list. If, on the other hand, the records are strewn all over the disk, then the read–write head will have to move a relatively long distance to access each new record, thus slowing things down.

On a hard disk, data on the same track or cylinder can be accessed without moving the read–write head. This means that in some cases, it is possible to considerably speed up a database application by storing the records of a particular data file contiguously on one or more disk cylinders.

If should be emphasized that many database systems rely on operating system routines for their input/output operations. This means that it may be the operating system that determines where data will be placed on the disk. This is important because many operating systems have no provision to assure that data will be stored contiguously. In fact, many operating systems will deliberately break up files and spread them all over a disk, putting their places into small empty spaces so that all areas of the disk are used and no space is wasted.

The need to store a file contiguously depends on the physical architecture of the database and its corresponding file-access method. If the database uses the sequential access method, then physically placing the records next to each other on the disk is desirable. For the indexed-access method, however, it is almost always desirable to place the indexes in contiguous storage, because these files are often read sequentially and in their entirety. But it may not be necessary to place the records in the related data files next to each other on the disk, because records in these files are randomly accessed in the two-stage lookup process described before. Sometimes, however, it might be desirable to batch process all the records in an indexed file (as is often done with ISAM files), and in such cases, contiguous storage for the primary file would be desirable. Finally, for the direct-access method, storing records next to each other would provide no improvement in response time. In fact, contiguous storage might be impossible due to the nature of the hashing approaches described before.

DATABASE MANAGEMENT SYSTEMS AND DATABASES IN PRACTICE

What Database Management Systems Do

Database management systems (DBMSs) are computer programs that enable a user to create and update files, to select and retrieve data, and to generate various outputs and reports.

All DBMSs contain three common attributes for managing and organizing data:

Data Description Language (DDL)

The DDL allows the database administrator (DBA) to define the logical structure of the database, called the **schema.** Defining the schema normally involves defining each of the following:

- the name of the data element
- the type of data (numeric, alphabetic, date, etc.) and the number of decimal positions if the data element is numeric
- the number of positions (e.g., nine positions for social security numbers)

The DDL may also be used to define **subschema,** which are individual user views of the database. For example, the sales order processing department might be able to view and edit the data elements DATE, CUSTOMER_NAME, ACCOUNT_NUMBER, QUANTITY, and PRICE. The production department might have a different view of the same database, seeing instead CUSTOMER_NAME, ACCOUNT_NUMBER, and SCHEDULED_DATE_OF_COMPLETION. Further, the production department might be restricted from editing CUSTOMER_NAME and ACCOUNT_NUMBER. Note that in this example, the application program (i.e., the accounting system) automatically generates the DDL statements required to create the subschemas.

The DDL may also be used to create, modify, and delete tables in a relational setting.

Data Manipulation Language (DML)

The DML consists of the commands for updating, editing, manipulating, and extracting data. In many cases, the user does not need to know or use the DML. Rather, the application program (e.g., the payroll program or interactive accounting system) automatically generates the DML statements to accomplish the user's requests. SQL is a common DML in relational settings.

Name	Account Number	Account Balance
		>1000

FIGURE 11.20 Selecting Accounts >$1,000 Using QBE.

Data Query Language (DQL)

The DQL is a user-friendly language or interface that allows the user to request information from the database. One such friendly interface is QBE (query by example), which allows the user to request information by simply filling in blanks. For example, a user might fill in the blanks in a form such as shown in Figure 11.20 to request all records with account balances greater than $1,000.

There also exist natural language interfaces, which allow users to make requests for information using ordinary, everyday English—for example, "May I please have a sales report for the month of June?" Such systems are capable of recognizing a variety of phrasings for the requests, and if the user makes an unintelligible request, the system will ask the necessary questions to resolve the problem.

Figure 11.21 depicts the processing of a user query as it relates to the schema, the subschema, the DDL, and the DML.

FIGURE 11.21 Logical Model for Processing User Queries.

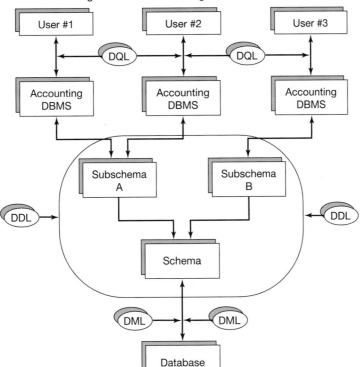

Example of DDL, DML, and DQL Statements Using dBase SQL

The following statements provide a rudimentary illustration of the use of DDL, DML, and DQL statements. This is accomplished by creating a dBase (version 4 or higher) relational database with two tables. The database is called AIS and has a path of f:\db4\ais. dBase has been installed and configured for the use of SQL. Statements beginning with asterisks are comments.

```
* Activate SQL
SET SQL ON;
* DDL—Create the database; call it AIS
CREATE DATABASE F:\DB4\AIS;
   Response from dBase: Database AIS created
* DDL—Activate from database
START DATABASE AIS;
   Response from dBase: Database AIS started
* DDL—Create table with three data elements; call it CUSTOMER
CREATE TABLE CUSTOMER (NAME CHAR(8), ACCT CHAR(6), AMOUNT DECIMAL(8,2));
   Response from dBase: Table CUSTOMER created
* DML—Add one row of data to CUSTOMER INSERT INTO CUSTOMER VALUES
("BODNAR", "222222", 125.25);
   Response from dBase: 1 row(s) inserted
* DML—Add another row of data to CUSTOMER INSERT INTO CUSTOMER VALUES
("HOPWOOD", "111111", 225.25);
   Response from dBase: 1 row(s) inserted
* DQL—Display the CUSTOMER table
SELECT NAME, ACCT, AMOUNT FROM CUSTOMER;
   Response from dBase:
   NAME          ACCT          AMOUNT
   BODNAR        222222        125.25
   HOPWOOD       111111        225.25
* DDL—Create second table called CUSTACCT
CREATE TABLE CUSTACCT (NAME CHAR(8), ACCT CHAR(6), BALANCE DECIMAL
(8,2));
   Response from dBase: Table CUSTACCT created
* DML—Add a row of data to CUSTACCT INSERT INTO CUSTACCT VALUES
("HOPWOOD", "111111", 900.10);
   Response from dBase: 1 row(s) inserted
* DML—Add another row of data to CUSTACCT INSERT INTO CUSTACCT VALUES
("JONES", "666666", 500.17);
   Response from dBase:1 row(s) inserted
* DML—Add another row of data to CUSTACCT INSERT INTO CUSTACCT VALUES
("BODNAR", "222222", 577.27);
   Response from dBase: 1 row(s) inserted
* DQL—Display the CUSTACCT table
SELECT NAME, ACCT, BALANCE FROM CUSTACCT;
   Response from dBase:
   NAME          ACCT          BALANCE
   HOPWOOD       111111        900.10
   JONES         666666        500.17
   BODNAR        222222        577.27
* DML—Update Bodnar's account
UPDATE CUSTACCT SET BALANCE=0 WHERE NAME="BODNAR";
Response from dBase: 1 row(s) updated
* DQL—Display the CUSTACCT table
* Note the new balance in Bodnar's account
SELECT NAME, ACCT, BALANCE FROM CUSTACCT;
   Response from dBase:
   NAME          ACCT          BALANCE
   HOPWOOD       111111        900.10
   JONES         666666        500.17
```

```
BODNAR        222222      0.00
* DQL—Display selected information
SELECT NAME, BALANCE FROM CUSTACCT WHERE NAME= "BODNAR";
 Response from dBase:
 NAME          BALANCE
 BODNAR        0.00
```

The DQL statements (i.e., the `SELECT` commands) in this example provide a very rudimentary way of querying the database. In an actual accounting application, the application program would automatically generate the `SELECT` statements (or their equivalent) to satisfy the user's request. In other words, the accounting system would be written in the dBase language, and would have embedded in it the statements to interact with the user and to generate the needed SQL statements. The best way to explain this is to first note that although dBase has the basic elements of a DBMS, it is not something that a business would use in its raw form. To make dBase more useful, extensive programs have to be written using dBase commands, and these programs in conjunction with dBase work together to form the working DBMS.

✓ Nonprogrammable Database Systems

Some database systems do not require any programming statements. With such systems, designers and programmers can create entire database management systems, accounting systems, and other applications by simply pointing and clicking with a mouse, that is, by using visual programming. But, of course, it takes many points and clicks of the mouse to get the job done, and in some cases it can actually take more effort and time to develop an application with a nonprogrammable database than with one that is programmable.

Microsoft Access is a good example of a nonprogrammable database system. Access is a fully relational system for point-and-click programming. Many sophisticated applications developed in Microsoft Access contain external program modules that are written in a high-level language such as Microsoft Visual Basic. Thus, in practice the current approach often is to develop accounting systems with less programming than was once required, but at least some programming is still needed.

Almost all database systems and languages on the market support some degree of visual programming. Some of these systems produce modifiable source code, while others do not. When working with a database system that does produce modifiable program code, it is possible to use the visual programming features to create the basic skeleton of the final application system. The skeleton can then be manually edited and modified to produce a final version of the application.

✓ Why Database Management Systems Are Needed

DBMSs **integrate, standardize,** and **provide security** for various accounting applications. In the absence of integration, each type of accounting application such as sales, payroll, and receivables will maintain separate, independent data files and computer programs for managing these files. Although maintaining independent files is simple, it has several disadvantages. First, the same data item may be used in several different application areas; with independent files, this data item has to be fed into each application file. A sale, for example, affects the inventory file, accounts receivable file, and various revenue and expense files. Inputting the same data element numerous times (once for each application it is used in) is time-consuming and potentially expensive; furthermore, there is a greater chance for errors and inconsistencies among the various representations of a piece of data in several independent files.

Second, because files must be rigidly defined early in the system implementation process, procedures may be constrained by the existing file structure rather than the evolving needs of applications. Finally, independence among files often leads to different structures for the same data, different coding systems, different abbreviations, and different field lengths, to name a few examples. Comparison and reconciliation of supposedly identical data may be difficult under these conditions. The result of inconsistent data is that inconsistent reports are produced from the various application programs. Such problems call into question the integrity of an information system.

In addition to the data management and storage problems just discussed, independent files each require their own processing and maintenance instructions, as neither the content nor the structure of the files is standardized. Inquiry capability concerning nonkey information is restricted because each individual application program must specify detailed instructions concerning the physical handling of data.

Data Independence

The solution to the problems with maintaining independent files lies in the separation of the physical handling of data from their logical use. This requires two fundamental changes: First, data storage is integrated into a single database, and, second, all access to the integrated set of files (database) is through a single software system designed to manage the physical aspects of data handling and storage. These are the essential characteristics of the database approach to data processing.

In a sense the word **file** loses meaning in a database environment. A single master file may be logically subdivided into numerous subsystem files and these files combined and recombined into numerous other files. Database software separates the physical and logical aspects of file use, and in doing so opens up a broad spectrum of information processing capabilities simply not feasible without such software.

Figure 11.22 illustrates these concepts with two independent application files, each containing four fields per record. Note that two data items, X and Y, are common to both files. Below these files is a database—a single file that contains all the nonredundant information previously found in the two physically independent files. This database file is structured and managed by a DBMS system. Upon requests from user programs, the DBMS structures logical application files (subschema) through a database dictionary file. A **database dictionary** is a collection of all data item names in a database, along with a description of the standardized data representation form of these data items (e.g., their size, type of data—numeric, alphabetical, etc.). The database dictionary is defined and controlled by the database administrator.

Logical files 1 and 2 (Figure 11.22) are temporary files constructed by the DBMS for use by applications one and two. At the completion of processing, the updated values in the logical files may be copied to the actual physical database. Logical file 3 is a new file created for a specific nonroutine use, such as a query (inquiry) or a special accounting data analysis. The ability to construct such special files quickly and efficiently is a major advantage of DBMSs. This ability is provided through the DBMS maintenance of inverted files, lists, rings, or other data structures designed to facilitate information retrieval by users.

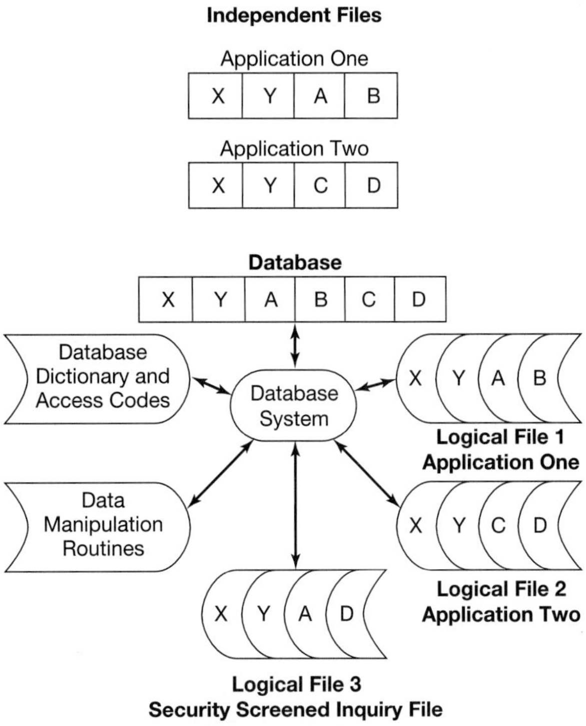

Independent Files

Application One

X	Y	A	B

Application Two

X	Y	C	D

Database

X	Y	A	B	C	D

Database Dictionary and Access Codes

Database System

X Y A B
**Logical File 1
Application One**

Data Manipulation Routines

X Y C D
**Logical File 2
Application Two**

X Y A D
**Logical File 3
Security Screened Inquiry File**

FIGURE 11.22 Database Management Concepts.

Security

Another advantage of DBMSs is their general ability to assign security codes to data items and their processing attributes. Part of the data dictionary file contains a list of authorized system users and their assigned security and access codes. Each of the six unique data elements in Figure 11.22 could be assigned a numerical priority code. These codes would specify which data items may be retrieved by each user of the DBMS; furthermore, such codes may also be used to restrict and define the processing a user may do to any data item.

Application one in Figure 11.22 could have authority to request only items X, Y, A, and B, and authority to modify/update only fields A and B. Application two could request X, Y, C, and D, and modify only C and D. Similarly, application 3 may have authority to access but not to modify any data items, and so on through a hierarchy of security or privacy coding applied to data items in the database.

Database Documentation and Administration

Database dictionaries are used both alone and with DBMSs to centralize, document, control, and coordinate the use of data within an organization. The data dictionary is simply another file, a sort of file of files, whose record occurrences consist of data item descriptions. Figure 11.23 illustrates some likely data items for a data dictionary occurrence of a field. Most of the items shown in the figure are self-explanatory or have been previously discussed. An **alias** arises when different users call the same field different names. For example, the warehouse may call "requisition number" the data item that purchasing calls "order number." Aliases also arise because the same data item is called different things in different programs written in different languages or by different programmers. Encoding

Items in a Data Dictionary Occurrence

Specifications
- Name
- Definition
- Aliases

Characteristics
- Size
- Range of values
- Encoding
- Editing data

Utilization
- Owner
- Where used
- Security code
- Last update

FIGURE 11.23 Data Dictionary Format.

refers to the physical form in which the data item will be stored, for example, BCD or EBCDIC. Owner refers to the user who has final responsibility or primary interest in the integrity of a data item occurrence.

The primary objectives of a data dictionary are to eliminate or at least control inconsistencies in usage that result from the processing of aliases and to eliminate data redundancies to the extent feasible. Responsibility for the data dictionary should be centralized in a **database administrator (DBA).** Database administration is responsible for resolving incompatibilities and coordination and communication problems between groups of users sharing a database. A major task of the DBA is to establish standards, conventions, and documentation of the data resource. The administration of the data dictionary is the major means by which the DBA accomplishes this task. Effective control of data is central to the database approach to data processing. Incompatibilities and redundancy abound in a traditional file-oriented system in which users maintain and process their own data files. It might be impossible to centralize all data usage. Users may be unwilling to give up responsibility for their data elements. Many of the problems the DBA faces are political. The DBA has to be a diplomat in coordinating usage among various users and in dealing with those users who might not obtain significant benefits from centralization and standardization of data. Accordingly, the DBA function needs to be sufficiently high in the organization, or at least directly responsible to someone sufficiently high, to be able to effectively deal with problems that cross organizational units.

The data dictionary might be maintained manually, but usually it is computerized and processed like other computer files. If the dictionary is used in conjunction with a DBMS, it can be maintained by the DBMS. In either case, it is the procedures surrounding the use of the dictionary, as well as the dictionary itself, that make the concept an important element of database administration.

SUMMARY

Database technology has developed in tandem with computer hardware and software. Three trends in particular have fueled the database revolution: an exponential growth in mass storage, the availability of better communications, and improvements in the technology for converting data into machine-readable format. Together these trends have contributed to a proliferation of data and a corresponding need for intelligent databases built of a combination of technologies, including hypertext, object-oriented database, expert systems, and database management systems.

Database management systems (DBMSs) still represent the mainstay of current technology, and their architecture exists at three levels: the conceptual level, the logical level, and the physical level. The conceptual architecture involves defining in general terms the contents of the database and the required uses of the data. The logical architecture involves defining the logical data structure, which can follow either a hierarchical, network, or relational model. The physical architecture involves defining the file-access methods, which may be either sequential, indexed, or direct. In practice, the overall architecture will be structured around the users' needs for information. In today's business environment, the relational model is dominant among the logical models, and is often implemented with either an indexed- or direct-access physical architecture. Still, all models are being used.

Two conceptual modeling methods were discussed. In the entity-relationship model, segments (entities) are connected to each other by general relationships. In the object-oriented modeling technique, segments (object classes) are related through the concept of inheritance.

Three logical models were discussed. In hierarchical models, logical records are chained to each other by embedded pointer fields. Accessing one record allows accessing of the next record in the chain. A hierarchical model is formed by chaining the records together in such a way that a graph depicting their interrelationships forms a tree. All records are ultimately interconnected to one common record that forms the top of the tree. Network models are similar to hierarchical models, but there is no constraint that the records be chained in such a way so as to form a tree. Finally, the relational model interrelates records sharing common attributes (fields) through the use of tables rather than embedded pointers.

Sequential file organization is the most basic physical architecture. In sequentially organized files, records are always accessed in the exact same sequence, from the first to the last. Such files are useful for batch processing, when a large percentage of the records need to be accessed. However, it is not an efficient file organization when, say, a single record needs to be accessed. A second type of physical architecture is an indexed file. An indexed, or inverted, file is used for faster access (relative to sequentially accessed files) to a single data record. To access an indexed file, the program first consults a directory (or index) and looks up the address of the desired record; it then directly retrieves this record. One special type of an indexed file is an ISAM (indexed-sequential access method) file. An ISAM file is a sequential file that is indexed and physically ordered on one key. Such a file can be processed either sequentially or through the use of the index. A third physical architecture is direct-access file organization. Direct access is accomplished by physically placing each record on disk in such a way that it can be located by one or more of its data values.

Database management systems (DBMSs) are computer software programs that include a data definition language (DDL), a data manipulation language (DML), and a data query language (DQL). The database administrator uses the DDL to define various fields and records, and create a data dictionary. Once data are input into the database, users can manipulate records and fields with a DML, and then view data and extract reports with a DQL. DBMSs provide for standardization, integration, flexibility, and security.

Glossary

activity ratio: the number of active records divided by the number of records in the file.

alias: different users call the same field different names.

attribute: synonym for field.

branch: the connection between children and parent(s) in a tree structure.

children: lower-level elements in a tree diagram of a data structure that are connected to (i.e., part of) the parent element.

database administrator (DBA): has overall responsibility for database administration.

database dictionary: a collection of all data item names in a database, along with a description of the standardized data representation form of these data items.

database management system (DBMS): computer programs that enable a user to create and update files, to select and retrieve data, and to generate various outputs and reports.

database model: synonym for schema.

data description language (DDL): the DDL is used to define the logical structure of the database (schema).

data item: synonym for field.

data manipulation language (DML): the commands for updating, editing, manipulating, and extracting data from a database.

data query language (DQL): a user-friendly language or interface that allows the user to request information from the database.

direct-access file: each record has a strong location (address) that bears some relationship to the record's key field, allowing direct retrieval of each record in the file.

disk access time: the time required for the CPU to retrieve a single block of data from the disk.

element: synonym for field.

entity-relationship (E-R) data model: a conceptual model for depicting the relationships between segments in a database.

field: the smallest block of data that will be stored and retrieved in the information system.

first normal form: relational tables that do not contain any repeating groups.

fixed-length record: both the number of fields and the length (character size) of each field are fixed.

fully inverted file: a file that is indexed for all its fields.

hypertext systems: systems that allow users to browse through databases in random fashion by selecting key words or objects.

indexed file: one where an attribute has been extracted from the records and used to build a new file whose purpose is to provide an index to the original file.

indexed-sequential file: a sequential file that is stored on a DASD and is both indexed and physically sorted on the same field.

inheritance: a relationship created when an object class is divided into subclasses.

instance: synonym of occurrence.

inverted file: synonym for indexed file.

ISAM: indexed-sequential access method; synonym for indexed-sequential file organization.

key: synonym for record key.

list organization: each record contains one or more pointers (fields) indicating the address of the next logical record with the same attribute(s).

logical data structure: the logical manner in which records and fields in the database are structured and organized.

multilist organization: a record may be part of several list organizations.

multiple-ring structure: several ring organizations pass through individual records.

network structure: a logical data structure that allows a child segment to have more than one parent.

node: synonym for repeated group.

normal forms: rules that govern the creation of relational tables in the relational database model.

normalization: the process of applying normal form rules in the relational database model.

object: corresponds to an instance in the object-oriented modeling technique (OMT).

object class: corresponds to a segment in the object-oriented modeling technique (OMT).

object-oriented modeling technique (OMT): a conceptual model for depicting the relationships between segments in a database that views the components of the system being modeled as object classes.

occurrence: a specific set of data values for a record.

parent: the highest-level element in a tree diagram of a data structure.

primary (sort) key: the first field used to sort the records in a file.

random access: synonym for direct access.

randomizing transformation: a widely used method of storing and locating records in a direct-access file.

record: a logical grouping of fields (data items) that concern a certain entity.

record key: a data item or combination of data items that uniquely identifies a particular record in a file.

relation: synonym for table in the relational model.

relational algebra: operations used to extract information from relational tables.

relational model: a logical data structure that views the database as a collection of two-dimensional tables.

relative random order: a field in which a file is not sorted.

repeated group: related groups of fields that repeat themselves in variable-length records.

ring structure: a list organization in which the last record in the ring-list points back to the first record.

schema: synonym for logical data structure of a database.

secondary (sort) key: a field used to determine relative position among a set of records when the primary key has the same value in each record of the set.

second normal form: no key in a relational table is allowed to determine the values of a nonkey field.

segment: synonym for repeated group.

sequential-access file: records in the file can be only accessed in their predefined sequence.

subschema: individual, logical user views of the database.

tertiary (sort) keys: additional fields beyond primary and secondary keys required to uniquely identify and sort records in a file.

third normal form: no nonkey field in a relational table is allowed to determine the values on another nonkey field.

trailer record: a fixed-length extension of a master record.

tree structure: a logical data structure where each node represents a segment, and each node is related to another node at the next highest level of the tree.

tuple: a row in a relational table.

variable-length record: both the number of fields and the length (character size) of each field are variable.

Chapter Quiz

Answers to the chapter quiz appear on page 471.

1. Which of the following is (are) "fixed" in a fixed-length record?
   (a) the number of fields
   (b) The length of each field
   (c) both a and b
   (d) neither a nor b

2. Which of the following types of files might be stored on a direct-access storage device (DASD)?
   (a) a sequential-access file
   (b) a direct-access file
   (c) both a and b
   (d) neither a nor b

3. Which of the following terms is *not* a synonym?
   (a) field
   (b) instance
   (c) data item
   (d) element

4. Which of the following terms is a synonym for "repeated group"?
   (a) attribute
   (b) segment
   (c) field
   (d) record key

5. In a(n) (_____) system, a user may browse an on-line database by selecting key words to retrieve information in a random fashion.
   (a) expert
   (b) object-oriented
   (c) segmented
   (d) hypertext

6. Which of the following conceptual database models views the components of the system being modeled as object classes?
   (a) object-oriented modeling technique
   (b) entity-relationship (E-R) data model
   (c) both a and b
   (d) neither a nor b

7. The (_____) should have overall responsibility for documentation and control of an organization's database.
   (a) database administrator
   (b) manager of programming
   (c) manager of operations
   (d) manager of systems analysis

8. Which of the following is the mainstay of current database technology?
   (a) expert systems
   (b) object-oriented systems
   (c) database management systems (DBMSs)
   (d) hypertext systems

9. Which of the following refers to the overall logical structure of a database?
   (a) alias
   (b) virtual data
   (c) schema
   (d) network

10. Which of the following would the database administrator utilize to define the overall logical structure of a database?
    (a) DBA
    (b) DDL—Data description language
    (c) DML
    (d) DQL

Review Problem

Consider the relation

```
BOOK (ISBN, TITLE, AUTHOR, AUTHOR-AFFILIATION, PRICE)
```

The underlining of ISBN indicates that it is the record key.
(a) Is this relation normalized? If so, is it in 1nf, 2nf, or 3nf?
(b) If it is not already in 3nf, what is necessary to attain this?

Solution to Review Problem

(a) Because the ISBN uniquely identifies each book, the relation is in 1nf. Because the key (ISBN) is a single key, the relation must be in 2nf as well as 1nf. Is the relation in 3nf? That is, are all the nonkey fields mutually independent? No. AUTHOR-AFFILIATION clearly depends on AUTHOR.

(b) To attain 3nf, we must separate this relation, giving two separate 3nf relations:

BOOK (ISBN, TITLE, AUTHOR, PRICE)

and

AUTHOR-AFFILIATION(AUTHOR, AUTHOR-AFFILIATION).

Review Questions

1. Distinguish between fixed- and variable-length records.
2. Distinguish between primary and secondary sort keys.
3. Identify major developments in the evolution of database technology.
4. What is a hypertext system?
5. Distinguish between the conceptual level, the logical level, and the physical level of database architecture.
6. Characterize each of the three major models of logical data structures:
   (a) tree or hierarchical models
   (b) network models
   (c) relational models
7. What is list organization? How does it differ from a ring structure?
8. Identify the basic operations of a relational algebra. What are they used for?
9. What is normalization? Distinguish between first, second, and third normal forms.
10. Distinguish between the following:
    (a) sequentially accessed files
    (b) indexed-sequential files
    (c) directly accessed files
11. What factors affect response time in database systems?
12. What are database management systems?
13. Distinguish between the following:
    (a) data description language (DDL)
    (b) data manipulation language (DML)
    (c) data query language (DQL)
14. What are the functions of the database administrator (DBA)?

Discussion Questions and Problems

15. Discuss some of the differences between the traditional approach to data processing and the database approach.
16. Discuss the advantages and disadvantages of having an industrywide standard to which all database software systems conform.
17. For each of the following applications, specify a file organization method (sequential, direct-access, indexed-sequential). Briefly justify your selection in terms of the anticipated activity ratio, processing time frame, file size, and response time to inquiries about file status.
    (a) General Motors stockholder file, updated weekly, and used for mailing dividend checks, quarterly reports, and proxy requests.
    (b) A salesperson commission file, updated at the time of sale from a point-of-sale data entry terminal.
    (c) A bank's customer account file, updated daily for deposits and withdrawals and used for mailing monthly statements of account.

(d) An inventory file, updated daily, that is also used to ascertain product availability and other related inquiries during daily operations.

(e) A master payroll file, used biweekly to process payroll and also quarterly to process various tax reports.

(f) A master scheduling file, used by a large airline to reserve seats on all its flights. The file is used heavily every day for scheduling and ad hoc inquiries concerning seat availability but is never processed to generate reports.

(g) A file of authors for a publishing company, processed quarterly to prepare royalty checks and once at year-end to prepare tax reports.

(h) A vendor file used by a large manufacturing company. The file is used heavily every day for ad hoc inquiries concerning orders and payments and is also processed once each week to generate payment checks for many of the company's 500 vendors.

(i) A master file of fixed assets for a small manufacturing firm, processed quarterly to produce depreciation for tax and accounting reports and once each year for insurance purposes.

18. The West Company maintains a master accounts receivable disk file. Approved applications for new charge accounts are keyed to disk. The resultant file is sorted and processed against the master file.

The current master disk file is strictly sequential. What are some advantages and disadvantages that might accrue from changing the file organization method to either a random or indexed-sequential structure?

19. For each of the following application files, discuss the relative merits of sequential, direct, and indexed-sequential file organization:

(a) open-order file in a large manufacturing firm
(b) accounts receivable file for a magazine publisher
(c) inventory file for a large automobile dealership
(d) accounts payable file for a retailing firm
(e) fixed-asset file in a manufacturing firm

20. Identify an inquiry for (1) a specific record and (2) a group of related records that might be made for each of the following files. Discuss how these inquiries might be satisfied if the file organization method was sequential, direct, or indexed-sequential:

(a) an employee master file
(b) an accounts receivable file
(c) a work-in-process file

21. Use the flowchart in Figure 11.13 to solve this problem. Assume that the master file and the transaction file are composed of the record numbers shown in the sequence given:

Master   11, 15, 31, 84, 87, 99

Transaction   11, 12, 31, 31, 15, 84, 99

The record number 99 in each file is used to indicate the logical end of the file.

Process these data, using the flowchart in Figure 11.13.

Indicate

(a) which master records are updated.
(b) which master records are not updated.
(c) the disposition of each transaction record (i.e., posted to the master or an error condition).

22. Consider an open-purchase order file in a manufacturing company. Identify several other files to which the purchase order file might be linked (chained) through the use of pointer fields.

23. A personnel file contains a record for each employee in an organization. Each record contains four fields: (1) name, (2) division, (3) specialty, and (4) age. The following are four sample records:

Storage Location	Name	Division	Specialty	Age
22	Ash	New York	Audit	30
28	Fox	New York	Audit	25
64	Luh	Chicago	Marketing	29
106	Smith	Los Angeles	Personnel	40

Each of the four fields is expected to be an important search parameter in the personnel application system. Design an index (directory) to invert this file fully.

24. Discuss the relative advantages and disadvantages of inverted files and lists or ring structures (pointer field structures) in answering inquiries of the following types:
   (a) Are there are any records that have both attribute 1 and attribute 2 (sales greater than $5,000 and location equal to the state of New York)?
   (b) How many records have attribute 1, attribute 2, . . . , attribute n?

25. Consider the following relation:

```
CLASS-LIST  (STUDENT#,  CLASS#,  STUDENT-NAME, STUDENT-MAJOR, CLASS-TIME,
CLASSROOM).
```

   Required
   (a) Suppose we wish to add a new class time and room (i.e., a new section) for a particular class number (#). Is this possible? If not, what is necessary before we can add a new class time and room to the file?
   (b) Suppose all students drop a particular class number (#) from their schedules. What effect would this have on the data stored in the CLASS-LIST relation?
   (c) Is CLASS-LIST in 1nf, 2nf, or 3nf?

26. An automobile manufacturer maintains a cumulative sales file in the following relation:

```
CUM-SALES (MAKE, BODY-STYLE, COLOR, SALES-REGION, SALES, OPEN-ORDERS)
```

   An example (tuple) would be

```
CUM-SALES, (Buick, Sedan, Red, West, 123400, 4500)
```

   Is this relation in 3nf?

27. Consider the two-record hierarchy

```
DEPARTMENT (DEPT#, DEPT-NAME, . . . , PROFESSOR) PROFESSOR (PROF#, PROF-
NAME, . . .)
```

   in which professors are linked to their department by the field PROFESSOR in the DEPARTMENT record.
   Does this relation have a repeating group? If so, how would you normalize this relation?

28. Organizing and maintaining a database is more complicated than organizing and maintaining independent files because a database provides more data retrieval functions and performs more operations. A DBMS may have three different types of languages associated with its use: a data manipulation language (DML), a data definition language (DDL), and a data query language (DQL). For each of the following illustrations, indicate which of these three languages would probably be used.
   (a) A programmer writes a COBOL program to update inventory records that are stored in the database.

(b) The database administrator (DBA) documents the content and structure of the database.

(c) A sales manager requests an ad hoc report on sales of a certain product over the past month.

(d) The field for customer address in the accounts receivable segment of the database is expanded to allow for a ten-digit zip code.

(e) The payroll manager requests a special report detailing those employees in the database who have college degrees.

(f) A programmer writes a COBOL program to prepare payroll checks for employees whose personnel records are stored in the database.

(g) A new field is added to employee personnel records in the database to allow for a new payroll deduction for health benefits.

(h) A programmer writes a COBOL program to update accounts receivable records that are stored in the database.

(i) The credit manager requests a special report detailing those customers in the database who have purchased more than $25,000 worth of goods in the past three months.

29. A data record is a collection of related fields or data elements. Record design is one of the fundamental problems of data management. A data record should include all the data elements that are essential to an application. In certain instances, however, a particular data element might be computed as needed on the basis of the other data elements stored in a record. In such cases, it is not really necessary to store this type of data element in a data record, because its value can readily be computed as needed. This type of data element is called *virtual data.*

For example, a payroll record might contain the following three data elements in addition to others:

- pay rate per hour
- hours worked
- gross pay

In this case, gross pay would be a virtual data element. Gross pay could be computed as needed based on the pay rate per hour and hours worked data elements.

Virtual data is an example of redundancy in data records. The elimination of virtual data has several advantages. One is to reduce the overall size of the data record and thus reduce the amount of storage space required. This would tend to reduce the total cost of storing a data record. Another advantage is that there are fewer data items in the data record that have to be maintained. This might lead to simpler application programs and would tend to reduce the possibility of having errors occur when the data record is modified. This becomes more important when a data element is contained in more than one data record. In such cases, a data element might be updated in one record but not in others. This results in inconsistent data in an information system.

Required

Consider the following data record for a work-in-process application system:

- work-in-process number
- materials cost
- direct labor cost
- applied overhead cost
- total cost
- units started
- units spoiled
- good units in process

Which of these data items is (are) virtual data? What types of advantages might be gained if virtual data elements are removed from the work-in-process record? Explain.

30. Ernst and Anderson is a manufacturer of power tools and other products used in the construction industry. The company was originally founded in the early 1900s as a manufacturer of quality hand tools such as hammers and screwdrivers, but such products have represented a decreasing percentage of total company sales for more than a decade. The company has been very successful in industrial power tools, which is its primary line of business. Several small companies were acquired in the late 1980s to broaden the company's product line to include a variety of commercial products such as small appliances and household cleaning equipment such as vacuum cleaners. Because their products are consumer oriented and thus do not compete with industrial power tools, these acquisitions have generally been allowed to operate as independent companies.

The company operates several manufacturing facilities that produce power tools, but the largest and oldest plant, based in Pittsburgh, accounts for almost 80% of total production. The Pittsburgh plant employs more than 1,000 people and manufactures more than 250 different types of power tools. Much of the company's success in maintaining its position in the marketplace in the face of intense international competition can be attributed to its long-standing policies concerning good employee relations and adequate plant maintenance. Although old in years, the Pittsburgh plant has been well maintained and the company has continuously invested in new manufacturing equipment.

A computer-based information system for production control has been used at the Pittsburgh plant since the early 1970s. Management of Ernst and Anderson was an early believer in the view that adequate information is an essential ingredient in the successful operation of a complex manufacturing operation. The production control system is organized into five major applications: production scheduling, materials management, labor cost reporting, work-in-process inventory, and finished goods inventory. These applications were developed separately and have been modified constantly over the years. The five different applications all utilize their own separate files and programs. Applications are linked together through separate batch processing runs. For example, periodically the work-in-process application is processed to generate a file of completed jobs. This transaction file of completed jobs is then reformatted as necessary and processed by the finished goods inventory application to update the finished goods inventory records. The reformatting is necessary because each application has been independently developed. This has resulted in some inconsistencies between identical data elements in the different applications.

These inconsistencies have become more and more bothersome as the company has expanded the role of its computer-based production control system. Management is convinced that the effectiveness of the information system can be significantly increased if the five separate, stand-alone applications are integrated in a DBMS. To this end, the company has established a project team to study the feasibility of using a DBMS. The company hired a large public accounting firm to assist them in this project. Upon the advice of their consultant, the project team has begun a study of the inputs, file structures, and outputs of the five separate applications to determine the data-definition ambiguities that exist in the present systems. These ambiguities will have to be eliminated if the production scheduling, materials management, labor cost reporting, work-in-process inventory, and finished goods inventory applications are to be integrated in a DBMS.

To date the project team has studied three of the five applications, and this has taken three times as long as it had originally expected. More than 400 different data names were discovered, but analysis of these data names indicated that only about 150 different data variables really existed. The difference is due to data redundancy. For example, the number of units being produced in a job is referred to by the data name "units started" in the production scheduling application but by "quantity" in the work-in-process application and "units" in the finished goods inventory application. These three different data names in the three different applications refer to the same real data element. As another example, the economic production quantity for a product is referred to by the data name "lot size" in the production scheduling application but by "minimum level" in the finished goods inventory application. These examples indicate one reason why data have to be reformatted when they are transferred from one application to another. The project team found many other similar instances of data redundancy in the three applications they have studied so far.

The problem of data redundancy is also complicated by the fact that the different data names for the same data element usually have different physical representations in the different applications. For example, "units started" in the production scheduling application has a length of eight characters, but "quantity" in the work-in-process application has a length of ten characters.

Inconsistency is another type of data ambiguity the project team discovered. Inconsistency occurs when the same data name is used to mean different things in different applications. For example, the data name "code" in the production scheduling application means department code. But "code" means transaction code in the work-in-process application and product number in the finished goods inventory application. This is yet another reason why data have to be reformatted when they are transferred from one application to another. The project team found several other similar instances of data inconsistency in the three applications they studied.

The five applications cannot be integrated while data ambiguities exist. Yet the project is taking considerably more time than expected. The status of the DBMS project is currently being reviewed by the management of Ernst and Anderson.

Required

(a) If a user requested the data name "lot size" in the production scheduling application, and the same user entered the data name "minimum level" in the finished goods inventory application, what would be the result? If a user requested the data name "units started" in the production scheduling application, then requested the data name "quantity" in the work-in-process application, and then requested the data name "units" in the finished goods inventory application, what would be the result? What additional consideration compounds this type of problem?

(b) If a user requested the data name "code" in the production scheduling application, then requested "code" in the work-in-process application, and then requested "code" in the finished goods inventory application, what would be the result?

(c) Discuss the role of a data dictionary in analyzing data ambiguity. Indicate how specific sections of a data dictionary can help resolve data ambiguity.

(d) What action should the management of Ernst and Anderson take concerning the status of the DBMS project? Should the project team complete its study of data ambiguity even though the project has taken considerably more time than expected? Should the DBMS project proceed in view of the large amount of data ambiguity that has been discovered? If so, what is the first database that should be implemented?

31. The database administrator (DBA) is not necessarily a single individual. In a large organization, several individuals may share overall responsibility for the DBA function. Discuss each of the following:

(a) Why is the DBA function crucial to the concept of data management?

(b) What administrative responsibilities should be vested in the DBA?

(c) What responsibilities and duties should not be vested in or permitted to the DBA function?

(d) Where should the DBA function be placed in the organizational structure of a firm?

32. Consider the following relation in 1nf:

```
ORDER (ORDER#, VENDOR#, PART#, DESCRIPTION, QUANTITY, PRICE,
TOTAL_AMOUNT)
```

CHAPTER 11 File Processing and Data Management Concepts **471**

The underlining indicates a combination key that consists of the concatenated fields ORDER#, VENDOR#, and PART#.
  (a) What is needed to attain 2nf?
  (b) What is needed to attain 3nf?

33. Consider the following relation:

    CLASS-LIST (<u>COURSE#</u>, CLASS-ROOM, STUDENT#, STUDENT-MAJOR)

  (a) Assuming that each student can have only one major, is this relation normalized? If so, is it in 1nf, 2nf, or 3nf? If it is not already in 3nf, what is necessary to attain this?
  (b) Would your answer to part (a) be different if a student can have more than one major? Discuss.

Answers to Chapter Quiz

1. C	**4.** B	**7.** A	**10.** B
2. C	**5.** D	**8.** C	
3. B	**6.** A	**9.** C	

CHAPTER 12

Distributed Information Systems and Electronic Data Interchange

LEARNING OBJECTIVES

Careful study of this chapter will enable you to:

■ Understand distributed computing concepts.

■ Describe how data and computing resources may be distributed in networks.

■ Describe how electronic data interchange (EDI) works and is utilized in business communications.

■ Characterize the electronic funds transfer (EFT) environment.

DISTRIBUTED INFORMATION SYSTEMS

Distributed Computing Concepts

A **distributed computing system** is a network of computers connected such that it appears to be a single computer to the individual user. Consider, for example, a LAN consisting of three personal computers, *A, B,* and *C.* In a fully distributed computing system, the files and programs of any one of these three computers would automatically be made available to the other two computers. By "automatically made available," we mean that the user of, say, computer *A* could access a file or database that resides on computer *B* or *C* without having to even be aware of the fact that this file or database resides in a different computer.

Distributed computing transforms many computers in a network into what is effectively a single computer, thus maximizing the use of computing resources. This not only means that any workstation in the network can conveniently access any data file in the network; it also implies that a computer program and its related data files can reside in different computers. For example, in a distributed system, it would be possible to run a database program on one computer that accesses a database stored on another computer. Furthermore, from the user's point of view, both the database program and its related database would appear to reside in one computer.

Distributed computing has implications for the processing of accounting and other data. Various files, databases, and programs can be dispersed over a wide area. For example, the accounts receivable transaction files for a given company might reside in Miami, whereas the related master file resides in Chicago. Files can be conveniently stored in the locations most accommodating to the company's organizational structure, thus minimizing communication costs and geographically diversifying the responsibilities of file maintenance.

Network transparency (or **location transparency**) means that the user is unaware of the distributed nature of the system. That is, all data and files in the network, regardless of their location, appear to reside on the user's computer. Distributed computing systems combine all the computers and resources in a network so that they effectively become one computer system. Note that all distributed computing systems are networks, but not all networks are distributed computing systems. A network only becomes a distributed computing system when it is organized to provide network transparency. The main idea behind network transparency is that data items, files, and computers in a network can be accessed by name rather than by physical location.

Data communications in distributed systems are facilitated by servers. A **server** is a constantly running computer program (i.e., a resident program) and related database (or data file) that provides one or more software or data services to other computers in the network. For example, a server might control a database containing all sales transactions. Other computers, called clients, might query and update this database through remote communications. A **client** is a computer or program that accesses data and programs located on network servers.

Server programs operate differently from other types of programs. First, servers execute continually while monitoring communications channels for requests from clients. In most cases, server programs execute the entire time the network is up and running. Ordinary programs, on the other hand, only execute long enough to complete a particular task. In some cases, an entire CPU is dedicated solely to one server program. In other cases, the CPU is shared with other applications, and the server program constantly runs in the background. More than one server can exist on the same computer.

Second, database servers typically support **remote procedure calls,** which allow a program on one computer to perform queries and updates on a database server elsewhere in the network. For example, in developing a database application, the programmer can insert a single line of code into the program (a remote procedure call) that requests data for a given field/record combination, without regard to the physical location of the desired data. When the program is executed, it can then automatically locate the desired data anywhere in the network.

Data and files are automatically located in one of several possible ways. The local database program itself can keep a record of the location of all relevant data items in the network. This approach, however, is inefficient because each program on each workstation has to keep its own records on the locations of all relevant data in the network. An alternative approach involves the user of a **name server,** a specialized server that maintains a centrally located directory of files and/or data. Whenever a program needs data or files, it first consults the name server to find the desired address, and then uses that address to access the desired data. By using this approach, the data on the name server are updated whenever relevant files and/or data are added or deleted.

Naming services (applications of name-server technology) are the foundation of any distributed computing system. They are so important that they have been standardized by **Open System Interconnection (OSI) standard X.500.** A good example of an implementation of this standard is Digital Equipment Corporation's Distributed Name Services (DECdns), which provides global-access facilities to all applications in the network.

In some cases, naming services might be provided to applications through a **distributed file system,** a portion of or extension to the operating system that controls the naming services. The operating system might be either a network operating system or a distributed operating system. In a **network operating system,** each computer in the network runs its own copy of an operating system that supports communications with other computers in the network. There is no requirement that each computer even use the same operating system that other computers in the network use, although in practice it is common for all network computers to use the same operating system. In a **distributed operating system,** however, there is one unified operating system that is distributed in pieces over all computers in the network.

The exchange of information between clients, servers, and application programs in distributed systems is called interprocess communication. A **process** is an executing program that communicates with one or more other concurrently executing programs. **Interprocess communication** refers to the direct program-to-program communication between two computer programs that are executing simultaneously, possibly on two separate computers in the network. Consider, for example, the case in which a user queries a sales database that, along with the database program, resides in his or her own computer. Further assume that the user requests June's sales totals, and that these data are not found in the database residing in the user's computer. Then the database program running in the user's computer might obtain the desired data through interprocess communication with the database program running on another computer. The program on the user's computer (process one) would send a request through the network to the program running on the second computer (process two). The second program would then transmit the requested data to the first program, which would in turn display them for the user. The user would not even be aware that data were retrieved from the second computer.

Interprocess communication can take place either through local or remote communications (e.g., through fiber-optic cables) or through **distributed shared memory** (Figure 12.1), common primary memory that is addressable by various computers in the network. Systems in which computers communicate through communications are called **loosely coupled systems.** Systems in which computers communicate through distributed shared memory are called **tightly coupled systems.**

FIGURE 12.1 Distributed Shared Memory.

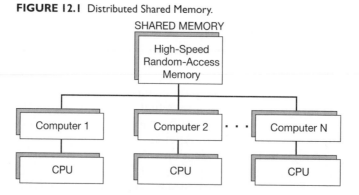

Network Processing Architectures for Distributing Data

There are three basic computer architectures for distributing data in a network. These three **network processing architectures** include the centralized nondistributed architecture, the client–server distributed architecture, and the peer-to-peer distributed architecture.

The network architecture selected by a particular company will depend on its organizational structure, geographical dispersion, and information needs. Distributing the company's computing and information functions is tantamount to decentralization. Companies differ widely in the overall degree of decentralization in their organizational structures. So it is understandable that distributed processing is a better option for some companies than others.

There are significant benefits to both centralization and decentralization of the computing and information functions. Favoring centralization are the economies of scale that accompany the concentration of resources in one place, as well as the benefits of centralized control. Furthermore, centralization reduces security risks by reducing exposures to potential intruders. On the other hand, centralized computers are more vulnerable to disasters, are further removed from end users, and may require more communication and other support costs. In the final analysis, each company must weigh the costs and benefits of the two approaches, although these are often difficult to estimate. In practice, the degree of decentralization is often based on selecting the system that is most compatible with the company's organizational and operational structures.

Nondistributed, Centralized Processing

Under a completely **nondistributed network processing architecture,** communications between computers may take place, but without network transparency and without interprocess communication. This means two things. First, the absence of network transparency implies that the user of one computer must use the physical address of another computer in order to communicate with it. Second, the absence of interprocess communication implies that there is no transparent transfer of data between computers.

One example of nondistributed architecture is a central computer that does not have any servers and is serviced by communications terminals. In this environment, personal computers might be attached to the central computer but only so that they can emulate communications terminals when they communicate.

In practice, however, most networks of more than one or two computers involve some elements of distributed processing. For example, in a central-computer environment, the user might first select a host processor (where several processors share the same disks) by name before logging on. Alternatively, he or she might send another user a message by name with an electronic mail program. Therefore, the distinction of distributed versus nondistributed computing systems is somewhat artificial, because distributed processing is often a matter of degree.

The term **distributed information system (DIS)** applies to distributed computing systems in which the databases exist in servers. **Distributed data processing (DDP)** refers to data processing in a distributed information system. DDP is of particular importance to accounting and is the primary focus of the remaining discussion in this chapter relating to distributed processing. Henceforth, the terms *distributed data processing* and *distributed processing* are used interchangeably.

Client–Server Processing

Under a **client–server network processing architecture** (Figure 12.2), various application programs in the network fulfill either one of two roles: client or server. Three types of servers are possible: file servers, DBMS servers, and repository servers. Each of these client–server architectures is discussed. First, some terminology is discussed. For our purposes, it is convenient to view a distributed database system as consisting of four components: the database management system (DBMS), the user task, the database, and the database policies. The DBMS is the "master program" that controls the database. The **user task** is a set of instructions telling the DBMS how to perform the processing tasks desired by the user such as queries and requests for updates. The database contains the actual data.

There are four types of **database policies:** security policies, integrity policies, trigger policies, and derivation policies. **Security policies** restrict access to authorized users for authorized purposes. **Integrity policies** protect that data from corruption by limiting updates to acceptable values. **Trigger policies** initiate processing when data values fall within preplanned ranges. For example, an aging report might automatically be initiated on the first of every month. Finally, **derivation policies** describe how some data fields or values are automatically calculated from other data fields or values. For example, a field called NET_PAY might be automatically calculated from fields containing the gross pay and the payroll deductions.

File Servers.   In a **file–server** environment, the DBMS, the user task, the database policies, and all processing capabilities reside on the client, and the database resides on the server. As needed, the client application requests data from the server, which in turn downloads blocks of data (often a file or an entire DBMS) to the client.

The file–server architecture is the least evolved of the client–server architectures. Accordingly, it possesses several major drawbacks. First, each workstation in the network must possess its own copy of the DBMS. This means possibly unwarranted duplication. Second, file servers must typically send the client more data than the client actually needs. For example, assume that the client wants to find all sales records for product X in sales district Y. The server has no processing capabilities of its own, so the client must request all sales records from the server and then search for the desired records locally. In a large database, this could mean downloading thousands of records from the server in a case in which only one record is really needed by the client. Finally, because file servers do not contain any processing capabilities, database security and integrity are typically minimal. For example, the server has no way of screening updates received from clients. Consequently, there is nothing preventing an errant client application from replacing records in the database with garbage.

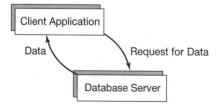

FIGURE 12.2 Client–Server Relationship.

File–server technology is provided with most simple network operating systems designed for LANs. Because it is so widely available, there may be a temptation to use it for mission-critical accounting applications. This is probably inadvisable, for the alternative client–server architectures discussed in what follows overcome many of the drawbacks of the simple file server.

A good use of the file servers is as a means of file distribution rather than as tools to facilitate data processing. File servers can maintain a library of files (programs, text files, graphic files, databases, etc.) and distribute individual files to users on request. In some systems (such as Listserve on the Bitnet network), users can automatically subscribe to a particular file on a file server. Whenever that file is updated, all subscribers are automatically sent a new copy.

DBMS Servers.   In a **DBMS–server** environment, the user task and database policies reside on the client, and the DBMS and database reside on the server. The DBMS server represents somewhat of an improvement over the file server. Because the DBMS resides on the server, it can perform some or all of the processing tasks and, in doing so, minimizes the amount of data that must be downloaded to the client. Assume, for example, that the client requests the account balance for customer X. The DBMS server can extract this one record and download it to the client.

Because the DBMS server's database policies all reside on the client, security and integrity cannot be ensured by the DBMS. Security and integrity must be maintained at the workstation level, and an errant workstation can cause the same problems as can a client of a file server.

Repository Servers.   In a **repository–server** environment, the server contains the DBMS, the database policies, and the database. The client contains the user application. This type of server is the most secure and overcomes the limitations of file and DBMS servers. Client programs can access and update data on the server with remote procedure calls but subject to the server's central policy constraints.

In a variation of the simple repository–server environment, clients also possess their own copies of the server's database policies, called **shadow policies.** The shadow policies allow the client the opportunity to check the validity of a request before forwarding it to the server. In some cases, this approach can save communication traffic and improve response time. Invalid requests are rejected immediately before being forwarded to the network. The repository–server architecture is widely supported among the higher-end database systems such as IBM's Repository Manager and DB2.

Peer-to-Peer Processing

With peer-to-peer processing, related versions of a common application program run on both the client and server computers. The database program and the policies reside on the server. The server may possess shadow policies. The client and server application programs exchange messages with each other regarding transaction updates and queries.

Peer-to-peer processing is useful when it is desirable to do both local processing on the client and remote processing on the server. The client and server can interact with each other as peers, which in some cases can reduce the number of messages required to commit a transaction that updates the database.

One form of peer-to-peer processing is **synchronized policy processing.** This type of processing involves the server transmitting its policies via messages to the client, thus assuring a synchronization of policies between the client and server. **Cooperative processing,** another form of peer-to-peer processing, is similar to synchronized policy processing, except that policies are maintained only on the server, unless a shadow policy is in effect. With cooperative policy processing, however, there is no built-in assurance that a shadow policy on the client is the same as the policy on the server.

Distributing Data and Computing Resources

Distributed processing technologies make it possible to distribute both data resources and processing power. Both of these issues are discussed, along with problems that arise from multiple users' concurrent access to data.

Distributing Data

We use the term **distributed database** to mean any database that is globally accessible throughout the network through some method such as remote procedure calls. Such a database can be distributed in one of three ways. First, it can exist in a single database server accessible from anywhere in the network. Second, it can be replicated so that multiple copies of it exist in more than one location. And third, it can be fragmented and distributed in pieces throughout the network. The important thing is that from the user's point of view, the physical location of the data is irrelevant. In all cases, the distributed nature of the system is invisible to the user.

From the accountant's point of view, however, the difference in the method used to physically distribute the database is important, so we discuss this topic further. We have already discussed the single database server, so we move on to the replicated database. A database is replicated when different identical copies of it exist in multiple locations. The simplest way to implement a **replicated database** is to require that all updates be made to a central copy. Once accepted, the updates can be multicasted to the replicated copies. **Multicasting** is similar to the ordinary concept of broadcasting (sending messages to all nodes in the network), the only difference being that multicasting involves sending messages only to a predetermined subset of the nodes in the network.

There are some obvious problems with multicasting messages to replicated databases. The most salient problem is that it is possible for one copy of the database to become unsynchronized with the others. For example, if for some reason one copy of the database becomes unavailable and cannot receive messages, it will not be up to date. When it does become available, it must be brought up to date before it can receive current messages. For example, assume that one database server is cut off from the network because of communication problems. Further assume that while this server is off-net, it misses a multicasted message instructing it to add a new customer record for, say, customer 123. Now assume that the disconnected database comes back on line and immediately receives a message to update the record for customer 123. It is unable to complete this task because customer 123 was never added due to the communications failure. There are various ways for dealing with system faults, but they are beyond the scope of this chapter.

If updates to the replicated database are infrequent, then it might be simpler and more efficient to periodically send entire copies of the updated database to individual nodes. The updated copy of the database would in each case entirely replace the outdated copy.

The number of possible ways to distribute data is endless. For example, there is no reason that updates to a database have to be multicasted only to replicated copies of the same database. The same updates could be multicasted to completely different databases that share some common data elements with the originating database. Alternatively, summary information from a given transaction might be sent to various servers. For example, only the totals from a sales transaction file might be sent to the master file. Finally, with peer-to-peer technology, there is no reason that a database cannot serve both as a server and client; that is, it might receive updates from some databases and send updates (such as financial totals) to others.

Distributing a database by **fragmentation** involves maintaining a name server of databases, their data items, and locations. Several fields from separate databases can be logically pieced together to form the appearance of a single database. This approach may achieve some of the benefits of a replicated database without the complex overhead brought on by replicated files.

In practice, because many companies use relational databases, fragmenting a database typically means partitioning relational tables into smaller tables. These smaller tables are then distributed to various physical locations. Application programs can then perform relational algebra on the smaller tables without having to worry about their physical locations.

Concurrency Issues.   In many cases, it is undesirable to allow two users to concurrently update the same data item, record, or database at the same time. Allowing such a thing might produce unpredictable results. This problem is normally managed with **record locking, file locking,** or **database locking.** When a data entity is locked, it cannot be modified. The locking can be for reading, writing, or both.

The extent of the locking will depend on the needs of the particular application. For example, an application that is making extensive updates to many records in a particular database might want to lock the entire database (to other applications) until the update is complete.

In some applications, the client application might download a copy of a particular record from the server and display it for the user so that he or she can update it. When the user is finished updating the record, the client application will then send it back to the server, which in turn will replace the old record in the database with the new one. In such a case as this, it is obvious that the record must be locked until the client finishes with it. Otherwise, another client on the network might subsequently send a copy of the record to the server that it obtained between the time that the first client obtained a copy and the time that the server applied the update. This subsequent copy of the record would not contain any of the updates made by the first client. The result would be that the first client's update would be completely undone. Transactions that require record locking for the reasons described here are called atomic transactions. **Atomic transactions** are transactions that must be completed in their entirety.

Another reason to enforce locking for atomic transactions is to protect against an abrupt failure (e.g., a disk crash) of either the client or server. A common approach to make the updating process fault-tolerant is to use the **two-phase commit** transaction approach. This works like the example in the previous paragraph. First, all relevant data values are downloaded to the client, where they are updated. When the updating is complete, the client commits the updated information and sends it back to the server, which in turn applies it to the database. The relevant data items are locked between the first and second phases. The essence of the two-phase commit procedure is that changes to the database are made on an all-or-none basis. This minimizes the possibility of a system crash when a transaction is only partially entered.

Distributing CPUs

It is also possible to distribute CPUs. This means that a user or application automatically can use any processor in the network if that processor is local. Distributing CPUs allows the automatic assigning of individual applications to CPUs from a pool of processors. This allows for the balancing of computing loads across multiple CPUs. For example, an application can automatically be assigned to the CPU with the most excess capacity.

ELECTRONIC DATA INTERCHANGE

Electronic data interchange (EDI) is the direct computer-to-computer exchange of business documents such as purchase orders and sales orders. By some estimates, 7% of all corporate spending is dedicated to sending invoices, processing purchase and sales orders, and related expenses. According to analysts, these costs might be cut in half by EDI. First National Bank of Chicago, for example, claims that because of EDI, it saves over $1 million a year in forms and supplies.

There are four typical benefits resulting from EDI. Costs are reduced by eliminating paperwork. Errors are minimized by reducing the amount of human data entry. For example, when one company electronically sends a purchase order to an **EDI trading partner,** the partner uses the incoming purchase order to automatically generate a sales order. This contrasts with the typical non-EDI purchase/sales transaction, in which the trading partner must manually key in the sales order.

A third benefit of EDI is that it allows companies to complete transactions more quickly. Digital Electronics Corporation, for example, was able to cut the administrative cycle for its inventories from five weeks to only three days. This sort of time saving makes a company more competitive. It also helps companies to reduce their inventories and implement just-in-time (JIT) delivery.

A fourth benefit of EDI is that it allows companies to rapidly take advantage of new business opportunities. With EDI, new business relationships can be rapidly formed by establishing EDI communication links. Once these links are established, bids and purchase orders can be exchanged quickly in standard EDI format.

How an EDI System Works

Before two companies interchange documents between each other, both companies must sign an **EDI partnership agreement** that sets forth in legal terms how electronic business will be transacted. This agreement will specify the medium through which EDI messages are transmitted. Examples include standard telephone lines, satellite links, ISDN, and vendors of public packet-switching services. The agreement will also specify the standardized computer formats to be used for various documents (e.g., purchase orders, invoices, and so on). Security measures, acknowledgment procedures, and error-handling procedures should also be specified.

Once the EDI agreement is in effect, the parties can send and receive EDI documents in one of three ways, as governed by their agreement. Documents might be exchanged through direct company-to-company communications (possibly via the Internet); indirectly through public networks such as Sprintnet, Tymnet, MCI, and AT&T; or indirectly through a third party that supplies EDI services. If the companies send and receive EDI documents through direct company-to-company communications (e.g., standard phone lines, VSAT, or ISDN), both companies must use the appropriate translation and communication software. The translation software converts in-house documents to and from the agreed-upon standardized EDI format, and the communications software sends and receives the EDI documents. Many software packages are available for personal computers and mainframes that provide the needed communications and translation services. Examples include American Business Computer's Electronic Data Exchange PC/Mini and Supply Tech Inc.'s STX.12 for the Mainframe. Some software packages even integrate EDI with other functions such as MRP and EFT.

A second alternative is for two companies to send and receive documents indirectly through a public **value-added network (VAN)** such as Sprintnet or MCI. One way to implement this approach is to send and receive EDI messages through the VAN's e-mail system using the OSI X.400 e-mail protocol. The **OSI X.400 e-mail protocol** is a very widely accepted broad protocol for the transfer of mail messages, text files, binary files, and graphics. Users of VAN systems still must have their own translation and communication software. The VAN simply provides the means to transfer EDI messages from one company to another.

The final alternative is to use a third-party turnkey system. Third-party EDI vendors provide a full range of communication and translation products and services. Examples of major vendors for EDI products and services include General Electric Information Services (GEIS), Digital Electronic Corporation (DEC), Western Union, and IBM. For example, as a component of its Network Application Support and DECnet architecture, DEC provides DEC/EDI, a comprehensive EDI software system. DEC/EDI runs on a single DEC VAX computer or can be distributed across a network of VAX computers. This software consists of three servers: the communication server, the translation server, and the application server. Figure 12.3 depicts the flow of EDI messages through the three servers. Collectively, the three servers provide for fully automatic, completely unattended, paperless processing.

The communication server automatically sends and receives EDI information. The company has a wide range of communication options, including direct X.400 company-to-company messaging, as well as multiple VANs, such as AT&T and MCI, and their X.400 services. All incoming and outgoing EDI messages are automatically logged to disk.

The translation server supports automatic translations from and into a wide variety of translation formats, including those widely used in the United States and Europe. Standards for translation formats are discussed in what follows.

The application server consists of a set of application-callable program routines that the accounting (or other) application can use to access incoming messages or send outgoing messages.

An example is given of how the system might work in a retailing firm. Assume that all sales come from POS terminals and that an inventory server automatically sends requisitions to the accounting application server when inventories are low.

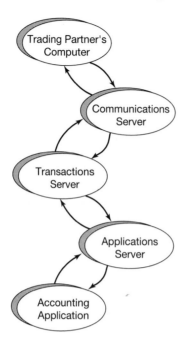

FIGURE 12.3 Flow of EDI Messages.

Assume that the accounting application server receives a request from the inventory server to order more goods. The application server then automatically generates a purchase order and sends it to the translation server, indicating the desired vendor and EDI format. Next, the translation server automatically converts the document into the vendor's EDI format and sends it to the communication server. The communication server then sends the purchase order to the vendor. Later, when an order confirmation is received from the vendor, the communication server forwards the incoming message to the accounting server, which then logs the confirmation into the purchasing database. This entire transaction might take as short a time as 5 or 10 minutes, or less.

Less sophisticated companies might use simpler methods that require more human intervention. For example, instead of the inventory and accounting servers, the company might use various electronic mailboxes. That is, the inventory department might send the requisition to the purchasing department via electronic mail. The purchasing department might then review and approve the requisition, and then send an electronic purchase order to the translation server. The rest of the transaction would be automatic.

In an even simpler approach, a company might key in the purchase order, manually run a program to convert it to EDI format, and then manually send the EDI message to the vendor via electronic mail. The purchasing department might even need to manually call the vendor's computer in order to send the message.

In general, EDI is made more effective by integrating it with other systems in the company. Furthermore, EDI integrates especially well with EFT, providing for instant payment to vendors.

EDI Standards

Public EDI standards have been developed to facilitate the electronic exchange of business data between independent companies. Such standards provide a common architecture for data interchange while ensuring that individual companies can maintain their own proprietary formats for internal processing of data. Some companies have gone a step further and adopted EDI standards for internal use.

In the United States and Canada, the most commonly used standard is **American National Standards Institute (ANSI) Standard X.12.** Overseas, especially in Europe, the most popular EDI standard is **EDIFACT.** Furthermore, many industries have developed their own standards. The various standards and groups of standards are discussed individually.

Ansi X.12. At the most general level, an ANSI X.12 EDI message comprises **transaction sets,** the electronic equivalent of standard business documents. Examples of X.12 transaction sets are depicted in Figure 12.4. Each transaction set is made up of **segments,** groups of data elements such as name, date, and account number. Multiple transaction sets are typically sent in a single transmission, all of them packaged together inside a single electronic envelope called the **interchange-level envelope.** Inside the interchange-level envelope, transaction sets are stored in **functional groups.**

To illustrate how X.12 transaction sets work, we illustrate the application of transaction set 810 (the invoice transaction set). Consider the following data from Figure 12.5:

Date	8/01/99
Invoice #	12345
Order Date	7/15/99
Customer Order #	10088

Each of these items is a part of a header information segment of an invoice. This segment (containing the data elements date, invoice #, order date, and customer order #) would be coded as follows:

```
BIG*990801*12345*990715*10088 N/L
```

The "*" serves as a field terminator, and the code N/L as a line terminator. These are defined as such in the standards. The code BIG identifies the header segment. Examination shows that the example data appears in the line, with the dates placed into year–month–day format.

The invoice total amount due:

| Invoice Total | $5,487.25 |

would be coded as follows:

```
TDS*5487.25 N/L
```

Transaction Set	Description
810	Invoice
819	Operating expense statement
840	Request for quotation
850	Purchase order
860	Purchase order change request

FIGURE 12.4 Examples of ANSI X.12 Transaction Sets.

Invoice	Format for EDI
	ST*810*1234 N/L
Heading Data: Date 8/01/99 Invoice # 12345 Order Date 7/15/99 Customer Order # 10088	BIG*990801*12345*990715*10088 N/L
Ship To: Rabare Company Harvard Hollow Road Houston, TX 77077-0129	N1*ST*Rabare Company N/L N3*Harvard Hollow Road N/L N4*Houston, TX 77077-0129 N/L

Items Ordered:
50 quilted cotton towels
  #t25 5.00 each
25 normal silk towels
  #t45 80.50 each
25 quilted silk towels
  #t48 128.99 each
	IT1**50*EA*5.00*CN*t25*FD*quilted cotton towels N/L
	IT1**25*EA*80.50*CN*t45*FD*normal silk towels N/L
	IT1**25*EA*128.99*CN*t48*FD*quilted silk towels N/L

Invoice Total: $5,487.25	TDS*5487.25 N/L
	SE*1234 N/L

Illustration based on *American National Standard for Electronic Business Data Interchange—Invoice Transaction Set (810)*

FIGURE 12.5 Coding a Document for EDI.

The code TDS identifies the following field (5487.25) as the Total Monetary Value Summary, the total amount due per the invoice. Again, the "*" serves as a field terminator, and the code N/L as a line terminator. All other data segments on the invoice are coded in similar fashion using the ANSI X.12 EDI format for an invoice.

In general, there are many possible segments that can be used for particular transactions, and in practice, individual industries develop their own X.12-compatible standards by agreeing to use a particular subset of segment codes and ignore others.

Edifact. Under the auspices of the United Nations, **EDIFACT** was developed as an international standard for EDI. Although EDIFACT has been most strongly supported by the European Economic Community, it has also been used by Pacific Rim countries such as Japan and Australia.

EDIFACT is somewhat similar to ANSI X.12, although X.12 focuses more on business documents, and EDIFACT focuses more on transaction data. In any event, there is some indication that in the future, EDIFACT might incorporate X.12 as a subset, in effect merging the two standards together.

Other EDI Standards. Many of the additional EDI standards pertain to particular industries in the United States. For example, the chemical industry uses **CDIX,** the grocery and warehousing industries use **WINS/UCS,** and the electrical industry uses **EDIX.** Similarly, in Europe, specific industries also use their own standards, such as **ODETTE** in the automobile industry and **CEFIC** in the chemical industry. Many of the industry standards are particular applications of X.12 or EDIFACT.

Electronic Funds Transfer

Electronic funds transfer (EFT) is a large group of methods for sending informational messages that electronically effect economic exchanges. Overall, EFT is similar to EDI in that it mainly involves sending an electronic message from one place to another. EFT is also similar to EDI in that it is also heavily influenced by public messaging standards.

EFT Messaging Standards

Some of the major EFT message formats are shown in Figure 12.6. In practice, CCDPlus is probably the most widely recognized standard used among banks. But some banks also recognize CTX, making it possible for corporate EDI systems to communicate directly with their banks' systems.

First Interstate of Los Angeles is an example of a bank that accepts EDI instructions for payment. The retailer desiring to pay a supplier sends a request for payment to First Interstate in ANSI 820 format. The bank then converts the ANSI 820 payment message into a CTX message and sends it to the supplier's bank, possibly through a VAN. The supplier's bank can then send the supplier either an electronic or printed copy of the message.

In this example, two types of message exchanges take place (see Figure 12.7). The first message, the company's request for payment, is an example of a retail EFT message. The second message, the bank-to-bank transfer of funds, is an example of a wholesale EFT message. There is also a third type of EFT message exchange, the public or private message exchange. All three major types of EFT messages are summarized as follows:

FIGURE 12.6 EFT Message Formats.

EFT Message Standard	Description
Cash Concentration and Disbursement (CCD)	A messaging format used for transferring funds into a central account. Messages contain a maximum of 94 characters.
CCDPLUS	An enhanced version of CCD that packs more information into the 94-character message. This format is sponsored by the National Automated Clearing House Association (NACHA).
Corporate Trade Payment (CTP)	A messaging format capable of including over 5,000 lines of information in a single transaction (i.e., message). This format is used by Sears to pay its suppliers.
Corporate Trade Exchange (CTX)	A NACHA-supported messaging format that is compatible with ANSI 820, a format compatible with ANSI X.14 and capable of carrying detailed remittance-advice information such as purchase order numbers, product descriptions, and so on.

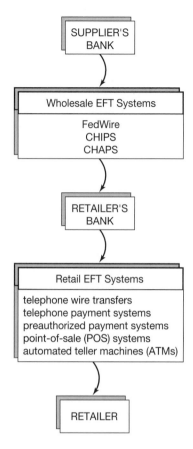

FIGURE 12.7 EFT Message Types.

EFT MESSAGE TYPE	MESSAGE PURPOSE
Wholesale EFT	For the immediate transfer of funds from one bank to another.
Retail EFT	For a company to send a request for payment to its bank.
Public and private message exchanges	For one bank to send instructions to another bank regarding the transfer of funds

Wholesale EFT Systems

The immediate transfer of funds from one financial institution to another is accomplished through **wholesale EFT.** This type of funds transfer is made between banks that have memberships (i.e., credit accounts) with some common central bank that acts as an **automated clearing house (ACH)** for EFT transactions. When one member bank wishes to send funds to another member bank, it sends a message to the central bank requesting that its account with the central bank be charged and that the other bank's account be credited. The central bank then forwards the message to the bank receiving the funds. The entire process typically takes 10 minutes or less.

Most U.S. banks use one or more of three clearing house systems for wholesale EFT: the Federal Reserve System (FedWire), the Clearing House Interbank Payment System (CHIPS), or the Clearing House Automated Payment System (CHAPS).

FedWire is used to transfer funds between members of the Federal Reserve System. One member bank sends funds to another member bank by sending a FedWire message to its district Federal Reserve Bank. The Federal Reserve then charges the account of the sending bank and credits the account of the receiving bank, and then automatically forwards the message to the receiving bank. All member banks must settle with the Federal Reserve at the end of each business day. Banks that receive more FedWire funds than they send in a given day are said to be in a net receiving position. On the other hand, banks that send more FedWire funds than they receive in a given day are said to be in a net paying position. Banks in a net paying position settle their account with the Federal Reserve by remitting funds. Those in a net receiving position settle their account by receiving funds from the Federal Reserve.

The FedWire message format allows the sending bank to include a customer account number. The receiving bank uses this account number as a basis for adding the incoming funds to the designated customer's account.

CHIPS is an ACH system used to transfer Eurodollar payments between U.S. and non-U.S. financial institutions. Its central clearing house is in New York. Many CHIPS participants, called **settling banks,** settle their accounts with CHIPS at the end of each day through their Federal Reserve accounts. Banks that do not settle through a Federal Reserve account are called **nonsettling banks.** Such banks settle their daily accounts with CHIPS through a bank that is a settling bank rather than through the Federal Reserve.

CHAPS is a clearing house system based in England. Settlements are effected through the Bank of England.

Retail EFT Systems

There are several ways in which companies and consumers may send EFT instructions to their banks. In a **telephone wire transfer,** the company (or consumer) places a telephone call to its bank, provides an appropriate identification number, and gives verbal instructions for an EFT payment. The bank charges the company's (or consumer's) account and then performs the EFT transaction through whatever means is convenient.

In a **telephone payment system,** commonly referred to as a **pay-by-phone system,** companies (or consumers) can call their bank and give verbal or computer instructions for making payments to particular merchants. A good example is Chase Manhattan's pay-by-phone service, in which bank customers make telephone calls to the bank and provide information for payees (e.g., payee name, account number, and payee address). The bank then sends a letter to the payee verifying the account information. When this process is complete, the bank customer thereafter can call the bank anytime (either by voice or by computer), give a prearranged password and payee code, and instruct the bank to pay an amount due to the payee. The bank will then make an EFT payment to the payee on the customer's behalf, or if this is not possible, send the payee a check through the mail with a memorandum requesting that the customer's account be credited.

In a **preauthorized payment** system, the bank customer gives the bank standing instructions for automatically making recurring payments. The bank then makes the payments in the same manner as that of pay-by-phone systems. Many pay-by-phone systems allow their customers to make preauthorized payments.

In a **POS system,** the company typically scans the customer's debit or credit card and receives immediate authorization for the sale. The company's bank account is credited the next business day after the sale.

ATMs are similar to POS systems. They work with both debit and credit cards and allow customers to make deposits, withdrawals, balance inquiries, transfers, and cash advances. Many ATMs are linked together in national or international packet-switched networks. Customers can make cash withdrawals at any ATM in the network. Transactions typically take effect the next business day.

Public and Private Message Exchanges

Some message systems are directed toward sending instructions to effect the transfer of funds. The transfer of funds typically does not take place simultaneously with the message's transmission. In many cases, a private bank is used as a clearing house. These types of systems are called **public and private message exchanges (PPMEs).**

Telex and SWIFT (Society for Worldwide Interbank Financial Telecommunication) are PPMEs. **Telex** is a very old system for the worldwide sending of hard-copy messages, and is sometimes used by smaller banks that cannot afford more expensive systems. The problem with this method is that authenticating messages involves a complex and time-consuming process.

SWIFT is often used by U.S. banks to effect overseas transfers. Assume, for example, that a company in Geneva, Switzerland, wants to send an EFT to a company in Pittsburgh, Pennsylvania. Assume that both companies have accounts in the XYZ bank in New York City. The sending bank would send a SWIFT message to the Pittsburgh bank through the XYZ bank in New York City, which would act as a clearing house. SWIFT can also interface with FedWire.

Digital Signatures

Data encryption is used to provide secrecy and security in electronic communication. Authentication builds on encryption methods. The purpose of authentication is not secrecy, however. It is to ensure that data such as bank account numbers, dollar amounts, or order quantities are not altered during transmission or storage.

Digital signatures can be used to provide authentication of electronic communications. A **digital signature** is a string of bits attached to an electronic document. The electronic document might be a spreadsheet or word processing file, an e-mail message, or an EDI transaction. This bit string is generated by the signer, and it is based on both the document's data and the signer's secret password. Someone who receives the document can prove to himself or herself that the signer actually signed the document. If the document is altered, the signer also can prove that he or she did not sign the altered document.

Public-key encryption can be used for digital signatures. Public-key encryption uses two different keys: a public key that everyone knows, and a private key that only one person knows. In practical implementations, public-key encryption is too inefficient to sign long messages directly. Instead, special cryptographic hashing algorithms are used to develop a hash value of the message—a one-way value analogous to a checksum. The hash value compactly represents the message and is used to detect changes in the message—much like a conventional hash control total over a set of transaction data. The sender digitally signs the hash of the document rather than the message itself.

Encryption and digital signatures can be combined to provide both privacy and authentication. A message is first signed with one's private key, and then the signed message is encrypted with the recipient's public key. The recipient reverses this procedure. First, the recipient decrypts the message with his or her private key, and then verifies the enclosed signature with the sender's public key.

SUMMARY

A distributed computing system is a network of computers connected such that it appears to be a single computer to the individual user. In distributed systems, files can be conveniently stored in the locations most adaptable to the company's organizational structure, thus minimizing communication costs and geographically diversifying the responsibilities of file maintenance. There are three computer architectures for distributing data in a network. These include the centralized nondistributed architecture, the client–server distributed architecture, and the peer-to-peer distributed architecture. Distributed processing technologies make it possible to distribute both data resources and processing power.

Electronic data interchange (EDI) is the direct computer-to-computer exchange of business documents. Public EDI standards have been developed to facilitate the electronic exchange of business data between independent companies. Such standards provide a common architecture for data interchange while ensuring that individual companies can maintain their own proprietary formats for internal processing of data. Electronic funds transfer (EFT) includes a large group of methods for sending informational messages that electronically effect economic exchanges. Overall, EFT is similar to EDI in that it mainly involves sending an electronic message from one place to another. EFT is also similar to EDI in that it is also heavily influenced by public messaging standards. Digital signatures can be used to provide authentication of electronic communications. Public-key encryption can be used for digital signatures.

Glossary

ACH: acronym for automated clearing house.

ANSI X.12: the American National Standards Institute (ANSI) standard for EDI.

atomic transactions: transactions that require record locking as they must be completed in their entirety.

Cash concentration and disbursement (CCD): An EFT message format used for transferring funds into a central account. Messages contain a maximum of 94 characters.

CCDPlus: An enhanced version of the CCD EFT message format that packs more information into the 94-character message. This format is sponsored by the National Automated Clearing House Association (NACHA).

Clearing House Automated Payment System (CHAPS): a wholesale EFT system based in England.

Clearing House Interbank Payment System (CHIPS): a wholesale EFT system used to transfer Eurodollar payments between U.S. and non-U.S. financial institutions. Its central clearing house is in New York.

client: a computer that accesses data and programs located on network servers.

client–server network processing architecture: various application programs in the network fulfill either one of two roles: client or server.

cooperative processing: form of peer-to-peer processing, similar to synchronized policy processing, except that policies are maintained only on the server, unless a shadow policy is in effect.

corporate trade exchange (CTX): A NACHA-supported EFT message format compatible with ANSI 820, a format compatible with ANSI X.14 and capable of carrying detailed remittance-advice information such as purchase order numbers, product descriptions, and so on.

corporate trade payment (CTP): an EFT message format capable of including over 5,000 lines of information in a single transaction (i.e., message). This format is used by Sears to pay its suppliers.

database derivation policies: describe how some data fields or values are automatically calculated from other data fields or values.

database integrity policies: protect data from corruption by limiting updates to acceptable values.

database security policies: restrict access to authorized users and for authorized purposes.

database trigger policies: initiate processing when data values fall within preplanned ranges.

DBMS server environment: the user task and database policies reside on the client, and the DBMS and database reside on the server.

digital signature: a string of bits attached to an electronic document.

distributed computing system: a network of computers connected in such a way that it appears to be a single computer to the individual user.

distributed database: any database that is globally accessible throughout the network through some method such as remote procedure calls.

distributed data processing (DDP): refers to data processing in a distributed information system.

distributed file system: a portion of or extension to an operating system that controls naming services in a network.

distributed information system (DIS): distributed computing systems in which the databases exist in servers.

distributed operating system: one unified operating system is distributed in pieces over all computers in a network.

EDIFACT: an international standard for EDI developed under the auspices of the United Nations.

electronic data interchange (EDI): the direct computer-to-computer exchange of business documents.

electronic funds transfer (EFT): methods that are either wholly or in large part electronic and are used to send messages (including money and information transfers) that effect economic exchanges.

FedWire: a wholesale EFT system used to transfer funds between members of the Federal Reserve system.

file–server environment: the DBMS, user task, database policies, and all processing capabilities reside on the client, and the database resides on the server.

fragmentation: method of distributing a database that involves maintaining a directory of databases, their data items, and locations.

interchange-level envelope: in ANSI X.12, an electronic envelope, which may contain multiple transaction sets, used in transmission.

interprocess communication: the exchange of information between clients, servers, and application programs in distributed systems.

location transparency: synonymous with network transparency.

loosely coupled systems: systems in which computers communicate through communications.

multicasting: sending messages only to a predetermined subset of nodes in the network.

name server: a specialized server that maintains a centrally located directory of files and/or data.

network operating system: each computer in a network runs its own copy of an operating system that supports communications with other computers in the network.

network transparency: all data and files in a network, regardless of their location, appear to reside in the user's computer.

nondistributed network processing architecture: communications between computers may take place, but without network transparency and without interprocess communication.

Open System Interconnection (OSI) standard X.500: a standard for naming services (applications of name-server technology) in networks.

OSI X.400 e-mail protocol: a widely accepted protocol for the transfer of mail messages, text files, binary files, and graphics.

pay-by-phone system: synonymous with telephone payment system.

peer-to-peer environment: related versions of a common application program run on both the client and server computers. The database program and the policies reside on the server.

preauthorized payment: retail EFT system where a bank customer gives the bank standing instructions for automatically making recurring payments.

process: an executing program that communicates with one or more other concurrently executing programs.

public and private message exchanges (PPMEs): message systems directed toward sending instructions to effect the transfer of funds. The transfer of funds typically does not take place simultaneously with the message's transmission.

remote procedure call: allows a program on one computer to perform queries and updates for a database server elsewhere in the network.

replicated database: one that maintains replicated copies.

repository–server environment: the server contains the DBMS, database policies, and the database, and the client contains the user application.

segments: groups of data elements such as name, date, and account number used in ANSI X.12 transaction sets.

server: a constantly running computer program and related database that provides one or more software or data services to other computers in a network.

shadow policies: copies of the server's database policies in a repository–server environment that are possessed by clients.

Society for Worldwide Interbank Financial Telecommunication (SWIFT): A PPME system used by U.S. banks to effect overseas transfer.

synchronized policy processing: form of peer-to-peer processing where the server transmits its policies via messages to the client, thus assuring a synchronization of policies between the client and server.

telephone payment system: retail EFT system where companies or consumers can call their bank and give verbal or computer instructions for making payments to particular merchants.

telephone wire transfer: retail EFT system where a company or consumer places a telephone call to its bank, provides an appropriate identification number, and gives verbal instructions for an EFT payment.

telex: A PPME system for the worldwide sending of hard-copy messages.

tightly coupled systems: network systems in which computers communicate through distributed shared memory.

transaction sets: the electronic equivalent of standard business documents utilized in ANSI X.12.

two-phase commit: updating procedure where the client first updates a record and then sends a copy of the updated information back to the server, which in turns applies it to the database.

wholesale EFT: funds transfer between banks that have memberships (i.e., credit accounts) with a common central bank that acts as an automated clearing house (ACH) for EFT transactions.

Chapter Quiz

Answers to the chapter quiz appear on page 498.

1. A (_____) is a constantly running computer program and related database that provides one or more software or data services to other computers in a network.
   (a) client
   (b) repository
   (c) server
   (d) peer

2. Open System Interconnection (OSI) standard X.500 is concerned with
   (a) naming services.
   (b) EFT.
   (c) EDI.
   (d) database security.

3. Systems in which the computers communicate through distributed shared memory are called (_____).
   (a) tightly coupled systems
   (b) loosely coupled systems
   (c) networked systems
   (d) telexed systems

4. Which of the following types of database policies protect data from corruption by limiting updates to acceptable values?
   (a) security policies
   (b) integrity policies

    (c) trigger policies

    (d) derivation policies

5. Which of the following types of database policies initiate processing when data values fall within preplanned ranges?

    (a) security policies

    (b) integrity policies

    (c) trigger policies

    (d) derivation policies

6. Which of the following have developed and published national standards for electronic data interchange (EDI)?

    (a) AICPA

    (b) ANSI

    (c) both a and b

    (d) neither a nor b

7. Which of the following methods might be used for electronic data interchange (EDI)?

    (a) a value-added network (VAN) service

    (b) direct company-to-company communication

    (c) both a and b

    (d) neither a nor b

8. Which of the following is a potential benefit of using electronic data interchange (EDI) to place orders with vendors?

    (a) increased speed of data communications

    (b) reduced clerical and administrative costs

    (c) both a and b

    (d) neither a nor b

9. Which of the following acronyms identifies a wholesale EFT system based in England?

    (a) CHIPS

    (b) CTP

    (c) CTX

    (d) CHAPS

10. Which of the following is a wholesale EFT system?

    (a) CCD

    (b) ATM

    (c) CTX

    (d) FedWire

Review Problem

Identify each of the items listed as belonging to one of the following categories of electronic funds transfer (EFT) messages:

    (a) wholesale EFT

    (b) retail EFT

    (c) public and private message exchange

___ automated teller machines (ATMs)

___ CHAPS

___ CHIPS

___ FedWire

___ point-of-sale (POS) systems

___ preauthorized payment systems

___ telephone payment systems

___ telephone wire transfer

___ SWIFT

___ telex

Solution to Review Problem

_b_ automated teller machines (ATMs)
_a_ CHAPS
_a_ CHIPS
_a_ FedWire
_b_ point-of-sale (POS) systems
_b_ preauthorized payment systems
_b_ telephone payment systems
_b_ telephone wire transfer
_c_ SWIFT
_c_ telex

Review Questions

1. Describe the concept of network transparency.
2. Distinguish between a distributed computing system and a computer network. Are they always the same?
3. Characterize the function of a name server.
4. Distinguish between "loosely coupled systems" and "tightly coupled systems" for intercomputer communication.
5. Describe each of the following architectures for distributing data in a network:
   (a) centralized nondistributed
   (b) client-server
   (c) peer-to-peer
6. Distinguish between the following types of servers:
   (a) file servers
   (b) DBMS servers
   (c) repository servers
7. Identify and describe four different types of database policies.
8. What is a replicated database?
9. How are concurrency issues typically handled in a database?
10. What are the potential benefits of using electronic data interchange (EDI)?
11. What steps are necessary to implement electronic data interchange (EDI)?
12. Identify several standards for electronic data interchange (EDI). Which is the most common in the United States?
13. Identify several messaging standards for electronic funds transfer (EFT).
14. Distinguish between wholesale and retail EFT systems. Given an example of each.

Discussion Questions and Problems

15. The Molly Company uses electronic funds transfer (EFT) in its cash disbursements functions. EFT is used to pay vendors.

    Required
    (a) Explain how a company might use EFT in its cash disbursements functions.
    (b) What advantages does a company gain by using EFT in its cash disbursements functions?

16. Executives of Molly Company have recently had some discussions concerning electronic data interchange (EDI). The president attended a presentation on EDI at a trade show in Pittsburgh, and wants to explore using EDI in the company's purchasing operations.

Even though the company uses computer processing, it seems that processing purchase orders is expensive and error-prone. The president is confident that the company's success with its use of electronic funds transfer (EFT) for vendor payments can be enhanced with EDI.

Required
(a) What steps does a company have to take to use EDI in its purchasing operations?
(b) What advantages does a company gain by using EDI in its purchasing operations?
(c) What options are available to send and receive EDI documents to vendors?

17. Multiple users access the same records in a database management system (DBMS). Consider the following sequence of events pertaining to two users, A and B, who are updating a record in the DBMS pertaining to customer X.

2:00 P.M.	Customer X's record shows a balance due of $200.
2:05 P.M.	User A, a clerk in the accounts receivable department, uses a data terminal to access customer X's record. After retrieving the record, user A must answer a telephone call.
2:07 P.M.	User B, a clerk in the accounts payable department, uses a data terminal to access customer X's record. User B posts a payment of $150 to customer X's record.
2:09 P.M.	User B returns customer X's record to the DBMS, causing it to be updated.
2:11 P.M.	User A, finished with her phone call, posts a new sale-on-account of $150 to customer X's record.
2:13 P.M.	User A returns customer X's record to the DBMS, causing it to be updated.

Required
(a) What is the ending balance of customer X's record? What should it be?
(b) How can concurrency problems such as just given be prevented?

18. The objectives of database technology—data shareability and nonredundancy of stored data—open the door for concurrency problems. Multiple users access the same records in a database management system (DBMS). Database administration should coordinate data sharing by proper use of locking mechanisms provided by the DBMS, with the goal of ascertaining that at all times any one user sees the database in a consistent state, and not in a possible temporarily inconsistent state that may be brought on by other concurrent processing not properly coordinated or locked.

Locking, however, can create its own problems. Consider the following sequence of events pertaining to three users, A, B, and C, who wish to access records in a DBMS.

2:00 P.M.	User A, a clerk in the sales department, uses a data terminal to access product X's record. User A is talking to customer D on the telephone. Customer D is considering a purchase of product X. To prevent the quantity-on-hand field from being altered during the processing of this transaction, user A places a lock on the product X record, preventing its access by anybody else.
2:02 P.M.	User B, a clerk in the purchasing department, is processing a purchase requisition for product X. User B uses a data terminal to attempt to access product X's record. User B receives a notice that the record is locked and currently unavailable. User B decides to wait for the record to be unlocked, as this is a rush order.
2:04 P.M.	User C, a clerk in the accounts payable department, uses a data terminal to access customer D's record. User C plans to post a sales return to customer D's account. To prevent the balance-due field from being altered during the processing of this transaction, user C places a lock on customer D's accounts receivable record, preventing its access by anybody else. The sales return involves product X. In order to determine the amount of the credit, user C must access the product X record in the database. User C uses a data terminal to attempt to access product X's record.

User *C* receives a notice that the record is locked and currently unavailable. User *C* decides to wait for the record to be unlocked.

2:06 P.M.   User *A* has sold some product *X* to customer *D*. In order to process the sale, user *A* uses a data terminal to access customer *D*'s accounts receivable record. User *A* receives a notice that the record is locked and currently unavailable. User *A* decides to wait for the record to be unlocked, as this is a big sales order.

4:50 P.M.   Users *A, B,* and *C* finally stop waiting, and log off the DBMS after a very unproductive day.

Required

(a) Explain what happened to users *A, B,* and *C.* Why were they unable to proceed with their processing?

(b) How can concurrency problems such as just given be prevented?

19. Code the following invoices into the ANSI X.12 EDI format illustrated in the chapter discussion and Figure 12.5. Additional coding information is as follows:

```
N2
```

Identifies an additional (second) name. (Not used in Figure 12.5.)

```
ST*810*1234
```

ST is the code for a transaction set header. 810 is the transaction set. 1234 is the transaction number (user-assigned).

```
IT1**50*EA*5.00
```

IT1 is the code for a baseline item data. This would be a line item in an invoice. Double asterisks indicate a skipped field (not used); subsequent fields are

- quantity (50)
- unit (EA, each; DZ, dozen; CAS, case)
- unit price (5.00)

```
CN*t25
```

CN indicates that the following item is a line item product code number (t25).

```
FD
```

FD indicates the following as descriptive data (quilted cotton towels).

```
SE*1234
```

SE is the code for a transaction set trailer. 1234 is the transaction number.

INVOICE				
Date 8/21/99				
Order Date 8/15/99		Invoice #66345		
Customer Order # 10058				
<u>Ship To:</u>				
Smith Company				
125 Main Street				
San Antonio, TX 76904				
Quantity	Unit	Product Code	Description	Price
50	case	BB004	large bolt	75.00
50	dozen	BB003	small bolt	1.45
			Invoice Total:	$3,822.50

INVOICE				
Date 8/24/99				
Order Date 8/12/99		Invoice #20767		
Customer Order # 32311				
<u>Ship To:</u>				
Tom Murphy				
The Duck Farm				
Route 9-W				
Lewisburg, PA 18019				
Quantity	Unit	Product Code	Description	Price
100	each	25021	duck food	11.00
10	dozen	30100	duck toys	5.50
			Invoice Total:	$1,155.00

```
┌─────────────────────────────────────────────────────┐
│                      INVOICE                        │
│  Date 8/31/99                                       │
│  Order Date 8/25/99              Invoice #10098     │
│  Customer Order # 10022                             │
│  Ship To:                                           │
│  Fred's Hats                                        │
│  2213 Sky Plaza                                     │
│  Philadelphia, PA 19019                             │
│                                                     │
│  Quantity   Unit   Product Code   Description  Price│
│  ─────────────────────────────────────────────────  │
│    150      each     50514        pirate hat   2.25 │
│     50      each     50524        sailor hat   3.45 │
│     10      case     BB004        mixed hats  25.22 │
│                          Invoice Total: $1,003.70   │
└─────────────────────────────────────────────────────┘
```

20. Vincent Malloy, director of special projects and analysis for Milok Company, is responsible for preparing corporate financial analyses and projections monthly and for reviewing and presenting to upper management the financial impacts of proposed strategies. Data for these financial analyses and projections are obtained from reports developed by Milok's systems department and generated from its mainframe computer. Additional data are obtained through terminals via a data inquiry system. Reports and charts for presentation are then prepared by hand and typed. Malloy has tried to have final presentations generated by the computer but has not always been successful.

   The systems department has developed a package utilizing a terminal emulator to link a personal computer to the mainframe computer. This allows the personal computer to become part of the current data inquiry system and enables data to be downloaded to the personal computer's disk. The data are in a format that allows printing or further manipulation and analyses using commercial software packages, for example, spreadsheet analysis. The special projects and analysis department has been chosen to be the first users of this new computer terminal system.

   Malloy questioned whether the new system could do more for his department than implementing the program modification requests that he has submitted to the systems department. He also believed that his people would have to become programmers.

   Lisa Brandt, a supervisor in Malloy's department, has decided to prepare a briefing for Malloy on the benefits of integrating personal computers with the mainframe computer. She has used the terminal inquiry system extensively and has learned to use spreadsheet software to prepare special analyses, sometimes with multiple alternatives. She also tried the new package while it was being tested.

   Required
   (a) Identify five enhancements to current information and reporting that Milok should be able to realize by integrating personal computers with the company's mainframe computer.
   (b) Explain how the utilization of computer resources would be altered as a result of integrating personal computers with the company's mainframe computer.
   (c) Discuss what security of the data is gained or lost by integrating personal computers with the company's mainframe computer.

   (CMA)

21. Generic Nutrition Company is a regional distributor of health foods, vitamins, and exercise equipment. The company operates several hundred retail stores, most of which are located in suburban shopping malls. To increase operating profitability with high inventory turnover ratios, Generic Nutrition tries to maintain minimum inventory stock in its retail stores. This necessitates frequent deliveries of stock to each retail store from one of the nine large warehouses the company operates. The nine ware-

houses also attempt to maintain minimum inventory stock. This necessitates careful monitoring of stock levels and frequent ordering from the firm's several hundred vendors. Much of the company's success in implementing its just-in-time purchasing system is due to its on-line computer system, which allows detailed monitoring of stock levels in the warehouses, automatic generation of purchase orders when stocks fall below predetermined reorder points, and quick processing of vendor's invoices.

Andrew Wyatt, controller of Generic Nutrition, is aware of the positive effect that smooth, uninterrupted operation of the on-line computer system has on the firm's profitability. It is because of this that he is somewhat concerned that Bill Katz, manager of computer operations, has decided to purchase a database management system for the company's computer system. Andrew met with Bill Katz to express his concern.

"Bill, I hope you've thoroughly thought through this purchase of a database management system. You know that the smooth, uninterrupted operation of our systems for inventory control and vendor processing is absolutely essential to our continued profitability. I realize that database management systems are supposed to have a lot of advantages over independent-file types of systems like the one we have now, but I'm not absolutely sure this will be the case in our type of operation.

"We enter a large number of transactions into these systems each and every day. Data terminals at each of our nine warehouses are constantly inputting data on deliveries and orders of merchandise, and terminals here at our central office are always busy entering vendor-related data to monitor orders and payments. What we have is a situation where ten different sources are entering vendor-related data at the same time. It is quite possible that one source is entering a delivery-received transaction from a particular vendor at the same time another source is entering an order to the same vendor. The delivery would decrease the quantity we have on order from the vendor, and the order would increase the quantity we have on order from the vendor. In our present independent-file system, each of these different transactions to the same vendor is posted to a different file, and the total effect is determined in a subsequent processing run of file activity. But as I understand it, in a database management system, there would only be one large file, the database, and each of these different transactions would update the same vendor data element. Doesn't this create the possibility of incorrectly recording such transactions? If this is indeed the case, then perhaps Generic Nutrition would be better off without a database management system."

Required

Consider a database environment with several users sharing the same physical database, such as discussed by Andrew Wyatt in the case of Generic Nutrition Company. What types of problems might arise in having two or more different users sharing and updating the same data element?

22. Imtex Corporation is a multinational company with approximately 100 subsidiaries and divisions, referred to as reporting units. Each reporting unit operates autonomously and maintains its own accounting information system. Each month, the reporting units prepare the basic financial statements and other key financial data on prescribed forms. These statements and related data are either mailed or telexed to corporate headquarters in New York City for entry into the corporate database. Top and middle management at corporate headquarters utilize the database to plan and direct corporate operations and objectives.

Under the current system, the statements and data are to be received at corporate headquarters by the twelfth working day following the end of the month. The reports are logged, batched, and taken to the data processing department for coding and entry into the database. Approximately 15% of the reporting units are delinquent in submitting their data, and three to four days are required to receive all of the data. After the data are loaded into the system, data verification programs are run to check footings, cross statement consistency, and dollar range limits. Any errors in the data are traced and corrected, and reporting units are notified of all errors by form letters.

Imtex has decided to upgrade its computer communication network. The new system would allow data to be received on a more timely basis at corporate headquarters and provide numerous benefits to each of the reporting units.

The systems department at corporate headquarters is responsible for the overall design and implementation of the new system. The systems department will utilize current computer communications technology by installing smart computer terminals at all reporting units. These terminals will provide two-way computer communications, and also serve as microcomputers that can utilize spreadsheet and other applications software. As part of the initial use of the system, the data collection for the corporate database would be performed by using these terminals.

The financial statements and other financial data currently mailed or telexed would be entered by terminals. The required forms initially would be transmitted (downloaded) from the headquarter's computer to the terminals of each reporting unit and stored permanently on disk. Data would be entered on the forms appearing on the reporting unit's terminal and stored under a separate file for transmission after the data are checked.

The data edit program would also be downloaded to the reporting units so the data could be verified at the unit location. All corrections would be made before transmitting the data to headquarters. The data would be stored on disk in proper format to maintain a unit file. Data would either be transmitted to corporate headquarters immediately or retrieved by the computer at corporate headquarters as needed. Therefore, data arriving at corporate headquarters would be free from errors and ready to be used in reports.

Charles Edwards, Imtex's controller, is very pleased with the prospects of the new system. He believes data will be received from the reporting units two to three days faster, and that the accuracy of the data will be much improved. However, Edwards is concerned about data security and integrity during the transmission of data between the reporting units and corporate headquarters. He has scheduled a meeting with key personnel from the systems department to discuss these concerns.

Required

Imtex could experience data security and integrity problems when transmitting data between the reporting units and corporate headquarters.
(a) Identify and explain the data security and integrity problems that could occur.
(b) For each problem identified, identify and explain a control procedure that could be employed to minimize or eliminate the problem.

Use the following format to present your answer.

Problem Identification and Explanation	*Control Procedure and Explanation*

(CMA)

Answers to Chapter Quiz

1. C	4. B	7. C	10. D
2. A	5. C	8. C	
3. A	6. B	9. D	

CHAPTER 13

Electronic Data Processing Systems

LEARNING OBJECTIVES

Careful study of this chapter will enable you to:

■ Describe how application controls are used in data processing systems to ensure accuracy and integrity. *input complete updates to m correct*

■ Characterize the various types of electronic systems used for transaction processing.

■ Describe the basic functions and operation of a computerized accounting application.

THE INPUT SYSTEM

Paper-Based Input Systems

In some computerized accounting systems, inputs to the accounting system are based on handwritten or typed source documents. These documents are then collected and forwarded to computer operations for error checking and processing. Each phase of input processing is discussed in what follows.

Preparation and Completion of the Source Document

The source documents, such as sales orders, are filled in manually. Errors at this stage can be minimized if the source document is well designed and easy to understand. Ideally, boxes should be provided to guide the user in placing characters in the correct places. Once the source documents are completed, they are periodically collected and transferred to the data processing department for entry into the computer system.

Transfer of Source Documents to Data Processing

Batch control totals and data transfer registers are fundamental controls over data transfer between user departments and data processing. The absence or inadequacy of procedures for the control of data transmitted between user departments and the data processing department could represent a significant weakness because it presents an opportunity for unauthorized and/or fraudulent transactions to be introduced into the processing system.

The use of batch control over the entire data processing input–process–output sequence is fundamental to organizational independence. Proof and control functions should be performed outside the data entry department. Original source documents should be retained for a period of time sufficient to facilitate error correction. Procedures should be designed to ensure that source documents are not processed more than once. Control practices such as the use of prenumbered forms, supervision, and approval apply to EDP applications as well as others.

Submission of input data should be accompanied by the completion of an **input document control form** similar to the one shown in Figure 13.1. Document counts are a simple form of batch control. In addition to document and/or record counts, batch totals may be taken for all or several numeric fields in the original data file. These totals may be used throughout the data processing cycle to monitor the completeness of processing.

The data entry group should not accept data unless an input document control form is present to evidence and reference the transfer of these data. The input document control form may be dated and time-stamped and the batch should be checked to ensure that it is complete and consistent with control procedures. Information in the input document control form is typically entered in a **data transfer log** (register) to provide a control over the disposition and use of these data. Batch control totals are fundamental to this process.

Figure 13.2 illustrates the development and use of batch control totals in a data processing application. User departments develop control totals over batches of input, and then forward the batches of documents along with an input document control form to the data processing department. The input document control form is logged in the data processing department, and then balanced to the output control totals that are developed during the processing of the batch of input. The output is returned to the user department, where it is batch balanced to the batch totals on the input document control form.

FIGURE 13.1 Input Document Control Form.

[Prenumbered]
150

Batch Control Form

Originating Department ______________

Date ______________

Preparer's Signature ______________

Control Totals

Batch Number |_|_|_|_|_|_|

Number of Documents |_|_|_|

Field Totals (list):

Field Number	***Name***	***Total***

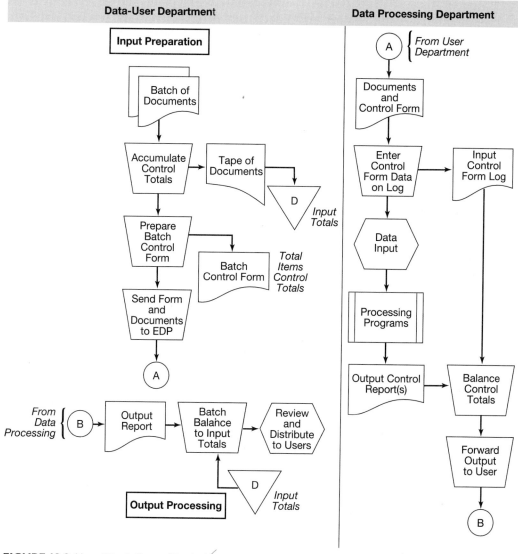

FIGURE 13.2 Use of Batch Control Totals.

Data Entry

After the source documents such as invoices are received by data processing, they are manually key-transcribed or keyed (i.e., typed) using a data terminal or personal computer, and then stored on disk. Next, the input file is key-verified. **Key verification** is a control procedure that detects errors in the keying operation. An error might occur, for example, when a customer account number is mistyped because the data entry clerk presses the wrong key or misinterprets a character on a source document. In key verification, each source document is key-transcribed a second time. The key-verification software compares the retranscribed data as they are being entered, key by key, to the input data already on the disk file. If these are the same, nothing happens and the operator proceeds with the next character of data. In the case of a mismatch, the operator is notified and may then correct the error. To reduce the costs associated with key-verifying input data, nonessential fields, such as a customer's name and street address (as opposed to account number or zip code), are often not verified. A second but less effective way to detect data entry error is **visual verification.** With this approach, someone compares the source documents to a printout of the key-transcribed file.

Program Data Editing

Verification does not edit data, so it is essential that data be thoroughly edited after entry to ensure valid content. **Program data editing** is a software technique used to screen data for errors prior to processing. It should be used in addition to verification for several reasons. First, input errors can occur that will pass verification. Incorrect recognition of a character on a source document is one possibility; another is the simple omission of a necessary input item by the individual preparing the source document. As this second example illustrates, data editing at the programming level is a control over the initial verification function. Last, the volume of data in EDP operations, coupled with the fact that once data are entered in the system they may be used without reconversion, necessitates a methodological screening of all input data.

Program Data Editing Techniques.   Data editing routines may be applied to each of the basic data structures: characters, fields, records, and files. The most basic editing technique ensures that all data fields contain only valid characters. For example, numeric data items should contain only digits and alphabetic data items should not contain any digits.

After data items have been edited at the character level, they can be checked for reasonableness. One way to edit for reasonableness is to establish a table file that contains a list of acceptable values for each field. The edit program then compares the actual value of each field to the acceptable values in the table. This is called a **table lookup.** For example, an actual value of the customer account field might be compared to a master list of customer account numbers stored in a table.

Numeric data values, as opposed to numeric codes, should in general fall within certain ranges; thus, checking numeric data as being within certain limits requires a check only against extreme values of the range. This is called a **limit test.** For example, the field payroll hours may typically not be less than zero or more than, say, 100 for a two-week pay period. Sales in a certain department generally should be within a range of zero to some upper limit based on historical data.

It is possible to edit numeric data with respect to being outside acceptable ranges; in such cases, the data are rejected. At times, it may be desirable to discriminate further among acceptable items as well. For example, a payroll field may contain a value that is acceptable but so high or low as to warrant investigation. This item may be accepted for processing but flagged for subsequent audit. Alternatively, such items may be held in suspense of processing until the data are reverified. The use of programmed edit tests to discriminate among acceptable data so that some items are either held in suspense of processing until audited or collected for audit after processing is called **continuous operations auditing.**

√ Numeric codes can be verified by using a check digit. A **check digit** is an extra, redundant digit added to a code number much as a parity bit is added to a byte. The check digit is computed when a code is initially assigned to a data element. Check digits are computed by applying mathematical calculations to the individual digits in a code number in such a way as to generate a result that is a single digit. This digit becomes the check digit and is added to the original code. In subsequent processing, this same mathematical operation can be performed to ensure that the code has not been incorrectly recorded.

There are numerous check digit procedures. The following illustration is one version of a technique known as Modulus 11:

Account Number	*1*	*2*	*4*	*0*
Multiply each digit separately by the corresponding digit in the sequence . . . 5 4 3 2:	× 5	× 4	× 3	× 2
Add results of digit multiplication digit by digit:	$5 + 8 + (1 + 2) + 0 = 16$			
Subtract results from the next highest multiple of 11:	$22 - 16 = 6$			
Check digit = 6				
Complete Account Number:	1 2 4 0 6			

The use of check digits is very common because of the high reliability of this procedure. Commercial check digit packages catch 100% of transposition errors and a very high percentage of random errors. No control system is perfect, and checks digits do not guard against all input errors.

Data Editing Terminology. The data edits just discussed, as well as several other types of data edits, are illustrated with examples in Table 13.1. The terminology illustrated in the table is typical, but there are many terms used to describe the same type of data edit. A **valid code check,** for example, is a particular type of table lookup in which the table file consists of valid codes. Other authors use terms such as *validity check* or *existence check* in describing the same type of data edit.

Paperless Input Systems

In **paperless input systems,** sometimes called **on-line input systems,** transactions are input directly into the computer network, and the need for keying in source documents is eliminated. Paperless systems therefore provide a higher degree of automation than do paper-based systems. Still, there are various degrees of automation in different paper-based systems. On one hand, for example, users might initiate purchase transactions by manually keying them into the computer. On the other hand, the computer might automatically originate these transactions and then process them with no human intervention. Alternatively, an EDI purchase order originating from a vendor's computer might be automatically received and processed with no human intervention.

One problem with paperless systems is the possible loss of segregation of duties and audit trail. In paper-based input systems, source document preparation and data entry are normally segregated, as they are in a manual system. In paperless input systems, however, these functions are performed by the same person. Therefore, the concentration of functions in paperless data entry eliminates controls associated with a segregation of duties. These controls—review and batch control of source documents and controls related to source document preparation, such as prenumbering, authorization, and review—are important to the integrity of the audit trail and must be compensated for in paperless systems.

The loss of paper-based internal controls can be compensated for by using transaction logs. **Transaction logs** or **transaction registers** are created by logging

TABLE 13.1 Data Edit Illustration

Data Edit	Description	Example
Completeness check	Check that entries exist in fields that cannot be processed blank.	Each field in a record is checked to assure the presence of data.
Field format check	Check that each character in a field is in proper mode (e.g., alpha or numeric).	Each character of a vendor number field is checked to assure it is numeric.
Field length check	Check the entry in a field for a specific number of characters.	A date field in a month–day–year format is checked that it contains six digits.
Field sign check	Check the sign (positive/negative) of a numeric field for the correct value.	The amount due field of a bill is checked that the sign is positive.
Limit check	The value of a numeric field is checked against a predetermined upper and/or lower limit.	The value of the hours worked field in a time card record is checked that it does not exceed a predetermined limit of 60 hours.
Reasonableness check	The value of a numeric field is compared to another numeric field in the same record.	Overhead costs in a work-in-process record are checked that they do not exceed 200% of the labor cost field.
Valid code check	Match the value of a code to a table file of acceptable code values.	A vendor code field is validated by matching it to a table file of valid vendor codes.
Check digit	Validate a numeric code through the use of a check digit algorithm.	A point-of-sale system validates a credit card by recomputing the check digit in the customer's account number.
Combination field check	The value of one field is compared or related to another field to establish validity.	A transaction code field is compared to a department code field. Certain transaction codes are only valid for certain departments.
Internal label check	An internal file label is read to validate the characteristics of a file.	The file code on an internal label is checked by a payroll program to assure that it is the payroll file.
Sequence check	A field in a series of records is checked for ascending or descending sequence.	The sequence of invoice numbers is verified as the invoice file is processed.
Record count check	The number of records in a file is counted during processing and balanced to input controls.	The record count of time cards processed is balanced to input totals from the payroll department.
Hash total check	The hash total of a field in a file is computed during processing and balanced to input controls.	The hash total of employee numbers is computed during processing and balanced to input controls from the payroll department.
Financial total check	The financial total of a field in a file is computed during processing and balanced to input controls.	The total dollar amount of invoices processed is computed and balanced to a total from the billing department.

all inputs to a special file that automatically contains tags to identify transactions. **Tagging** means that additional, audit-oriented information is included with original transaction data. Such information as date and user authorization codes can be included to provide an extensive audit trail. Transaction logs also provide an important backup, as well as a source for control totals.

Paperless Input Systems Requiring Human Intervention

There are many types of paperless input systems in which users enter transactions directly into the computer. These systems include, for example, on-line manual data entry systems and automatic identification systems such as point-of-sales (POS) systems.

In on-line **manual data entry systems,** users manually type transactions into the computer system. For example, a plant manager (possessing appropriate access codes) might manually type a purchase requisition into a data terminal. The requisition then would be automatically forwarded to purchasing for additional processing. The purchase order would be generated with no rekeying of data. In **automatic identification systems,** merchandise and other items are tagged with machine-readable codes. One example of automatic identification is the **automated POS system** in which salespersons use an optical scanner to scan the bar coded merchandise for sale, as well as the customer's credit card. The transaction information is then automatically forwarded to the billing and inventory systems for additional processing, and no additional human intervention may be required. Another application of automatic identification involves the electronic tagging of containers in the shipping industry. For example, DEC and Amtech Corporation have developed a system of remote radio tagging that will identify the location and contents of a container in seconds.

Automatic identification can be especially useful if two trading partners agree on a standard method of tagging cartons and boxes. The tags on incoming cartons can be scanned, facilitating their identification and matching with the related purchase order.

Transactions in paperless input systems involving human intervention typically proceed through two phases: data entry and data editing, and transfer to the host application system. Both of these phases are discussed.

Data Entry and Data Editing.   In paperless input systems, complete program data editing is often performed when the transaction is entered. Once the transaction is accepted, it might be processed either immediately or at a later time. If it is processed at a later time, additional data editing may be performed.

Transfer to the Host Application System.   In centralized paperless systems, transactions are usually input directly into the central computer through some type of remote data terminal. In decentralized and distributed systems, transactions might be entered into one computer and then either immediately or later transferred to another computer for processing. As was discussed in the chapter on distributed processing, data editing (i.e., database policy implementation) might be performed on more than one computer.

Paperless Systems Requiring No Human Intervention

In some systems, transactions are processed from beginning to end without any human intervention: completely automated transaction processing. One application of this technology is the **networked vending machine (NVM).** The POS gasoline pump is a good example of NVM technology. With this system, the customer inserts a credit card or ATM card into the gas pump. The pump then delivers the gas, and the customer's credit card company or bank is billed electronically. Another interesting application is the automated slot machine. The customer inserts an ATM card into the POS slot machine, enters a PIN code, and pulls the handle. Losses and gains are immediately charged or credited to the customer's bank account.

Another important application of completely automated transaction processing is electronic data interchange (EDI). With EDI and the appropriate database servers, incoming purchase orders and outgoing sales orders can be handled with no human intervention. For example, when inventories are low, the inventory servers sends a purchase order message to the EDI translation server. The translation server then translates the message into the ANSI X.12 format and sends it to the communications server. The communication server then forwards it electronically to the desired vendor. The remainder of the entire transaction cycle, including payment, can also be automated with EDI, EFT, and automatic identification.

THE PROCESSING SYSTEM

Paper-Based Processing Systems

Virtually all paper-based systems for processing transactions are batch-oriented. In **batch-oriented processing systems,** transactions are entered into the computer (as was discussed before) in batches. These batches are then processed periodically. Examples of batch processing include processing weekly time reports to produce paychecks, processing groups of checks to update accounts payable master files, and processing invoices to update an accounts receivable master file.

Batch processing is economical when large numbers of transactions must be processed. It is best suited to situations in which files do not need to be updated immediately to reflect transactions, and reports are required only periodically. Payroll is a good example. Payroll is prepared periodically. It is not calculated every day. The major disadvantage of batch processing is that files and reports might be out of date between periodic processing. A good example of this is an inventory file. If the inventory file must be used frequently to determine the availability of product for sale, the file will often be out of date if sales are processed only periodically in batches. It is primarily for this reason that many companies utilize real-time processing systems. Batch processing is still widely used, however, because that are still many situations in which it is a very efficient method of processing data.

Batch processing can be performed with either sequential or random-access (i.e., direct or indexed) file updating. Both approaches are discussed in what follows.

Batch Processing with Sequential File Updating

Many paper-based, batch-oriented systems use **sequential file processing** to update the master file. Processing in such a system usually involves the following steps:

- Preparing the transaction file. First, any additional data editing and validation are performed. Then the records in the transaction file are sorted into the same sequence as the master file.

- Updating the master file. The records in both the transaction and master files (i.e., subsidiary ledgers) are read one by one, matched, and written to a new master file that reflects the desired updates.

- Updating the general ledger. The general ledger is updated to reflect changes in the master files.
- Preparing general ledger reports. Trial balances and other reports are produced.

Figure 13.3 outlines the processing of transaction data in a typical paper-based, batch processing accounting system. Each of the transaction cycles generates batches of transactions for processing. Examples are sales transactions generated by the sales order application system in the revenue cycle and payroll transactions generated by the payroll application system in the expenditure cycle. Batches of transactions from each application system are processed against the relevant application files in separate computer runs. The computer runs post the transactions to subsidiary ledgers and also generate the information necessary to prepare journal entries (journal vouchers) for posting to the general ledger. The journal vouchers are accumulated and processed as a batch against the general ledger in a separate computer run.

As indicated before, batch processing often involves maintaining a sequentially organized master file. This file—an accounts receivable master file for illustration—commonly resides on a direct-access storage device. Sales transactions affect the information on the accounts receivable file. These transactions and others—such as new accounts and payments on account—must be reflected in the master file. Figure 13.4 outlines the procedural steps in paper-based batch pro-

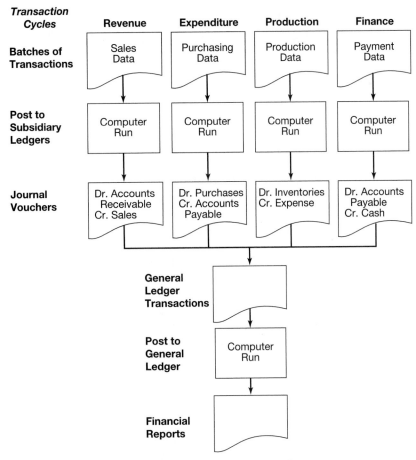

FIGURE 13.3 Overview of Batch Processing of Accounting Data.

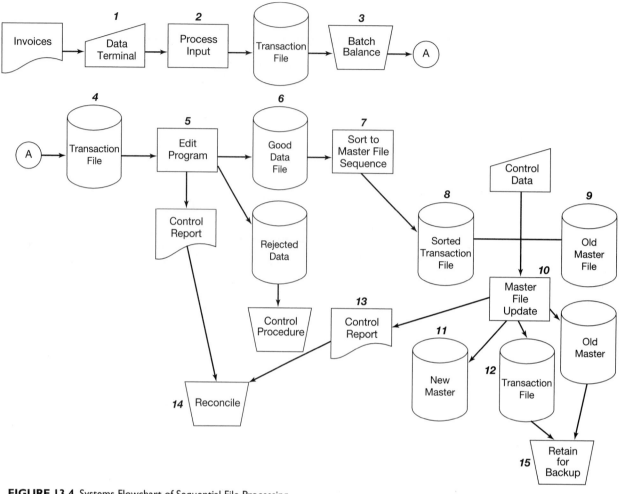

FIGURE 13.4 Systems Flowchart of Sequential File Processing.

cessing with sequentially organized files, beginning with data input. The numbers in this figure are keyed to the following discussion.

Preparing the Transaction File As Figure 13.4 illustrates, batches of documents are input (1), processed to build a transaction file (2), and subjected to batch balancing procedures (3) to ensure that all documents are accounted for prior to computer processing. The batch control totals would normally be supplied by the user along with the input data and reconciled by the data entry function prior to further processing. The resultant file of transactions is on disk (4). This file is processed with an edit program (5) to screen the data before further processing. Data editing of the source documents prior to input is essential to ensure the reliability of the data processed.

In addition to screening data, the edit program (5) must accumulate revised batch control totals for the input data. This is necessary, as the figure shows, because the input data have been divided into good data—those that have passed the edit program—and rejected data. The rejected data must be held in suspense until they are corrected. To facilitate processing, the rejected data are usually reentered for processing as a separate batch at a later date. The control report that is output by the edit program provides the data necessary to reconcile the results of the edit program to user-supplied batch control totals.

The file of edited transactional data (6) is sorted to master file sequence (7) to facilitate the matching process necessary for efficient sequential file processing. It should be noted that Figure 13.4 shows data editing performed at the earliest possible point in the flow of processing, that is, before the transactions are sorted. At times, however, depending on the particular circumstances, data editing may be performed after the transactional data have been sorted to master file sequence. This allows input editing to detect duplicate transactions or to check the sequence of records to be processed. Therefore, either sequence, "edit and sort" or "sort and edit," is possible, with the best sequence determined by the particular circumstances surrounding the application (Figure 13.5).

Updating the Master File   Once the transaction data have been edited and sorted (8), they are processed against the old master file (9) in the accounts receivable application program(s) run (10). This master file update program (or set of programs) posts the detail of accounts receivable transactions to the accounts receivable master file. The new updated master file (11) is the basis for generating reports and other detailed information. This master file is a subsidiary ledger, the accounts receivable subsidiary ledger in this illustration. The transaction data (12) and the old master file are retained for backup control, as illustrated in Figure 13.4. The control report (13), which is printed at the completion of the processing,

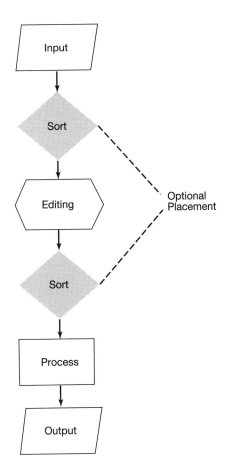

FIGURE 13.5 Placement of Editing in the Flow of Processing.

is reconciled (14) with the batch totals/control report produced by the edit program. These control totals must be reconciled to user-supplied batch control totals before any output is returned to the user. Reconciliation must allow for any transactions that were rejected by data editing. This reconciliation of input to output control totals is performed by the user department, a special control unit, or the internal audit function. The control report (13) would normally include a detailed listing of transactions processed against the master file. This transaction register is the equivalent of a journal produced in a manual system.

As Figure 13.4 shows, the old master and the transaction file should be retained for backup (15). If the new master file is lost or found to be in error, the processing run may be repeated using the old master and the transaction file. This concept is often referred to as **son–father–grandfather retention,** with each version of the master file being a "generation." As Figure 13.6 shows, the old master file that is used as input to a file update is the "father." The processing yields a "son"—the new master file. The new master is another generation of information. The "son" file then becomes the input master file for the next file update. Thus, the "son" file becomes a "father"; there is a new "son"; and the old master file that is the backup master from the previous file update becomes a "grandfather" file, that is, a file that is at least two processing cycles old. Several generations of backup files may be kept, depending on the control objectives.

Updating the General Ledger. Every organization must maintain some type of general ledger accounting system. Data must be collected, recorded, properly classified, and entered into the appropriate records for further financial report summations. A general ledger system is the cornerstone of an accounting system.

There are two major aspects to the operation of a computerized general ledger system. One concerns the direct processing of the general ledger programs, most of which takes place on a monthly basis. The second aspect concerns the processing in other computer application systems to prepare the inputs to the general ledger sys-

FIGURE 13.6 Son–Father–Grandfather Master Files.

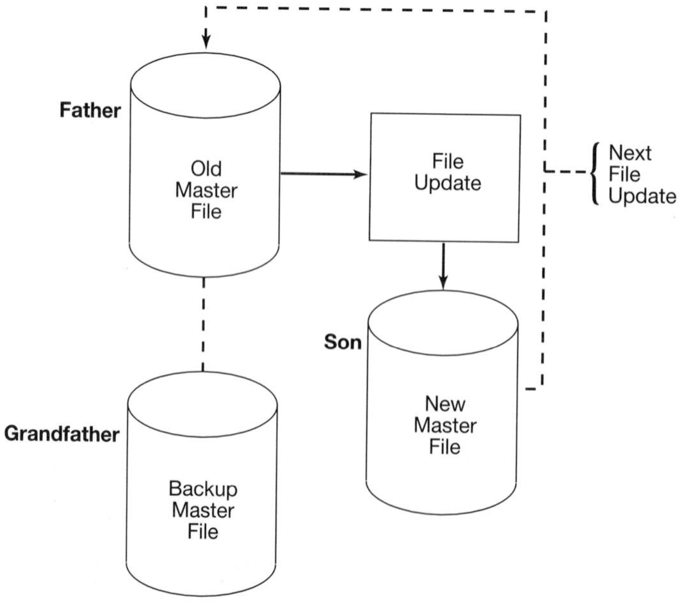

tem. One of the tasks to be undertaken in designing a general ledger system is the creation of a pro forma set of journal entries providing for the collection and updating of all data needed for financial reports. The typical approach is to have each relevant application system (such as payroll or accounts payable) generate general ledger transactions (standard journal entry data) to be used as input at the proper time. Doing this implies the use of a separate transaction file in the general ledger system.

The processing procedure described in detail before posts transactions to subsidiary ledgers maintained for accounts receivable. The general ledger has not yet been updated. The summary information needed to prepare journal entries may be printed at the completion of processing the subsidiary ledgers and used to update a manual general ledger, or subsequently this information may be input for processing against a computerized general ledger system. Alternatively, the standard journal entries may be output initially in machine-readable form.

All entries into the general ledger should be documented with journal vouchers. Responsible departments originate the input data to the general ledger system. This may entail the manual preparation of journal vouchers or, in cases where these data are provided by other application programs, the review and adjustment (if required) of these data into journal voucher format.

The journal voucher format (Figure 13.7) is similar in most organizations and includes the journal voucher number and date, the control and subaccounts (as applicable), and the debit and credit amounts. There may be one or several accounts entered on one journal voucher, depending on the complexity of the transaction and the system design. Journal voucher numbers are established to code the type of transaction (cash, receivables, sales, and the like). The column headed by ID designates that the journal is an original entry or the reversal of a prior entry. The account and debit/credit amounts are self-explanatory. This basic format may be expanded to include other information relevant to a particular system. Examples of such data are detailed cost ledger information (to support a subsidiary cost file) and details of expenses by organizational unit for responsibility reports. Either of these data items might be used in conjunction with a separate master budget file to produce reports showing "budget vs. year to date," and so forth.

Journal Voucher			
Number	*Month*	*Year*	*ID*
Accounts		Debit	Credit
		Received from:	

FIGURE 13.7 Journal Voucher Format.

General Ledger File Update. Figure 13.8 provides a systems flowchart overview of a typical general ledger file update. As they are released by the general ledger department, journal vouchers are used to build a journal voucher file (the transaction file). This file is program data edited to check for the proper journal and account numbers and to determine whether the accounts are correctly associated with their related journals. Invalid data are reported as exceptions and returned to their originating sources for correction and reentry. The edited journal voucher file may be sorted and structured to produce a variety of reports. The current journal voucher transactions are processed against the previous month's general ledger master file (the old master) in order to update that file and produce the current period's general ledger register.

Computer processing of accounting data is typically a two-step procedure. The first step produces preliminary reports, which are forwarded to the accounting department for review and audit relative to the journal voucher listings and general ledger listing. After the audit and submission of corrections and any additional data, the second step is a run that produces the final listings and financial schedules. Numerous reports may be prepared.

Preparing reports requires a link between the general ledger accounts and the report(s) in which they appear. This process is called line coding.

Line coding is a procedural step, typically accomplished by a table-lookup (matching) process between the updated general ledger file and a line-coding table file. Table files function as reference files. Table files contain items or records that are not a part of data files but are an integral part of the processing function. Tax tables and line-coding assignments are examples of table files stored on direct-access storage devices in accounting applications. The result of line-coding procedure is several report files, which are ultimately printed and distributed to users.

Figure 13.9 illustrates a line-coding assignment. A specific general ledger account, such as "marketable securities," is located in the line-coding file. The line code is then used to structure the report. In Figure 13.9, the first field (one digit) indicates the type of schedule—a financial one in this illustration. The second field identifies the specific report—a balance sheet in our example. The third and fourth fields locate the item in the report structure. Marketable securities is the third line item on the balance sheet, and this account value is placed in column 2. A balance sheet typically has four columns of data: (1) actual this period, (2) beginning-of-year balance, (3) budget, and (4) variance between (1) and (3). As an alternative to the procedure just described, line codes could be stored within the general ledger file itself. The line code for the marketable securities account could be stored as a separate field within the marketable securities record structure.

Common General Ledger Reports. In addition to financial reports and schedules, common reports from a general ledger system would include the following five items:

1. Journal voucher in sequence
2. Journal voucher within general account
3. General ledger by account
4. General ledger summary
5. Working trial balance

Item 3, general ledger by account, is a summary of this month's activity in the general ledger; item 4 is a year-to-date summary; and item 5 is a sort/summarization of the year-to-date general ledger in trial balance format. Typically, finan-

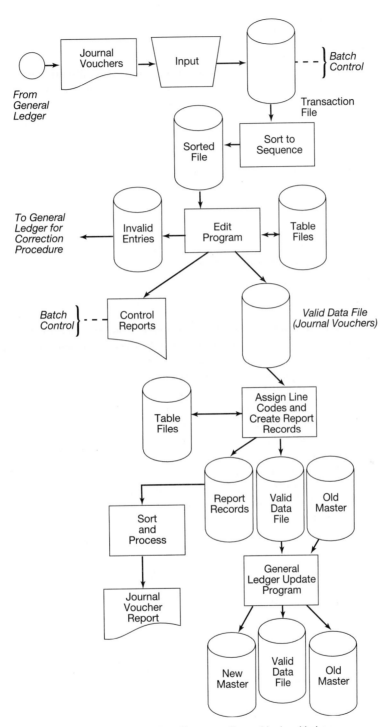

FIGURE 13.8 Systems Flowchart Showing a General Ledger Update.

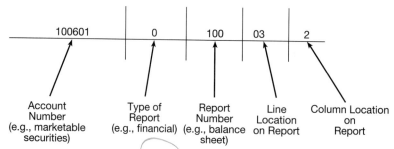

FIGURE 13.9 Example of a Line Code.

cial statements and trial balances contain details summarized from the general ledger rather than a listing of all the individual accounts. Detailed reports for lower levels of management may be prepared from the relevant subsidiary ledger files.

Batch Processing with Random-Access File Updating

Although the updating in the previous example is done with sequential file updating, random-access updating is also possible, even desirable, with batch processing. In many systems (especially DBMS-oriented accounting systems as opposed to file-oriented accounting systems), indexes are maintained for both the subsidiary and general ledger files. Maintaining these indexes serves the primary need of allowing users to quickly access a particular account. For example, an interactive query program might use an index file to help the end user to quickly locate a customer's account. But given that an index is present, it can also be used for file updating.

Random-access file updating is simpler than sequential-access updating. With random-access updating, it is not necessary to sort the transaction file into the same order as the master file, and there is no need to generate a new master file. Instead, individual records are read one by one from the transaction file and used to update the related records in the master file *in place*. The following steps are followed:

- A record is read from the transaction file.
- The key value of the transaction record is used to randomly access (by using the index) the related record in the master file.
- The record in the master file is updated in memory and then rewritten back to the data file.

Of course, a backup of the master file should exist before the updating begins, and a transaction register must be generated as the update proceeds.

Illustration of Batch Processing with Random-Access File Updating

This section depicts an on-line cash receipts application. Batches of customer remittances on account are entered via data terminals and posted with random-access file updating directly to the accounts receivable file. Figure 13.10 presents a system flowchart of the on-line cash receipts application.

New Invoice Application.   The application maintains on open-item accounts receivable file. New invoices are periodically posted to the open-item accounts re-

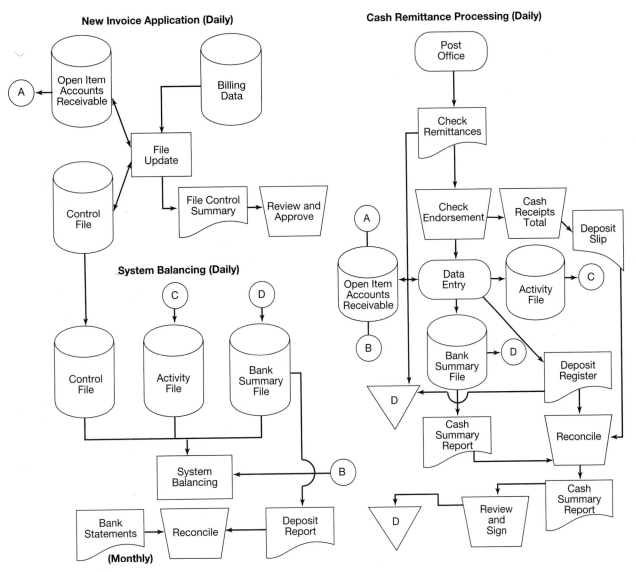

FIGURE 13.10 Cash Receipts Application.

ceivable file. A control file is updated to reflect the addition of the new batch of invoices to the accounts receivable file. The control file is a summary of the accounts receivable file by type of account (such as installment or net 30 days). A file control summary report is generated, reviewed, and approved by management prior to the processing of daily cash remittances. This procedure ensures that the accounts receivable file and the control file are in balance after the new billing data are added.

Cash Remittance Processing.   Customer payments are remitted to a special post office box number. This approach separates the checks from other mail received by the organization, thereby eliminating manual sorting of the checks and reducing the number of individuals handling them when they are received.

When the checks are brought from the post office, they are given to a control desk, where a clerk restrictively endorses them. This stamped endorsement prevents the deposit of the remittance to any unauthorized bank account. The clerk then totals all checks by adding machine and prepares a deposit slip. This ensures the accountability of checks received and their subsequent disposition. When the checks are deposited, the bank-validated deposit slip and adding machine tape are filed to be later reconciled to a cash summary report.

For ease of handling, controlling, and reconciling, the payments are batched into groups of 30 or fewer checks. When the checks are ready to be processed, a terminal operator requests access to the accounts receivable system through a network terminal. The operator keys into the terminal a unique security code and employee number and identifies the type of transaction to be processed.

A security application, which controls access to all applications, verifies that the operator is an authorized user of the system and that his or her personal profile of clearances includes the transaction he or she has requested. Accounts receivable management may delegate or remove authority to process transactions, but the security application limits management to the delegation of transactions within the scope of its authority (as defined by a similar type of manager's security profile) and to transactions that will not compromise good separation of duties when processed in combination with existing transaction authorities.

The terminal operator enters from the remittance advice the invoice number and check amount as an individual line item for as many lines as the terminal is capable of displaying. The accounts receivable system then compares the individual line items against the records in the accounts receivable file. For those line items where an invoice number and check amount match a corresponding record in the file, the check amount is applied using random-access file updating. If there are line items that do not completely match an invoice number and check amount, or if the accounts receivable system notes that an entered invoice number was previously cleared, an error message is immediately transmitted back to the input terminal, indicating the line item in error and the reason for rejection (e.g., no unpaid invoice number on file, or the check amount entered is under or over invoice amount of file).

As payments are applied against the unpaid invoice records on the accounts receivable file, the invoice records are updated to reflect the payment date, activity code (e.g., check payment, invoice adjustment), and a sequential check number generated by the system. The paid customer invoice records are retained on-line for 1 year and are available for inquiries.

The terminal operator is restricted by application controls within the system to applying cash remittances to a single customer account. The terminal can access only one customer account for each check remittance. The entire check remittance amount must be applied to that customer account. The terminal operator cannot apply the remaining check amount of one customer's payment to another customer's account. If a terminal operator is unable to apply a customer remittance because the customer's account is not on the file (usually the result of a check misrouted by the customer), then accounts receivable management follows up with the customer. If it is appropriate to do so, the check amount is subtracted from the batch total and the check is returned to the customer.

All check remittances within a batch must be applied except those that were erroneously sent to the company. If a check remittance is for some reason not entered into the system and not subtracted from the batch control totals, the discrepancy will be highlighted by the cash balancing procedure employed at the end of the daily application of remittances.

System Balancing.   All cash remittance activity is logged on an activity file to provide an audit trail of all cash transactions processed. The activity file is used in the daily balancing of the accounts receivable system and for preparing, upon request, listings that assist data processing personnel in tracing any lost activity that may have resulted from a system error.

After a batch of checks has been applied, the system updates a bank summary file for the dollar amount of the batch of checks. Also, a deposit register, detailing and totaling the invoice numbers and invoice amounts in the batch, is printed.

Daily, upon completion of the application of cash remittance, the accounts receivable system prints a cash summary report from the bank summary file. This report lists the total number of checks and total dollars applied during that day. The deposit register is compared to the cash summary report to ensure that the cash applied to the system is in balance. In addition, the bank-validated deposit slip is reconciled to the cash summary report. This reconciliation ensures that the cash deposited was applied by the accounts receivable system. After the deposit register and the cash summary report are balanced, the cash summary report is given to management for review and signature, and is filed for future reference. The deposit register is filed with the day's customer remittance advices for future reference or reconciliation.

Daily, the activity file is summarized and compared to the totals in the bank summary file. Also, the activity file totals by type of accounts receivable are subtracted from the control file totals, which reflect the previous day's accounts receivable file data by type of accounts. Finally, the current accounts receivable file is accumulated by type of accounts. These accounts receivable system processing steps are made daily before the accounts receivable file is updated with new billing data or invoice adjustment data.

Comparing the activity file and the bank summary file ensures that all cash that has been deposited has been applied and recorded on the activity file. The total derived from subtracting the activity file from the control file should equal the sum of the totals by type of the current accounts receivable file. This system balancing imposes a three-way check to ensure that each file within the accounts receivable system is in balance. As a result, any out-of-balance condition is readily identified and appropriate corrective action initiated prior to proceeding with the next day's accounts receivable processing procedures.

Bank statements are received each month and reconciled to reports prepared from the bank summary file. Also, at the end of each month, the total amount of cash activity on the activity file is summarized and forwarded to the general ledger application system. This information, which is used as a standard journal entry, is output in machine-readable form and as such is directly entered into the month's journal voucher file for posting to the general ledger.

Paperless Processing Systems

In paperless processing systems, either batch or real-time processing is possible. With **real-time processing**, sometimes called **on-line real-time processing**, transactions are processed as they are input into the system. Both batch and real-time processing are discussed in the context of paperless processing systems.

Batch Processing in Paperless Processing Systems

Batch processing in paperless systems is similar to batch processing in paper-based systems. The main difference is that journal vouchers are replaced by their electronic equivalents, and the general ledger is updated automatically in periodic batch runs. Either sequential or random-access file updating is possible.

Real-Time Processing in Paperless Processing Systems

A primary advantage of paperless systems is that they make possible real-time processing. On-line, real-time systems (OLRSs) process transactions immediately after they are input and can provide immediate output to users. Transactions are not accumulated into batches, but rather upon input they are immediately applied to updating the master file using random-access file updating. The processing of individual transactions as opposed to groups of transactions is called **immediate, direct,** or **real-time processing.** Immediate processing is the primary characteristic of the OLRS. Master files are always up-to-date because they are updated as soon as transaction data are input. Responses to user inquiries are immediate because information in randomly accessible files can be quickly retrieved.

Types of Real-time Processing in the OLRS. Many types of real-time processing are possible in the OLRS. In **inquiry/response systems,** users do not input data for processing; rather, they only request information. Inquiry/response systems are designed to provide users with quick responses to their requests for information. A common example is when a bank clerk wishes to find out if a customer has a sufficient balance to cover the check she wishes to cash.

In **data entry systems,** users interactively input data. The data are stored by the OLRS but are processed periodically in batches. For example, stores may capture sales transactions in real time during the day and then process them at night in batches.

In file processing systems, users also interactively input data as they do in data entry systems. However, **file processing systems** differ from data entry systems in that they go one step further and immediately process the data against the relevant master files. For example, a retail store might collect and process sales transactions immediately, charging the customer's account within moments of the sale. The transaction, however, would be incomplete until the customer is billed at the end of the month.

In **full processing systems,** or **transaction processing systems,** users also interactively input transactions. However, full processing systems differ from file processing systems in that they go even further and complete the entire transaction when it is input. For example, in the case of the retail store example in the previous paragraph, the customer would also be billed immediately, thus completing the transaction. Sometimes in practice, however, the terms file processing system and full processing system are used interchangeably.

The Economics of the OLRS. Most of the attributes of OLRS, such as immediate processing of transactions and quick response to inquiries, are relative advantages when compared to batch processing systems. The OLRS is desirable in many situations. On-line reservation systems, inventory control in retail stores, and customer account files in a bank are some familiar examples. The relative disadvantages of the OLRS stem from the increased costs and complexity of systems operation. In particular, the OLRS is more sensitive to hardware and software errors, and is much more susceptible to processing errors that arise from erroneous or fraudulent input. Whereas a hardware or software malfunction in a batch system might have little or no effect on users because they are not directly using the system, a hardware or software malfunction in an OLRS immediately affects users. An incorrect transaction in a batch processing system might be corrected prior to processing or detected in a review of the results of processing. In an OLRS, however, an incorrect transaction is immediately processed and might contaminate several different files that are updated at the same time. In addition, the results of processing an incorrect transaction are immediately available to users of the OLRS.

Control of transaction processing is much more involved in OLRSs than in batch-oriented systems. Application system files are integrated, and transactions are directly entered by users through remote network terminals (e.g., POS terminals) or personal computers for immediate processing. Application system interfaces are handled automatically; once a transaction has been input, it may be posted immediately to several different files. Printed output concerning transaction processing is not usually produced, because transactions are processed individually in real time rather than as a batch. As a result, a transaction may generate no directly human-verifiable evidence of its processing. The audit trail must be carefully considered in the design of such systems. The high degree of concentration of functions characteristic of on-line systems necessitates the use of special control techniques to ensure that data are accurately and reliably processed.

THE OUTPUT SYSTEM

The output system can be paper-based, paperless, or something in between. Most paper-based, batch-oriented systems with sequential file processing produce very large volumes of output. Because such systems do not provide random-access user queries, they typically generate printouts or microfiche copies of all files for reference. For example, a printout of the accounts receivable file might be used to look up individual customer balances.

On the other hand, on-line, real-time paperless systems tend to produce very little output. Such systems are almost imperative in very large companies for this reason, as it would be impractical to continually print what may be hundreds of thousands, or even millions, of records.

Output controls are designed to check that processing results in valid output and that outputs are properly distributed. Reports should be reviewed critically by supervisory personnel in user departments for general reasonableness and quality in relation to previous reports. Control totals should be balanced to control totals generated independently of the data processing operation, as discussed earlier. Furthermore, program data editing checks should be performed on all outputs. This can prevent problems such as those that once occurred in the Social Security System when social security numbers were accidentally printed in the amount fields on Social Security benefit checks.

A separate **EDP control group** is often established to monitor EDP operations. The EDP control group is frequently part of the internal audit function. Procedures should be established to provide assurance that errors are reported to the EDP control group. These procedures must assure that such errors are entered into controls, corrected, and properly reentered into the system for further processing. Corrections should be subject to the same testing as original data. The distribution of output should be controlled so as to minimize the danger of unauthorized access to confidential data. Output distribution is controlled through documentation and supervision. Typically, an **output distribution register** is maintained to control the disposition of reports. This register and its attendant documentation should be periodically reviewed in the internal audit function.

SUMMARY

Data processing systems vary in the degree to which they are computerized. Some systems, although computerized, rely heavily on paper documents. Other systems can process transactions from beginning to end without a shred of paper. There are a variety of application controls that might be utilized in a data processing system, including batch controls, programmed data editing, and transaction logs.

Batch processing of transactions is a common approach to data processing. Representative examples of batch processing include processing weekly time reports to produce paychecks, processing groups of checks to update accounts payable files, and processing invoices to update an accounts receivable file. In a paper-based, batch processing accounting system, batches of transactions from each application system are processed against the relevant application files in separate computer runs. The computer runs post the transactions to subsidiary ledgers and also generate the information necessary to prepare journal entries (journal vouchers) for posting to the general ledger. The journal vouchers are accumulated and processed as a batch against the general ledger in a separate computer run. Computer processing of accounting data is typically a two-step procedure. The first step produces preliminary reports, which are forwarded to the accounting department for review and audit relative to the journal voucher listings and general ledger listing. After the audit and submission of corrections or additional data, the second step is a run that produces the final listings and financial schedules.

Many EDP systems maintain indexes for both subsidiary and general ledger files. These indexes allow users to quickly access particular accounts. When an index is present, it can also be used for random-access file updating. With random-access updating, it is not necessary to sort the transaction file into the same order as the master file, and there is no need to generate a new master file. Individual records are read one by one from the transaction file and used to update the related records in the master file in place. Batch processing with random-access file updating was illustrated in the context of an on-line cash receipts application.

On-line, real-time processing systems are transaction-oriented rather than file-oriented. Individual transactions may be input for processing by users through network terminals rather than being batched and submitted to a processing center as a group of source documents. Extensive control and audit trails may be implemented in such systems, but these features must be included within the design of the system during development. Standard application controls over system inputs and processing in an on-line, real-time processing system were discussed in the context of a purchasing application.

Glossary

application controls: ensure that the recording (input), processing, and reporting (output) of data are properly performed.

batch processing: accumulating source documents into groups for processing on a periodic basis.

check digit: an extra digit added to a code number that is verified by applying mathematical calculations to the individual digits in the code number.

continuous operations auditing: the use of programmed edit tests to discriminate between acceptable and nonacceptable data values so that some items are either held in suspense of processing until audited or collected for audit after processing.

direct processing: the processing of individual transactions in real time as opposed to groups of transactions.

hash totals: sums that are nonsensical (e.g., the total sum of department codes) but are nevertheless useful for batch balancing.

header label: the initial record in a file that contains relevant identification and control information.

input document control form: documents batch control totals for batches of input data transmitted between user departments and the data processing department.

interactive processing: the use of an OLRS to seemingly work directly with the computer.

key verification: a control procedure to ensure the accuracy of key-transcribed input data.

limit test: an edit program checks the value of a numeric data field as being within a range of certain predefined limits.

line coding: assigning codes to items in the general ledger that indicate the item's use and placement in financial statements.

on-line, real-time systems (OLRSs): computer systems that process input data immediately after they are input and can provide immediate output to users.

output controls: designed to check that processing results in valid output and that outputs are properly distributed to users.

output distribution register: a log maintained to control the disposition of output and reports.

passwords: an authorization code or number, which is verified before access to some system is permitted.

processing controls: used to provide reasonable assurance that a file or record has been processed according to intended specifications.

program data editing: a software technique used to screen data prior to computer processing.

real time: immediate or fast-response processing occurs.

son–father–grandfather retention: retaining the old master (i.e., father) and the transaction file for backup over the new master file (i.e., son).

table lookup: an edit program compares the value of a field to the acceptable values contained in a table file.

tagging: audit-oriented information that is included with original transaction data when they are recorded.

transaction processing system: a system that collects and processes transactions, and provides immediate output concerning processing.

updated in place: updated records on a DASD are physically rewritten over the original record, destroying the original record.

valid code check: a table-lookup procedure in which the table file consists of valid data codes.

Chapter Quiz

Answers to the chapter quiz appear on page 539.

1. Which of the following is (are) a typical example of batch processing?
   (a) processing weekly time reports to produce paychecks
   (b) processing groups of checks to update accounts payable files
   (c) both a and b
   (d) neither a nor b

2. Accumulating source documents into groups prior to processing is a character of
   (a) batch processing.
   (b) on-line, real-time processing.
   (c) both a and b.
   (d) neither a nor b.

3. Which of the following errors would probably be corrected by key verification of data input?
   (a) a salesperson manually enters an incorrect product number on a sales invoice,

which is subsequently given to a data entry operator in the information systems department for key transcription to machine-readable format

(b) a data entry operator in the information systems department mistypes a product number on a sales invoice when keying the document to machine-readable format

(c) both a and b

(d) neither a nor b

4. Which of the following controls would prevent the following situation? A worker's paycheck was incorrectly processed as he had transposed letters in his department identification code, having entered "ABC," an invalid code, instead of "CAB."

(a) control total

(b) limit test

(c) internal label check

(d) table-lookup procedure

5. The son–father–grandfather concept of backing up master files can be used when master files are stored on

(a) magnetic tape.

(b) magnetic disk.

(c) both a and b.

(d) neither a nor b.

6. A review of an EDP system reveals the following items. Which of these is a potential internal control weakness?

(a) backup master files are stored in a remote location

(b) users must verbally approve all changes to be made to application programs

(c) computer operators have restricted access to system programs and data files

(d) computer operators are required to take vacations

7. For control purposes, data clerks total up the employee social security numbers in each batch of payroll transactions. Which of the following terms best describes the resulting total?

(a) hash total

(b) financial total

(c) parity total

(d) record count

8. In an on-line computer system, which of the following may be used to ensure that users have proper authorization to perform a task?

(a) check digits

(b) passwords

(c) control totals

(d) limit tests

9. For control purposes, data clerks total up the employee gross pay amounts in each batch of payroll transactions. Which of the following terms best describes the resulting total?

(a) hash total

(b) financial total

(c) parity total

(d) record count

10. A customer inadvertently orders part number 1234-8 instead of 1243-8. Which of the following controls would detect this error during processing?

(a) hash total

(b) financial total

(c) limit check

(d) check digit

Review Problem

The computer system most likely to be used by a large savings bank for customers' accounts would be
(a) an on-line, real-time system.
(b) a batch processing system.
(c) a generalized utility system.
(d) a direct-access database system.

(CPA)

Solution to Review Problem

The answer is a.
(a) An on-line, real-time system is characterized by data that are assembled from more than one location and records that are updated immediately. A large savings bank would likely have several different branches from which transactions on customer accounts are likely to be entered and it is desirable that records be processed immediately in order that customer account data reflect their current financial positions.
(b) A batch processing system is characterized by data that are assembled at a centralized location and processed against records periodically as batches of sufficient size are accumulated. A large savings bank could utilize a batch processing system to post transactions on customer accounts, but it is desirable that such records be processed immediately rather than periodically as a batch in order that customer account data reflect their current financial positions.
(c) A generalized utility system is not a defined term in data processing.
(d) A direct-access database system sounds good but this is not a defined term in data processing as is an on-line, real-time system.

Review Questions

1. Identify and describe several controls over data transfer between user departments and data processing. Why are such controls necessary?
2. Describe key verification of input data. What types of errors does key verification control?
3. Describe program data editing. Is program data editing necessary if input data have been key-verified? Explain.
4. Identify and describe several program data editing techniques.
5. Describe how the loss of paper-based internal controls can be compensated for in paperless input systems.
6. Give an example of automatic identification in a paperless input system that requires human intervention.
7. Give an example of a paperless input system that requires no human intervention.
8. Describe batch processing of transactions in a paper-based processing system. When is batch processing most economical?
9. Identify several points where reconciliation of control totals should occur in the batch processing of transactions against a master file.
10. Explain son–father–grandfather file retention.
11. What is a journal voucher? Describe how computer batch processing of journal vouchers may be used to update the general ledger.

12. Identify several general ledger reports that might be prepared after updating the general ledger with computer processing.
13. Explain how random-access file updating differs from sequential-access updating.
14. Characterize several different types of real-time processing in an OLRS.
15. Identify and describe several output controls. Why are such controls necessary?

Discussion Questions and Problems

16. What type of EDP system is characterized by data that are assembled from more than one location and records that are updated immediately?
    (a) microcomputer system
    (b) minicomputer system
    (c) batch processing system
    (d) on-line, real-time system
    (CPA)

17. An EDP technique that collects data into groups to permit convenient and efficient processing is known as
    (a) document-count processing.
    (b) multiprogramming.
    (c) batch processing.
    (d) generalized audit processing.
    (CPA)

18. Which of the following is not a characteristic of a batch processed computer system?
    (a) The collection of like transactions that is sorted and processed sequentially against a master file.
    (b) Key transcription of transactions, followed by machine processing.
    (c) The production of numerous printouts.
    (d) The posting of a transaction, as it occurs, to several files, without intermediate printouts.
    (CPA)

19. What is the computer process called when data processing is performed concurrently with a particular activity and the results are available soon enough to influence the particular course of action being taken or the decision being made?
    (a) real-time processing
    (b) batch processing
    (c) random-access processing
    (d) integrated data processing
    (CPA)

20. The real-time feature normally would be least useful when applied to accounting for a firm's
    (a) bank account balances.
    (b) property and depreciation.
    (c) customer accounts receivable.
    (d) merchandise inventory.
    (CPA)

21. An EDP input control is designed to ensure that
    (a) machine processing is accurate.
    (b) only authorized personnel have access to the computer area.
    (c) data received for processing are properly authorized and converted to machine-readable form.
    (d) electronic data processing has been performed as intended for the particular application.
    (CPA)

22. When erroneous data are detected by computer program controls, such data may be excluded from processing and printed on an error report. This error report should be reviewed and followed up by the
    (a) computer operator.
    (b) systems analyst.
    (c) EDP control group.
    (d) computer programmer.

    (CPA)

23. Which of the following would lessen internal control in an EDP system?
    (a) The computer librarian maintains custody of computer program instructions and detailed program listings.
    (b) Computer operators have access to operator instructions and detailed program listings.
    (c) The control group maintains sole custody of all computer output.
    (d) Computer programmers write and debug programs that perform routines designed by the systems analyst.

    (CPA)

24. An internal administrative control sometimes used in connection with procedures to detect unauthorized or unexplained computer usage is
    (a) maintenance of a computer tape library.
    (b) use of file controls.
    (c) maintenance of a computer console log.
    (d) control over program tapes.

    (CPA)

25. A procedural control used in the management of a computer center to minimize the possibility of data or program file destruction through operator error includes
    (a) control figures.
    (b) crossfooting tests.
    (c) limit checks.
    (d) external labels.

    (CPA)

26. If a control total were to be computed on each of the following data items, which would be best identified as a hash total for a payroll EDP application?
    (a) net pay
    (b) department numbers
    (c) hours worked
    (d) total debits and total credits

    (CPA)

27. In designing a payroll system, it is known that no individual's paycheck can amount to more than $300 for a single week. As a result, the payroll program has been written to bypass writing a check and will print out an error message if any payroll calculation results in more than $300. This type of control is called
    (a) a limit or reasonableness test.
    (b) error review.
    (c) a data validity test.
    (d) a logic sequence test.

    (CPA)

28. Where disk files are used, the son–father–grandfather updating backup concept is relatively difficult to implement because the
    (a) location of information points on disks is an extremely time-consuming task.
    (b) magnetic fields and other environmental factors cause off-site storage to be impractical.

   (c) information must be dumped in the form of hard copy if it is to be reviewed be-
       fore being used in updating.
   (d) process of updating old records is destructive.

(CPA)

29. A customer inadvertently ordered part number 12368 rather than part number 12638.
    In processing this order, the error would be detected by the vendor with which of the
    following controls?
    (a) batch total
    (b) key verifying
    (c) self-checking digit
    (d) an internal consistency check

(CPA)

30. In the weekly computer run to prepare payroll checks, a check was printed for an em-
    ployee who had been terminated the previous week. Which of the following controls,
    if properly utilized, would have been most effective in preventing the error or ensur-
    ing its prompt detection?
    (a) a control total for hours worked, prepared from time cards collected by the time-
        keeping department
    (b) requiring the treasurer's office to account for the numbers of the prenumbered
        checks issued to the EDP department for the processing of the payroll
    (c) use of a check digit for employee numbers
    (d) use of a header label for the payroll input sheet

(CPA)

31. Accounting functions that are normally considered incompatible in a manual system
    are often combined in an EDP system by using an EDP program, or a series of pro-
    grams. This necessitates an accounting control that prevents unapproved
    (a) access to the magnetic tape library.
    (b) revisions to existing computer programs.
    (c) usage of computer program tapes.
    (d) testing of modified computer programs.

(CPA)

32. Totals of amounts of computer-record data fields that are not usually added for other
    purposes but are used only for data processing control purposes are called
    (a) record totals.
    (b) hash totals.
    (c) processing data totals.
    (d) field totals.

(CPA)

33. The use of a header label in conjunction with magnetic tape is most likely to prevent
    errors by the
    (a) computer operator.
    (b) data entry clerk.
    (c) computer programmer.
    (d) maintenance technician.

(CPA)

34. Where computers are used, the effectiveness of internal accounting control depends,
    in part, on whether the organizational structure includes any incompatible combina-
    tions. Such a combination would exist when there is no separation of the duties be-
    tween the
    (a) documentation librarian and the manager of programming.
    (b) programmer and the console operator.
    (c) systems analyst and the programmer.
    (d) processing control clerk and the data entry supervisor.

(CPA)

35. The basic form of backup used in magnetic tape operations is called
    (a) an odd parity check.
    (b) dual-head processing.
    (c) file protection rings.
    (d) the son–father–grandfather concept.

(CPA)

36. When an on-line, real-time (OLRT) EDP system is in use, internal control can be strengthened by
    (a) providing for the separation of duties between data entry and error listing operations.
    (b) attaching plastic file protection rings to reels of magnetic tape before new data can be entered on the file.
    (c) preparing batch totals to provide assurance that file updates are made for the entire input.
    (d) making a validity check of an identification number before a user can obtain access to the computer files.

(CPA)

37. Which of the following most likely constitutes a weakness in the internal accounting control of an EDP system?
    (a) the control clerk establishes control over data received by the EDP department and reconciles control totals after processing
    (b) the application programmer identifies programs required by the systems design and flowcharts the logic of these programs
    (c) the systems analyst reviews output and controls the distribution of output from the EDP department
    (d) the accounts payable clerk prepares data for computer processing and enters the data into the computer

(CPA)

38. An effective control designed to provide reasonable assurance that hourly payroll information has been entered accurately into the computer system is to
    (a) establish the use of batch control totals for total hours to be processed.
    (b) review the contents of the computer master file.
    (c) limit access to the on-line terminals.
    (d) circulate to user departments periodic reports containing the contents of the master file.

(IIA)

39. Which of the following activities would most likely be performed in the EDP department?
    (a) initiation of changes to master records
    (b) conversion of information to machine-readable form
    (c) correction of transactional errors
    (d) initiation of changes to existing applications

(CPA)

40. Garmela Department Stores has a fully integrated EDP accounting system and is planning to issue credit cards to credit-worthy customers. To strengthen internal control by making it difficult for one to create a valid customer account number, the company's independent auditor has suggested the inclusion of a check digit that should be placed
    (a) at the beginning of a valid account number, only.
    (b) in the middle of a valid account number, only.
    (c) at the end of a valid account number, only.
    (d) consistently in any position.

(CPA)

41. One of the major problems in an EDP system is that incompatible functions may be performed by the same individual. One compensating control for this is use of
    (a) a tape library.
    (b) a self-checking digit system.
    (c) computer-generated hash totals.
    (d) a computer log.

    (CPA)

42. The primary documentation upon which a company should rely for an explanation of how a particular program operates is the
    (a) run manual.
    (b) periodic memory dump.
    (c) maintenance of three generations of master files.
    (d) echo check printout.

    (CPA)

43. The use of external labels in conjunction with magnetic tape storage is most likely to prevent errors that might be made by which of the following?
    (a) a computer programmer
    (b) a systems analyst
    (c) a data entry clerk
    (d) a computer operator

    (CPA)

44. An on-line sales order processing system most likely would have an advantage over a batch sales order processing system by
    (a) detecting errors in the data entry process more easily by the use of edit programs.
    (b) enabling shipment of customer orders to be initiated as soon as the orders are received.
    (c) recording more secure backup copies of the database on magnetic tape files.
    (d) maintaining more accurate records of customer accounts and finished goods inventories.

    (CPA)

45. Which of the following is a general control that would most likely assist an entity whose systems analyst left the entity in the middle of a major project?
    (a) son–father–grandfather record retention
    (b) input and output validation routines
    (c) systems documentation
    (d) check digit verification

    (CPA)

46. This question requires using the check digit formula presented in this chapter (page 503).
    (a) Calculate checks digits for the following hypothetical account numbers: 4388, 5100, 9106.
    (b) Verify the following codes (which include a check digit): 10307, 50008, 22222.

47. Consider the following numerical input data utilized in an accounts receivable application:

Account Number 4 Digits	Invoice Number 4 Digits	Gross Amount 7 Digits	Discount 5 Digits	Net Amount 7 Digits
4012	1003	265000	15000	250000
4810	1007	321550	27130	294420
7188	1008	108010	11500	96510

Required

(a) For these data, calculate an example of each of the following: hash total, financial total, record count.

(b) You are to design an edit program that will be used to screen these data before they are processed against a sequentially organized accounts receivable master file. Assuming that the input data the edit program receives will be sorted in ascending order by account number, what detailed editing procedures would you include in the design of the edit program?

48. The Foxx Company is designing a standard postings file to be used in the editing of transactions to be posted to the general ledger. The file (relation) as designed has the following format:

```
STANDARD-ENTRIES (CODE#, DESCRIPTION, DR-or-CR, ACCOUNT#, ACCOUNT-NAME)
```

Is this relation a flat file? If not, how would you normalize this relation?

49. Indicate the objective of the following questions, which are abstracted from an EDP internal control questionnaire. What error or weakness might exist if the answer to a specific question is "No"?

(a) Do management and user departments review and approve all new systems design work?

(b) Have backup procedures been documented and are the arrangements up-to-date?

(c) Is there an organizational chart of the EDP function?

(d) Are computer operators required to take vacations?

(e) Does more than one programmer or a supervisor have a working knowledge of each specific program?

(f) Are internal file labels tested by computer programs to validate file setup?

(g) Are check digits used where appropriate?

(h) Are changes to master files, such as pay rates or price changes, properly authorized and is their posting to the file verified by the originating department?

(i) Are output reports viewed critically by supervisory personnel in user departments for general reasonableness and quality in relation to prior periods?

50. What control or controls would you recommend in a computer processing system to prevent the following situations?

(a) Working through the main control console, the night-shift computer operator made a change in a payroll program to alter his rate of pay in his favor.

(b) A customer payment recorded on a remittance advice as $55.05 was entered into the computer from a data terminal as $550.50.

(c) A new program to process accounts receivable was unreliable and would not handle common exceptions. The programmer who wrote the program recently quit the organization because he was repeatedly asked to document this program (which he never did do).

(d) The payroll master file was incorrectly loaded on a disk drive that was supposed to hold the accounts receivable master file. The accounts receivable program was nevertheless run, destroying the payroll master file.

(e) A weekly payroll check issued to an hourly employee was based on 96 hours rather than 46.

(f) The master inventory file, contained on a removable magnetic disk, was destroyed by a small fire next to the area where it was stored. The company had to take a special complete inventory in order to reestablish the file.

(g) The magnetic tape containing accounts receivable transactions could not be located. A data processing supervisor said that it could have been put among the scratch tapes available for use in processing.

(h) In preparing payroll checks, the computer omitted 12 of a total of 1,570 checks that should have been processed. The error was not detected until the supervisors distributed the checks.

(i) A sales transaction document was coded with an invalid customer account code (seven digits rather than eight). The error was not detected until the updating run, when it was found that there was no such account to which the transaction could be posted.

(j) During data entry of customer payments, the digit 0 in a payment of $123.40 was mistakenly entered as the letter *O*. As a result, the transaction was not correctly processed.

(k) A systems analyst entered a special routine one evening after work. The next day she obtained the program that calculates interest payments on customer accounts and processed it to add her routine to the program's logic. Her routine adds the fraction of a cent of each customer's interest, which would otherwise be rounded off, to her own account at the bank.

(l) A salesman entering a customer order from a portable data entry terminal entered an incorrect but valid product number. As a result, the customer received a delivery of 100,000 kilograms of industrial salt rather than industrial sugar.

(m) A customer called to inquire as to why he received a bill for five cents amount due, when postage cost is more than a quarter.

51. You have been engaged by Central Savings and Loan Association to examine its financial statements for the year ended December 31, 19X7. The CPA who examined the financial statements at December 31, 19X6, rendered an unqualified opinion.

In January 19X7, the association installed an on-line, real-time computer system. Each teller in the association's main office and seven branch offices has an on-line, input–output terminal. Customers' mortgage payments and savings account deposits and withdrawals are recorded in the accounts by the computer from data input by the teller at the time of the transaction. The teller keys the proper account by account number and enters the information in the terminal keyboard to record the transaction. The accounting department at the main office also has input–output devices. The computer is housed at the main office.

In addition to servicing its own mortgage loans, the association acts as a mortgage servicing agency for three life insurance companies. In this latter activity, the association maintains mortgage records and serves as the collection and escrow agent for the mortgagees (the insurance companies), who pay a fee to the association for these services.

Required

You would expect the association to have certain internal controls in effect because an on-line, real-time computer system is employed. List the internal controls that should be in effect solely because this system is employed, classifying them as

(a) those controls pertaining to input of information

(b) all other types of computer controls.

(CPA)

52. Peabock Company is a wholesaler of softgoods. The inventory is composed of approximately 3500 different items. The company employs a computerized batch processing system to maintain its perpetual inventory records. The system is run each weekend so that the inventory reports are available on Monday morning for management use. The system has been functioning satisfactorily for the past 15 months, providing the company with accurate records and timely reports.

The preparation of purchase orders has been automatic as a part of the inventory system to ensure that the company will maintain enough inventory to meet customer demand. When an item of inventory falls below a predetermined level, a record of the inventory item is written. This record is used in conjunction with the vendor file to prepare the purchase orders.

Exception reports are prepared during the updating of the inventory and the preparation of the purchase orders. These reports identify any errors or exceptions identified during the processing. In addition, the system provides for management approval of all purchase orders exceeding a specified amount. Any exceptions or items requiring management approval are handled by supplemental runs on Monday morning and combined with the weekend results.

Figure 13.11 presents a system flowchart of Peabock's inventory and purchase order procedure.

Required

(a) The illustrated system flowchart of Peabock's inventory and purchase order system was prepared before the system was fully operational. Several steps that are important to the successful operation of the system were inadvertently omitted from the chart. Now that the system is operating effectively, management wants the system documentation complete and would like the flowchart corrected. Describe steps that have been omitted and indicate where the omissions have occurred. The flowchart does not need to be drawn.

(b) In order for Peabock's inventory purchase order system to function properly, control procedures would be included in the system. Describe the type of control procedures Peabock would use in its system to assure proper functioning, and indicate where these procedures would be placed in the system.

(CMA)

53. Tune Fork, Inc., is a large wholesaler of sheet music, music books, musical instruments, and other music-related supplies. The company acquired a midrange computer system last year, and an inventory control system has already been implemented. Now the systems department is developing a new accounts receivable system.

Figure 13.12 is a diagram of the proposed accounts receivable system as designed by the systems department. The objectives of the new system are to produce current and timely information that can be used to control bad debts, to provide information to the sales department regarding customers whose accounts are delinquent, to produce monthly statements for customers, and to produce notices to customers regarding a change in the status of their charge privileges.

Input data for the system are taken from four source documents: approved credit applications, sales invoices, cash payment remittances, and credit memoranda. The accounts receivable (A/R) file is maintained on magnetic disk by customer account number. The record for each customer contains identification information, last month's balance, current month's transactions (detailed), and current balance. Some of the output items generated from the system are identified and described briefly:

1. Accounts receivable register (weekly)—a listing of all customers and account balances included in the accounts receivable file.
2. Aging schedule (monthly)—a schedule of all customers with outstanding balances, detailing the amount owed by age classifications—0–30 days, 30–60 days, 60–90 days, over 90 days old.
3. Delinquency and write-off registers (monthly)—(a) a listing of those accounts that are delinquent and (b) a listing of customers' accounts that have been closed and written off; related notices are prepared and sent to these customers.

Required

Tune Fork's systems department must develop the system controls for the new accounts receivable system. Identify and explain the system controls that should be instituted with the new system. When appropriate, describe the location in the flowchart where the control should be introduced.

(CMA)

54. Consider the on-line cash receipts application discussed in this chapter. Modify the cash application procedure to allow the operator to process customer remittances with multiple payments or no payments (invoice numbers) referenced on them. Your

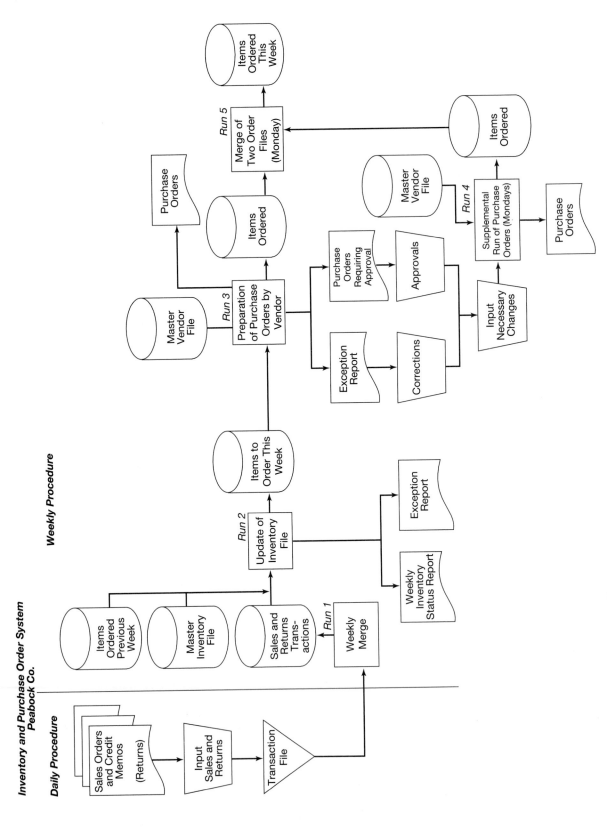

FIGURE 13.11 Flowchart for Problem 52.

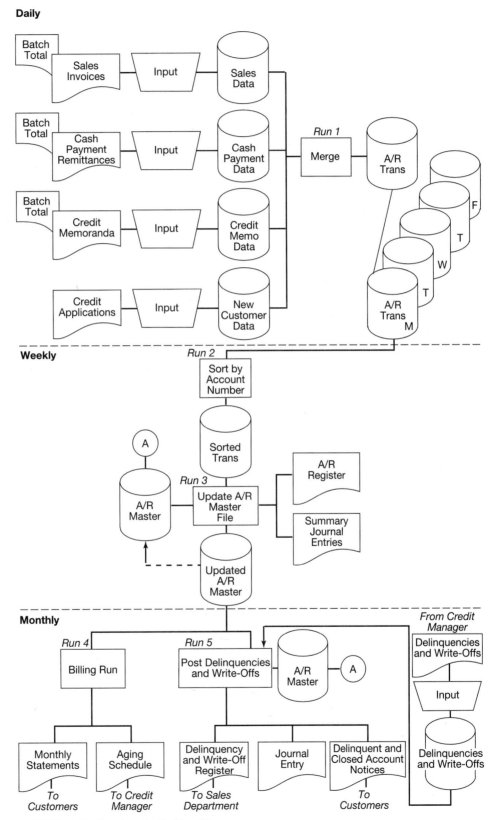

FIGURE 13.12 Flowchart for Problem 53.

comments should specify in detail the options that your procedure gives to the terminal operator.

55. Until recently, Consolidated Electricity Company employed a batch processing system for recording the receipt of customer payments. The following narrative and Figure 13.13 describe the procedures involved in this system.

The customer's payment and the remittance advice (an optically scanned turn-around document) are received in the treasurer's office. An accounts receivable clerk in the treasurer's office enters the cash receipt onto the remittance advice and forwards the document to the EDP department. The cash receipt is added to a control tape listing and then filed for deposit later in the day. When the deposit slips are received from EDP later in the day (approximately 2:30 P.M. each day), the cash receipts are removed from the file and deposited with the original deposit slip. The second copy of the deposit slip and the control tape are compared for accuracy before the deposit is made and then filed together.

In the EDP department, the remittance advices received from the treasurer's office are held until 2:00 P.M. daily. At that time, the customer payments are processed to update the records on magnetic tape and to prepare a deposit slip in triplicate. During

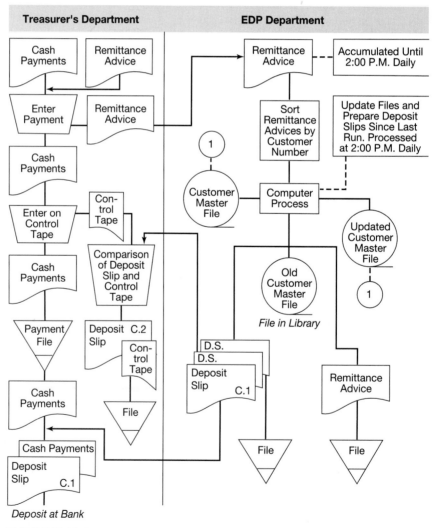

FIGURE 13.13 Flowchart for Problem 55.

the update process, data are read, nondestructively, from the master accounts receivable tape, processed, and then recorded on a new master tape. The original and second copy of the deposit slip are forwarded to the treasurer's office. The old master tape (former accounts receivable file), the remittance advices (in customer-number order), and the third copy of the deposit slip are stored and filed in a secure place. The updated accounts receivable master tape is maintained in the system for processing the next day.

Consolidated has reviewed and redesigned its computer system so that it has on-line capabilities. The new cash receipts procedures, described in what follows, are designed to take advantage of the new system.

The customer's payment and remittance advice are received in the treasurer's office as before. A terminal is located in the treasurer's office to enter the cash receipts. An operator keys in the customer's number and payment from the remittance advice and checks. The cash receipt is entered into the system once the operator has confirmed that the proper account and amount are displayed on the screen. The payment is then processed on-line against the accounts receivable file maintained on magnetic disk. The cash receipts are filed for deposit later in the day. The remittance advices are filed in the order in which they are processed; these documents will be kept until the next working day and then destroyed. The computer prints out a deposit slip in duplicate at 2:00 P.M. for all cash receipts since the last deposit. The deposit slips are forwarded to the treasurer's office. The cash receipts are removed from the file and deposited with the original deposit slip; the duplicate deposit slip is filed for further reference. At the close of business hours (5:00 P.M.) each day, the EDP department prepares a record of the current day's cash receipts activity on magnetic tape. This tape is then stored in a secure place in the event of a systems malfunction; after ten working days, the tape is released for further use.

Required

(a) Prepare a systems flowchart of Consolidated Electricity Company's new on-line cash receipt procedures.
(b) Have the new cash receipt procedures as designed and implemented by Consolidated created any internal and systems control problems for the company? Explain your answer.

56. Tel-Zet, a long-distance communications company, uses direct, on-line processing in its customer payments application system. Data entry terminals in the cashier's department allow direct entry of customer payments data into the computer system for processing.

Customer payments are delivered from the mailroom to the cashier's office for processing. Clerks working under the supervision of the customer payment supervisor open the customer payments to ensure that both a remittance advice and a check are enclosed. If either of these is missing, the payment is set aside in a batch that is subsequently delivered to the chief cashier for reconciliation. Payments containing both a remittance advice and a check are grouped into batches of about 50. The customer payment supervisor attaches a batch control form to each batch and assigns the batches to the data entry operators for processing.

Data entry operators sign onto the computer system using their own unique password. Operators enter customer account numbers from the remittance advices. When an account number match is made, the system prompts the operator to key in the other information—such as check number and the amount of the payment—as required. These data are taken directly from the customer's check. In all cases where input is not possible, the remittance advices and customer payments are returned to the customer payment supervisor for resolution.

After each batch of payments has been entered, the operator terminates the session with a special command. The system then presents a summary report of terminal activity on the monitor. The operator copies the total amount of payments from the summary report onto the batch control form and then returns the batch to the supervisor. The supervisor keeps a cumulative total of payments applied by the operators; as each batch is returned, the total amount of payments shown on the batch control form is added to the running total. At the end of the shift, the customer payment supervisor prepares a payments received report (three copies). The customer payments and two copies of the payments received report are forwarded to the chief cashier for verification and deposit. The customer remittance advices, in batches, are filed with the payments received report by date.

Required
(a) Identify deficiencies and/or weaknesses in the data entry procedures described.
(b) Suggest an improvement to remove each weakness/deficiency that you note in part (a). Use the following format to answer this question.

a. Deficiency/weakness   b. improvement suggest

57. VBR Company has recently installed a new computer system that has on-line, real-time capability. Terminals are used for data entry and inquiry. A new cash receipts and accounts receivable file maintenance system has been designed and implemented for use with this new equipment. All programs have been written and tested, and the new system is being run in parallel with the old system. After two weeks of parallel operation, no differences have been observed between the two systems other than data entry errors on the old system.

Al Brand, data processing manager, is enthusiastic about the new equipment and system. He reveals that the system was designed, coded, compiled, debugged, and tested by programmers utilizing an on-line terminal installed specifically for around-the-clock use by the programming staff. He claimed that this access to the computer saved one-third in programming elapsed time. All files, including accounts receivable, are on-line at all times as the firm moves toward a full database mode. All programs, new and old, are available at all times for recall into memory for scheduled operating use or for program maintenance. Program documentation and actual tests confirm that data entry edits in the new system include all conventional data error and validity checks appropriate to the system.

Inquiries have confirmed that the new system conforms precisely to the flow-charts. A turnaround copy of the invoice is used as a remittance advice (R/A) by 99% of the customers; if the R/A is missing, the cashier applies the payment to a selected invoice. Sales terms are net 60 days, but payment patterns are sporadic. Statements are not mailed to customers. Late payments are commonplace and are not vigorously pursued. VBR does not have a bad-debt problem because bad-debt losses average only 0.5% of sales.

Before authorizing the termination of the old system, Cal Darden, controller, has requested a review of the internal control features that have been designed for the new system. Security against unauthorized access and fraudulent actions, assurance of the integrity of the files, and protection of the firm's assets should be provided by the internal controls.

Required
(a) Describe how fraud by lapping of accounts receivable could be committed in the new system and discuss how it could be prevented.
(b) Based on the description of VBR's new system and the systems flowchart that has been presented in Figure 13.14:
   1. Describe any other defects that exist in the system.
   2. Suggest how each other defect you identified could be corrected.

(CMA)

58. The flowchart in Figure 13.15 depicts part of a client's revenue cycle. Some of the flowchart symbols are labeled to indicate control procedures and records. For each symbol numbered 1 through 13, select one response from the answer list that follows. Each response in the list may be selected once or not at all.

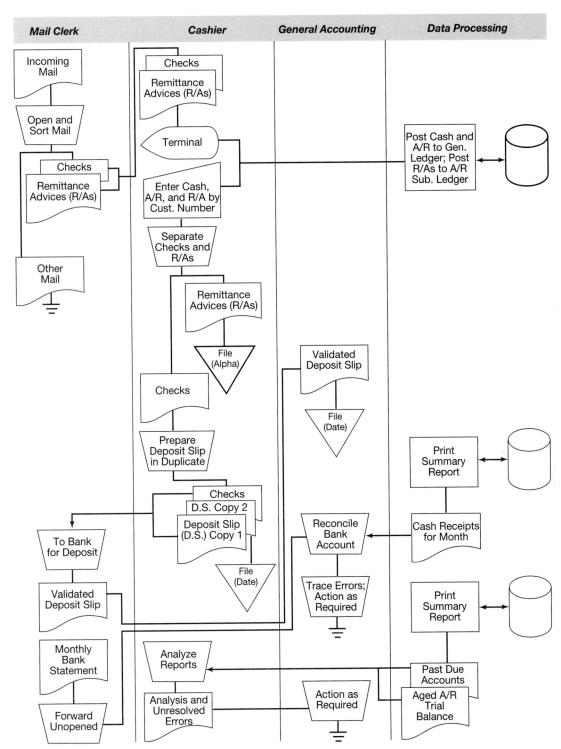

FIGURE 13.14 Flowchart for Problem 57.

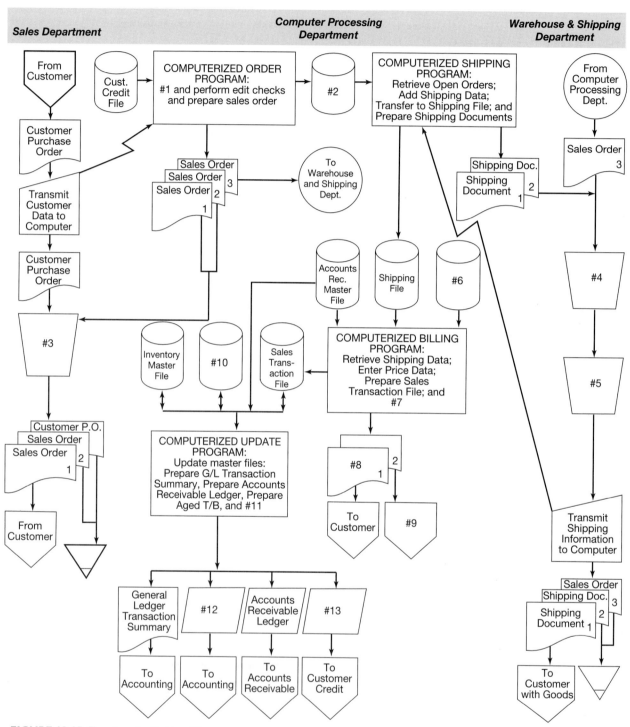

FIGURE 13.15 Flowchart for Problem 58.

Answer List

OPERATIONS AND CONTROL PROCEDURES

A. Enter shipping data
B. Verify agreement of sales order and shipping document
C. Write off accounts receivable
D. To warehouse and shipping department
E. Authorize accounts receivable write-off
F. Prepare aged trial balance
G. To sales department
H. Release goods for shipment
I. To accounts receivable department
J. Enter price data
K. Determine that customer exists
L. Match customer purchase order with sales order
M. Perform customer credit check
N. Prepare sales journal
O. Prepare sales invoice

DOCUMENTS, JOURNALS, LEDGERS, AND FILES

P. Shipping document
Q. General ledger master file
R. General journal
S. Master price file
T. Sales journal
U. Sales invoice
V. Cash receipts journal
W. Uncollectable accounts file
X. Shipping file
Y. Aged trial balance
Z. Open order file

Answers to Chapter Quiz

1. C	**4.** D	**7.** A	**10.** D
2. A	**5.** C	**8.** B	
3. B	**6.** B	**9.** B	

CHAPTER 14

Quick-Response Sales and Manufacturing Systems

LEARNING OBJECTIVES

Careful study of this chapter will enable you to:

■ Understand why bar codes have become the dominant technology for automatic identification of transactions.

■ Characterize the key components of quick-response retail sales systems.

■ Identify and describe key components of computer-integrated manufacturing (CIM) systems.

■ Depict the flow of processing necessary to support manufacturing resource planning (MRP II) systems.

■ Describe why activity-based costing is particularly relevant to CIM systems.

AUTOMATIC IDENTIFICATION TECHNOLOGY

A **quick-response system** utilizes contemporary information technology to maximize system performance. Automatic identification technology is central to the design and performance of a quick-response system. Automatic identification (henceforth abbreviated AI) of transactions provides improved efficiency, reduced data processing costs, and elimination of the handling and storage problems associated with information that is recorded on paper. There are many potential applications of AI in organizations. AI can be used anywhere a pencil and paper is used—remote data collection, ticket identification systems, security checkpoint verification, file folder tracking, inventory control, and identifying work-in-process in repair or manufacturing environments. Many organizations are using bar codes to physically tag assets for AI. The bar codes replace traditional paper-based identification labels, which must be hand-copied during the physical inventory count. AI can be used to identify product numbers during an inventory count. AI might even be utilized by auditors to identify and subsequently control audit workpapers and other documentation.

There are several different types of AI. Optical character recognition (OCR), optical mark recognition (OMR), and magnetic-ink character recognition

(MICR) devices have existed for several decades. OCR involves scanning characters printed in special typefaces, and OMR involves scanning marks made in predefined fields. MICR is an input method commonly used by banks to read the numbers at the bottom of checks. MICR and OCR fonts have the advantage of being readable by both people and machines. Bar code scanning is similar to OCR and MICR, but characters are encoded with a graphics symbology that is not as directly human-readable.

More recent methods of AI include radio frequency and magnetic-strip identification. Of the different AI technologies, radio frequency identification has the unique advantage that the item being automatically identified does not have to be visible to the scanner. This is because radio waves, unlike light rays, may pass unaffected through most packaging or protective coverings. AI is frequently used to "license plate," that is, tag, something such as a product for identification. Only ID information is coded. The UPC, for example, identifies a product but does not contain its price. Magnetic-strip identification is generally used when a "license plate" approach is not being used, that is, more information is to be coded and perhaps even updated on the item. Although bar codes might be used in such instances, magnetic-strip identification has a much greater data density.

Bar Coding Technology

Bar codes have become the dominant AI technology for several reasons. Foremost is that machine-readable bar codes can be successfully printed easily. "Successfully" means that the printed bar codes may be subsequently scanned with high accuracy and reliability. "Easily" means that no special equipment or paper is required. Even reasonable-quality dot-matrix printers may be used. Printing on paper is extremely cheap; thus bar codes may be produced at minimal cost compared to any other AI technology.

A second significant reason is that bar codes are inherently more reliable than OCR when damage or wear and tear in use is a factor. Experience and studies have been shown that AI labels that use bar codes can withstand much more wear and tear than the same label that is coded in OCR. Thus, bar codes have replaced OCR in many applications.

A **bar code** is a grouping of parallel dark (usually black) bars of varying widths separated by light (usually white) spaces of varying widths. Information is encoded in the bar code by varying the presence or absence of bars and by varying the widths of the bars and the spaces between them. What makes a bar code readable is that light is reflected from a light surface and is absorbed by a dark surface. The spaces between bars reflect light and the bars absorb light. The width of a space or bar is "read" by the amount of time the light is reflected or absorbed, respectively.

Scanners come in a variety of forms, such as hand-held lightpens, fixed-beam stationary units, and moving-beam stationary units. Touch ("pen type") scanners must be in contact; laser scanners read from a distance. Early scanners were "hardwired" and confined to the identification of a single bar code symbology. Microprocessor-based scanners are autodiscriminating among a variety of symbologies.

The light beam from the scanner is focused into a tiny spot that scans the bar code label. The output from the scanner is an analog waveform with maximum amplitudes proportional to the white spaces between bars and minimum or near-zero amplitudes proportional to the dark bars. The total duration of a signal representing a space or a bar is determined by the width of that space or bar. The information contained in the waveform is converted into digital information by a decoder that assigns a binary value of "1" to wide bars and spaces and a binary value of "0" to narrow bars and spaces. The combination of the binary values is the basis for all of the bar code symbols in use today.

Two of Five

Human reading of a bar code is possible if one knows how the data characters in the bar code were encoded. Two of Five is one of the simplest bar codes in use. It consists of a numeric character set with different start and stop characters (characters that provide the scanner with start and stop reading instructions as well as code orientation).

Two of Five is detailed in Table 14.1. Two of Five is a discrete code: Only bars contain information. Spaces are not part of the code and thus may vary in width. Wide bars are read as "1," narrow bars as "0." The fifth digit in each encoded character is a parity bit. The fifth digit is set at either 0 or 1, whichever is necessary to make the total number of 1 bits even. As indicated in Table 14.1, each digit encoded in Two of Five requires five bars, two of which are wide, that is, 1's; thus, the name "Two of Five."

In addition to the 0 through 9 character coding, a start character at one end of the bar code and a different stop character at the other end enable bidirectional decoding of the symbol. The scanning system can read the bar code label in either direction. If the label is read in the reverse direction, the software in the system merely reverses the sequence of the characters.

Figure 14.1 illustrates the coding of the number "02." Note the correspondence of the bars to the character set shown in Table 14.1. As shown, the bars code the start symbol, then the digit "0," then the digit "2," and then the stop code. Leading and trailing edges of the bar code symbol are identified by start and stop characters included in the symbol. The start character is positioned at the normal left end by the symbol adjacent to the most significant digit. The stop character is positioned at the normal right end adjacent to the least significant

TABLE 14.1	Two of Five Code	
Character set:	0	00110
numeric	1	10001
	2	01001
	3	11000
	4	00101
	5	10100
	6	01100
	7	00011
	8	10010
	9	01010
	start	110
	stop	101
Discrete	Only bars contain information. Spaces are not part of the code. Wide bars read as a "1," narrow bars as a "0." Wide bars are usually three times as wide as narrow bars.	
Self-checking	Each digit in the code has a parity bit.	
Density: relatively low	With a 3:1 wide bar to narrow bar ratio, equal size spaces, and each space the same width as the narrow bar, each character requires 14 modules.	

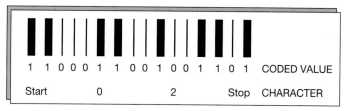

FIGURE 14.1 Two-of-Five Code Illustration.

digit. An area known as the quiet zone is an area that is clear and free of all printed matter preceding the start character and following the stop character.

Characteristics of Bar Code Symbology

A variety of bar codes are in use today. Some provide for the encoding of a small amount of information; others contain a great deal of information. The specific application determines which available bar code is needed. Several characteristics of bar code symbology are summarized in Table 14.2.

Interleaved 2 of 5 (also known as USD-1) uses the same coding technique as Two of Five except both bars and spaces are coded. In USD-1, two characters are paired together using bars to represent the first character and spaces to represent the second. This interleaved technique permits information to be encoded in both the bars and the spaces, and results in a higher code density.

When both bars and spaces are part of the code, the bar code symbology is said to be continuous. The interleaving process necessitates an even number of characters. Therefore, if an odd number of characters are to be encoded, a leading 0 changes the number of characters to an even number to allow character pairing. An example would be the number 127. It would be encoded as 0127. Similarly, the number 2 would be encoded as 02.

Many other bar codes exist. The most familiar is the UPC. EAN (European Article Number) is similar to UPC. Codabar is a discrete, self-checking code that is frequently utilized in libraries. The Codabar character set is numeric, and also includes several special symbols (:,/,.,+). Code 39 (code 3 of 9) is one of several alphanumeric codes that are available.

TABLE 14.2 Characteristics of Bar Code Symbology

Character set	Number of characters.
	Alphanumeric or numeric.
Discrete or continuous	Whether or not spaces between bars are part of the code.
Self-checking	Errors (substitution of characters) occur from printing defects. Parity increases to two or more the number of independent substitution errors required for substitution of characters in a code.
Symbol tolerances	Printing tolerances determine the type of printing devices that can be used (i.e., dot matrix or laser). Printer errors such as too much or too little ink might cause spaces to be read as lines or vice versa, causing substitution errors.
	Scanning tolerances affect accuracy and speed of reading codes.
Density	Number of characters per inch.
	Also may be measured in modules per character, where a module is defined as the narrowest bar or space width.

The Automatic Identification Manufacturers product section of The Material Handling Institute, Inc. (MHI), in Pittsburgh, issues Uniform Symbol Descriptions of the bar codes in use industrially. Interleaved 2 of 5, discussed before, is also known as USD-1 as it is described in USD-1, that is, Uniform Symbol Descriptions Number One.

QUICK-RESPONSE SALES SYSTEMS

In quick-response sales systems, purchase orders for inventory items are made on a "demand–pull" basis rather than a fixed interval (e.g., monthly or weekly) "push" basis to restock inventory levels. New goods arrive when they are needed, that is to say, "just in time." Orders to vendors are placed on the basis of actual sales to quickly replenish stocks of items that are selling. Current sales demand pulls (i.e., automatically generates) orders for inventory. Retailers order on the basis of current buying trends. This is critical in retailing, where fads (i.e., customer demand for certain products) can and do change rapidly. What sold last year, last month, or maybe even last week may no longer be what the customer wants.

Quick-response sales systems are central to the competitive strategy of mass retailers such as Sears, Wal-Mart, and J.C. Penney. These systems are also central to the competitive strategy of major vendors to mass retailers, such as Levi, Haggar, and Wrangler (all brand-name suppliers of men's clothing for retail outlets). This is because major vendors to mass retailers are themselves operating sales systems, and they face exactly the same problems. If Levi, for example, is out of stock of a popular item when it is ordered, the delay or inability to satisfy the order is lost revenue. In a competitive market, this revenue is lost forever. Sears will buy similar merchandise from a competitor who can fill the order when it is needed. The customer, in turn, will purchase a competitor's product.

Levi, Haggar, and Wrangler in their turn must issue purchase orders to their vendors to stock the items that they in turn manufacture and/or resell to retailers. The suppliers face the same situation in their sales systems. If they are out-of-stock when items are ordered, the delay or inability to satisfy the order is lost revenue. And so on, the situation repeats for each trading partner. If a major competitor participates in a quick-response retail sales system, then one is likely to be in a position of competitive disadvantage unless one also participates.

A significant degree of cooperation among trading partners is required to implement quick-response sales systems. Companies, their suppliers, and buyers often enter into close, noncompetitive trade partnership agreements. In some cases, customers and suppliers coordinate their production schedules so that goods can be manufactured just-in-time. Prior to quick-response systems, trading partners have customarily worked at arm's length from each other, sharing the minimum information required to make a deal. Reveal more information, and your trading partners might take advantage of you. The development of mutual trust among trading partners is essential to the operation of quick-response retail sales systems. The retailer must trust the supplier, to whom he supplies current data from his POS terminals. The retailer trusts that the supplier will use these data to ship the right product to the right store at the right time. The supplier must, in turn, trust that the retailer is providing accurate data, and that the retailer will accept shipments when they arrive. All trading partners must trust their data are being used solely for the intended purposes, and are not being sold or supplied to direct competitors.

Components of Quick-Response Sales Systems

Two technologies have combined to make quick-response retail sales systems feasible (Figure 14.2): the POS (point-of-sale) system and the EDI (electronic data interchange) ordering system. Each of these systems is discussed.

The POS System

The UPC bar code scanned by POS technology at the checkout counter of a retail store is the initial event in a chain of events that ends with the right item being quickly replenished in the store's inventory so that it can be sold again.

A consideration of the type of information useful to the management of a retail store would include numerous summaries of sales transaction data, such as total sales, total cash sales, total sales on credit, sales returns, total purchases, and current inventory status. Further consideration of a retailing store would indicate that a large percentage of transactions originate at the cash registers—the point of sale in the merchandising cycle. Enhancing of the traditional cash register to allow it to function as a source data entry device for sales transactions is the essence of a POS system.

A system that collects data on retail sales in this fashion is referred to as a **point-of-sale (POS) system** because data are collected at the point where the sale is completed. The specially designed cash registers are called point-of-sale retail terminals. Data may be entered manually through a keying operation by the sales clerk or automatically, using special codes and sensing devices. Sensing devices include wands and scanners for OCR (optical character recognition) and UPC bar code recognition. Bar code scanners have performed more reliably than OCR equipment, and have become the most prevalent form of POS technology.

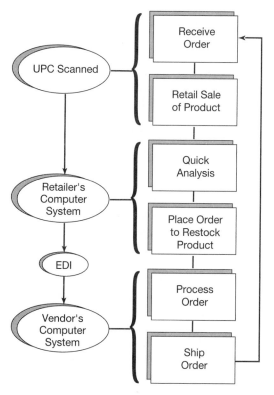

FIGURE 14.2 Chain of Events in a Quick-Response Sales System.

POS terminals record both cash and charge sales. Data relating to either type of sale are transmitted to a computer network where they may be processed immediately. In a cash sale, the customer pays cash and receives the goods. In addition, a sales slip is printed by the terminal. Data relating to the transaction—such as inventory codes for the items purchased, number of items purchased, cost of each item, date, total sales amount, and any sales taxes—are recorded via the terminal and made available to the store's computer network for immediate processing. For example, the number of items on inventory of the goods purchased by the customer will be reduced by the units sold. The sales tax, cost of the items sold, and total sales price will be posted to daily sales records.

Sales on account require that a customer's charge account number and credit standing be verified prior to releasing goods. The customer's charge account number is input to the POS terminal, allowing the computer system to access the customer's record, examine it, and determine the status of the account. If the charge sale is authorized, the system automatically completes the transaction. The sale on credit will be automatically posted against the appropriate records in the same manner as a cash sale. The status of the customer's charge account will also be updated to a new charge balance, and an update of the credit available to the customer and a record of the items purchased will be made.

Point-of-sale systems have a major impact on the management of a retail firm, providing a wide variety of timely and detailed reports concerning operations. Various reports may pinpoint areas of responsibility and accountability. Typical reports that may be obtained include checker settlement, deposits and receipts, checker cash list, department sales, store dollars, hourly activity, price-lookup file, and check authorization file.

An hourly activity report offers management detailed statistics about customer activity, average sale per customer, average number of items sold per customer, and total items sold within a specified period of time. Such a report summarizes sales data by hourly time intervals and enables store management to monitor customer traffic patterns throughout the store and at checkout lanes. POS systems provide detailed information on stock turnover, which is useful to management in assessing profitability. In grocery stores, for example, POS system data on the sale of generic food items have sometimes indicated a profit rate lower than expected because of the low turnover rate of these items. Such detailed data are not available without a POS system, and management has to guess or presume the profitability rate associated with the sale of specific items. Such guesses or presumptions often turn out to be incorrect.

Bar Coding Technology

Automatic identification of sales input is essential to a quick-response system; thus, machine-readable bar codes and scanner technology are critical components of quick-response retail sales systems. Maximum benefit is obtained when the standard, widely used UPC bar code system is utilized. Originally used in grocery retailing, UPC coding is now commonplace on consumer products. When UPC coding is utilized, all participants in the quick-response system chain share and process the same basic data. Without code standardization, each agent in the chain uses its own codes, which must be cross-referenced to everyone else's codes. While cross-referencing codes is possible, it is both time-consuming and error-prone. Neither of these attributes facilitates quick response.

Using UPC as a base, all agents use the same product code, eliminating cross-referencing problems. But this is a relatively minor consideration when compared to the other benefits that are obtained from UPC standardization. The UPC product identification code can be scanned and used for automatic identification throughout the chain of quick-response events. Cartons or other containers in transit or in inventory can be coded and scanned as well as individual items at the POS checkout counter. Cartons are UPC coded when shipped by the vendor. Cartons are scanned when received by the retailer, and the data input to the store information system. Cartons can be scanned when in inventory, to easily identify the items contained within. UPC coding also lets the vendor code individual products for sale in the retailer's store. A retailer no longer has to code its own inventory; it arrives precoded with UPC.

The EDI Ordering System

EDI (electronic data interchange) is the direct computer-to-computer exchange of business documents via a communications network. The EDI link between the retailer's computer system and the vendor's computer system in Figure 14.2 allows near instantaneous placing and processing of the purchase order, facilitating quick shipment. The vendor could also invoice the retailer using EDI. In some cases, EFT payment might be made by the retailer to the vendor's account. All of these events, including the picking of the order from the vendor's inventory, might take place without any human intervention.

Public EDI standards, in particular ANSI X.12, also provide maximum benefit when used in quick-response systems. Without standardization, each agent in the chain must cross-reference everyone else's codes. Public EDI standards provide a common architecture for data interchange, and thus eliminate costly and error-prone cross-referencing. Many early users of EDI started with their own proprietry codes for electronic data interchange, then switched to the X.12 standard.

In addition to purchase order and invoicing data, EDI can also be used to transmit retail sales data captured from the retail store to vendors. These data can then be analyzed by the vendor and directly input to purchasing and production applications to provide maximum inventory planning and control. This is feasible because both the retailer and vendor utilize the UPC product code. Actual retail sales data at the size and color level may be instantaneously known by the vendor due to the integration of UPC coding, scanner technology, and EDI.

EDI might also be used by vendors to electronically transmit electronic catalogs with current price information to retailers.

The quick-response retail sales system just described might be considered to be an ideal system. This ideal system has already been achieved by some organizations. Although the ideal system is indeed feasible, several variations are common. One variation is to use bar codes and scanning technology, but to forward computerized retail sales and purchase orders data to the vendor by nonelectronic means, such as ordinary mail services. Although similar processing is possible, the non-EDI link slows the system considerably. Another type of variation is to implement EDI without POS scanning. Retail sales and inventory data must be manually processed by the retailer, but the results can be transmitted with EDI. This variation might be the only feasible way for some small retailers to participate in a quick-response system operated by major vendors, as POS scanning technology is still relatively expensive. Other variations incorporate proprietary coding systems, substituting proprietary codes for the UPC or ANSI X.12. This type of variation might persist for early EDI users, who continue to use their established systems rather than switch to common UPC and X.12 coding standards.

Such variations might also occur in cases where an organization finds UPC coding inadequate for its own purposes, or chooses not to use UPC coding for competitive reasons. The UPC code is public knowledge, and some organizations may wish to keep their data codes secret.

Price-conscious mass merchandising retailers are currently the largest users of quick-response sales systems. Many large retailing organizations have set themselves up as the central hub in their own EDI networks. Several of these organizations originally developed their own proprietary code systems, but most have since switched to UPC and ANSI X.12.

Transaction Processing in Quick-Response Sales Systems

Although the exact sequence of events will vary somewhat from system to system, the processing of an order will typically involve seven steps. These include sending the customer an electronic catalog, forecasting the customer's sales order, receiving and translating the incoming order, sending an acknowledgment, sending the order to inventory or production (as applicable), generating and transmitting an advance shipping notice, and shipping the goods (see Figure 14.3). Each of these events is discussed in turn.

Sending the Customer an Electronic Catalog

The customer is periodically sent (via EDI) an electronic catalog of the company's products. A special version of this catalog might be made for each customer to reflect any possible contract prices agreed on through competitive bidding.

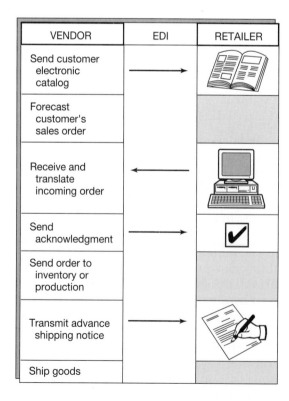

FIGURE 14.3 Transaction Processing in Quick-Response Sales Systems.

Sending the catalog electronically has three major advantages over sending it in paper form. First, the information in the electronic catalog can be used by the customer to generate an EDI purchase order. This minimizes errors that might arise from the manual keying of data that would otherwise be required. Second, the catalog allows the company to almost instantly bring the customer up to date with new prices and other information. Third, the electronic catalog can obtain UPC product codes that can be subsequently used by both companies for automatic identification and tracking.

Forecasting the Customer's Sales Order

In many cases, the company will analyze the customer's sales trends and predict future needs. Even in a JIT system, predicting demand can facilitate production planning.

Receiving and Translating the Incoming Order

The initial processing of the incoming EDI order involves several phases. These include the physical receipt of the order, validation and authentication, and decryption and translation. Each phase is discussed.

Physical Receipt of the Order   There are several ways that an order may arrive, depending on the system. It can arrive as an electronic mail message, either in the company's internal mail system or in a third-party mail/EDI system. Alternatively, the company might have its own dedicated EDI communications server.

Validation, Decryption, and Authentication   Regardless of how the incoming message physically arrives, it must be validated, decrypted, and authenticated. Even if the message itself is encrypted, its electronic envelope generally will not be. As an initial check, the return address in this envelope will be checked to see if the message originated from a recognized customer. Next, the message will be decrypted (if necessary) and authenticated. Authentication is accomplished through the use of authentication codes that ensure the message has not been altered in transit.

Once decrypted, the message is checked for internal consistency and completeness. EDI documents typically contain **dual control numbers,** one control number at the beginning of the message and another at the end. The correctness of internal passwords is also verified. Then the message is translated into a format recognized by the company's accounting system, and, finally, the document is assigned an internal sequence number.

Sending an Acknowledgment

Next the sender of the message is sent an acknowledgment. Three types of acknowledgments are possible. A **transmission acknowledgment** simply indicates that a message was received. A **functional acknowledgment** not only acknowledges receipt of the message, but also reports in detail the items in the received message. Finally, a **transactional acknowledgment** provides full verification of all data (e.g., the correctness of the part numbers) in the message.

Sending the Order to Production/Inventory

The order is sent to production or inventory for processing. Transaction processing in the production and/or inventory department is discussed.

Generating and Transmitting an Advance Shipping Notice

The advance shipping notice will alert the customer to the planned delivery date. This notice will typically include the customer's purchase order number, the quantities being shipped, and bar codes for automatic identification. In many companies, the advance shipping notice also serves as an invoice.

Shipping the Goods

The shipping department scans items as they are packed. This permits automatic matching of the bar codes on the packed items against those in the advance shipping notice. The packing slip is then automatically generated.

Special Internal Control Considerations

Certain internal control problems particularly pertain to quick-response sales systems. First, customer orders may be processed without human intervention or approval. In effect, the customer may have the ability to generate his or her own sales order because generation of the sales order is automatically performed when a valid EDI purchase order is received. Second, the traditional separation of duties in transactions is completely obliterated. The computer handles the transaction from beginning to end. Finally, many traditional documents may be eliminated in EDI-based systems. For example, as was discussed before, in such systems it is common practice to dispense with invoices. The various special control problems in quick-response systems can be compensated for by careful program data editing checks and transaction logs, and also by good computer security.

QUICK-RESPONSE MANUFACTURING SYSTEMS

A **computer-integrated manufacturing (CIM) system** integrates the physical manufacturing system and the manufacturing resource planning (MRP II) systems. A **quick-response manufacturing system** is a CIM system in which the physical manufacturing system and the manufacturing resource planning (MRP II) systems are integrated with advanced integration technologies (Figure 14.4). **Advanced integration technologies** consist of EDI, automatic identification, and distributed processing.

Components of Quick-Response Manufacturing System

The Physical Manufacturing System

Two subsystems directly support the physical manufacturing system. These include the CADD (computer-aided design and drafting) and CAM (computer-aided manufacturing) systems, discussed in what follows.

Computer-Aided Design and Drafting (CADD)   CADD is the use of computer software to perform engineering functions, and is principally intended to increase the design engineer's productivity. This productivity increase, in turn, allows the organization to be more responsive to market demands for new and improved product offerings. In addition, CADD systems allow the automation of repetitive design tasks, further increasing productivity, as well as accuracy.

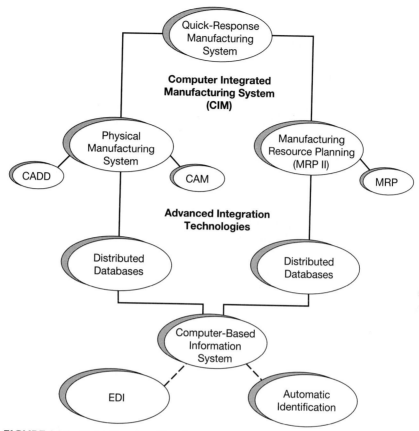

FIGURE 14.4   Quick-Response Manufacturing System.

CADD was developed initially to be used in manufacturing aircraft and missiles and other complex products. It is now widely used in the manufacture of consumer-oriented products like refrigerators and televisions. Engineers, designers, and drafters work at CADD stations—personal workstations dedicated to assisting in their jobs. A CADD station usually consists of a monitor with graphics capability, a light pen or mouse for placing lines and other details on the screen, and a plotter or printer for hard copy. Details on product design are stored by the computer and can be recalled and manipulated by the user. Various estimates suggest that CADD improves productivity by as much as 20 to 1.

CADD systems provide several different types of support functions. **Solids modeling** is the mathematical representation of a part as a solid object in computer memory. These models are represented as volumes enclosed by surfaces. Part models can be used to predict properties of finished products, such as weight, stability, or moments of inertia. **Finite-element analysis** is a mathematical method used to determine mechanical characteristics, such as stresses of structures under load. The structure is reduced to a network of simple geometrical elements, such as rods, shells, or cubes. Each of these elements has stress characteristics that are easily obtained from well-established theory. The behavior of the structure is predicted by having a computer solve a resulting set of simultaneous equations for all elements.

Automated drafting produces engineering drawings and other hard-copy documentation. Drawings are produced by plotting various views of the geometric model previously created and stored in computer memory.

Computer-Aided Manufacturing (CAM)   CAM systems include software for defining the manufacturing process, tools to improve process productivity, decision support systems to aid in the control and monitoring of the production process, and in some implementations, elements of shop floor process control such as robotics, programmable logic controllers, and machine vision systems. Such devices might be called "intelligent tools." In robots or other intelligent tools, the sequence of instructions for guiding equipment through the steps of the manufacturing process is provided by a computer. An **industrial robot** is a device designed to move material, parts, tools, or specialized devices through variable programmed motions for the performance of a variety of tasks. Industrial robots are flexible manipulators whose actions can be altered through programming rather than mechanical changes.

CAM systems typically include modules to facilitate process planning, line analysis, statistical process control, quality analysis, and maintenance monitoring. On-line process controllers are used to feedback process data to each of these systems for subsequent manipulation and analysis. Process planning considers the sequence of production steps required to make a part from start to finish, generally with successive operations on several machines. The plan that is developed describes the routing through the shop floor and its state at each work center. Logic flow diagrams and information such as part specifications received from a CADD system, tooling requirements, assembling, and machining conditions are used to develop a production sequence for fabricating the part in the fastest, most economical manner. Line analysis for existing manufacturing operations can be used to predict the work centers that require improvement tools.

CAM systems collect and process data from programmable manufacturing processes to provide decision support. The data are used to generate reports and to analyze the performance of the manufacturing process. The system monitors status conditions and processing parameters from production machines, quality gauges, and in-process material handling systems. The information collected from these systems includes machine status, fault alarms, part counts, machine efficiency, float counts, cycle times, quality levels, and part characteristics. This information is input to production monitoring, quality analysis, and maintenance monitoring systems.

Many CAM systems use statistical process control. **Statistical process control** is used to determine whether or not a manufacturing process is under control. The process outputs are compared to the engineering specifications. Usually, an average variation value and range from highest to lowest variation are calculated. These values are plotted on control charts and compared to statistical control limits. The process is considered under control when the points fall within the limits and are randomly located around the desired average.

Some CAM systems, called **flexible manufacturing systems (FMSs),** incorporate programmable production processes that can be quickly reconfigured to produce different types of products. An FMS can significantly contribute to the overall speed in which a system responds, for it can greatly speed up time-consuming retooling.

The Manufacturing Resource Planning (MRP II) System

The **MRP II system** comprises the **materials requirements planning (MRP)** system and the related systems for sales, billing, and purchasing. But the MRP system is the heart of the MRP II system.

Initial applications of computers in manufacturing concentrated on materials control systems. The acronym MRP was coined to describe the use of computers in production planning and control systems. MRP systems utilize the computational ability of computers to process the vast amount of detail data necessary to plan and schedule materials usage requirements. The M in MRP is used comprehensively to include all inventories: raw materials, work-in-process, and finished goods. Work-in-process inventory includes direct labor and overhead costs in addition to raw materials, so all manufacturing elements are included in MRP systems. MRP systems integrate four subsystems (Figure 14.5): production planning, production scheduling, cost accounting, and reporting.

Advanced Integration Technologies

A manufacturing system's flexibility and speed of response depend largely on the degree to which its components are integrated. Automatic identification enhances integration because electronically tagging products and materials effectively makes them machine-readable and thus physically part of the organization's computer-based information system. EDI enhances integration because it effectively integrates the company's system with the systems of its suppliers and customers. Distributed processing enhances integration because it logically and physically combines geographically dispersed information resources into a single coherent system. Each of these integrating technologies is discussed.

Automatic Identification   Automatic identification of production activities is essential to factory automation; thus, machine-readable bar codes and scanner technology are indispensable elements. If you look under the hood of a new car, you will see bar code symbols on many parts, the bar symbol being similar to the bar code that is now commonplace on consumer products. A bar code symbol for use in factories and warehouses has been developed and standardized, although some large firms use their own unique codes. The bar codes, which are as commonplace on factory goods as they are on consumer goods, allow a computer or robot to identify materials, process information, and initiate whatever procedures are necessary.

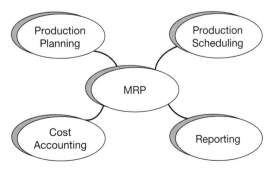

FIGURE 14.5 Materials Requirements Planning (MRP).

A manufacturer can obtain significant benefits by utilizing the standard UPC bar code system. UPC coding is as commonplace on commercial products as on consumer products. Products such as General Electric Information Services' *UPC*Express Catalog,* an electronic listing of UPC bar codes, facilitate UPC bar code identification of products. Without UPC code standardization, one has supplier-assigned numbers for every product as well as customer-assigned numbers for every product. These codes must be cross-referenced during processing, which is both time-consuming and error-prone. With UPC, both customer and supplier use the same product code, eliminating cross-referencing problems. UPC coding is **vendor-based coding,** which can be applied at any point. Problems with vendor-based coding usually result from different vendors using the same code for their different items. UPC assigns a unique six-digit code to each vendor. Thus, a duplication problem cannot occur as long as these six unique digits are included in the product code. Using UPC coding, one no longer has to code one's own inventory, as it arrives precoded with UPC.

EDI   In manufacturing as in most environments, a typical EDI application links a vendor and a customer electronically. EDI thus is a continuation of the integration of computerized applications inherent in CIM. EDI impacts manufacturing and inventory efficiency by simplifying the logistical chain of events in placing and filling orders and by making such systems more responsive to current needs. Inventory levels can be reduced simply by using EDI to shorten order filling and placement times. Errors are also reduced. Although useful in any type of manufacturing environment, EDI can be a critical component of a JIT (just-in-time) manufacturing environment.

UPC bar code identification of products and scanning technology are essential to obtain maximum benefit from EDI. Commerce is moving toward common pools of information, based on scanned UPC bar codes, that manufacturers, shippers, retailers, banks, and other trading partners can use to track goods and create the necessary documentation. Documents such as invoices will become superfluous as this type of open flow intercompany exchange of information becomes commonplace.

Distributed Processing   Distributed processing eliminates physical distances in information systems, thus increasing the overall system's responsiveness.

Transaction Processing in Quick-Response Manufacturing Systems

The discussion in this section focuses on transaction flow through the manufacturing process. We concentrate on production planning, production scheduling, cost accounting, and reporting. Activity-based costing and the relationships between JIT and CIM/MRP II are also discussed.

Production Planning

Production planning involves the determination of which products to produce and the scheduling of production to make optimal use of production resources. The determination of which products to manufacture requires an integration of the demand for a product, its production requirements, and the production resources that are available to the firm.

Figure 14.6 is a diagram of the data flows involved in production planning. Demand requirements for a product depend on whether the item is manufactured per customer order or routinely manufactured for inventory. If the item is manu-

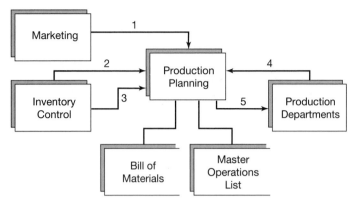

Data Flow Key

1 Sales Forecast
2 Finished Goods Status
3 Raw Materials Status
4 Factor Availability Report
5 Production Schedule

FIGURE 14.6 Data Flow Diagram: Production Planning.

factured for inventory, production requirements depend on a sales forecast. The sales forecast (data flow 1 in Figure 14.6) will generally be prepared by the sales or marketing department as part of the firm's budget preparation. Upon being authorized by management, the sales forecast is sent to the production planning function to indicate the expected demand for products.

The sales forecast must be related to the amount of each product that is currently held in inventory. Such information is provided in a finished goods status report (data flow 2 in Figure 14.6). A finished goods status report is sent to production planning from inventory control. The finished goods status report lists the quantities of finished product that are in inventory. The amount of resources that is available for production is communicated to production planning through raw materials status reports (data flow 3 in Figure 14.6) and factor availability reports (data flow 4). A raw materials status report details the amount of raw materials that is available for production. A factor availability report communicates the availability of labor and machine resources.

The production requirements of products are specified in a bill-of-materials file and a master operations file. A bill of materials lists the raw materials that are necessary to produce a product, and identifies the part number and the quantity of each part that is used to make a product. A bill of materials provides a structured, level-by-level listing of the components of a product, including part number, part description, quantity used, and a linkage from each level of the assembly to subassemblies and components. In similar fashion, a master operations list identifies and specifies the sequencing of all labor operations and/or machine operations that are necessary to produce a product. The information contained in both the bill-of-materials file and the master operations file will generally be specified by the engineering or product planning department when a product is first designed.

The integration of all of these factors results in a master production plan for the firm. The master production plan is implemented through the issuance and subsequent accounting of production orders. Processing of production orders results in a master production schedule (data flow 5 in Figure 14.6). Generation of the master production schedule is the focal point of MRP systems.

Implementing the Production Plan   Figure 14.7 illustrates the processing required to implement the master production plan. The master production plan is processed against the production status, bill-of-materials, and master operations files. This processing generates production order files, materials requisitions, and routings, and also updates the production status file. The **production status file** contains both accounting data and operational data pertaining to the status of production orders. This file integrates production order data pertinent to the stage of completion of projects; the production status file is a major input to the scheduling and cost accounting applications.

The **bill-of-materials file** contains a record for each product manufactured. Each record contains the detailed material requirements and standard material cost of the product identified by the record's key field value. The **master operations file** contains similar data related to each product's detailed labor and machine operation requirements and their sequencing through the production process. Standard times and costs are also contained in the master operations file.

The **production planning application program** integrates data from the master production plan, bill-of-materials file, and master operations file and generates the necessary production order documents—detailed production orders, materials requisition forms, and **routings (RTGs)** to guide the flow of production. RTGs indicate the sequence of operations required to manufacture a product. RTGs contain information about the work center, length of time, and tooling required to perform each task. These documents are distributed to the factory departments along with up-to-date production schedules. The production planning application program also updates the production status file. This file contains information found on the production order and establishes a production status (work-in-process) record for each production order. This file is an essential input to the production scheduling and cost accounting applications discussed in what follows.

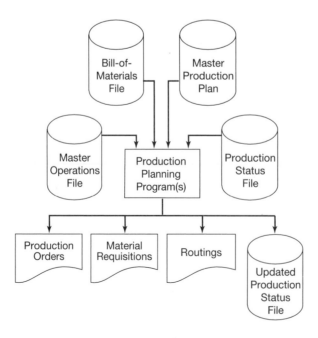

FIGURE 14.7 Production Planning.

Production Scheduling

As Figure 14.7 illustrates, the production status file is updated by the production planning application. The production status file contains a record for each open production order. This file is also used to accumulate both cost and operational data pertinent to production status. It integrates functions relating to production order status and cost accounting. This integration results from the use of production-status file in both the scheduling and cost-accounting applications.

Production scheduling is detailed in Figure 14.8. Routing (RTG) data concerning current production status is collected in the factory departments as work progresses. RTG data may be collected in different ways. RTGs may be output as turnaround documents by the production planning application. RTGs are filled in by the factory departments as work progresses on specific production orders. Each RTG contains a production order number and a format for specifying the work completed on an order. A separate RTG might be generated for each specific operation required on a production order. As each operation is completed, the corresponding RTG is completed by adding such information as units produced, scrap count, and actual time required. The RTGs are then forwarded to computer operations for input and processing. Alternatively, RTG data may be input directly from factory operations by having employees use data terminals to input RTG data at the completion of tasks. Employees might enter data such as production/work order code, operation code, employee code, machine/department code, materials used data, and time accumulated on the task.

CIM architectures provide the ability to tie factory floor machines directly to MRP systems. Automated data collection techniques may be used to electroni-

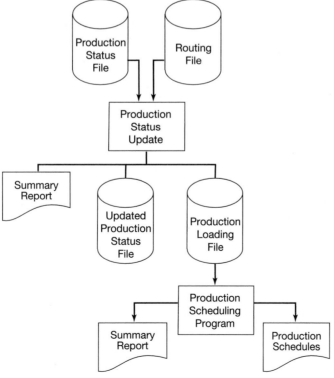

FIGURE 14.8 Production Scheduling.

cally collect production data from the shop floor as production occurs. Sensors on production lines may be used to count production or identify completed operations, whereas data entry stations are used by workers to manually enter codes indicating downtime and other production conditions.

RTG data received from the factory are used to update the production status file. RTG data are posted to the corresponding production order record in the production status file. Outputs of this operation include a summary report, the updated production status file, and a production loading file that details the production requirements associated with open production orders.

The **production loading file** is the major input to the production scheduling application. This file is processed by the scheduling application program to produce production schedules. The scheduling application program simply may accumulate and print reports showing total labor and machine operation requirements for each department/work center. In MRP systems, the scheduling application program would include the use of linear programming or other decision-support techniques to relate resource availabilities within each department or work center to overall production requirements to generate a schedule that represents an optimal assignment of available resources to production.

Cost Accounting

Figure 14.9 presents a diagram of the cost accounting application within an MRP system. The central feature of the cost accounting application is the updating of the production status (work-in-process) file.

Material requisitions data are transmitted from the inventory department for processing. Material requisitions data document the issuance of materials to specific production orders. Job time data and machine time data are included in the RTGs forwarded from the production departments. RTG data show the distribution of labor and machine time to specific production orders within a production department or work center. Both material requisitions data and RTG data are input to build a production data file. This transaction file is processed by the cost accounting application program, along with the production status file. This

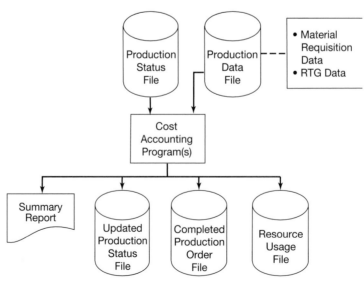

FIGURE 14.9 Cost Accounting.

processing accumulates material and labor usage shown by material requisitions data and RTG data and posts them to the work-in-process record maintained for each open production order. Overhead is applied to work-in-process on the basis of burden rates maintained in the cost accounting program. The program monitors the status of each production order and also prepares a file that summarizes the variances between standard cost and operational data maintained in the work-in-process record and the actual cost and operational data posted to each production order. As orders are completed, the related work-in-process record is closed and a record is created to update the finished inventory file. The outputs of the cost accounting program include the following items:

- an updated production status file
- a completed production order file
- a resource usage file
- a summary report

The updated production status file contains current information on the status of all open production orders. This file is used in the next cycle of production planning and scheduling. The summary report includes batch and application control information, as well as the summary journal entry data debiting work-in-process for standard material, labor, and overhead costs; crediting stores, accrued payroll, and applied overhead; and debiting or crediting the necessary variance accounts. The completed production order file and the resource usage file are described in the next section.

Reporting

The completed production order file lists all cost data for completed production orders. This file is used to update the finished goods inventory file, as shown in Figure 14.10. Outputs of this processing include an updated finished goods inventory file, a finished goods stock status report, a completed production order cost summary, and a summary report that includes batch and application control information as well as the summary journal entry data debiting finished goods and crediting work-in-process for the standard cost of goods completed.

The resource usage file that is output from the cost accounting application contains both the actual and standard material, labor, and operation costs for work completed, as shown by the materials requisitions data and RTG data. The standard quantities, times, and costs are copied to this file from the production status file. This file is input to a computer application program that accumulates material and operation costs by department or work center and prints resource usage reports. These reports detail variances between standard and actual cost data. Resource usage reports are distributed to department supervisors to assist in the overall production function.

Activity-Based Costing

Traditional cost accounting techniques may be inadequate in a CIM environment. Three major elements enter into the cost of manufacturing a product. These are direct material, direct labor, and overhead. Overhead is best described as the portion of manufacturing cost that is neither direct materials nor direct labor. Overhead costs cannot be readily identified with the manufacturing of specific products; rather, overhead costs are identifiable to the production process itself. In addition to indirect materials and indirect labor, overhead includes such items as factory rent or depreciation, heat, power, insurance, maintenance, supervision, machinery costs, and material handling costs.

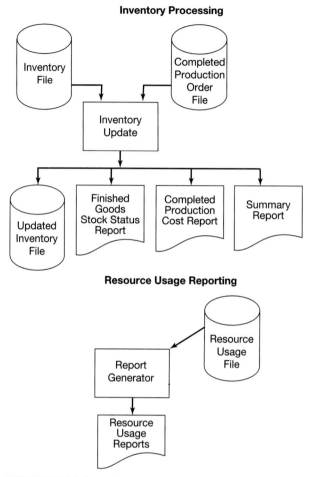

FIGURE 14.10 Reporting.

CIM Changes Cost-Behavior Patterns   The term *applied overhead* describes the familiar cost accounting technique in which the overhead charge to a product is calculated using a predetermined overhead application rate. Predetermined overhead rates traditionally have been based on either total expected direct labor hours or total expected direct labor cost. A predetermined overhead rate is computed as follows:

$$\text{Predetermined rate} = \frac{\text{budgeted overhead cost}}{\text{budgeted activity}}$$

For example, if overhead is budgeted as $200,000 and activity is budgeted as 5,000 direct labor hours, the predetermined overhead rate would be $200,000 divided by 5,000 hours, a rate of $40 per hour. Predetermined overhead rates may be computed on either a plantwide or a departmental basis. A plantwide rate is a rate that is used throughout the firm. That is, the rate does not differ from one department or division to another. A plantwide rate is usually inappropriate in a large firm that produces a variety of products or services and that has several distinct departments or divisions. In such cases, better control is achieved when overhead costs and activity are budgeted on a departmental or divisional basis.

CIM significantly alters a manufacturer's cost-behavior patterns by causing a substitution of capital equipment for direct labor. Direct labor is reduced, perhaps totally eliminated, as computer-controlled machinery manufactures products. Overhead costs increase and direct labor costs decrease. The costs of computer-controlled machinery, like the costs of all other capital resources, are indirect rather than direct to production. They are primarily "fixed" relative to volume of production. Thus, CIM causes decreased variable costs by reducing direct labor and increased fixed costs of production (cost of CIM technology). In addition to equipment costs, many other overhead items may be significantly increased with CIM. Total supervision costs, for example, may increase even though there is less direct labor to supervise. The computer-controlled machinery that replaces workers needs to be "supervised" by skilled technicians, who likely earn significantly higher wages than the employee-oriented supervisors whom they replace.

Traditional cost accounting systems allocate overhead on a single base that all products have in common. This base has typically been direct labor hours or direct labor cost, as direct labor was a critical manufacturing component common to all products. However, this method is deficient for a CIM environment because products manufactured with costly automated machinery, which contributes greatly to overhead costs, typically have the lowest number of direct labor hours associated with their production. If direct labor is used to allocate overhead, products that use relatively more manual labor will unfairly be charged more overhead than products that use relatively more automated, high-overhead machinery.

Activity-based costing (ABC) calculates several overhead rates, one for each manufacturing activity, and uses these rates to build product costs from the costs of the specific activities that are undertaken during production. Activities might be machine centers, material handling, inspection stations, or any other type of manufacturing operation. A single department might contain several different activities. For example, an assembly department where some products are assembled using robotics equipment while other products are assembled manually might have two activities, robotics and manual assembly. Different overhead bases then could be used to more accurately assign these different activity costs to products.

Figures 14.11 and 14.12 provide an illustration. Figure 14.11 shows the costing of products A and B in a traditional cost accounting system where all overhead is allocated to products on the basis of direct labor hours. Note that product A, which requires five more hours of direct labor, costs more to produce than product B. Product B, however, requires more parts than product A, which means that product B requires relatively more usage of high-overhead, robotics equipment during assembly.

Figure 14.12 shows the costing of the same two products in an activity-based cost accounting system where robotics equipment is identified as a separate activity. Several different overhead bases are used. Robotics equipment overhead is allocated to products on the basis of the number of parts in a product. All other overhead is allocated on the basis of direct labor hours. Note that product B, which requires 50 more parts, costs more to produce than product A according to the activity-based cost accounting system.

Cost Drivers   A **cost driver** is an element that influences the total cost of an activity. Typically, several cost drivers influence the total cost of an activity. Materials handling costs are influenced by the total number of items handled, the types

Traditional Cost Accounting (single overhead base)		
Overhead	$2,400,000	
Activity Base (labor hours)	100,000	
Rate per labor hour	$24	
	Product A	**Product B**
# Parts	*50*	*100*
# Labor Hours	*25*	*20*
Material cost	$800	$800
Labor cost ($20 per hour)	$500	$400
Overhead ($24 per hour)	$600	$480
Total cost	$1,900	$1,680

FIGURE 14.11 Traditional Cost Accounting.

of items handled (i.e., small, big and heavy, hazardous, etc.), the type of equipment used, and worked efficiency, to name just a few examples. Cost drivers might be measured by production volume, number of employees, number of forms completed, or the number of parts in a product. Time-in-process measures, such as direct labor hours, machine hours, or clock time, are frequently used as cost drivers.

Activity-Based Cost Accounting (several overhead bases)		
	Robotic Assembly	All Other
Overhead	$400,000	$2,000,000
Activity	40,000 (parts)	100,000 (hours)
Rates	$10 per part	$20 per hour
	Product A	**Product B**
# Parts	*50*	*100*
# Labor Hours	*25*	*20*
Material cost	$800	$800
Labor cost ($20 per hour)	$500	$400
Overhead ($10 per part)	$500	$1,000
Overhead ($20 per hour)	$500	$400
Total cost	$2,300	$2,600

FIGURE 14.12 Activity-Based Cost Accounting.

The significance of activity-based costing as a management tool depends largely on the accuracy of the cost drivers that are selected as the allocation bases for activity costs. The greatest benefit is obtained when the principal cost driver for an activity is selected as the overhead allocation base for that activity. This then links cost incurrence to product costing, and meaningful managerial decisions may be based on product cost information. Statistical regression analysis is often used as a means for identifying cost drivers.

MRP II versus MRP

An MRP II system includes the major processing modules of MRP (Figure 14.13). The bill-of-materials module is used to communicate the structure of a product, as in MRP. Extensions to bill-of-materials processing in MRP II might include maintenance of engineering/product drawings from a CADD system. The routings file module indicates the sequence of operations required to manufacture a component or assembly, as in MRP. Extensions to routings file processing in MRP II might include expanded data concerning work center capacity data, maintenance of machine tooling data, and maintenance of numerical machine control data from the CADD system. The master production scheduling module maintains the assembly schedule for specific configurations, quantities, and dates based on product mix and material availability, much as in MRP. A production order module releases orders for manufacturing after evaluating material, capacity, and tooling availability. If availability is adequate, a packet is prepared that contains the order, material list, routing, and drawing information, much as in MRP. The packet is forwarded to the plant floor. Extensions to production order processing in MRP II might include the creation of transaction files and numerical machine control tapes for the plant floor. As in MRP, an inventory control module maintains accurate and timely status of on-hand balances. To maintain accuracy, techniques such as obsolescence analysis and cycle counting should be implemented to ensure accuracy on a continual basis. Finally, a production activity control module is used to implement the production plan developed in the master production scheduling module. As in MRP, this module reduces delays and waiting time by effective monitoring and feedback of production and shop floor status data. Typical functions include attendance reporting, collecting direct labor and machine hours, and revision of production status and priority data based on actual usage of material, labor, and machine resources.

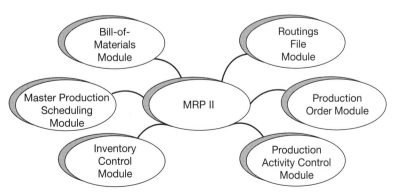

FIGURE 14.13. Major Processing Modules in MRP II.

Implementing JIT in an MRP II/CIM Environment

In a batch production environment, manufacture of specific products is sporadic. Batches of similar products are periodically assembled to satisfy present and planned future needs. Setup costs are usually incurred every time a batch is produced, and these costs are typically the same regardless of the proposed size of the batch production run. As the word "planned" indicates, a batch environment fosters a "push" concept of manufacturing efficiency. Economic (i.e., efficient) batch size is derived by using formulas (i.e., economic order quantity models) or is output from a computer simulation or computational model.

MRP II is directed at the synchronization and scheduling of the type of events that occur in batch environments. Batch size is determined from the production planning module. The scheduling model organizes and/or optimizes the timing of events necessary for production. The bill-of-materials model is used to forecast materials requirements, and so on until the actual production orders are issued.

A just-in-time (JIT) manufacturing environment is a continuous flow environment. A JIT environment requires economical production of small lots—essentially the operation of production on a continuous basis—to minimize or totally eliminate inventories. JIT advocates the elimination of waste in the manufacturing process and stresses continuous improvement in operation. In a JIT environment, products are manufactured under a "pull" concept. Production occurs only when it is needed to fill a customer order. In contrast to a batch environment, there is no advance scheduling in a JIT environment. The customer order "pulls" product from the production line; in effect, demand schedules production. This type of operation requires rapid setups, high-quality production, continuous elimination of wasted motion, and inventory flow improvements.

As a manufacturer moves from a batch to a JIT continuous flow manufacturing environment, less emphasis might be placed on a complete MRP II system. The de-emphasis on advanced scheduling in JIT and the associated reduction in inventories eliminate much data and computation toward which MRP II is directed. But many aspects of MRP II might be used. Scheduling modules might generate level production schedules. Material requirements planning might generate estimated procurement quantities to support the demand–pull system. CADD and CAM applications can support quality requirements by allowing greater amounts of process control technology on the plant floor. Adaptive, self-correcting decision-support systems can become an integral part of the manufacturing process. Statistical process controls can monitor production to assure that products are produced within quality control limits.

Special Internal Control Considerations

Quick-response manufacturing systems, similar to other totally computerized systems, intensify certain internal control problems. Transactions may be processed without human intervention or approval. This eliminates conventional controls associated with separation of duties in transactions. Thus, a major consideration is to ensure that such controls, or their equivalents, are an integral part of a quick-response manufacturing system. Computer processing in general, and EDI in particular, eliminates human-oriented paper documents. There are challenging validation and authenticity problems concerning the operation of paperless processing systems, both within a firm (e.g., electronic production order) and in its exchanges with its trading partners (EDI and EFT).

Extensive control and audit trails may be implemented in quick-response manufacturing systems, but these features must be included within the design and development of the system. It is neither feasible nor desirable to install controls in a computer-based information system after it has been implemented. Programmed controls and audit trails can be highly effective, but their integrity must be established during system development. A control may look good on paper, but it will be ineffectual if its operation is incorrectly programmed. Also, a programmer might deliberately code a program incorrectly. Thus, internal controls over system operation must be complemented with increased control over the systems development process. Audit trail and control techniques such as transaction logs and programmed edit checks require extra developmental resources and extra processing. The costs of their use must be balanced against overall system objectives. Because audit trails and controls require direct and obvious expenditures, underusage is perhaps more likely than overusage.

Systems development is a major concern in any computer-based system, but systems development is mission-critical in quick-response manufacturing systems. A major deterrent to the proliferation of automation in factories is the same one that has plagued the application of computers to other application areas—programming and software. The lack of "turnkey systems"—robots or other automated tools that can be bought and immediately turned on and used—has constrained the application of hardware technology that has been available for years. The same types of systems development problems that occur in information systems development occur in the application of computers to production processes. The cost of programming an industrial robot, which frequently involves extensive engineering or systems development, can easily exceed the purchase cost of the robot system.

SUMMARY

Automatic identification of transactions provides improved efficiency, reduced data processing costs, and elimination of the handling and storage problems associated with information that is recorded on paper. Bar codes have become the dominant AI technology as machine-readable bar codes can be printed easily and bar codes are very reliable in use. A variety of bar codes are in use. Several characteristics of bar code symbology were discussed and illustrated.

A quick-response sales system is the retailing equivalent of JIT (just-in-time) inventory systems used in manufacturing. Purchase orders for inventory items are made on a "demand–pull" basis rather than a fixed-interval (e.g., monthly or weekly) "push" basis in order to restock store inventory levels. New goods arrive when they are needed. Orders to vendors are placed on the basis of actual sales to quickly replenish stocks of items that are selling. Machine-readable bar codes and scanner technology are critical components of quick-response retail sales systems. Maximum benefit is obtained when the standard, widely used UPC bar code system is utilized. An EDI (electronic data interchange) link between a retailer's computer system and a vendor's computer system allows quick placing and processing of orders, invoices, and payments.

Computer-integrated manufacturing (CIM) is an integrated approach to the use of information technology in manufacturing enterprises. Components of a CIM system typically include CADD workstations, real-time production monitoring and control systems, and order and inventory control systems. CIM components are connected by a network and equipped with software systems designed to support distributed operation. CIM can support product evolution from initial design and drafting through planning to manufacturing and assembly, while also incorporating management accounting systems. CIM reduces information costs and through EDI, brings the producer, the supplier, and the customer closer together.

Glossary

activity-based costing (ABC): a system that calculates several overhead rates, one for each manufacturing activity, and uses these rates to build product costs from the costs of the specific activities that are undertaken during production.

advanced integration technologies (AITs): consist of EDI, automatic identification, and distributed processing.

computer-aided design and drafting (CADD): the use of computer software to perform engineering functions.

computer-aided manufacturing (CAM): includes software for defining the manufacturing process, tools to improve process productivity, and decision-support systems to aid in the control and monitoring of the production process.

computer-integrated manufacturing (CIM): integrates the physical manufacturing system and the manufacturing resource planning (MRP II) systems.

cost driver: an element that influences the total cost of an activity.

dual control numbers: EDI documents typically contain two control numbers, one at the beginning of the message and another at the end.

finite-element analysis: a mathematical method used to determine mechanical characteristics, such as stresses of structures under load.

flexible manufacturing system (FMS): CAM systems that incorporate programmable production processes that can be quickly reconfigured to produce different types of products.

functional acknowledgment: both acknowledges receipt of a message and also reports in detail the items in the received message.

industrial robot: a device designed to move material, parts, tools, or specialized devices through variable programmed motions for the performance of a variety of tasks.

manufacturing resource planning (MRP II): comprises the materials requirements planning (MRP) system and the related systems for sales, billing, and purchasing.

materials requirements planning (MRP): the use of computers in production planning and control systems, particularly applications in materials control systems.

point-of-sale (POS) system: technology that enhances the traditional cash register to allow it to function as a source data entry device for sales transactions.

quick-response manufacturing system: a CIM system in which the physical manufacturing system and the manufacturing resource planning (MRP II) systems are integrated with advanced integration technologies (AITs).

quick-response system: a system that uses contemporary technology to minimize order lead time, manufacturing time, and inventories.

routings (RTGs): documents that indicate the sequence of operations required to manufacture a product.

solids modeling: the mathematical representation of a part as a solid object in computer memory.

statistical process control: procedures used to determine whether a manufacturing process is under control that involves comparing process outputs to engineering specifications.

transactional acknowledgement: both acknowledges receipt of a message and provides full verification of all data in a message.

transmission acknowledgement: indicates only that a message was received.

vendor-based coding: having a purchaser (i.e., retailer) utilize a vendor's product codes as its own product codes for the same products.

Chapter Quiz

Answers to the chapter quiz appear on page 574.

1. Which of the following is (are) **not** identified by the PC bar code?
   (a) retailer
   (b) product
   (c) vendor
   (d) both a and c

2. In a quick-response sales system, the UPC bar code may be utilized by
   (a) the retailer.
   (b) the vendor.
   (c) both a and b.
   (d) neither a nor b.

3. Which of the following is a technology that enhances the traditional cash register to allow it to function as a source data entry device?
   (a) ABC
   (b) CIM
   (c) MRP
   (d) POS

4. Which type of acknowledgement both acknowledges receipt of a message and also reports in detail the items in the received message?
   (a) functional
   (b) transactional
   (c) both a and b
   (d) neither a nor b

5. Which of the following is an element of CADD technology?
   (a) solids modeling
   (b) statistical process control
   (c) both a and b
   (d) neither a nor b

6. (_____) integrates the physical manufacturing system and the manufacturing resource planning (MRP II) systems.
   (a) MRP
   (b) AIT
   (c) CIM
   (d) RTG

7. In a production planning system, the bill-of-materials file would be an input to which of the following?
   (a) production planning program(s)
   (b) cost accounting program(s)
   (c) both a and b
   (d) neither a nor b

8. In a production planning system, the production status file would be an input to which of the following?
   (a) production planning program(s)
   (b) inventory update program(s)
   (c) both a and b
   (d) neither a nor b

9. In a production planning system, the master operations file would be an input to which of the following?
   (a) cost accounting program(s)
   (b) inventory update program(s)

    (c) both a and b

    (d) neither a nor b

10. Cost drivers for activity-based costing might be identified with (_____).

    (a) solids modeling

    (b) finite-element analysis

    (c) statistical regression

    (d) statistical process control

Review Problem

CIM architectures provide the ability to tie factory floor operations directly to computer-based information systems. Automated source data collection techniques may be used to electronically collect production data from the shop floor as production occurs. Sensors on production lines may be used to count production or identify completed operations, whereas data entry stations are used by workers to manually enter data concerning completed operations.

Required

(a) What types of data might be entered by production workers concerning completed operations?

(b) Describe programmed edit checks that might be made on the data indicated in part (a).

(c) Assume that all necessary files are direct-access organization. What on-line processing might result from a worker entering data on completed operations?

Solution to Review Problem

(a) Workers might enter the following types of data at the completion of an operation:

    1. production/work order code

    2. operation code

    3. worker code

    4. machine/department code

    5. materials used data

    6. time accumulated on the task.

(b) Possible edit checks include

    1. a label check on files.

    2. a data access matrix to verify worker authorization.

    3. check digit verification where appropriate.

    4. valid code checks.

    5. limit tests where appropriate.

    6. a validity check on the operation code entered relative to the production order file.

(c) The following files might be updated to reflect the data entered:

    1. raw materials inventory file

    2. finished goods inventory file

    3. production order (work-in-process) file

    4. production scheduling file

    5. employee data file (a production scheduling file for workers)

    6. summary costing files

Review Questions

1. Identify technologies that are utilized in quick-response systems.
2. What degree of cooperation among trading partners is required to implement quick-response sales systems?
3. Characterize the key components of quick-response retail sales systems.
4. Describe the operation of a POS retail sales terminal. What types of data might be collected?
5. Identify benefits that might be obtained by a retailer that adopts the UPC product identification code for use in its own operations.
6. Describe the general sequence of events in transaction processing in quick-response sales systems.
7. Identify special internal control considerations in quick-response sales systems.
8. Identify and describe key components of computer-integrated manufacturing (CIM) systems.
9. Distinguish between MRP and MRP II.
10. Describe several different types of support functions that are typically provided by CADD.
11. Describe support functions that are typically provided by CAM.
12. Describe several uses of automatic identification in production activities.
13. Describe the flow of processing necessary to support manufacturing resource planning (MRP II) systems.
14. What is activity-based costing (ABC)? Why is ABC particularly relevant to CIM systems?

Discussion Questions and Problems

15. How might the following employees in a large retail store be affected by the installation of a point-of-sale (POS) system?
    (a) checkout clerk
    (b) inventory clerk
    (c) sales manager
    (d) staff analysts for the financial vice president
    (e) president of the store
    (f) customer making a purchase on credit
16. Point-of-sale systems (POS) are a key component of quick-response sales systems. Data are collected manually through keying by the sales clerk, or automatically, using special codes and sensing devices. POS terminals record both cash and charge sales. Data relating to either type of sale may be transmitted to a computer network where it may be processed immediately.

    Required
    Identify application controls that might be utilized in POS in a large retail store, which has many terminals in daily operation. Limit your comments to the operation of the POS terminals, including the input of data items by salespersons.
17. The Wadswad Corporation manufactures both standard and customized electrical control boards for automated manufacturing machinery. The company was started by an electrical engineer and a salesman for a machinery company when they saw a demand for systems integration support by companies who were purchasing customized electrical control boards. Neither of their former employers seemed interested in providing systems integration support for customized electrical control boards, so they

started manufacturing control boards and offered complete systems integration support to companies desiring this service.

The firm was successful from the start and grew quickly. As the number of employees and sales increased, management began to computerize the firm's accounting system. First, payroll was computerized, and then accounts receivable and accounts payable. The company is now ready to implement a new computer system to control its work-in-process inventory. The firm utilizes a job costing system. Work-in-process numbers are established to control the manufacture of both standard and customized control boards. Boards are usually produced in batches of ten to several hundred units.

Fred Beam, the controller of Wadswad, has just returned from a meeting with the programmer who is implementing the new computer system for work-in-process. The programmer explained the proposed structure of the master work-in-process file and the type of transactions that will be processed against the file. These structures are outlined in what follows:

Each record in the master work-in-process file will contain the following data:

Field 1	Work-in-process number
Field 2	Units started
Field 3	Units spoiled
Field 4	Materials cost
Field 5	Direct labor cost
Field 6	Total cost
Field 7	Expected completed data

The work-in-process number, number of units started, and expected completion date will be entered into the computer when a job is authorized to begin production. The following four types of transactions will be processed:

1. **Materials requisitions.** The cost of materials requisitioned for each job will be posted to field 4 of the master work-in-process file, which accumulates the total materials cost of a job. The cost of materials requisitioned for each job will also be posted to field 6 of the master work-in-process file, which is used to accumulate the total cost of each job.
2. **Job time tickets.** The direct labor cost for each job will be posted to field 5 of the master work-in-process file, which accumulates the total labor cost of a job. The direct labor cost for each job will also be posted to field 6 of the master work-in-process file, which is used to accumulate the total cost of each job.

   Applied overhead will be computed as a percentage of direct labor cost. Applied overhead will be posted to field 6 of the master work-in-process file, which is used to accumulate the total cost of each job.
3. **Spoiled-production reports.** Units spoiled in production for each job will be posted to field 3 of the master work-in-process file, which accumulates the total units spoiled in production for each job. Special messages will be printed during processing if the spoilage rate exceeds management's expectations.
4. **Completed production reports.** When a job is complete, the computer system will report the total cost of the job and also the per unit cost. The date of completion will be compared to the expected date of completion, field 7 in the master work-in-process file. Special messages will be printed during processing if a job is completed late.

Required

(a) The new computer-based work-in-process system will provide summary accounting data that must periodically be posted to the firm's general ledger. Prepare the standard journal entries that Fred Beam, the controller of Wadswad, could use to document how the expected outputs of the new system will impact the general ledger.

(b) Are accounting-related data the only type of output this system will provide? Discuss.

18. Deake Corporation is a medium-sized, diversified manufacturing company. Fred Richards has been promoted recently to manager, property accounting section. Richards has had difficulty responding to some of the requests from individuals in other departments of Deake for information about the company's fixed assets. Some of the requests and problems Richards has had to cope with are as follows:

(a) The controller has requested schedules of individual fixed assets to support the balances in the general ledger. Richards has furnished the necessary information, but he has always been late. The manner in which the records are organized makes it difficult to obtain information easily.

(b) The maintenance manager wished to verify the existence of a punch press that he thinks was repaired twice. He has asked Richards to confirm the asset number and location of the press.

(c) The insurance department wants data on the cost and book values of assets to include in its review of current insurance coverage.

(d) The tax department has requested data that can be used to determine when Deake should switch depreciation methods for tax purposes.

(e) The company's internal auditors have spent a significant amount of time in the property accounting section recently, attempting to confirm the annual depreciation expense.

The property account records that are at Richards' disposal consist of a set of manual books. These records show the date the asset was acquired, the account number to which the asset applies, the dollar amount capitalized, and the estimated useful life of the asset for depreciation purposes.

After many frustrations, Richards has realized that his records are inadequate and he cannot supply the data easily when they are requested. He has decided that he should discuss the problems with the controller, Julie Castle.

RICHARDS: Julie, something has got to give. My people are working overtime and can't keep up. You worked in property accounting before you became controller. You know I can't tell the tax, insurance, and maintenance people everything they need to know from my records. Also, that internal auditing team is living in my area and that slows down the work pace. The requests of these people are reasonable, and we should be able to answer these questions and provide the needed data. I think we need an automated property accounting system. I would like to talk to the information systems people to see if they can help me.

CASTLE: Fred, I think you have a good idea, but be sure you are personally involved in the design of any system so that you get all the information you need.

Required

(a) Identify and justify four major objectives Deake Corporation's automated property accounting system should possess in order to provide the data that are necessary to respond to requests of information from company personnel.

(b) Identify the data that should be included in the computer record for each asset included in the property account.

(CMA)

19. FasterCard, a large credit card company, operates several regional processing centers where it processes customer statements. FasterCards are issued to customers by individual banks who participate in the FasterCard program. Customers who have complaints concerning their FasterCard statement of account contact the bank that issued their card. The bank then sends a request to a regional processing center for the docu-

mentation (credit slips) concerning any transactions that are disputed by the customer.

One problem with this system is the time delay in mailing the necessary documentation. When a customer disputes a purchase, the necessary receipts are mailed by the regional processing center and often do not arrive at the bank in time to stop fraudulent claims. FasterCard estimates that it loses several million dollars each year because of the lack of documentation to refute false customer claims.

Required

FasterCard is considering the implementation of a document imaging system in its regional processing centers. What effect might a document imaging system have on FasterCard's problem concerning the lack of documentation to refute fraudulent customer claims for refunds?

20. Yard Company is a family-owned, medium-sized manufacturing company that has been in operation for more than 30 years. The company makes moldings and related parts for other manufacturing firms. Yard Company's manufacturing operations include machining, welding, and assembly. The company has always employed skilled artisans and has been able to maintain a reputation for high-quality production.

Moldings are made to order and sold through contract with the purchasing party. The uniqueness of its product had allowed the company to avoid automating its production processes until just last year. Realizing that labor costs were going to escalate steadily for the foreseeable future, management purchased three numerically controlled machines to automate some of its production processes. A numerically controlled machine is a computer-oriented workstation that is programmed to operate tools and to perform a sequence of manufacturing operations in conjunction with one or more human operators. For example, the machine might be programmed to drill several holes of specific sizes in a certain sequence. The human operator manipulates the part, pressing a button to let the machine know when to drill a hole.

Programming the numerically controlled machines requires skills that are most readily obtained by studying computer science in college or a trade school. Because none of the artisans employed by the Yard Company had the necessary background, it was necessary to hire two recent college graduates to program the machines. The two programmers were much younger than most of the artisans and had very different backgrounds and career objectives. It was very difficult for the two groups to communicate.

Relations between the artisans and the programmers quickly deteriorated because the numerically controlled machines operated very inefficiently, mostly due to programming errors. For example, a drill bit would withdraw several feet into the air so that an artisan could rotate a part, when it was only necessary for the drill bit to withdraw several inches. In addition to the time delay, errors of this type lessened the artisans' confidence in the programmers' work. This situation has existed for more than a year. One of the original programmers quit the company and another was hired to take his place. Rumor has it that both programmers are currently seeking other positions.

The management of Yard Company is aware there is a problem but does not know how it should proceed. The numerically controlled machines were a sizable investment for the company and were expected to make production more efficient. Management expected some start-up problems, but the problems that have been encountered have been much more severe than expected. Total production costs have increased rather than decreased, and management is aware that both the programmers and the artisans are blaming each other for the company's problems.

Required

(a) What factors have contributed to the problem Yard Company is experiencing in implementing numerically controlled machines in its production operations?

(b) Suggest a solution to Yard Company's problem.

21. Molly Company manufactures both standard and customized electrical control boards for automated manufacturing machinery. The company recently completed installation of a robotic assembly unit. This automated unit completely eliminates direct labor in the production of several types of standard electrical control boards.

    Molly utilizes a job costing system. Boards are usually produced in batches of 10 to several hundred units. Overhead is applied to products based on direct labor hours.

    Sally Seed, the controller of Molly Company, recently met with Sam Nut, the production supervisor, concerning the cost of producing several of the firm's products. The following discussion took place.

    SAM: Sally, I'm perplexed by your most recent cost figures for products X, Y, and Z, our big sellers. Before we installed the robotic assembly unit, the following data applied:

Product	X	Y	Z
Number of parts	10	15	20
Labor hours	4	4	2
Costs:			
Material	$200	$200	$200
Labor ($30/hour)	120	120	60
Overhead	80	80	40
Total Cost	**$400**	**$400**	**$300**

    Products X and Y had identical unit costs, and Product Z was the cheapest to produce.

    SALLY: That was correct, Sam. Our total budgeted overhead was $600,000. Given our expected 30,000 hours of direct labor, we had an applied overhead rate of $20 per direct labor hour. You can see, then, how these costs were calculated, as our direct labor costs $30 per hour.

    SAM: According to your latest report, the first since we installed the new automated equipment, the following data apply:

Product	X	Y	Z
Number of parts	10	15	20
Robot hours	3	0	1
Labor hours	0	4	2
Costs:			
Material	$200	$200	$200
Labor ($30/hour)	0	120	60
Overhead	0	200	100
Total Cost	**$200**	**$520**	**$360**

    Sally, I'm not sure that these cost representations are believable. We purchased expensive automated equipment, and overall eliminated almost a third of our labor cost, yet product Y, which does not use the new equipment, has increased more than 25% in cost. On the other hand, product X, which does use the new equipment, has decreased 50% in cost.

SALLY: Well Sam, our total budgeted overhead has increased to $1 million. But our expected hours of direct labor drops from 30,000 to 20,000. This gives an applied overhead rate of $50 per direct labor hour. You can see, then, how these costs were calculated, as our direct labor cost $30 per hour.

SAM: Well that may be Sally, but something just doesn't make sense about using direct labor as the only allocation base for all overhead items. There are other things beside labor that increase production cost. Consider parts per product, for example. We spend a lot of effort in material handling, and it seems to me that more parts make more work which means to me that it costs more.

SALLY: Sam, you may be right. I wanted to investigate activity-based costing, and this conversation has convinced me to do so. I'm going to collect some data, and recompute these cost figures using activity-based costing. I'll get back to you soon, and we can see if these new figures seem to make more sense.

Required

Sally collected the following data for activity-based costing.

	Activity		
	Material Handling	Robotic Assembly	All Other Overhead
Overhead	$200,000	$400,000	$400,000
Base	40,000	5,000	20,000
	(Parts)	(Robot Hours)	(Labor Hours)
Rate	$5	$80	$20

(a) Compute product costs under activity-based costing, using the three activities and their associated allocation bases shown in the tables.

(b) How might allocation bases for activity costs be identified?

Answers to Chapter Quiz

1. A	4. A	7. A	10. C
2. C	5. A	8. A	
3. D	6. C	9. D	

CHAPTER 15

Auditing Information Technology

LEARNING OBJECTIVES

Careful study of this chapter will enable you to:

- Distinguish between "auditing through the computer" and "auditing with the computer."

- Describe and evaluate alternative information systems audit technologies. ~~Table 15.1 P580~~

- Characterize various types of information systems audits.

INFORMATION SYSTEMS AUDITING CONCEPTS

The term *information systems auditing* is commonly used to describe two different types of computer-related activity. One use of the term is to describe the process of reviewing and evaluating the internal controls in an electronic data processing system. This type of activity is normally undertaken by auditors during compliance testing, and might be described as **auditing through the computer.** The other general use of the term is to describe the utilization of the computer by an auditor to perform some audit work that otherwise would have to be done manually. This type of activity is normally undertaken during substantive testing of account balances, and might be described as **auditing with the computer.** Many audits involve both compliance testing and substantive testing. Both types of information systems auditing might be undertaken by both internal auditors and external auditors.

Structure of a Financial Statement Audit

The primary objective and responsibility of the external auditor is to attest to the fairness of a firm's financial reports. Whereas the internal auditor serves a firm's management, the external auditor serves a firm's stockholders, the government, and the general public. Despite this clear difference of purpose, internal and external auditors do similar things in the area of information systems auditing. This is not to say that much audit work is duplicated. Generally, the opposite is true, due to the large degree of cooperation and interaction that frequently exists between a firm's internal and external auditors. Internal auditors commonly undertake audits that are reviewed and relied upon by external auditors as they audit a firm's financial statements.

Various types of professional certifications are applicable to auditing. At the most general level, the American Institute of Certified Public Accountants, in conjunction with the individual state boards of accountancy, provides the designation of CPA (certified public accountant). As a general rule, an audit report signed by a CPA is required for all publicly traded companies. But CPA audits are also applicable to a wide range of situations for privately held companies, partnerships, and sole proprietorships. For example, many banks will make loans only with an audit report signed by a CPA.

The CISA (certified information systems auditor) is a second type of professional certification relating to auditing. This type of certification is provided by the Information Systems Audit and Control Association, and is a general broad-based program applicable to auditing in a wide range of situations. A third type of audit certification is the CIA (certified internal auditor), as provided by the Institute of Internal Auditors. This type of certification places the heaviest emphasis on internal auditing.

All auditor certification programs provide for not only rigorous testing of those to be certified, but also for codes of ethics that help to ensure professional and ethical conduct of their members. Thus, members of the organizations agree to live up to professional standards that transcend those of their daily work environments.

In an audit directed toward the attestation of financial statements, the auditor could, in theory, ignore the system of internal control and still obtain sufficient evidence to justify a professional opinion of the financial statements. This approach is generally impractical because the cost of obtaining enough substantive evidence to be sufficient without using the internal control system is prohibitive. Total audit cost can usually be significantly reduced if some audit resources are directed at reviewing and verifying the internal controls in the system that generated the financial statements. Then, relying on the client's internal control system, a lesser degree of assurance is necessary in direct substantive tests of financial statement figures.

For this reason, an audit is almost universally divided into two basic components (Figure 15.1). The first component, usually called the **interim audit,** has the objective of establishing the degree to which the internal control system can be relied upon. This usually requires some type of **compliance testing.** The purpose of compliance testing is to confirm the existence, assess the effectiveness, and

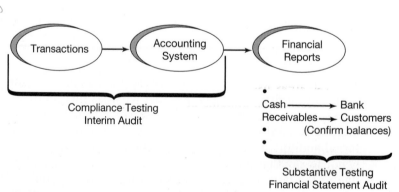

FIGURE 15.1 Structure of a Financial Statement Audit.

check the continuity of operation of those internal controls on which reliance is to be placed. The second component of an audit, usually called the **financial statement audit,** involves **substantive testing.** Substantive testing is the direct verification of financial statement figures, placing such reliance on internal control as the results of the interim audit warrant. For example, as shown in Figure 15.1, substantive testing of cash would involve direct confirmation of bank balances. Substantive testing of receivables would involve direct confirmation of balances with customers. In an audit directed at the attestation of financial statements, the direct purpose of the audit is served by substantive testing in the financial statement audit phase, while an indirect purpose (achieving overall economy through permitting reliance on internal control) is served by compliance testing in the interim audit phase.

Auditing Around the Computer

During the early years of information systems development, computerized accounting systems provided auditors with very little need to significantly alter audit approaches and technology used in manual systems. Batch processing was the dominant method used in computers, and an "around-the-computer" approach provided for an adequate audit.

In general terms, an accounting system is comprised of input, processing, and output. In the **around-the-computer** approach, the processing portion is ignored. Instead, source documents supplying the input to the system are selected and summarized manually so that they can be compared to the output. As batches are processed through the system, totals are accumulated for accepted and rejected records. Auditors emphasize control over rejected transactions, their correction, and then resubmission.

Given advances in information technology, the around-the-computer approach is no longer widely used. This approach implicitly assumes that the computer does not exist. Assumptions about the system are drawn by examining the source documents and the output, comprised of error listings, reports, and so on. This approach also assumes that a computer cannot be used to falsify records without being detected by manual procedures.

Auditing Through the Computer

Auditing through the computer may be defined as the verification of controls in a computerized system. Consideration of the nature of information technology (IT) and internal control in an IT environment yields the framework shown in Figure 15.2. General controls are relevant to the information systems themselves, as well as to the systems development aspect of IT. Application controls are related to specific computer application systems. A thorough information systems audit involves verifying both general and application controls in a computerized system. More generally, an individual information systems audit would be directed at one of these areas, usually a specific application system such as accounts receivable.

Information systems audits to verify compliance with internal controls are performed by both internal and external auditors. The objectives of the external auditor are usually directed toward the attestation of financial statements. Frequently, internal auditors embrace the same objectives; at other times, internal auditors perform compliance audits that are responsive to the desires of top management and the particular needs of their company. The general conduct of an information systems audit is subject to the same professional standards relevant

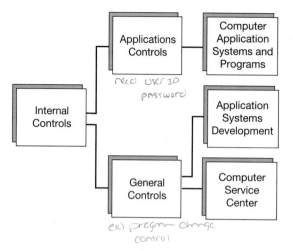

need user ID password

ex) program change control

FIGURE 15.2 Control Framework in IT Environment.

to any audit. For the external auditor, these standards are specified in AICPA's Statements of Auditing Standards. Internal auditors have professional auditing standards promulgated by the Institute of Internal Auditors, which are similar to the AICPA standards. Basic auditing standards are not altered by the technology employed in the system to be audited.

Auditing with the Computer

Auditing with the computer is the process of using information technology in auditing. Information technology is used to perform some audit work that otherwise would have to be done manually. The use of information technology by auditors is no longer optional. It is essential. Most of the data that auditors must evaluate are already in an electronic format. It is senseless to convert electronic data to a paper format strictly for audit purposes. Furthermore, auditing itself is not immune from competitive pressures to be more productive. The use of information technology is essential to increase the effectiveness and efficiency of auditing.

The potential benefits of using information systems technology in an audit include the following:

Benefits the individual auditor.

- Computer-generated working papers are generally more legible and consistent. Such working papers also may be easily stored, accessed, and revised.
- Time may be saved by eliminating manual footing, cross-footing, and other routine calculations.
- Calculations, comparisons, and other data manipulations are more accurately performed.
- Analytical review calculations may be more efficiently performed, and their scope may be broadened.
- Project information such as time budgets and the monitoring of actual time versus budgeted amounts may be more easily generated and analyzed.

Benefit the manager.

- Standardized audit correspondence such as questionnaires and checklists, proposal letters, and report formats may be stored and easily modified.
- Morale and productivity may be improved by reducing the time spent on clerical tasks.
- Increased cost-effectiveness is obtained by reusing and extending existing electronic audit applications to subsequent audits.
- Increased independence from information systems personnel is obtained.

The benefits identified in the first four points accrue primarily to the individual auditor who is actually performing the audit. Clear and obvious benefits are obtained from the calculating and data analysis capability provided by information technology. Properly programmed, totals and the like should be accurate. More complicated calculations such as statistical regressions are easily performed. The other benefits may be realized by the management of the internal audit function. Management of internal audit, like managers in other organizational functions, has much to gain from the efficient application of information technology. The ability to analyze time budget and other types of project control information facilitates managerial control, a quality necessary to the internal audit function as well as to all other organizational functions. The ability to standardize work papers, questionnaires, and other such documents utilized in audits performed by the audit staff also enhances managerial control and helps to ensure uniform and consistent application of practice by the audit staff. The reusability of electronic audit technology increases overall cost-effectiveness. The potential positive effects on staff morale and subsequent productivity gains should make the use of information technology a goal of every audit manager.

INFORMATION SYSTEMS AUDITING TECHNOLOGY

Information systems audit technology has evolved along with computer system development. There is no one overall auditing technology (Table 15.1). Rather, there is a variety of tools and techniques that may be used as appropriate to accomplish an audit's objectives. These technologies differ widely as to the amount of technical expertise required for their use. Several of the technologies entail significant costs to implement, whereas others may be implemented with relatively little cost.

Test Data

Test data is auditor-prepared input containing both valid and invalid data. Prior to processing the test data, the input is manually processed to determine what the output should look like. The auditor then compares the test output with the manually processed results (Figure 15.3). If the results are not as expected, the auditor attempts to determine the cause of the discrepancy.

Historically, test data represented the first attempt to audit through the computer. Although it might be impractical for an auditor to be able to understand the detailed logic of a computer program, she or he can understand the general specifications of a system and use this knowledge to determine whether or not a system works.

The test data technique is widely used by auditors as well as computer programmers to verify the processing accuracy of computer programs. Test data may be used to verify input transaction validation routines, processing logic, and computational routines of computer programs and to verify the incorporation of program changes. The technique is particularly good for testing programs in which calculations such as interest or depreciation are involved. The technique requires minimal computer expertise and is usually inexpensive to implement as it requires no modification to existing computer applications.

In using test data, regular live production programs are used, and it is essential to ensure that the test data do not affect the files maintained by the system.

TABLE 15-1 Information Systems Auditing Technologies

Technique	Description	Example
Test data	Test data are input containing both valid and invalid data.	Payroll transactions with both valid and invalid employee identification numbers.
Integrated test facility (ITF)	ITF involves both the use of test data and the creation of fictitious records (vendors, employees) on the master files of a computer system.	Payroll transactions for fictitious employees are processed concurrently with valid payroll transactions.
Parallel simulation	Processing real data through audit programs. The simulated output and the regular output are then compared.	Depreciation calculations are verified by processing the fixed-asset master file with an audit program.
Audit software	Computer programs that permit the computer to be used as an auditing tool.	An auditor uses a computer program to extract data records from a master file.
Generalized audit software (GAS)	GAS is audit software that has been specifically designed to allow auditors to perform audit-related data processing functions.	An auditor uses GAS to search computer files for unusual items.
PC software	Software that allows the auditor to use a PC to perform audit tasks.	A PC spreadsheet package is used to maintain audit working papers and audit schedules.
Embedded audit routines	Special auditing routines included in regular computer programs so that transaction data can be subjected to audit analysis.	Data items that are exceptions to auditor-specified edit tests included in a program are written to a special audit file.
Extended records	Modification of programs to collect and store data of audit interest.	A payroll program is modified to collect data pertaining to overtime pay.
Snapshot	Modification of programs to output data of audit interest.	A payroll program is modified to output data pertaining to overtime pay.
Tracing	Tracing provides a detailed audit trail of the instructions executed during the program's operation.	A payroll program is traced to determine if certain edit tests are performed in the correct order.
Review of system documentation	Existing system documentation such as program flowcharts are reviewed for audit purposes.	An auditor desk checks the processing logic of a payroll program.
Control flowcharting	Analytic flowcharts or other graphic techniques are used to describe the controls in a system.	An auditor prepares an analytic flowchart to review controls in the payroll application system.
Mapping	Special software is used to monitor the execution of a program.	The execution of a program with test data as input is mapped to indicate how extensively the input tested individual program statements.

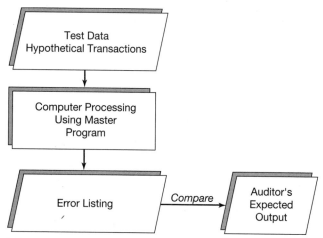

FIGURE 15.3 Test Data Approach.

This requires coordination between the auditor and computer personnel. It would be ironic if an audit procedure designed to detect errors were to introduce its own errors. It is important to note that test data can only evaluate programs. Other tests of the integrity of input data and output files are usually needed as well.

Test data are prepared after the system to be audited has been reviewed and transactions (test data) are designed to test selected aspects of the system. The test data might be generated by completing input forms to generate fictitious test transactions or alternatively by reviewing actual input data and selecting several real transactions for processing as test data. A less common technique is to create test data using test data generators—specially designed computer programs that create comprehensive test data based on input parameters that describe the nature of the program to be tested.

As an audit technology, test data have several limitations. A test can be run only on a specific program at a specific point in time. The test data may become obsolete because of program changes. The use of test data must be announced; the data are processed in a test run, rather than concurrently with actual live transactions. Thus, an auditor cannot always ensure that the program being tested is the one that is used regularly. Finally, test data generally cannot cover all combinations of conditions that a computer program might encounter in usage.

Integrated-Test-Facility Approach

Integrated test facility (ITF) approach involves the use of test data and also the creation of fictitious entities (e.g., vendors, employees, products, accounts) on the master files of a computer system. The technique is integrated as the test data are processed concurrently with real transactions against live master files that contain the real as well as fictitious entities. Accordingly, audit checks are made as a part of the normal processing cycle, ensuring that the programs being checked are identical to the programs that process real data (Figure 15.4).

Test data are identified by special codes and must be excluded from the normal system outputs, either manually or by modifying or initially designing the application programs to perform this function. The need to exclude the fictitious

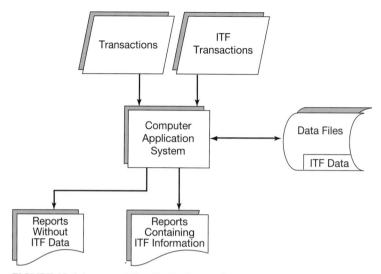

FIGURE 15.4 Integrated-Test-Facility Approach.

[Handwritten margin note: The initial cost of the development increases normal cost. However, once implemented, operating costs are low.]

data from normal output reports is the major disadvantage of ITF, but this is an unavoidable consequence of the objective of the technique, which is to process test data concurrent with real data. Careful planning is necessary to ensure that ITF data are properly segregated from the normal outputs.

ITF is a popular technique. If carefully planned, costs of using ITF are minimal. This is because no special processing or other interruption of normal computer activity is involved. An ITF will normally be developed at the same time as the application system and will increase the normal cost of systems development. However, once implemented, operating costs are low. ITF is commonly used to audit large computer application systems that use real-time processing technology. Concurrent testing is appropriate to concurrent, real-time processing of transactions.

ITF is a powerful audit technology. Ironically, one of the earliest publicized computer-fraud cases—the Equity Funding scandal—involved the modification of computer programs to separately process thousands of bogus insurance policies, which is essentially the same concept used in ITF. The bogus policies were identified by a special code and were routinely excluded from reports provided to auditors but were included in all other reports. Similarly, test data differ from fraudulent data only in that test data are processed under controlled conditions by auditors.

Parallel Simulation

The test data and ITF methods both process test data through real programs. **Parallel simulation** processes real data through test or audit programs. The simulated output and the regular output are compared for control purposes. The amount of redundant processing undertaken by the test or audit program is usually limited to sections that are of major interest to the audit. For example, parallel simulation of a cost accounting program may be limited to the functions that update work-in-process records. Other functions, such as scheduling or performance reporting, may not be included in the simulation program as they are not of direct interest to the audit. This is illustrated in Figure 15.5.

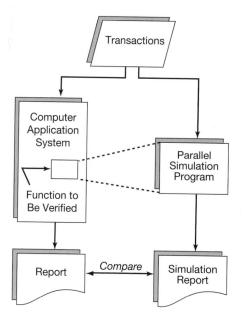

FIGURE 15.5 Parallel Simulation.

Parallel simulation—the redundant processing of all input data by a separate test program—permits comprehensive validation and is appropriate where transactions are sufficiently important to require a 100% audit. The audit program used in parallel simulation is typically some type of generalized audit program that processes data and produces output identical to the program being audited. The same actual data are processed by both programs and the results compared. This approach is expensive and time-consuming but, unlike the other approaches, it uses real data. Furthermore, it can be used off-site.

Benefits

Audit Software

Audit software includes computer programs that permit the computer to be used as an auditing tool. The computer is programmed to read, select, extract, and process sample data from computer files. There are many types of audit software that may be utilized to varying degrees in both mainframe and PC environments. Conventional software such as system utility programs, information retrieval programs, or high-level languages might be used. More common is the use of specially designed audit software packages, known as generalized audit software (GAS), and personal computer software packages. These are discussed separately.

Generalized Audit Software (GAS)

Generalized audit software (GAS) is software that has been specifically designed to facilitate the use of information technology in auditing. GAS was originally developed by public accounting firms in the late 1960s, and has a long history of usage. GAS are specifically designed to allow auditors with little computer expertise to perform audit-related data processing functions. These packages can perform such tasks as selecting sample data from the files, checking computations, and searching the files for unusual items. They also incorporate many special features that are useful to auditors, such as the statistical selection of sample data and the preparation of confirmation requests.

PC Software

The low cost of PCs coupled with the wide variety of software packages available has made the PC an important tool in administrating an audit. General-purpose **PC software** packages such as word processing and spreadsheet software have many audit applications. In addition, special-purpose, audit-oriented software packages have been developed specifically for use in audit administration.

One example of a PC-based audit software package is ACL™ (published by ACL Software), which allows the auditor to connect a personal notebook computer to the client's mainframe or PC and then extract and analyze the various accounting files.

ACL accesses the client's files in their native format without any need to convert them. It then provides a wide range of functions that allows the auditor to do the following:

- Recalculate and verify account balances
- Test for unauthorized relationships between employees and suppliers
- Locate errors and pinpoint fraud possibilities by comparing the data in the accounting files to preestablished criteria
- Age and analyze accounts receivable
- Identify trends and pinpoint exceptions

ACL also runs on IBM mainframe computers, thus in some cases allowing the auditor flexibility of either working through or around the client's computer. The trend, however, seems to be more in the direction of the auditor running the audit software on a personal computer.

The large public accounting firms typically use their own proprietary audit software systems. One example is the Deloitte & Touche AuditSystem/2™ software designed for the Microsoft Windows™ operating system (Figure 15.6). Deloitte & Touche's total investment in this audit system (including hardware, software, and training) initially exceeded $220 million.

AuditSystem/2 performs a wide range of services for the auditor, including the following:

- Smart audit support: helps the auditor answer specific auditing questions
- Work papers: generates the necessary work papers required to document the audit
- File interrogation: interfaces with ACL for data extraction and analysis
- Multilocation support: helps working with companies whose accounting data are spread over more than one site.

An important feature of AuditSystem/2 is that it is designed to work with teams of auditors. Specifically, it allows the various members of the audit team to work cooperatively and exchange information through standard Windows applications such as Microsoft Word™ (for word processing), Microsoft Excel™ (for spreadsheet processing), Microsoft Access™ (for database applications), Lotus cc:Mail™ (for electronic mail), and ACL (for data extraction and analysis).

Embedded Audit Routines

Embedded audit routines are an audit technology that involves the modification of computer programs for audit purposes. This is accomplished by building special auditing routines into regular production programs so that transaction data or

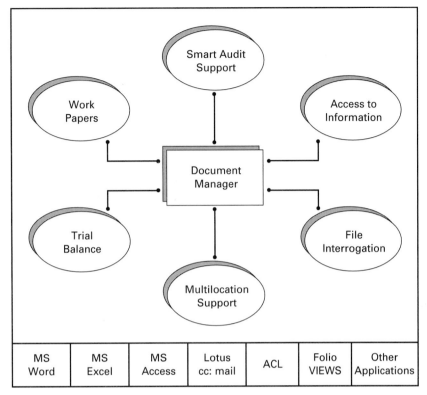

FIGURE 15.6 Deloitte & Touche AuditSystem/2™.

some subset of them can be subjected to audit analysis. One such technique has been called embedded audit data collection. Embedded audit data collection uses one or more specially programmed modules embedded as **in-line code** within the regular program code to select and record data for subsequent analysis and evaluation (see Figure 15.7). The use of in-line code means that the application program performs the audit data collection function at the same time as it processes data for normal production purposes. Embedded routines are more easily included in a program as it is being developed rather than added as a modification later on.

Audit criteria for selecting and recording transactions by the embedded modules must be supplied by the auditor. This can be done in different ways. In an approach called the **system control audit review file (SCARF),** auditor-determined, programmed edit tests for limits or reasonableness are included in the program as it is initially developed. During the normal operation of the program, data items that are exceptions to these edits are written on a file. This file of exceptions may be reviewed by the auditor and any appropriate actions may be undertaken. Values used in such limit or reasonableness tests may be set when the module is originally developed; alternatively, the module may be programmed so that the test limits may be altered by the auditor as desired. Transactions might be selected randomly rather than as exceptions to programmed edit tests. The objective of this approach is to generate a statistical sample of transactions for later audit. This approach has been called the **sample audit review file (SARF).**

How it
works

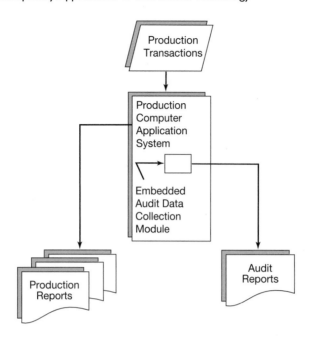

FIGURE 15.7 Embedded Audit Data Collection.

Extended Records

Extended records refers to the modification of computer programs to provide a comprehensive audit trail for selected transactions by collecting in one extended record additional data concerning processing that are not normally collected. Because many different processing steps may be combined within a single program, the intervening steps that make up the audit trail are often lost. Several different files might have to be reviewed to follow the processing of a specific transaction.

With the extended record technique, specific transactions are tagged and the intervening processing steps that would not normally be saved are added to the extended record, permitting the audit trail to be reconstructed for these transactions. The extended record includes data from all of the separate application programs that may process a transaction, thus providing a complete audit trail. Transactions might be identified by special codes, selected randomly, or selected as exceptions to edit tests.

Snapshot

Snapshot, as the name implies, attempts to provide a comprehensive picture of the working of a program at particular points in time. Snapshot is a common program debugging technique. Snapshot involves the addition of program code to cause the program to print out the contents of selected memory areas at the time during processing that the snapshot code is executed. This provides a hard copy of the operation of the program that otherwise would not be available and is very useful in locating bugs in a program. As an audit tool, snapshot code may be added to areas of the program that are of interest to the audit and executed only for transactions that are exceptions to predetermined edit tests. Snapshot and extended records are very similar technology, with snapshot generating a printed audit trail and extended records incorporating snapshot data in the extended record rather than on hard copy.

Tracing

Tracing is another audit technique that originated as a program debugging aid. Tracing a program's execution provides a detailed audit trail of the instructions executed during the program's operation. Tracing is normally executed using an option in the program source code language (such as COBOL). The audit trail provided by the trace is dependent on the particular trace package. High-level languages are traced at the source statement level; lower-level languages are traced at a more detailed level. Tracing provides a detailed listing of the sequence of program statement execution. A trace can produce thousands of output records, and care must be exercised that an excessive number of transactions are not tagged for tracing. For audit purposes, tracing might be used to verify that internal controls within an application program are executed as the program processes live or test data. A trace may also indicate sections of unexecuted program code, a situation that has in some instances resulted in the discovery of incorrect or unauthorized modifications to a program.

All embedded audit routine techniques require a high level of technical expertise when they are first set up, and a moderate to high level of knowledge to use them effectively. They are far easier to implement when a program and/or files for an application are first designed rather than after the system has begun operation. The degree of independence that auditors can maintain while developing such systems will depend largely on the level of technical expertise that they possess. Even when the auditor possesses a high level of technical expertise, development still requires a good deal of cooperation between the auditor and systems personnel.

Review of Systems Documentation

Review of systems documentation, such as narrative descriptions, flowcharts, and program listings, is probably the oldest EDP auditing technique, and is still a widely used one. This approach is particularly appropriate in the initial phases of an audit as preparation for the selection and utilization of other more direct audit technology.

Many types of reviews are possible. An auditor may request computer personnel to "dump" a computer file, that is, to provide the auditor with a complete listing of the file's contents. Alternatively, the auditor may request dumps of program source language listings. These listings may be reviewed manually by the auditor. Programs might be **desk checked** by the auditor. In desk checking, the auditor manually processes test or real data through the program logic. Program flowcharts might be reviewed in the same manner. A more sophisticated review of a program might be undertaken by requesting a dump of the object code, that is, machine-language version of a program. Review of this form of system documentation provides the greatest assurance that what is checked is actually what does the processing, but this form of review requires considerable technical expertise and patience. The auditor might review the manufacturer's blueprint of the software and compare it to the software in use. The auditor might verify a hash total of the object code of the software to detect modifications to the software.

Another type of documentation that may be examined is the operating documentation generated by many computer systems as a routine part of operations. Software that monitors the performance of computer operations is commonly available on large systems to provide technical statistics useful in tuning the system for efficient operation. Although these statistics are oriented toward the operating functions of the system, such as channel and disk usage, they might also be used for specialized auditing purposes. Job accounting routines are frequently part of a computer's operating system. These routines collect and summarize statistics concerning program (job) resource utilization. Again, such statistics may be of interest to the auditor because they show who used the system and also when and which resources and programs were involved.

Control Flowcharting

In many cases, specific documentation for auditing purposes is reviewed and developed to show the nature of application controls in a system. This documentation has been called **control flowcharting.** Analytic flowcharts, system flowcharts, or other graphic techniques are used to describe the controls in a system. A major advantage of flowcharts is that they are understandable to auditors, users, and computer personnel, and thus facilitate communication between these different parties.

Mapping

More direct audit evidence concerning programs may be obtained by monitoring the running of a program with a special software measurement package. This audit technique is called **mapping.** Special software is used to monitor the execution of a program; in doing so, the software counts the number of times each program statement in the program is executed and provides summary statistics concerning resource utilization. Mapping originated as a technique to assist program design and testing. Auditors can use the same software to determine whether specific program statements have been executed. Mapping can help assure that program application control statements that appear in the source language listing of a program actually execute when the program runs, and that they have not inadvertently or otherwise been bypassed by a logic not readily apparent in the source code listing of the program. Although software measurement packages can ensure that certain program steps have been executed, they do not ensure that execution was performed in the proper sequence. Counts of the number of times each program statement was executed do not imply that the total program executes in accordance with the intent of the programmer (i.e., that the program does the right thing).

Mapping can be used effectively in conjunction with a test data technique. The execution of a program with test data as input can be mapped. Evaluation of the output of the software monitor can indicate how extensively the input tested individual program statements. Statements that have not executed have not been tested.

TYPES OF INFORMATION SYSTEMS AUDITS

General Approach to an Information Systems Audit

Most approaches to an information systems audit follow some variation of a three-phase structure. The first phase consists of an initial review and evaluation of the area to be audited and audit plan preparation. The second phase is a detailed review and evaluation of controls. The third phase involves compliance testing and is followed by analysis and reporting of results.

The initial review phase of an information systems audit determines the course of action the audit will take and includes decisions concerning specific areas to be investigated, the deployment of audit labor, the audit technology to be used, and the development of a time and/or cost budget for the audit. The primary control over the conduct of an information systems audit, like that of any other organized activity, centers on documentation and review of performance. Each general phase of an audit, as well as specific steps within each phase, should have as an objective the preparation of documentation. Such documentation provides a tangible output and goal for each audit step, allows effective supervision, and facilitates review.

Audit resources are usually limited, so it will generally not be possible to audit each application every year. Applications that are more subject to fraud or serious financial error are likely targets for audit. Frequently, a rotating system of selection is used to select audit areas, with each application being audited according to some multiyear schedule.

Decisions concerning the deployment of auditing labor, the audit technology to be used, and the time/cost budget for the overall audit should also be made according to some systematic procedure. The outcome of all these decisions and the product of the initial review phase of an information systems audit is the audit program. An **audit program** is a detailed list of the audit procedures to be applied on a particular audit. Standardized audit programs for particular audit areas have been developed and are common in all types of auditing. The use of a standardized information systems audit program is often possible, with modifications made to reflect the particular situation subject to audit.

The second general phase of an information systems audit is detailed review and evaluation. In this phase of the audit, effort is focused on fact-finding in the area(s) selected for audit. Documentation of the application area is reviewed and data concerning the operation of the system collected by interviews, administration of internal control questionnaires, and direct observation. Transaction files, control logs, program listings, and other data are reviewed as necessary to confirm the scope of the audit set in the audit program and to design the test procedures to be subsequently used.

The third phase of the audit is testing. The testing phase of an audit produces evidence of compliance with procedures. Compliance tests are undertaken to provide reasonable assurance that internal controls exist and operate as prescribed in system documentation. The nature of compliance tests that might be included in an information systems audit are discussed in the following sections.

Information Systems Application Audits

Application controls are divided into three general areas: input, processing, and output. An information systems application audit generally involves reviewing the controls in each of these areas. In addition to the usual manual tracing and vouching techniques, all of the information systems audit technologies discussed earlier are relevant. The specific technology used will depend on the ingenuity and resources of the auditor. Test data, ITF, or parallel simulation might be used to test processing controls. Transactions to be selected for audit might be generated by an embedded audit module or by a separate audit program. GAS might be used to review transaction and/or output files. The nature of an information systems application audit will be heavily influenced by the amount of audit involvement in the systems development process. ITF and embedded audit modules can be used only if they already exist in the application.

Application Systems Development Audits

Systems development audits are directed at the activities of systems analysts and programmers who develop and modify application programs, files, and related procedures. Controls governing the systems development process directly affect the reliability of the application programs that are developed. Three general areas of audit concern in the systems development process are systems development standards, project management, and program change control. The primary audit technique in each of these areas is a review and testing of the related documentation. This is accomplished by directly observing the documentation and by collecting relevant information through interviews and/or questionnaires.

Systems development standards are the documentation governing the design, development, and implementation of application systems. The existence of systems development standards is a major general control in computerized systems. Development standards ensure that appropriate application controls are considered, selected, and implemented in application systems, that an adequate audit trail is provided, and that suitable levels of operability and maintainability are achieved after implementation. The primary audit technique is to review such documentation, assess it for sufficiency, and then determine compliance with it. This is done by reviewing application system documentation. Application system documentation, such as flowcharts, system narratives, and test data, should conform to the specifications set forth in the organization's systems development standards.

Project management controls measure and control progress during application systems development. Project management consists of project planning and project supervision. A project plan is a formal statement of the project's detailed work plan. Project supervision monitors the execution of project activities. Auditors can evaluate the adequacy of project management controls by comparison of criteria available in the systems development literature. Compliance testing involves reviewing project planning and supervision documentation—such as PERT/CPM charts, GANTT charts, schedules, time reports, and status reports—and interviewing users and systems personnel.

Program change controls concern the maintenance of application programs. The objective of such controls is to prevent unauthorized and potentially fraudulent changes from being introduced into previously tested and accepted programs. Elements of control include documentation of change requests and a register of program changes with dates and appropriate approvals for authorization, programming the change, testing and certification of test results, and revision of the production program and its related documentation. Appropriate segregation of programmers, operations, and the program/tape library is necessary in the process. Program maintenance is more subject to error than normal program development and represents a major loss exposure in terms of both fraud and access to sensitive programs.

Compliance testing might involve the review of documentation of maintenance procedures, review of systems job accounting information, and source language and object code comparison techniques. The common technique for code comparison has the audit function retain custody of duplicate program copies and periodically compare its copies to the actual production programs. This is commonly done at the source statement level; object code comparison is less common. Any differences detected between the test program and the production program are reconciled by tracing back to the program change documentation file. Test data utilized in program maintenance should also be reviewed for completeness. If testing of program modifications is incomplete, the probability of introducing errors to an application program is increased.

Information systems audits of the systems development process are more common to large organizations, as many small organizations may not have a formal systems development process. The essence of a formal systems development process is documentation. If none exists, a potential audit is necessarily terminated, as the audit consists primarily of the review and testing of such documentation.

Computer Service Center Audits

Normally, an audit of the computer service center is undertaken before any application audits to ensure the general integrity of the environment in which the application will function. The general controls that govern computer service center operations complement application controls that are developed in specific application systems. The general controls that govern computer operations also help to ensure the uninterrupted availability of computer service center resources.

Audits might be undertaken in several areas. One area concerns environmental controls. Mainframe systems associated with large computer service centers generally have special temperature and humidity requirements that necessitate air conditioning. Another area that is closely related to environmental controls is physical security of the center. There are many concerns and thus many potential controls in this area. Controls are necessary to maintain a stable power source, and also to provide for an alternative power source in the case of failure. Fire protection must be provided, and the center must be protected from water damage. Controls must assure controlled physical access. Controls over the release of data, reports, and computer programs are also of concern. Provisions for casualty insurance and business interruption insurance might be reviewed.

The center's disaster recovery plan might be reviewed. A disaster recovery plan would include items such as management responsibility statements—specifying who is responsible for what in the event of a disaster, emergency action plans, facilities and data backup plans, and recovery process controls. Another area concerns controls over malfunction reporting and preventative maintenance. This area includes failure reporting and logging, preventative maintenance scheduling, and malfunction correction.

Management controls over the operation of the computer service center are also an area of concern. This area includes techniques used to budget equipment load factors, project usage statistics, budget and plan staffing requirements, and plan equipment acquisitions. Job (i.e., computer resource) accounting systems are another general control over operations. Job accounting systems may contain user billing or charge-out procedures. Billing algorithms might be reviewed, and periodic user billing statements might be reconciled to usage.

The only compliance tests that would be utilized in all of the foregoing audit areas would be review of documentary evidence; corroborating interviews with users, management, and systems personnel; direct observation; and inquiry. Audits of computer service center operations require a higher degree of technical training and familiarity with computer operations than do audits of computerized applications.

SUMMARY

The term *information systems auditing* is commonly used to describe two different types of computer-related activity. One use of the term is to describe the process of reviewing and evaluating the internal controls in an electronic data processing system. This type of activity is described as auditing through the computer. The other general use of the term is to describe the utilization of the computer by an auditor to perform some audit work that otherwise would have to be done manually. This type of activity is described as auditing with the computer.

Information systems audit technology has evolved along with computer system development. There is no one overall information systems auditing technology. Rather, there are several technologies that may be used as appropriate to accomplish an audit's objectives. Technologies discussed include test data, integrated test facility (ITF), parallel simulation, and generalized audit software, among others. Information systems audit technologies differ widely as to the amount of technical expertise required for their use. Several of the technologies entail significant costs to implement, whereas others may be implemented with relatively little cost.

Most approaches to an information systems audit follow some variation of a three-phase structure. These phases are initial review and evaluation of the area to be audited, detailed review and evaluation, and testing. Three general types of information systems audits might be undertaken. These are information systems application audits, application systems development audits, and computer service center audits.

Glossary

around-the-computer: information systems auditing approach in which the processing portion of a computer system is ignored.

auditing through the computer: the process of reviewing and evaluating the internal controls in an electronic data processing system.

auditing with the computer: the utilization of the computer by an auditor to perform some audit work that otherwise would have to be done manually.

audit program: a detailed list of the audit procedures to be applied on a particular audit.

audit software: computer programs that permit the computer to be used as an auditing tool.

compliance testing: testing to confirm the existence, assess the effectiveness, and check the continuity of operation of internal controls.

control flowcharting: analytic flowcharts or other graphic techniques are used to describe the controls in a system.

desk checking: the auditor manually processes test or real data through the logic of a computer program.

embedded audit routines: special auditing routines included in regular computer programs so that transaction data can be subjected to audit analysis.

extended records: modification of programs to collect and store additional data of audit interest.

financial statement audit: the second stage of a financial statement audit that uses substantive testing for direct verification of financial statement figures.

generalized audit software (GAS): audit software that has been specifically designed to allow auditors to perform audit-related data processing functions.

in-line code: an application program performs an embedded audit routine function such as data collection at the same time that it processes data for normal purposes.

integrated test facility (ITF): concurrent information systems audit technology that involves the use of test data and also the creation of fictitious entities on the master files of a computer system.

interim audit: first stage of a financial statement audit that has the objective of establishing the degree to which the internal control system can be relied upon.

mapping: special software used to monitor the execution of a program.

parallel simulation: the processing of real data through audit programs, with the simulated output and the regular output compared for control purposes.

review of systems documentation: existing systems documentation such as program flowcharts are reviewed for audit purposes.

sample audit review file (SARF): use of in-line code to randomly select transactions for audit analysis.

snapshot: modification of programs to output data of audit interest.

substantive testing: direct verification of balances contained in financial statements.

system control audit review file (SCARF): auditor-determined programmed edit tests for audit transaction analysis are included in a program as it is initially developed.

test data: auditor-prepared input containing both valid and invalid data.

tracing: provides a detailed audit trail of the instructions executed during the program's operation.

Chapter Quiz

Answers to the chapter quiz appear on page 600.

1. Which of the following is a potential problem when using test data?
   (a) testing a program that is not the actual program used for processing
   (b) introducing errors into the program being tested
   (c) both a and b
   (d) neither a nor b

2. Which of the following is a potential problem when using integrated test facility (ITF)?
   (a) testing a program that is not the actual program used for processing
   (b) introducing errors into the program being tested
   (c) both a and b
   (d) neither a nor b

3. Which of the following is a concurrent auditing technology?
   (a) test data
   (b) integrated test facility (ITF)
   (c) both a and b
   (d) neither a nor b

4. Which of the following is a concurrent auditing technology?
   (a) parallel simulation
   (b) generalized audit software
   (c) both a and b
   (d) neither a nor b

5. Which of the following is a concurrent auditing technology?
   (a) embedded audit routines
   (b) control flowcharting
   (c) both a and b
   (d) neither a nor b

6. Which of the following is used to test the functioning of computer programs?
   (a) test data
   (b) parallel simulation
   (c) both a and b
   (d) neither a nor b

7. Which of the following is used to select data for audit analysis?
   (a) generalized audit software
   (b) embedded audit routines
   (c) both a and b
   (d) neither a nor b

8. Which of the following would most likely be implemented with generalized audit software?
   (a) embedded audit routines
   (b) parallel simulation
   (c) both a and b
   (d) neither a nor b

9. Mapping is a technology that provides the auditor
   (a) assurance that program instructions are executing in proper sequence.
   (b) summary information regarding which program instructions are executed.
   (c) both a and b.
   (d) neither a nor b.

10. Normally, an audit of the computer service center is undertaken (_____) any application audits.
    (a) during
    (b) before
    (c) after
    (d) instead of

Review Problem

In the past, the records to be evaluated in an audit have been printed reports, listings, documents, and written papers, all of which are visible output. However, in fully computerized systems that employ daily updating of transaction files, output and files are frequently in machine-readable forms, such as tapes or disks. Thus, they often present the auditor with an opportunity to use the computer in performing an audit.

Required

Discuss how the computer can be used to aid the auditor in examining accounts receivable in such a fully computerized system.

(CPA)

Solution to Review Problem

Testing Extension and Footings

The computer can be used to perform simple summations and other computations to test the correction of extensions and footings. The auditor may choose to perform tests on all records instead of just on samples, because the speed and low cost per computation of the computer enable this at only a small extra amount of time and expense.

Selecting and Printing Confirmation Requests

The computer can select and print out confirmation requests on the basis of quantifiable selection criteria. The program can be written to select the accounts according to any set of criteria desired and using any sampling plan.

Examining Records for Quality (Completeness, Consistency, Valid Conditions, etc.)

The quality of visible records is readily apparent to the auditor. Sloppy record keeping, lack of completeness, and so on, are observed by the auditor in the normal course of the audit. If machine-readable records are evaluated manually, however, a complete printout is needed to examine their quality. The auditor may choose to use the computer for examining these records for quality.

If the computer is to be used for the examination, a program is written to examine the record for completeness, consistency among different items, valid conditions, reasonable amounts, and so forth. For instance, customer file records might be examined to determine those for which no credit limit is specified, those for which account balances exceed the credit limit, and those for which credit limits exceed a stipulated amount.

Summarizing Data and Performing Analyses Useful to the Auditor

The auditor frequently needs to have the client's data analyzed and/or summarized. Such procedures as aging accounts receivable or listing all credit balances in accounts receivable can be accomplished with a computer program.

Selecting and Printing Audit Samples

The computer may be programmed to select audit samples by the use of random numbers or by systematic selection techniques. The sample selection procedures may be programmed to use multiple criteria, such as the selection of a random sample of items under a certain dollar amount plus the selection of all items over a certain dollar amount. Other considerations can be included, such as unusual transactions, dormant accounts, and so forth.

(CPA)

Review Questions

1. What is meant by the expression "auditing around the computer"?
2. What are the two meanings of the term *information systems auditing?*
3. List and briefly describe the three phases of an information systems audit.
4. Distinguish between auditing through the computer and auditing with the computer.
5. What is a computer audit program?
6. What types of documents are examined in an information systems audit?
7. List five embedded audit routine techniques.
8. Compliance testing tests what?
9. How have microcomputers affected information systems auditing?
10. Identify the characteristics that are common to a typical information systems audit.
11. How would you select areas that should be audited in an information systems system?
12. Why do computer service center audits require the greatest expertise of an information systems auditor?

Discussion Questions and Problems

13. Auditors' initial response to computer systems was to audit around the computer. This strategy is *least* likely to be successful in an audit of
    (a) a batch processing system for payroll.
    (b) a card-based system for inventory.
    (c) an on-line system for demand deposit accounts.
    (d) a mark-sense document system for utility billing.

(IIA)

14. Normally, auditors using the ITF technique enter immaterial transactions to minimize the effect on output. This is a disadvantage because
    (a) certain limit tests cannot be attempted.
    (b) the transaction will not appear normal.
    (c) a special routine will be required in the application system.
    (d) designing the test data can be difficult.

(IIA)

Use the following information to answer Questions 15, 16, and 17.

Management has requested a special audit of the recently established electronic controls systems division because the last three quarterly profit reports seem to be inconsistent with the division's cash flow. The division sells customized control systems on a contract basis. A work-in-process (WIP) record is established for each contract on the WIP master file, which is kept on magnetic disk. Contract charges for material, labor, and overhead are processed by the WIP computer program to maintain the WIP master file and to provide billing information.

The preliminary audit has revealed that not all costs have been charged against the WIP records. Thus, when contracts are closed, reported profits have been overstated. It is now necessary to determine the reason(s) for this loss of control.

15. Which of the following information systems auditing techniques would be most appropriate to audit the processing accuracy of the WIP computer program in posting transactions to the master WIP file?
    (a) control flowcharting
    (b) test data
    (c) review of program documentation
    (d) embedded audit source code

16. Which of the following information systems auditing techniques would be most appropriate to audit the content of the WIP master file that is stored on magnetic disk?
    (a) control flowcharting
    (b) test data
    (c) generalized audit software
    (d) embedded audit source code

17. Which of the following information systems auditing techniques would be most appropriate to audit the overall business control context of the WIP computer processing system?
    (a) control flowcharting
    (b) test data
    (c) generalized audit software
    (d) embedded audit source code

(IIA adapted)

18. Smith Corporation has numerous customers. A customer file is kept on disk storage. Each customer file contains name, address, credit limit, and account balance. The auditor wishes to test this file to determine whether credit limits are being exceeded. The best procedure for the auditor to follow would be to
    (a) develop test data that would cause some account balances to exceed the credit limit and determine if the system properly detects such situations.
    (b) develop a program to compare credit limits with account balances and print out the details of any account with a balance exceeding its credit limit.
    (c) request a printout of all account balances so they can be manually checked against the credit limits.
    (d) request a printout of a sample of account balances so they can be individually checked against the credit limits.

(CPA)

19. When an auditor tests a computerized accounting system, which of the following is true of the test data approach?
    (a) test data are processed by the client's computer programs under the auditor's control
    (b) test data must consist of all possible valid and invalid conditions
    (c) testing a program at year-end provides assurance that the client's processing was accurate for the full year
    (d) several transactions of each type must be tested

(CPA)

20. An auditor's objective is to verify the processing accuracy of an application. An EDP audit approach for achieving this objective that avoids contaminating client master files or requiring substantial additional application programming is the
    (a) embedded data collection technique.
    (b) integrated test facility.
    (c) test data method.
    (d) snapshot method.

    (IIA)

21. Headquarter's auditors are reviewing a payroll application system via the ITF technique. Which of the following would be used by the auditors?
    (a) fictitious names processed with the normal payroll application of the corporation to a dummy entity
    (b) fictitious names processed in a separate run through the payroll application of the corporation
    (c) a sample of last month's payroll reprocessed through the audit software package to a dummy entity
    (d) fictitious names processed through the generalized audit software package with the same company codes

    (IIA)

22. Which of the following is true of generalized audit software packages?
    (a) they can be used only in auditing on-line computer systems
    (b) they can be used on any computer without modification
    (c) they each have their own characteristics, which the auditor must carefully consider before using in a given audit situation
    (d) they enable the auditor to perform all manual compliance test procedures less expensively

    (CPA)

23. The most important function of generalized audit software is the capability to
    (a) access information stored on computer files.
    (b) select a sample of items for testing.
    (c) evaluate sample test results.
    (d) test the accuracy of the client's calculations.

    (CPA)

24. When auditing around the computer, the independent auditor focuses solely on the source documents and
    (a) test data.
    (b) information systems processing.
    (c) compliance techniques.
    (d) information systems output.

    (CPA)

25. In auditing through a computer, the test data method is used by auditors to test the
    (a) accuracy of input data.
    (b) validity of the output.
    (c) procedures contained within the program.
    (d) normalcy of distribution of test data.

    (CPA)

26. Which of the following methods of testing application controls utilizes a generalized audit software package prepared by the auditors?
    (a) parallel simulation
    (b) integrated testing facility approach
    (c) test data approach
    (d) exception report tests

    (CPA)

27. A primary advantage of using generalized audit software packages in auditing the financial statements of a client that uses a computerized system is that the auditor may
    (a) substantiate the accuracy of data through self-checking digits and hash totals.
    (b) access information stored on computer files without a complete understanding of the client's hardware and software features.
    (c) reduce the level of required compliance testing to a relatively small amount.
    (d) gather and permanently store large quantities of supportive evidential matter in machine-readable form.

    (CPA)

28. When testing a computerized accounting system, which of the following is *not* true of the test data approach?
    (a) test data are processed by the client's computer programs under the auditor's control
    (b) test data must consist of all possible valid and invalid conditions
    (c) test data need consist of only those valid and invalid conditions in which the auditor is interested
    (d) only one transaction of each type need be tested

    (CPA)

    Question 29 is based on the flowchart in Figure 15.8.

29. The flowchart in Figure 15.8 depicts
    (a) program code checking.
    (b) parallel simulation.
    (c) integrated test facility.
    (d) controlled reprocessing.

    (CPA)

    Question 30 is based on the flowchart in Figure 15.9.

30. In a credit sales and cash receipts system flowchart, the symbol *X* could represent
    (a) auditor's test data.
    (b) remittance advices.
    (c) error reports.
    (d) credit authorization forms.

    (CPA)

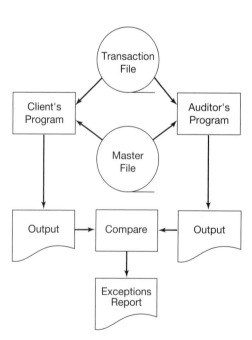

FIGURE 15.8 Flowchart for Problem 29.

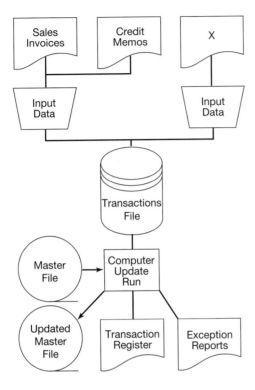

FIGURE 15.9 Flowchart for Problem 30.

31. Which of the following computer-assisted auditing techniques allows fictitious and real transactions to be processed together without client operating personnel being aware of the testing process?
    (a) parallel simulation
    (b) generalized audit software programming
    (c) integrated test facility
    (d) test data approach

    (CPA)

32. An auditor who is testing information systems controls in a payroll system would most likely use test data that contain conditions such as
    (a) deductions **not** authorized by employees.
    (b) overtime **not** approved by supervisors.
    (c) time tickets with invalid job numbers.
    (d) payroll checks with unauthorized signatures.

    (CPA)

33. An auditor most likely would test for the presence of unauthorized information systems program changes by running a
    (a) program with test data.
    (b) check digit verification program.
    (c) source code comparison program.
    (d) program that computes control totals.

    (CPA)

34. You decided to use a newly acquired audit software package in auditing accounts payable. The accounts payable system has been computerized for several years, and the transaction records are recorded on magnetic disk.

Required

(a) Briefly describe five of the major functions of the typical generalized audit software package.
(b) List three important steps in auditing of accounts payable for which generalized audit software can be used.
(c) Briefly describe how the generalized audit software should be used to perform these audit steps.

(IIA)

35. An auditor is conducting an examination of the financial statements of a wholesale cosmetics distributor with an inventory consisting of thousands of individual items. The distributor keeps its inventory in its own distribution center and in two public warehouses. An inventory computer file is maintained on a computer disk and, at the end of each business day, the file is updated. Each record of the inventory file contains the following data:

- Item number
- Location of item
- Description of item
- Quantity on hand
- Cost per item
- Date of last purchase
- Date of last sale
- Quantity sold during year

The auditor is planning to observe the distributor's physical count of inventories as of a given date. The auditor will have available a computer tape of the data on the inventory file on the date of the physical count and a general-purpose computer software package.

Required

The auditor is planning to perform basic inventory auditing procedures. Identify those procedures and describe how using the general-purpose software package and the tape of the inventory file data might be helpful to the auditor in performing such auditing procedures.

Organize your answer as follows:

Basic Inventory Auditing Procedure	*How General-Purpose Computer Software Package and Tape of the Inventory File Data Might Be Helpful*
1. Observe the physical count, making and recording test counts where applicable.	Determine which items are to be test counted by selecting a random sample of a representative number of items from the inventory file as of the date of the physical counts.

(CPA)

Answers to Chapter Quiz

1. A	4. D	7. C	10. B
2. D	5. A	8. B	
3. B	6. C	9. B	

CHAPTER 16

Systems Planning and Analysis

LEARNING OBJECTIVES

Careful study of this chapter will enable you to:

■ Describe the relationship of systems analysis to systems development as a whole.

■ Describe the various stages of systems analysis.

■ Discuss the major techniques for gathering and organizing data for systems analysis.

■ Describe some of the human problems involved in systems analysis.

OVERVIEW

Systems planning involves identifying subsystems within the information system that need special attention for development. The objective of systems planning is to identify problem areas that either need to be dealt with immediately or some time in the future. Systems analysis begins after systems planning has identified subsystems for development. Its primary objectives (Figure 16.1) are to understand the existing systems and problems, to describe information needs, and to establish priorities for further systems work.

Once a particular subsystem of the organization is targeted for development, systems analysis focuses on defining the information needs and system requirements that are necessary in order for the system to implement management's objectives. Therefore, systems analysis emphasizes the study of the decisions that managers make and their associated information requirements. These requirements are then translated into specific applications during the design and implementation phases of the systems development life cycle.

The importance of the systems analysis process can be seen in Figure 16.2. The majority of development cycle costs are tied up in the design and implementation phases. This means that major errors in the analysis phase can become quite costly later. It is, therefore, very important that the systems analyst gain a thorough understanding of the situation in terms of management's problems and information needs.

Objectives

1. Gain an understanding of the existing system (if one exists).
2. Identify and understand problems.
3. Express identified problems in terms of information needs and system requirements.
4. Clearly identify subsystems to be given highest priority.

Focus
■ Identify critical success factors.
■ Give special attention to these factors.

FIGURE 16.1 Objectives of Systems Analysis.

SYSTEMS PLANNING AND FEASIBILITY ANALYSIS

It is essential that a top-down, total systems approach be taken to systems development. Careful attention must be given to developing an overall systems plan and strategy. Such a plan must include the overall support and approval of top management. Without such an overall plan, the information system is likely to develop as a maze of patchwork. An overall plan seeks to ensure the following objectives:

- Resources will be targeted to the subsystems where the needs are greatest.
- Duplication and wasted effort will be minimized.
- Systems development in the organization will be consistent with the overall strategic plan of the organization. Value Added System!

Systems planning and feasibility analysis involve seven phases:

1. Discussing and planning on the part of top management.
2. Establishing a systems planning steering committee.
3. Establishing overall objectives and constraints.
4. Developing a strategic information systems plan.
5. Identifying and prioritizing specific areas within the organization for the systems development focus.
6. Setting forth a systems proposal to serve as a basis of the analysis and preliminary design for a given subsystem.

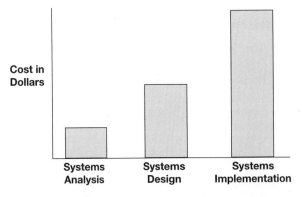

FIGURE 16.2 Cost Patterns at Varying Development Stages.

7. Assembling a team of individuals for purposes of the analysis and preliminary systems design.

Notice that these seven steps operate in a top-down fashion. The planning effort begins with top management and ends with a specific team of individuals charged with the task of analyzing a particular system and coming up with a preliminary systems design. In the following sections, each of the seven phases is discussed individually.

Systems Planning and Top Management

It is crucial that all major systems development efforts have the support of top management. A major task of the systems developer is to communicate with top management regarding its strategic plans, key success factors, and overall objectives. The systems developer must do a lot more than simply ask top management what its problems are. The role of the systems developer is much like that of a doctor with regard to a patient. The patient is only able to describe symptoms of the problems; it is the doctor who must determine the underlying problem and its causes. Picture what a doctor would say if a patient said, "I have a bad headache, and I want you to give me a shot of penicillin." The doctor would take note of the patient's problems and suggested solution but would make an independent diagnosis and analysis of the underlying cause and the best treatment. The same approach must be taken by the systems developer. In practice, management often misdiagnoses problems. This, of course, varies considerably from company to company, because some managers have more expertise than others. However, it is not uncommon for the systems developer to confront a situation where management requests the developer to do certain things that are not in the best interest of the company.

One example of this problem relates to computers. It is common for managers to think that fundamental information systems problems are simply computer problems. For example, a manufacturing company may have severe problems delivering its finished products to customers within a reasonable time frame. In such situations, management might immediately conclude that new computers would solve the problem. In this situation, the systems developer would be responsible for finding out the basic problem and its underlying causes. In doing this, the developer often finds a number of fundamental problems that have to be solved whether or not a new computer is installed. In this example, it might be found that the production supervisor does not have a systematic scheduling procedure. The developer therefore would recommend such a procedure be implemented whether or not a new computer is installed.

The systems developer runs a considerable risk by simply taking statements of management as fact at all times. The ultimate responsibility for the success or failure of the new system will be on the shoulders of the systems developer. If a systems developer installs a new computer, but the fundamental problems of management do not go away, then management will ultimately blame the developer.

In summary, the systems developer is a professional and is ultimately responsible for the success or failure of the system. It cannot be overemphasized that development efforts must be conducted while in close communications with top management. The only way to avoid spending months on a development project and having top management say, "This isn't what we want" after the project is finished is through continuous communication with management throughout the entire project.

Steering Committee

A useful approach to guiding the overall systems development effort is to have a **steering committee,** representing top management and all major functional areas within the organization. A primary responsibility of this committee should be to focus on the overall current and future information needs of the company. Such a committee must have representation by top management because it is essential that the information system fit within the overall strategic plan of the corporation. This entails taking a long-run view. Failure to take a long-run view can be very costly to the company. For example, if it is known that the company plans to launch a new product within the next five years, the information systems plan should allow for growth of the existing system in such a way that it can easily accommodate a new product. In fact, it might prove cost effective to include plans for the new product in the current systems development effort instead of adding them later.

The steering committee should be responsible for the overall planning and control of the systems development effort of the company. An ideal person to be in charge of such a committee would be a vice president of information systems. The steering committee should not, however, become involved in the details of specific development projects. Individual projects should be supervised and managed by an individual who reports periodically to the steering committee.

Developing Objectives and System Constraints

Effective, overall sound planning calls for the development of general objectives for the company and specific objectives for individual subsystems within the company. General objectives include the overall strategic objectives relating to the company's long-run planning cycle. Subsidiary to the strategic objectives are tactical objectives. These correspond to tactical planning and typically relate to about a one- to three-year time horizon.

Also important are the company's **key success factors.** These factors are those characteristics that distinguish a company from its competitors and are the keys to its success. For example, some companies emphasize speed of service; others emphasize product quality; still others emphasize low prices. Whatever the key success factors are, they must be incorporated into the objectives for systems design. A company that has an overall key objective relating to fast delivery times would want to make information relating to late deliveries an important part of its shipping/delivery system.

It is extremely important that specific objectives be set for systems before commencing a full development effort. Without such objectives, it is very difficult to evaluate a completed system. In addition, with no objectives, it is very difficult for the systems analyst and designers to work efficiently.

As an example of specific subsystem objectives, consider a production control system. For production control, a company might set the following objectives:

- Ensure that all jobs are completed by the promised delivery date.
- Minimize waste of raw materials.
- Minimize idle time.
- Ensure a high level of quality control.

From these objectives, a systems designer can develop specific reports. For example, the quality control objective might be satisfied by a periodic report relating to rejected units.

Developing a Strategic Systems Plan

A major output of the steering committee or individual in charge of systems development should be a **strategic systems plan.** This plan should take the form of a written document that incorporates both short-run and long-run goals relating to the company's systems development effort. Key elements of a plan should include the following:

- An overall statement relating to key success factors of the company and overall objectives.
- A description of systems within the company for which development efforts are needed.
- A statement of priorities indicating which areas are to be given the highest priority.
- An outline of required resources, including costs, personnel, and equipment.
- Tentative timetables for developing specific systems.

Identifying Individual Projects for Priority

As stated previously, the strategic plan should identify specific areas to be given the highest priority. Setting priorities is crucial, because financial resources are always limited. Prioritizing projects should be done in the same way as in capital budgeting. Specific benefits should be defined for projects, and their costs should be estimated as closely as possible and set forth in financial budgets. These financial budgets should be done as accurately as possible.

Because the benefits of systems development are often difficult to quantify, it is easy to lose sight of financial considerations when prioritizing systems development projects. However, it is almost always possible to quantify the costs, and this should be done before commissioning a project. In addition, even though benefits may be difficult to quantify, they should be stated in formal written terms. For example, a company might consider a sales order system that would allow its salespeople to check on the status of incomplete orders. Such a system would allow salespeople to better deal with customers when there is a question about the status of a possibly overdue order. Such a system might allow a salesperson to immediately find the current or revised delivery date. This information could be conveyed to the customer, and the customer could plan accordingly. In this situation, it might be very easy to identify the costs. However, what are the financial benefits of being able to provide information to the customer on short notice? There is an obvious benefit in terms of customer relations. This benefit might result in sales increases. If so, such increases should be estimated and incorporated into the formal system proposal.

Developing a Systems Project Proposal

The systems project proposal should serve as a tentative project budget. A final budget cannot be made until the systems analysis and preliminary systems design phases have been completed because the exact specifications for the system cannot be determined until an actual design plan is proposed. Therefore, the project proposal should include an estimate of the cost of developing a system analysis and preliminary design. In addition, the proposal should set forth a statement of overall objectives and preliminary estimates of the ultimate cost and benefits of the project.

Commissioning the Systems Project

In many respects, commissioning the systems project is like constructing a building. A building project requires carpenters, plumbers, bricklayers, electricians, and metalworkers. Similarly, a systems development project requires individuals from several disciplines. The actual personnel requirements will depend on the specific project; however, it is common to require management, accountants, systems users, computer programmers, and various types of technical support individuals.

It is important that the project development team have a leader that reports to upper-level management, such as the vice president of information systems or possibly the chairperson of the systems development steering committee. It is also important that there be a high degree of communication between individual members of the project development team, users of the system under development, and top management. This implies that there should be regular meetings where ideas are communicated and progress to date is discussed. One of the most important objectives in this communication process is to ensure that there are no surprises when the development project is completed.

THE STEPS OF SYSTEMS ANALYSIS

Figure 16.3 depicts the major steps or phases of the systems analysis effort.

Phase 1: Survey the Present System

Objectives of Surveying

There are four objectives of the system survey.

1. Gain a fundamental understanding of the operational aspects of the system.
2. Establish a working relationship with the users of the system.
3. Collect important data that are useful in developing the systems design.
4. Identify specific problems that require focus in terms of subsequent design efforts.

The systems development team must become very familiar with the workings of the system under consideration for change. It is dangerous to try to modify an existing system that you do not understand thoroughly. In addition, the developer must become familiar with the people who work in the system on a daily ba-

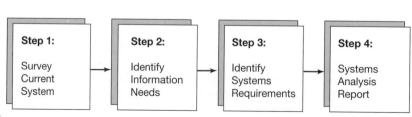

FIGURE 16.3 Steps Involved in Systems Analysis.

sis. This familiarity allows the developer to gain an understanding of problems with which top management may be completely unaware.

The objective of establishing a relationship with individuals who work within the system under development is especially critical. *The success or failure of a development project will to a large extent depend on the quality of the relationship between the development team and the individuals working in the system.* A poor relationship can result in misunderstandings and misplaced design efforts. The individuals working in the system must live with the development results on a long-term basis. More specifically, it is a very real possibility that the new system can be rejected by the individuals for whom it is designed. If these individuals do not respect the development team, they may resist implementation of the completed design. Such resistance can come in many forms, including complaints to top management, strikes, or sabotage.

Behavioral Considerations

The human element is of key importance in conducting the system survey. The fact that systems development involves changing the existing system poses many problems. Most people do not like change. In many situations, an individual may have been at a certain job and routine and has not changed for many years. This individual is very likely to see you as a threat. Other individuals might be concerned about losing their jobs, possibly to a computer. Still other individuals might see you as a "front office spy." Figure 16.4 depicts these problems in terms of a communication gap between the systems analyst and management. It is the responsibility of the systems analyst, not management, to bridge this communication gap. Therefore, the first task of the analyst conducting a systems survey should be to establish a good working relationship between the project team and management.

Certain approaches can help bridge this communication gap:

- Get to know as many people involved in the system as soon as possible.
- Communicate the benefits of the proposed system to the individuals involved.
- Provide assurances, to the degree possible, to all individuals that there will be no losses of jobs or major changes in job responsibilities.

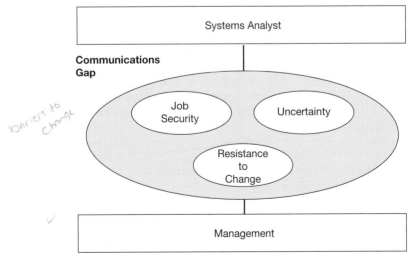

FIGURE 16.4 Communication Gap Problem.

- Provide assurances that you are genuinely concerned with making life better for those involved in the system.

✓ One useful thing you can do is show individuals that you will help them improve their job performance. Individuals are more likely to view you favorably if you are perceived as someone who can help them achieve their goals. These goals usually include job satisfaction, compensation, and job security. Therefore, the systems developer should communicate to the users how the systems development project will favorably impact these factors. For example, you might indicate to them that substantial cuts in operating costs may make it feasible for management to give pay raises, if this is in accordance with management's objectives.

It is also essential that the systems developer be completely honest and open with the users. This means that the developer should communicate, as soon as possible, the scope and purpose of the development project to all affected individuals. If the project contains some undesirable elements when viewed from the standpoint of the employee, the developer should try to find a way to put a positive light on these things—to the extent that this can be done honestly.

Communication at the earliest possible stage is also important for preventing rumors. A natural response of employees to unknown changes in the work environment is apprehension. Apprehension normally translates into rumors, which are likely to be inaccurate. Inaccurate rumors can turn into hostility toward the developers. Once a cycle of hostility begins, it may be difficult to get any work done or change attitudes. Therefore, early and open communication can establish a bridge by which a successful development effort can be completed.

Sources for Gathering Facts

A variety of techniques can be used to gather facts relating to the information subsystem under study. These techniques are discussed in a subsequent section of this chapter; however, we note here that all available sources of information should be used. These include interviews, questionnaires, observations, and reviews of various types of documents such as corporate minutes, charts of accounts, organization charts, financial statements, procedure manuals, policy statements, job descriptions, and so on. In addition, sources of information outside the company should not be overlooked. These include industry and trade publications as well as professional journals. Finally, the customer should be viewed as a vital component of the system and included in any analysis.

Analysis of Survey Findings

When the survey has been completed, the strengths and weaknesses of the subsystem under study should be thoroughly analyzed. The survey focuses on understanding the nature and operation of the system (with its associated problems), and the analysis of the survey findings focuses on strengths and weaknesses of the system. Some of the following questions might be asked in evaluating the present system:

- Is a given procedure necessary?
- Does the procedure involve unnecessary steps?
- Is the procedure cost-effective?
- Is a given report clear and easy to read?
- Are the source documents well designed?
- Are reports being generated that are not needed or used?
- What causes a particular problem?

- What additional reports might be useful to management?
- Is the system documentation adequate?

Overall, these questions should result in a report that summarizes the strengths and weaknesses of the existing system. In making such an evaluation, certain standards must be used as benchmarks. These standards relate to effectiveness and efficiency. Effectiveness here simply means that the system accomplishes the objectives set forth in the systems planning phase. Efficiency relates to whether or not these objectives are achieved at the lowest possible cost.

Evaluation of the effectiveness of the system's ability to achieve the overall planned objectives should focus on bottlenecks. **Bottlenecks** represent weaknesses in the system where small changes can result in major improvements. For example, a company may have difficulty delivering its goods to its customers within a reasonable time. An analysis of the situation might reveal that the job scheduling system is ineffective and that there are times when employees are idle, even though there is a backlog in the production schedule. In this case, the results of the analysis would indicate a need to focus on the production scheduling system.

Phase 2: Identify Information Needs

The second major phase of systems analysis involves identifying information requirements for managerial decision making. In identifying information needs, the analyst studies specific decisions made by managers in terms of the information inputs. This process, called **information needs analysis,** is depicted in Figure 16.5. The heart of this diagram is the study of decisions made. An important step in information needs analysis is the identification of decisions.

How are the decisions made by managers identified? You might think it is good enough simply to ask managers what decisions they make. Unfortunately, managers are often not able to specifically answer this question. One reason for this is that managers often think in terms of getting certain jobs done. For example, a product engineer might view her job responsibility as being the designer of a particular new product. If you ask her what decisions she makes, she might respond, "I simply design new products." Your responsibility as a systems developer would be to ask more detailed questions that would get at the nature of some of the decisions she makes in the process. For example, you might ask her, "What are some of the design considerations you have to take into account?" and "How do you make these considerations?" Answers to these questions might reveal that safety considerations are an important factor. From all of this, you might conclude that this particular individual might need certain product safety reports. In conclusion, you have to become intimately familiar with the problems of a particular manager in order to understand the decisions that are made and the corresponding information needs.

Fortunately, some systematic techniques can be used to gain an understanding of decisions and information needs. Several basic approaches can be followed:

- Identify the manager's primary job responsibilities.
- Identify the means by which the manager is evaluated.
- Identify some of the major problems the manager faces.
- Identify the means by which the manager evaluates personal output.

The first two approaches suggest that you get an understanding of the manager's position and related responsibilities in a company. The means by which the

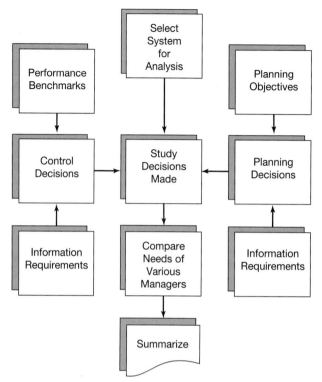

FIGURE 16.5 Information Needs Analysis.

manager is evaluated are especially important because they will determine, to a large extent, the approaches a manager takes in dealing with day-to-day problems. Another way of looking at this is that the criteria used to evaluate a manager should be a statement of goals regarding the manager's performance. For example, an advertising manager might be evaluated on the responsiveness of customers to the company's advertising campaign. Therefore, such a manager would want specific reports relating to advertising expenditures and the associated customer responses.

Although the approach of asking managers about their problems can often be very helpful, you cannot simply walk up to a manager and ask, "What kind of problems do you have here?" First, managers are often reluctant to discuss their problems with someone they do not really know. Second, a given manager might feel that admitting a problem is somehow admitting failure. Therefore, it is often helpful to take an approach that involves asking the managers a lot of questions about what they do and then listening carefully. If you can get managers to talk long enough, their problems will come out. All of this points to the importance of establishing a good working relationship between the systems developer and the manager.

Phase 3: Identify the Systems Requirements

The third phase of the system analysis project involves specifying systems requirements. Such requirements can be specified in terms of inputs and outputs. The input requirements for a given subsystem specify the specific needs that must be met in order for that subsystem to achieve its objectives.

For example, the information requirements of a production control system might include short-run sales forecasts, reports on availability of materials, specifications of quality control and standard costs, and information needed to prioritize individual jobs. For the same system, the following might be considered as output requirements:

- daily progress reports
- daily finance reports
- reports on defective units
- reports on problems with raw materials

The input requirements for one subsystem will specify, in turn, output requirements for another subsystem. In this case, the input requirements of sales forecasts would be an output requirement for some other system within the company (such as marketing).

Phase 4: Develop a Systems Analysis Report

The final output of the systems analysis project is a report. This report is extremely important because it often serves as a basis for further decision making on the part of top management. In addition, this report organizes and documents all the findings of the three phases of the analysis project. Without such careful documentation, a lot of information would be lost in the long run. If the analysis is not carefully documented at the time it is conducted, when the time rolls around for doing the design and implementation work, a lot can be forgotten. Also, to develop a design report all of the analysis findings must be carefully organized within some consistent framework.

Some of the key elements of the systems analysis report should include the following:

- a summary of the scope and purpose of the analysis project
- a reiteration of the relationship of the project to the overall strategic information systems plan
- a description of any overall problems in the specific subsystem being studied
- a summary of the decisions being made and their specific information requirements
- specification of system performance requirements
- an overall cost budget and timetable for the project to date
- recommendations for improving the existing system or for designing new systems
- recommendations relating to modifying objectives for the subsystem under study

The systems analysis report, when completed, is presented to the vice president of information systems, the information systems steering committee, or, if appropriate, directly to top management. The report is then reviewed and discussed among the relevant individuals, who decide whether a preliminary systems design should be undertaken. The preliminary systems design, if undertaken, provides a complete budget for the design and implementation parts of the development project.

FACT-GATHERING TECHNIQUES

A large portion of the systems analyst's job is to collect and organize facts. Fortunately, there are a number of techniques that help the analyst perform these difficult tasks. Table 16.1 summarizes some of the major tools used by analysts in fact gathering.

TABLE 16.1 Techniques for Gathering Facts for Analysis

Technique	Objective
Depth interview	Gain a fundamental understanding of the system.
Structured interview	Systematic follow-up based on depth interviews.
Open-ended questionnaire	Same as depth interview.
Closed-ended questionnaire	Same as structured interview.

Document reviews
  Flowcharts
  Organization charts
  Procedure manuals
  Operation manuals
  Reference manuals
  Historical records
	Gain an understanding of the existing system. (*Caution:* Sometimes the system does not operate as documented.) It is often helpful to review system documents before conducting interviews and distributing questionnaires.

Observation	Familiarity with the system.

Depth Interviews

Depth interviews are useful for familiarizing the analyst with individual decision makers and their problems. The objective of a depth interview is not to answer a specific set of questions, but rather to allow the conversation to be guided largely by the feelings and interests of the manager. The analyst does not go into a depth interview with many preset questions but rather with several broad topics for discussion. This type of interview has the advantage of being flexible in that the manager has the opportunity to discuss any issues that may be of particular importance to him or her.

Depth interviews also allow the systems analyst to establish a personal working relationship with the manager. The emphasis should be on building trust and opening lines of communication, not on collecting specific facts. A depth interview should not be completely unstructured, however. Specifically, the analyst should attempt to direct the conversation to areas that will be productive in terms of the systems analysis project. If the manager were to bring up the topic of raw material shortages, for instance, the analyst's job would be to direct the conversation to the underlying causes of the shortages.

The important thing to remember about depth interviews is that they provide only a partial picture of the system under study, because it is possible to conduct these interviews and completely omit discussing some important issues. Therefore, you should be very careful in drawing conclusions about a system on the basis of depth interviews only. Furthermore, the results of depth interviews should be taken collectively—the analyst should interview all managers involved and then assemble the information from these various interviews into an overall picture.

Structured Interviews

The objective of **structured interviews** is to answer a specific set of questions. After an initial round of depth interviews, it is often useful to do more detailed follow-up interviewing. In fact, the results of a depth interview might provide a detailed set of questions to be used on a follow-up basis. For example, a number of managers might have mentioned problems relating to raw material shortages during the depth interviews. After reviewing the results of these depth interviews, the analyst might develop a list of specific questions that, if answered, would help understand the causes of the problem: "How often do these shortages occur?" "What is the effect, in terms of time delay, on completing customer orders?"

In both depth and structured interviews, it is necessary to take written notes either during or immediately following the interview. Research has shown that as much as 80% of the content of an interview can be forgotten within 24 hours of its completion.

After the initial depth and structured interviews are completed, key members of the systems analysis team should meet and discuss the results. During this discussion, additional questions can be defined for use in additional interviews. Overall, the interview process never ends. The analysis team should work constantly with management throughout the entire project. This helps build a foundation for a system that will ultimately be accepted and favorably viewed by management.

A couple of final points on interviewing should be noted. First, it is possible that an interviewee will be uncooperative. If this happens, there may be nothing to do but find someone else to interview. A second problem is that managers may give biased answers if they perceive the systems analyst as an intruder into their environment or as a threat to their existing job position. Such problems can be minimized by a good initial public relations campaign. Finally, interviewing involves the art of listening. An effective interviewer will let the interviewee do most of the talking.

Open-Ended Questionnaires

Open-ended questionnaires are a fact-gathering technique where persons provide written answers to general rather than specific questions. Open-ended questionnaires serve the same purpose as depth interviews, asking very general questions such as, "Do you have any suggestions for improving the system? Please explain." The open-ended questionnaire gives managers a chance to say whatever is on their minds. This type of questionnaire, however, has the disadvantage of being less personal than the depth interview and does not establish a working relationship with the manager. On the other hand, written questionnaires have some advantages over depth interviews. First, the manager may have a lot more time to think about a particular question before responding. This often produces better answers. Second, in many situations, it is not feasible to conduct depth interviews with all employees, especially when the number of employees is large. In such cases, it might be useful to have depth and structured interviews with certain key managers but written questionnaires for other managers. Finally, the written questionnaire can be administered anonymously. In many situations, employees feel more comfortable suggesting changes when they know their comments can be made anonymously. This is especially true in situations where suggestions for improvement might be viewed as criticisms of a supervising manager.

Closed-Ended Questionnaires

Closed-ended questionnaires are a useful technique for gathering answers to a large number of questions. They require considerably less time on the part of the systems analyst than interviewing techniques do. Such questionnaires are very effective in many situations, including collecting information about internal control.

There are, however, a number of pitfalls that can occur when using closed-ended questionnaires. One problem is that an excessively large number of questions might result in frivolous answers. A second danger is that employees are typically restricted to a narrow response list. Such forced responses can sometimes produce a misleading picture of the situation. For example, if a production manager were asked to respond "Yes" or "No" to "Are the raw material shortages caused by the purchasing department?" misleading results might be obtained. The production manager might feel that the purchasing system is at fault and not the purchasing manager; however, there would be no way to indicate this with a simple yes or no answer. Finally, a major limitation of detailed questionnaires is that there is a risk of important questions being omitted. A major problem might go completely undetected by the questionnaire simply because no pertinent questions relating to that problem are included.

Document Reviews

In many organizations, a large number of documents are available for review: flowcharts, organizational charts, procedure manuals, operation manuals, reference manuals, and historical records. Depending on the organization, these documents can be either easy or difficult to obtain. In good situations, all the needed documents can be obtained through a central library. However, in many situations, documents must be collected piece by piece from individual managers.

If at all possible, key documents should be reviewed before commencing interviews. This is especially true for charts of accounts, organizational charts, and minutes of the board of directors. These documents can help the analyst gain an overall understanding of the organization. It is also sometimes helpful to study industry or trade journals to become familiar with the nature and operations of the business to be analyzed.

When reviewing documents, it is important to remember that systems commonly do not operate and perform as documented. In some situations, changes might be made in the systems without any updating of the relevant documents. Therefore, the analyst should never rely only on the documentation when attempting to describe the performance or operation of a system.

In some cases, discrepancies between actual systems performance and documented systems performance can indicate problems. Therefore, the analyst should make an overall assessment regarding the status of a particular document in terms of its importance to company policy. If the document does in fact represent current company policy, then a policy violation is evident.

Observation

There is no substitute for directly observing the activities under study. You can conduct interviews and review documents to gain a basic understanding of procedures and operations; however, observing the actual operations of the system being studied will provide insight that can be obtained in no other way. In addition, observations can be useful for confirming information obtained in questionnaires and interviews.

One useful observation technique is to watch a transaction being processed through the entire system; for example, to observe a sales order being taken, then to physically follow the flow of the sales order through the entire production and shipping processes. This can be especially useful if it is done unannounced, where you can see things as they are normally done.

TECHNIQUES FOR ORGANIZING FACTS

The systems analyst needs formal techniques for organizing facts. Table 16.2 presents a number of techniques that are helpful in summarizing and organizing facts.

Work Measurement Analysis

An important aspect of systems analysis is the measurement of work activities. One useful technique for analyzing the activities of a particular system is work measurement. The purpose of **work measurement** is to analyze a particular task and summarize the required number of inputs to complete the task. For example, the analyst might measure the number of documents processed by an accounts receivable clerk in a 1-hour period. A primary objective of work measurement analysis is to study and measure the efficiency of a particular job task. For example, consider a situation in which there are two accounts receivable clerks. One clerk may be utilized at full capacity, and the other clerk might be utilized only to 50% capacity. Given this situation, management might find it practical to redistribute some of the work from one clerk to the other clerk. As a result, the overall efficiency and effectiveness of the processing operations could be improved.

Table 16.3 is an example of a work measurement summary. In this case, there are four employees who work both morning and afternoon. The analysis reveals that one employee (Gordon) requires a considerably shorter amount of time to serve a customer than do the other employees. In this situation, management might want to redistribute the workload or take some other corrective action.

In an especially complicated situation, where there are many transactions, it is not possible to observe every single occurrence of a particular task. For example, an accounts receivable clerk might process hundreds of invoices in a given day. It would not be an effective use of the analyst's time to observe the process-

TABLE 16.2 Techniques for Fact Organization

Technique	Objective
Work measurement	Summarize resources required for various tasks.
Work distribution	Summarize employee time utilization for tasks.

Flowcharting
  General
  Decision flow
  Logical data flow
  Systems
  Detailed
	Graphically depict flows and relationships and process requirements, with a focus on modularity.

Decision analysis	Summarize decisions and needed information.
Functional analysis Hierarchical function	Summarize functions and related information.
Matrix analysis	Summarize related data inputs/outputs.
Narratives	Written summarization.
File/report summaries	

TABLE 16.3 Example of Work Measurement Summary

Employee Name	Average Time in Minutes for Employee to Serve Customer	
	Morning	Afternoon
Wells	9.2	8.4
Janson	4.5	6.4
Gordon	3.6	2.9
Hill	5.0	6.1

ing of each invoice. Therefore, analysts often use statistical sampling in which random samples of transactions are periodically observed. Based on these samples, general conclusions can often be made.

Work Distribution Analysis

Work distribution analysis is very similar to work measurement analysis. The major difference is that work distribution analysis focuses on several tasks for a given individual, whereas work measurement analysis focuses on one particular task. Table 16.4 gives an example of work distribution analysis. In this report, there are five employees and four tasks. The analysis reveals the amount of time each employee spends on each task. This information can be useful in evaluating the effectiveness of the work assignment system. In addition, it can be very helpful in identifying bottlenecks in the production system. For example, Lee has only 1 hour of idle time during the average week. On the other hand, Young, Mills, and Hills each has an average total of 9 hours of idle time. Further analysis might indicate that some jobs are being delayed at the grinding stage. Based on this information, management might find it useful to assign Young, Mills, and Hills to additional grinding duties in order to alleviate the bottleneck.

Together, work measurement analysis and work distribution analysis can provide an effective means of studying the utilization of company resources. In addition, these techniques provide the analyst with an in-depth insight into the workings of the system under investigation.

TABLE 16.4 Example of Work Distribution Analysis

Employee	Work Times and Task Utilization in Hours					
	Packaging	Assembly	Machining	Grinding	Idle	Total
Young	10	5	10	6	9	40
Mills	10	5	8	8	9	40
Kent	10	5	11	9	5	40
Hills	12	4	9	6	9	40
Lee	14	6	12	7	1	40
Average	11.2	5	10	7.2	6.6	

Information Flow Analysis

An important part of the information system analysis effort involves analyzing the flows of information both between and within subsystems. A number of techniques are useful for this kind of analysis. Document and analytic flowcharts can be helpful in giving an overall picture with regard to transaction processing within the organization. Another useful technique, depicted in Figure 16.6, is the **decision flow diagram.** A decision flow diagram emphasizes the chain of decisions relating to a particular subsystem within the company. In addition, the information requirements for each particular decision within the overall chain are shown. Figure 16.6 shows one possible chain of decisions relating to credit policy.

Another useful technique is the **logical data flow diagram,** or **data flow diagram (DFD).** This type of diagram emphasizes the logical flow of events that must occur in a given system. A DFD uses a small set of symbols to illustrate data flows through interconnected processes. Typically, DFDs are constructed in a hierarchical fashion, with successive DFDs showing more and more detail. Figure 16.7 shows the overall logical flow of events for a textbook author royalty payment system. This DFD is quite general, showing only the basic entities and data flows in the system. DFDs of this type are called **context diagrams.**

The context diagram for the author royalty system begins with customers and ends with the senior editor. The box-shape symbol for customers and the senior editor is a **terminator symbol,** which is used to indicate a source or destination of data in the system being described. The **data flow symbol,** used to indicate a flow of data, is an arrowheaded flowline. As shown, data concerning textbook sales flows from customers to the author royalty system for processing, and the results of processing flow to the senior editor. The author royalty system is a process, something that transforms inputs into outputs. The **process symbol** used in DFDs is either a circle, as shown, or a rectangle with curved edges. The **data store symbol,** either an open-ended rectangle, as shown, or an oval, is used to indicate a store of data (i.e., file). The author royalty process outputs the data flow "royalty report" to the senior editor. As a result of processing, the data flow "royalty details" updates the data store "author royalty file."

Logical data flow diagrams differ from decision flow diagrams in that they focus on the operational steps required to complete a particular task or function.

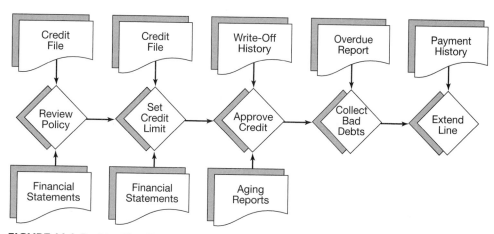

FIGURE 16.6 Decision Flow Diagram.

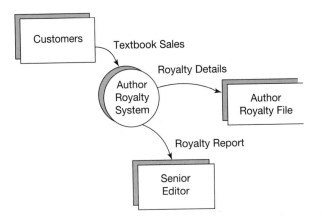

FIGURE 16.7 Context Diagram.

DFDs stress the relationship between data flows and processes. DFDs are simple and natural to use. As a result, they are a popular systems technique. DFDs generally do not specify details as to the type of technology that will be used in processing, nor do they typically specify the exact data that will be processed.

Warnier–Orr methodology is another useful technique. This methodology is based on analyzing the outputs of an application and factoring the application into a hierarchical structure of modules to accomplish the necessary processing. It uses a diagramming technique that is illustrated in Figure 16.8.

Warnier–Orr methodology uses brackets or braces to show hierarchy. The highest level is to the left of the figure, and the lowest level is to the right. The diagram is produced using only three basic constructs: sequence, selection, and repetition. The processes included in a sequence are enclosed in brackets and are executed from top to bottom. To compute the total amount due for a set of invoices, the following sequence is followed: first, determine the discount for an individual invoice, then determine the amount due as gross amount less discount, and then accumulate the total amount due. Note that these three steps are enclosed in a single bracket. Selection is necessary when there are two or more alternatives. Mutually exclusive alternatives are enclosed in a bracket, and separated by the exclusive symbol $\oplus$ (a plus sign enclosed in a circle). A discount is available if the due date is greater than or equal to today's date. There are two mutually exclusive

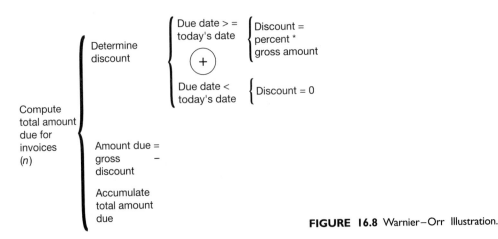

FIGURE 16.8 Warnier–Orr Illustration.

alternatives, enclosed in a bracket and separated by the exclusive symbol. The discount calculation in either case is indicated by the next-lower bracket in the hierarchy. If no processing is required, the world "null" or "skip" is used to indicate this in the diagram. Repetition is indicated by subscripts. If a process is to be repeated only once, subscript (1) would be used. In our illustration, we have an unknown number of invoices, so subscript *(n)* is used.

Warnier–Orr methodology is easy to understand and use. It can be used to document any type of system, from a top-level overview to detailed program logic. Most significant, the left-to-right pattern forces a structured, top-down approach to analysis.

Functional Analysis

Functional analysis differs from information flow analysis in that no inputs, outputs, or processes are specified. Instead, transactions are described in terms of performing particular functions. One very useful application of this kind of technique is hierarchical functional analysis. An example of this approach is given in Figure 16.9. In this example, a purchase transaction is hierarchically broken down into a number of related subtransactions. In this case, the purchase transaction is divided into four basic subtransactions: (1) originating the transaction, (2) receiving the goods, (3) paying the vendor, and (4) generating the reports. Furthermore, each of the four basic transactions is then divided into several other transactions. This type of analysis is a good example of applying a top-down, modular approach to systems analysis.

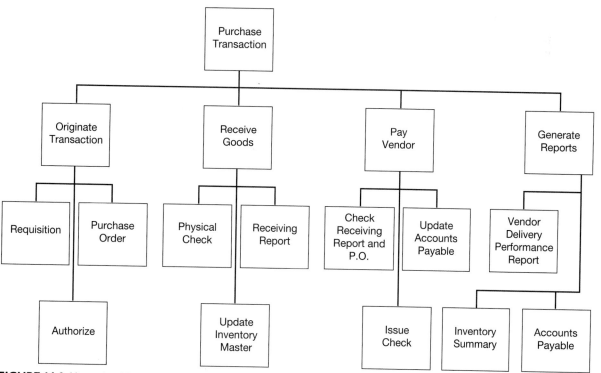

FIGURE 16.9 Hierarchical Function Diagram.

A very useful way to improve the hierarchical function analysis approach is to supplement it with logical data flow diagrams and document flowcharts. In particular, it is possible to provide a **blow-up** for each function given in Figure 16.9. These detailed flowcharts can provide useful supplementary information that includes inputs, processes, and outputs. Hierarchical function diagrams that contain supplementary flowcharts showing inputs, outputs, and processes are called **HIPOs** (hierarchy, plus input–process–output).

Overall, HIPOs have a distinct advantage over simple flowcharts because they show the information system in terms of clear-cut modules and relate these modules to the flows of the information within the organization. The modular analysis is especially helpful in terms of focusing design efforts in particular areas. In fact, HIPO modules provide natural divisions that are useful for assigning individual system design teams to specific tasks.

Matrix Analysis

A final technique for organizing facts is matrix analysis. In Table 16.5 an input/output matrix is given for a typical purchasing procedure. In the left-hand column, a number of data items are given. Across the top, a number of uses for these data items are given. Both sources and uses of information are given, so this type of diagram is sometimes referred to as a **sources and uses of information diagram.**

TABLE 16.5   Input/Output Matrix for Typical Purchasing Procedure

Data Item \ Data Output	Purchase Order	Receiving Report	Invoice Register	Daily Summary	Weekly Summary	Bid	Inventory Register	Vendor Performance Report	Overdue Deliveries	Inventory Summary
Stock number	X	X	X	X	X	X	X	X		X
Data ordered	X		X					X	X	
Vendor code	X	X	X			X	X			
Purchase order number	X	X		X			X		X	
Promised delivery date							X	X		
Quantity received		X	X	X	X		X	X	X	X
Account code		X		X	X	X	X			
Unit price	X		X	X	X	X	X	X	X	X
Quantity ordered	X	X	X				X	X	X	
Department originating order		X		X	X	X	X			

In practice, the systems analyst employs a wide variety of matrices. For example, both work measurement and work distribution analysis involve matrices. In addition, there is a wide range of possible uses for the input/output diagram. For example, the analyst might show all the information inputs and outputs of a particular department. An input/output diagram might even be used to depict the information used and generated by a given decision maker.

Input/output matrices can be very helpful to the systems designer. One important problem facing the systems designer is the specification of record layouts and file structures. Input/output diagrams provide a useful reference point for these types of design considerations.

Input/output diagrams have the disadvantage of not depicting the information flows. Therefore, these types of diagrams would normally be used in addition to flowcharts and hierarchical function charts.

STRUCTURED SYSTEMS ANALYSIS

Thus far, the discussion has focused on the general steps of systems analysis and the techniques for collecting and analyzing facts. In this section, the focus is on the analysis of specific systems. **Structured systems analysis** is an approach to systems analysis that begins with a very general description of a particular system and then proceeds through a logically related set of steps, each increasing in detail, and ends with computer program code (and other details). Perhaps the best way to view structured systems analysis is as a system of documentation. This includes several levels of documentation, where each level is a logical blow-up or "explosion" of the previous level. At the first level, logical data flow diagrams describe the system. They are then supported by additional logical flow diagrams that provide more detail. Other documentation describes the process logic and data components of these diagrams.

Logical Flow Diagrams versus Flowcharts

The previous description of structured systems analysis incorporates logical data flow diagrams as opposed to document or analytic flowcharts. In practice, either type of diagram might be used. Each approach has its unique advantages. As discussed in Chapter 2, the primary difference between the two approaches is that the flowchart gives a physical description of a system, whereas the logical data flow diagram gives a logical description of a system. Specifically, an analytic flowchart specifies input/output devices such as a data terminal or printer. It also specifies storage devices, such as magnetic tape or disk. The logical data flow diagram incorporates these same elements but leaves the exact physical description open.

In designing new systems, the logical data flow diagram is especially helpful because it does not require a commitment to a particular physical implementation. In addition, it is often useful to analyze an existing system without referring to physical input/output and storage devices. For example, an analyst might have to decide whether an existing accounts receivable system should be on-line or batch. The logical data flow diagram would be the same for either system, but the document flowcharts would vary considerably across the two situations. The logical data flow diagram would help the analyst conceptually separate the two problems of data flow and physical implementation.

Document and analytic flowcharts are indispensable tools. It is always necessary to document the physical implementation of a system. In addition, all other types of documentation, such as HIPOs, file matrices, and so on, should be used as needed.

In summary, similar documentation is used for both design and analysis. In designing new systems or analyzing existing systems, logical data flow diagrams are especially helpful because they separate the problems of logical flow and physical implementation. On the other hand, document flowcharts are important in documenting physical implementation.

Systems Design versus Systems Analysis

Structured systems analysis and structured systems design are very similar processes. Strictly speaking, design refers to the creation of a new or modified system, whereas analysis involves the critical evaluation of a particular problem or existing system. However, practically speaking, systems analysis and design are often indistinguishable. For example, in order to better understand and document a particular problem, the analyst will often develop logical data flow diagrams, document flowcharts, and specific process logic. All of this documentation can also serve as the basis for a new system.

In conclusion, structured systems analysis must be studied simultaneously with structured systems design. The documentation and working steps of the two problems involve common elements.

The Steps in Structured Systems Analysis

Develop Logical Data Flow Diagrams

The system is first described in general terms using a logical data flow diagram. Figure 16.10 gives a context diagram for a purchasing system. This diagram does not show the details of the logical processes or any error conditions. These types of details should be given in supporting diagrams. For example, Figure 16.11 provides additional details, exploding the "Purchasing System" process in Figure 16.10 into two subprocesses, "Validate Requisition" and "Prepare Purchase Order." It should be possible to provide even more detail in support of the original purchasing system context diagram by exploding the subprocess in Figure 16.11

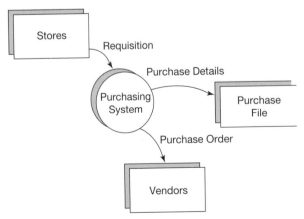

FIGURE 16.10 Purchasing System Context Diagram.

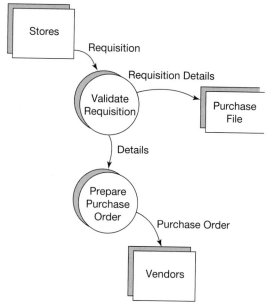

FIGURE 16.11 Expansion of Purchasing System Context Diagram.

into lower-level subprocesses. This procedure should continue until the system is adequately described.

Define Data Dictionaries

The next step is to define data dictionaries corresponding to the data stores referenced in the logical data flow diagrams. This involves giving a description of the data structure and data elements involved. For example, Figure 16.12 gives data dictionary details for the data store "Purchase File" in Figure 16.11. In this case, the data structure incorporates several categories, including "Account-Identifiers," "Validation-Information," "Financial-Information," and "Vendor-Information." Within each major category, individual data elements are listed. For

---

Purchase File Description

Account-Identifiers
  account-no-1   . . .   primary account number
  account-no-2   . . .   secondary account number
  person-responsible   . . .   person in charge of account
  expiration-date   . . .   account termination date

Validation-Information
  signature-required   . . .   name of required signer
  maximum-charge   . . .   maximum limit per requisition

Financial-Information
  account-balance   . . .   current balance
  last-purchase   . . .   most recent transaction

Vendor-Information
  vendor-1   . . .   list of approved vendors
  vendor-2   . . .
  vendor-3   . . .

FIGURE 16.12 Data Dictionary for Purchase File.

example, the "Financial-Information" category includes the data items "account-balance" and "last purchase."

Note that no physical detail is given at this point. At a subsequent time (the design and implementation stages), it would be necessary to provide specifics on forms layout, storage media, and so on.

Define Access Methods

It is also necessary to specify how the data stores will be accessed. This typically involves defining primary and secondary access keys. For example, the purchase file in Figure 16.12 might have "account-no-1" as the primary key and "person-responsible" as the secondary key.

Define Process Logic

There are many approaches to documenting the process logic. These include various types of decision trees and decision diagrams, as well as structured English. The latter approach is discussed here because it is particularly easy to understand, flexible, and useful in the development of computer programs.

Structured English is a special language for describing process logic that uses several key words, including IF, THEN, ELSE IF, and SO. Figure 16.13 gives an example of structured English describing account number validation in the "Validate Requisition" subprocess in Figure 16.11. The logic is structured in a format that a nontechnical person can understand. This approach, therefore, has the additional benefit that it can be read and modified by system users.

Another very useful aspect of structured English is that it very closely resembles source code in structured programming languages, such as COBOL, or FORTRAN V. Therefore, structured English can greatly reduce the task of programming.

Structured English does not include provisions for error conditions and data file access. If these are added, the resulting documentation is sometimes referred to as **pseudocode**. It is sometimes desirable to develop pseudocode as a final step before program coding.

SUMMARY

Systems planning involves decisions on the part of top management with respect to prioritizing system development needs. The output of systems planning is a written document that states the overall information systems objectives for the company. In addition, the document specifies general areas of need for systems development work. A general plan is given for implementing these needs. The systems analysis plan is dynamic and must be continuously revised. Systems develop-

```
Access purchase file
For each purchase requisition
IF   account no. on requisition equals account-no-1
                    THEN   flag account-no-1 field
ELSE  IF   account no. on requisition equals account-no-2
                    THEN   flag account-no-2 field
ELSE   (none of the above)
SO   void the transaction and generate error code
```

FIGURE 16.13 Structured English for Account Validation Related to Purchase Routine.

ment is a never-ending process because the business environment and corporate information needs are constantly changing.

Systems analysis begins with a system or systems specified in the overall company information systems plan. The systems analysis effort involves three distinct phases: (1) surveying the current system, (2) identifying information needs, and (3) identifying systems requirements. After these steps are completed, a systems analysis report is written and conveyed to top management. This report should focus on particular problems discovered and should suggest general approaches to solving them. In addition, a specific proposal for developing a new system (or modifying an old system) should be included.

The systems planning and analysis portions of the development cycle are extremely crucial, because mistakes made at these levels can be extremely costly. Design and implementation costs can often run into millions of dollars. Therefore, the analysis phase should give management a clear picture of where it needs to go.

Many techniques can aid in the systems analyst's work, including questionnaires, interviews, and direct observation. The analyst also uses work measurement and work distribution techniques. These analyses are accompanied by narratives, input/output matrices, data flow diagrams, hierarchical function diagrams, and flowcharts.

A particularly useful approach is structured systems analysis. This approach begins with a general logical data flow diagram, which is then supported with detailed data flow diagrams, data dictionaries, access method descriptions, and specifics on process logic.

In conclusion, an effective systems analysis can be extremely helpful when it comes to the systems design phase. The analysis highlights areas to be given special attention. In addition, systems analysis can establish a working relationship between the manager and the systems analyst. This relationship can serve as a bridge that can pave the way to a systems design specification that will be completely satisfactory to the managers involved.

Glossary

blow-up: a detailed flowchart for a function specified in another higher-level chart.

bottleneck: a weakness in a system where small changes can result in major improvements in performance.

close-ended questionnaire: a fact-gathering technique where persons provide written answers to specific questions.

context diagram: a data flow diagram that shows only the basic entities and data flows in a system.

data flow diagram (DFD): synonymous with logical data flow diagram.

data flow symbol: an arrowheaded flowline used to indicate a flow of data in a data flow diagram.

data store symbol: either an open-ended rectangle or an oval used to indicate a store of data (i.e., file) in a data flow diagram.

decision flow diagram: graphic technique that emphasizes the chain of decisions relating to a particular subsystem.

depth interview: an interviewing technique where the objective is not to answer a specific set of questions but rather to allow the conversation to be guided largely by the feelings and interests of the interviewee.

functional analysis: transactions are described in terms of performing particular functions rather than in terms of inputs, outputs, or processes.

HIPO: hierarchy, plus input–process–output charts. Hierarchical functions diagrams that contain supplementary flowcharts showing inputs, outputs, and processes.

information needs analysis: analysis of specific decisions made by managers in terms of the information inputs.

key success factors: characteristics that distinguish a company from its competitors and are the keys to its success.

logical data flow diagram: graphic technique that illustrates data flows through interconnected processes.

open-ended questionnaire: a fact-gathering technique where persons provide written answers to general rather than specific questions.

process symbol: either a circle or a rectangle with curved edges used to indicate a process in a data flow diagram.

pseudocode: structured English type of system documentation that includes provisions for error conditions and data file access.

sources and uses of information diagram: an input/output matrix where the rows are data items and the columns of the matrix indicate uses for these data items.

steering committee: committee representing top management and all major functional areas within the organization that is charged with guiding the overall systems development effort.

strategic systems plan: a written document that incorporates both short-run and long-run goals relating to the company's systems development effort.

structured English: a special language for describing process logic that uses several key words, including IF, THEN, ELSE IF, and SO.

structured interview: an interviewing technique where the objective is to answer a specific set of questions.

structured systems analysis: an approach to systems analysis that begins with a very general description of a particular system and then proceeds through a logically related set of steps, each increasing in detail.

systems analysis: the process of understanding existing systems and problems, describing information needs, and establishing priorities for further systems work.

systems planning: identifying subsystems within the information system that need special attention for development.

terminator symbol: box-shape symbol that is used to indicate a source or destination of data in a data flow diagram.

Warnier–Orr methodology: a methodology and diagramming technique for analyzing the outputs of an application and factoring the application into a hierarchical structure of modules to accomplish the necessary processing.

work distribution analysis: analysis of the assignment of work tasks to entities (individuals, departments, etc.).

work measurement: the quantitative analysis of tasks to study and measure their efficiency.

Chapter Quiz

Answers to the chapter quiz appear on page 632.

1. It is crucial that all major systems development efforts have the support of (the) (_____).
   (a) steering committee
   (b) top management
   (c) chief systems analyst
   (d) controller

2. Which of the following should be responsible for the overall planning and control of the systems development effort of a company?
   (a) steering committee
   (b) top management
   (c) chief systems analyst
   (d) controller

3. Which of the following terms describes the analysis of specific decisions made by managers in terms of information inputs?
   (a) HIPO
   (b) work measurement
   (c) functional analysis
   (d) information needs analysis

4. The third phase of the systems analysis project involves specifying systems requirements. Such requirements are usually specified in terms of (_____).
   (a) reports
   (b) inputs and outputs
   (c) decisions
   (d) processes

5. Which of the following fact-gathering techniques best allows the systems analyst to establish a personal working relationship with a manager?
   (a) depth interviews
   (b) structured interviews
   (c) open-ended questionnaires
   (d) closed-ended questionnaires

6. Which of the following fact-gathering techniques will often provide the analyst with insight into system activities that can be obtained in no other way?
   (a) depth interviews
   (b) structured interviews
   (c) document reviews
   (d) observation

7. An overview logical data flow diagram, which shows only the basic entities and data flows in a system, is called a
   (a) decision flow diagram.
   (b) sources and uses of information diagram.
   (c) context diagram.
   (d) HIPO chart.

8. In a logical data flow diagram, which of the following symbols would be used to represent a file of data?
   (a) terminator
   (b) data flow
   (c) data store
   (d) process

9 In a logical data flow diagram, which of the following symbols is drawn either as a circle or as a rectangle with curved edges?
   (a) terminator
   (b) data flow
   (c) data store
   (d) process

10. Which of the following is not one of the three basic constructs used in constructing a Warnier–Orr diagram?
    (a) redundancy
    (b) sequence
    (c) selection
    (d) repetition

Review Problem

Bird Manufacturing produces electronic components that are used in various products including computers, television sets, and microwave ovens. At present, the company employs approximately 50 individuals, most of whom are involved in the production process. The overall corporate structure includes the president (Mr. Bird), a chief accountant, a production engineer, two clerks, and two full-time salespeople. All work is done on a custom order basis. Both of the salespeople give bids to prospective customers. The bids are based on such factors as overhead, raw materials, production engineering time, and planned profit margin. A major problem of Bird Manufacturing has been its inability to assess the profitability of completed jobs. Although bidding is based on estimates that should lead to profitable operations under good conditions, there is no follow-up that investigates a job's actual profitability. Furthermore, Bird Manufacturing has been having cash flow problems, as evidenced by a number of bills that are 90 days overdue. Mr. Bird does not understand this, because the company is operating at full capacity, and he is reasonably sure that the profit margins built into the bid specifications are sufficient to allow for substantial errors in the cost estimates.

Required

(a) Given the previous set of facts, what are some likely areas that a management steering committee should focus on?

(b) You estimate that a full systems analysis will cost the company $30,000. Mr. Bird says the company does not have the funds to conduct such an analysis. What do you recommend?

(c) Assume that this company's problems can be solved by a standard cost accounting system. Would you recommend the installation of such a system without a formal systems analysis?

Solution to Review Problem

(a) The management steering committee should review the entire accounting system with a special emphasis on the cost of accounting, sales/bidding, and cash management systems.

(b) It is often the case that a company, once in trouble, is unable to afford a solution to its problem. The real question is how did the company get into this situation to begin with? It is evident that the basic accounting system did not go through a rigorous systems development. Fortunately, it generally is not a major problem to implement a simple cost collection system that will help management assess the profitability of individual jobs.

(c) It is generally preferable to do a thorough analysis before installing any system. However, this is one of those cases where the expedient approach is justifiable. In order to keep the company out of bankruptcy, something has to be done. Therefore, the best solution is probably to help the company set up a cost collection system and temporarily bypass a review of the overall accounting information system. Unfortunately, this expedient approach is taken far too often in practice. In the hurry to get something done now, companies never manage to deal with the overall picture.

Review Questions

1. Define and explain each of the following terms:
   (a) systems planning
   (b) systems analysis
   (c) communications problem
   (d) information needs analysis
   (e) depth interview
   (f) open-ended questionnaire
   (g) closed-ended questionnaire
   (h) structured interview
   (i) work measurement
   (j) work distribution
   (k) hierarchical function diagram
   (l) input/output matrix
   (m) logical flow diagram

2. Is the systems analysis phase of systems development more expensive than the systems design phase?

3. Which individuals should be involved in systems planning?
4. What is the function of the systems steering committee?
5. What are the primary phases of systems analysis?
6. What are some of the major hurdles that the systems analyst must overcome?
7. Discuss the primary advantages of depth interviews.
8. Discuss the primary advantages of structured interviews.
9. Under what situations would a closed-ended questionnaire be appropriate?
10. What should be included in the contents of the systems analysis report?
11. What is the difference between work measurement analysis and work distribution analysis?
12. What is the primary advantage of hierarchical function analysis?
13. Where are the limitations of hierarchical function analysis?
14. What is a HIPO?
15. When would the use of a decision flow diagram be important?
16. What are the key elements of a logical data flow diagram?
17. Give three examples of matrix-oriented analysis.
18. Why is systems analysis an important first step preceding systems design?
19. What are some of the key behavioral considerations that are important in systems analysis?

Discussion Questions and Problems

20. Discuss some of the major problems often encountered in systems analysis. How can these problems be avoided?
21. Why is observation needed? Can the analyst save a considerable amount of time by simply relying on the system as documented?
22. How do you deal with the situation in which a manager claims not to understand departmental information needs?
23. In a company too small for an information systems steering committee, which individual would be the most appropriate to oversee the systems development function?
24. For each of the following systems, develop a hierarchical function diagram:
    (a) purchasing system
    (b) production system
    (c) inventory management system
25. Assume that you have been hired as a consultant for a small company that has problems with its payroll system. Describe the steps you would take in developing a solution.
26. Discuss the major goals of systems analysis.
27. Discuss the importance of the systems analysis report.
28. Following is a list of problem situations. In each case, discuss some of the major steps you would follow in systems analysis.
    (a) a company has problems with raw material shortages
    (b) a company has production bottlenecks and is not able to manage production according to a preset schedule
    (c) a company has severe problems with credit losses
    (d) overall production employee morale is low
    (e) there are large quantities of units in inventory that have been sitting there for many years.
29. Describe several systems analysis techniques that would be helpful for purposes of gathering and organizing the facts needed in studying an accounts receivable system.

30. Which of the following systems analysis techniques—(1) work measurement analysis, (2) work distribution analysis, (3) questionnaire, (4) logical data flow diagram, (5) interview, (6) input/output diagram—would be the most appropriate for each of the following cases?
    (a) analyzing the information needs of a production manager
    (b) analyzing the information flows within the sales department
    (c) analyzing an inventory management system
    (d) analyzing a purchase order system

31. Describe structured systems analysis.

32. Herman Manufacturing has been having many difficulties. This company manufactures caps and gowns used for graduation ceremonies in both high schools and colleges. Most of the company's problems have revolved around its inability to generate sufficient sales to maintain overall profitability. The president of the company, Barbara Novel, feels that this situation has been caused by poor relations between the company and its customers. Barbara has confided in some of the company's major customers about this matter, and they have advised her that they are very happy with the quality of the company's products. However, they mentioned a number of problems. Among the problems given were late deliveries and incomplete orders. Further discussion with some of the company's production employees has revealed a wide range of production problems exist, including (1) low-quality raw materials, (2) bottlenecks in production due to a general lack of coordination in job scheduling, and (3) mixups in customer's orders.

    You have been called in as an independent consultant and have been asked to advise Barbara Novel.

    Required
    (a) Where do you begin dealing with this company's problem?
    (b) What type of systems analysis techniques would be useful in this situation?

33. Central Manufacturing produces custom-made kitchen cabinets. This is a medium-sized, family-owned corporation with approximately 150 employees. Joe Starr has been the president for the past five years. The company presently serves a wide range of customers in the Ft. Lauderdale–Miami area of south Florida. The organizational structure is reasonably simple. Under Joe Starr are three vice presidents (all of whom are major shareholders in the company): Mary Noddle (vice president of production), Ron Hill (vice president of sales), and Kim Debe (vice president of accounting).

    Under Ron Hill are seven sales managers, each of whom represents a particular segment of the Dade–Broward County areas. As sales orders are received, the production department processes a custom manufacturing order, which specifies the exact materials to be used. In the next phase, the raw materials are pulled, and the job is assigned to a team of workers. The size of this team depends on the size of the job.

    At present, Joe Starr is concerned with a number of problems but primarily with bad-debt losses. A superficial analysis of accounts receivable indicated that a large number of accounts are more than 90 days overdue. Mr. Starr is sure that these will be collected eventually; Central Manufacturing has, however, had difficulty in paying its bills due to these late collections.

    Joe Starr has asked the chief accountant, Jim Wdeve, for an explanation of the problem. Mr. Wdeve explained that he periodically reviews the accounts receivable records, making notes on overdue accounts, which he uses as a basis for telephoning customers and asking for explanations.

    Mr. Wdeve recommended that the problem be solved by implementing a network of microcomputers throughout the company. He suggested that, with a microcomputer on each employee's desk, everyone would have instant access to any information needed.

    Required
    Comment on Mr. Wdeve's suggestion for installing a network of microcomputers.

34. John Needles has been hired as a systems consultant for Arco Manufacturing. The company's president, Barbara Arco, has told John that the company has been having numerous problems with late deliveries on customers' orders. The problem has been very acute because the competition has taken away a lot of business by offering faster delivery times.

   John sets up an interview with the production supervisor to discuss the problem. The interview goes as follows:

> JOHN: I have been hired to help alleviate any bottlenecks leading to late deliveries.
>
> SUPERVISOR: I appreciate your offer to help, but I'm afraid that our problems can only be solved by someone with a considerable amount of experience doing this type of work.
>
> JOHN: I agree. That's why I hope I can rely on you and your experience.
>
> SUPERVISOR: I'm still afraid there isn't much I can do for you. Perhaps it would be better if you work directly with Ms. Arco. I have an awful lot of work to do and need to make a production deadline this afternoon.
>
> JOHN: Perhaps I can come back later this afternoon?
>
> SUPERVISOR: You're welcome to come back, but, again, I don't think I can help you.

Required

John Needles seems to be having trouble communicating with the production supervisor. Discuss some possible causes of this problem and make suggestions for overcoming it.

35. The General Company has an accounting staff of five employees: a supervisor and four clerks. The daily tasks of each employee are as follows:

SUPERVISOR (MARY WILD)

- Checking paperwork—5 hours
- Filing documents—5 hours
- Preparing invoices—4 hours
- Other activities—1 hour

ACCOUNTS PAYABLE CLERK (JOE FREEDMIRE)

- Preparing monthly statements—4 hours
- Preparing aging report—3 hours
- Checking invoices—4 hours

HELPER CLERK (BOB STANS)

- Checking invoices—3 hours
- Preparing aging report—2 hours
- Account posting—5 hours

DOCUMENT VERIFICATION CLERK (MARGARET LEE)

- Preparing disbursement vouchers—4 hours
- Checking invoices—2 hours
- Other activities—3 hours

CLERK-TYPIST (DEBBIE CHASE)

- Typing invoices—4 hours
- Assisting in verification of invoices—3 hours

Required

(a) Prepare a work distribution chart using tasks such as aging of accounts receivable, voucher preparation, and so on.

(b) Identify any weaknesses in the distribution of tasks. In addition, note any internal control problems.

36. Systems analyst, Jack Blount, has been hired as a consultant to a large national distributing company to develop a new system for inventory control. The company is extremely large and has manufacturing plants and offices throughout the country. Mr. Blount decided to initially focus his attention on the Chicago plant.

He initially interviewed the plant manager. The discussion was very productive and, after several meetings, he felt that he was in a position to make suggestions for improving the system. Based on this, he prepared a systems analysis report for review by the company's chief accountant.

In his meeting with the chief accountant, a number of problems arose. The chief accountant told him that a number of employees had complained to him, "Mr. Blount said he was going to have a number of employees laid off." Several supervisors complained that they were being replaced by computers. The situation had gotten so out of hand that a number of employees were on the verge of striking. Such a strike could cost the company thousands of dollars in a very short time. For this reason, the chief accountant informed Mr. Blount that the company did not wish to proceed with systems design and implementation. Mr. Blount was very disappointed to hear this, because he felt that a few simple changes to the existing system could be very helpful in terms of solving the company's problems.

Required

Has Mr. Blount made any mistakes? If so, what did he do wrong?

Answers to Chapter Quiz

1. B	4. B	7. C	10. A
2. A	5. A	8. C	
3. D	6. D	9. D	

CHAPTER 17

Systems Design

LEARNING OBJECTIVES

Careful study of this chapter will enable you to:

■ Describe the various steps involved in specifying systems design alternatives.

■ Discuss the various considerations relevant to preparing design specifications.

■ Describe the content of a systems design proposal.

■ Summarize several major design techniques.

■ Discuss the usefulness of systems design packages.

OVERVIEW

Chapter 16 discussed systems planning and analysis. These activities form the basis of an overall framework for targeting specific systems design projects. This chapter focuses on considerations and problems surrounding the design of a specific system.

A systems design is very similar to the architectural layout of a house. In the planning phase, the architect determines the basic functions that the house should perform and formulates a general plan with regard to the overall layout. In the design stage, however, the architect prepares a specific blueprint of a house that can be used by electricians, plumbers, and carpenters. In a similar fashion, the systems designer prepares a blueprint that can be implemented by accountants, computer programmers, and management.

Small errors made at this stage can result in large amounts of wasted dollars and expenditures at later stages. Consider what would happen if, in building a house, an architect forgets to include plumbing in the kitchen. Further assume that such a house was built as designed. Upon discovering this error, the owners would have to pay to have the walls (and possibly the floors) ripped out in order to retrofit the omitted plumbing. Needless to say, this process would be quite painful and expensive. Similar problems can and often do occur in the design of accounting information systems. For example, a company might implement a systems design plan that calls for purchasing a particular computer network and certain accounting software packages. After using this system for a year or two, the company might find that the software packages no longer meet the changing information needs of management. Furthermore, it might be impossible to modify these software packages, necessitating replacing the entire system after a short period of use.

There are other pitfalls. One of the most dangerous is user rejection of the system. Because of lack of adequate involvement of users in the design plan, the implemented system could become unpopular and ultimately be rejected by the individuals for whom the system was designed.

STEPS IN SYSTEMS DESIGN

Systems design can be defined as the formulation of a blueprint for a completed system. Systems design proceeds from the general to specific. This is the nature of the top-down approach. The general functions and objectives that a specific system will accomplish must first be identified. Given these objectives, it is then possible to prepare detailed specifications, such as database structures, record layouts, and specific report forms. Therefore, systems design can be viewed as either preliminary or detailed. In most cases, the design effort actually begins during the systems planning and analysis phases of the development cycle. The design effort should be viewed as a process of continuously increasing detail that begins during the analysis and planning phases and ends with the beginning of the implementation phase of the development cycle. Furthermore, the entire development cycle, including the design phase, is a never-ending process. During implementation, problems are often encountered with the design specifications. When this happens, it is necessary to go back to the design process and make the necessary changes. Furthermore, the business environment is always changing and, as new system requirements arise, the systems design must be restructured as needed.

Figure 17.1 defines these major steps in systems design. The first is the evaluation of various design alternatives, the second is the preparation of design specifications, and the third is the preparation of systems design specifications.

Evaluating Design Alternatives

In every case, the systems design project arises out of a specific need as determined by the systems planning and analysis phase of the development cycle. The systems design should provide a solution to a specific problem. Systems design problems are much like many other problems in life. There is usually no single solution that perfectly solves the problem. The systems designer is usually faced with a number of solutions, all of which may appear very attractive upon superficial examination. Therefore, a very important aspect of systems design is the enumeration and consideration of the various major design alternatives.

Enumeration of Design Alternatives

At the most general level, the designer is faced with the alternatives of either developing a completely new system or modifying the existing system (Figure 17.2). If the company has no existing system, the choice is easy. For example, if a company has no cost accounting system at all, it would not be necessary to consider various modifications to the existing system; the designer could build a new system from the ground up.

In designing a completely new system, there are two general approaches. One approach is to design the system completely from scratch. The other approach is to

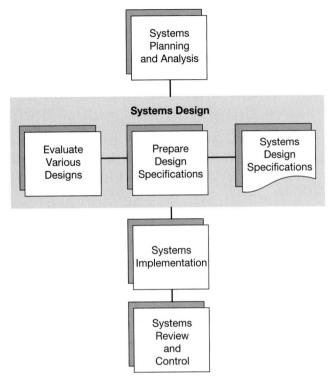

FIGURE 17.1 Systems Design.

have the designer select and recommend a premade system. For example, a given company might find it very economical to purchase one of the many computerized accounting packages that are available. However, some software packages may be inappropriate for a given application. In addition, many packages give the user a wide range of alternatives for data items, report formats, and so on. It is often neces-

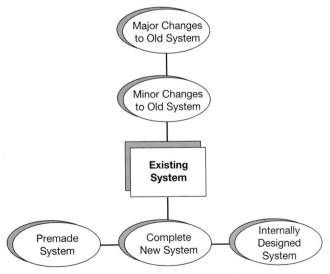

FIGURE 17.2 General Design Approaches for an Existing System.

sary to do a substantial amount of design work anyway, because even predesigned packages do not completely solve design problems. This is an important point because there is a tendency on the part of managers to feel that either a computer or a computer package alone will solve their information needs.

Computer packages can sometimes meet the specific needs of an individual situation with minimal design work. This is particularly true when a computer package has been written for a specific industry. For example, there are a number of **turnkey systems** available for lawyers, doctors, the construction industry, and so on. Such systems can very closely meet the needs of management. However, as firms increase in complexity and in the number of their products, it becomes increasingly difficult to find a predesigned system that adequately meets the needs of management.

A second situation often faced in systems design is an existing system that is not adequately functioning. In this case, it is necessary to design changes into the existing system. As a general rule, it is more difficult to modify an existing system than to implement a new one. This is especially true because of a tendency for individuals to resist change.

In modifying an existing system, there are several basic approaches that can be taken. The first of these is that of simply modifying the data collected and reports generated. This is the simplest approach because it involves little or no redefining of individual job responsibilities. A second approach to redesigning existing systems involves reorganizing job responsibilities. This approach is substantially more drastic than the first and is much more likely to be resisted by existing employees. Employees usually feel comfortable in a particular job after working at it for several months. The possibility of changing job responsibilities can introduce considerable uncertainty into an employee's life. This uncertainty alone can make an individual uncomfortable, and the result could be resistance to the change. Therefore, systems designers should be careful to recommend organizational changes only in situations where changes are really needed. Although organizational changes should be recommended with caution, it is often desirable to either completely reassign employees or make dramatic changes in their job responsibilities. Such changes occur when clear-cut costs/benefits or internal control considerations are involved. In these situations, every effort should be made to alleviate employee uncertainty and discomfort.

Finally, a number of design alternatives might apply either to a new system or to a modification of an already existing system. One general alternative might involve considering whether a particular system should be computerized. Another general alternative could involve deciding whether to create a centralized or decentralized system. Table 17.1 lists a number of commonly encountered design alternatives.

Describing the Alternatives

Once a list of major alternatives has been made, each alternative should be documented and described. For example, a computer network for data collection and report distribution might be either centralized or decentralized. In a centralized design alternative, each division supplies accounting data to the central computer system. The central computer system then produces and distributes reports to each of the divisions. In a decentralized design alternative, each division has its own computers and collects its own data. The completed reports are transmitted to company headquarters. The description of each alternative should incorporate its relative advantages and disadvantages. Relevant cost information should also

TABLE 17.1 Typical Design Alternatives

Design Consideration	Typical Design Alternatives
Data processing	Manual versus automated; batch versus on-line; microcomputer versus mainframe
Computer network	Centralized versus decentralized
File organization	Random versus sequential
Data-access method	Direct versus sequential
Update frequency	Daily versus monthly
Storage media	Disk versus tape
Input approach	Batch versus on-line
Processing approach	Batch versus on-line
Input media	MICR versus OCR
Output media	Monitor versus printout
Report frequency	Daily versus weekly
Report trigger	Demand versus periodic reporting

be provided so that cost/benefit comparisons can be made on design alternatives. For example, the centralized computer system might cost $1,000,000 and the decentralized computer system $1,250,000. On the surface, the centralized computer system appears cheaper. However, the decentralized system might provide a number of additional functions. Furthermore, the total capacity of the individual decentralized computers might substantially exceed that of the centralized system. This would be particularly important if there were a possibility that the capacity of the centralized system might be reached in the near future.

Evaluating the Alternatives

Once each alternative has been carefully laid out and documented, it is possible to compare alternatives. The primary criteria for selecting an alternative for implementation should be cost versus benefits. In addition, the selected alternative should satisfy all major systems objectives.

Another important factor that must be considered is **feasibility.** A given design proposal must be both technically and operationally feasible. It must be possible for a given company to actually implement the design specifications. For example, if a company is to acquire a sophisticated mainframe computer, it must be prepared to administer it. This may involve upgrading the job responsibilities of existing individuals. When such an approach is to be taken, the company must ensure that the targeted individual is capable of managing the new system. *It is very easy to underestimate the requirements of maintaining, managing, and operating sophisticated information systems.*

The best major design alternative is normally selected by top management. Furthermore, the major designs presented to top management are typically not highly detailed. Once management selects a design, the design team prepares detailed design specifications.

Preparing Design Specifications

The primary rule in developing design specifications is that the designer should work backward from outputs to inputs. Working with the system objectives, the designer should design all management reports and operational output docu-

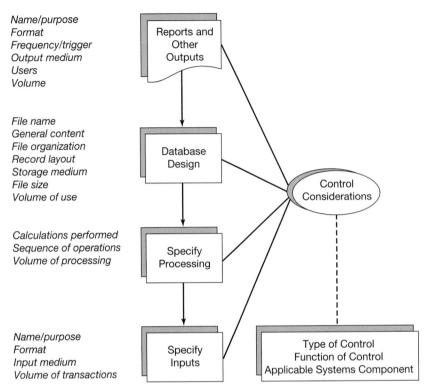

Attribute

Name/purpose
Format
Frequency/trigger
Output medium
Users
Volume

Reports and
Other
Outputs

File name
General content
File organization
Record layout
Storage medium
File size
Volume of use

Database
Design

Control
Considerations

Calculations performed
Sequence of operations
Volume of processing

Specify
Processing

Name/purpose
Format
Input medium
Volume of transactions

Specify
Inputs

Type of Control
Function of Control
Applicable Systems Component

FIGURE 17.3 Design of System Elements.

ments as a first step in the process. Once all of these outputs are specified, the data inputs and processing steps are automatically determined. Once these decisions have been made, the designer then builds in the appropriate controls. Figure 17.3 shows this process. In each phase of the design sequence, specific considerations must be made. In designing the reports and other outputs, such factors as the reporting frequency, the output medium, and the actual report format must be considered. In developing a database, design considerations regarding file organization, record layout, storage media, and volume of usage must be made. For the processing phase, the exact calculations to be performed and the appropriate sequence of operations must be specified. Finally, in specifying the inputs, precise input formats, the input medium, and volume of transactions must be considered.

Preparing and Submitting Systems Design Specifications

The completed design specifications should take the form of a proposal. If the project is large, the proposal should be reviewed by top management before approval. However, proposals that are relatively inexpensive might be approved by a department or division manager. The **detailed design proposal** should include everything necessary to actually implement the design project. In general, it will include specific timetables for completion, a budget, and a description of personnel requirements as well as flowcharts and other diagrams that describe the systems to be implemented. A copy of all proposed system outputs would be incorporated as well as specifics on any databases to be created or modified. The database specifications would include the exact contents of specific data items as well as file organization and file-access methods. In addition, details relating to storage requirements, file size, and updating frequency should be provided.

With regard to data processing, details regarding required hardware and software should be provided. Hardware normally includes the computer itself as well as communications equipment, printers, and input/output devices. On the software side, specifications regarding processing operations should be included. Furthermore, specific processing cycles and times should be given.

Next, specific details relating to the input of data in the system should be provided. These should include the method of input, procedures for screening input data, and the content of data inputs.

Finally, in all cases, specific volume and cost information should be provided. For example, if the system calls for manual entry of sales orders into a computer system, details regarding the personnel and cost and time requirements for data entry should be given. This information should be provided in terms of peak volume (e.g., during the busy season) and average volume.

It is also important that a detailed analysis of control and security measures be incorporated into the design proposal, because a number of the design considerations may involve trade-offs between internal control and efficiency. For example, a design might specify that a particular data item be entered into the system twice so that the computer can cross-compare the two entries for accuracy and consistency. In this case, the design proposal should clearly state that this is being done for internal control purposes.

GENERAL DESIGN CONSIDERATIONS

The previous section focused on specific factors to consider in developing a systems design proposal. This section considers objectives pertinent to each phase of the design process. Table 17.2 summarizes these general considerations for each major system element in the design phase.

Output Design

The first and foremost consideration for output design is **cost-effectiveness.** The principle of cost-effectiveness should be applied to all elements of the system because an investment in the information system is like any capital budgeting expenditure—it should be evaluated on a cost/benefit basis. The intent is to maximize the ratio of the benefits to cost while satisfying the objectives for a given system.

The properties of relevance, clarity, and timeliness are essential to managerial reports. Reports should include only information that is relevant to a particular decision maker. However, this principle cannot be strictly adhered to because some reports must be generated for more than one manager, and different managers have different preferences for information. Nevertheless, both unneeded or missing information can decrease the value of a report. A report that is cluttered with irrelevant information might be ignored by a manager who is unwilling to wade through a lot of useless data. The inclusion of irrelevant information in a report may also result in excessive information costs.

TABLE 17.2 Design Considerations for System Elements

System Element	Design Consideration
Outputs (report or document)	Cost-effectiveness Relevance Clarity Timeliness
Database	Cost effectiveness Integration Standardization Flexibility Security Accuracy Efficiency Organization
Data processing	Cost effectiveness Uniformity Integration Accuracy
Data input	Cost effectiveness Accuracy Uniformity Integration
Controls and security measures	Cost-effectiveness Comprehensiveness Appropriateness

One very important factor relating to clarity involves including appropriate titles and captions within a report. Far too often, information systems produce reports that are not adequately titled and captioned. The justification that managers know the contents of the reports and do not need detailed explanations is often offered. The danger in this line of reasoning is that many companies have a high rate of turnover in their management staff, which means that a new manager might either misinterpret a report or ignore it altogether because of its lack of clarity.

Database Design

Several important principles apply to database design. Of particular importance is that a company's databases be integrated. **Integration** means the avoidance of collecting and maintaining the same data items in more than one place in the company. In an integrated system, various phases of business operations can share the same data. For example, the sales department, shipping department, and billing department might all need the customer's name and address. In a fully integrated system, this information might be entered into the system once in the credit department. It then could be accessed by the sales department for generating orders and by the shipping department for shipping to the correct address. In a system without integration, this information might have to be typed three separate times. This would not only produce higher costs, but would result in a higher error rate.

Another important consideration in database design is that of **standardization,** which means that all data items be entered in a standard format and assigned a common name when used in more than one place. For example, if a departmental expense budget shows the item "automobile expense," it should have the same definition throughout the entire company. Therefore, it would be undesirable to have automobile expense include depreciation in one department but not in another. Flexibility and security are other important features of a database design. Databases should be designed in such a manner that users can structure a wide variety of queries. For example, one manager might want sales broken down by district and then by product, and another manager might want sales broken down by product and then by district. A flexible database design would allow for either type of report.

Data Processing

One important consideration in data processing relates to uniformity and integration. It is important that the company's overall data processing system develop according to some general plan. For example, it would often be undesirable for one department to acquire a PC accounting package that would not run on any of the other computers within the same company.

Data Input

One often difficult consideration in designing the data input system is that of accuracy. The use of well-defined source documents can encourage employees to record data accurately without omissions. For example, if a customer's telephone number is a needed data input, the sales order document should have a specific line that is clearly labeled "customer telephone number." A document that simply includes several lines with a label "customer information" would be less desirable because some employees would leave out the telephone number.

Controls and Security Measures

Implementing adequate controls is too often overlooked. Comprehensive, appropriate controls should be established for each phase of the system's design process. This is one area in which the accountant can play a critical role while working with a design team. In many cases, the design team may involve primarily information systems specialists who might have an appreciation for controls but not detailed expertise in this area. In this case, the accountant can review the overall plan and discuss inadequacies in controls with the individual team members.

DESIGN TECHNIQUES

Designing a system is a creative activity. It is unlikely that two design teams will produce the same solution to a given problem. Therefore, systems design can be viewed somewhat as an art, although one in which various refined techniques have been developed. As an artist needs special tools for painting, the designer needs certain tools to assist in the design process. Many of these tools are also used in systems analysis, and were discussed in Chapter 16. These include such techniques as input/output analysis, systems flowcharting, data flow diagrams, and Warnier–Orr diagrams.

Whereas all of the systems analysis techniques pertain to systems design, certain special problems relate more to information systems design. These relate primarily to forms (document) and database design, which are discussed.

Forms Design

The process of designing specific forms is called forms design. The area of **forms design** should be given very careful attention by the systems design team because forms are the interface between the users and the system itself. Therefore, forms design should focus on producing documents that provide effective interfaces between managers and the information system. Because of its importance, a number of specialized techniques have been developed for forms design and analysis. These techniques are discussed in what follows.

Forms Analysis Sheet

Figure 17.4 gives an example of a **forms analysis sheet** for a typical purchase order. This sheet summarizes all relevant properties of the purchase order. In addition, certain vital information related to cost and usage of the form is included. Taken together, all of this information can be useful for the designer in evaluating the existing form or designing a new one.

Data Hierarchy Diagram

The focus of a **data hierarchy diagram** is on data elements and their hierarchical relationships to each other. This type of diagram logically relates similar data items to each other, which makes it easier for the designer to consider the addition or deletion of additional data elements to a given layout.

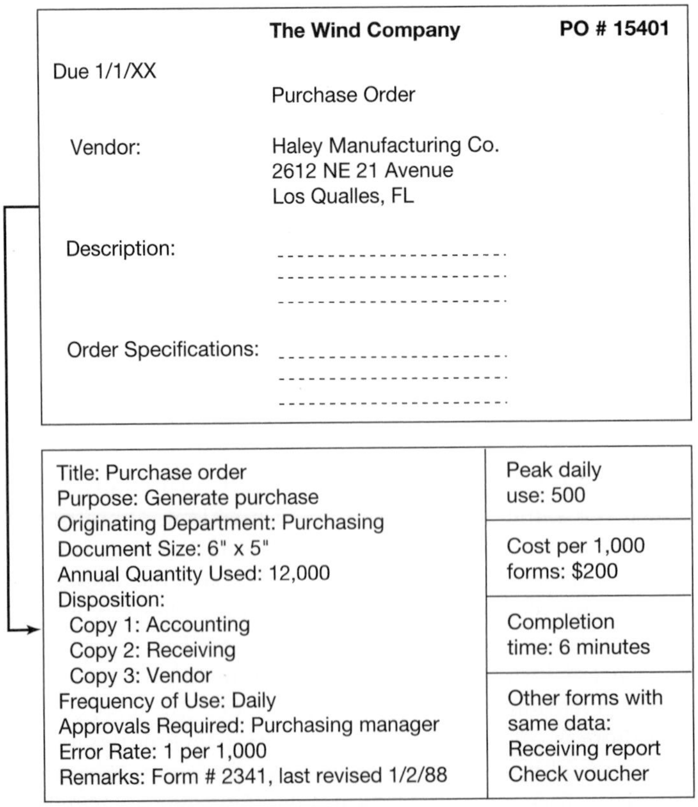

FIGURE 17.4 Forms Analysis for a Typical Purchase Order.

Forms Layout Chart

The **forms layout chart** involves using a grid on which each item in the grid corresponds to a particular location on a video screen, computer printer, or other medium where the form is to be displayed. The grid is divided into the appropriate number of rows and columns. A typical line printer grid is 66 lines by 132 columns, whereas many video screens have 24 lines by either 80 or 132 columns.

Database Design

There are a number of useful techniques for designing databases: data structure diagrams, record layouts, file analysis sheets, and file-related matrices. Data structure diagrams show the relationships between various kinds of records. For example, a manufacturing company may have several records in various databases relating to a given customer. One record may contain sales order information, another record production status information, and another information relating to billing. The data structure diagram defines the relationship among these different data records.

A record layout diagram shows the various data fields within a record. Both record layout and data structure diagrams are discussed in detail in Chapter 11 on file processing and data management concepts.

File analysis sheets provide the system designer with all major points of relevant information regarding the contents of a particular file. Such information would include record layouts, the purpose of the file, the expected number of records, and so on.

File-related matrices show the interrelationship between files, their contents, and their uses. File-related matrices can be helpful in determining the effective and efficient usage of data items within files, eliminating unneeded or redundant data items, and optimizing file structure in general. For example, one file-related matrix might show a list of data items on one side versus a list of files in which these data items are used on the other side. Another example of a file-related matrix would be one that lists data items on one side and reports on the other side. This type of matrix would be helpful in assessing the usage of particular data items in reports. If a data item does not appear in any of the reports, the company might consider eliminating it from the file.

Systems Design Packages

A number of prepackaged design methodologies are available to assist in the systems development cycle. The purpose of these packages is to assist the designer in systematically approaching a given problem. These packages help the designer structure the design problem, and can result in considerable time savings.

CASE (computer-aided software engineering) is computer software technology that supports an automated engineering discipline for software development and maintenance. CASE can produce data flow diagrams, narrative documentation, screen and report prototypes, and data dictionary descriptions. CASE can increase productivity, improve software quality through introduction of rigorous standards and analysis, and decrease the cost of developing, documenting, and maintaining software. Most CASE products include some elements of prepackaged design methodologies.

Prepackaged design systems have the advantage of assisting the designer in structuring a particular problem; however, most design packages have certain shortcomings. In particular, the packages do not assist in specifying the desired outputs, nor do they deal adequately with the problem of system response time. The design packages may provide some assistance but not total solutions to all problems.

Choosing Software and Hardware

At some point, the decision must be made as to whether the computer software is to be built from scratch or purchased. Although this seems to be a design decision, it should be made at the end of the analysis phase. Much of the design phase may be omitted if a purchase decision is made. Once the requirements of any new system have been specified, one can then look at available software packages to see which ones most closely fit a company's needs—all without actually "designing" that system.

On the other hand, nothing pleases computer professionals more than the freedom of designing and building a new system from scratch. This is what they have been trained to do, so they tend to ignore the multitude of good software packages already available on the market. It is economically more feasible for many businesses, especially smaller ones, to buy rather than build software.

Purchased software packages have several advantages:

- They are cheaper. The cost of development is carried by many purchasers rather than just the creator.

- They are already debugged. If several other organizations have been using the package for some months, it is reasonably safe to assume that most of the bugs have been found and exterminated.

- The company can try the product before investing a great deal of money. With in-house software, it is possible to put months of development time into a program only to discover that it does not produce the desired results when it is done.

The main disadvantage of **canned software packages** (i.e., purchased software packages) is that they rarely exactly meet a company's needs. It may be necessary to modify the software (which can be expensive, if not impossible) or modify a company's procedures to match what the package requires.

A **dedicated software package** is one intended for a narrow audience, such as retail stores or accounting firms. To find a good dedicated software package, talk to people who work for other companies in the same industry. Someone who works for another manufacturing organization, for example, may know of a good production control package. Trade magazines for an industry also tell what is available (e.g., software packages for florists are advertised in *Florist's Review*). General computer publications—*Computer World, Datamation, InfoWorld,* and the like—have advertisements and reviews of the more general-purpose packages like spreadsheets and word processors.

When evaluating purchased software, it is helpful to use a decision table format to consider the following:

- How close is the fit to what is needed? Will the programs or our procedures or both have to be modified?

- How stable is the software vendor? Will it still be in business in a year or two when problems arise? Does it give prompt support when problems arise? A toll-free, 24-hour telephone line is a good indicator.

- Is there a trial period, where everything can be returned for full refund after a month or so?

- How many other installations have used the software? For how long? Who are they?

Some people get a list of users' names from the vendor but do not ask those users for evaluations because they know the evaluation will be good or the vendor would not have supplied them. Instead, ask them for second-level references—other organizations that they know are using the package but whom the vendor failed to mention. Here is where the skeletons can be uncovered.

- How flexible is the software? Can it change along with the changing business environment? Are there any growth limits on file size, number of transactions, or embedded tables?

- Is it user-friendly? Does the software guide the operator through each program, with adequate explanations and error messages? Is the documentation clear, complete, and easy to read?

- Are source programs supplied? If not, the company will be forever dependent on the vendor for modifications at whatever price is named.

Only after collecting data on the various software packages available is it time to worry about choosing the hardware. Because the software is what determines how well the computer meets the company's needs, it is usually fairly safe to be content with the hardware on which that software runs. There are a few constraints in hardware selection that are much the same as those detailed in the preceding points. In addition, try to get machinery that is **upwardly compatible**— easily upgradable to a larger or faster model in the future without losing existing data or programs.

One last note on purchasing any computer hardware or software: It is a mistake to put off a purchase in the belief that either the price will drop shortly or a new version will be available soon. In most cases, the price drop is negligible compared to the inconvenience caused by not having the computer in the meantime. And the state-of-the-art methods of the newer version are not usually required; mere adequacy has its merits. It might be better to buy the system now, when it is needed, than to try to outguess the computer market, which is so unpredictable that no one has a very good batting average for forecasting.

SUMMARY

Systems design is an orderly process that begins at a very general level with the setting of objectives for a particular system. The process then proceeds to the more detailed level with the specification of file structures, processing operations, and forms design. The major steps in system design include evaluating design alternatives, preparing design specifications, and submitting a completed systems design report. Once a particular design alternative has been selected, it can be presented to top management. Top management then reviews the proposed design, along with its budget, and decides whether the project should proceed in more detail. If management does decide in favor of selecting a particular design project, the design team can specify the design details. Detailed design considerations would include things such as output design, database design, data processing operations, data inputs, and controls and security measures. The preferred procedure is to first design the system outputs and then work backward to define the inputs.

A number of systems design techniques are very helpful. These include standard systems design techniques, such as flowcharting, data flow diagrams, and input/output analysis. There are, however, a number of techniques that are particularly useful in systems design. These include forms analysis sheets, data hierarchy diagrams, forms layout charts, data structure diagrams, record layouts, file analysis sheets, and file-related input/output matrices. The first three techniques assist the systems designer in preparing and analyzing forms. The latter techniques are useful in the design and layout of databases.

Systems design packages provide a structured approach to systems design. The more sophisticated packages allow the designer to specify the desired inputs, outputs, and processing operations. The design package then generates a working database system. Such packages save the designer a considerable amount of time. Many decisions must be made, however, that the design package cannot help with. For example, the design package cannot tell the designer what the desired outputs should be. In addition, the design package may be inadequate with regard to specifying the optimal database structure and file-access methods.

In conclusion, systems design is a process that involves a considerable amount of creativity. Success comes with good communication between the design team and management. In addition, all feasible alternatives must be carefully considered. Special emphasis should be given to system integration and security measures.

Glossary

canned software package: a software package purchased from a vendor.

cost-effectiveness: the benefits of a design should exceed its costs.

data hierarchy diagram: identifies data elements and their hierarchical relationships to each other.

dedicated software package: a commercially available software package that is intended for a narrow audience.

detailed design proposal: everything necessary to actually implement a design project, including timetables, a budget, personnel requirements, and design documentation.

feasibility: design criterion that it must be possible to actually implement the design specifications.

forms analysis sheet: a summary of all relevant properties of a form.

forms design: the process of designing specific forms.

forms layout chart: a grid on which each item in the grid corresponds to a particular location on a video screen, computer printer, or other medium where the form is to be displayed.

integration: design criteria that means the avoidance of collecting and maintaining the same data items in more than one place.

standardization: design criteria that all data items be entered in a standard format and assigned a common name when used in more than one place.

turnkey system: computer packages that meet the specific needs of an individual situation with minimal design work.

upwardly compatible: computer hardware that is easily upgradable to a larger or faster model without losing existing data or programs.

Chapter Quiz

Answers to the chapter quiz appear on page 653.

1. Which of the following design criteria holds that the benefits of a design should exceed its costs?
   (a) feasibility
   (b) cost-effectiveness
   (c) standardization
   (d) integration

2. Which of the following design criteria holds that it must be possible to actually implement the design specifications?

(a) feasibility
(b) cost-effectiveness
(c) standardization
(d) integration

3. In a certain company, the data item "automobile expense" includes depreciation in one department but not in another. This violates which of the following design criteria?
   (a) flexibility
   (b) security
   (c) standardization
   (d) integration

4. In a certain company, the data item "customer address" is entered and maintained in separate databases by both the billing and sales departments. This violates which of the following design criteria?
   (a) flexibility
   (b) security
   (c) standardization
   (d) integration

5. Forms design should be given very careful attention by the systems design team because
   (a) forms are expensive to produce in volume.
   (b) forms are the interface between users and the system.
   (c) forms are the first step in detailed systems design.
   (d) forms are the final step in detailed systems design.

6. Computer packages that meet the specific needs of an individual situation with minimal design work are called
   (a) turnkey systems.
   (b) CASE systems.
   (c) integrated systems.
   (d) database systems.

7. Which of the following tools uses a grid on which each item in the grid corresponds to a particular location on a medium where a form is to be displayed?
   (a) input/output matrix
   (b) forms layout chart
   (c) data hierarchy diagram
   (d) forms analysis sheet

8. The main disadvantage to canned software packages is
   (a) they rarely exactly meet a company's needs.
   (b) they are more expensive than developing in-house software.
   (c) they need to be debugged.
   (d) they cannot be tried without investing a great deal of money.

9. When evaluating purchased software, a good indicator of vendor support for the package is
   (a) a toll-free telephone number.
   (b) the relative price of the package.
   (c) the number of installations using the package.
   (d) how user-friendly the package is.

10. Computer hardware that is easily upgradable to a larger or faster model without losing existing data or programs is said to be (_____).
    (a) a super-flexible system
    (b) an upwardly compatible system
    (c) a user-friendly system
    (d) a turnkey system

Review Problem

Alda Manufacturing produces and sells printing equipment. The company does not do any retail business but sells strictly to office supply businesses, who in turn sell the equipment to the customers. Most equipment sells for less than $5,000; therefore, the company is able to reach a high volume of sales.

In each sales district, the sales manager has approximately 40 accounts with retail outlets. Associated with these accounts is a file of historical information that profiles the specialized needs of each individual retail store. In addition, all sales are done on a credit basis, according to preapproved credit lines. Presently, the overall sales volume of the company is approximately 19,000 units per month.

The existing accounting system involves running all sales transactions on a batch basis. The current approach is to use a key-to-tape machine to enter all transactions directly onto a magnetic tape. The magnetic tapes are then processed by the accounting system periodically, and a new master file is created.

A number of difficulties have arisen with the present system. First and foremost is that the batch-oriented system does not allow for up-to-date on-line inquiries about customer accounts and customer orders. In addition, salespeople working in the field would like to be able to dial into the company's computer and gain access to information about particular orders and customer histories. This is especially useful to new salespeople, who have less experience.

Required

(a) What files would be required to implement an on-line, real-time sales and billing system?
(b) Describe the record layouts in each file.
(c) Describe the appropriate file organization and file access methods in each case.

Solution to Review Problem

(a) The choice of files will depend on the overall design and the company's need to integrate the sales database with other functions such as billing and shipping. The importance of this case is that students should recognize some of the different options, including the following:
   (1) Store the sales and history both in the same file, with one record per customer. This especially makes sense if the history fields are updated at the same time as the sales fields. For example, assume that two of the history fields include the number of sales transactions and largest purchase to date. These two fields would be involved in any updating to the sales fields. In this system, this file also serves as an accounts receivable master file and open order file.
   (2) The sales and history files are kept separately. The sales file would serve as an open order and accounts receivable master file.
   (3) The sales file and history file are kept separately. In a completely different approach than in (2), the sales file would simply be a transaction file that would be used to update both the accounts receivable master and history files. This latter system is more appropriate for on-line input with batch processing. Alternative (2) might be more appropriate for real-time processing.
(b) The record layouts would vary, depending on the alternative selected. The history file is pretty much judgmental, given the information in the case. History-related fields might be used to store such items as the customer's shipping address, credit limit, statistics on previous purchases, and so on. The sales fields would describe open orders in detail and include items such as the promised delivery date. An accounts receivable master file would primarily contain the customer's name, account number, and outstanding account balance. Other fields might include previous purchases and payments, although these could be kept in the history file.

(c) For on-line queries needing completely up-to-date information on histories, open orders, and account balances, random file organization would be required. The access method would need to be something more sophisticated than plain sequential, at least indexed-sequential, and this method would probably suffice. However, there are plenty of arguments for a direct-access scheme involving a hierarchical or network data structure. This latter approach might be discussed by instructors who like to delve into the more complicated data structures.

Review Questions

1. Define each of the following terms:
   (a) design alternatives
   (b) forms analysis sheet
   (c) file-related matrices
   (d) operational feasibility
2. What are the major steps in the systems design process?
3. What are some of the major considerations that must be incorporated into the systems design process?
4. Which step in the design process is the most important?
5. In what ways can the accountant contribute the most to the systems design team?
6. Discuss the purpose of systems design packages.
7. Discuss the limitations of systems design packages.
8. At what stage should the systems design proposal be reviewed by top management?
9. Describe the major components of the systems design report.
10. Describe several major considerations involved in database design.
11. Describe several major considerations involved in output document design.

Discussion Questions and Problems

12. List several important data fields that would be found in a database design for accounts receivable.
13. In evaluating design alternatives, the costs versus the benefits of a particular design proposal should be weighed; however, it is often difficult to quantify the benefits associated with a particular proposal. Give several examples of systems design problems where the benefits would be difficult to quantify.
14. Consider a small manufacturing company that has taken on the project of designing databases for sales orders, inventory, and accounts receivable. List several data fields that these three databases might have in common.
15. A problem that can sometimes occur in systems design is that the final users of the system will fight its implementation. What can be done during the design phase to avoid this problem?
16. Assume that you have been assigned the job of designing a system for a medium-sized clothing manufacturing company. This company maintains raw material inventories for about 19 different fabrics. These fabrics are dyed and cut according to pre-specified patterns. The plant manager has been advocating the introduction of a standard cost control system. Your job as the systems designer is to help the plant manager describe the various reports that would be required from a new system. The plant manager is specifically interested in reports for production cost control and inventory management.

Required
Describe at least three reports that could be produced by the new system.

17. A systems design team is considering the development of a system for sales orders. With what members of management should this team communicate throughout the design project?

18. Does the size of a company have any impact on the approach taken to the systems design project? If your answer is yes, explain.

19. What would be some unique problems associated with systems design in the automobile manufacturing industry?

20. You are in the process of designing an accounts receivable system for your company. A local computer retailer hears that you are designing a system and calls on you. He tells you that he can sell you a computer and software package that will solve all your problems. What is your response to the computer salesman?

21. You have been charged with the responsibility of heading up a design team. The team's responsibility will be to design a production control system. The team consists of you and four other members, including two systems analysts, a database designer, and the production manager. To initiate the project, you call a meeting of all individuals on the design team. At the first meeting, however, you find that the two systems analysts and the database designer have already made up their minds regarding the structure of the system under consideration. As head of the team, you feel that several major design alternatives should be considered before selecting a particular system. How do you deal with this problem?

22. A medium-sized grocery store has point-of-sale cash registers. The cash registers automatically summarize sales of all items sold in the store. One major problem facing the store is that of keeping adequate amounts of all grocery items on the shelves. Therefore, the store is searching for a way to monitor inventories and place daily orders for new goods, as needed.

Required
Give two major alternatives for the design of a system that accounts for and controls inventory for this grocery store.

23. The *Daily Times* newspaper company serves a small community. A considerable portion of the newspaper's revenues come from advertising. At present, all advertising orders are taken by salespeople, usually at the customers' place of business. At the end of every three days, all advertising orders are processed in a batch. Therefore, it normally takes four days between the time the orders are taken and the time the ad appears in the newspaper. Recently, however, a competitive newspaper has offered faster service to its customers.

Required
Present two major design alternatives for processing sales orders for the *Daily Times.*

24. The Good Burger Company owns and operates a chain of fast food restaurants located throughout the southeastern portion of the United States. The company's main headquarters is in Atlanta. A major problem of the company is that of delivering food products to all of the individual company stores. This involves loading up warehouse trucks and then stopping at individual stores on a weekly basis. Each store has a large refrigerator room where a considerable amount of food supply inventory can be maintained. Charles Hill, the general manager of food distribution, has noted that the company should develop a formal system for determining the amount of food to be delivered to each store. In addition, he has questioned whether it is necessary to deliver food to each store on a weekly basis. His rough calculations indicate that some stores might be visited less often. The major problem is that of communication between individual stores and the central office. At present, there is no way for the central office to know how much food to deliver to the individual stores.

Required
Design a system that would collect data on a daily basis at the central office regarding the need for food supplies to the individual stores. Your system should incorporate a

database that keeps track of the sales and inventories of food supplies at individual stores. Your answer should be expressed in general terms. It is not necessary to develop a detailed database design.

25. Green Hardware Manufacturing produces and sells hardware products throughout the western portion of the United States. The primary source of revenue for the company comes from sales to individual hardware stores. The company has divided its sales territory into seven districts, with a sales manager in charge of each district. The individual sales managers try to travel from store to store and take sales orders directly from store owners. The sales orders are then sent to company headquarters in Los Angeles, where they are processed. The present procedure is for the sales manager to write his or her own name on the sales order. At the end of each month the company's accountant prepares a summary of sales by each district and for each product. This process, however, is extremely difficult and usually takes the accountant about four days to complete.

Required
Compose a general design alternative for collecting sales data and producing sales reports in a timely fashion.

26. Assume that you are the information systems manager for a medium-sized department store. At present your company does all of its customer billing manually. Your responsibility is to design a computerized database for customer accounts receivable.

Required
Exactly what data fields are needed for the accounts receivable database?

27. The Fund Travel Agency operates four offices in a medium-sized metropolitan area. Each office has several individuals who plan trips and make reservations for clients. In order to optimize the use of employee time, all reservationists are shifted from office to office as needed. The company's telephone system operates such that customers can dial a central number and then be connected to the office where a reservationist is then assigned to that particular customer. A problem in the system is that because the reservationists do not stay at one office, they do not always have the customer's records when a customer calls in to review or change a reservation.

Required
Design a centralized reservation system for the Fund Travel Agency. Create a computerized system such that a customer's file can be accessed from any location.

28. Brown Chemical Manufacturing produces a single product called CRX. The company's product is sold mainly to food processing manufacturers who use it as a preservative. The production process for CRX is quite complicated. The product goes through four different stages, and each stage is carefully controlled with regard to temperature and moisture. At the first stage, two basic chemicals are mixed together and heated to 1,500 degrees. At stage two, the product is cooled and an additional chemical is added when it reaches just the right temperature. At the third and fourth stages, the resulting chemical is successively refined. Therefore, the company has to maintain raw materials inventory for three different chemicals. In addition, the finished goods inventory for CRX has to be maintained. Almost all the cost of producing CRX is for raw materials and overhead. The process is fully automated, so there is no direct labor cost. Another major cost, however, is that of storing the finished product. In order to increase the product's shelf life, the finished chemical is stored under specially controlled temperature conditions. These conditions require refrigeration to zero degrees, with essentially no moisture. This refrigeration process is fairly expensive, because the company manufactures a very large quantity of CRX.

Recently, the management of the company has been evaluating the overall systems design. Several comments have been made with regard to the manufacturing and inventory systems:

(a) it has been determined that a large number of production batches of CRX have to be discarded due to inadequate environment conditions during processing. At present, there is no management reporting for the costs of the lost materials or time.

(b) Management suspects that the company is incurring too high a cost in the refrigeration of finished goods. It would prefer that production batches be run as customer orders are placed. This way the finished CRX chemical could be shipped directly to the customer, without a need for refrigerated storage in inventory. However, the problem is that the company has never been able to successfully implement this type of system for several reasons: (1) delays in processing of customer orders, (2) difficulty with efficiently scheduling production, and (3) problems with distribution. It is often the case that when a production order is ready, the company's trucks are all out of state making deliveries. It would be disastrous if a production batch were completed and there was no truck to deliver it. This would result in the loss of the entire shipment.

Required
Present a systems design alternative for dealing with Brown Chemical's problems.

29. The Honest Law Firm is made up of five partners who specialize in various areas of law. The oldest partner, Bill Brown, originally founded the firm 30 years ago. His original practice consisted primarily of writing business contracts and helping businesses incorporate. In the early days, Mr. Brown had one secretary who did all the billing. Most of his work was done on a flat-fee basis, and there was no need to provide detailed accounting on time spent on individual clients. However, with the addition of the new partners, the business has become quite complicated. The newer partners specialize in areas such as criminal law, bankruptcy, real estate, and family law. The trend of the business has been such that most of the billing needs to be done on an hourly basis. At present, each partner submits a weekly billing report to the head partner's secretary. These reports are used as a basis for billing individual clients and providing weekly "salary" reports for the partnership.

The partnership's main problem is that most of the partners are having a difficult time recording all the necessary information to bill clients. As a result, it is estimated that only about 75% of the lawyers' actual time is billed to clients. Furthermore, it has been determined that a very weak area for collecting billing information is the telephone system. Several discussions among the partners revealed that the lawyers often spend a lot of time on the telephone with clients, but the information is not recorded into the system for appropriate measures of billing the client.

Required
Design a system that efficiently and effectively records and processes 100% of the firm's billing costs.

30. You are the partner in charge of management services for a medium-sized public accounting firm. You have contracted with a local manufacturing system to develop a specialized production control system. Several of your younger staff accountants have been involved in the actual systems design. A problem has arisen. They have reported to you that top management is very enthusiastic about the design of the new system. However, they are very confused about the response of the production managers and other key employees. The major problem is that the production manager and other employees keep missing meetings with the design team.

On one occasion, the production manager told members of the design team that she liked what they were doing but just did not have time to work with them in detail.

Required
Discuss several possible causes for the problems encountered by the design team. What steps might have been taken to facilitate a better working relationship between the design team and management?

APPENDIX[1]

System Modeling

Systems designers use system models to test their ideas. As discussed in this chapter, it is cheaper to abandon a bad design than a finished system. Furthermore, the modeling process, briefly described in this appendix, leads systematically from the current system to a logical model of a new and improved one.

Before going further, a few critical terms must be defined. The *essence* of a system, or *essential* activities, means the parts that justify the very existence of the system, and that will remain in any new version. For instance, in an invoice payment application, paying the invoice is an essential activity. Essential activities are the most logical part of the system, because they need to be done regardless of the actual implementation of technology.

On the other hand, the incarnation of the system is the actual physical form, or implementation, that it takes. The essential activity of paying invoices could take one of several incarnations: Someone could write the checks manually, a computer could write them automatically, or the funds could be transferred directly from one bank account to another. Hence, the essential activities are the most logical, whereas the incarnation is the actual physical form of the essential activities (see Figure 17A.1).

Four system models are used to work from the old system to the new, and from physical (incarnation) to logical (essential) and back to physical again. A DFD of the process is shown in Figure 17A.1. The four system models are as follows:

1. Current physical model (CPM)—shows the incarnation of the current system. Only by understanding the existing system can we attempt to better it.

2. Current logical model (CLM)—shows the essence of the current system. The essential functions are distilled from the CPM because those activities will remain the same in the new system.

3. New logical model (NLM)—shows the essence of the new system. Here, any new functions that the user requires are added to the essential parts of the old system (CLM).

4. New physical model (NPM)—shows the incarnation of the new system. This presents the actual physical form that the aggregate essential functions (the old plus the new of the NLM) will take in the new system.

---

[1]Adapted from Penny A. Kendall, *Introduction to Systems Analysis and Design: A Structured Approach*, Chapter 10. Englewood Cliffs, N.J.: Prentice Hall. Copyright © 1987 by Prentice Hall. Reprinted with permission.

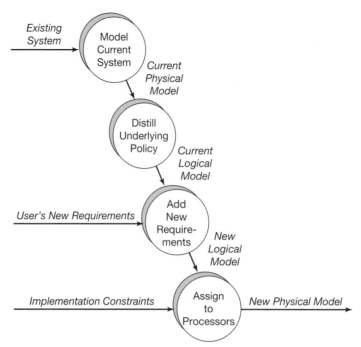

FIGURE 17A.1 Modeling the System.

In summary, the basic idea is to determine what currently exists (CPM), throw out anything unnecessary (CLM), add in any new functions the user wants (NLM), and, finally, determine how to implement the new design (NPM). The sections that follow discuss each model in depth.

CURRENT PHYSICAL MODEL

This model presumes the existence of a current system. If instead a new system is being created from scratch, as in the case of a brand new business, bypass this and the following model and start with the new logical model.

Even if the current system is going to be discarded anyway, it must still be diagrammed because the process of researching and diagramming helps one understand the current system. A new system cannot be created without understanding the old.

The model of current procedures also starts the partitioning of the problem while still working with something that is concrete and verifiable. It is hard enough to partition without working in the abstract realm of essence at the same time.

Finally, the CPM serves as an excellent reference throughout the life of the project. It will be referred to many times to find out exactly how something is presently being done. In the actual model, data flow diagrams reflect the system as it currently exists.

One common mistake is to overspecify the current physical model. It would be easy to spend months tracking down every last detail of the existing system, but there would be no time left for creating the new one. The intent is not to know every minute aspect, but to understand the entirety in a reasonable amount of time.

When the current physical model is complete, walk through it with the user, who can spot errors and omissions while they are correctable with an eraser rather than with reprogramming. If the user is not familiar with DFDs, teach him or her how to read them. After all, a completed DFD is little more than a picture of the system. The only complicated part is in knowing the terminology and construction rules, and the user need not be concerned with all that.

CURRENT LOGICAL MODEL

The CLM still reflects the current way of doing business but shows only the essential functions. Remove all nonessential functions in order to reveal the underlying policy.

The nonessential functions, called *administrative activities,* are adjuncts to the essential activities. They are the more physical aspects of the system incarnation and usually change depending upon the incarnation.

NEW LOGICAL MODEL

The NLM builds upon the CLM, adding any new functions the user wants. For the first time, the process of design is entered, where it is decided what actually needs to be done and a logical way of doing it.

If a requested function is merely a modification of an existing activity, alter the overview diagram and the process's lower-level DFD to reflect the change. If, instead, the request reflects an entirely new activity, draw a lower-level DFD for it and then add the new process to the overview. Either way, of course, the detailed system design and data dictionary must be changed to reflect any new access paths, entities, or data elements.

NEW PHYSICAL MODEL

The new physical model shows the actual physical requirements, including such details as hardware and software specifications, for the new system.

In returning to physical requirements, it is necessary to replace the administrative functions, particularly formats and writes, that were deleted back in the current physical model. They should be put on the lower-level diagrams because, as trivial functions, they should not appear on the overview.

Then divide work among available *processors.* A processor is anything—human or machine—capable of performing work. If a system has eight people and one computer available, it has a total of nine processors.

Dividing the activities among processors is, at the same time, showing the "human–machine boundary," indicating the automated and manual portions of the system.

Now that the processors have been allocated, it is necessary to specify a few more details about any processors that are computer hardware. Try to avoid getting into such detail of specifying the exact machinery, however. Instead of saying,

"We need six Kluge 2s networked to a single Kluge hard disk, along with a Brightmodem and a Fastprint model B printer," say something more like, "We need six 32-bit microcomputers networked to a single 100-megabyte hard disk, along with an auto-dial auto-answer modem and a 300-character-per-second dot-matrix printer." This leaves the option of researching the exact equipment at a later time, while still being able to come up with reasonable cost estimates now.

Part of the NPM includes an estimate of the costs and benefits inherent within the new system. Only then can management realistically evaluate any solution presented.

At this point, one of the options might be to buy a software package to handle all of the computer's duties. If that turns out to be the final decision, most of the design phase, as such, will be eliminated, and the time will be spent evaluating packages instead.

The new physical model has been discussed as if it were just one set of DFDs; in reality, it is multiple models. There is never just one "perfect" solution to a problem. In fact, there are many solutions, some better than others, to each problem encountered.

Complete models are developed for each alternative, including DFDs, data dictionary, data structure diagram, selected process specifications, and cost–benefit analysis. One handy way of summarizing the alternatives is to present them in a decision table format, with benefits used as decision variables and costs used in the action rows so that one alternative occupies each vertical column.

Regardless of which solution seems to be the best, present all alternatives to management, and let it make the final decision. The system analyst is far from objective as to which is the most appropriate—the analyst has been working with the system too closely. Only the people who will have to live with the system on a daily basis and who also have the most complete business experience should make the final decision.

CHAPTER 18

Systems Implementation, Operation, and Control

LEARNING OBJECTIVES

Careful study of this chapter will enable you to:

- ■ Describe the major phases of systems implementation.

- ■ Recognize some of the major human factors involved in systems implementation.

- ■ Describe the major forms of documentation involved in the implementation of a new system.

- ■ Discuss various factors involved in financial control over computer-based accounting information systems.

- ■ Describe several approaches for control over nonfinancial systems resources.

OVERVIEW

This chapter deals with the implementation of the systems design plan. If the systems design process has been done carefully and thoughtfully, the systems implementation phase should proceed quite smoothly. It is impossible to anticipate all potential problems that might occur during the implementation phase. Because of this, delays and problems with implementation are routine. For example, a design plan might call for the installation of a new computer system. If the delivery of the new system is delayed beyond the delivery date specified in the general plan, the entire implementation project might be delayed.

Because of the many problems that can occur during systems implementation, formal plans and controls for the implementation phase should be established. Figure 18.1 shows three major steps in systems implementation: (1) establish plans and controls, (2) execute activities as planned, and (3) follow up and evaluate the new system. Finally, the implemented system must be reviewed and controlled.

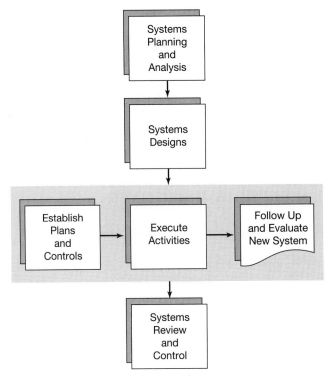

FIGURE 18.1 Systems Implementation.

SYSTEMS IMPLEMENTATION

Establishing Plans and Controls for Implementation

Project management is a key concept in systems implementation. In order to adequately manage the implementation project, specific plans need to be developed. These plans should incorporate three major components: (1) a breakdown of the project into various phases, (2) specific budgets applicable to each phase, and (3) specific timetables applicable to each project phase. There are several different scheduling techniques that might be used to control implementation.

Figure 18.2 shows a **Gantt chart,** which graphically depicts the major activities of a hypothetical systems implementation project. This chart shows both the actual and planned times for a given activity. Gantt charts can be very helpful; however, they are limited in that they cannot show the relationship between various project activities. They do not show the order in which the activities must be performed.

Figure 18.3 shows a **network diagram,** which depicts the order in which the activities must be performed. For example, notice that employees cannot be trained until the software is selected. The network diagram approach can be expanded to include estimated times for each of the individual activities. Given these times, it is possible to use the Program Evaluation and Review Technique (PERT) or Critical Path Method (CPM) to estimate the critical path for a project. The **critical path** is a list of activities that are critical to the project in the sense that if any one of them is delayed, the entire project will be delayed.

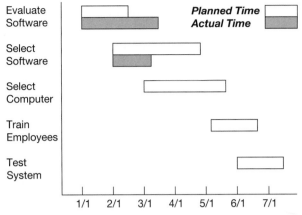

FIGURE 18.2 Gantt Chart Example.

Executing Implementation Activities

Executing implementation activities involves the actual carrying out of the design plan. Typical activities during execution include selecting and training personnel, installing new computer equipment, detailed systems design, writing and testing computer programs, system testing, standards development, documentation, and file conversion. Each of these activities is discussed in detail in this section.

In carrying out the implementation plan, certain measures should be taken to provide a smooth transition and ensure acceptance on the part of company employees. It is normally desirable for management and the systems team to make a formal announcement regarding the execution of the project. Care should be taken to assure employees that the transition will be smooth, and, when possible, employees should be assured that their jobs will be protected. A formal announcement process should have the benefit of minimizing rumors. This is impor-

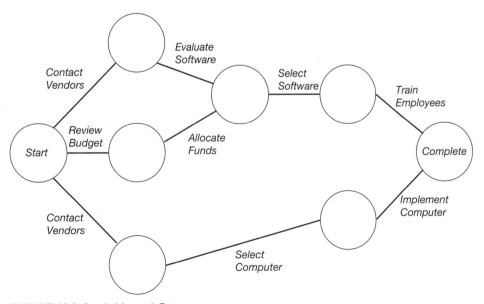

FIGURE 18.3 Simple Network Diagram.

tant because rumors can generate a considerable amount of uncertainty and employee unrest.

Another important aspect of the execution phase is the organization of a special project team. Ideally, the team should consist of individuals who also participated in formulating the design specifications and plans for implementation. Affected managers should also participate.

Employee Training

Virtually any successful systems implementation requires that considerable attention be devoted to employee training. In some cases, new employees must be hired and trained. In other cases, existing employees must be taught to work with new forms, reports, and procedures.

The importance of adequate training cannot be overemphasized. You should never assume that employees will learn to use the system by themselves. If employees are not adequately trained, it is likely that they will simply ignore the new system. Therefore, the success of the entire systems development project is affected by the adequacy of training.

The company will typically face a number of options relating to utilizing and training employees. For example, management often has to decide whether the company should hire a new employee for a given position or retrain an existing employee. In many cases, it is best to retrain an existing employee. There are several reasons for this:

- Recruiting costs relating to hiring a new employee are avoided.
- Existing employees are already familiar with the firm's operations.
- Employee morale is often enhanced, especially in cases where the new position would be a promotion for an existing employee.

There are also many training approaches available to the company. These include the following:

- Hiring outside training consultants
- Using training manuals
- Videotape presentations
- Audiotape presentations
- Training seminars
- Individualized hands-on instruction
- Computer-assisted training

Acquiring and Installing New Computer Equipment

The installation of new computer equipment can sometimes be a monumental task. For installations of any appreciable size, the computer manufacturer normally provides engineers and other personnel to assist in the installation. There are, however, many problems that can be encountered. First, adequate facilities must be available. Most large computers require controlled environments that keep humidity and temperature within specified ranges. In addition, these installations require rooms with false floors, where large bundles of wires can be run. Other requirements typically include specialized security measures, such as special fire extinguishing systems, video monitoring systems, or specialized door locks.

Detailed Systems Design

During the implementation phase, it is almost always necessary to do some additional design work. This might include various kinds of forms or reports design. Also, it is not uncommon for the implementation phase to reveal that certain parts of the design plan are unworkable; therefore, it is always necessary to do some last-minute fine-tuning of the systems design plan.

A very important part of detailed design execution during the implementation phase involves computer programming. In some cases, the design plan might call for prepackaged computer programs; however, most large installations require custom programming. In addition, if the company is switching to a new computer system, it might be necessary to change existing programs so they will run on the new system.

The design specifications for a computer program are determined by the design team, not the programmer. The programmer's primary function is to implement a specific plan; however, it is important for the programmer to work in conjunction with the design team. Finally, computer programs should be very carefully tested before being put into operation. One powerful means of testing computer programs involves processing test data. Test data can be either made up or come from real data. In either case, the test data should include a large number of different kinds of errors. In addition, the test data should include a wide range of conditions, because a defective program will often work with no problems given that there are no errors in the input data file, or where the test data represent the average operating conditions. Therefore, the approach should be taken to "break" the program; the individual doing the testing should do everything possible to find something wrong with the program.

Finally, all computer programs should be adequately documented, both internally and externally. Internal documentation would include various kinds of comments (embedded within the program) that describe different segments of the program code and define the various program variables. External documentation should be written both from the programmer's and user's points of view. Programmer's documentation would include structured English, flowcharts of the program logic, definitions of various subprograms, functions, and program variables. The documentation should be usable by a different programmer, working several years later, to modify the program. Programs without adequate documentation may be worthless when the programmer who wrote them leaves the company.

In addition to testing programs individually, it is also important to test related programs as a group. For example, a given system may have four programs that access the same data file. In this case, all four programs should be tested together. This type of testing would uncover errors relating to integration. Such errors might occur when one program makes faulty assumptions regarding the tasks performed by another program.

Documenting the New System

Documentation is one of the most important parts of systems implementation, but it is often overlooked. One reason for the neglect in documenting systems adequately is that programmers typically receive substantial amounts of training in programming languages but little or no training in documentation. Of course, some educational institutions do an excellent job in teaching documentation skills; however, the opposite is too often true.

It has often been said that a good computer programmer will write several lines of program code per day. One reason for the small number is that a good programmer will spend a substantial portion of time developing plans and documentation. The development of computer software without documentation is an almost worthless exercise. Good documentation can serve a wide range of useful purposes, including (1) training new employees, (2) providing programmers and analysts with useful information for future program evaluation and modification activities, (3) providing auditors with useful information for evaluating internal controls, and (4) assisting in assuring that systems design specifications are met.

File Conversion

A typical problem involved in systems implementation is that of data conversion. In many cases, files maintained manually must be converted to computer format.

Conversion can be an expensive, time-consuming process. This is especially true in the case of converting manual files to computerized files. In such cases, it is often necessary to do a lot of data screening after entering the information into the computer, because errors are typically made in the data input process.

Test Operations

Before the system is actually implemented, it must be thoroughly tested as a whole. There are three basic approaches to the final testing of the system: (1) the direct approach, (2) parallel operation, and (3) modular conversion. The **direct approach** involves switching to the new system and abandoning the old system at a fixed point in time called the **cutover point.** The direct approach, although relatively inexpensive, has the distinct disadvantage of allowing for the possibility of major system problems impairing the actual operation of the company. For example, it could be disastrous to find that a new accounts receivable system bills all of the company's customers for incorrect amounts. The second approach, **parallel operation,** involves running the new and old systems simultaneously. All transactions are processed by both systems. The results of operations based on the two systems are compared. Any discrepancies probably indicate a problem in the new system. Parallel operation has the advantage of being extremely safe; however, it is very expensive and may not be cost effective in all applications. The final approach, **modular conversion,** involves phasing in a new system in segments. For example, the new accounting system might include modules for accounts receivable, accounts payable, inventories, and general ledger. A modular conversion approach might implement the inventory module itself. After the company feels comfortable with this module, other modules could be brought on-line. A major drawback of the modular conversion process is that it can involve a greatly extended checkout period. This might delay implementation of a new system far too long to be practical.

Evaluating the New System

Once the new system has been implemented, more work remains. Follow-up is necessary to ensure that the new system operates as planned. There are many approaches that can assist in follow-up and evaluation, including observation, questionnaires, performance measures, and benchmarks. In summary, almost any system implementation will involve some problems and require adequate follow-up.

FINANCIAL CONTROL OVER INFORMATION SYSTEMS

Financial control of computer-based information systems is concerned with the magnitude of information systems as a composite line item in an organization's budget and/or financial statements and with the operation of information systems as a support, cost, or profit center within an organization's responsibility accounting system. Financial control calls for planning, reporting actual performance against the plan, evaluating variances from planned activities, and undertaking appropriate corrective actions.

The Information Systems Budget

The general objective of financial control is not usually reducing costs per se, even though there has been a steady growth in absolute terms of total information systems costs within organizations. Rather than reduction of overall costs, the usual goal of financial control is to increase the benefits gained from information systems expenditures in the sense of return on costs. There are several reasons why reducing overall costs is not a major goal. First is the essential nature of information systems as a service activity within a firm. Data processing is the neural system of an organization; without it, many organizations would not be able to function. Some "fat" or excess capacity in the budget can be desirable if it reduces the risk of information systems not being able to function continuously. Second, in perspective to other major costs, information systems costs are not that large to begin with. A third reason concerns the nature of costs, which are almost entirely fixed in the short run and remain largely unchanged across a wide level of processing activity. A final reason is that information systems offer many opportunities to increase the effectiveness of managerial decisions. Information is a valuable resource, and information systems can provide a wide variety of information relevant to managerial decisions.

Total information systems costs have increased steadily for most organizations. Within this overall pattern of increase, a significant change has occurred in the general composition of the budget. Prior to PCs, computer equipment expenditures (hardware) were generally the largest component of a typical information systems budget, averaging over 50% of the total budget. Personnel costs have since replaced hardware as the largest component of a typical information systems budget. This change in budget composition reflects the general trend of decreasing unit hardware costs and increasing unit personnel costs that has characterized the information systems environment.

The Nature of Information Systems Costs

One major determinant of cost controllability is whether costs are primarily fixed or variable. Most information systems personnel are professional and are paid on a salary rather than on an hourly basis. Salaries and hardware expenditures together can be expected to account for 75% or more of a typical budget. Hardware is either purchased outright or leased at a fixed price per month, regardless of usage. The net result is that the typical budget consists primarily of fixed costs. Although cost categories other than hardware and personnel, such as supplies and utilities expense, might be variable, their effect on the overall cost/activity relationship is negligible.

The previous discussion refers to the cost of current operations. When new applications are to be developed, the related costs may warrant special consideration. If applications are developed in-house, the major costs are salaries and computer time. If no new staff or equipment are required, total development costs would be included within total information systems operating costs because, as just discussed, personnel and hardware costs tend to be fixed over a wide range of activity. Laying off staff as new application development diminishes is usually not desirable unless a permanent reduction in developmental efforts is expected. While laying off staff might save salary costs in the short run, the costs of recruiting and training new staff when it is subsequently needed are frequently greater than any short-run cost savings gained from laying off experienced personnel. If new staff or equipment are required because of new applications development, then the extra costs incurred are variable with respect to the new developments but become fixed in the context of overall operations, unless the extra staff and equipment can be eliminated once the new application is completed. Most firms maintain an applications development staff at a fixed or slowly growing size, delaying any new applications that cannot be handled by their staff or contracting some or all new application development to outside consultants. The use of consultants is attractive because their services can be eliminated at the completion of the new application development. This same line of reasoning applies to most other categories of computer expenditures as well, such as data entry, programming, and site management. Rather than perform all services in-house, an organization should consider **outsourcing,** procuring services as necessary on a consulting or contract basis to keep the size of staff and equipment to that essential to smooth operations. All types of hardware, software, and related services may be procured externally as well as developed in-house. External procurement may be desirable if internal development would require the addition of resources that might later on be idle.

Acquisition and Insurance Controls

Financial control of information systems includes determining the most advantageous method(s) to finance equipment acquisition and also acquiring appropriate insurance to control potential loss exposure. A common method of financing mainframe system hardware is to rent it from the vendor. This approach requires the least commitment on the user's part, because most rental agreements can be canceled on short notice. Rental contracts usually call for overtime charges if equipment is used above a certain number of hours and frequently include regular maintenance of the equipment by the vendor. If a firm expects to use a piece of equipment for a long time, a long-term lease with a vendor or other party for use of equipment can bring about a sizable reduction in monthly rental charges. With a long-term lease, some of the risks of ownership are transferred to the lessee because the long-term lease may not be canceled as easily as a rental agreement. Third-party leasing firms frequently interface between a vendor and user by purchasing equipment from a vendor with the specific intention of subsequently entering into a long-term lease for this equipment with a user. Computer leasing from third parties, rather than vendors, is a significant percentage of total hardware acquisition financing.

Long-term leasing is a financing alternative to outright purchase of the equipment. The pattern of cash flow is quite different for a lease than a purchase, although the user's obligations under a long-term lease might be similar to those that it would have with outright ownership. Frequently, long-term leases include a purchase option, which allows the lessee to purchase the equipment at a favorable price after several years of use. The conceptual similarity between long-term leases with purchase options and outright purchases is recognized by generally accepted accounting principles. Many long-term leases have to be accounted for as purchases in financial statements, even though the tax effects and, hence, cash flow, are very different from that of an outright purchase.

Financially, the relative advantages of leasing over purchasing are based on traditional capital budgeting considerations, such as cost and availability of capital, useful life, and depreciation rates. Lease rental payments are tax deductible in entirety, and leasing does not require that the firm initially invest any capital. By contrast, the cash flow effects of a purchase are dependent on existing interest rates for capital and depreciation rates. Both interest rates and depreciation rates change frequently.

In addition to cash flow effects, other considerations are relevant to the lease or purchase decision. Charges for regular equipment maintenance and other support services, any charges for overtime usage in a lease, purchase and sale options, lease cancellation fees, and other factors may be important. An important concern is technological obsolescence. A long-term lease or purchase commits the user to equipment that may become technologically obsolete when new equipment models are introduced. The rate of technological change in the computer industry has made technological obsolescence a recurring problem, but one that is difficult to predict with accuracy. Despite this problem, it is usually cheaper to lease equipment and cheaper still to purchase it rather than to rent it for any significant period of time.

A related financial consideration is that of insurance for equipment and services. Customary insurance coverage may not provide the protection necessary to cover loss exposure. At a minimum, insurance coverage of equipment is desirable. Standard insurance policies may not cover accidental damage, loss while the equipment is in transit from the vendor, flood, electrical damage, or, most important, damage done purposely by employees (computer crime). A firm's insurance policies should be reviewed to see what coverage already exists, and extra insurance should be obtained as necessary. Specific information systems insurance policies are available, but even these are likely to exclude damage due to dishonest and criminal actions by employees. Firms leasing or renting equipment sometimes mistakenly believe that loss or damage is assumed by the supplier of the equipment under the terms of the lease. This may not be the case. Differences in the terms of rental and lease agreements require a careful analysis on the part of the user to determine the extent of liability.

Insurance coverage for information systems equipment may not cover the related data storage media (tapes, disk packs, and the like) unless the policy is specifically endorsed to do so. Loss of information stored on tapes and other media can be very expensive to reproduce or replace. Care should be taken to ensure that coverage of information systems media includes reproduction costs, not only the nominal value of blank media.

Other types of insurance may be relevant in special circumstances. A firm that is highly dependent on information systems for daily operations may be interested in obtaining business interruption insurance for loss of information systems operations. Business interruption insurance might be obtained as a separate policy or added to an existing policy. Firms that sell excess information systems capacity may wish to obtain insurance coverage for liabilities that might arise in providing this service to outside interests. Managerial analysis of risk and financial exposures related to information systems should result in a contingency plan to protect equipment and records and an insurance program that minimizes the possibility that a large financial loss will not be covered.

Financial Control Strategies

The conceptual similarity between information systems operations and other manufacturing or production operations suggests that traditional financial controls, such as responsibility accounting and standard costs, might be applied to information systems operations as well. There are, however, several important differences, the most notable being that the product—information—is often quite difficult to measure and evaluate. Another problem is that costs tend to be fixed or at best semivariable with output. The integrated nature of information systems also creates difficulties in establishing costing relationships between inputs and outputs.

Difficulties such as these have led some firms to view information systems costs in the same light as research and development costs, which are notoriously difficult to control. Expenditures are planned with a conventional line item budget, detailing such items as hardware costs, personnel costs, and supplies. If actual expenditures keep within their budget, then "management by exception" governs. With this type of "global control" strategy, information systems are viewed as a single function, and there is little need for detail utilization and cost records, because there is no attempt or desire to account for costs in detail. Users are not charged for costs, and next year's budget tends to be set at last year's amount plus 1, 10, or some other percentage increase, allowing for obvious exceptions, such as new equipment purchases.

This type of control structure is generally unsatisfactory in any medium- to large-sized system. At a minimum, a more detailed classification of costs by cost center within the overall information systems department is needed to facilitate managerial review. The department is segmented into several cost centers, such as administration, programming and analysis, operations, and data entry. Global budget line items, such as hardware and salaries, are allocated within the department to each relevant cost center.

The cost center approach provides more detailed information for managerial review but does not by itself relate costs incurred to actual usage. Relating costs to usage is the objective of **chargeback systems.** Chargeback systems are used to bill or allocate costs to users within an organization. The theory of chargeback systems is that pricing mechanisms are the most effective means for allocating resources to alternative uses.

A common view of information systems holds that it is a support service and that users should not be charged for it, or that users should receive only "awareness allocations." In this case, costs are allocated to users based on their consumption of services, but these allocations or charges are not formally a part of the financial control system. If users are not charged for services, or are charged only in the sense of receiving awareness reports that are not actually financially significant for the user, then control mechanisms other than price must govern the use of resources.

- All jobs with more than 1,000 records must be run after 3 P.M.
- All jobs requiring three or more tapes must be run on Saturdays.
- All jobs needing 600K or more must be cleared with the operations supervisor.

Chargeback Systems

A chargeback system is a mechanism used to allocate costs to users in an organization within the overall framework of a responsibility accounting system. In this framework, both users and information systems are considered as cost or profit centers, and the chargeback system transfers appropriate charges between these entities to reflect the consumption of information systems services. The objective of a chargeback system is to facilitate communication of the costs of operating information systems and to motivate users to exercise control over the costs.

Chargeback systems take one of two general forms. The more sophisticated involves establishing predetermined rates or charges (prices) for unit services (such as a minute of computer time) and billing or charging users for their actual usage at these predetermined rates. The predetermined rate approach to chargeback is an explicit managerial control system and more than an accounting technique. The second form is more of an accounting technique. Usage statistics are collected and total actual costs are allocated periodically to users based on these usage statistics. Allocation of service center costs (such as information systems) to user departments is a common accounting technique that is necessary to the development of full unit costs or full cost overhead rates for use by the producing departments. The cost allocation approach to chargeback does not establish an explicit pricing mechanism, but as costs are allocated to users on the basis of usage statistics, these usage statistics may be perceived by users as surrogates for prices.

Transfer Prices

Transfer pricing systems are used to generate prices for internally produced goods and services that are exchanged between profit centers in an organization. If information systems are to be controlled as a profit rather than cost center in the context of the organization's responsibility accounting system, then predetermined rates should be set according to the theory of transfer prices. Transfer pricing theory is rooted in microeconomic price theory. Accordingly, setting transfer prices analytically involves using marginal cost or opportunity cost, because this equates marginal revenue to marginal cost and thus maximizes the profit of the profit center. This is consistent with the objective of establishing profit centers within an organization. If certain conditions concerning the nature of the commodity are satisfied, then optimal managerial control and the most efficient distribution of the transferred goods within the firm are attained.

The ideal situation in transfer pricing theory occurs when all profit centers are highly independent and completely autonomous with respect to decision making. In this situation—an analogy to the "perfect competition" model of microeconomic theory—the good in question (information systems services) is available externally as well as internally, and the supplier and the consumers may use the external, as well as internal, market in satisfying their demands. As restrictions are added—such as forbidding information systems to sell services to outsiders or forbidding users to independently purchase information systems services outside the firm—the transfer pricing problem becomes more complex. The result of this complexity is that it is very unlikely that transfer prices can be established in a way that simultaneously generates efficient resource allocation within the firm and maintains the decision-making autonomy of the decentralized profit centers. Thus, although conceptually appealing, the transfer price approach to information systems chargeback is fraught with difficulties and is rarely implemented in practice.

Cost Recovery Systems

The majority of chargeback systems are cost recovery systems. In a **cost recovery system,** information systems operates as a cost center and sets rates with the objective of charging its costs to users, not with the objective of maximizing its own profits.

Although there are many approaches to setting cost-based rates, the common approach is to initially budget information systems expenditures in a cost center budget. These cost center budgets are then related to the units that will be used for charging purposes by cost allocation techniques. A typical calculation is shown in Tables 18.1 through 18.3.

The first step is to reallocate information systems administration in the cost center budget to the other chargeable categories, because information systems administration is not directly used by users. This might be done in several ways. The common approach is to allocate administration in proportion to the total direct costs of the other cost centers, as shown in Table 18.1.

The next step is to allocate the revised cost figures for each chargeable information systems cost center to chargeable activities within each cost center. These chargeable activities within each cost center are selected on practical grounds relating to the measurement of user services. Table 18.2 illustrates this process for the operations cost center of Table 18.1. Total operations costs are suballocated to its chargeable activities, either directly or through the use of an allocation technique. This process involves the reallocation of operations cost center overhead to its chargeable activities. The process shown in Table 18.2 for the operations cost center would need to be done for each separate cost center.

The final step is to calculate the charging rates by dividing the budgeted cost of each chargeable activity by its budgeted or standard usage as measured by some item such as "number of lines printed," "number of minutes used," and so on. This process is shown in Table 18.3 for the chargeable activities of the operations cost center shown in Table 18.2.

Practically, the technique of developing cost recovery rates is straightforward, but the resultant rates lack support in economic theory. This is particularly

TABLE 18.1 Reallocation of EDP Administration to Other Cost Centers

	Cost Center			
Cost Before Allocation	*Administration*	*Analysis and Programming*	*Data Entry*	*Operations*
Direct	$30,000	$200,000	$ 75,000	$125,000
Overhead	$20,000	$ 50,000	$ 30,000	$ 20,000
Total	$50,000	$250,000	$105,000	$145,000
Allocation[a]	($50,000)	$ 25,000[b]	$ 9,375	$ 15,625
Total cost after allocation	0	$275,000	$114,375	$160,625

[a]Allocation based on direct cost ratio;

$$\text{Allocation} = \frac{\text{total administration costs}}{\text{total direct costs of chargeable cost centers}} \times \text{direct cost of cost center}$$

[b]$25,000 = \dfrac{\$50,000}{\$400,000} \times \$200,000$

TABLE 18.2 Allocation of EDP Operations Costs to Chargeable Activities

Cost Item	*Chargeable Activity in Operations*						
	CPU	*Tapes*	*Disk*	*Printer*	*Terminals*	*Overhead*	*Total*
Hardware	$55,000	$12,000	$14,000	$ 4,000	$2,000	$ 3,000	$ 90,000
Salaries	0	$10,000	$10,000	$ 2,000	$2,000	$11,000	$ 35,000
Supplies	0	$ 1,000	$ 1,000	$ 1,000	$1,000	$ 1,000	$ 5,000
Facility	$ 4,000	$ 2,000	$ 1,000	$ 1,000	$1,000	$ 1,000	$ 10,000
General	0	0	0	0	0	$ 5,000	$ 5,000
Administration allocation	0	0	0	0	0	$15,625	$ 15,625
Subtotal	$59,000	$25,000	$26,000	$ 8,000	$6,000	$36,625	$160,625
Reallocation of overhead[a]	$17,426	$ 7,384	$ 7,679	$ 2,363	$1,773	($36,625)	0
Total chargeable cost	$76,426	$32,384	$33,679	$10,363	$7,773	0	$160,625

[a]Based on direct cost ratio shown in the subtotal.

true if the budgeted costs used to develop the rates include fixed costs, as is the usual case. The process then results in an average cost whose magnitude is highly dependent on budgeted usage, and many of the conceptual limitations inherent in average costing from a control viewpoint again apply. In fact, the process just illustrated to develop predetermined rates can be and actually is used to allocate actual information systems costs to users based on actual usage at the end of a period. One difference is that cost allocations used to develop predetermined rates usually involve more detailed chargeable activities within each cost center than would be used if costs were only being allocated after the fact.

There are many variations in cost recovery chargeback systems. Rather than total costs, variable costs, standard costs, or only selected costs may be used to develop rates. Rates might be set at external market prices for similar services. Although conceptually appealing (this is a principle of transfer pricing approach), it is usually very difficult to find external prices for all the information systems services provided in-house. Modifications to the total cost approach have the objective of making the resultant rates more meaningful in an economic theory sense, but modifications are difficult to implement because of the predominantly fixed cost of information systems services. The result is that most cost recovery systems are based on total budgeted information systems costs.

TABLE 18.3 Calculation of Charging Rates for the Operations Cost Center

Chargeable Unit	Unit of Measure	Budgeted Cost	Budgeted Usage	Charging Rate
CPU	CPU minutes	$76,426	43,200	$1.7691
Tapes	Drive minutes	$32,384	227,000	$0.1427
Disk	Track days	$33,679	73,224,680	$0.0005
Printer	1,000 lines printed	$10,363	177,000	$0.0585
Terminals	1,000 minutes used	$ 7,773	33,600	$0.2313

One significant variation is to separate costs of current operations from costs of new systems development and to develop separate rates for each type of service. Or, only costs of current operations may be charged to users, and new systems development costs are absorbed as information systems overhead.

Another significant variation is to develop **flexible rates.** In this case, all or selected charging units are further factored into priority classes, and each class is assigned a priority/price factor to reflect its relative value to the user. For example, a CPU minute may have a base rate of $10, which is adjusted up or down for the priority class of processing provided. There might be five priority classes of processing, with the highest priority priced at two times the base rate and the lowest priority class priced at one-half the base rate. Flexible rates are set to affect the user's demand for services rather than to strictly reflect the cost of service provided. Although this objective is also embraced by transfer pricing theory, flexible pricing may be implemented even if information systems services are accounted for as a cost center. The intent is to make flexible rates meaningful in influencing user demand for information systems services but not necessarily to make the rates meaningful as economic prices.

Without some form of chargeback system, information systems services are a "free good" within the organization. There is no incentive for users to be concerned about the efficiency and effectiveness of information systems services. Organizations often use some type of chargeback system, perhaps quite simple in nature, to extend the degree of financial control by motivating users to control the costs of information systems services. There are several conceptual approaches to chargeback. The methods implemented in practice are usually cost-based and lack support in economic price theory. Despite this ambiguity in meaning, chargeback systems affect the way people's performance is measured in an organization and, accordingly, can contribute to effective and efficient use of the information systems resource.

CONTROL OVER NONFINANCIAL INFORMATION SYSTEMS RESOURCES

A number of factors relating to information systems are important to management from a control point of view but are not measured in terms of dollars. These include performance measures for hardware, software, and personnel.

Measuring hardware performance involves system utilization, system downtime, and system responsiveness. Measures of systems utilization typically include ratios such as CPU time actually used to that available. Also, statistics can be derived for the individual components of the computer system, such as terminals, tape drives, and so on. Utilization statistics are very important, because they can indicate bottlenecks or needs for systems expansion. In addition, utilization statistics reported for various times of the day can assist management in scheduling major computer runs at times when system utilization is low.

In many systems, downtime is a major concern. **Downtime** is the percentage of the time that all or part of the network is unavailable for use. In addition, the mean time between failures and the mean time to repair the system are also reported. Downtime statistics are helpful in evaluating overall hardware effectiveness. A system that is down too much can cause a number of problems—including lost business.

A second major nonquantitative factor important to control is software performance. A very sound overall approach to evaluating software performance is to survey systems users, asking a large number of questions relating to ease of use, functionality, and user friendliness. Software performance must be constantly monitored because environmental changes can produce changes in the satisfaction of users.

Finally, it is necessary to apply controls relating to personnel. Therefore, reports need to be prepared for a large variety of factors. For example, programmers might be evaluated in terms of the quality of documentation written. Various other types of reports needed for evaluating personnel performance might include the following:

- Performance reports for data entry specialists. These reports might include statistics such as the number of keystrokes per hour or number of data records entered per hour.
- Reports evaluating the efficiency of systems operators. These reports might include statistics relating to the effectiveness in running prescheduled jobs on time.
- Reports relating to the efficiency of hardware repair persons. Such reports might include statistics on the number of repair jobs and the average length of time required for each repair job, broken down by various types of repair categories.

Auditing the Information System

Most firms employ either internal or external auditors to audit the information system. The audit's focus should be on the information system itself and on the validity and accuracy of data as processed by the system. The accountants' interests in auditing the information system tend to focus on internal control. The general approach followed by the auditor is to obtain first a detailed description of the internal control system, typically using internal control questionnaires. Once a description of an internal control system has been obtained, the auditor then performs tests of compliance. During this process, the auditor ascertains the degree to which the company actually applies the internal controls as documented in the internal control evaluation. Finally, the auditor performs tests of specific transactions as they flow through the system. The amount of testing required depends on the degree to which an adequate set of internal controls exists and is in effective operation. In systems with a high degree of internal controls, the auditor can rely on a statistical sampling of transactions.

Maintaining and Modifying the System

In all operational systems, it becomes necessary to make changes. One reason for changes is that it is not possible to foresee all contingencies during the design phase. In addition, environmental conditions and information needs change. Finally, almost any computer program contains some "bugs." **Bugs** are computer programming errors that might not be detected until the system actually begins operation.

For control purposes, it is very important that all modifications to the system's software and data schema be formally reviewed and approved. Ideally, users should have the opportunity to make requests for systems modifications. These requests should be reviewed by a committee of managers and systems specialists. Upon approval, they should be referred to the appropriate systems or applications programmers for implementation. Systems and applications programmers should work according to a preestablished set of priorities. In addition, these programmers should not have access to the operational copy of software being modified. Instead, programmers should apply the modifications to a copy of the original software. This software, after being modified, should be reviewed very carefully and then installed by an independent person. All modifications of the system should be carefully documented. The documentation should include the reason for changes, the exact changes made, and the person approving the changes. In addition, documentation standards should apply. This means that user manuals and systems programming documentation should be updated.

SUMMARY

Critical to success in systems implementation is the need to establish a systems implementation plan. This plan should include a detailed timetable and budget showing all key activities in the implementation plan. The implementation plan then must be continuously monitored, and any discrepancies relating to the timetable or budget should be reported.

Many implementation activities are required. These include personnel training, physical preparation, detailed systems design, program testing, standards development, documentation, file conversion, and systems cutover. In addition, the implemented system must be evaluated for ongoing control purposes.

Financial control of information systems is concerned with the magnitude of information systems as a composite line item in an organization's budget and/or financial statements and with the operation of information systems as a support, cost, or profit center within an organization's responsibility accounting system. A number of factors relating to information systems are important to management from a control point of view but are not measured in terms of dollars. These include performance measures for hardware, software, and personnel. Formal procedures should be developed for maintaining and modifying the existing system.

Glossary

bug: a computer programming error that is not detected until the program is in use.

chargeback systems: techniques used to bill or allocate costs to users of information systems within an organization.

cost recovery system: the information system operates as a cost center and sets rates with the objective of charging its costs to users rather than with the objective of maximizing its own profits.

critical path: a list of activities that are critical in that if any one of them is delayed, the entire project will be delayed.

cutover point: the point in time under the direct approach to implementation where the switch to a new system is made.

direct approach: an approach to implementation that involves switching to a new system and abandoning the old system at a fixed point in time.

downtime: the percentage of time that equipment is unavailable for use.

flexible rates: charging units are factored into priority classes, and each class is assigned a priority/price factor to reflect its relative value to the user.

Gantt chart: a scheduling technique that graphically depicts both the actual and planned times for activities, but does not show the relationships between various activities.

modular conversion: an approach to implementation that involves phasing in a new system in segments.

network diagram: a scheduling technique that depicts the order in which the activities must be performed.

outsourcing: procuring information systems services on a consulting or contract basis.

parallel operation: an approach to implementation that involves running the new and old systems simultaneously before final conversion.

Chapter Quiz

Answers to the chapter quiz appear on page 678.

1. Which concept is the most important to systems implementation?
   (a) Ashby's law of requisite variety
   (b) Grosch's law
   (c) project continuity
   (d) project management

2. The Gantt chart shows
   (a) planned activity times.
   (b) relationships between activities.
   (c) both a and b.
   (d) neither a nor b.

3. The conversion approach that is most risky to a company's operations is
   (a) the direct approach.
   (b) parallel operation.
   (c) modular conversion.

4. The conversion approach that involves phasing in a new system in segments is
   (a) the direct approach.
   (b) parallel operation.
   (c) modular conversion.

5. The largest component of a typical information systems budget is
   (a) computer hardware.
   (b) software.
   (c) personnel.
   (d) utility expense.

6. The general objective of financial control of information systems is usually
   (a) to reduce costs.
   (b) to increase return on costs.
   (c) to increase costs.
   (d) to reduce return on costs.

7. Technological obsolescence is a factor that encourages
   (a) the outright purchasing of computers.
   (b) the long-term leasing of computers.
   (c) both a and b.
   (d) neither a nor b.

8. The statement "All jobs with more than 1,000 records must be run after 3 P.M." is indicative of
   (a) explicit control of information systems services.
   (b) financial control of information systems services.
   (c) a chargeback system for information systems services.
   (d) total absence of control of information systems services.

9. In a cost recovery chargeback system, rates for information systems services are established with the objective of
   (a) charging users' costs to information systems.
   (b) charging information systems' costs to users.
   (c) maximizing information systems' profits.
   (d) maximizing users' profits.

10. Computer programming errors that are not detected until the system actually begins operation are called
    (a) nuts.
    (b) bugs.
    (c) moths.
    (d) crackers.

Review Problem

Some companies operate their information systems departments as profit centers. The department earns revenue by charging users for the services they receive. Standard rates are set for the services provided by the computer department and charged to users as they receive services.

Required
(a) How might this encourage users to consider the value of information?
(b) Suppose a user finds that a special report can be prepared outside the organization for a lower cost than would be charged for the same service by the organization's own information systems department. Should the user department have the authority to take this work outside? Would the absence of this authority weaken the viability of the profit center as a control technique?
(c) Rather than set standard usage rates for computer services, many companies charge out (allocate) the actual costs of their information systems to users. These allocations are commonly based on relative usage of information systems services. Discuss the relative merits of this approach versus that of charging users a standard rate for the services they receive. (Note that a standard rate may charge out more or less than the information systems department's actual costs, depending on use.)

Solution to Review Problem

(a) If users were profit centers, rationally they would only request processing that had a benefit greater than its cost. For nondiscretionary processing, charging costs should tend to have users try to minimize their cost to any extent possible.
(b) Although a complex consideration, a simple answer is yes to both questions. Access to transferred goods at market price is widely held as a necessary condition for the viability of the profit center concept. If cost is correctly specified (some surrogate for marginal cost), then both the user and the overall organization profit from the use of the outside service.
(c) This part raises the issue of transfer prices for information systems services—a subject that has been discussed in many academic articles. Allocations based on relative usage have been widely criticized as supporting dysfunctional behavior, as a unit's cost becomes dependent on the actions (relative usage) of other units. Yet, at the end of a period, allocations based on relative usage seem an intuitively fair way to charge out the information systems service centers cost to users.

   The basic argument against the allocation of actual costs to users is that these charges are arbitrary and unavoidable. Standard rates, even at or near market prices, raise another set of problems. Use of a standard rate allows user groups and information systems to be profit centers. Theoretically, this is appealing, but in practice, users often resent seeing information systems make profits at their expense. Setting the rates can be very difficult; they should not exceed market, yet the firm (or at least information systems management) does not want to lose money on its information systems function. Should information systems be allowed to perform work for other firms? How independent should the information systems function be? These and other questions raised by transfer pricing defy a definitive textbook solution.

Review Questions

1. Define each of the following terms:
   (a) PERT chart
   (b) Gantt chart

    (c) critical path
    (d) parallel operation
    (e) modular conversion
    (f) test data
    (g) transfer price
    (h) chargeback system
    (i) systems modification

2. Identify the major steps in systems implementation.

3. Identify several key activities in systems operation. Briefly discuss the components of the systems implementation plan.

4. Why is detailed systems design work necessary during the systems implementation phase?

5. Contrast and compare the modular versus parallel operations approaches to conversion.

6. Discuss several functions of systems documentation.

7. What is the relative magnitude of the typical information systems budget to the budget of the entire organization?

8. What is the nature of information systems costs? Are they mostly fixed or mostly variable with respect to information systems activity?

9. Identify several types of insurance a firm might carry to minimize information systems-related loss exposure.

10. What are the relative merits of purchasing information systems equipment over leasing it or renting it from a vendor?

11. Identify several financial control strategies that may be used in the management of information systems.

12. What is a chargeback system? Distinguish between a predetermined rate system and a cost allocation system for chargeback of information systems costs to users.

13. How does a cost recovery system for information systems chargeback differ from a transfer pricing approach to information systems chargeback?

14. What are the likely consequences of not charging users for their consumption of information systems resources?

Discussion Questions and Problems

15. Bonn Company recently reorganized its computer and data processing activities. The small installations located within the accounting departments at its plants and subsidiaries have been replaced with a single data processing department at corporate headquarters, responsible for the operations of a newly acquired large-scale computer system. The new department has been in operation for two years and has been regularly producing reliable and timely data for the past 12 months.

    Because the department has focused its activities on converting applications to the new system and producing reports for plant and subsidiary managements, little attention has been devoted to the costs of the department. Now that the department's activities are operating relatively smoothly, company management has requested that the departmental manager recommend a cost accumulation system (to facilitate cost control) and the development of suitable rates to charge users for service.

    For the past two years, the departmental costs have been recorded in one account. The costs then have been allocated to user departments on the basis of the computer time used. The accompanying schedule reports the costs and charging rate for 19XX.

Data Processing Department Costs for the
Year Ended December 31, 19XX

1. Salaries and benefits	$622,600
2. Supplies	40,000
3. Equipment maintenance contract	15,000
4. Insurance	25,000
5. Heat and air conditioning	36,000
6. Electricity	50,000
7. Equipment and furniture depreciation	285,400
8. Building improvements depreciation	10,000
9. Building occupancy and security	39,300
10. Corporate administrative charges	52,700
Total Costs	$1,176,000
Computer hours for user processing*	2,750
Hourly rate ($1,176,000 ÷ 2,750)	$ 428
*Use of available computer hours	
Testing and debugging programs	250
Setup of jobs	500
Processing jobs	2,750
Downtime for maintenance	750
Idle time	742
	4,992

The department manager recommends that the department costs be accumulated by five activity centers within the department: systems analysis, programming, data preparation, computer operations (processing), and administration. He then suggests that the costs of the administration activity should be allocated to the other four activity centers before a separate rate for charging users is developed for each of the first four activities.

The manager made the following observations regarding the charges to the several subsidiary accounts within the department after reviewing the details of the accounts:

1. Salaries and benefits—records the salary and benefit costs of all employees in the department.
2. Supplies—records paper costs for printers, and a small amount for miscellaneous other costs.
3. Equipment maintenance contract—records charges for maintenance contracts. All equipment is covered by maintenance contracts.
4. Insurance—records costs of insurance covering the equipment and the furniture.
5. Heat and air conditioning—records a charge from the corporate heating and air conditioning department estimated to be the incremental costs to meet the special needs of the computer department.
6. Electricity—records the charge for electricity based on a separate meter within the department.
7. Equipment and furniture depreciation—records the depreciation charges for all owned equipment and furniture within the department.
8. Building improvements depreciation—records the amortization charges for the building changes required to provide proper environmental control and electrical service for the computer equipment.
9. Building occupancy and security—records the computer department's

share of the depreciation, maintenance, heat, and security costs of the building. These costs are allocated to the department on the basis of square feet occupied.

10. Corporate administrative charges—records the computer department's share of the corporate administrative costs. They are allocated to the department on the basis of number of employees in the department.

Required

(a) For each of the ten cost items, state whether it should be distributed to the five activity centers, and for each cost item that should be distributed, recommend the basis on which it should be distributed. Justify your conclusion in each case.

(b) Assume that the costs of the computer operations (processing) activity will be charged to the user departments on the basis of computer hours. Using the analysis of computer utilization shown below the department cost schedule presented in the problem, determine the total number of hours that should be employed to determine the charging rate for computer operations (processing). Justify your answer.

(CMA)

16. Wright Company employs a computer-based data processing system for maintaining all company records. The present system was developed in stages over the past five years and has been fully operational for the last 24 months.

When the system was being designed, all department heads were asked to specify the types of information and reports they would need for planning and controlling operations. The systems department attempted to meet the specifications of each department head. Company management specified that certain other reports be prepared for department heads. During the five years of systems development and operation, there have been several changes in the department-head positions due to attrition and promotions. The new department heads often made requests for additional reports according to their specifications. The systems department complied with all of these requests. Reports were discontinued only on request by a department head, and then only if it was not a standard report required by top management. As a result, few reports, in fact, were discontinued. Consequently, the data processing system was generating a large number of reports each reporting period.

Company management became concerned about the quantity of information that was being produced by the system. The internal audit department was asked to evaluate the effectiveness of the reports generated by the system. The audit staff determined early in the study that more information was being generated by the data processing system than could be used effectively. They noted the following reactions to this information overload.

(a) Many department heads would not act on certain reports during periods of peak activity. The department head would let these reports accumulate with the hope of catching up during a subsequent lull.

(b) Some department heads had so many reports that they did not act at all on the information, or they made incorrect decisions because of misuse of the information.

(c) Frequently, action required by the nature of the report data was not taken until the department head was reminded by someone who needed the decision. These department heads did not appear to have developed a priority system for acting on the information produced by the data processing system.

(d) Department heads often would develop the information they needed from alternative, independent sources, rather than utilizing the reports generated by the data processing system. This was often easier than trying to search among the reports for the needed data.

Required

(a) For each of the observed reactions, indicate whether they are functional or dysfunctional behavioral responses. Explain your answer in each case.

(b) Assuming one or more of the reactions were dysfunctional, recommend procedures the company could employ to eliminate the dysfunctional behavior and to prevent its recurrence.

(CMA)

17. The Able Company has decided to calculate charging rates for its computer operations department as follows:

Chargeable Activities	Budgeted Usage
Processor	56,000 CPU minutes
Tapes	315,000 drive minutes
Disks	100,000,000 cylinder days
Printers	250,000 10,000 lines printed
Terminals	500,000 terminal minutes

Required

Using the following data compute charging rates for each of the five chargeable activities. To do this, first reallocate overhead to the chargeable activities on the basis of their direct cost ratios, as shown in Table 18.2. Then divide the resulting total chargeable cost for each chargeable activity by its budgeted usage to compute the charging rates, as shown in Table 18.3.

Cost Item	Processor	Tapes	Disks
Hardware	$31,250	$ 5,100	$5,400
Salaries	$33,000	$ 375	$4,850
Supplies	$ 9,000	$ 2,550	$1,800
Facility	$49,500	$ 1,200	$ 700
Other	$16,200	$19,000	$6,600

Cost Item	Printers	Terminals	Overhead
Hardware	$3,750	$1,550	$28,700
Salaries	$ 400	$ 600	$32,100
Supplies	$5,250	$2,250	$35,750
Facility	$ 450	$ 650	$35,850
Other	$8,900	$3,675	$43,500

Answers to Chapter Quiz

1. D	4. C	7. D	10. B
2. A	5. C	8. A	
3. A	6. B	9. B	

Index